WOMEN'S STUDIES ENCYCLOPEDIA

Women's Studies Encyclopedia

Volume II

LITERATURE, ARTS, AND LEARNING

EDITED BY Helen Tierney

GREENWOOD PRESS

New York • Westport, Connecticut • London

Library of Congress Cataloging-in-Publication Data

Women's studies encyclopedia.

Bibliography: p.
Includes index.
Contents: v. 1. Views from the sciences —
v. 2. Literature, arts, and learning.
1. Women—United States—Dictionaries.
2. Women—Dictionaries.   I. Tierney, Helen.
HQ1115.W645 1990   305.4'03   88-32806
ISBN 0–313–24646–7 (set)
ISBN 0–313–26725–1 (v. 1 : lib. bdg. : alk. paper)
ISBN 0–313–27357–X (v. 2 : lib. bdg. : alk. paper)

British Library Cataloguing in Publication Data is available.

Library of Congress Catalog Card Number: 88–32806
ISBN: 0–313–24646–7 (set)
ISBN: 0–313–26725–1 (v. 1)
ISBN: 0–313–27357–X (v. 2)

First published in 1990

Greenwood Press, 88 Post Road West, Westport, CT 06881
An imprint of Greenwood Publishing Group, Inc.

Printed in the United States of America

The paper used in this book complies with the
Permanent Paper Standard issued by the National
Information Standards Organization (Z39.48–1984).

10 9 8 7 6 5 4 3 2 1

Contents

Consultants and Contributors

CONSULTANTS

Susan K. Ahern, Language and Literature, Department of English, University of Houston-Downtown Houston, Texas

Susan G. Cole, Classics, Department of History, University of Illinois at Chicago, Chicago, Illinois

Carol Klimick Cyganowski, American Literature, Department of English and Women's Studies Program, DePaul University, Chicago, Illinois

Helene P. Foley, Classics, Classics Department, Barnard College, Columbia University, New York, New York

Geraldine Forbes, Indian History and Literature, Department of History, State University of New York at Oswego, Oswego, New York

Marilyn Gottschalk, Fine Arts, Women's Studies Department, University of Wisconsin-Platteville, Platteville, Wisconsin

Mary Gomez Parham, Iberian and Latin American History and Literature, Department of Humanities, University of Houston-Downtown, Houston, Texas

Annis Pratt, Language and Literature, Department of English, University of Wisconsin-Madison, Madison, Wisconsin

Ann Waltner, East Asian History and Literature, Department of History, University of Minnesota, Minneapolis, Minnesota

CONTRIBUTORS

Laura Niesen de Abruña, Department of English, Ithaca College, Ithaca, New York

Marjorie Agosin, Department of Spanish, Wellesley College, Wellesley, Massachusetts

Susan K. Ahern, Department of English, University of Houston-Downtown, Houston, Texas

Kathleen Ashley, Department of English, University of Southern Maine, Gorham, Maine

Marina Astman, Department of Russian, Barnard College of Columbia University, New York, New York

Charlene Ball, Department of English, Georgia Institute of Technology, Atlanta, Georgia

Tarcisio Beal, Departments of History, Religious Studies, and Peace and Justice Studies, Incarnate Work College, San Antonio, Texas

Marianne Berardi, Kansas City Art Institute, Kansas City, Missouri

Paal Björby, Department of Scandinavian Studies, University of Oregon, Eugene, Oregon

Janice M. Bogstad, Chalmer Davee Library, University of Wisconsin-River Falls, River Falls, Wisconsin

Edith Borroff, Department of Music, University Center at Binghamton, State University of New York, Binghamton, New York

Betsy Bowden, Department of English, Camden College of Arts and Sciences, Rutgers University, Camden, New Jersey

Jane Bowers, Department of Music, University of Wisconsin-Milwaukee, Milwaukee, Wisconsin

Laurie Buchanan, Department of English, Illinois State University, Normal, Illinois

Albrecht Classen, Department of German, University of Arizona, Tucson, Arizona

Jane Crisler, Department of English, DePaul University, Chicago, Illinois

Ralph Croizier, Department of History, University of Victoria, Victoria, British Columbia

Leo C. Curran, Department of Classics, University at Buffalo, State University of New York, Buffalo, New York

Carol Klimick Cyganowski, Department of English and Women's Studies Program, DePaul University, Chicago, Illinois

Josephine Donovan, Department of English, Boston University, Boston, Massachusetts

Penelope J. Engelbrecht, Department of English, DePaul University, Chicago, Illinois

Peter Erickson, Sterling and Francine Clark Art Institute, Williamstown, Massachusetts

Virginia Eskin, Concert Pianist, Boston, Massachusetts

Claire R. Farrer, Department of Anthropology, California State University, Chico, California

Nona Fienberg, Department of English, Millsaps College, Jackson, Mississippi

Ruth Firestone, Department of Foreign Languages, Fort Hays State University, Hays, Kansas

Kathy Fletcher, Department of Theatre Arts and Dance, University of Nebraska-Lincoln, Lincoln, Nebraska

Lucy M. Freibert, Department of English, University of Louisville, Louisville, Kentucky

Carole Ganim, Core Faculty, Union Institute, Cincinnati, Ohio

Julia M. Gergits, Department of Communications, Oregon Institute of Technology, Klamath Falls, Oregon

Mary Ellis Gibson, Department of English, University of North Carolina at Greensboro, Greensboro, North Carolina

Janet N. Gold, Department of Foreign Languages and Literatures, Bates College, Lewiston, Maine

Clia M. Goodwin, University Library, University of New Hampshire, Dover, New Hampshire

Karen Gould, Department of Romance Languages, Bowling Green State University, Bowling Green, Ohio

Nancy Gray, Department of English, California State Polytechnic University, Pomona, California

Elizabeth Grossman, Department of Art and Architecture, Rhode Island School of Design, Providence, Rhode Island

Nan Hackett, Department of English, Iowa State University, Ames, Iowa

Susan Hawkins, Department of English, Oakland University, Rochester, Michigan

Nancy G. Heller, Department of Art, University of Maryland, College Park, Maryland

Melissa Hensley, St. Louis, Missouri

Carolivia Herron, Department of Afro-American Studies and Comparative Studies, Harvard University, Cambridge, Massachusetts

Kathleen Hickok, Department of English, University of Iowa, Iowa City, Iowa

Anne S. Higham, Norfolk, Virginia

Sharon Shih-jiuan Hou, Department of Modern Languages and Literatures, Pomona College, Claremont, California

Faith Ingwersen, Scandinavian Studies, University of Wisconsin-Madison, Madison, Wisconsin

Lorna Irvine, Department of English, George Mason University, Fairfax, Virginia

Naomi Jacobs, Department of English, University of Maine at Orono, Orono, Maine

Natalie Boymel Kampen, Department of Art, University of Rhode Island, Kingston, Rhode Island

Lynn Keller, Department of English, University of Wisconsin-Madison, Madison, Wisconsin

Carol Farley Kessler, Department of English and American Studies, Delaware County Campus, Pennsylvania State University, Media, Pennsylvania

Jean Kittrell, Department of English Language and Literature, University of Southern Illinois at Edwardsville, Edwardsville, Illinois

Helga Kress, University of Iceland, Reykjavik, Iceland

Amelia Howe Kritzer, Department of Theater and Drama, University of Wisconsin-Madison, Madison, Wisconsin

Laifong Leung, Department of East Asian Languages and Literatures, University of Alberta, Edmonton, Alberta

Carole Levin, Department of History, State University of New York, New Paltz, New Paltz, New York

Joan H. Levin, Department of Italian, Vassar College, Poughkeepsie, New York

Naomi Lindstrom, Department of Spanish and Portuguese, University of Texas at Austin, Austin, Texas

Sharon Locy, Department of English, Loyola Marymount University, Los Angeles, California

Nellie McKay, Department of Afro-American Studies, University of Wisconsin-Madison, Madison, Wisconsin

Marylou Martin, Department of Foreign Languages, Hendrix College, Conway, Arkansas

Susan Matisoff, Department of Asian Languages, Stanford University, Stanford, California

Elizabeth A. Meese, Department of English, University of Alabama, Tuscaloosa, Alabama

Amalia Mondríquez, Department of Foreign Languages, Incarnate Word College, San Antonio, Texas

Ruth Nadelhaft, University College, University of Maine at Orono, Bangor, Maine

Vasudha Narayanan, Department of Religion, University of Florida, Gainesville, Florida

Usha Nilsson, South Asia Studies Program, University of Wisconsin-Madison, Madison, Wisconsin

Mary Kay Norseng, Scandinavian Section, University of California, Los Angeles, Los Angeles, California

Judith W. Page, Department of English, Millsaps College, Jackson, Mississippi

J. Bernardo Pérez, Department of Spanish, Portuguese and Classics, Rice University, Houston, Texas

Carol O. Perkins, Women's Studies Department, San Diego State University, San Diego, California

Elizabeth Petroff, Department of Comparative Literature, University of Massachusetts at Amherst, Amherst, Massachusetts

Cyrena N. Pondrom, Department of English, University of Wisconsin-Madison, Madison, Wisconsin

Annis Pratt, Department of English, University of Wisconsin-Madison, Madison, Wisconsin

Edith E. Pross, College of Humanities, Houston Baptist University, Houston, Texas

Sherry Reames, Department of English, University of Wisconsin-Madison, Madison, Wisconsin

Betsy Cogger Rezelman, Department of Fine Arts, St. Lawrence University, Canton, New York

Bette B. Roberts, Department of English, Westfield State College, Westfield, Massachusetts

Paul S. Ropp, Department of History, Clark University, Worcester, Massachusetts

Norma L. Rudinsky, Department of English, Oregon State University, Corvallis, Oregon

Rinaldina Russell, Department of Romance Languages, Queens College, Flushing, New York

Ute Margarete Saine, Woodside, California

Jo O'Brien Schaefer, Department of English, University of Pittsburgh, Pittsburgh, Pennsylvania

Mary Anne Schofield, Department of English, St. Bonaventure University, St. Bonaventure, New York

Sally Schwager, Director, Women's History Institute, Harvard Graduate School of Education, Cambridge, Massachusetts

Carol A. Senf, Department of English, Georgia Institute of Technology, Atlanta, Georgia

Victoria L. Shannon, Chicago, Illinois

Paul Smith, Department of English, Carnegie Mellon University, Pittsburgh, Pennsylvania

Eva Stigers Stehle, Department of Classics, University of Maryland, College Park, Maryland

Gloria Stephenson, Department of English, University of Wisconsin-Platteville, Platteville, Wisconsin

Phyllis H. Stock-Morton, Department of History, Seton Hall University, South Orange, New Jersey

Mary Rose Sullivan, Department of English, University of Colorado at Denver, Denver, Colorado

Freida High Tesfagiorgis, Department of Afro-American Studies, University of Wisconsin-Madison, Madison, Wisconsin

Dominique Thévenin, Department of Foreign Languages, University of Wisconsin-Eau Claire, Eau Claire, Wisconsin

Elizabeth Boyd Thompson, Department of English, Purdue University, West Lafayette, Indiana

Lasse T. Tiihonen, Department of Spanish and Portuguese, Baylor University, Waco, Texas

Rima de Vallbona, Department of Spanish, University of St. Thomas, Houston, Texas

Tomás Vallejos, Department of English, University of Houston-Downtown, Houston, Texas

Annette Van Dyke, Associate Director of Women's Studies, University of Cincinnati, Cincinnati, Ohio

Nancy Vedder-Shults, Women's Studies Program, University of Wisconsin-Madison, Madison, Wisconsin

Victoria V. Vernon, Department of Comparative Literatures, Hamilton College, Clinton, New York

Ronald H. Wainscott, Department of Theatre Arts and Dance, University of Nebraska-Lincoln, Lincoln, Nebraska

Cheryl Walker, Department of English, Scripps College, Claremont, California

Elizabeth Webby, Department of English, The University of Sydney, Sydney, New South Wales

Marsha Weidner, McIntire Department of Art, University of Virginia, Charlottesville, Virginia

Marta Weigle, Department of American Studies, University of New Mexico, Albuquerque, New Mexico

Robin Wheeler, President, Performing Arts Consultants, Boston, Massachusetts

Maya Bijvoet Williamson, American University in Cairo, Cairo, Egypt

Katharina M. Wilson, Department of Comparative Literature, University of Georgia, Athens, Georgia

Kaye Winder, Department of Fine Arts, University of Wisconsin-Platteville, Platteville, Wisconsin

Introduction

The emphasis in this volume of the *Women's Studies Encyclopedia* is on women as producers of literature, art, and music. There are also articles on other aspects of women's relationships to writing and the fine arts and on women's education, since women's participation in a society's "higher culture" has depended upon the extent and quality of their education. The primary focus is on the United States and on literature in English, but greater attention is given both to other Western and to non-Western women than was possible in the first volume of the *Encyclopedia*.

Most articles present the results of current research on a topic, with, in many cases, a short bibliography following the article. In a few cases, in which the current state of research on the topic or the nature of the topic itself seems to warrant it, the articles themselves are mainly bibliographic.

Since the arrangement of articles presented several problems that seemed to have no completely satisfactory solutions, some rather arbitrary decisions were made. In general, for the period from the Reformation to the present, articles about women writers and artists of specific countries or regions other than the British Isles and the United States are listed under national or regional rubrics (e.g., African, Chinese, Eastern European, Swedish). Since the culture of the United States originated directly from English roots and was, through the nineteenth century, heavily dependent upon Britain, the articles about British and United States' writers are grouped together under generic rubrics and are listed chronologically, with articles about British women preceding those about women from the United States. Articles about the portrayal or image of women in literature and art are generally under the rubric of the period (e.g., Romantic period literature, Victorian literature).

Space limitations alone would prevent any single volume from giving adequate coverage to the relationships between women and literature and the arts. It was impossible to get articles on all countries and regions and to cover all aspects of the arts. The predominance of articles about literature reflects both the greater participation by women in literature than in the other arts and the greater concentration of feminist scholarship in this area.

All articles are signed by the contributors. Those that carry no signature were written by the editor.

WOMEN'S STUDIES ENCYCLOPEDIA

A

AESTHETICS, FEMININE (also known as female aesthetics or feminist aesthetics). Debates continue as to whether there is such a thing, what it is or might be, and what it might do. Of central importance to such debates are the questions of what "woman" is and what happens to traditional notions of art when women become subjects and creators as well as objects of artistic expression. In addition, once feminine aesthetics is claimed and given shape, there arises the question of whether it pertains exclusively to women or whether it incorporates those concerns and practices shared by any group of people marked "other" and marginal by dominant culture.

Aesthetics is that which provides a theory of the beautiful and of art. In Western patriarchal culture, it is assumed that art and beauty are universal categories of truth. Feminist theory, however, reveals the extent to which such universals are actually androcentric (man-centered) specifics coded as the norm and thus not accessible to women within the system of cultural expectation. This fact holds true in parallel fashion for identifications of race and class (among others) as well as gender. Woman marks the sexual category of Man; it is a culturally produced image bearing little resemblance to, though powerfully influential for, actual women. As muse, primordial origin, eternal mystery, object of desire and loathing, Woman constitutes the enabling inspiration as well as the raw material of art; beauty can scarcely be encountered without evoking Woman. Feminist theory demystifies this Woman-image to reveal her existence as myth or ideological construct and to enable women to enact themselves as subjects and artists. Such enactments are variously described as nonlinear processes based on subjectivity, as shifting and multiple rather than stable and monolithic, as prepatriarchal ideals of female-centered experience, or as invisible and unspoken realities breaking through barriers of repression and silence. Important to the debate over feminine aesthetics is the argument between essentialism (woman by nature is . . .) and production (culture assigns and teaches gender), with most current feminist theory eschewing the all-too-familiar traps of essentialism.

Feminine aesthetics is a problematic term precisely because, in a male-dominant culture, anything feminine is understood as "other" and inferior. Many current female artists and writers, therefore—especially if they are avant-garde or feminist—purposely call attention to Woman in order to unmask the myth. Women's performance art and " *écriture féminine*" (a means to female-centered language through "writing the body") are but two examples of women using the female body, for instance, to claim female subjectivity while disrupting the androcentric codes. Because so much of women's art and writing, purposely or not, functions in the world to change the world, the term perhaps most appropriate to its accompanying theory is feminist aesthetics.

Further References. Gisela Ecker (ed.), *Feminist Aesthetics,* trans. Harriet Anderson (Boston, 1985). Teresa de Lauretis, *Alice Doesn't: Feminism, Semiotics, Cinema* (Bloomington, Ind., 1984). Rachel Blau Du Plessis and Members of Workshop 9, "For the Etruscans: Sexual Difference and Artistic Production—The Debate over a Female Aesthetic," in Hester Eisenstein and Alice Jardine (eds.), *The Future of Difference* (Boston, 1980).

NANCY GRAY

AFRICAN ARTISTS. Women artists assume an important role in art production throughout Africa. They create artworks in a wide range of techniques including weaving, pottery, basketry, mural painting, fabric dyeing, beadwork, body decoration, and, more recently, metalwork and woodcarving. In general, African women artists can be divided into two broad categories: traditional and modern. Traditional artists work within the limitations of gender proscriptions and prototypes that are imposed by society, while modern artists produce works within and outside of such structural boundaries and are far more flexible in their selection of materials and personal expression. Both groups constitute the historical continuum in the art of African women. The first group sustains artistic traditions that are centuries old, while the second intervenes in society to add modern dimension to culture indicative of social transformation. Women artists, whether traditional or modern, complement male artists in formulating the essential female-male duality that has long been established in African art and life.

Within their particular societies, traditional women artists produce functional artworks that are highly valued. Their creativity centers around their own household responsibilities and is, therefore, primarily produced within domestic settings, where they acquire their skills from older women, usually relatives. Functionally, however, artworks serve both domestic and public spheres. For example, pottery is used in the home for cooking and storage, yet it is also used in ceremonies of the larger community. Public demands for such works, which meet religious, social, and political needs, provide women with some degree of economic independence. Additionally, such demands emphasize their value as participants in the life-sustaining practices of their society.

Modern African women artists work in contexts and systems that are radically different from those of the traditional artists. They develop their artistic skills through formal education in institutions controlled by men, including foreigners. As in most modern societies, their artworks are not central to everyday life and, therefore, fall to the periphery of life's activities. Consequently, modern women artists, like their male counterparts, must create a place for themselves in their various societies as they confront the global arena of exhibitions, reviews, etc. Some preparation to meet this challenge is made in the educational institutions where the artists interact in a social climate that is characterized by competitiveness in teacher-student roles and in peer associations. Perhaps the primary compensation for the artist's marginal status and competitive life-style is her "freedom" to choose materials, forms, and themes to produce artworks according to the dictates of her intellect.

In general, African women artists remain virtually unknown to the Western world. Indeed, few traditional women artists have become recognized outside of their indigenous societies; however, a number of modern women artists are beginning to develop reputations in African and European countries. Those who are achieving recognition are artists of the current generation, although some are known to have been active in and outside Africa for several decades. Suzanna Ogunjami, a Nigerian, for example, is listed in a 1935 Harmon Foundation catalogue as having an exhibition at Delphic Studio in New York during the same year. Artists' works are commanding more attention today because artists are more active on the European art scene. At this point, it would be premature to suggest the most significant modern African artists because of the dearth of scholarship in this area of contemporary art. It is appropriate, however, to identify some who are periodically presented in the literature. They are Miranda Burney-Nicol of Sierra Leone (b.1928), E. Betty Manyolo of Uganda (b.1938), Kamala Ishag of Sudan (b.1939), Clara Ugbodaga of Nigeria, Afi Ekong of Nigeria, Rosemary Karuga of Uganda, Helen Sebidi of South Africa (b.1943), Theresa Musoke of Uganda (b.1944), Assa Djionne of Senegal/France, Oyenike Olaniyi (Nike) of Nigeria, Sokari Douglas Camp of Nigeria (b.1957), and Kate Appiah of Ghana (b.1962).

The artists noted above work in a wide range of materials and styles that defy traditional restrictions. Metal sculpture, oil, and batik painting are among their various techniques. It is difficult to classify their styles since they do not fall into Western established categories. Many works, however, are figurative and share a common thread—a thematic focus on humanity in its various manifestations. Images, ranging from aspects of traditional life to urban political unrest, suggest the diversity in their social consciousness. Although the artists themselves tend to reject the notion of a feminist quality in their works, many compositions, oppositionally, exhibit some element of womanist interpretations. Women subjects, for example, assume active, positive, and multiple roles that significantly transform the prevailing nurturing prototype of women in the works of men.

Another characteristic in these works is the influence of traditional African art that emerges in stylized figuration, patterning, and color.

Historically, African women artists have met the demands of social change in both traditional and modern contexts. Whether these artists remain central or marginal to society, they give shape to ideas that illuminate their own psychological, cultural, social, and political situation, as well as their assessment of global issues. While they do not profess a feminist perspective, their works are enlivened with knowledge gained from women's personal experience. They present to the world an exciting new dimension in contemporary art that expands its pluralist character and challenges the modern scholar to de-Europeanize and demasculinize the pervasive territorial boundaries of art historical inquiry.

Further References. Lisa Aronson, "Women in the Arts," in Margaret S. Hay and Sharon Stichter (eds.), *African Women South of the Sahara* (London, 1984). Kojo Fosu, *Twentieth Century Art in Africa* (Zaria, Nigeria, 1986).

FREIDA HIGH TESFAGIORGIS

AFRICAN WRITERS. Since 1960, publications by *black African women writers* have experienced rapid increase and accelerating respect within and beyond the African continent. The most prominent sub-Saharan and Sahelian nations and their writers in this flourishing of black African women's writing are Cameroon (Werewere Liking), Congo (Cécile-Ivelse Diamoneka, Amelica Néné, Marie-Léontine Tsibinda), Ghana (Christiana Ama Ata Aidoo, Asare Konadu, Efua Theodora Sutherland), Kenya (Micere Githae Mugo, Rebeka Njau, Grace Ogot), Mozambique (Noémia de Sousa), Nigeria (Buchi Emecheta, Flora Nwapa, Zulu Sofola, Adaora Lily Ulasi), Senegal (Mariama Bâ, Annette M'baye d'Erneville, Aminata Maïga Ka, Aminata Sow Fall), South Africa (Jane Chifamba, Bessie Head, Miriam Tlali), Tanzania (Martha Mvungi), and Zaire (Ikole Bolumbo, Marie-Eugénie Mpongo, Tol'Ande Myeya, Madiya Nzuji). These novelists, poets, and dramatists write and publish their work primarily in French and English, although some such as Efua Theodora Sutherland in the Akan language and Martha Mvungi in Swahili also publish in African languages. Writers working primarily in African languages include Jane Chifamba (South Africa) in Shona and Beverly B. Mack (United States), who has edited a volume of Hausa women's poetry ("Walcokin Mata: Hausa Women's Oral Poetry"[diss., University of Wisconsin-Madison, 1981]). Very little African women's writing is available in Portuguese, although respect for the widely anthologized poetry of Noémia de Sousa has been well established since 1960.

The life and work of Mariama Bâ of Senegal have become emblematic of the power and creativity of black African women writers. When her *Une si longue lettre* (So Long a Letter) was published in 1979, she achieved almost instantaneous audience and respect for her work, which was awarded the Noma Prize at the 1980 Frankfurt Book Fair. This first novel focuses on acts of cultural independence by a Senegalese woman, Ramatoulaye, who suffers from the effects of polygamy and who, upon widowhood, refuses to marry her brother-in-law, Tamsir, as is dictated by tradition. Bâ died in 1981, prior to the publication of her second novel, *Un chant écarlate* (A Scarlet Cry).

The literary concern with the choices available to black African women as well as the depiction of African intracultural, colonial, and postcolonial conflict is also powerfully present in the writings of Buchi Emecheta, Aminata Sow Fall, Flora Nwapa, and Grace Ogot. Emecheta's *The Bride Price* and *The Slave Girl* are concerned both with gender conflicts and with tensions of intracultural influence and change. The tensions of such changes are also emphasized in Aminata Sow Fall's *Le Revenant* (The Spector), in which a young African man chooses to fake his own death in response to local pressure. Nwapa and Ogot, while giving acute attention to the details of women's lives in their novels, focus thematically on the effects of cross-cultural change on individuals, male and female, within local African communities. Bessie Head, a South African who wrote from exile in Botswana until her death in 1986, has written novels of intense artistic power that focus on themes of exile, racial mixture, racism, cultural exclusion, insanity, African oral tradition, and love.

Black African women dramatists such as Aidoo, Micere Mugo, Sutherland, and Liking have focused primarily on political and cultural issues. Christiana Ama Ata Aidoo's *The Dilemma of a Ghost* details conflicts between African and African-American heritage for the protagonist. Efua Sutherland's *Edufa*, on the other hand, is meticulously circumscribed within the local African community.

Alongside the rapid growth of imaginative literature by black African women there has been a surge in the publication of oral narrative and autobiography. Such works as *Nisa*, edited by Marjorie Shostak, *Three Swahili Women*, edited by Sarah Mirza and Margaret Strobel, and *Die Swerfjare van Poppie Nongema* (*Poppie*, in Eng. trans.), a collaboration between a black South African woman (Poppie Nongema) and the white South African woman Else Joubert, are examples not only of interest in autobiography but of focus on native African languages.

The most prominent *North African women writers* are Fatima Mernissi (Morocco), Alifa Rifaat (Egypt), Nawal el Saadawi (Egypt), and Fettouma Touati (Algeria). All of these women have elaborated and analyzed problems of male-female conflict in Muslim society. El Saadawi is highly prolific in fiction and nonfiction and is dedicated to depicting, analyzing, and helping to correct the problems of Arab women. Mernissi has published several works of nonfiction concerned primarily with women's issues. Autobiography is also rapidly developing in North African countries as evidenced by the work of Fadhma Amrouche and Wédád Zenié-Ziegler and Fatima Mernissi's own edition of interviews with Moroccan women (*Doing Daily Battle*).

Among *white African women writers living in Africa* Nadine Gordimer is the most prominent. Her South African tales and novels, which focus thematically on the tensions and dire prophecies evoked by aparthied, provide imaginative, provocative, creative, and complex renderings of her country's racial and personal tensions. Her insistence upon examining racial and social problems in literary form separates Gordimer dramatically from earlier white African women writers such as Beryl Markham and Isak Dinesen, who rarely depicted racial tensions explicitly. Olive Schreiner (1855–1920) is the earliest internationally recognized white African woman novelist, and her work focuses thematically on issues of race and cultural conflict. White African women writers living outside of Africa include Doris Lessing, who is treated more fully under NOVELISTS, BRITISH (TWENTIETH-CENTURY).

Several *diaspora African women writers* living in Africa are contributing to the rapidly developing canon of African literature. Among these are Peggy Appiah (England/Ghana), Maryse Conde (Guadeloupe/Sahelian Africa), Elizabeth Delaygue (France/Comores), and Myriam Warner-Vieyra (Guadeloupe/Senegal).

CAROLIVIA HERRON

AFRICAN-AMERICAN ARTISTS. The earliest known artworks by African-American women are crafted objects produced by anonymous slave women during the antebellum period. Crafted art production continued after the emancipation of slaves and remains a vital component of African-American culture today. Predominant techniques are textile and basketmaking traditions, which are directly linked to artworks in African societies, especially to those located in West and Central Africa, where the American slave population originated.

In accordance with American colonial practices, which maintained gender divisions in art production, slave women created works in materials and techniques that were prescribed to female artistry, such as weaving, embroidery, quiltmaking, and basketmaking, functional art creating objects specifically designed for household purposes. There is substantial evidence that some of these skills were brought from Africa to America (e.g., coiled basketmaking techniques of South Carolina and Georgia). Although African-American female and male art production differed (men employing techniques in blacksmithing, woodcarving, pottery, and architecture, among others), a complementary pattern functioned to sustain the rich cultural memory of the African heritage.

Luiza Combs (1853–1947) and Harriet Powers (1837–1911) are the earliest identified women artisans. Combs, born in Guinea (West Africa), was taken as a child into slavery to Hazard, Kentucky. Powers was born into slavery in Athens, Georgia. Both produced works that significantly link African heritage to American experience in women's creative expression. Little is known about their lives and works: only a woven blanket dated c.1890 remains of Combs's work; two quilts appliquéd with biblical, social, and personal imagery and dated c.1886 and c.1895–1898 are attributed to Powers. Combs's blanket demonstrates technical expertise in dyeing and weaving that is directly connected to Guinea. Strip weaving, earth colors, and poly-rhythmic broken line motifs convey particular aesthetic modes of that African continuum. Similar characteristics are present in Powers's quilts; however, more of an African and European blend in aesthetic canon and technique is apparent. Particular influences of appliqué textiles of the

Fon people in the Republic of Benin (formerly Dahomey) are recognizable in the color scheme, stylized figuration, technique, and narrative character that merges religious, social, and personal histories. European influences are evident in the technique and in the type of religious and social history depicted.

While crafted artworks by African-American slave women are valued for their preservation of the African heritage and for their distinctive African and European mixture, they are also important because they explicitly demonstrate that African-American women ingeniously engaged in aesthetic evaluation and creative expression as they met domestic responsibility.

Freeborn Edmonia Lewis (c.1843–1900), of African-American and Native American parentage, began to make her mark prior to emancipation and later became the first African-American sculptor to gain recognition. Her style was neo-classical, but her subject matter often departed from neo-classical references in favor of people and circumstances relevant to her dual heritage. *Forever Free* (1867) and *Hagar* (1875) are two of her best-known works. Of marble (as are most of her works), both project statements about struggles and triumphs over slavery and oppression. Although she expatriated to Rome in 1865 and associated with the White Mamorean flock (American women sculptors who lived in Rome and worked in marble), Lewis remained conscious of her personal identity while producing a body of thematically diverse sculpture. Exhibitions, reviews, commissions, and an honorable mention in the 1876 Centennial Exhibition in Philadelphia attest to her achievement. Her works can be found in various collections including those of the National Museum of American Art, Howard University, and Harvard University.

African-American women artists emerged in significant numbers during the twentieth century. Their art production encompasses a variety of styles and media, and their professional experience is diverse. In general, their lives and works are best understood within the matrix of the cultural, social, and political experience of two major epochs particularly significant for African-American artistic expression, the New Negro of the 1920s and 1930s (also known as the Harlem Renaissance) and the Civil Rights/Black Power of the 1950s and 1960s. Both periods were charged with a social and political fervor that reaffirmed African-American cultural pride and spirit of self-determination. The postsixties period might be considered as a third era that marked a significant stage of development, particularly for African-American women artists. Works of these later decades suggest that many women artists were more cognizant of womanist experience. While their works do not fall into Euro-American feminist paradigms, an interesting Afrifemcentrist (African-female-centered) mode is prevalent that has yet to be examined. (*Afrifemcentrist* is a term that was coined by the writer and presented as *Afrofemcentrist* in 1984.)

Meta Vaux Warrick Fuller (1877–1967), May Howard Jackson (1877–1931), Annie Walker (1855–1929), and Laura Wheeler Waring (1887–1968) were artists who worked just prior to and during the New Negro movement. Sculptors Fuller and Jackson produced forms enlivened with feelings of strength and pride while

Waring and Walker presented a similar consciousness in painting. Little is known about Walker, but Waring is noted for her mastery of portraiture, especially of prominent figures of the Harlem Renaissance. Fuller has the highest reputation of the women artists of the period. Her imagery, in Romantic and Impressionist styles, is infused with racial uplift, cultural identity, and Pan-American politics, all of which foreshadowed major ideological developments in the African-American art of her time and influenced that of successive generations.

Elizabeth Prophet (1890–1960), Alma Thomas (1894–1978), Augusta Savage (1900–1962), Selma Burke (b.1901), Delilah Pierce (b.1904), Lois Jones (b.1905), Elizabeth Catlett (b.1915), and Margaret Burroughs (b.1917) are prominent among the artists who followed. Prophet, Savage, Burke, and Catlett were/ are sculptors; the others, painters. In addition, Catlett has mastered various printmaking processes, and Burroughs also produces prints. Much like their predecessors, each artist created works that reaffirmed a commitment to African-American life. (It is important to say at this point that, although themes of African-American art centered on African-American life and experience, the artworks often present universal emotions, i.e., celebration, grief, anger, pride, etc.) Foremost, artists sought to master their medium while expressing ideas about social, cultural, political, and/or personal issues, in styles that ranged from realism to abstraction. Their success is implicit in their exhibits, awards, and general ability to achieve in spite of the Euroethnic pallocratic slant of the art establishment. Invariably, these women created challenges, not only for themselves, but also for their successors who gained strength through their triumphs. Interestingly, several founded art institutions: Savage established the Savage School of Arts and Crafts in New York in 1932; Burroughs, the DuSable Museum of African-American History in Chicago in 1961; and Burke, the Selma Burke Art Center in Pittsburgh in 1968.

Artists without formal art education are also important in African-American art. Prominent are Clementine Hunter (1885–1988), Minnie Evans (1892–1987), and Gertrude Morgan (1900–1980). Hunter and Evans were domestics while Morgan was a preacher. All turned to painting late in life and command great respect as visionary artists.

The most prominent of the artists listed above is Catlett, who began to emerge in the 1940s. Catlett's sculpture and prints have long sustained a vision of women's diversity, activism, and strength and thus stand on the cutting edge of Afrifemcentrist and general feminist orientations. *Homage to My Young Black Sisters* (1968) is one of her most popular works. A stylized, organically robust female form sculpted in wood, *Homage* depicts woman's powerful presence in the struggle against oppression, emphasized by its upwardly thrusting clenched fist. Celebrating the involvement of Women of Color in the battle for human rights, it exemplifies Catlett's commitment to the working class and her ability to speak universally for women in an idiom influenced by African and Mexican aesthetics.

Many artists have become visible since Catlett, some of her generation and far greater numbers of later generations. While their technical approaches to creativity have broadened to include video, performance, and multimedia installations, their struggles for success do not differ much from those of their predecessors. Their styles, however, are more acceptable within the art establishment, partly because of general postmodernist trends that overlap with ongoing African-American social consciousness and artistic variation. Among the many artists who have or are developing national and international reputations are Marie Johnson-Calloway (b.1920), Samella Lewis (b.1924), Betye Saar (b.1926), Barbara Chase Riboud (b.1930), Faith Ringgold (b.1934), Camille Billops (b.1934), Mildred Thompson (b.1936), Margo Humphrey (b.1924), Mary O'Neal (b.1924), Howardina Pindell (b.1943), Evelyn Terry (b.1946), Freida High W. Tesfagiorgis (b.1946), Winnie Owens (b.1949), Martha Jackson-Jarvis (b.1952), Adrian Piper (b. c.1950s), Virginia Meek (b.1950), and Allison Saar (b.1956). Samella Lewis is particularly significant as a painter who has placed her painting in the background of art historical discourse and curatorial practice. Through her research, publications (a journal, *International Review of African-American Art*, and book [see below]), and Museum of African-American Art in California, founded in 1976, the art of African-American women and men has been documented and exhibited. Like Savage, Burke, and Burroughs, she has become an institution. Billops, too, is significant in the preservation of art and culture through the Hatch-Billops Collection that she and her husband, James Hatch, officially established in New York in 1974.

Altogether, these artists are producing some very exciting works that are largely autobiographical, sociological, cultural, political, and psychological. While the artists vary in style and technique, an impressive common strand is evident in their self-defined, self-directed visual statements about life as they know it, statements about identity that defy any feminine stereotype. Equally as impressive are their dynamic sense of color and dramatic manipulation of rhythm, which, however abstract, build upon long-established principles in African-American culture.

Further References. David Driskell, *Two Hundred Years of African-American Art* (New York, 1976). Jacqueline Fonvielle-Bontemps and Arna A. Bontemps, *Forever Free: Art by African-American Women 1862–1980* (Normal, Ill., 1980). Samella Lewis, *Art: African-American* (rev. ed. Miami, Fla., 1978). John Vlach, *The Decorative Tradition in Afro-American Art* (Cleveland, 1978).

FREIDA HIGH TESFAGIORGIS

AFRICAN-AMERICAN POETS. Women poets are significant in numbers and are leaders in the African-American literary tradition. The earliest extant writing by an American black, "Bars Fight," is a short poem in tetrameter couplets by Lucy Terry, describing an Indian raid on an English settlement near Deerfield, Massachusetts, in 1746. Today, Terry's verse is important as an historical document, not for its aesthetic value. In 1773, Phillis Wheatley's *Poems on Various Subjects, Religious and Moral* was published in London, making her the first black living in America to author a book. The American edition appeared in 1786. Wheatley, a Senegalese slave woman, was brought to America as a child. She benefited from living with a Boston family that encouraged her literary interests. Her poetry, eighteenth-century neo-classical in style, belongs to the tradition of Alexander Pope.

Prominent eighteenth- and nineteenth-century black writers included approximately a dozen black women poets. The most important was Frances Watkins Harper, who lived from 1825 to 1911. Between 1854 and 1901 Harper published at least five volumes of poetry, one novel, and political essays. A teacher and abolitionist lecturer with strong religious beliefs, she was a staunch feminist and vigorously supported the temperance movement. Her writings reflect these concerns. Nineteenth-century black women also published poetry anonymously in religious journals, magazines, and newspapers, most of which are lost. No book-length collections by individual women writers of the eighteenth or nineteenth centuries exist except for those of Wheatley and Harper.

Black women poets of the twentieth century extend and enrich the earlier tradition. The writings of Alice Dunbar Nelson, Georgia Johnson, Anne Spencer, Jessie Redmonn Fauset, Angelina Weld Gimke, and Helen Johnson represent the period between the early part of the century and the Harlem Renaissance of the 1920s, a stimulating time of artistic and cultural expression. These well-educated women wrote conventional poetry, rejecting racial themes and the social protest of their predecessors. Critics generally consider them among the minor writers of the time.

A second group of black women poets emerged between the end of the 1930s and the beginning of the 1960s. They too wrote mainly in traditional forms, but they chose the black experience for their theme. Gwendolyn Brooks, who has earned numerous awards for her work, is the most widely celebrated of them. In 1950 she received the Pulitzer Prize for *Annie Allen*, the first black American to be so honored. Others in this group include Margaret Alexander Walker, also the recipient of several awards, Margaret Burroughs, and Pauli Murray.

Influenced by the Civil Rights movement in America and simultaneous political upheavals in other parts of the world, a younger generation of women and men changed black writing drastically from the end of the 1950s through the 1960s. Combining political activity, racial consciousness, and creative expression, they produced a race-conscious literature that was visionary, immediate, nationalistic, and extremely energetic. For the poets, the symbol of the revolution became the rejection of traditional white poetic forms for the blues, jazz rhythms, and other manifestations of black vernacular speech. The oral folk tradition provided them usable patterns that expressed black pride, beauty, and strength. Deviations from traditional Western poetry such as musical accompaniments to spoken texts, the typographical variations in the uses of punctuation, the lengthening or shortening of words, and other visual changes in written texts were quickly incorporated into their style. Earlier black poets had experimented with blues and jazz rhythms, but the power of the shift in racial sensibility in the 1950s and 1960s led to what became known as the "new black poetry." Some older poets, including Gwen-dolyn Brooks, discarded the forms that had brought them fame in the white world and joined their younger colleagues in the search for a distinct black aesthetic.

The number of published black women poets has dramatically increased since the beginning of the new literary movement in the late 1950s. While many appear primarily in anthologies, magazines, and journals, others have several individual collections. Some are also outstanding for their fiction, autobiographies, and drama as well. Among the most prominent with multiple volumes of poetry and works in other genres are Maya Angelou, Nikki Giovanni, June Jordan, Audre Lorde, Ntozake Shange, Alice Walker, and Shirley Anne Williams.

Further References. Gloria T. Hull, "Black Women Poets from Wheatley to Walker," in Roseann P. Bell et al., *Sturdy Black Bridges: Visions of Black Women in Literature* (New York, 1979), 69–86. Erlene Stetson, (ed.), *Black Sister: Poetry by Black American Women, 1746–1980* (Bloomington, Ind., 1981).

NELLIE MCKAY

AFRICAN-AMERICAN PROSE WRITERS. The first published works by black women prose writers were religious autobiographies, slave narratives, and essays and speeches condemning slavery in the early part of the nineteenth century. Religious autobiography was launched with the 1836 publication of *The Life and Religious Experiences of Jarena Lee*, an evangelist, while the first black female slave narrative was Harriet Jacobs' *Incidents in the Life of a Slave Girl* in 1861. Lee spoke for the spiritual authority of black women, Jacobs for re-sistance to and triumph over slavery. Autobiographies and nonfiction prose con-demning slavery, lynching, and other racial injustices dominated black women's writings in the nineteenth century.

In contrast, twentieth-century African-American women's autobiography is a disparate body of works characterized by careful selectivity in self-revelations. These works range from childhood remembrances of slavery, written in the early 1900s, to the conscious novel that emphasizes growth and development. Women in all walks of life write about themselves, including teachers, nurses, social workers, ministers, politicians, sports figures, entertainers and writers. Excluding writers, who author few autobiographies and who are less self-revelatory in this genre than in others in which they write, most texts represent model lives. Writer Maya Angelou is unique in having written five volumes of her life story.

In the early 1830s, the publication of an antislavery tract by Maria W. Stuart, the first American woman to make a profession of the lecture circuit, launched the essay tradition in black women's writings. For many decades, the essay was relegated to magazines and newspapers. Since the late 1970s changes have occured as collections of essays by individual writers such as June Jordan and Audre Lorde have appeared.

The first printed drama by a black woman was Alice Dunbar Nelson's *Mine Eyes Have Seen*, published in *Crisis* in 1918. This publication occured at the beginning of the Harlem Renaissance, a period of intense black artistic and cultural activity that lasted until 1930. *Mine Eyes* examined black men's military obligations to America in times of war. By 1930, ten additional black women had published 20 one-act plays, mainly in journals and magazines. Several won prizes. Themes range from folk drama to comedy to lynching, birth control for poor women, and women's social roles. Contemporary critics consider Marita Bonner, a Radcliffe graduate and prize-winning essayist, the most impressive of these playwrights, especially for her expert use of Expressionist techniques in *The Purple Flower*, published in 1929. As dramatists, black women came of age with the Broadway debut of Lorraine Hansberry's acclaimed *A Raisin in the Sun* in 1959. In the wake of the Civil Rights movement of the 1960s and 1970s and the search for a distinctive black aesthetic, contemporary black women's drama reflects avant-garde experimental techniques, black theatre history, spiritual sensibilities, and the celebration of black heritage and black women's heritage. The most well-known dramatists include Alice Childress, Adrienne Kennedy, Sonia Sanchez, Maya Angelou, and Ntazake Shange.

In 1859, *Our Nig*, the first novel by a black woman, Harriet Wilson, was published in Boston. By 1900, four novels by black women had been published. The most important were *Our Nig* and Frances Watkins Harper's *Iola Leroy, or Shadows Up-lifted*. Both addressed white racism. For most of the twentieth century, short stories and novels have been the primary literary forms to engage black women writers. Most of the former continue to be published in anthologies, journals, and magazines, and few black women have collections of their own. Women's magazines that target black women audiences and anthologies published by small and/or feminist presses since the 1970s have significantly increased the number of short stories that black women publish.

Between 1900 and 1920 two novels were published by black women. Between 1920 and 1930 the number was eight, reflecting the increase in black women's literary production during the Harlem Renaissance. Zora Neale Hurston, one of the most important black women novelists of the century, wrote short fiction during the 1920s. Jessie Fauset and Nella Larsen concentrated on urban, black, middle-class women's lives and wrote two novels each. They were among the most productive members of the Renaissance. Their works, neglected for many years as products of the "genteel tradition," received wide critical appraisal in the 1980s.

Between the early 1930s and the mid–1950s, Hurston, Dorothy West, Gwendolyn Brooks, and Ann Petry were the most successful black women novelists. Hurston, who published four novels, rejected themes of racial oppression then popular in black writing in favor of exploring the internal strengths and weaknesses of the black folk culture. Critically ignored for decades, Hurston's work underwent a dramatic revival in the 1970s as the voices of black women critics joined the literary discourse. Janie, in Hurston's most celebrated work, *Their Eyes Were Watching God* (1937), a black woman in search of independent love and personal wholeness, is the first fictional black feminist heroine. West, a journalist, wrote short stories and one novel, *The Living Is Easy* (1948), examining black middle-class aspirations in early twentieth-century Boston. In 1953, Brooks, better known for her poetry, published a novel, *Maud Martha*, in which an "ordinary" young woman in Chicago discovers her positive self. Petry, also a journalist, wrote stories for children, three novels, and short fiction. *The Street* (1946), her first novel, received wider critical attention in its time than any previous black woman's novel. Her protagonist, a black working-class single mother, struggles unsuccessfully against urban ghetto deterioration.

Black American writing changed drastically in the 1960s, a time now called the Second Renaissance. The Civil Rights movement at home, the liberation of several formerly colonized African nations, and the struggle for freedom by oppressed peoples in different parts of the world had a pronounced effect on the life and literature of African Americans. Black militancy, black nationalism, and the search for dignity penetrated all areas of black endeavor. Poetry and drama responded immediately to the political situation; fiction assumed a reflective role in expressing the hopes and aspirations of a people who had suffered long because of their race. Black women's fiction since then has thoroughly explored black women's lives in relationship to race and gender. Writers consistently convey pride in black female selfhood and seek to liberate black women from the psychological restrictions black males and white males and females have imposed on them. Models come from the lives of foremothers who had no opportunity to write fiction but were nevertheless artists in other ways. The number of contemporary black women novelists and short story writers grows impressively, and includes Toni Morrison, Alice Walker, Gloria Naylor, and Jamaica Kinkaid. Black women writers have produced some of the most exciting American fiction of the last two decades.

Further References. Barbara Christian, *Black Women Novelists* (Westport, Conn., 1980). Mari Evans, *Black Women Writers (1950–1980), A Critical Evaluation* (New York, 1984). Marjorie Pryse and Hortense Spillers, *Conjuring, Black Women, Fiction, and Literary Tradition* (Bloomington, Ind., 1985).

NELLIE MCKAY

AMERICAN CLASSICAL CANON. Those writers whom the critical, publishing, and scholarly communities establish as the most significant in the national literature. As taste and critical standards are educated through the canon, it defines literary merit and promotes what it finds meritorious.

The American, or more rightly, the United States, canon has been driven by nationalist urges to assert a native literature distinct and separate from the British. While changing national identity and critical standards continually reshape the canon, it has generally been a list of Great Books by Great Men, selected and organized through chronological periods and associated with particular socio-philosophic world views, for example, Romanticism, realism, modernism. Women writers seldom neatly fit such categories, and the canon's selection of representative writers has tended to privilege males in defining the works, authors, subject matter, and techniques that are kept in print, anthologized, taught, and discussed in journals. Despite occasional brief spurts of attention to women writers, the proportion of women represented in standard anthologies of American literature hovered around 10 percent until the 1960s–1970s. Women's representation gradually increased to near 15 percent and sometimes reached 25 percent, occasionally more, in the 1980s. Across the anthologies, course syllabi, and established critical journals, however, the consensus on classic American women writers revolves around a very few names: Anne Bradstreet and often Phillis Wheatley (for the colonial era), Emily Dickinson (for the nineteenth century), and (for the twentieth century) Willa Cather, Edith Wharton, Edna St. Vincent Millay, and a sampling of poets—typically, Elizabeth Bishop, H. D., Amy Lowell, Marianne Moore, Sara Teasdale and Elinor Wylie. Women writers who were major figures in the nineteenth-century canons—Harriet Beecher Stowe, Sarah Orne Jewett, Helen Hunt Jackson, and Mary Wilkins Freeman—have essentially disappeared from the establishment lists. Only recently has critical consideration turned to assessing whether the classical canon accurately represents the history and diversity of American literature in terms of writers or readers.

From the beginnings of the United States to about 1825, the primary impetus in canon formation was defining a native literature. Early U.S. literary journals, like the *North American Review*, were established specifically to identify and advance American writing. Women writers who represented unique native contributions were included.

Anne Bradstreet was the first woman with a place in the canon, perhaps ironically because British reviewers acknowledged her as one of the first North American poets. Phillis Wheatley, the black slave poet, enjoyed international celebrity in the eighteenth century and intermittent canonization. While American critics saw her poetry as largely derivative, British attention and her singular social role ensured Wheatley's prominence. In the early period, canonization had an ambiguous relationship with literary merit and with American critics. Many early American writers were identified and developed by British reviewers and accepted because they fit the vaunted goal of a native literature.

In the midnineteenth century, other women moved into the canon when they represented distinctive features in the developing literature. Harriet Beecher Stowe was granted temporary inclusion because of her association with defining national social and political issues. Initially recognized for the national influence and international reception of her antislavery novels, *Uncle Tom's Cabin* and *Dred*, Stowe retained continuous popularity and status with her New England local color fiction. In the elite circles of nineteenth-century eastern publishing, Stowe was often the only female face. Despite Stowe's standing, editors and reviewers never treated her works with the respect generally accorded a canonical author. Her magazine editors considered themselves free to rewrite, usually without consultation. Critics have treated her works more as sociological artifact than as literature.

Later nineteenth-century women writers continued Stowe's attention to national issues and local color. In the 1870s and 1880s, new regional subjects and technical innovations brought Sarah Orne Jewett, Helen Hunt Jackson, and Mary Wilkins Freeman into the canon. Jewett, first published in the *Atlantic Monthly*, revealed rural New England deserted by young males gone west in search of opportunity. Helen Hunt Jackson (who often published under the pseudonym Saxe Holm) opened new social issues, especially mistreatment of Native Americans. Mary Wilkins Freeman displayed the dialect and repression of poor rural New England. Nineteenth-century popular and critical interest focused on their contributions of novel characters and subjects and on their realism, but they were not promoted with the force devoted to now classic male writers. Then, as now, literary reputation was established not only by acceptance and publication but by critical reviews and essays. *The Century Illustrated Monthly Magazine* solicited extended critical treatments of Henry James and Mark Twain to bolster and enlarge their reception, but no similar reputation building was devoted to their women contemporaries.

Throughout the nineteenth century, women, and especially women fiction writers, held the popular audience in volume publication, while now classic male writers found selling their work extremely difficult. Nathaniel Hawthorne even complained to his publisher that "scribbling women" monopolized the American audience. The perception that the American popular audience dismissed, or at least failed to buy, books lauded by the growing critical establishment led to the development of magazines specifically designed to promote and to provide a market for American writers. *Harper's Monthly*, the *Atlantic Monthly*, and the *Century Illustrated Monthly Magazine* provided income, markets, audience, and prestige for the writers who would comprise the classical canon. The magazines' impetus to educate the popular taste brought a firm and continuing distinction between great literature and popular literature, a distinction that would prove damning to the majority of women writers.

Magazine editors acknowledged that they promoted writers who had not succeeded with the larger reading public. Recognizing that women were the primary readers of literature, the magazines set out to educate their taste. The national magazines' power to award canonical acceptance was generally reserved for a small nucleus of male writers with strong personal and professional liaisons to each other and to the major magazines and their editors. Initially, sustained attention to writers like Henry James and Nathaniel Hawthorne came from editors' feeling the need to sell and explain these less popular writers. The liability of women writers' popularity thus became a two-edged sword. The separation between popular and critical acceptance ensured that popular writers were less likely to be ranked as classic and to be promoted through solicited reviews and essays. Decisions regarding promotion, unfortunately, were often decisions regarding prestige and status, as affected by reception as they were by critical standards.

In the last half of the nineteenth century, the editors and reviewers of literary magazines, a small group of eastern publishers, and the growing literature departments of northeastern universities effectively became the canon's arbiters. On the eastern seaboard, with the majority of publishers, presses, and journals, social factors impacted canon formation. Writers, critics, editors, and publishers comprised a sort of brotherhood, from which women were largely excluded. Quasi-institutionalized networks of old boys published and reviewed, and novices came to worship at the seats of power. While William Dean Howells and a few others became supporters of women writers, they worked within the restraints of an entrenched insider tradition of literary practice. When editors and critics groomed in the New England tradition found a place for women colleagues, that place was defined by distinctive subject matter or approaches, which established a separate place from that reserved for the male pantheon.

While the women writers of the 1870s–1890s lacked full acceptance in the canon-established male literary circles, they formed for themselves a strong and effective community. Though often geographically separated and hampered by the difficulties of travel and lack of funds, they supported each other, aesthetically, personally, and professionally.

Resentment of the popularity of women writers remained a continuing problem. The habit of decrying the American audience's tastes died hard, in part because of the general understanding that the majority of American readers were women. After 1870, as the literary marketplace failed to support growing numbers of male writers, traditionalist writers and critics grew especially misogynist in their critical preferences.

The male network of friendship and authority, tied to the national journals and major universities, did lead to the promotion of Emily Dickinson. While Dickinson's life was notably sequestered, she responded to an *Atlantic* column, "Advice to the Young Contributor." Its author, Thomas Wentworth Higginson, wielded considerable influence in promoting the fortunes of new writers, and Dickinson asked not for publication but for Higginson's response to her poetry. While Higginson hardly knew what to do with Dickinson's untraditional metrics, he recognized her genius. When volumes of Dickinson's verse were eventually published, Higginson promoted her singular voice through a series of critical articles, placing Dickinson before the canon's arbiters and pointing to qualities that made her a unique voice in American literature.

Encouraged by George Santayana's 1917 indictment of a feminine literary "genteel tradition," critics of the 1920s and 1930s redefined the canon. Women's writing on regional subjects was ejected as nostalgic, delicate, unworthy of a striving nation. Castigating the American audience who had rejected robust masculine writers, this criticism canonized masculine innovators. Walt Whitman and Samuel Clemens came into the canon; women, by and large, went out.

Despite deletions from the historical canon, the twentieth century's less centralized literary marketplace created openings for new women writers, although again women were admitted into the canon primarily because of distinctive subject matter. Willa Cather's regional subjects—Nebraska pioneers, frontier heroism, Roman Catholicism in New Mexico—placed her squarely in the tradition of her predecessors. Her early magazine writing and editing served as traditional means to belonging and recognition. *My Antonia* (1918) and *Death Comes to the Archbishop* (1927) became early classics, though Cather's inclusion in the canon lagged far behind her male contemporaries.

Edna St. Vincent Millay, like Emily Dickinson, wrote her first poems separate from the tradition and without echoes of imitation. Though her emotionally charged verse and drama were noticed for originality and technical skill, Millay was also distinctive for her cynicism, her surprising turns on expectation.

Edith Wharton broke new ground when her highly detailed portraits of society met the spirit of twentieth-century arbiters while also selling well and garnering international attention. Wharton quickly joined the American literary pantheon, even becoming, in 1920, the first woman to win the Pulitzer Prize. Along with St. Vincent Millay and Wharton, a number of women poets represent the canon's modern period. The six most frequently included—Elizabeth Bishop, H. D., Amy Lowell, Marianne Moore, Sara Teasdale, and Elinor Wylie—are all significant for technical innovation and virtuosity. Lowell and H. D. are practically synonymous with imagism, and all are masters of unconventional and unduplicated poetic systems.

While open to Wharton's portraits of society life, the canon's sense of universality and defining American subjects excluded black and other minority writers. Black women actively published and won prizes throughout the twentieth century, but only Gwendolyn Brooks has enjoyed some peripheral inclusion in the classical canon. Brooks established black life as a subject for traditional literary audiences. Brooks's status derives from her subject matter, her technical virtuosity in traditional forms, and the overwhelming number and prestige of the literary prizes she has won.

Since widely available anthologies, required reading lists, and library purchases tend to reproduce the classical canon, lack of canon status has made women's writing less available. The classical canon's concepts of a representative national literature and disdain for popular literature often belie the experiences and preferences of women readers.

Women's studies scholars of the 1970s and 1980s have focused on reconstructing the canon, rediscovering lost women writers, or creating a countercanon of women writers. While this scholarship has abated the canon's exclusiveness and increased the numbers of women writers in standard courses and texts, women remain distinctly underrepresented in the classical canon. Some feminist scholars also are concerned that reconstructing the canon or establishing alternative canons reifies the values of traditional canonical exclusion, buying into a process by which a few writers are elevated and established, to the exclusion of multiple voices.

Further Reference. Robert von Hallberg (ed.), *Canons* (Chicago, 1984).

CAROL KLIMICK CYGANOWSKI

AMERICAN LITERATURE: IMAGES OF AMERICAN WOMEN IN. In 1975, when Cheri Register identified the "Image of Women" approach as "the earliest form of feminist criticism and . . . thus the most fully developed, having already produced its own hardcover texts" ("American Feminist Literary Criticism: A Bibliographical Introduction," in Josephine Donovan [ed.], *Feminist Literary Criticism* [1975]), critical interest had already shifted. As Toril Moi pointed out ten years later in *Sexual/Textual Politics* (1985), the "image" approach—"the search for female stereotypes in the work of male writers and in the critical categories employed by male reviewers commenting on women's work"—gave way in about 1975 to analyses of works of women writers.

Earliest among "image" studies in American literature was Leslie Fiedler's *Love and Death in the American Novel* (1960), which delineates two stereotypes—the light (spiritual) and the dark (sexual) heroine. Feminist studies developed rapidly in the sixties. Katharine M. Rogers in *The Troublesome Helpmate* (1966), which traces literary misogyny from Judeo-Christian and classical to modern time, cites numerous examples from American literature. Mary Ellmann in *Thinking About Women* (1968) observes that "thought by sexual analogy" permeates Western culture. Ellmann shows how male writers and critics attribute to women characteristics such as formlessness, passivity, instability, confinement, piety, materiality, spirituality, irrationality, and compliancy and identify women as "incorrigible figures," such as the shrew and the witch. Kate Millett's *Sexual Politics* (1969) gained popularity among both academic and general readers, partially, at least, because it analyzed images of women as sex objects in works by two of the decade's most controversial American writers—Henry Miller and Norman Mailer—and did so with an authoritative aplomb that made four-letter words critically respectable.

During the seventies journal articles, anthologies, and collections of essays expanded the "image" tradition. Kimberley Snow's "Images of Women in the American Novel" (*Aphra* 2 [Winter 1970]: 56–68) and Wendy Martin's "Seduced and Abandoned in the New World: the Image of Women in American Fiction" (Vivian Gornick and Barbara K. Moran [eds.], *Women in Sexist Society* [1971]) applied the "image" approach specifically to American literature. Anthologies such as Mary Anne Ferguson (ed.), *Images of Women in Literature* (1973); Michele Murray (ed.), *A House of Good Proportion* (1973); and Carol Pearson and Katherine Pope (eds.), *Who Am I This Time?* (1976) revealed the inadequacy of negative and ideal stereotypes and thus the need to examine works by both men and women. Two collections of essays—Susan Koppelman Cornillon (ed.), *Images of Women in Fiction* (1972) and Marlene Springer (ed.), *What Manner of Woman* (1977)—pointed the same way. Koppelman Cornillon criticized the "unreal" female characters in works by both men and women, challenged the techniques of modernist writers and formalist critics, and called for new ways of reading and writing literature.

The earliest images of women in American literature by men picture woman as evil and frivolous. Thomas Weld's description of Anne Hutchison in his introduction to the second edition of John Winthrop's *A Short Story of the Rise, reign, and ruine of the Antinomians . . . And the lamentable death of Ms. Hutchison* (1644) employs satanic and serpentine imagery and finds her murder by Indians at Hell-gate providential punishment. Nathaniel Ward's *Simple Cobler of Aggawam* (1647) satirizes the Puritan woman preoccupied with fashion, labeling her "the epitome of nothing."

Eighteenth-century writers continue the pattern but focus more directly on woman's sexuality. Benjamin Franklin's treatment of his mother and of Deborah Read (*Autobiography*, 1868) reveals how minimally he regarded them. His satires also illustrate his sexist attitude, except when he allows his garrulous widow Silence Dogood and the promiscuous Polly Baker to voice his criticism of the double standard regarding sexual morality and property rights. His "Old Mistresses Apologue" (1926) reduces woman to sex object. John Trumbull's *The Progress of Dullness* (1772–1773) satirizes women as clothestrees, gossips, and readers of Samuel Richardson's sentimental novels.

When Americans begin writing novels, the virgin turns whore, falling prey to the wiles of the rake. Abandoned, she dies in childbirth, while the rake loses not a degree of social status. In the first American seduction novel, William Hill Brown's *The Power of Sympathy* (1789), stories of seduction fit into each other like Chinese boxes, the outermost dissolving when the would-be seducer repents, only to learn that the woman he loves and now wishes to marry is his sister by his father's early philandering. Although the heroine resists seduction, she dies, appalled at the near incest.

A variation on the seduction theme emerges in Charles Brockden Brown's gothic novels. Believing that higher education and financial independence would raise women's status, Brown introduces such ideas into his works. Constantia, the central female character in *Ormond* (1799), well educated and financially secure, resists Ormond's advances and kills him when he attempts rape, though as in others of Brown's novels, the woman merely reacts to circumstances.

The image of the fallen woman persists in the nineteenth and twentieth centuries, the heroine suffering either ostracism or death. Nathaniel Hawthorne's Hester Prynne wears her scarlet letter to her grave and Zenobia of *The Blithedale Romance* (1852), fallen in grace and fortune, takes her own life, as does the blemished heroine of Stephen Crane's *Maggie, A Girl of the Streets* (1893). In the twentieth century Ernest Hemingway's Catherine Barkley (*A Farewell to Arms*, 1957), like her predecessors, dies after childbirth, punished for her affair with Frederic Henry.

Generally, women characters play small parts in nineteenth-century fiction by men, except as stereotypes or as symbols. The women intended as wives and mothers in Washington Irving's stories fail even in those roles. Dame Van Winkle, described as a termagant, never appears to prove or disprove the label; Katrina Van Tassel, whose wealth and beauty beguile Ichabod Crane, slips from his grasp. Not all of James Fenimore Cooper's women are "sappy as maples and flat as a prairie," as James Russell Lowell describes them in "A Fable for

Critics'' (1848). Child-maidens, such as Alice Munro in *The Last of the Mohicans* (1826) and spirited, self-sacrificing, and conventional young women such as Elizabeth Temple in *The Pioneers* (1823), enjoy limited action, but Cooper prematurely kills off independent, strong, and sexual Cora of *The Last of the Mohicans*.

Premature death—either literal or figurative—is, in fact, commonplace for women in nineteenth-century works by men. Light and dark heroines so assigned include Hawthorne's Priscilla and Zenobia of *The Blithedale Romance* and Hilda and Miriam of *The Marble Faun* (1860), Herman Melville's Yillah and Hautia of *Mardi* (1849), and Lucy Tartan and Isabel of *Pierre* (1852). Ironically, in *Pierre,* the hero, characterized throughout the novel by female imagery, suffers an untimely death. Edgar Allan Poe's maidens, with the exception of Rowena and Ligeia, seldom appear in pairs, but whether they represent ideals of beauty (Helen), intelligence (Ulalume), or sexuality (the wife in ''The Black Cat''), they meet death early. Virgins in Melville's ''The Tartarus of Maids'' (1855) appear destined to be worn out either as millworkers or as childbearers. Some of the girls and women created by Mark Twain, who idealized the female as the guardian of home and culture, survive; others do not. Roxanne, the strong, passionate black woman of *Pudd'nhead Wilson* (1894), for example, disintegrates as a person and is sold down the river by her son.

The mature woman or mother figure in the early nineteenth century usually remains in the background, supporting and protecting husband and children, guarding the morals and asserting that things will turn out right. At mid-century Walt Whitman, sometime champion of sexual equality, errs blatantly when attempting to exalt women with the remark: ''There is nothing greater than the mother of men.'' As the century wanes, however, the mother becomes overly protective and rigidly moralistic, as illustrated by the hypocritical, drunken Irish mother in Crane's *Maggie,* who self-righteously drives her daughter into the streets. Marginally, she resembles the bitch figure that emerges as the century ends.

Three stereotypes of women appear in Henry James's *The Bostonians* (1886): the clairvoyant young woman, the lesbian, and the spinster reformer. Verena Tarrant, exploited by her parents as a public speaker and ''sold'' to Olive Chancellor, eventually finds her ''true nature'' in marriage to Basil Ransom. Olive Chancellor, the wealthy feminist reformer, who seems to have personal as well as political designs on Verena, loses out to Ransom. Miss Birdseye, a venerable spinster past her prime as an abolitionist, succumbs, like Verena, to the wills of stronger people.

Toward the end of the century, William James delineates the Bitch Goddess Success, an image that in various forms continues into the twentieth century. In ''They Shall Have Faces, Minds, and (One Day) Flesh: Women in Late Nineteenth-Century and Twentieth-Century American Literature,'' (Marlene Springer (ed.), *What Manner of Woman* [New York, 1977]), Martha Banta points out two forms—the bitch of conscience (moral tyranny) and the bitch of avarice (the greed to possess). *The Portrait of a Lady* (1881) and *The Wings of the Dove* (1902) provide examples of both. Trina Sieppe in Frank Norris's *McTeague* (1899) combines the two forms. In Theodore Dreiser's novel *Sister Carrie* (1900), Carrie Meeber represents the "sweet" bitch, luring men to her as she rises to success unmindful of the wrecks she leaves behind.

Cultural changes brought about by the first wave of the feminist movement and later aggravated by the social impact of World War I led to the development of the New Woman, one who seeks suffrage, increased sexual freedom, and a career. Male writers quickly reflected this change. Scott Fitzgerald's flapper of *This Side of Paradise* (1920) develops into a variety of bitch figures—the golden Daisy Faye Buchanan (*The Great Gatsby*, 1925), who lures Jay Gatsby to his death; Brett Ashley of Hemingway's *The Sun Also Rises* (1926), who continually teases Jake Barnes and wrecks the life and art of the young bullfighter Romero; Margot Macomber of Hemingway's "The Short Happy Life of Francis Macomber" (1938), who shoots her husband fatally; the mindless, heartless Faye Greener of Nathanael West's *The Day of the Locust* (1939), who destroys father, friends, and acquaintances as she tries to ease her own despair; and Mrs. Lillian Taylor, the black matriarch in Chester Himes's *The Third Generation* (1954), who, through her emulation of white culture, drives her doctor husband to poverty, her sons to self-destruction and crime, and herself to prostitution.

Not all women in twentieth-century novels by men are aggressive. Characters such as Dorothy in *The Fifth Column* (1938) and Maria in *For Whom the Bell Tolls* (1940) continue to represent passive servants. Examples of formlessness— soft body, soft mind—include Doris Hollis in Hemingway's *To Have and Have Not* (1937) and Elena Esposito in Norman Mailer's *The Deer Park* (1955).

Twentieth-century mother figures come in various forms, none favorable. William Faulkner's creations are either cold mothers—Mrs. Compson of *The Sound and the Fury* (1929)—or earth mothers—Lena Grove of *Light in August* (1932) and Eula Varner of *The Hamlet* (1940). Destructive mothers akin to the bitch figure include the deadly "Mommy" in Edward Albee's *The American Dream* (1961) and the comically destructive mother in Philip Roth's *Portnoy's Complaint* (1969). Black mothers range from the passive mother in James Baldwin's *Go Tell It on the Mountain* (1951), who submits herself and her children to her husband's violence, to the nagging mother in Richard Wright's *Native Son* (1940).

The most stark image to emerge in the twentieth century is woman as sex object. Promiscuous characters like Candace and Quentin Compson in Faulkner's *The Sound and the Fury* and Temple Drake in his *Sanctuary* (1931) combine whore and bitch, provoking violence and hatred in male characters that make past misogyny seem mild. The works of Henry Miller, such as the *Tropic of Cancer* (1934), *Tropic of Capricorn* (1939), *Plexus* (1949), *Sexus* (1953), and *Nexus* (1960), contain seemingly endless images of woman as cunt, sewer, whore, and bitch. Kate Millett characterizes Mailer as a "prisoner of the virility cult" who sees and depicts sex as war and war as sexual. Quoting extensively from his works, she illustrates his view of women primarily as recipients of male aggression, a salient example being Rojack's impregnating, then sodomizing Cherry, the maid, after having strangled Deborah, his wife.

Besides raising women's consciousness, the "images" approach, which gave way in the midseventies to the study of women authors, produced a generation of "resisting readers," to borrow Judith Fetterly's term, readers who would demand that literature more accurately reflect women's experience and model their possibilities.

LUCY M. FREIBERT

ARCHETYPAL CRITICISM, FEMINIST, engages literary critics in the analysis of texts to determine the impact of gender upon the way archetypes structure literary works. Archetypes are images, symbols, and narrative patterns that recur over hundreds of years, in art and religion as well as in literature, with certain constant features. They are not rigid givens, however, but complex variables modified by the personal and cultural signature of the author. For example, the Aphrodite/Venus archetype always retains the connotation of a powerful feminine sensuality as a constant, but this characteristic will be interwoven with attitudes toward it varying according to gender and culture. In the period before 1700, for example, women were considered as sensual as men, though lacking in control; after that time men and women were defined as essentially different, men experiencing strong sexuality and women ideally sexless. Thus a male poet's structuring of a poem on the Aphrodite archetype during the Renaissance would be determined, in part, by his culture's definition of women's sensuality; in the nineteenth century he would be more likely to value sexlessness in women and consider sensual women deviant. Correspondingly, a woman poet writing in the nineteenth century would punish herself for ''monstrous'' sexual desires more readily than her Renaissance counterpart. The archetypal experience of authentic feminine sensuality is interwoven in each text with overlays of cultural and gender determinants.

The feminist archetypal theory that emerges from this criticism is not dependent upon the archetypal theories of Carl Gustav Jung and his followers, nor does it conform rigidly to the theory of literary archetypes of Northrop Frye. Although aspects of Frye's and Jung's theories prove useful to feminist archetypal methods, other aspects have been critiqued and discarded. Thus when examining an archetypal narrative like the quest pattern (the journey of self-discovery undertaken by a young hero), feminist archetypal critics have noted significant differences between the quests of women and the quests of men heroes.

Some feminist archetypal critics define women writers' use of archetypes as a process of "revisioning" materials understood as basically masculine in origin, a process of usurpation of nonfeminine images and symbols and reworking them in manners appropriate to women's psychological experiences. Some of these critics assume that not only myths but language itself are masculine products. Other critics define Western European culture and its mythologies as only the most recent layer of archetypal materials in a long series of layers, tracing

Aphrodite, for example, back to the literature of Inanna in Sumeria of 2000 B.C. These critics approach the use of the archetype in a single text as the product of a dialectical relationship between recent responses and earlier responses to it, taking into consideration such mythic systems as that of Old Europe as a factor in classical mythology.

Feminist archetypal criticism draws upon the rich field of feminist theology and upon women's studies scholarship in psychology and anthropology as well as in history and the arts. Since archetypes can be understood as recurrent ways that the psyche responds to such key life experiences as sexuality, they form a useful basis for classroom discussions appropriate to women's studies emphasis on experiential pedagogy.

Further References. Estella Lauter, *Women as Mythmakers: Poetry and Visual Art by Twentieth-Century Women* (Bloomington, Ind., 1984). Estella Lauter and Carol Rupprecht, *Feminist Archetypal Theory* (Knoxville, Tenn., 1985). Annis Pratt, *Archetypal Patterns in Women's Fiction* (Bloomington, Ind., 1981).

ANNIS PRATT

ARCHITECTURE, AMERICAN: A BIBLIOGRAPHIC ESSAY. In the mid–1970s, as American women architects fought against the institutional barriers that had marginalized them, limited their numbers, and, historically, kept them out of the architectural profession altogether, so too feminists interested in the relation of women and architecture began the task of rewriting American architectural history. By the early 1980s these writers had produced a body of works that, taken together, challenged on all fronts the professed gender neutrality of the canon and methodologies of traditional architectural history.

Although women architects have succeeded in overturning the most overt discriminatory practices of the architectural profession and have continued to organize and monitor their status as designers in the fields of architecture, landscape architecture, and planning, the pioneering writings on women and architecture did not, after all, initiate a rewriting of the history of American architecture. In fact, as the publication dates of most of the entries in this bibliographical essay suggest, there seems to have been, by the mideighties, a loss of momentum in this feminist project of architectural history.

Anthologies were the quintessential literature of architectural activists in the late 1970s. With essays by practicing architects and historians, and also sociologists and anthropologists, this type of publication efficiently and effectively brought out new research, mapped the heterogeneity of the issues about women and architecture, and launched the inquiry about what a feminist history of women and architecture might be.

From the first, the concern of women designers, combined with the tradition of monographic writing in architectural history, led to an interest in identifying "forgotten" women architects. The biographical essays in Susana Torre (ed.), *Women in American Architecture: A Historic and Contemporary Perspective* (New York, 1977) showed that it was possible to construct a history of women designers of the nineteenth and twentieth centuries like that written about male architects. (The bibliography in Natalie Kampen and Elizabeth Grossman, "Feminism and Methodology: Dynamics of Change in the History of Art and Architecture" [Wellesley College Center for Research on Women, 1983] lists numerous short articles on specific women architects written in the late 1970s and early 1980s.) This tradition of writing about particular women architects has been extended by the anthology edited by Ellen Perry Berkeley, *Architecture: A Place for Women* (Washington, D.C., 1988).

At the same time the essays on architectural education in the Torre anthology taken with Gwendolyn Wright's essay, "On the Fringe of the Profession: Women in American Architecture," in Spiro Kostof (ed.), *The Architect* (New York, 1977) and with Ellen Perry Berkeley's "Architecture: Towards a Feminist Critique" in Judy Loeb (ed.), *Feminist Collage: Educating Women in the Visual Arts* (New York, 1979) added to the heroic achievements of women architects by exposing the barriers, both institutional and ideological, that they had to overcome to practice architecture at all.

By no means have all the writings on women and architecture focused on individual women architects, however. As its title suggests, Doris Cole's pioneering study *From Tipi to Sky-scrapers: A History of Women in Architecture* (Boston, 1973) urged a retrieval of the tradition of women working as collective designers. The essays in "Making Room: Women and Architecture," *Heresies* 11 (1981) consider the diverse ways in which particular buildings and public spaces may be related to class, race, and gender constructions. The articles in "Women and the American City," *Signs* (1979–1980) and Gerda R. Wekerle, Rebecca Peterson, and David Morley (eds.), in *Space for Women* (Boulder, 1980) treat the issue from the perspective of sociologists and historians. Whereas the *Heresies* essays emphasize female design strategies, these other two collections consider the impact of women as social reformers and the problems facing women as users of urban and suburban environments.

There have been few book-length studies on the subject of women and architecture. The notable exceptions, however, fall into the categories proposed by the anthologies. Doris Cole has written a monograph on the modern designer, *Eleanor Raymond Architect* (Philadelphia, 1981), and Virginia Grattan one on the southwestern architects who designed railroad hotels, *Mary Colter, Builder Upon the Red Earth* (Flagstaff, 1980). Dorothy May Anderson's *Women, Design, and the Cambridge School* (West Lafayette, Ind., 1980) is a study of an institution that was the exception to the sorry history of women and architectural education.

Although we can expect more monographs—I think particularly of Sara Boutelle's much awaited study of the prolific Beaux-Arts designer Julia Morgan—their limited number to date may suggest that the monograph has not proved effective in writing women into architectural history. It is hard, after all, to make the "marginal" integral unless the parameters for significance are altered, and the monographs to date have not effected that alteration.

By far the largest number of books on women and architecture has dealt with the impact of the design of domestic architecture on women and the family. This topic is engaged in two books by Gwendolyn Wright—*Moralism and the Model Home: Domestic Architecture and Cultural Conflict in Chicago 1873–1913* (Chicago, 1980) and *Building the Dream: A Social History of Housing in America* (New York, 1981). Dolores Hayden focuses more directly on this issue in *Redesigning the American Dream: The Future of Housing, Work and Family Life* (New York, 1984). Her analysis is informed by her work on the alternatives to the single family home offered by communitarian Socialism—*Seven American Utopias: The Architecture of Communitarian Socialism 1790–1975* (Cambridge, 1976)—and by her study of the material feminist tradition—*The Grand Domestic Revolution* (Cambridge, 1981). The problem of women's access to housing is the subject of Eugenie Ladner Birch (ed.), *The Unsheltered Woman: Women and Housing in the 80's* (New Brunswick, N.J., 1985).

In contrast to the monographs on individual women, these writings have become an integral part of the history of American domestic architecture. Disappointingly, however, there are almost no extended studies of the relation among design, women, and *public* institutions. The notable exceptions are the documentary history by Jeanne M. Weimann, *The Fair Women* (Chicago, 1981), in which women are shown to be organizers, clients, designers, and users of the Women's Building at the 1893 Chicago World's Fair, and Helen Lefkowitz Horowitz's *Alma Mater* (New York, 1984), which considers how women as users of buildings can revise the stereotypes imposed on them by gender-based design. Although these two works deal with buildings designed exclusively for women, they suggest the utility of studying the ideology of institutions from the perspectives of both gender and design. Yet despite the analyses being done by feminist cultural historians, social scientists, and theorists in other fields and the foundation provided by the works in this bibliography, the complex relations of women and architecture still remain, for the most part, unexamined.

ELIZABETH GROSSMAN

ART EDUCATION, EUROPE (NINETEENTH-CENTURY), underwent progressive changes, allowing women for the first time to receive professional artistic training comparable to men's. Throughout the century middle- and upper-class families supported their daughters' efforts to learn to draw and paint, as these aesthetic accomplishments were considered suitable for a role as guardian of culture and domestic affairs. Until the closing decades, however, male artists were protected from serious female competition by the belief that women lacked the intellectual and physical qualities necessary to excel beyond the amateur level and by the social stigma attached to women earning incomes outside the home. Equally important, women were denied admittance to the prestigious art academies and study from the life model, a prerequisite for figure drawing and the high-status historical and religious genres. Before 1900 the majority of females who obtained recognition continued to come from artistically oriented bourgeois and upper-class families or were connected by birth or association with a male artist. Some exceptional women artists, for example Anna Lea

Merritt, Camille Claudel, and Suzanne Valadon, taught themselves. Others received instruction from family members or private instructors. Yet, after mid-century, newly established art schools figured prominently in the history of women's art education, traditionally male schools were forced to change their admission policies, and the number of professional female artists visibly increased.

Until 1860, when Laura Hertford's admission to the Royal Academy (RA) Schools opened the door for others of her sex, English women's options were limited. As in France, most schools, including the National Art Training School, South Kensington, trained women for commercial work and teaching. Only Henry Sass's School of Art and Mr. Dickinson's Academy (founded 1845) specifically catered to those wishing to paint professionally. The curriculum at Dickinson's (later Leigh's and then Heatherley's) was particularly progressive: Kate Greenaway, Louise Jopling, and Anna Blunden all studied there. Other schools that were popular with serious women artists and served as good training grounds for the RA Schools were The Lambeth School of Art (founded 1853) and St. John's Wood Art School (founded 1880). By the 1890s mixed classes were available to women as was study from the nude model. However, the Royal Academy and St. John's Wood were typical in maintaining segregated life classes in which the males posed with covered loins. Even at the Slade School (founded 1871), which prided itself on offering equal opportunities to both sexes, women worked from a draped male model probably until the late 1890s.

The Metropolitan School of Art, Dublin, accepted women by the 1870s and was the most important school for Irish women, though many continued their studies in London and Paris. The continental art centers attracted students from all over the world. At the Royal Academy, Antwerp, Charles Verlat's classes included a large international contingent, but women do not appear to have been accepted. Native and foreign female students did attend the German Verein der Kunstlerinnen, which were established in Berlin, Munich, and Karlsruhe in 1869. Since women were excluded from the state-sponsored art academies, Käthe Kollwitz and Paula Becker sought art instruction at the Berlin branch in the mideighties and late nineties respectively. The only other alternative to the Verein der Kunstlerinnen was to rent a studio and pay for private lessons. Elizabeth Forbes, a Canadian, found this alternative an isolating experience, appropriate only for advanced students, and left for France after only five months.

By 1880 Paris was acknowledged to be the art student's mecca, for its atelier system (private studio instruction) was considered the exemplary method of training. For women the ateliers offered an opportunity to be taken seriously and have their particular talents and interests encouraged. They could study with reputable artists either individually or in one of the popular, and cheaper, academies, like Julian's or Colarossi's. By 1877 Julian's expanding student population induced him to create separate ateliers for men and women, yet the course of instruction remained the same for both, and in later years he instituted joint competitions. Frenchwomen achieved important, if belated, victories when in

1896 the Union des Femmes Peintres et Sculpteurs succeeded in integrating the life classes at Colarossi's and, more critically, in gaining women's admittance into the École des Beaux Arts.

Serious women art students had to possess considerable ambition, confidence, and independence. Even these qualities did not allow them to escape their dependence on male role models and the social constrictions dictated by their sex. In France, particularly, students felt their true education resulted from the ability to travel freely, experience cultural life fully, and share the companionship of like-minded peers. This view is the reason why the comparatively egalitarian atmosphere of the art colonies in Grez-sur-Loing, Brittany, Normandy, and Worpswede was so important to female students like Becker, Armstrong, Helen Trevor, and Cecilia Beaux.

Major institutional barriers did crumble for women in the late nineteenth century. Nevertheless, important psychological and social ones remained.

Further References. Marie Bashkirtseff, *Marie Bashkirtseff: The Journal of a Young Artist, 1860–1884*, trans. Mary J. Serrano (New York, 1889). Paula Modersohn-Becker, *The Letters and Journals of Paula Modersohn-Becker*, trans. and annot. J. Diane Radycki (Metuchen, N.J., 1980). Charlotte Yeldham, *Women Artists in Nineteenth-Century France and England*, 2 vols. (New York, 1984).

BETSY COGGER REZELMAN

ART STUDENTS LEAGUE. A New York institution that has been encouraging both men and women students to explore a broad range of stylistic and technical approaches to the visual arts for more than 100 years and a pioneer in the field of arts education for women. The league was established in 1875 by pupils from the National Academy of Design who were tired of the latter's rigid, conservative policies—in particular, its emphasis on drawing the human body from plaster casts of noted ancient sculptures (for centuries, the standard method in both European and American academies). Instead, the students wanted to be able to work from the living model, and they did—under Lemuel E. Wilmarth, a noted painter of his time—beginning that fall. The league's life classes were the first ones available to women students (who were restricted until the midtwenties to their own, gender-segregated sessions) in New York City and only the second in the United States (after those offered at Philadelphia's Pennsylvania Academy of Fine Arts; other schools, notably the Cooper Union in lower Manhattan, had provided earlier art classes—but not life classes—for women).

Today, as in 1875, the Art Students League (ASL) remains a highly democratic organization, emphasizing flexibility and accessibility to students from a variety of academic and economic backgrounds. There are no entrance requirements or examinations, no prescribed courses of study, and no semesters; students may enter or withdraw from the league whenever they like, and the modest tuition is paid on a month-by-month basis.

From the start, women have played an important role in the league's administration, faculty, and student body. Women have generally formed the majority of the Board of Control, the 12-member body (one-third of whom must be current ASL students) that governs the league, and there has always been both a men's and a women's vice president. Whereas, during the nineteenth century, female art teachers tended to be assigned only those subjects considered appropriate for their sex (fashion illustration, miniature painting, and classes for young children), early women teachers at the league—such as sculptor Mary Lawrence Tonetti—taught their specialties. Today, roughly one-sixth of the league's 65 teachers and more than one-half of its 2,000 students are women.

As one of New York's longtime artistic landmarks, the league counts an impressive list of well-known professional artists among its alumni. Prominent painters and sculptors who have studied and/or taught at the league include Thomas Hart Benton, Isabel Bishop, Alexander Calder, Thomas Eakins, Audrey Flack, Helen Frankenthaler, Red Grooms, Lee Krasner, Jacob Lawrence, Roy Lichtenstein, Marisol, Louise Nevelson, Georgia O'Keeffe, Jackson Pollock, Ben Shahn, John Sloan, and David Smith.

Further References. Kennedy Galleries, *The Hundredth Anniversary Exhibition of Paintings and Sculptures by 100 Artists Associated with the Art Students League of New York* (New York, 1975). Ronald G. Pisano, *The Art Students League, Selections from the Permanent Collection* (Hamilton, N.Y., 1987).

NANCY G. HELLER

AUSTRALIAN AND NEW ZEALAND WRITERS. Women have made notable contributions to their country's literatures, though these have not always received full recognition. Writing was introduced to both countries with European settlement: from 1788 in Australia, a few decades later in New Zealand. The Australian Aborigines and the New Zealand Maoris both had oral literatures to which women contributed. White invasion destroyed much of this literature, particularly in Australia, where there were many different tribes with their own languages and cultures. There have been recent attempts to revive the indigenous languages and literary traditions. In New Zealand Maori is now taught in schools, and many Maori writers are choosing to write in their own language or jointly in English and Maori. A work in the latter category, Keri Hulme's (b.1947) *the bone people* (1983), won the prestigious Booker Prize for Fiction in 1985.

In the early days of white settlement, most writing was functional or descriptive. Letters sent to maintain the links with relatives and friends sometimes found their way into the columns of newspapers or even between the covers of a book. Diaries or journals might eventually also be sent "home" to England and occasionally published. Many unpublished letters and diaries have been printed more recently, especially since the 1970s and the increasing interest in both social history and women's writing. Notable letter writers and diarists from Australia include Elizabeth Macarthur (1769–1850), Annie Baxter (1816–1905), Georgiana McCrae (1804–1890), and Rachel Henning (1826–1914); from New Zealand, Sarah Selwyn (1809–1867), Mary Taylor (1817–1893), and Charlotte Godley (1821–1907). Some of these women also wrote books based on their pioneering experiences, as did Australia's Louisa Anne Meredith (1812–1895) and New Zealand's Mary Anne Barker (1831–1911).

Women began contributing to local newspapers and magazines as they became established. Since most of these contributions were made anonymously or under a pseudonym, and little detailed research has yet been undertaken in this area, many nineteenth-century women writers remain to be discovered. Most women in this period contributed fiction or poetry though a few, like South Australia's Catherine Helen Spence (1825–1910), made the breakthrough into journalism, writing lead and political articles as well as criticism and reviews.

There was almost no commercial book publishing in either Australia or New Zealand until the twentieth century. Authors, or their friends and relations, paid to have a book printed and hoped to recover expenses through sales. The first novel by a woman to be written and published in Australia, Anna Maria Bunn's *The Guardian* (1838), was, however, intended only for private circulation. Spence's *Clara Morison* (1854), the first novel by a woman to be written and set in Australia, was published in Britain. She was writing to earn money and did make a few pounds from the novel, despite being charged for its abridgment, without her consent, to fit into a series. Like Spence, most later women writers from Australia and New Zealand published abroad from financial necessity. Many others, such as Miles Franklin (1879–1954) with *My Brilliant Career* (1901), found that the published novel was substantially different from what they had intended.

The fact that so many women writers became expatriates, particularly in the period from 1880 to 1950, is, then, hardly surprising. Nor is it surprising that expatriate writers were the first to achieve international reputations. Rosa Praed (1851–1935) moved from Queensland to London before publishing her first novel, *An Australian Heroine* (1880). She went on to produce over 40 more, besides plays, stories, and autobiography. Melbourne's Henry Handel Richardson (Ethel Florence Richardson, 1870–1946) traveled to Germany in 1888 to study music; after many years writing in relative obscurity, she wrote a bestseller, *Ultima Thule* (1929), final volume of the trilogy *The Fortunes of Richard Mahony* (1930). Katherine Mansfield (Kathleen Beauchamp, 1888–1923) was sent from Wellington to London for her education; determined to become a writer, she realized that London was the only place for her. Despite her fairly small output of stories and tragically early death, Mansfield is probably still the woman writer best known to those outside New Zealand and Australia, increasingly acknowledged as a pioneer of the modern short story. Later notable expatriate writers include the Australians Christina Stead (1902–1983), Shirley Hazzard (b.1931), and Germaine Greer (b.1939) and the New Zealanders Ngaio Marsh (1899–1920) and Fleur Adcock (b.1934).

Many of the writers who remained at home became involved in the fight for women's rights and other types of social reform. Louisa Lawson (1848–1920) published *Dawn* (1888–1905), the first feminist journal in Australia, and was a leading suffragette. In 1893, New Zealand became the first country to give women the vote; Australia followed suit in 1902. There was, however, still much to criticize. Australian novelists Catherine Martin (1847–1937) and Jessie Couvreur ("Tasma," 1848–1897) and the poet and novelist Ada Cambridge (1844–1926) queried the institution of marriage. So did Jane Mander (1877–1949) in *The Story of a New Zealand River* (1920). Mander, like her compatriot Edith Searle Grossman (1863–1931), also brought a woman's perspective to bear on pioneering life, as did the Australians Barbara Baynton (1857–1929) and Miles Franklin. Women writers, particularly Mary Gilmore (1864–1962), Katharine Prichard (1883–1969), and Eleanor Dark (1901–1985) in Australia and Blanche Baughan (1870–1958) in New Zealand, were in the vanguard of attempts to write sympathetically about Aborigines and Maoris and to expose the effects on them of white settlement of their lands. These same writers and others, such as New Zealanders Jean Devanny (1892–1962) and Robin Hyde (Iris Wilkinson, 1906–1939) and Australians Lesbia Harford (1891–1927), Marjorie Barnard (1897–1987), Dymphna Cusack (1902–1981), and Kylie Tennant (b.1912), kept alive the radical critique of society's treatment of other marginalized groups, especially women and workers.

In the post–World War II period the major women novelists have undoubtedly been Christina Stead and New Zealand's Janet Frame (b.1924). Though Stead began publishing in the 1920s, her reputation did not consolidate until the 1960s and the rediscovery of her *The Man Who Loved Children* (1940). Frame's reputation as the greatest living New Zealand writer, which had been steadily growing since the 1950s, was fully established in the 1980s by her three volumes of autobiography. Other important novelists who began writing during this period include, in New Zealand, Sylvia Ashton-Warner (b.1908), Marilyn Duckworth (b.1935), Joy Cowley (b.1936), and Margaret Sutherland (b.1941) and, in Australia, Thea Astley (b.1925) and Elizabeth Harrower (b.1928). Since 1975 women have been major producers of new fiction in both countries. In Australia, Jessica Anderson, Elizabeth Jolley (b.1923), Olga Masters (1919–1986), Barbara Hanrahan (b.1939), Beverley Farmer (b.1941), Helen Garner (b.1942), and Kate Grenville (b.1950) have won many local awards and seen their books increasingly distributed in Europe and the United States. Colleen McCullough (b.1937) had a major international success with *The Thorn Birds* (1977). While Keri Hulme is the only contemporary New Zealand writer to be well known overseas, another Maori novelist and story writer, Patricia Grace (b.1937), has been widely published in New Zealand, and Sue McCauley's *Other Halves* (1982) was a local best-seller.

Women are also becoming increasingly prominent in the poetry of both countries. There has, indeed, always been a strong tradition of women poets in New Zealand, from Jessie Mackay (1864–1938), Blanche Baughan, and Mary Ursula Bethel (1874–1945) through Eileen Duggan (1894–1972), Robin Hyde, and Ruth Dallas (b.1919) to present-day writers. Lauris Edmond (b.1924), who began publishing only in 1975, won the Commonwealth Poetry Prize in 1985. Among her contemporaries are Rachel McAlpine (b.1940), Elizabeth Smither (b.1942), and Cilla McQueen (b.1949). Judith Wright (b.1915) has long been the leading Australian woman poet, though both Rosemary Dobson (b.1920) and Gwen Harwood (b.1920) have increased their reputations with each new collection. *We Are Going* (1964) by Kath Walker (b.1920), the first collection of poems by an Aboriginal, was a national best-seller. A significant group of younger poets come from non-English backgrounds: Antigone Kefala (b.1936), Anna Couani (b.1948), and Ania Walwicz (b.1951).

Since 1975 poet Dorothy Hewett (b.1923) has also become the first Australian woman to win widespread recognition as a dramatist, though many earlier women wrote for amateur and fringe companies. Plays by the New Zealand expatriate Alma de Groen (b.1941) are also increasingly being performed by mainstream companies in Australia. In New Zealand, where the development of local drama has taken even longer than in Australia, women have been making a mark only since the 1980s, most notably the Maori feminist Renée (b.1929).

Specialist feminist presses, journals, and magazines have been established in both countries since the 1970s, with varying degrees of success. In Australia, the most prominent are *Hecate* (1975–   ), *Refractory Girl* (1979–   ), and *Australian Feminist Studies* (1985–   ); in New Zealand, *Spiral* (1976–   ), *Broadsheet* (1971–   ) and *Women's Studies Journal* (1985–   ). Melbourne's Sybylla Press (named after Miles Franklin's heroine) and the now defunct Sisters, along with Sydney's Redress Press, have concentrated on publishing contemporary writing. Auckland's New Women's Press has also reprinted works by earlier women writers. Interestingly, the major English feminist presses were founded by expatriates from Australia and New Zealand: Virago by Carmen Callil, Pandora by Dale Spender, and Women's Press by Stephanie Dowrick. All have reprinted works by Australian and New Zealand women; Penguin Australia has also recently begun a reprint program.

Further References. Carole Ferrier (ed.), *Gender, Politics and Fiction: Twentieth Century Australian Women's Novels* (St. Lucia, Queensland, 1985). Drusilla Modjeska, *Exiles at Home: Australian Women Writers, 1925–1945* (Sydney, 1981).

ELIZABETH WEBBY

AUTOBIOGRAPHIES AND DIARIES, BRITISH, are as diverse as British women themselves. Therefore, it is hard to characterize this vast and ever growing area of study. In the past 30 years, as literary critics began to embrace works formerly considered outside literature, feminist scholars have promoted what some categorize as personal prose, pieces perhaps not originally intended for publication. Despite some obvious differences, it is difficult to distinguish among autobiography, memoir, journal, diary, and personal essay. Many authors mix the forms within their works, placing segments of journals in their autobiographies or addressing their diaries to particular readers. The autobiography is the most consciously literary form; it requires plotting out a discrete part of the author's life, selecting events to present a consistent character, and having an awareness of the reader. However, besides the public figures who expect a large readership, many women wrote for only their immediate families; other texts are discovered in attics, presumably unread except by the writer. On the other hand, journals and diaries, supposedly composed with the self as audience, either to record events or provide an outlet for speculation or simply to keep the writer company, have in the twentieth century become a popular form of publication for novelists and poets.

Women's studies scholars have been in the forefront of the movement to study personal prose, frequently characterizing it as an especially feminine form; it certainly is an outlet for authors barred from traditional publication and discouraged from "serious writing." Women's studies scholars have worked in two directions. The first has been to recover lost and forgotten works. Many autobiographies and journals have been resurrected from attics, historical societies, library stacks, and general obscurity to be published, promoted, and studied. Feminist scholars point out that literary critics have focused on autobiographies written by men, ignoring many important works by women. Other scholars have looked for gender differences, claiming that women are more likely to combine forms of personal prose into nonlinear works or to emphasize others rather than themselves in their autobiographies. However, differences in life histories by men and by women seem slight and may be related to how well the author fits into the mainstream of the culture rather than to gender; characteristics of women's self-writing can be found in works by the working class and other excluded groups. However, since women who wanted to write for publication or for themselves were frequently blocked from other literary outlets, a study of women's autobiographies, journals, and diaries provides an especially fruitful look at women's lives and women's prose.

What follows is not a comprehensive bibliography of British autobiographies and published diaries and journals. This field is constantly growing, with more works rediscovered and added to bibliographies every year. Only the best known are noted. Although autobiographies and diaries have been separated, following traditional distinctions between books that appear to be overviews of lives and works that consist of daily or sporadic entries, the distinction is fuzzy.

Some scholars have claimed that the first autobiography written in English was by a woman, Margery Kempe, in 1438. Other medieval and mystical texts, besides *The Book of Margery Kempe,* include *Showing of God's Love* by Julian of Norwich and St. Brigitta's *Revelations.*

Because dissenting religions emphasized a close, personal relationship with God and the importance of conversion, many Quakers and Puritans wrote spiritual autobiographies, stressing religious belief and minimizing daily life.

By the seventeenth century, women were writing secular autobiographies as well. From the upper class, most of these women held traditional views. Although some delayed marriage, nearly all eventually married and treated domestic matters as the focus of their lives. Unusual among the predominantly male diarists of the century, Celia Fiennes describes the English countryside in her diary, *Through England on a Side-Saddle in the Time of William and Mary* (1888).

The authors and so their works in the eighteenth century show more social, economic, and occupational diversity. These women were not always fulfilled by domestic or religious concerns alone. Although some worked as novelists or actresses, social and economic factors pressured most into marriages, frequently uncongenial. Paralleling scenes from contemporary sentimental novels, women portrayed themselves besieged by unscrupulous and treacherous men and complained about the disparity of power. Spiritual autobiographies, secular autobiographies by upper-class women, and gossipy social diaries were still composed. More influential in the development of autobiography were the ''apologies'' by women of questionable reputation, Laetitia Pilkington, Frances Anne Vane, Con Phillips, and actresses George Anne Bellamy and Charlotte Clarke. Fanny Burney and Hester Thrale, who established themselves as part of the eighteenth century literary scene, kept extensive journals.

A central work of the nineteenth century is Harriet Martineau's *Autobiography* (1855), in which she details her intellectual and personal development. Margaret Oliphant, Mrs. Humphrey Ward, and Mary Mitford were minor novelists whose autobiographies display the tensions between the expected Victorian woman's role and their profession. Of the many diarists, the most famous was Queen Victoria herself. Other diarists of note include Caroline Fox, friend of Thomas and Jane Welsh Carlyle and John Stuart and Harriet Taylor Mill; Elizabeth Fry, prison reform worker; Fanny Kemble, actress probably best known in the United States for the 1863 volume of her diary criticizing southern plantation life, *Journal of a Residence on a Georgian Plantation*; Mary Shelley, novelist; Elizabeth Barrett Browning, poet; George Eliot, novelist; Dorothy Wordsworth, sister of the poet; and a transplanted American, Alice James.

Women who were politically active in the late nineteenth and early twentieth century such as Annie Besant, Hannah Mitchell, Annie Kenney, and Emmeline Pankhurst championed a variety of social causes, including women's rights, in their autobiographies. Beatrice Webb published a multivolumed diary: *My Apprenticeship* (1926), *Our Partnership* (1945), *Beatrice Webb's Diaries, 1912–1924* (1952), *Beatrice Webb's Diaries, 1924–1936* (1956).

Texts proliferate in the twentieth century. Virginia Woolf's and Katherine Mansfield's diaries (*The Diary of Virginia Woolf*, 4 vols. [1877–1982]; Mansfield's *Journal* [1927; rev. and enl. ed. 1954]) are prototypes for literary notebook-journals. The turn of the century, and later World War II, produced a spate of nostalgic looks at bygone times. These autobiographies and reminiscences usually focus on childhood, especially in rural and working-class areas. One of the most extensive is Flora Thompson's trilogy, *Lark Rise to Candleford*.

Interest in British women's autobiographies and diaries no doubt will continue to grow. Autobiographies and diaries have remained a popular form of expression for women writers, popular reading for the public, and a popular area of study for feminist scholars.

Further References. Cynthia Pomerleau, ''The Emergence of Women's Autobiography in England'' in Estelle C. Jelinek (ed.), *Women's Autobiography: Essays in Crit-*

icism (Bloomington, Ind., 1980), 21–39. Patricia Meyer Spacks, *The Female Imagination* (New York, 1975). Donna Stanton, "The Female Autograph," *New York Literary Forum* (1984): 12–13.

NAN HACKETT

AUTOBIOGRAPHIES AND DIARIES, U.S., are nonfiction narratives that record the personal lives and the historical significance of their authors. Genres closely related include letters, journals, memoirs, reminiscences, travel accounts, and fictionalized diaries and autobiographies. The female and, at times, feminist perspective is clearly present.

The motivating factor in these writings is the impetus toward claiming and proclaiming one's identity. For women, as for men, this process means a restating of the eternal "I am," but for women, more often than for men, it also means "I am in relation to You."

Autobiographies. Women's autobiographies have such purposes as self-revelation, self-justification, propaganda, apologia, self-knowledge, and historical record. Closely related to the interest in psychology and the women's movement, women's autobiographies have proliferated in the latter part of the twentieth century. The writer's translation of subjective, introspective experience into a public text provides a language for and a substantiation of the reader's private experience. Thus, women's autobiographies become a source of political feminist power. They contribute dramatically to an understanding of the history, psychology, and sociology of American women. Women's autobiographies emphasize human relations, the personal, the domestic, and inner, rather than outer, reality and action.

Autobiographies have several major contentual emphases: (1) personal, spiritual, psychological; (2) political; (3) minority; and (4) career.

1. Personal, spiritual, psychological. Some autobiographies emphasize more than others the development of the self, the growth of an identity. *The Living of Charlotte Perkins Gilman* (1935) chronicles Gilman's personal and emotional life within the context of political and social activities. Mary McCarthy's *Memoirs of a Catholic Girlhood* (1957) is a series of analytic memoirs about her past and her family; *The Long Loneliness* (1972) by Dorothy Day is a philosophical and spiritual autobiography. Kate Millet's *Flying* (1974) is representative of the personalization of contemporary feminist issues.

2. Political. Political autobiographies often have a persuasive as well as a personal tone. They function as propaganda, reminiscence, or charismatic message. See *Living My Life* (1931) by anarchist Emma Goldman, *This I Remember* (1949) and *On My Own* (1958) by president's wife and United Nations representative Eleanor Roosevelt, *With My Mind of Freedom* (1975) by black activist Angela Davis, and *Bella! Ms. Abzug Goes to Washington* (1972) by hatted congressional representative Bella Abzug.

3. Minority. Autobiography is an effective medium for the minority voice because the genre can personalize and individualize her larger concern. Maya Angelou's four-volume autobiography begun by *I Know Why the Caged Bird Sings* (1970), Zora Neale Hurston's *Dust Tracks on a Road* (c.1942), and Anne Moody's *Coming of Age*

in Mississippi (1968) are significant texts by black women, as are those by Lorraine Hansberry and Coretta Scott King, among others.

The Asian-American women's voice is heard in *The Woman Warrior* (1976) by Maxine Hong Kingston. The American Indian woman is found in the autobiography of Mountain Wolf Woman, Helen Sekaquaptewa's *Me and Mine* (1969), and Louise Abeita's *I Am a Pueblo Indian Girl* (1939).

Joan Baez's *Daybreak* (1968) and *And a Voice to Sing with: A Memoir* (1987) and *The Education of the Woman Golfer* (1979) by Nancy Lopez are three popular texts written by women of Mexican background.

4. Career. Career autobiographies are interesting because the autobiographer is typically more interested in telling about her personal and emotional life than about her professional achievements and successes. A popular enterprise, career autobiographies are as varied as the careers of their authors, from actress to zoologist. A sampler includes *Blackberry Winter* (1972) by anthropologist Margaret Mead, *Pentimento* (1973) by playwright Lillian Hellman, *The Story of My Life* (1903) by the blind and deaf scholar and writer Helen Keller, and *The Fabric of My Life* (1946) by Hannah Solomon, Jewish and feminist activist.

Diaries. Diaries may be classified as either private or public. They are usually chronological and episodic. Private diaries record women's daily lives and private thoughts and feelings. Public diaries provide historical records, pass on family traditions, or justify one's life and actions.

Women's diaries may document both American history and female experience. In general, diaries can be organized into five major categories of experience: (1) pioneering and travel; (2) personal, spiritual, psychological; (3) political; (4) minority; and (5) career.

1. Pioneering and travel. Colonial and pioneer women's diaries provide an invaluable account of largely ignored aspects of American history. Not typically introspective, the diarists keep records of domestic life. They occasionally reflect an awareness of the historical significance of their lives. The diaries are substitutes for the writers' absent female network. The travel diaries of the westward movement appear in multiple collections. Other travel diaries are accounts of pleasure or adventure trips. Some have historical significance. In others, overtones of "innocents abroad" or "the ugly American" appear. The first known travel diary by a woman was written by Madam Sarah Knight, who traveled on horseback from Boston to New York in 1704. The feminist perspective is well represented in Julia Holmes's *A Bloomer Girl on Pike's Peak, 1858* (1949) and in Eslanda Robeson's *African Journey* (1945).

2. Personal, spiritual, psychological. As society recognized the value of the individual and women saw themselves as more than adjuncts to their fathers, husbands, and sons, the diary as a form of personal ratification gained importance. For many women the diary was an outlet for their private thoughts, since they were not free to enter into the larger world occupied by men. Important texts here include the *Journal and Correspondence of Miss Adams* (1841) by Abigail Adams, *Pilgrim at Tinker Creek* (1974) by Annie Dillard, *The Diary of Alice James* (1964), *I, Mary MacLane* (1917), *The Diaries of Sylvia Plath* (1982), and May Sarton's *Journal of a Solitude* (1973).

3. Political. The diaries of such well-known political women as Elizabeth Cady Stanton, Dorothy Day, Lucretia Coffin Mott, Angela Davis, and Barbara Deming are important as both personal narrations and political argument.

The texts evidence their authors' consciousness of participating in history and their desire to interpret and explain the events in which they are involved. Political diaries also include works by women who kept records of a period with a consciously historical intention, for example, Mary Lydia Daly, whose *Diary of a Union Lady, 1861–1865* had as its purpose "to preserve, for rereading in the future, the immediate impressions of a coming national emergency." Mary Chesnut, Fanny Kemble, and Miss Emma Holmes all produced diaries detailing the painful loss of a way of life.

4. Minority. Minority women's diaries trace the experience of being both female and a member of a minority group in white male America. Important texts include *The Journal of Charlotte L. Forten* (1953), *The Cancer Journals* (1980) by Audre Lorde, and *Give Us Each Day: The Diary of Alice Dunbar-Nelson* (1985).

5. Career. Career diaries generally chronicle the rise of women successful in a certain profession. Many of these are written on the popular level. Some are primarily anecdotal, even gossipy. Others are more reflective and philosophical, sometimes serving as notes for further work.

Interesting career diaries include *The Notebooks of Martha Graham* (1973), writer Janet Flanner's *Paris Journal* (1965, 1971), *The Adolescent Diaries of Karen Horney* (1980), *Dear Josephine: The Theatrical Career of Josephine Hull* (1963), *Katherine Dunham's Journey to Accompong* (1946), and *Stay With It, Van: From the Diary of Mississippi's First Lady Mayor* (1958) by Dorothy Crawford.

Further References. Margo Culley (ed.), *A Day at a Time: The Diary Literature of American Women from 1764 to the Present* (New York, 1985). Estelle Jelinek (ed.), *Women's Autobiography: Essays in Criticism* (Bloomington, Ind., 1980). Mary Jane Moffat and Charlotte Painter (eds.), *Revelations: Diaries of Women* (New York, 1974). Lillian Schlissel, *Women's Diaries of the Westward Journey* (New York, 1982).

CAROLE GANIM

B

BLACK ARTISTS. See AFRICAN-AMERICAN ARTISTS

BLACK WRITERS. See AFRICAN-AMERICAN POETS; AFRICAN-AMER-
ICAN PROSE WRITERS

BLOOMSBURY GROUP. A loose association, based on close friendship, of
writers, painters, critics, and economic and political theorists in London's
Bloomsbury; its women members included the sisters Virginia Woolf (1882–
1941) and Vanessa Bell (1879–1961). Although its own participants and later
historians all disagree about its exact nature, time span, and very membership,
the Bloomsbury group strongly influenced British fiction, biography, art, criticism, economics, and politics in the twenties and thirties. While its members
insisted that they gathered for conviviality and conversation and that they embraced no single philosophy or aesthetic, their ideas and attitudes overlapped in
complex patterns. Detractors of the group saw its members as snobbish intellectuals who scoffed at artistic, social, and sexual conventions.

The group, mostly children of eminent Victorians, began in 1904 around the
four children of Julia and Leslie Stephen, Vanessa, Thoby, Virginia, and Adrian.
Thoby welcomed his Cambridge friends, especially Lytton Strachey, Clive Bell,
Desmond MacCarthy, and Saxon Sydney-Turner; slightly later, Molly Mac-
Carthy, Duncan Grant, Roger Fry, Leonard Woolf, and Maynard Keynes com-
pleted the stable core.

Friendship was highly valued and became accepted as possible between men
and women. Eroticism never permanently damaged friendship, although openly
acknowledged heterosexual and homosexual liaisons recombined often over the
years. Of the women, Virginia Woolf was closest to Vanessa Bell, Lytton
Strachey, and Leonard Woolf, to whom she was happily married, although she

was in love at different times with women such as Violet Dickinson and Vita Sackville-West. Vanessa Bell married Clive and had two sons. She then had an intense affair with Roger Fry before settling permanently with Duncan Grant, who was primarily homosexual and with whom she had one daughter. Bell and Fry remained her loyal friends.

The individual achievements of the Bloomsbury Group are impressive, and Virginia Woolf was one of its most brilliant members. Her best-known novels were written in her middle period. *Mrs. Dalloway* (1925) follows a day in Clarissa Dalloway's life while shifting among characters' minds and memories to elicit the whole beneath the surface. *To the Lighthouse* (1927) is both critical portrait of Woolf's stifling patriarchal family and lyrical tribute to an angelically giving mother and a gifted father. Woolf then romped through English history in *Orlando* (1928), which celebrated Woolf's love for Vita Sackville-West. *The Waves* (1931) presented phases from the lives of six consciousnesses in a stylized, dramatic form. In these novels Woolf experimented with narrative form, voice, and style. Her recurrent themes include the importance of androgyny; absence, decay, and death, which are barely opposed by human creativity and love; and the opposition of fact and truth, the latter being attainable through art and during mystical moments of vision or being or unity. She often used the imagery of houses, the ocean and flora, and the structure of natural cycles.

Woolf's other novels include *The Voyage Out* (1915) and *Night and Day* (1919), which are now attracting feminist criticism for their biographical implications and their submerged feminist agendas; *Jacob's Room* (1922), Woolf's first experiment with form; *The Years* (1937), an historical novel; and *Between the Acts* (1941).

Besides her novels, Woolf also wrote several short stories, two biographies, and volumes of diaries and letters. She regularly reviewed books for the *Times Literary Supplement* and wrote elegant essays on subjects ranging from the Greeks to contemporary fiction.

Although Woolf never considered herself a political activist, because she believed that as an artist she was unable to influence society directly, she did over the years work quietly for the Women's Co-operative Guild and the women's suffrage cause. Her major direct contribution to feminism, however, came in two essays. *A Room of One's Own* (1929), an essay on "women and fiction," calling for androgynous, enriched writing from both sexes, while pointing out that women will require what men have had, income, privacy, and education, to release the "Shakespeare's sister" within them. *Three Guineas* (1938) is more direct, more strident. Woolf links the patriarchal oppression of women with the black threat of Hitler's fascism.

The strain of the war that followed, added to profound unhappiness with her current fiction writing and fear of another bout of madness, which had plagued her intermittently since her mother's death in 1895, drove her to suicide in the River Ouse in March 1941.

Vanessa Bell was as dedicated and prolific a painter and designer as her sister was a writer, although Bell never achieved similar fame and is not now considered a major talent. Having studied briefly with Sir Arthur Cope and then with John Singer Sargent at the Royal Academy Schools from 1901 to 1904, she came in 1910 under the influence of Picasso, Derain, and especially Matisse, whose color, curvilinear shapes, and decorative approach to painting appealed to her.

From 1910 to 1920, Bell was at the forefront of English Post-Impressionism. She exhibited four paintings at the Second Post-Impressionist Exhibition (1912), which stormed London. In her landscapes, still lifes, and portraits, with subjects drawn from her own surroundings, experience, and friends, she concentrated on flat color areas and on the formal relationships within each picture.

Design also interested her. She decorated Virginia Woolf's books and others at the Woolfs' Hogarth Press. In 1913, she became codirector of Roger Fry's Omega Workshops and decorated furniture, textiles, pottery, murals, and interiors, often in collaboration with Duncan Grant. After 1920, Bell's work returned to a more conventional Impressionism, but she remained concerned with formal relationships and color. In the 1920s she exhibited with the London group and later at the Anthony d'Offay Gallery and the Lefevre Gallery. Posthumous shows include those at the Adams Gallery, London (1961), the Arts Council Gallery, London (1964), and Davis and Long Company, New York (1980).

Vanessa Bell was not an active feminist, but, having totally rejected conventional society, she led a radically free personal life. Strachey considered her the most complete human being of the Bloomsbury Group.

The last woman member of Bloomsbury was Molly (Mary Warre-Cornish) MacCarthy (1882–1953), married to Desmond, who wrote the popular book *A Nineteenth-Century Childhood* (1924) and who founded for Bloomsbury the highly successful Memoir Club, devoted to frank, personal reminiscence.

Three other women were peripheral to Bloomsbury. Karin Costelloe Stephen (1889–1953), married to Adrian Stephen, practiced psychoanalysis and published *The Wish to Fall Ill: A Study of Psychoanalysis and Medicine* (1933, 1960). Dora Carrington (1893–1932) was a promising Slade School-trained painter. She worshiped Lytton Strachey from 1915 and relinquished her own identity to become his platonic companion until his death and her subsequent suicide in 1932. Lydia Lopokova (1892–1981) was a Russian-born ballerina with the Imperial Russian Ballet and Diaghilev's company; she married Maynard Keynes in 1925.

Many non-Bloomsbury people are now associated in the public mind with some Bloomsbury member. These include Lady Ottoline Morrell (1873–1938), a wealthy patron of the arts who ran a salon; Vita Sackville-West (1892–1962), a poet, novelist, and gardener; and Dame Ethel Smyth (1858–1944), composer, conductor, feminist, memorialist, and ardent admirer of Virginia Woolf in the thirties. Smyth, imprisoned in 1911 for militant suffrage activities, composed the campaign song "The March of the Women."

Further References. Elizabeth Abel, "Narrative Structure(s) and Female Development: The Case of *Mrs. Dalloway*," in Elizabeth Abel, Marianne Hirsch, and Elizabeth

Langland (eds.), *The Voyage In: Fictions of Female Development* (Hanover, N.H., 1983), 161–85. Quentin Bell, *Virginia Woolf: A Biography* (New York, 1972). Jane Marcus (ed.), *New Feminist Essays on Virginia Woolf* (Lincoln, Neb., 1981). Frances Spalding, *Vanessa Bell* (New Haven, Conn., 1983).

ANNE S. HIGHAM

BLUES. A solo black folk music (contrasting to the group music of the spiritual) that developed after the Civil War out of male southern field workers' hollers and street cries and spread throughout the South and Midwest by male itinerant musicians. By the 1900s traveling tent and vaudeville shows included acts featuring young, black, female blues singers. The blues, with their plaintive melodies using flatted thirds and sevenths, were taken up by brass bands and orchestras in New Orleans, which were already playing syncopated rag tunes, and became an essential element of jazz (see JAZZ: THROUGH THE 1950s). Southern women dominated blues performance and recording in the decade of the 1920s, the classic blues era.

Gertrude Pridgett ("Ma") Rainey, the "Mother of the Blues," stayed close to country blues style even though, on tours with the Theater Owners' Booking Agency (TOBA) ("tough on black ass," as the entertainers called it), she wore flamboyant satin gowns and jewelry of real gold coins. She recorded 92 sides.

Bessie Smith, the greatest of the early blues and vaudeville singers, traveled like Rainey in tent shows and with TOBA. Writing many songs herself, Smith, the highest paid black entertainer of her time, soon headed her stage shows as the "Empress of the Blues," carrying Rainey's country blues and her own humorous vaudeville tunes into the big theaters of Atlanta, New York, Philadelphia, and Chicago. She made 160 records for Columbia (all reissued in 1970), accompanied by such jazz greats as Louis Armstrong, Don Redman, and James P. Johnson.

Ida Cox ranks third among the classic blues singers because of her unique style and impressive career: composer of almost 100 songs and performer in road shows for nearly 50 years.

Other important vocalists of this blues decade include Mamie Smith, the first black vocalist to record a blues; Clara Smith, "The World's Champion Moaner" (there were 13 Smiths who recorded blues, all unrelated); Sara Martin, who recorded more than 130 songs; Sippie Wallace, the "Texas Nightingale," wailing high C blues; Victoria Spivey, the "Texas Moaner," playing organ, piano, and ukulele, briefly owning her own club, establishing her own jazz/blues label, and performing until the year of her death; Alberta Hunter, first black singer to record with a white band, not restricted to singing blues and jazz, performing in New York nightclubs and European cabarets; Edith Wilson, appealing to white patrons in Broadway houses more than to blacks, popular on both sides of the Atlantic; Ethel Waters, "Sweet Mama Stringbean," singing popular music as well as vaudeville tunes and the blues, with an enduring career on stage and screen; Memphis Minnie and Lucille Bogan, country blues; Lizzie Miles, Creole songs and vaudeville ballads as well as blues; Lucille Hegamin and her Blue Flame Syncopaters.

Performers strongly influenced by the blues though not generally considered blues or jazz singers include Sophie Tucker, Mae West, Helen Morgan, and Ruth Etting.

Carrying the blues into the 1940s were Bertha ("Chippie") Hill, Blue Lu Barker, and Lil Green.

Rhythm and Blues (R&B). R&B was a new name announced in *Billboard* in 1949 for "race" records (blues and jazz intended for sale in black communities). R&B music offers more 16- than 12-bar blues and more varied harmonies and uses new electrical instruments to emphasize bass lines. Julia Lee and Dinah Washington were rhythm and blues stars. Lee reigned over the blues in Kansas City for 40 years with numerous Top Ten hits on the R&B charts, accompanying herself on piano, often with a boogie beat. Washington, "Miss D," the "Queen of the Blues," recorded 450 songs in 20 years of singing, with numerous R&B Top Ten hits and unique interpretations of pop songs. In the sixties and seventies Willie Mae ("Big Mama") Thornton, dancer, comedian, singer, and composer, brought new life to the blues, inspiring Janis Lyn Joplin (as did Leadbelly, Odetta, and Bessie Smith), to her fiery, intensely emotional delivery. In the seventies and eighties Linda Hopkins toured with her *Me and Bessie* show, based on Bessie Smith songs, and Koko Taylor reached audiences in clubs, on radio, and in U.S. and European concerts.

Blues Lyrics Sung by Women. Written by women and men to express sorrow caused by poverty, frustrating work, imprisonment, unfaithful lovers, and by natural disasters such as floods, boll weevils, tuberculosis, old age, death; the majority concerned mistreatment by lovers. Many of Ma Rainey's earliest lyrics describe the misery of a passive, suffering woman, accepting any kind of treatment from a man, with no hope to change her life; or the desperation of a woman deserted by her man, obsessed with the need to get another one, any kind of man. By the 1920s, many blues lyrics exhibit a woman's awakening to the possibility of different responses to a man's mistreatment, a change from passive acceptance to active resistance. The focus remains, however, on male-female relationships. A woman whose man is unfaithful may return to her family, seek a fortune-teller to help her reclaim her man, stay with him but take on another lover, or give him up completely and move on to a new man. She may become aggressive, kill her female rivals, or, the ultimate revenge, kill him. Whatever choice she makes, her realistic, resilient humor underlies her complaints, enabling the singer to laugh ironically at herself and her desire for a man.

The blues queens of the 1920s enlarged the themes of the blues, in nonblues vaudeville tunes that they often wrote themselves, to declare a woman's hard won freedom from a man's mistreatment, based on her new financial independence. Now able to pay her own household bills, she requires two actions of any man she allows to be around: to share his money with her and to be faithful to her; otherwise, she kicks him out. If the man cannot perform sexually on cue, she may cruelly taunt him with being nothing but a good old wagon that's broken down and needs an overhaul. This frank new woman does not promise faithfulness to male or female friends. If she wants a friend's beau, she may go after him, take him part time when she can get him, and try to make him all hers. Or she may adopt infidelity as a way of life and keep several men around. By not getting too emotionally involved with any one man, she has no blues if one misbehaves. A few independent women kick all men out of their lives and exult in their freedom from the ball and chain of marriage, from the male demand for a maid, nurse, mama, and lover in one. Some even suggest a preference for another woman.

The realistic depiction of male/female relationships and the independent attitudes of women expressed in blues and vaudeville lyrics of the 1920s contrast sharply with the romanticized expressions of happy fidelity and uncomplicated love in the popular music of the period, where female submissiveness to mistreatment remains a constant theme. A wife begs her wandering husband to please come home, she accepts all blame for his leaving, and hopes he won't be mean to her because she loves him, even when he beats her. By the 1930s and 1940s some popular music and Broadway songs reduce the adult female in love to a simpering, whimpering, childlike person whose heart belongs to her Daddy dear in exchange for the financial and emotional support he provides. This arrangement contrasts vividly with the straightforward sexual pleasure anticipated, indeed demanded, by the lyrics of the lusty blues.

Further References. Daphne Duval Harrison, *Black Pearls: Blues Queens of the 1920s* (New Brunswick, N.J., 1988). Sandra Lieb, *Mother of the Blues: A Study of Ma Rainey* (Amherst, Mass., 1981). Rosetta Reitz, Liner Notes for Records in Women's Heritage Series, Rosetta Records (New York, 1980–1987).

JEAN KITTRELL

BLUESTOCKINGS. A name applied, for about a century (c.1750–c.1850), to Englishwomen who had, or who affected to have, literary and other intellectual interests. The term implied that such women were unfeminine, careless of their appearance, and neglectful of their proper domestic role.

The term itself refers to men's plain worsted stockings, usually blue or grey, and was first used to deride men who wore worsted instead of black silk stockings in public. The Little Parliament (aka Barebones Parliament) of 1653, made up of 140 Puritan worthies nominated by the independent churches, was also referred to as the Bluestocking Parliament.

Bluestocking came to be applied to women, apparently because Mr. Benjamin Stillingfleet, one of the scholars who attended Mrs. Elizabeth Montagu's "conversation parties," often showed up not in proper evening attire. From 1750, Mrs. Elizabeth Montagu (1720–1800), in her bid to be London's social leader, began giving evening assemblies at which card playing, the usual entertainment, was replaced by conversations on literary topics. Other hostesses followed her lead, and some say it was Admiral Boscawen, husband of one of them, who derisively dubbed the "conversation party" the Bluestocking Society. The name was proudly taken up by the women who attended these salons, and *bluestocking Ladies*, *bluestockingers*, or simply *blues* came to be used to designate, first, female habitués of the literary salons, then, any woman who dared to show interest in other than trivial subjects outside her proper domestic sphere.

In her 50 years as undisputed leader of intellectual society, Mrs. Montagu is credited with helping to introduce a healthier note into London society by breaking the grip of card playing (and its attendant gambling) on social occasions. Regular guests at her evenings included Horace Walpole, Samuel Johnson, Sir Joshua Reynolds, and Edmund Burke. Women writers Elizabeth Carter (1717–1806), Hester Chapone (1727—1801), and younger contemporaries Fanny Burney (1732–1840) and Hannah More (1745–1833), leading bluestocking of the next generation, were members of her circle. Among other bluestocking hostesses were the Mesdames Boscawen, Vesey, Ord, and Greville, and Dorothy Bentwick, duchess of Portland. Hannah More celebrated Mrs. Montagu's beneficent effect on society in her 1781 poem "Bas Blue."

In the early nineteenth century the term was used with frequency and condescension by reviewers of women writers. Lord Byron's satire "The Blues: A Literary Epilogue" (1821) pours ridicule on bluestocking hostesses and the male writers who frequented their salons.

BRAZILIAN WRITERS. Brazilian literature traces its origins to the highly literate and descriptive letter written to the king of Portugal by the scribe Pêro Vaz de Cominha, who chronicled the discovery of Brazil by Pedro Álvares Cabral in 1500. The subsequent 400 years of maturation of letters in the New World were the exclusive domain of men writers, with the notable exception of *As aventuras de Diófanes* (1725; The Adventures of Diophanes), considered by some scholars to be the first Brazilian novel. The author, Teresa Margarida de Silva e Orta, by using an anagrammatic pseudonym (Dorothea Engrassia Tavareda Dalmira), confused the issue of authorship. The editor of the third edition erroneously attributed the work to Alexandre de Gusmão. In general, women, until the twentieth century, had had scant opportunity for higher education and were, thereby, precluded from participating in the intellectual and public life of the country in general. However, this century has brought a profound change and a vindication of women's roles in society.

The turning point in the status of women may be placed in the first 30 years of the twentieth century, which were marked by social and political unrest. Specifically, the pressure for change was manifest in the arts as evidenced by a series of concerts, exhibits, and lectures collectively called *The Week of Modern Art* held in São Paulo in February 1922. This event gave rise to an artistic and literary movement best known as modernism. European artistic ideas and literary vanguard currents, such as cubism, dadaism, and surrealism, as well as the new psychoanalytical Freudian and Jungian insights, provided a new dimension and direction for the arts. These concepts were incorporated into the resurgence of nationalism, which emphasized Brazilian character, values, and themes. For the first time in Brazilian intellectual history, women were to play a highly visible and significant part. Modernism made possible the emergence of two women painters, Anita Malfatti and Tarsila do Amaral, and an internationally recognized pianist, Guiomar Novaes, all of whom became influential in artistic circles in Brazil. This first phase of modernism (1922–1930) was characterized by conflicting and competing literary, political, and ideological debate.

The second phase of modernism (1930–1945) focused its attention on a socially conscious literary "regionalist" current that utilized the novel as the primary vehicle to transport ideas. Its themes were derived from social ills and maladjustment of a region in decline and consequent psychological trauma. Among a clearly defined northeastern regionalist group we find a woman writer, the initiator of the modernist novel, Rachel de Queiroz, whose plays, novels, and journalism have exerted a powerful influence on Brazilian ideas. Some of her novels are *O quinze* (1930; The Fifteen), *João Miguel* (1932), *The Three Marias* (1939; Eng., 1985). Her plays include *Lampião* (1953) and *A beata Maria do Eqito* (1950; The Pious Mary of Egypt). She portrayed legendary characters, some extracted from local folklore, with intense interest in ethical concerns such as good and evil, honor and duty. The local settings often serve as points of departure into the universal. Her works illustrate individual adaptation to the environment, the relativity of truth, and the tragedy of life itself.

The 1930s witnessed the appearance of Lúcia Miguel-Pereira, who for two decades was the country's foremost woman literary critic. In poetry there were two noteworthy women, Adalgisa Nery and Henriqueta Lisboa. However, of all the poets of this time period, Cecília Meireles (1921–1964) is the best known and most critically acclaimed, having been named for the Nobel Prize twice. Meireles's poetry is timeless, as she was concerned with the problem of fleeting time, the abstraction of the moment that only had meaning as it faded into memory. This introspective poetry led to doubt and cynicism, a melancholy verse almost mystical in character. Her principal works include *Espectros* (1919; Specters), *Viagem* (1939; Voyage), *Vaga música* (1942; Vague Music), *Romanceiro da inconfidência* (1953; Collection of Poems of the Inconfidência). In English a bilingual selection of her poetry is available: *Cecília Meireles: Poems in Translation* (1977).

The third phase of modernism (1945–1964) was oriented toward the search for the universal in the human condition, and the themes stressed existential anguish in contemporary society. Several major women writers emerged during this third generation. In 1944, Clarice Lispector (1925–1977) began her literary career with *Perto do coração selvagem* (Close to the Untamed Heart), and Lygia Fagundes Telles began hers with *Praia viva* (Living Beach). Both authors describe characters in their introspective intimacy. Lispector, through her novels, develops a psychoanalytic study of human behavior and emotional states in an attempt to decipher the metaphysical reason for existence. Her heroes suffer the existential anguish caused by the freedom that each has to choose in a universe that is at the same time absurd and indifferent. The metaphysical and psychological concerns are evident in *Alguns contos* (1952; A Few Stories), *Family Ties* (1960; Eng., 1984), *The Apple in the Dark* (1961; Eng., 1986), *Foreign Legion* (1964; Eng., 1986), *The Passion According to G.H.* (1968; Eng., 1988), *An Apprenticeship or the Book of Delights* (1969; Eng., 1986), and *The Hour of the Star* (1977; Eng., 1986). Lygia Fagundes Telles, in her short stories and novels, elaborates her characters' futile attempts to live authentically only to be doomed by memories or some obscure remorse from the past. Themes of extreme futility and frustration bordering on the morbid and even the macabre abound in *Marble Dance* (1954; Eng., 1986), *Verão no aquario* (1963; Summer in the Aquarium), *O jardim selvagem* (1965; Savage Garden), *Antes do baile verde* (1970; Before the Green Masquerade), *The Girl in the Photograph* (1973; Eng., 1986), and *Tigrela: And Other Stories* (1977; Eng., 1986). Both women have secured their position among the ranks of major Brazilian writers. Many of Lispector's works are widely available in the United States.

Nélida Piñon is another talented woman writer who began her career in the fifties. Her more recent works are notable for the creation of an almost surreal atmosphere that rivets the reader's interest in tales that are at the same time allegorical and fablelike. Illustrative works include *Sala de armas* (1973; Weapons Room), *O calor das coisas* (1980; The Heat of Things), and *A república dos sonhos* (1984; The Republic of Dreams).

Each succeeding generation of writers has produced an increasing number of women among its ranks. The increase of women writers has brought the development of feminist themes to the forefront along with a wide experimentation in literary techniques, topics, and styles in general. Of particular interest is the appearance of a highly vocal and articulate feminism. It seems that at last women are expressing their concerns and experiences of what it is to be a woman in a conservative, male-dominated society. In this new wave of women writers are Maria Alice Barroso, Maura Lopes Cançado, Sônia Coutinho, Marina Colasanti, Márcia Denser, Tânia Jamardo Faillace, Lélia Coelho Frota, Yone Gianetti Fonseca, Judith Grossman, Hilda Hilst, Lya Luft, Ana Maria Martins, Maria Geralda do Amaral Mello, Adalgisa Nery, Marly de Oliveira, Adélia Prado, Diná Silveira de Queiróz, Edla Van Steen, Socorro Trindade, and Dinorath do Valle.

With the exception of Hilda Hilst, who has been writing since the 1950s and has produced 28 works, the last group of women writers has not been critically studied. However, these are names that merit further scrutiny, and perhaps many will permanently enrich Brazilian cultural and intellectual life.

Further References. Assis Brasil, *A nova literatura*, 4 vols. (Rio de Janeiro, 1973–1976). Wilson Martins, *The Modernist Idea: A Critical Survey of Brazilian Writing in the Twentieth Century* (New York, 1970). Massaud Moisés, *História da literatura Brasileira*, 4 vols. (São Paulo, 1983). Samuel Putnam, *A Marvelous Journey: A Survey of Four Centuries of Brazilian Writing* (New York, 1971).

LASSE T. TIIHONEN

C

CANADIAN WRITERS, ANGLOPHONE. Women writers are prominent in Canadian anglophone letters, particularly in fiction and poetry. A woman novelist, Frances Brooke, wrote *The History of Emily Montague* (1769), the first novel about Canadian life. In the nineteenth century, the sisters Susanna Moodie and Catherine Parr Traill documented the adventures of British gentlewomen in the wilds of Upper Canada. At the turn of the century, the social realist Sara Jeanette Duncan wrote *The Imperialist* (1904), a novel that dramatizes political and economic tensions between Canada and the United States from the perspective of a passionate, independent female hero. Twentieth-century women writers have relied on these literary precursors to portray women in various kinds of crises. Martha Ostenso, in *Wild Geese* (1925), uses the main female character to expose a patriarchal misanthrope whose daughter demonstrates how female wildness and independence can free a family from male tyranny. Ethel Wilson, in both short stories and novels, explores twentieth-century women's social and spiritual values.

From the mid–1950s on, women writers have dominated Canadian fiction. Because Canadian literature and the women's movement blossomed simultaneously in the 1960s, women writers often use female identity quests to parallel Canada's quests for identity. Many have gained international followings. Margaret Laurence, probably Canada's major twentieth-century novelist, in such novels as *The Stone Angel* (1964), *Rachel, Rachel* (1966), and *The Diviners* (1974), centers on strong prairie women whose roots are deeply Canadian and who are beginning to produce a distinctive Canadian literary mythology. Like other women writers, Laurence dramatizes female development from various chronological perspectives and in different classes.

Five other fiction writers deserve special mention: Sheila Watson, Mavis Gallant, Marian Engel, Audrey Thomas, and Alice Munro. Sheila Watson's *The Double Hook* (1959), considered by many to be Canada's first contemporary novel, presents, cryptically and poetically, Canada's West as a wasteland controlled in many ways by female characters. Mavis Gallant, best known for her many *New Yorker* short stories, although resident for years in Paris, frequently describes Canadian landscapes. Two novels, *Green Water, Green Sky* (1959) and *A Fairly Good Time* (1970), illustrate female characters struggling to emerge whole from cultural patterns designed to defeat them. The novellas ("Its Image on the Mirror" and "The Pegnitz Junction") and the autobiographical Linnet Muir stories (*Home Truths*, 1981) emphasize the development of the female artist from various perspectives. Marian Engel is best known for her novel *Bear* (1976), an ironic commentary on such male-centered stories as Faulkner's "The Bear." In this poetic, mythic novel, the female narrator gradually learns about the world through her intense relationship with a male bear. Somewhat more realistic, but also marked by Engel's frequently bizarre imagination, are the domestic novels, *The Honeyman Festival* (1970) and *Lunatic Villas* (1981). In each of these, and in many of her short stories, Engel focuses on women whose considerable wit allows them to survive crises with style. Audrey Thomas, the most stylistically experimental of this group, dramatizes, in the connected novels *Mrs. Blood* (1970), *Songs My Mother Taught Me* (1973), and *Blown Figures* (1974), unconscious fantasies and delusions, not only by realistic description, but by interrupted narrative, fragmented by interjections from newspapers, unattached voices, and floating memories. The content of her fiction is profoundly female, emphasizing relationships between mothers and daughters and demonstrating women's thoughts as they experience pregnancy. Finally, Alice Munro, in short story collections like *The Moons of Jupiter* (1982) and *The Progress of Love* (1986), as well as in the connected stories of *Lives of Girls and Women* (1971), dramatically illustrates female desire in narrative plot and structure. Munro's stories are intricately detailed, evoking the specificity of particular times and spaces while also ironically questioning the nature of realism.

Margaret Atwood is Canada's best-known writer. Novelist, short story writer, poet, essayist, and critic, she has been concerned, throughout her career, in clarifying national literary characteristics. Her 1972 guide to Canadian literature, *Survival*, emphasizes victimization (with survival) as distinctively Canadian; this theme is reflected particularly in women's writing and through female characters. In *Surfacing* (1972), the unnamed narrator passes through various victim positions in an epic quest designed to teach her what it means to be a Canadian woman. Increasingly political, later Atwood novels like *Bodily Harm* (1981) and *The Handmaid's Tale* (1986), are radical, subversive analyses of patriarchal cultures that can damage women physically and spiritually.

Atwood is also Canada's major poet. Like her novels, her poetry is political. *Power Politics* (1971) dramatically correlates American imperialism with patriarchal power, situating Canada in a female position. *You Are Happy* (1974), *Two-Headed Poems* (1978), *True Stories* (1981), and *Interlunar* (1984) metaphorically present border disputes (between Canada and the United States and between French Canada and English Canada) as battles between the sexes, demonstrating, in a world on the verge of extinction, the dangers of rigid gender terminology.

Other important women poets are Dorothy Livesay, Gwen MacEwen, Margaret Avison, and Phyllis Webb. Dorothy Livesay's interest has moved from historically focused political poetry to poetry directed toward women's issues. *The Unquiet Bed* (1967) and *Plainsongs* (1969) demonstrate this interest, while she celebrates aging in *Ice Age* (1975) and *The Woman I Am* (1977). She has edited a collection of poetry by women, *Forty Women Poets of Canada* (1972). MacEwen's work is marked by history and myth. Her latest poetry, *The T. E. Lawrence Poems* (1982), in which Lawrence's voice is vividly evoked, and *Earthlight* (1982), use fantasy to create subtle images. Phyllis Webb continues to publish work of remarkable technical virtuosity, particularly notable in *Wilson's Bowl* (1980) and *The Vision Tree* (1982). Margaret Avison's second collection, *The Dumbfounding* (1966), established her as a major poet. *Sunblue* (1978) further demonstrates an intense religious conviction as well as considerable social sensitivity.

Canadian drama is less advanced than either fiction or poetry. Nonetheless, several important Canadian playwrights are women. Gwen Ringwood, author of more than 60 plays, has influenced the development of Canadian drama. *The Collected Plays of Gwen Pharis Ringwood* (1982) reveals her skill in establishing place. Five other women dramatists pay particular attention to women: Carol Bolt, Joanna M. Glass, Sharon Pollock, Erica Ritter, and Margaret Hollingsworth. In *Red Emma* (1974), Bolt examines Emma Goldman's Marxist politics and her concern with women's rights. *Shelter* (1975) and *One Night Stand* (1977) dramatize issues of particular concern to women. Joanna M. Glass frequently explores male-female relationships in contemporary society. *Canadian Gothic* and *American Modern* (1977) concentrate on domestic despair, while *To Grandmother's House We Go* (1981) explores often frightening connections among three generations. Sharon Pollock began by satirizing specific political problems in British Columbia but, as *Blood Relations and Other Plays* (1981) demonstrates, has become increasingly broader in dealing with the effects of public events on private lives. Best known for *Automatic Pilot* (1980), Erica Ritter often writes of female characters in comic situations. Like other plays of hers, *The Passing Scene* (1982), an exposé of journalism, is a satire. Margaret Hollingsworth, in plays like *Ever Loving* (1980) and *Mother Country* (1980), demonstrates the difficulties that face women who attempt to speak out. Her plays treat women's voices symbolically.

Further References. Lorna Irvine, *Sub/Version* (Toronto, 1986). M. G. McClung, *Women in Canadian Life and Literature* (Toronto, 1977).

LORNA IRVINE

CANADIAN WRITERS, FRANCOPHONE. Women's contributions to the development of French Canadian literature, particularly since the latter part of the nineteenth century, have been substantial and influential. Contemporary women writers in Quebec are well aware of the formidable accomplishments of their literary foremothers and often remember them publicly and in their own writings.

The novel became the preferred medium of artistic expression for many French Canadian women writers until the late 1960s. The popularity and literary merit of novels by Laure Conan (Félicité Angers; 1845–1924), Germaine Guèvremont (1893–1968), Gabrielle Roy (1909–1983), Anne Hébert (b. 1916), and Marie-Claire Blais (b.1939) are well established. More recently, Acadian writer Antonine Maillet (b.1929) has attracted international attention for her imaginative historical novels about the epic struggles of the Acadian people dispersed by the English between 1755 and 1762 from the original French settlements of L'Arcadie.

Women novelists have often critiqued the culturally acceptable ideals of womanhood and the ideological forces that dominated Quebec culture until the "Quiet Revolution" of the 1960s. Laure Conan's *Angéline de Montbrun* (1882), commonly considered the first important psychological novel in French Canada, explores the emotional strength, idealism, and psychological complexity of a young woman who suffers disfigurement and subsequently decides to break her engagement to a man who no longer loves her. Themes of marriage, solitude, and autonomy are central to Conan's feminine characterization. In *Le Survenant* (1945), a best-seller in the 1940s and a radio series from 1953 to 1955, Germaine Guèvremont examines the lingering force of rural values in Quebec society, especially the patriarchal nature of familial relations and the pervasive authority of the Catholic church. Her rebellious male protagonist subverts the existing order by rejecting the conventional wisdom that happiness flourishes only in the traditional family unit and in an agrarian landscape that never changes.

Equally recognized for her contributions to the short story and the novel, Gabrielle Roy is most widely known for her realistic portrayal of working-class life in *Bonheur d'occasion* (1945), a novel that depicts the effects of urban poverty, particularly on women who, as mothers of large families in dismal urban dwellings, become the double victims of urbanization and rural patriarchal values. Marie-Claire Blais, whose novel *Une saison dans la vie d'Emmanuel* (1965) has been translated into 16 languages, has used both urban and rural Quebec landscapes for her haunting portraits of impoverished children, social outcasts, lesbians, and a seemingly lost generation of adolescents, all of whom fall prey to the disapproving gaze of a patriarchal and wantonly self-destructive society. Virtually all of Blais's protagonists—primarily young women—are engaged in various stages of subconscious or conscious revolt against the repressive structures and moral hypocrisy of the dominant culture.

Anne Hébert, whose works span five decades and mark four genres, has distinguished herself as Quebec's poet-novelist par excellence. The troubled young women in her fictional works are tormented by both sexual yearnings and the fear of punishment. In the claustrophobic and decaying worlds of *Les Chambres de bois* (1958), *Kamouraska* (1970), and *Les Fous de Bassan* (1982), women are brutalized, raped, and closeted away or murdered so as to prevent any undermining of the precarious social order, a patriarchal and heavily masculine order that will crumble nevertheless because of its rigidity and hypocrisy, its inherent taste for violence, and the sexual repression of women. Hébert's novels have enjoyed a wide reading public in Quebec and France, and both *Kamouraska* and *Les fous de bassan* have been adapted to the cinema.

In the late 1960s, the Quebec novel began to yield its position of influence to more open-ended forms of literary expression, which appeared to coincide with a new era of political awareness and artistic experimentation, an era of particularly rapid changes in the legal, social, and cultural status of women in Quebec. During the 1960s and early 1970s, postmodern writers (women and men alike) were challenging the intent and efficacy of representational art as well as the restrictive categories of literature. Feminist writers began to produce new literary forms, creating a growing number of "mixed texts" that combined fiction, autobiography, poetic fragments, theory, and political reflections.

The new generation of self-consciously feminist writers that emerged in the mid–1970s includes many writers who, despite differing attitudes regarding the wide range of political issues facing contemporary women, are attempting to incorporate feminist political concerns and recent theories of women's place in language, culture, and history into their writing. Nicole Brossard, Madeleine Gagnon, Louky Bersianik, France Théoret, Yolande Villemaire, and Jovette Marchessault are among the most critically acclaimed writers in the 1970s, although their reading public is relatively small because of the highly experimental nature of their works.

The most widely read of recent feminist texts in Quebec, Louky Bersianik's *L'Euguélionne* (1976), is a humorous woman-centered antibible that recounts the arrival of an extraterrestrial female being who, dissatisfied with the sexual politics on her own distant planet, has come to earth in search of a more "positive planet" and a male species that is more feminist in outlook. She is greatly troubled and disappointed by what she discovers on earth.

Two other ground-breaking texts are Nicole Brossard's *L'Amèr ou le chapitre effrité* (1977), a poetic search for the lost warmth, regenerative power, and repressed speech of the mute mother, and Madeleine Gagnon's *Lueur* (1979), which combines Gagnon's own personal quest for origins with a psychoanalytic journey back to the mother's womb in search of a lost female language, a language that Gagnon links to the historically silenced maternal body and primeval forms of life.

During the 1970s and 1980s, women writers also gravitated toward the theatre in increasing numbers. Denise Boucher's controversial *Les Fées ont soif* (1976) sent a shock wave through Quebec's theatrical establishment for its "disrespectful" and all too human representation of the Virgin Mary. The collaborative feminist play *La Nef des sorcières* (1978) also broke new ground with its six female monologues in which women denounce various male myths about who they are and struggle to construct an identity on their own terms. The feminist plays of Jovette Marchessault, particularly *La Saga des poules mouillées* (1981), have been well received by the critics and general public, no doubt because of their unusually creative mixture of poetry, history, and sexual politics. In *La Saga*, Marchessault brings four of Quebec's most influential women writers together—Laure Conan, Germaine Guèvremont, Gabrielle Roy, and Anne Hébert—to discuss their accomplishments and collective dreams as artists and to mourn the censorship of their works and the oppression they suffered as women.

Women writers in Quebec today have a solid feminine literary tradition behind them. In their current experimental efforts to rename and rewrite women's experience they continue to carve new paths for women writers in general and for French Canadian literature.

Further References. Mary Jean Green, Paula Gilbert Lewis, and Karen Gould, "Inscriptions of the Feminine: A Century of Women Writing in Quebec," *American Review of Canadian Studies* 15 (1985): 363–388. Paula Gilbert Lewis (ed.), *Traditionalism, Nationalism, and Feminism: Women Writers of Quebec* (Westport, Conn., 1985).

KAREN GOULD

CARIBBEAN WRITERS IN ENGLISH (TWENTIETH-CENTURY). Women writers of the former British West Indies live in a society of extreme diversity and cultural fragmentation. The insecurity of human relationships, particularly between man and woman and mother and daughter, and uneasiness about personal identity are the most common concerns of the prominent writers: Phyllis Shand Allfrey (Dominica), Zee Edgell (Belize), Merle Hodge (Trinidad), Jamaica Kincaid (Antigua), Paule Marshall (Barbados), Jean Rhys (Dominica), and Sylvia Wynter (Jamaica).

Although these women come from different countries, their writing explores the shared problem of establishing personal and cultural identity within a small community that has suffered the conquest and genocide of its aboriginal people, the enslavement of Africans, absentee landlordism and imperialistic control, racism, isolation, claustrophobia, and tension between indigenous African and imported European cultural elements. During the colonial era, Caribbean literature was based on models derived from European, and particularly British, attitudes. However, with independence there was an increasing consciousness of the African and distinctively Creole elements in West Indian culture. A new literature that reflected this great awakening was needed. Many writers questioned the importance of European literary models, but no easy solutions have been found as the area struggles to find a new language and a new literature that genuinely express a Caribbean sense of reality. In the last ten years, only an ambivalent balancing of European and African cultures has been achieved.

Women sometimes write with great anxiety, since their models are usually male, and their societies emphasize that women's vocation lies in nurturing relationships with men and with children. Nevertheless, these writers have created characters who are self-supporting, often single parents of great strength and endurance. They struggle and survive because of their basic respect for life, and they depend on no man for success in their fight for basic survival.

Women writers have investigated the problems women experience in growing up in the West Indies. Jean Rhys's best novel, *Wide Sargasso Sea* (1966), and Phyllis Shand Allfrey's first novel, *The Orchid House* (1953), examine the identity problems that destroy the descendants of white Creole families, disliked by blacks as the descendants of slave owners and patronized by the British as colonials, not genuine Europeans. Rhys shows that the lack of a sense of identity with the West Indian community, combined with tenuous relationships within the family, leads to despair, alcoholism, and suicide. Novels focusing on the African-Caribbean woman's passage into maturity are more positive. The adolescent Beka in Zee Edgell's *Beka Lamb* (1982) learns to survive rejection by males, while her pregnant friend Toycie disintegrates when her Mexican boyfriend rejects her because she is not light-skinned. Beka's survival shows a strength similar to that of Télumée Miracle in Guadeloupean Simone Schwarz-Bart's *Bridge of Beyond* (1972). Télumée survives desertion because the Toussine women teach each generation the endurance and self-reliance needed for survival.

Paule Marshall and Jamaica Kincaid, who have lived for long periods in the United States, have examined both the problems of a young woman's adolescence and the tension she experiences between life in the United States and in the West Indies. In Paule Marshall's *Brown Girl, Brownstones* (1959), Selina Boyce, who grows up in Brooklyn, rejects the coldness of the other Barbadian exiles who have embraced the worst of North American values and decides to return to Barbados, her parents' birthplace, to seek the human values they have lost through their emigration. Jamaica Kincaid's characters move in the opposite direction in *At the Bottom of the River* (1978) and *Annie John* (1983). Both explore the close but alternatively suffocating relationship between a daughter and her mother. In the latter book, Annie John as a child adores her mother but during adolescence comes to hate the older woman and, finally, after near death, leaves the island to start a career.

Both Sylvia Wynter, whose *The Hills of Hebron: A Jamaican Novel* (1962) explores the culture of Afro-Jamaicanism, and Merle Hodge, in *Crick Crack Monkey* (1981), examine the tension between the African-Caribbean and metropolitan cultures. In Hodge's novel, Tee must choose between Aunt Beatrice's attempts to imitate British upper-class society and language and Tantie's more honest acceptance of Creole manners and dialect. Although Tee feels more comfortable with Tantie, her earlier contact with Beatrice's values makes it impossible for her ever to identify completely with the black Creole culture. Hodge deals with this traditional theme of male writers, the problem of cultural identification, perhaps best of all the women writers. Although the women do not, any more than the men, offer a convincing alternative to the present ambivalent balancing of the two cultures, they do offer many more positive models of strength and endurance. Their women characters who survive, physically and psychologically, do so because they have formed strong and supporting bonds with other women in their families and communities.

Further References. Edward Kamau Brathwaite (ed.), *Savacou: Caribbean Woman* (Washington, D.C., 1977). Barbara Comissing and Marjorie Thorpe, "A Select Bibliography of Women Writers in the Eastern Caribbean (excluding Guyana)," *World Literature Written in English* 17 (1978): 274–304. Donald E. Herdeck, Maurice A. Lubin, and John Figeroa (eds.), *Caribbean Writers: A Bio-Bibliographical Critical Encyclopedia* (Washington, D.C., 1979). Leota S. Lawrence, "Women in Caribbean Literature: The African Presence," *Phylon* 44 (1983): 1–11.

LAURA NIESEN DE ABRUÑA

CHAUCER'S WOMEN derive from the religious, classical, and continental chivalric traditions yet create a native English tradition less tied to stereotypically opposed roles. The tradition of biblical exegesis poses an opposition between the Old Testament Eve and the New Testament Mary. The classical tradition opposes Philosophia and Fortuna. The continental tradition opposes the courtly love lady, Fin Amour, and the fabliau lady, False Amour. In Chaucer's work, such figures as Dame Alisoun, the Wife of Bath, and Criseyde of *Troilus and Criseyde* expose the limitations of those stereotypical roles to suggest a richer sense of women's lives.

The Wife of Bath's prologue opens with an examination of terms from the medieval debate on knowledge: "Experience, though noon auctoritee/ Were in this world, is right ynogh for me/ To speke of wo that is in marriage" (ll. 1–3). The Wife of Bath, however, soon demonstrates that the dichotomy between the patriarchy's authority found in books and women's experience does not contain the complexity of feeling and awareness of human knowledge. She is able, through challenging Jankyn's learning and using her experience, to dissolve simple distinctions. Her achievement of "maistrye," like that of the old wife in her tale of a callow Arthurian knight's education, provides a model for heroic womanhood. Neither Eve nor Mary, neither Lady Philosophy nor Lady Fortune, neither Fin Amour nor False Amour, the Wife of Bath epitomizes the complexity of Chaucer's representation of women.

In *Troilus and Criseyde*, Chaucer's debt to Boethius's *Consolation of Philosophy* is revealed in the tension between Lady Philosophy's and Lady Fortune's control of the fates of the characters. Yet in Criseyde's fate as a political pawn in the Trojan War, abandoned by her father, torn from her lover, and then reconciled to life in the Greek camp with Diomede, a new lover, only men seem to wield effective power. Here her representation derives from the passive role of the Fin Amour love object of the chivalric tradition. Yet just as Chaucer reevaluates that tradition, so he reexamines the women's role in it. Criseyde, a widow, not without experience, declares, "I am myn owene woman, wel at ese" (1. 750). Although Pandarus violates her independence through manipulating his niece into an amorous relationship with Troilus, Criseyde retains sufficient resourcefulness in difficult circumstances to survive, and perhaps thrive.

In every instance, Chaucer's women reevaluate the limiting roles to which their lives have traditionally been ascribed. In "The Clerk's Tale," Griselde triumphs over and questions the part of the "patient Grissel." Alison, the wife of "The Miller's Tale," alone of all her community escapes punishment, apparently beyond judgment in her vitality. The poor widow and her two daughters in "The Nun's Priest's Tale" preside like a kind of communal female divinity over their paradisal barnyard, a universe marred only by Chaunticleer's male pride and folly.

Yet the darker side of women's position in late medieval England remains a subject of Chaucer's poetry. In both "The Franklin's Tale" and "The Physician's Tale" virtuous women become the sacrificial victims of male allegiance to false vows. Dorigen of "The Franklin's Tale" submits to her husband, Arveragus's, inflexible conception of "trouthe." In "The Physician's Tale," Virginia, like Jephthah's daughter, to whom Chaucer alludes, is sacrificed to her father's false justice. Chaucer's treatment of these traditional views of women as victim leads to a vigorous reevaluation of the patriarchal structure that perpetuates them.

Further References. Ruth M. Ames, "The Feminist Connections of Chaucer's *Legend of Good Women*," in J. N. Wasserman and Robert N. Blanch (eds.), *Chaucer in the Eighties* (Syracuse, 1986), 57–74. Robert W. Hanning, "From *Eva* and *Ave* to Eglentyne and Alisoun: Chaucer's Insight into the Roles Women Play," *Signs* 2 (1977): 580–599. H. P. Weissman, "Antifeminism and Chaucer's Characterization of Women," in G. Economou (ed.), *Geoffrey Chaucer: A Collection of Criticism* (New York, 1975), 93–110.

NONA FIENBERG

CHICANA WRITERS. Women of Mexican descent who live in the United States and write from that perspective. Among the most recent arrivals to the American literary world, they made their first appearance as part of the Chicano literary outburst of the early 1970s, the peak of the Chicano movement. Thus, writings by Chicanas are best understood if read in the same historical, societal, and cultural contexts as those of their male counterparts. However, since Estela Portillo Trambley published her first play (*The Day of the Swallows*) in 1971, it has been clear that sexism was to be an important theme among Chicana writers.

Chicanas' experiences are unique in that they have been subjected to a threefold oppression. First, the Chicana has been victimized by racism, since she is of mixed Indian and Spanish blood in a society dominated by Anglo-Americans. She has also been the victim of economic exploitation as a member of an ethnic group historically relegated to poor working-class status. Finally, she has been subjected to a double dose of discrimination against women by both American and Mexican traditions of male domination.

However, there is a positive side to this threefold experience. Cordelia Candelaria shows this is Chicano Poetry: A Critical Introduction (Westport, Conn., 1986) by not only explaining the Chicana's "triple jeopardy," but also stressing her "triple joy," namely the advantages of her Spanish/English bilingualism, the three cultures she has at her disposal (Indian, Spanish, and U.S. American), and the traditions of feminism in Mexican and, even more, in American history (172). Chicana writers draw from all aspects of this "triple jeopardy/triple joy," giving the best Chicana writing distinctiveness and freshness.

According to Tey Diana Rebolledo in her article "The Maturing of Chicana Poetry: The Quiet Revolution of the 1980s" (in Paula A. Treichler et al. [eds.], *Alma Mater: Theory and Practice in Feminist Scholarship* [Chicago, 1985]), Chicana writers began to express themselves in much the same manner as male Chicano movement poets, in angry protest. Much of their poetry in the 1970s was an explosion aimed primarily at males in the Chicano movement who pressed for liberaticn but denied Chicanas equal status. They also expressed frustration with and alienation from middle-class feminism, which they felt excluded them. Their anger gave rise to protest, says Rebolledo, but much of the poetry it generated paid little heed to the craft itself and did not express a full range of Chicana experience.

Since the initial outburst of the 1970s, Chicana writers have waged what Rebolledo calls a "quiet revolution." Although this historical summary overlooks two poets of the 1970s, Bernice Zamora and Marina Rivera, who were writing much more than angry protest, it provides a generally valid description of Chicana writers' evolution from the beginning of the movement to the present. Rebolledo also offers a good overview of major themes found in Chicana writing: growing, identity, reflection and creation of self through female family members, especially mothers and grandmothers, the search for and adaption of myth and tradition, the depiction of everyday life, love and passion, the craft and function of writing, and, of course, social criticism. One should also add the philosophical themes commonly found in literature: reflections on nature, life, death, and the supernatural.

Many themes developed by Chicanas are common to all Chicano writing: cultural conflicts, suppression of the Spanish language, the exploitation and struggles of Chicano workers, the immigration authorities, social mobility, conditions in the *barrios* (Chicano neighborhoods), and the effects of U.S. society on *barrios*, families, and traditions. Some writers also express resentment toward Anglo-Americans' expropriation of Mexican lands after the Mexican-American War.

However, unlike Chicanos, Chicanas are often critical of traditional Mexican patriarchy and its suppression of women. Perhaps one theme Chicana writers have in common is the assertion of self against sexism. Chicana literature is often a necessary response to rape, sexual exploitation, domestic violence, rigid gender roles, suppression of sexual desires, and other injustices against women.

The first published Chicana writer, and the most prolific, is Estela Portillo Trambley, the only notable Chicana playwright and the best-known Chicana fiction writer. Her lyrical play *The Day of the Swallows*, vivid and rich in metaphor, stirred much controversy because of its depiction of lesbianism and denunciation of traditional Mexican male domination. Her book of short stories,

Rain of Scorpions (1976), also has feminist themes, whose dimensions are deepened by tapping Greek, Catholic, and ancient Mexican Indian myths and worldviews. Her other drama includes *Sun Images* (1976) and *Sor Juana and Other Plays* (1983). Her first novel *Trini* was published in 1986.

Only a few other fiction writers have emerged. Most notable is Sandra Cisneros, whose *House on Mango Street*, an American Book Award winner, is a finely wrought, poetic collection of sketches narrated by and revolving around a young Chicana coming of age in an urban *barrio*. With humor and moving sensitivity, Cisneros depicts the hopes, joys, and often sad realities of *barrio* people, especially women. Other Chicana fiction includes *There Are No Madmen Here*, a novel by Gina Valdés, *The Last of the Menu Girls*, a collection of memoirs by Denise Chávez, and *The Moths and Other Stories*, by Helena Viramontes.

Although recent trends show Chicana writers moving into other genres, most are poets. Among the most important are Lorna Dee Cervantes, Evangelina Vigil, Bernice Zamora, Lucha Corpi, Angela de Hoyos, Inés Tovar, and Pat Mora. Cervantes's *Emplumada* stands out as the only Chicana book of poems published by mainstream academia, the University of Pittsburgh's Pitt Poetry Series. Bernice Zamora's *Restless Serpents*, Corpi's *Palabras de Mediodia/Noon Words*, Inés Tovar's *Con razon corazon*, Evangelina Vigil's *Thirty an' Seen a Lot*, De Hoyos's *Arise, Chicano, Selected Poems*, and *Woman, Woman*, and Pat Mora's *Chants* and *Borders* are also noteworthy.

Summarizing Chicana writers' themes is impossible, for theirs are multifaceted expressions of women who are, as Pat Mora says in *Chants*, ''sliding back and forth/between the fringes of both worlds'' (52). Portillo Trambley urges a personal and societal balance and wholeness. Zamora seeks an alternative to greed and racial purity, a ''deeper, wider mind'' that ''knows itself to be muddy with adobe'' (*Restless Serpents*, 58). Marginalized by both American and Chicano societies, Chicanas have learned, to paraphrase Cervantes, to trust only what they have built with their own hands (*Emplumada*, 14). Perhaps Cisneros sums the Chicana writer's perspective when she tells of her desire to have her own house. ''Not a man's house. Not a daddy's. A house all my own . . . quiet as now . . . clean as paper before the poem'' (*House on Mango Street*, 100).

Further References. Roberto J. Garza, *Contemporary Chicano Theatre* (Notre Dame, Ind., 1976). Marta E. Sanchez, *Contemporary Chicana Poetry: A Critical Approach to an Emerging Literature* (Berkeley, 1985).

TOMÁS VALLEJOS

CHINESE ARTISTS (BEFORE 1912). In premodern China some of the daughters and wives of professional artists painted, but only a few became famous enough to attract the attention of leading collectors and connoisseurs. Most of the Chinese women painters known through textual accounts and extant works either belonged to scholar-official families, China's gentry, or were courtesans who served gentlemen of this class. They were counterparts to the male scholar-amateur painters whose theories and practices came to dominate Chinese painting in the Ming (1368–1644) and Qing (1644–1912) dynasties. The story of these women belongs to the history of the scholar-amateur tradition that modern writers have characterized as almost exclusively male.

Recognizing the calligraphic roots of their art, Chinese scholar-painters, men and women, counted calligraphers among their artistic ancestors. A model for women was Madame Wei (272–349), an early teacher of China's most celebrated calligraphy master, Wang Xizhi. During the Song period (960–1279), when the theoretical foundation for scholar-amateur painting was established, a number of leading literati families boasted artistically gifted ladies. These women painted the same subjects and employed the same styles as their male relations. The younger sister of Li Chang (1027–1090) made excellent copies of paintings of pines, bamboo, and rocks; the third daughter of the bamboo painter Wen Tong (1019–1079) learned her father's methods and transmitted them to her son. The foremost female poets of Song, Li Qingzhao (1084–c.1151), and Zhu Shuzhen (twelfth century) are said to have sketched blossoming plum and "ink bamboo." Ink-monochrome bamboo was a staple of the scholar-amateur tradition, and, according to one account, it originated with a tenth-century woman. Sitting alone in a garden pavilion one moonlit night, she noticed the shadows cast by the bamboo and used her writing brush to trace them on the paper window.

The full flowering of scholar-amateur or literati painting came in the Yuan dynasty (1279–1368) with the revolutionary achievements of the "Four Great Masters" and their predecessor, the statesman, calligrapher, and painter Zhao Mengfu (1254–1322). Artists of later times constantly looked to the works of these men for inspiration, producing countless imitations of their compositions and brush styles. They also revered the work of Zhao Mengfu's wife, Guan Daosheng (1262–1319), the most famous female artist in Chinese history. Like her husband, Guan was known as a calligrapher as well as a painter, and their son Zhao Yong (c.1289–c.1362) was similarly accomplished. Their talent was recognized by an emperor who proclaimed that he wished later generations to know that his reign "not only had an expert female calligrapher, but a whole family capable in calligraphy—an extraordinary circumstance."

In painting, Guan Daosheng excelled at various subjects, including Buddhist figures and landscape, but she is remembered especially for her ink bamboo. In this genre she contributed a variation—the depiction of bamboo groves in mist after rain. This depiction is the subject of one of the best paintings today attributed to her, *Bamboo Groves in Mist and Rain*, a horizontal composition mounted in a collective handscroll of Yuan works, now in the National Palace Museum, Taipei. Guan Daosheng's reputation continued to grow down through the centuries, and both men and women frequently painted bamboo in her manner. As a bamboo painter she was as highly regarded as any male artist except the Song master Wen Tong.

Other women artists were active during the Yuan period, but women began to enter the Chinese art-historical record in significant numbers only in the Ming dynasty (1368–1644). This timing was due to a combination of social developments, especially the growth of female literacy. Women increasingly acquired the education prerequisite to scholarly artistic activities. They went from reading "improving" literature, their primary course of study, to composing poetry and pursuing the sister arts of calligraphy and painting. They exchanged poems and paintings, formed poetry clubs, and were encouraged by fathers, husbands, and lovers.

Most of the celebrated female painters of the Ming resided in the coastal provinces of the Yangzi River region, China's cultural heartland, and were active in the sixteenth and early seventeenth centuries. Compared to the women artists of earlier and subsequent times, they were a socially diverse group. The daughter of the professional artist Qiu Ying (c.1492–c.1552) was one of the few women of the artisan class to achieve enduring fame for her painting. Like her father she specialized in figures, especially Buddhist deities and palace women. Wen Shu (1595–1634), on the other hand, was the descendant of the literati luminary Wen Zhengming and married into an old Suzhou gentry family. Wen Shu depicted scenes from the residential gardens of Suzhou. Typically she created restrained compositions of eroded garden rocks, flowers, and butterflies in cool colors on paper. Handsome examples are in the Freer Gallery and the Metropolitan Museum. Like Guan Daosheng, Wen Shu had a substantial following in later times, but unlike Guan's it was primarily female. Critics even suggested that the refinement of Wen's style could be imitated only by women.

Equally well known in the seventeenth century was Li Yin (1616–1685), the concubine of a respected scholar of Haining. After her husband died in 1645, Li supported herself by selling her decorative flower-and-bird compositions. Most were boldly brushed in ink on satin. Her work was so popular that some 40 local artists found it profitable to turn out paintings under her name.

Lower on the social ladder, yet still within the literati cultural sphere, were the courtesan-painters, most notably Ma Shouzhen (1548–1604) and Xue Susu (Wu) (c.1565–1635). Both were romantic figures, and painting was just one of the entertainments they offered their clients. Xue Susu, for instance, was also skilled in poetry, calligraphy, embroidery, and archery; upon occasion she performed crossbow stunts on horseback. In painting, her subjects included landscapes, Buddhist figures, plants, insects, and flowers—especially orchids. Her works can be seen in the Honolulu Academy of Arts and the Asian Art Musuem of San Francisco. Ma Shouzhen painted orchids in delicate ink monochrome and colored styles. The Metropolitan Museum has a fine ink study, *Orchid and Rock,* by Ma. Orchids were a popular theme long treated by male and female artists alike, but they were especially favored by courtesan-painters, no doubt because courtesans were likened to these fragrant plants that blossom in seclusion.

The Ming-Qing transition period of the seventeenth century was a great age in the history of the women painters of China, and many more individuals might be introduced, such as the landscape painters Lin Xue (early seventeenth century) and Huang Yuanjie (midseventeenth century); the literatus Mao Xiang's painter-concubines Dong Bai (1625–1651), Jin Yue (later seventeenth century), and Cai Han (1647–1686); the famous concubines Gu Mei (1619–1664) and Liu Shi (1618–1664); and the sister teams of Chai Jingyi and Zhenyi, Zhou Xi and Hu (midseventeenth century). Their works were well received by contemporary scholars, and their biographies testify to the widespread acceptance of female participation in the scholarly artistic life of the period.

Chen Shu (1660–1736) was one of the leading women artists of the early Qing dynasty. Another was Wang Zheng, and the two invite comparison because, unlike so many female painters, neither was born into a prominent family of artists. Their artistic development seems to have been self-motivated. Moreover, their flower paintings suggest that their taste was similar. Both left Impressionistic sketches of the sort popular with the literati, as well as tightly executed, detailed nature studies. Chen Shu also painted figures and landscapes. In landscape, she aligned herself with the "orthodox school" and imitated the styles of the Yuan masters. This position was a popular but conservative one for the period. On the whole, Chinese women painters did not pursue the individualistic paths opened by some of their male contemporaries.

Because of the efforts of her son, who presented her paintings at court, Chen Shu became the woman artist best represented in the Qing dynasty imperial collection. (Most of her extant works are in the National Palace Museum.) She also instructed men who became well-known artists, accepted female pupils, and, through her art, touched painters of subsequent generations.

The famous eighteenth-century artists Yun Bing, Jiang Jixi, and Ma Quan all came from celebrated scholarly families of painters who specialized in floral subjects. These families were, moreover, closely associated socially and artistically. Yun Bing was a descendant of the master Yun Shouping (1633–1690); Jiang Jixi was the younger sister of the master Jiang Tingxi (1669–1732), a Yun Shouping follower; Ma Quan was the daughter of Ma Yuanyu (1669–1722). The painters of the Jiang and Ma families were greatly influenced by Yun Shouping, so works of these three women have much in common. They all bring garden flowers to life in rich, shimmering colors and fine detail, in a manner reminiscent of the realistic courtly traditions of the Song dynasty. An outstanding example is Yun Bing's flower album of flowers and insects in the Musée Guimet.

The late eighteenth century saw the continued growth of women's participation in the poetic and visual arts. Fang Wanyi, Luo Qilan, and Wang Yuyan, to cite just three examples, were accomplished in both arts. By the nineteenth century noteworthy female painters were active all over the country, from the art circles of Guangdong in the south, to the court at Beijing in the north. Miao Jiahui, a lady of southwestern China, for instance, was summoned to the court to serve as a painting instructor and "substitute brush" for the Empress Dowager Cixi (1835–1908). The empress dowager had some artistic ability and a genuine enthusiasm for painting and calligraphy. Many of the works that bear her name, however, were actually the work of Miao and other court ladies.

The paintings produced at the late Qing court, although entertaining, were

CHINESE ARTISTS (MODERN)   61

determinedly backward-looking. The foundation of modern Chinese painting was laid not in official circles, but in the thriving commercial centers of Guangdong and Shanghai. Prominent in the former were Wu Shangxi, the daughter of a famous art collector; Yu Ling, the concubine of the painter Su Liupeng (c.1814–1860); and Ju Qing, a descendant of a distinguished family of flower-and-bird painters. In Shanghai, Wu Shujuan (1853–1930) was considered the equal of the leading male flower painter of the city, and Ren Xia (1876–1920) carried on the figure, bird, and animal painting methods of her enormously influential father Ren Yi (Bonian, 1840–1896), occasionally signing his name to her own works to make them sell better.

The Rens were professional artists who painted for the affluent merchants of Shanghai, but by the nineteenth century commercialism had long been a reality in literati painting circles as well. Not a few of the women mentioned above, after learning to paint as amateurs, went on to use their art, as their male relatives did, to contribute to the support of their families. In sum, the amateurism of Chinese women painters must be understood in its peculiarly Chinese art-historical context, where it was esteemed far more than professionalism, yet was often more posture than fact.

Further References. Ch'en Pao-chen, "Kuan Tao-sheng and the National Palace Museum 'Bamboo and Rock,' " in *Ku-kung chi-k'an* (National Palace Museum Quarterly) 11, 4 (Summer 1977): 51–84 (English summary: 39). Marsha Weidner (ed.) *Flowering in the Shadows:Women in the History of Chinese and Japanese Painting* (Honolulu, 1990). Marsha Weidner and Ellen Laing (eds.), *Views from Jade Terrace: Chinese Women Painters, 1300–1912* (Indianapolis, 1988). Tseng Yu-ho, "Hsüeh Wu and Her Orchids in the Collection of the Honolulu Academy of Arts," *Ars Asiatiques* 2 (1955): 197–208.

MARSHA WEIDNER

CHINESE ARTISTS (MODERN). Women have achieved considerable recognition, both in traditional-style Chinese painting and in new Western-inspired art forms, but none have been accorded the status given the most famous twentieth-century masters.

This fact is somewhat paradoxical in view of the emphasis on sexual equality in the ideology of the Chinese revolution and the fame of such women writers as the novelist Ding Ling. Moreover, in traditional Chinese society women had already established their ability to use the brush, usually in what was considered the more appropriately feminine genre of flower-and-bird painting. But neither this secure, if minor, niche in the art of old China nor the transvaluation of sexual attitudes that has marked the birth of new China has been sufficient to lift women to a position approaching equality in the Chinese art world.

The reasons for this situation lie partly in the general failure to achieve sexual equality after the success of the Communist revolution and partly in the particular social and cultural conditions surrounding modern Chinese art. The decline of the traditional ideal of the upper-class amateur scholar-painter by the beginning of the twentieth century and the rise of neoliterati professional painters in the major urban centers affected women artists in two ways. First, women had more opportunity to study with famous masters, usually as personal disciples but sometimes in the new art school environment. Yet at the same time even the most talented of the new women artists encountered serious social obstacles to pursuing the kind of professional artistic career that brought maximum recognition. For most women artists in the first half of the twentieth century, painting was a polite accomplishment, but not a full-time career.

This description was particularly true for the numerous upper- and middle-class women who painted in the traditional style and usually painted the traditional feminine subjects, but it can also be seen among the young urban women who entered the more radical world of Western-style painting. The careers of two of the most prominent women oil painters of the pre-Communist period illustrate this point.

Pan Yuliang (1905–1979) was a "kept woman" in Shanghai who happened into the first coeducational school for Western art and became a star pupil of its founder, Liu Haisu. At his urging, she studied in Paris and took up the position of instructor in oil painting in the Art Department at the National Central University in Nanking. A superb draftsperson, she was in the forefront of the small group of "modernists" in urban China. But her career in China was short-lived. Hounded by scandal over her personal life as a "second wife," caught in factional rivalries within art circles, and hampered by the lack of a market for modern European-style paintings, she returned to France and lived the rest of her life there in relative obscurity.

Fang Junbi (b. c.1908), another Paris-trained oil painter, came from a more respectable social background and did not have the same economic problems. But, although she had some rather minor teaching positions in Canton in the 1930s, she failed to receive the kind of teaching and administrative appointments that could have made her a major force in modern Chinese art. She, too, withdrew from China to live in the West. In other words, the diploma from L'École des Beaux Arts, which was a ticket to fame and sometimes fortune for male artists, did not open the same doors for women painters.

With the founding of the People's Republic of China in 1949, the social basis of art changed, and supposedly the obstacles facing women artists disappeared. In the new government-sponsored art colleges, women formed a significant portion of the student body, continuing a trend started in the progressive private schools before the revolution. However, women were less numerous in the nationwide Chinese Artists Association or in the academies for recognized artists that were set up in most major cities. The prestigious Shanghai Academy of Traditional Painting, for instance, as of 1981 had only 13 women among its 81 full members. This underrepresentation becomes even more striking at the very top of the Chinese art world—the artists in key administrative teaching posts and those who have been honored with individual exhibitions and reproduction volumes by the state-controlled art institutions.

He Xiangning (1878–1972) is certainly the most widely publicized woman artist in the People's Republic, before and after her death. Associated with the revolutionary Cantonese School of Painting, she was an unusually vigorous painter in the traditional style, painting fierce lions, soaring pines, and lofty landscapes in addition to the more standard female subjects of birds and flowers. But the acclaim for her had political overtones, for she was widow of the martyred revolutionary leader Liao Zhongkai. She is the only woman in the modern painters section of the *Dictionary of Chinese Art* (Peking, 1984), but the spotlight on her is partly reflected glory.

Xiao Shufang (b.1911) is another well-known artist, married to a better-known man, the artist and art administrator Wu Zuoren. She combines her prerevolutionary training in English watercolor technique with traditional Chinese flower painting to produce some of modern China's freshest and most vigorous painting in that genre. But she is usually linked to her more famous husband.

In the post-Mao era, women artists have been somewhat more prominent in the freer artistic atmosphere that has generally prevailed since the late 1970s. Some, still working with flower-and-bird or female figure painting, have pushed these traditional female genres into new directions. In Shanghi, Chen Peiqiu (b.1923) does bold and lyrical bird painting. At the Peking Painting Academy, Zhou Sicong (b.1939) has given the often insipidly treated subject of national minority women more substance and dignity, while her younger colleague, Zhao Xiuhuan (b.1946) has attracted attention with her marvelously detailed nature studies.

Perhaps most significant, however, are the women painters such as Yang Yenping (b.1934), Nie Ou (b.1948), and Shao Fei (b.1954) who go beyond the traditional feminine genres to do powerfully innovative landscapes and figure paintings. They are expanding the scope of women's art in China, but it remains to be seen how far they will rise in the strict and seniority-conscious hierarchy of the Chinese art world.

Since at least the 1920s, the talent, the promise, and the positive example of female success in the literary world have been there for Chinese women artists. But, to date, even through revolutionary periods, social and cultural conservatism has been too strong for that promise to be realized.

Further References. Joan Lebold Cohen, *The New Chinese Art, 1949–1986* (New York, 1987). Ellen Johnston Laing, *The Winking Owl: Essays on Art in the People's Republic of China* (Berkeley, 1988). Cao Xingyuan, "Nine Women Artists," *Chinese Literature* (Winter 1987): 165–167.

RALPH CROIZIER

CHINESE TRADITIONAL FICTION constitutes a massive written resource for the study of the cultural ideals, popular images, and actual lives of women throughout China's long history. In portraying women, Chinese storytellers were far more curious and comprehensive than Confucian historians and far less bound by Confucian stereotypes of vice and virtue. Most authors, including patriarchal conservatives, wrote works that vividly illustrate the social and psychological pressures on women in traditional China. Their image of women is extremely complex and diverse; the following brief survey only suggests some of this diversity.

Water Margin (*Outlaws of the March* [Beijing and Bloomington, 1981]), written in the fifteenth century, is a loosely structured Robin-Hood-style adventure tale. Women are only minor characters, but their portrayal illuminates some of the negative stereotypes of women in Chinese popular culture. Although usually weak and dependent upon men, the women are also seen as potentially very dangerous in their cunningness and sexuality. Often criticized as a thoroughly misogynist work, *Water Margin* contains chilling descriptions of brutality toward women without exhibiting very much sympathy for their plight.

A much more detailed description of ordinary women's lives is found in *Jin ping mei* (*The Golden Lotus,* 4 vols., repr., London, 1972; abridged trans.: *Chin P'ing Mei* [Toms River, N.J., 1960]), a late sixteenth-century novel of manners and one of the most graphically erotic works in the Chinese tradition. A work of sophisticated social and psychological realism, *Jin ping mei* chronicles the rise and fall of a wealthy merchant, Ximen Ching, his six wives, and their house full of servants and maids. Totally dependent on their playboy husband's whims and insecure unless they produce him a male heir, the women in this household must use sex as a major weapon in their struggle for survival. Much more than a simple work of pornography, this novel is the most complex and intimate portrait of women's lives in China (and perhaps in any country except for Japan's *Tale of Genji*) before the eighteenth century.

Jin ping mei is surpassed in both psychological realism and feminist concerns by China's greatest novel, *Dream of the Red Chamber* (*A Dream of Red Mansions,* 3 vols. [Beijing, 1978–1980]; *The Story of the Stone,* 5 vols. [New York, 1973–1986]), written in the mideighteenth century by Cao Xueqin. Although framed as a Buddhist allegory, the bulk of *Dream of the Red Chamber*'s 120 chapters describes in meticulous detail the long, painful decline of a very prominent aristocratic family. Featured are the young male protagonist (a partial self-portrait of the author) and dozens of his female relatives, friends, and servants, all described in a leisurely, realistic, almost Proustian style. Nearly all the major female characters meet a tragic end: some commit suicide to escape and protest their mistreatment by the family; some live in quiet desperation with unloving and unlovable husbands; some seek solace in joining Buddhist nunneries and renouncing earthly ties; and some strive to submit to the authority of their elders and to serve the family through Confucian self-sacrifice. Despite the novel's occasional bow to Confucianism and the Buddhist proclamations of its narrative framework, none of these strategies appears to succeed in saving the family or in providing individuals with much meaning or satisfaction in life. No other novel in the Chinese tradition is as encyclopedic in its theme, as sympathetic and insightful in its portrayal of women, or as sharp in its social criticism as *Dream of the Red Chamber*.

In the early nineteenth century, a little-known amateur painter and poet, Shen

Fu, wrote *Six Chapters of a Floating Life* (*Six Records of a Floating Life* [New York, 1983]), a poignant autobiographical memoir detailing, among other things, Shen's intense lifelong love affair with his wife Yun. Although technically not fiction, Shen's memoir is so self-consciously artful that its truth, like the truth of fiction, depends far more on its plausibility than on its facticity. Because they are romantics and in love, Shen and his wife are ostracized by his family, and she eventually dies in poverty and despair. Among her chief sins, Yun had fallen in love with a singing girl, with Shen Fu's sympathetic consent! Shen Fu is no modern-style feminist—he has an open affair with a singing girl himself—but his memoir beautifully illuminates the dilemmas of romantic conjugal love in a pragmatic, hierarchical, Confucian, family-centered society.

A more famous, and also more conventional, early nineteenth-century work is *Flowers in the Mirror* by Li Ruzhen (abridged trans. [Berkeley, 1965]). An inventive travelogue-style fantasy designed to show off Li's encyclopedic knowledge, *Flowers in the Mirror* is a clever satire of many facets of traditional Chinese society. Its most famous part portrays a Kingdom of Women where traditional Chinese sex roles are completely reversed. When a Chinese merchant visits the Kingdom of Women to sell cosmetics, he is captured and properly "feminized" (complete with the most painful binding of his feet), so that he can be a concubine for the female emperor. Li Ruzhen's feminism is easily overstated (he approved of widow suicide, for example), but he does illustrate that some traditional Chinese males could be both Confucians and staunch critics of such practices as concubinage and footbinding.

The above are only the most famous traditional Chinese works that serve to illuminate the lives of women from the fifteenth to the nineteenth century. Thousands of other works from this time and earlier are equally revealing. Use of these sources promises to provide a much fuller understanding of the evolution of women's lives, expectations, roles, and status in China over the centuries.

Further References. Frederick P. Brandauer, "Women in the *Ching-hua Yuan*: Emancipation toward a Confucian Ideal," *Journal of Asian Studies* 36 (1979): 647–660. Anna Gerstlacher et al. (eds.), *Woman and Literature in China* (Bochum, FRG, 1985).

PAUL S. ROPP

CHINESE WRITERS (CLASSICAL PERIOD). Women have played a less important role in Chinese literature than the far more numerous male writers. This difference may be attributed largely to restrictions that the Confucian-based Chinese society imposed on women. Confucianism, which emphasized social order and relations, defined women's role as the fulfillment of three major responsibilities, that is, performing household duties, attending to the needs and comfort of the husband and elders, and raising children. The activities of women were generally confined to the home. Though Confucianism advocated female education, this was mainly to prepare women for their prescribed familial responsibilities. Reading or writing literary works was discouraged, for imagination and spontaneity stood against the Confucian doctrine of restraint and decorum as moral correctives. Thus, Chinese women writers generally regarded literature as a mere amusement or distraction. Many even destroyed their own manuscripts, a practice that resulted in a serious loss of women's literature.

Few works dated before the Han period (206 B.C.–A.D. 220) can be ascribed to female authorship with certainty. Among women writers of the Han, Zhuo Wenjun (fl.150–115 B.C.), Ban Zhao (?–c.A.D. 116), and Cai Yan (fl.A.D. 162–239) were the most noteworthy. Zhuo achieved distinction in literature through a single poem entitled "Baitou yin" (A Song of White Hair) written in protest against her husband's intention to take a concubine. For centuries, this poem has been a symbol for wives abandoned because of old age and waning beauty. Ban was renowned for her accomplishments in both historical scholarship and literary creation. Erudite and well-informed, she had a share in the completion of *Han shu* (History of the Han). She was also a skillful writer in the prose and *fu*, or rhyme-prose, forms. Cai's fame arose from her extraordinary personal experience, powerfully embodied in three poems attributed to her, "Huqie shiba pai" (Eighteen Verses Sung to a Barbarian Reed Whistle) and "Beifen shi" (Poems [two] of Lament and Resentment). In a tone of wrath and agony, each poem chronicles her abduction by the Huns, then China's most threatening enemies, life among the barbarians, and return to China.

The most celebrated woman writer during the Jin period (265–420) was Zuo Fen (fl.275). Her writings include poetry, prose, and *fu*.

Women's literature of the Southern Dynasties (420–589) is best represented by *yuefu*, a type of song poetry. These songs deal almost exclusively with love. Couched in characteristically fluent and conversational language, feelings are usually expressed with little restraint. The most notable of the *yuefu* is "Ziye ge," a group of 42 poems attributed to a girl named Ziye (fl.third and fourth centuries). These poems were emulated by later generations.

During the Tang period (618–907), usually considered the Golden Age of Chinese poetry, many court ladies, upper-class women, courtesans, and Taoist nuns wrote poetry. Most renowed were Xue Tao (768–831) and Yu Xuanji (fl.844–871). Xue favored such conventional subjects as friendship, lovesickness, the passage of time, and the vicissitudes of history. The overall tone of her poetry was one of resignation and acquiescence. In poetic talent and skill, Yu was the equal of Xue. Yu, however, demonstrated in her works an awareness, rarely seen among other women poets, of the sexual inequality in society. In some poems, she clearly demanded that women be allowed to take more than one lover and to participate in state examinations leading to officialdom.

In the Song period (960–1279), many women composed *ci*, a type of poetry with a musical origin. The most celebrated was Li Qingzhao (1081–c.1141), generally recognized as China's greatest woman poet. In accordance with two distinct stages in her life, Li describes in her poetry one of two contrary moods: either that of a happily married young woman or that of a distressed, aging widow. In either mood her poetry had an intimacy, accuracy, and immediacy rarely surpassed by China's other writers. She was especially skillful in experimenting with difficult prosodic devices.

During the Yuan (1234–1368) and Ming (1368–1644) periods, *sangu* poetry, a variation of the *ci*, became the dominant form. Women poets of this time were noted for their successful exploration of the female mind. Huang E (fl.1535) was especially remarkable because of her undisguised descriptions of love and sex.

The multiplicity of women's literature in the Qing period (1644–1911) is reflected by the presence of both elite forms, such as poetry and drama of the literati, and those of folk origin, such as *tanci*, stories put into rhyme for chanting with musical accompaniments. In poetry, Gu Taiqing (1799–1876?) was the most noteworthy. She was skillful in the employment of simple language to create an atmosphere of sublimity and the manipulation of rhymes to achieve desired sound effects. Famous female dramatists include Ye Xiaowan (1613–?), Liang Yisu (fl.1644), and Wang Yun (dates unknown). Their works concern separation, lovesickness, and the vicissitudes of life. In *tanci* literature, of greatest renown was Chen Duansheng (fl.1785), whose work reveals strong feminist thought in demanding equal career opportunities for women.

Considered as a whole, Chinese women's literature of the classical period consisted of poetry as the major genre and fiction, drama, and prose as minor ones. Works written in the literary language outnumbered those in the vernacular, and the focus of creative attention was on the individuality of the writers, rather than their surrounding society.

Further Reference. Sharon Shih-jiuan Hou, "Women's Literature," in William H. Nienhauser, Jr. (ed.), *The Indiana Companion to Traditional Chinese Literature* (Bloomington, Ind., 1986), 176–195.

SHARON SHIH-JIUAN HOU

CHINESE WRITERS (MODERN). The first significant women writers of modern China appeared during the 1920s in connection with the May Fourth Movement (named after the widespread demonstration on May 4, 1919, protesting concessions given to Japan by the victorious Western Allies at the Versailles Peace Conference). The movement witnessed the upsurge of antitraditionalism and political consciousness among Chinese intellectuals, as well as the adaptation of vernacular language as a literary medium and the introduction of Western literature with its techniques and sentiments. Amid the male-dominated literary scene, there emerged a small number of women writers (Bing Xin [Xie Wanying, b.1900], Lu Yin [Huang Ying, 1896–1934], Ling Shuhua [b.1904], Ding Ling [Jiang Bingzhi, 1907–1986], Xie Bingying [b.1906], Xiao Hong [Zhang Naiying, 1911–1942], Cao Ming [Wu Xuanwen, b.1913]) who were mostly from the elite class, some even educated in the West. Their works were mainly short stories and novellas that were characteristically autobiographical and often written from the first-person point of view. Besides revealing the psychology of the frustrated, lonely, and love-seeking urban intellectual female (such as Ding Ling's "The Diary of Miss Sophie"), they also deal with the plight of Chinese women in the overwhelmingly oppressive social milieu (such as Ling Shuhua's "The Embroidered Pillowcase"). There were very few women poets, and those who did write poetry (such as Bing Xin and Lin Huiyin) produced mainly love poems and poems on nature. Play writing was rarely attempted by women writers.

In the late twenties and early thirties, the increasing influence of Marxism led to different groupings of Chinese writers. Of the women writers, Ding Ling was the most conspicuous in her drastic change to include themes of class struggle (as shown in the novella *Water* [1931]). During the Sino-Japanese War (1937–1945), many patriotic and Communist-oriented intellectuals from the coastal cities made their way to Yan'an, then the revolutionary base of the Communist party led by Mao Zedong. Mao's *Yan'an Talks on Literature and Art* (1942) laid down the rules for Chinese writers for the following several decades (among these rules are "Literature and art serve politics" and "Literature and art serve the workers, peasants, and soldiers"). Ding Ling was the most outstanding woman writer in Yan'an, and because of her artistic conscience and social obsession, she was the earliest to be criticized during the rectification campaign (1942). She was sent to "experience" life and later came up with the novel *The Sun Shines over the Sangang River* (1953), which won her a Stalin Prize.

While some women writers turned to the Communists during the Sino-Japanese War, others continued to produce works of nonpolitical content, stressing instead their personal artistic sensibility. Examples are the novella *The Golden Cangue* by Eileen Zhang (Zhang Ailing), who left China in 1952 for Hongkong and then went to the United States in 1955, and the works of Yang Jiang, who, after a long silence, resumed writing in the early 1980s.

After the Communist victory in 1949, many women writers (Yang Mo [b.1914], Liu Zhen [b.1930], Ru Zhijuan [b.1925] and Ke Yan [b.1929]) nurtured by the Communists wrote mainly within the confines of Party ideology. During the fifties, the Party's successive campaigns for ideological conformity among intellectuals brought criticism to at least two female writers, Yang Mo and Ding Ling. Yang Mo was criticized because of her novel *The Song of Youth*, which focuses on urban intellectuals. Ding Ling, because of her allegedly "bourgeois" influence among young writers, was condemned more severely than the first time and sent to labor reform in northeast China, to be rehabilitated only in 1979. She died in 1986.

During the Cultural Revolution (1966–1976), literature and art were reduced to a mere propaganda role. Most Chinese writers were silenced, purged, or forced to commit suicide. Chinese literature revived only in 1979 with the new pragmatic government led by Deng Xiaoping. The literary thaw (and other reasons) facilitated the emergence of an unprecedented number of women writers (prominent names include Chen Rong, Zhang Jie, Dai Houying, Wang Anyi, Zhang Xinxin, Zhang Kangkang, Lu Xing'er, Yu Luojin, Zhu Lin, Liu Suola).

The vigorous call for "writing the truth" and the re-recognition of the value of a human being in the post-Mao era have enabled Chinese women writers realistically and, to a considerable extent, artistically to depict various aspects of the life of Chinese women. The sensational appeal and psychological depiction in their works overshadow those of the male writers. These women writers reveal the vulnerability of women to exploitation and abuse by vicious and corrupt officials (as shown in many stories of young women sent to the countryside during the rustication campaign from the late 1960s to the mid–1970s), the loss of feminine identity because of ultraleft dogmatism and extreme puritanism (as shown in many stories about female Red Guards), the search for romantic love and sexual equality (as shown in many stories on love), and the boredom and hopelessness of domestic life (as shown in many stories on marriage). All these themes were discouraged, if not banned, in Maoist literature. As far as poetry is concerned, it is no longer dominated by male poets as in the May Fourth Period. Prominent women poets (such as Shu Ting and Wang Xiaoni) have produced modernistic poetry with profound individuality and artistry. On the whole, for Chinese women writers, this period is the most prosperous one in Chinese literary history.

Further References. Yi-tsi Mei Feuerwerker, *Ding Ling's Fiction: Ideology and Narrative in Modern Chinese Literature* (Cambridge, Mass., 1982). Howard Goldblatt, *Selected Stories of Xiao Hong* (Beijing, 1982). Margery Wolfe, *Revolution Postponed: Women in Contemporary China* (Stanford, 1985). *Seven Contemporary Chinese Women Writers* (Beijing, 1982).

LAIFONG LEUNG

COMPOSERS (TWENTIETH-CENTURY). The twentieth century has witnessed three distinct generations of women composers.

The first of these can be represented by the American Amy Marcy Cheney (later Mrs. H.H.A. Beach), who was trained as a pianist by prominent teachers in Boston but was denied the study of composition because of her gender. She was educated in composition outside the system, as women would have to be in the United States until after World War II. Beach is known especially for her sensitive song settings and her instrumental works, including a Piano Trio and the *Gaelic* symphony. Like most of her generation, she aimed to work in the mainstream, establishing herself as a powerful exception to the rule but not committing herself to changing the rule.

In this group were a few spectacular successes, such as Lili Boulanger, whose fine music had a supreme spokesperson in her sister Nadia, who held a vital pulpit as the great seminal teacher at the American Conservatory at Fontainebleau. Boulanger is representative: no threat to any man because she was safely dead (at 25) and her music was advertised with persistent conviction by someone else. Exceptionally, Dame Ethel Smyth was more active in fighting for herself and for other women in music but she worked in Great Britain, a land much more tolerant of eccentrics. These composers produced scores of unquestioned value but were granted limited (and insufficient) recognition.

The second generation can be represented by Ruth Crawford (later Seeger), trained outside the system but having joined it by marriage (her husband was a professor of ethnomusicology) and latterly (and, to greatest effect, posthumously) accepted within it. Whereas earlier composers had seen themselves as working outside the system, this generation wanted to work inside and to be a part of it. Some women of this group, such as Marcelle de Manziarly, Dorothy James, Undine Smith Moore, Grazyna Bacewicz, Peggy Glanville-Hicks, Rebecca Clarke, and Miriam Gideon, have commanded universal respect. Their music is vibrant and strong: one thinks of the String Quartet of Crawford; the Song Cycles and Piano Trio of Manziarly; the operas of Glanville-Hicks, Moore, and James; and the choral and orchestral works of Gideon.

But with this generation, even genuine success as a composer could not open the door to positions as professor of composition, still reserved exculsively for males. The success of the women in this group is not to be measured in their own careers, but in the careers of the women who followed them, for whom they had won their victories.

The third generation can be represented by Ellen Taaffe Zwillich, educated within the system and therefore eligible for recognition (she won the Pulitzer Prize) within the system. Her graduation in composition, from Juilliard in 1975, was the first anywhere for a female. She joins a growing cadre of women already working for the first time within the system, though trained outside of it, fine composers such as Joan Tower, Thea Musgrave, Dorothy Rudd Moore, Jean Eichelberger Ivey, and Nancy Van de Vate. This generation may contain women who will breach the fastness of university professorships of composition and bring women into full citizenship as composers.

Further References. Jane Bowers and Judith Tick, *Women Making Music: The Western Art Tradition, 1150–1950* (Urbana, Ill., 1986). Aaron I. Cohen, *International Encyclopedia of Women Composers* and *International Discography of Women Composers* (Westport, Conn., 1982 and 1984). Jane Frasier, *Women Composers—A Discography* (Detroit, Mich., 1983). Judith Lang Zaimont, *The Musical Woman*, 2 vols. (Westport, Conn., 1984, 1987).

EDITH BORROFF

CONCERT ARTISTS. Among beginning piano students, girls outnumber boys about 25 to 1. From then on, the ratio changes radically: by the time students reach large regional piano competitions, the ratio is perhaps 6 women to 4 men; in major international competitions, about 1 woman to 15 men. New York management companies usually have only a token number of women to 20–30 men.

The larger number of girls and their much higher attrition rate compared with boys in the early years of study attest to the fact that the tradition of women's "accomplishments" lives on. Parents think that playing the piano is a "nice" thing for girls to learn how to do. The relatively few who continue study may attend a conservatory, enter competitions, win prizes, and give public concerts, but they find the career possibilities so daunting that they turn to teaching. They usually marry. If they become mothers, they discover that it is extremely difficult to combine motherhood and career as a concert artist.

Women concert artists, like women in other professions, have to try harder. In the conservatory, teachers take boys more seriously than they do girls. It is easier for young men to find patrons to support them in international competitions, to secure their first recording contract, and to find a good manager. Managers let females know that in their experience women are less dependable, less reliable, less dedicated, and much harder to sell. The same kinds of discrimination that are found in the business world operate in the music world. Women who complain are weak, fussy, aggressive, "bitchy," in the same situations in which men are assertive or "true artists." Women who have careers in music manage to grit their teeth, never cancel, never change their minds, are consistently reliable, and don't get fussy and balk at playing on bad instruments.

There is another factor unique to the arts: women more frequently than men foster the arts, are the major force in fund raising, sell tickets, arrange benefit perfomances, actually attend concerts—and generally prefer a male performer. Further, the bulk of the concert repertoire was composed by men and originally played by men; the male tradition is well rooted and familiar.

The women performers who are the role models for the concert artists of the late twentieth century coped with the problem of a career usually with the help of supportive husbands or other family members. Alicia de Larrocha's husband (also a pianist) took care of the children while she was on tour. Myra Hess and Gina Bachauer had no children, but Bachauer's husband, conductor Alec Sherman, left his career to manage hers and travel with her. Erica Morini's brother was her agent. A number of women musicians today have close relatives who manage their careers; most, however, are doing it on their own.

Trying to juggle family needs and a concert career is a special problem for women with children. The most careful planning cannot take childhood diseases, which seem to come at the worst possible times, into account. Another hindrance is competition juries who still believe that since a long career is less likely for a woman, when big prizes are awarded, it is better to give them to men.

The scarcity of concert opportunities is a serious problem for the careers of both women and men. Men complain that in the competition for concert dates, women have an advantage they do not—there are only a few women concert artists whereas male artists tend to be swamped by other men.

The great tradition of solo concert artists probably peaked in the 1920s. By the 1930s radio broadcasts and musical recordings were already affecting the market for touring artists. Hofman, Rachmaninoff, and Paderewski traveled with a retinue in private railway cars. Today the soloist hangs out alone in desolate airports, waiting for the weather to break to make connections to the next concert date.

A woman preparing for a career as a concert pianist needs to be ready for any opportunity to play, to be able to sight-read accurately and artistically, to be diligent about learning the chamber music repertoire, and to be ready to accompany or be part of an ensemble. Conservatories would do well to teach a course in the business aspects of music. It helps to work part-time for a recording company or concert management. Otherwise it comes as a shock to a pianist to find herself a "product" to be sold. There are relatively few concert dates and crowds of competent men and women eager to fill them.

What keeps serious pianists going is the sheer love of playing. The satisfaction derived from the beauty of the music and the ability to share this beauty are basic. There has to be a belief in performance as a vocation or calling that cannot be refused or denied. Students should think of themselves as sharing and serving when they perform and think of music as a tool for life.

The material in this article was abstracted from concert pianist Virginia Eskin's article "Why Should a Woman Play Like a Man?" (*Keynote* 10, 9 [November 1986]: 14–17), with permission from the author and the publisher.

VIRGINIA ESKIN AND HELEN TIERNEY

CONDUCTORS. In the late nineteenth and early twentieth centuries, women, to play in professional orchestras, had to form their own orchestra, thereby allowing a few women the chance to conduct. Among the best known were founder/conductors Caroline B. Nicholas, Women's Fadette Orchestra in Boston, 1888–1920; Ethel Leginska (Ethel Liggins), Women's Symphony of Boston, 1920s–1930s; Frederique Petrides, Orchestrette Classique (later Orchestrette of New York), 1933–1945; and Antonia Brico, New York Women's Symphony Orchestra, 1934.

The heyday of all-woman orchestras was from 1925 to 1945, but after World War II most disappeared and, with them, their women directors. The number of women conductors began to grow slowly in the 1970s. In 1971, 1.4 percent of the orchestras registered in *The Musicians Guide* were led by women (Kay D. Lawson, "A Woman's Place Is at the Podium," *Music Educators Journal* 70, 9 [May 1984]: 49). In 1981, 32 of 737 (4.3 percent) orchestras in the annual American Orchestra League Directory published by *Symphony Magazine* had women directors; in 1988, the number was 56 out of 845 (6.6 percent). But no woman headed any of the 35 major United States symphonies, and only 7 (12.5 percent) led larger ensembles (3 urban, 2 metropolitan, 2 regional orchestras). The rest directed community/college (27) or youth/training (22) orchestras. A few women who have gained national or international recognition also appear as guest conductors with major orchestras.

Although the attitude toward women conductors is more favorable than it once was, forces working against hiring women have not disappeared. The dominating, European-trained male is still part of the American image of the conductor. Boards of directors and women's committees have been charged with considering qualities such as stamina, which women are sometimes thought to lack, and male sex appeal (the "Leonard Bernstein Syndrome"), which they do lack, in choosing conductors. Attractive women, on the other hand, may not be considered seriously—the more attractive, the less seriously—by hiring agencies or by players. The assertiveness that is expected of the male conductor tends to be translated as aggressiveness in a woman (Lawson, 47–49). Whatever the initial response to the conductor, once she has proven herself, prejudice among players disappears. If, however, the woman conductor does not succeed, sex figures prominently in discussions of her failure.

Several women conductors gained national and international recognition during the 1970s. Antonia Brico (1902–1988) ties women conductors of the 1930s with those of the 1970s. In the early 1930s she was a successful guest conductor, but by 1937 the novelty of a woman's conducting men had worn off, and job offers had dried up. Then in 1975, at age 72, she began a second career as a result of the documentary *Antonia: A Portrait of a Woman*. Appearances as conductor of major orchestras included a concert at the Hollywood Bowl, where she had made her American debut in 1930.

Sarah Caldwell (b.1924) has reinvigorated American opera through her Opera Company of Boston, founded in 1957 as the Boston Opera Group. In the early years of struggle her refusal to be other than herself, despite abundant advice to the contrary, helped build her legend. In 1970 she became the first woman to conduct the Metropolitan Opera Orchestra, and she has also directed the Central Opera Company of Peking.

Eve Queler (b.1930) founded the Opera Orchestra in 1967 and developed it into a highly acclaimed orchestra that presents seldom performed operas in concert, giving singers and instrumentalists experience with operatic repertoire and expanding audience knowledge beyond the standard U.S. operatic fare.

Judith Somogi (b.1937), like Eve Queler, has remained primarily interested in opera. In 1982 she was named first conductor of the Frankfurt Opera. Other successful operatic conductors include Paulette Haupt-Nolan, the first woman to receive an Affiliate Artists Exxon/Arts Endowment residency, and Doris Lang Kosloff, named musical director of the Connecticut Opera in 1983.

Margaret Hillis (b.1921), one the world's premier choral conductors, in the latter 1950s organized the Chicago Symphony Chorus, the best of its kind in the world, then added orchestral conducting to her repertoire (Kenosha [Wisconsin] Symphony Orchestra [1961–1968] and Elgin [Illinois] Symphony [1971–1985]). In 1977 she directed the Chicago Symphony Choir, the Elgin Symphony Orchestra, the Civic Orchestra of Chicago, and the Department of Choral Activities at Northwestern University. That same year she won a Grammy for her recording of Verdi's Requiem and rave reviews when she stepped in to conduct the Chicago Symphony's New York performance of Mahler's Symphony no. 8 on a few hours' notice.

In the 1960s both Sylvia Caduff (b.1933) of Switzerland and Delia Atlas of Israel chose international competitions as the route to recognition and employment. Sylvia Caduff was a winner in the Guido Cantelli Competition in Novarro,

Italy, and in 1966 won first prize in the Demetri Mitropolis International Conducting Competition in New York—the rules had to be changed to allow a woman to enter. In 1977 she was appointed Generalmusikdirektor of the orchestra of Soligen, Germany. Delia Atlas's prizes in the Guido Cantelli Competition (1963), the Royal Liverpool Philharmonic Competition (1964), the Dimitri Mitropolis Competition (1964), and the Villa-Lobos Competition (1978) opened up conducting opportunities worldwide.

The rising women conductors of the 1980s include Iona Brown, who in 1986 became one of two women to lead regional U.S. orchestras (Los Angeles Chamber Orchestra); Jo Ann Falletta (b.1954), who in 1985 won the Leopold Stokowski Conducting Competition and became musical director and conductor of the Denver Chamber Orchestra in 1983, and musical director in 1986 of the Bay Area Women's Philharmonic Orchestra; and five women recipients of Affiliate Artists conducting residencies between 1977 (the first year of the program) and 1986.

The Affiliate Artists Exxon/Arts Endowment Program, established in 1973, funds a residency of up to three years with a cooperating orchestra. By 1986 three women had been chosen to participate in this highly competitive program: Victoria Bond, 1979–1980; Paulette Haupt-Nolan, 1978; and Catherine Comet, 1982–1984. In 1980 Affiliate Artists also established a one- to two-year program for promising candidates with little or no experience. In its first five years, two of the conducting assistants in the program were women: Antonia Joy Wilson, 1982–1983 and Rachael Worby, 1983.

Victoria Bond (b.1949), the first woman to earn a doctorate in conducting from the Juilliard School of Music, is a composer as well as a conductor. In 1986 she was named music director and conductor of the Roanoke Symphony Orchestra. Catherine Comet, born in France, had her first professional experience in the orchestra pit of the Paris Opera's National Ballet Company. In 1986 she became the first woman conductor of a regional U.S. symphony orchestra, the Grand Rapids Symphony. After her Artists Affiliate experience Antonia Joy Wilson returned to formal training for a year, then became musical director of the Johnson City (Tennessee) Symphony. Rachael Worby in 1986 was named music director/conductor of the Wheeling (West Virginia) Symphony Orchestra.

Further References. Jane Weiner LePage, *Women Composers, Conductors, and Musicians of the Twentieth Century*, 3 vols. (Metuchen, N.J., 1980–1988). Judith Lang Zaimont et al. (eds.), *The Musical Woman*, 2 vols. (Westport, Conn., 1984–1987).

COURTLY LOVE. A concept invented in 1883, one year after the contraceptive diaphragm, in an attempt to systematize the male/female relationships portrayed in twelfth-century vernacular romances and some other medieval literature. During the late nineteenth and early twentieth centuries, many scholars believed that between 1100 and 1500 there existed a pan-European code of *amour courtois*, by which a knight declared abject humility and servitude to his chosen lady. Supposedly he was to tremble and turn pale in her presence, sigh, have trouble eating and sleeping, compose songs offering to die for her, and keep his passion secret from all—particularly from the lady's husband, for courtly love and marriage were mutually exclusive.

In 1883, Gaston Paris articulated this concept while reporting on a twelfth-century romance of King Arthur and his Knights of the Round Table, *Lancelot* by Chrétien de Troyes. In his article "Étude sur les romans de la Table Ronde. Lancelot du Lac. II" (*Romania* 12 [1883]: 459–534), Paris found supporting evidence for the concept in two places: first, a Latin prose treatise from the same era and region as Chrétien's Old French poem, *De amore* (About Love) by Andreas Capellanus; second, some songs in a different vernacular, from the south of France a century before Chrétien.

Paris's formulation inspired other scholars to seek courtly love elsewhere in medieval literature. By 1936 C. S. Lewis, in *Allegory of Love*, declared the abrupt emergence in about 1100 of an entirely new human emotion, romantic love. Ever more fascinated, scholars devoted their careers to study of unpublished manuscripts in dusty libraries. Study led to publication of variorum editions, soon followed by abridgments and translations suitable for classroom use. Thus new generations of medievalists could read far more primary material than had ever been accessible to their teachers and grand-teachers. They could see that courtly love describes only one among the rich variety of male/female relationships portrayed in literature and furthermore that male/female relationships are only one among many social, political, psychological, and artistic concerns of medieval authors.

For example, anyone who now reads a paperback translation of Chrétien's *Lancelot* can see that Gaston Paris was focusing on just one particular relationship. Throughout the poem Lancelot dotes on Queen Guinivere, the lawful wife of his lawful overlord. In private, she sometimes encourages Lancelot and sometimes scorns him; in public, at her commands, he humiliates himself in various ways such as losing jousts.

By treating Lancelot's obsequious attitude as the key to the poem, however, Paris was neglecting much of its action. As it opens, for example, Gawain and Lancelot set out to rescue the queen from abductors. They spend the first night at a castle owned and operated by a fair maiden. At her mocking challenge, Lancelot sleeps successfully in a forbidden bed, despite a flaming lance hurled at him at midnight. Lancelot arrives the second night at the castle of another fair maiden, who extends hospitality only if he will promise to have sex with her. And so on, day by day and night by night: fictional men confront a series of unpredictable but absolute rules, prohibitions, and challenges in their behavior toward women.

Since about 1960 literary scholars have increasingly pointed out that although terms meaning "love" and "courtesy" do sometimes occur together in medieval texts, little evidence exists for the codification into *amour courtois* as posited by Paris in 1883. In addition, historians including Georges Duby now provide a social context for fictional knightly adventures like Lancelot's. Estates in twelfth-century France were passed entire from eldest son to eldest son. French

younger brothers could acquire land only by searching out a bride with no
brothers, a girl who would inherit her father's land. These knights without land
or wives roamed France in high-spirited, sometimes destructive gangs referred
to as *juventi* (youth).

Old French romances would have appealed to audiences of *juventi*. The verse
narratives feature unmarried, landless knights triumphing over arbitrary rules
concerning women—though never quite triumphing totally. Lancelot may survive
one heiress's spear bed and scorn another's advances, but Guinivere scorns him
in turn. His affair with a married woman fails, that is, no matter how hard he
tries to please her.

Recent studies likewise provide context for the other evidence of courtly love
posited by Gaston Paris: songs in the vernacular of southern France and Andreas's
Latin prose treatise. Songs, treatise, and romances all have links to one wealthy
family that decided to use expensive parchment to write down secular literature.

Themes and images resembling courtly love occur in tenth-century Arabic
literature. They could have passed through Moorish Spain to the south of France
with Guillaume IX, duke of Aquitaine (1071–1127), who used writing materials
for songs by himself and other composers (i.e., troubadours). A few songs feature
a male narrator who declares himself willing to die for love; other songs treat
other subjects.

The custom of writing down secular songs may have come north with Guil-
laume's granddaughter, Eleanor of Aquitaine. She married the king of France;
after a divorce, she married the king of England. While queen of England,
Eleanor would visit her French daughter, Marie, who had married the count of
Champagne. It is to Marie of Champagne that Chrétien de Troyes dedicates
Lancelot.

Marie appears also in the treatise on love by Andreas, who claims to be her
court chaplain. Reworking Ovid's *Art of Love*, written 12 centuries earlier,
Andreas replaces Ovid's practical seduction techniques with a series of debates
in which men attempt to argue women into sexual intercourse by declaring
themselves pale, trembling, sleepless, near death, and so on. Scholars now
question whether courtly love was taken seriously even as a theme in fiction in
the twelfth century, since Andreas's treatise has lately been proven riddled with
obscene Latin puns.

By the fifteenth century social conditions had altered, but the literature on
paper remained, paper having replaced expensive parchment so that more and
more secular literature could survive. Readers looked back to a golden age of
chivalry, as portrayed in books. In one of the clearest cases on record of life
imitating art, knights in the real world began imitating those in the stories.

Historical knights' activities mostly involved politics, war, sports such as
jousting, and any behavior that might substantiate a property claim by demonstrating that one's ancestors behaved the same way on the same land. It may
well be, however, that in the fourteenth and fifteenth centuries some men imitated
fictional knights' behavior toward fictional ladies, even including Lancelot's

servile idealization of Arthur's wife. Several works by Geoffrey Chaucer, such as the "Knight's Tale" and *Troilus and Criseyde*, show complications that arise when human men and women try to behave like "courtly lovers."

In the twentieth century, it is still quite possible to find songs and other literature in which a male narrator offers to die for his love. It is indeed possible to meet real, live men who, supposing that women want to be worshiped, humbly present themselves as inferior and unworthy of love. Apparently some twentieth-century women even respond positively to an attitude of fawning obsequiousness. Perhaps some medieval women did the same.

Further References. Richard Barber, *The Knight and Chivalry* (1970; rep. New York, 1982). Larry D. Benson, *Malory's Morte d'Arthur* (Cambridge, Mass., 1976). Betsy Bowden, "The Art of Courtly Copulation," *Medievalia et Humanistica*, n.s., 9 (1979): 67–85. Joan M. Ferrante, " *Cortes' Amor* in Medieval Texts," *Speculum* 55 (1980); 686–695. F. X. Newman (ed.), *The Meaning of CourtlyLove* (Albany, N.Y., 1968).

BETSY BOWDEN

D

DANCE. The present article deals with women's contributions, as dancers and choreographers, to the principal forms of Western theatrical dancing—ballet and modern dance.

Ballet developed from court dances performed by the nobility in Renaissance Italy. By the seventeenth century ballet had evolved into a professional art form, presented in theatres and attended by the general public.

In 1661 the French king, Louis XIV, gave ballet its first official recognition by creating the Académie Royale de Danse, which codified ballet techniques and taught them to both men and women. (Earlier, female roles had been danced by male courtiers; the first professional ballerina was Mlle. de la Fontaine [1655–1738], who made her debut in 1681.)

The eighteenth century marked the rise of the ballet star–including Gaetano Vestris and his female counterparts, Marie-Anne de Cupis de Camargo (1710–1770) and Marie Sallé (1707–1756). Famed for her technical prowess, Camargo shortened her skirt to midcalf to show off her mastery of *entrechats*, jumps in which the feet are crisscrossed quickly in the air, while Sallé developed a reputation for dramatic roles and for replacing the usual, cumbersome wigs and hooped underskirts with simple, loose hairstyles and gowns. Other important eighteenth-century ballerinas were Marie-Madeleine Guimard (1743–1816); Teresa Vestris (1726–1808) (Gaetano's sister); Marie Allard (1742–1802); Barbara Campanini (1721–1799); and Anna Friedrike Heinel (1753–1808).

The nineteenth century is known as the Age of the Ballerina. As female dancers were called upon to portray mysterious, supernatural characters (sylphs, wilis), their costumes and techniques changed—most notably, through the introduction of *pointe* shoes, enabling them to dance on tiptoe, creating an otherworldy effect. Three of the most famous ballerinas of the day were Italians: Marie Taglioni (1804–1884), whose father Filippo choreographed *La Sylphide* (1832) for her; Carlotta Grisi (1819–1899), who created the title role in *Giselle* (1841); and

Fanny Cerrito (1817–1909), a particularly dramatic performer. This trio, plus the Danish dancer Lucile Grahn (1819–1907), made a tremendous hit in *Pas de quatre* (1845). It was during the Romantic period, too, that the Viennese ballerina Fanny Elssler (1810–1884) popularized so-called character dances (combining ballet technique with steps taken from Spanish, Hungarian, and other folk forms) and Augusta Maywood (1825–1876) became the first American ballerina to achieve international fame.

It was neither Europeans nor Americans, but a group of dancers from Russia who generated the most excitement during the early twentieth century. In 1910 Anna Pavlova (1881–1931), a *prima ballerina* with the Maryinsky Theatre (a forerunner of Lenningrad's Kirov Ballet), formed her own company and toured the world, introducing the classical repertoire to many parts of the world where ballet had never been seen before.

Meanwhile, in 1909 Russian impresario Serge Diaghilev organized the Ballets Russes, which presented Michel Fokine's innovative works—many performed to the radical music of Igor Stravinsky—in Paris. Diaghilev's roster included Tamara Karsavina (1885–1978); Felia Doubrovska (1896–1981); and Alexandra Danilova (b.1904), plus the celebrated Vaslav Nijinsky. (His sister, Bronislava Nijinska [1891–1972], was also an important Ballets Russes dancer and choreographer.)

After Diaghilev's death a new generation of Russian dancers toured widely as the Ballet Russe de Monte Carlo, which boasted three young stars called "baby ballerinas": Irina Baronova (b.1919); Tatiana Riabouchinska (b.1917); and Tamara Toumanova (b.1919).

Both major ballet companies in the Soviet Union—the Kirov and Moscow's Bolshoi Ballet—have featured outstanding ballerinas, most notably Galina Ulanova (b.1910) and Maya Plisetskaya (b.1925). And several notable Soviet dancers have defected to the West in recent years, including Natalia Makarova (b.1940) and Galina Panov (b.1949).

Two former Diaghilev dancers—Dame Marie Rambert (1888–1982) and Dame Ninette de Valois (b.1889)—can be credited with reviving ballet in England, the former through her Ballet Rambert, which nurtured many prominent dancers and choreographers. De Valois's Vic-Wells Ballet began in 1926 and formed the basis of Britain's Royal Ballet, which featured such luminaries as Dame Alicia Markova (b.1910) and Dame Margot Fonteyn (b.1919).

The United States was slow to accept the idea of homegrown ballet. It is not surprising, therefore, that the School of American Ballet was established (in New York in 1934) by a Russian—George Balanchine. His company (later christened the New York City Ballet [NYCB]) has produced an impressive list of ballerinas, including Melissa Hayden (b.1923); Maria Tallchief (b.1925); Allegra Kent (b.1938); Patricia McBride (b.1942); Kay Mazzo (b.1946); Suzanne Farrell (b.1945); and Gelsey Kirkland (b.1953). Another venerable company, American Ballet Theatre (ABT), was founded by Lucia Chase (1907–1986) and Oliver Smith in 1940. Whereas NYCB made its reputation with Balanchine's cool, abstract ballets, ABT became known for its productions of probing, psychological compositions by Anthony Tudor and the quintessentially American story ballets of Agnes de Mille (b.1909). Principal female dancers with ABT have included Janet Reed (b.1916); Nora Kaye (1920–1987); Lupe Serrano (b.1930); Toni Lander (b.1931); Sallie Wilson (b.1932); Martine van Hamel (b.1945); Cynthia Gregory (b.1946); and Marianna Tcherkassky (b.1955).

Other notable twentieth-century ballerinas are Frenchwoman Violette Verdy (b.1933), who served as artistic director of both the Paris Opera Ballet and the Boston Ballet; Brazilian Marcia Haydée (b.1939), since 1961 the star of the Stuttgart Ballet, which she now directs; Alicia Alonso (b.1921), prima ballerina and director of the National Ballet in her native Cuba; Celia Franca (b.1921) and Dame Peggy van Praagh (b.1910), former artistic directors of the National Ballet of Canada and the Australian Ballet, respectively; Vivi Flindt (b.1943) of the Royal Danish Ballet; and Lydia Abarca (b.1951), a principal with the Dance Theatre of Harlem.

The early twentieth century was a period of rebellion in all the arts, as painters, writers, and composers searched for innovative forms appropriate to contemporary life. One result of this rebellion was the development of modern dance, a radical new form intended to subvert the bases of classical ballet; instead of melodious music and sumptuous costumes, modern dance typically featured atonal music—or none at all—and accompanying barefooted dancers in unadorned leotards. Equally important, modern dance tended to tackle difficult, serious themes—not tales of enchanted dolls or swans, but violence-filled myths from ancient Greece or hard-hitting sociopolitical commentary.

Interestingly, most of the giants of modern dance have been women—primarily Americans. The immediate forerunners of modern dance were Isadora Duncan (1877–1927) and Ruth St. Denis (1880–1968), who rejected the rigidity and artifice of ballet, choosing instead to develop their own extremely personal types of movement.

The first true exemplar of modern dance was the German Mary Wigman (1886–1973). Her intense, expressionist choreography was seen all over Europe and the United States during the 1920s and 1930s, until the Nazis closed her school. In 1936 a Wigman pupil, Hanya Holm (b.1898), formed her own New York company, which produced a number of important dancers (Valerie Bettis [1920–1982], Glen Tetley, Alwin Nikolais). Another influential modern dance pioneer was the American Doris Humphrey (1895–1958), who danced with denishawn (the company founded by St. Denis and her husband, Ted Shawn), then established her own company with Charles Weidman. One of Humphrey's most famous protégés was José Limón.

The undisputed *grande dame* of modern dance for over a half-century is Martha Graham (b.1894). In 1929 Graham established a company for which she has choreographed well over 150 works and through which have emerged such eminent figures as Erick Hawkins, Merce Cunningham, and Paul Taylor. "Graham technique," taught the world over, is based on the principles of muscular contraction and release; her powerful dance-dramas emphasize striking, angular positions and often feature a female protagonist.

Many members of the next generation of female modern dancers were Graham students, including Anna Sokolow (b.1912); Jean Erdman (b.1917); Sophie Maslow (b.?); and Jane Dudley (b.1912). Younger artists such as Yvonne Rainer (b.1934) also received their formative training from Graham. Ann Halprin (b.1920), an important exponent of dance "happenings," was a Humphrey student, and others followed different paths: Bella Lewitzky (b.1915), a leading West Coast choreographer/dancer, trained with Lester Horton, and Helen Tamiris (1905–1966) was a ballet dancer until the age of 22.

While they did not form their own groups, certain artists have left indelible marks on the companies with which they created key roles: Betty Jones (b.1926) as Desdemona in José Limón's wrenching *Moor's Pavane*; Carolyn Adams (b.1943) in Paul Taylor's athletic, exuberant *Esplanade*; and the regal Judith Jamison (b.1944), for whom Alvin Ailey choreographed the powerful solo *Cry*.

Over the last quarter-century modern dance has continued to prosper, largely through the work of small, experimental companies—many headed by women. Two particularly innovative choreographers are Pina Bausch (b.1940), a leading German Expressionist, and Japanese choreographer Kei Takei (b.1946), whose ambitious dance cycle, *Light,* was begun in 1969. Among younger Americans, Trisha Brown (b.1936), a founder of the innovative Judson Dance Theatre, has been one of the most successful "postmodern" choreographer/dancers; others include Lucinda Childs (b.1940); Deborah Hay (b.1941); Senta Driver (b.1942); Molissa Fenley (b.1954); and Johanna Boyce (b.1954). Since the early 1970s Laura Dean (b.1945) has been creating intriguing arrangements of obsessively repeated sounds and gestures; Twyla Tharp (b.1942) has developed a kind of dry, physical humor by combining seemingly casual movements with music by such varied artists as Frank Sinatra and the Beach Boys; and Meredith Monk (b.1943) has produced remarkably complex theatre pieces involving dance, singing, and spoken words.

Further Reference. Jack Anderson, *Ballet and Modern Dance: A Concise History* (Princeton, N.J., 1986).

NANCY G. HELLER

DANISH WRITERS echo the voice of women in premedieval oral tradition. The folktales often feature a female protagonist whose development from childhood through arduous trials, which constitute a rite of passage, brings her to maturity and "happiness ever after" ("King Whitebear"); a passive young woman turns into a person resourceful enough to forge her own destiny. Women, who were often eloquent storytellers, preserved, transmitted, and thereby altered the genre. Those stories inevitably became vehicles for the women's experiences and hopes and perhaps—in the spirit of their Old Nordic ancestresses—even for their prophecies.

The ballad—of which Denmark has one of Europe's largest collections—is a late medieval genre dealing predominantly with the lives of the feudal aristocracy. The first collectors—and possible editors—were women of noble birth, Karen Brahe, Sofia Sandberg, and Ida Gjøe, who recorded the ballads in the late 1500s. Many a ballad features as its central character a woman who is neither pliant nor passive. A few ballads express a female point of view: in "Hr. Ebbe's døtre" (Sir Ebbe's Daughters), the violated young women take revenge in kind.

The Lutheran Reformation brought about the unity of monarchy and state church. Luther's *Cathecismus* (1529) would honor those in authority, and within the family structure that was the male. Latin schools were intended to educate boys of the middle class; girls were limited to little or no education and their mother tongue.

The daughters of the aristocracy were not so limited, and one such was Leonora Christina (1621–1698), a king's daughter who, because of her husband's condemnation for treason, spent 22 years in prison. Her journal, *Jammers Minde* (1674, pub. 1869; A Remembrance of Woe), was written in an honest, direct style that, oral in tone, was eloquent in its description of her imprisonment. There exists only the first of a three-part work, *Hæltinners Pryd* (1684; Heroines' Adornment), on women's contribution to history, demonstrating their natural equality with men with regard to common sense, the ability to learn, the wisdom to govern oneself, and the authority to rule.

Dorothe Engelbretsdatter (1634–1716), born in Norway (see NORWEGIAN WRITERS), which was then a part of Denmark, was the first published poet. Her collections of baroque hymns were enormously popular.

Anna Margrethe Lasson (1659–1738) wrote the first "original" novel in Danish: *Den Beklædte Sandhed* (c.1715, pub. 1723; The Disguised Truth). In the French baroque tradition, the love story became central. Charlotte Dorothea Biehl (1731–1788) wrote in many genres, but her play *Den listige Optrækkerske* (1765; The Cunning Extortionist), in which there appears a new woman—a deceiver of men—aroused discussion; *Mit ubetydelige Levnetsløb* (1787; My Unimportant Course of Life) described not only her early battles to read and to make her own choices but also her later years of isolation.

The nineteenth century, which turned from rationalism to romanticism and finally to realism/naturalism, was typified by the bourgeois family. Among the women famous for their intellectual salons was Karen Margrethe Rahbek (1775–1829), whose letters to male friends reflected her belief in intimate, but platonic, relationships. Thomasine Gyllembourg (1773–1856), the mother of the famous playwright and critic Johan Ludvig Heiberg (1791–1860), made her debut at 53. Her slightly romantic stories discuss problems of love and marriage in the homes of the bourgeoisie. *Ægtestand* (1835; Marriage) and "Maria" (1839) support the patriarchal ideal of woman but maintain a belief in women's right to an education, the freedom to choose a husband on the basis of love, and the economic independence of self-support. Gyllembourg's daughter-in-law, Johanne Luise Heiberg (1812–1890), was one of the age's most admired actresses (with 270 roles). The four-volume work *Et liv genoplevet i erindringen* (1855–1890, pub.

1891; A Life Recalled through Memory) was meant to honor her husband's contribution to literature. In articles she declared that the male should be the female's disciplinarian and the family, her school and that female emancipation would break the sexual biologic order. She interpreted her own longing and melancholy as proceeding from a religious instinct. Mathilde Fibiger (1830–1872) and Pauline Worm (1825–1883) viewed marriage as a type of women's welfare and recommended a brotherly-sisterly spiritual and intellectual relationship. Fibiger in *Clara Raphael. 12 breve* (1850; Clara Raphael: Twelve Letters) and Worm in *De fornuftige* (1857; The Sensible) stressed the function of art in spiritual liberation, as well as the many shortcomings of female education. Fibiger's book influenced parliamentary debate, which led to the law to give unmarried women the rights of adulthood (1857).

Adele Marie (Adda) Ravnkilde (1862–1883) was one of the women encouraged by, and a pupil of, Georg Brandes (1842–1927), the famous critic who translated John Stuart Mill's *The Subjection of Women* (1869) and who introduced into Scandinavia a new literary program, which came to be known as the "Modern Breakthrough," according to which authors were to place society's problems under debate. Ravnkilde, who wrote three stories—stressing equal rights for women but portraying the sexually masochistic—saw only *Judith Fürste* (1884) published before she committed suicide.

A bitter Nordic debate on men's morals opened the eyes of many female writers to the erotic double standard that existed in "free love," just as in traditional marriage. The next objective for many was to obtain an identity for woman as someone with an independent position.

Thit Jensen (1876–1957), however, felt that women had to choose love or work and that love was bound to the motherly, which represented the world's creative energy. Jensen debuted with *To søstre* (1903; Two Sisters) and by 1928 had written 25 books. She was also a zealous promoter of birth control. Agnes Henningsen (1868–1962) made her own life a work of art based on sexuality, the source of creativity, but she thought the Breakthrough's "free love" degrading to women. She wrote a three-volume autobiography, *Kærlighedens åårstider* (1927–1930; Love's Seasons), and an eight-volume memoir, *Let gang på jorden* (1941–1955; Stepping Lightly through Life).

Karin Michaëlis (1872–1950) wrote 70 books, the best known of which were translated into 20 languages. The book arousing greatest notice was *Den farlige alder* (1910; The Dangerous Age), in which a woman tries to escape society's decree that sexual desire is unsuitable for a woman of middle age.

Karen Blixen/Isak Dinesen (1885–1962) first published *Seven Gothic Tales* (1934) in the United States. Though raised in Denmark's upper bourgeoisie, she lived in Africa for many years. *Den afrikanske farm* (1937; *Out of Africa*, 1937) was an autobiographical work about her love and loss of that life. Blixen resumed life in Denmark and wrote with fantasy and an aristocratic understanding of other places and other ages. Believing in destiny, she rejected woman's role in bourgeois life. In her writing, which combines Gestalt and Jungian psychology, her characters seem to be living through the mythic and representing the archetypal.

Tove Ditlevsen (1918–1976), a child of the working class who dreamed of the security and tenderness of a middle-class marriage, was nevertheless a realist. Her lyric writing was reflective of her painful life, from her four marriages (in *Gift* [1971; Poison/Married]), through psychic breakdown (*Ansigterne* [1968; Faces]), to a prophecy of suicide (in *Vilhelms værelse* [1975; William's Room]). She has been called a symbol of the pain of being a woman.

Cecil Bødker (b.1927), Inger Christensen (b.1935), and Ulla Ryum (b.1937) belong to post–World War II modernism. Bødker, who has written several collections of poetry—such as *I vædderens tegn* (1968; In the Sign of the Ram)— short stories, experimental radio plays, and children's books, has received the Critics' Prize for the best prose writer. Her novels include *Tænk på Jolande* (1981; Remember Jolande). Christensen's most famous poetry collection, *Det* (1969; It), has won special praise. *Det* is the story of creation, which begins with "the word," but words begin to obscure the reality they would describe; new words must be found for a new beginning. Ulla Ryum is a novelist, dramatist, and short-story writer. Her novels—such as *Natsangersken* (1963; Night Singer) and *Latterfuglen* (1965; The Bird of Laughter)—stress psychoanalytic symbolism and absurdist techniques in tales of sexual cruelty. Elsa Gress (1919–1988), one of the few female members of the Danish Academy (1975), has written novels, essays, memoirs, plays, and film scripts. *Fuglefri og fremmed* (1979; Fancy Free and Foreign) treats the Occupation years.

There was a burst of increased authorial activity in the decade of the 1970s. Among the newer authors are Kirsten Thorup (b.1942) and Dorrit Willumsen (b.1940). Thorup's poetry collection *Love from Trieste* (1969) and novel *Baby* (1973) attempt to combine modernism with social realism, both of which tend to "object"-ify the individual. In Willumsen's universe, the women are childish in their dependence, and they seem unable to develop as human beings. Two of her works are the short story collection *Hvis det virkelig var en film* (1978; If It Really Were a Film, 1982) and the novel *Manden som påskud* (1980; The Man as an Excuse).

Artist and socialist Dea Trier Mørch (b.1941), most famous for *Vinterbørn* (1976; *Winter's Child*, 1986), pictures without mystification, in woodcuts as well as in text, birth and the sisterhood of the hospital. Hanne Marie Svendsen (b.1933) writes of women who are successful—like Ellen in *Dans under frostmånen* (1979; Dance Beneath the Frost Moon)—but who have suppressed certain aspects of their characters to be so. Inge Eriksen (b.1935) in *Fugletræet* (1980; The Bird Tree) warns against a woman's using her new freedom simply to escape.

If Vita Andersen (b.1944)—in her poetry *Tryghedsnarkomaner* (1977; Safety Addicts) or short stories *Hold kæft og vær smuk* (1978; Shut Up and Be Beautiful)—reveals women's lives as consisting of superficiality and brutal sexual encounters, Suzanne Brøgger (b.1944) would transform their limited lives into ideally erotic relationships encompassing mind and body. Brøgger debates modern morals in *Fri os fra kærligheden* (1973; *Deliver Us from Love*, 1976) and describes her effort to live "erotically" in *Creme fraiche* (1978; Sour Cream).

Women writers have tried to describe the "self" as well as to achieve both a communality and a general "fellowship." To that end they have not primarily sought integration into men's histories but have first demanded a recognition of their own history and that of their international sisterhood. There is now a burgeoning generation of critics as well as artists.

Among the new prose writers—Vibeke Grønfeldt, Iris Garnov, Vibeke Vasbo, Suzanne Giese, Jette Drewsen, etc.—and poets—Juliane Preisler, Merete Torp, and Pia Tafdrup—are the following critics: Mette Winge, Pil Dahlerup, Jette Lundbo Levy, Karen Syberg, Lisbet Møller Jensen, Lisbet Holst, Annagret Heitman, and Anne-Marie Mai.

Further References. Stig Dalager and Anne-Marie Mai, *Danske kvindelige forfattere*, 2 vols. (Copenhagen, 1982). Susanna Roxman (ed.), *Kvindelige forfattere. Kvindernes litteraturhistorie fra antikken til vore dage* (Copenhagen, 1985). Bodil Wamberg (ed.), *Out of Denmark: Isak Dinesen/Karen Blixen 1885–1985 and Danish Women Writers Today* (Copenhagen, 1985).

FAITH INGWERSEN

DETECTIVE FICTION. Soon after Poe's Dupin tales introduced the detective story proper to English literature in the 1840s, women writers took up the form and have remained in the forefront of the genre ever since. The first two Englishwomen to add to gothic mystery and crime plots the new concept of a central detecting intelligence were Mrs. Henry Wood, née Ellen Price (1814–1887), and Mary Elizabeth Braddon, later Maxwell (1835–1915). Wood, known for the popular *East Lynne* (1861), in *Mrs. Halliburton's Troubles* (1862) used a police sergeant and in *Within the Maze* (1872) used Scotland Yard officials to solve thefts and embezzlements. Braddon's equally popular *Lady Audley's Secret* (1862) borrowed from Wilkie Collins the amateur detective hero who confronts the villain after exhaustive examination of evidence and interviewing of witnesses. Her Robert Audley, an eccentric idler, foreshadows Sherlock Holmes by relying on inference and deduction. *Henry Dunbar* (1864), *Birds of Prey* (1867), and *Charlotte's Inheritance* (1868) are other Braddon novels featuring detectives.

Historians usually credit the American Anna Katharine Green (1846–1935) with writing the first detective novel—Braddon's and Wood's novels having initially appeared in serial form—and her first book, *The Leavenworth Case* (1878), used many elements later to become staples of the form: the suspects all of one household, with the least likely one guilty; an inquest employing ballistics; a diagram of the murder scene. Her police detective Ebenezer Gryce— patient, wise, and looking "not like a detective at all"—set a pattern for fictional professionals. He appears in other novels and in *That Affair Next Door* (1897) has a female assistant, Amelia Butterworth, who proves invaluable for her feminine perceptiveness.

Other writers had shown women occasionally detecting, like Collins's clever Marian Halcombe in *The Woman in White*, and even in a professional capacity, as with W. S. Hayward's ladylike police investigator Mrs. Paschal in *The Experiences of a Lady Detective* (1884). Hungarian-born Baroness Emmuska Orczy (1865–1947), whose main contribution to the genre is the armchair detective in *The Old Man in the Corner* (1909), also wrote *Lady Molly of Scotland Yard* (1910) about a beautiful aristocrat who with her woman assistant solves crimes while trying to free her imprisoned husband. Like Mrs. Paschal, Lady Molly is intrepid, ingenious, and respected—in her sphere—by male colleagues.

In *The Circular Staircase* (1908) American Mary Roberts Rinehart (1876–1958) has her inquisitive spinster narrator risk her life to unmask a criminal, in what was to become known as the Had-I-But-Known formula, after the heroine's hindsight realization. The novel was dramatized (as *The Bat*) in several stage and movie versions, and Rinehart used the formula in other novels, such as *Miss Pinkerton* (1932), which featured the nurse-sleuth Hilda Adams. Of a number of women adapting the formula to the gothic mystery, best known is Mignon Eberhart (b.1899), whose principal sleuth is nurse Sarah Keate in *The Patient in Room 18* (1929) and other novels.

The "Golden Age" of detective fiction following World War I was dominated by two British women, Dame Agatha Christie (1890–1976) and Dorothy L. Sayers (1893–1957). Between her first novel, *The Mysterious Affair at Styles* (1920), which introduced the Belgian detective Hercule Poirot, and her last published work, *Curtain* (1975), Christie wrote over 80 novels and became the most popular twentieth-century mystery writer. Admired for her skill at constructing puzzles, lively dialogue, and ingenious crimes, as in *Murder on the Orient Express* (1934), she was also criticized for allegedly breaking the rules of fair play in *The Murder of Roger Ackroyd* (1926) by having the narrator turn out to be the murderer. Her other series detective is spinster Jane Marple, seen first in *The Murder at the Vicarage* (1930). In contrast, Sayers wrote only a handful of full-length mysteries, beginning with *Whose Body?* (1923), which introduced her stylishly eccentric Lord Peter Wimsey. In *Gaudy Night* (1935) Wimsey shares the detecting with mystery writer Harriet Vane, whom he marries in *Busman's Honeymoon* (1937). Sayers also wrote many Wimsey short stories, presided over the famous Detection Club, wrote essays on the art of detective fiction, and edited mystery anthologies.

Notable in the next generation of writers are Englishwoman Margery Allingham (1904–1966), whose Albert Campion, "a trifle absent-minded" detective of vaguely aristocratic origins, appears as early as *The Crime at Black Dudley* (1929) and as late as *The Mind Readers* (1965); the New Zealander Dame Ngaio Marsh (1899–1982) whose Superintendent Roderick Alleyn, also of aristocratic stock, appears in innumerable novels between *A Man Lay Dead* (1934) and *Grave Mistake* (1978), often in theatrical settings where the murders are gruesome; and Scottish-born Elizabeth Mackintosh (1897–1952), who, as Josephine Tey, has rung some original changes on the form in *Miss Pym Disposes*

(1946), a moral and psychological study of a student crime, and in *The Daughter of Time* (1951), in which Inspector Alan Grant unravels the fifteenth-century murder of the Princes in the Tower.

Among current British writers Ruth Rendell (b.1930) has departed somewhat from tradition in making her Chief Inspector Reginald Wexford married, hypertensive, and stationed in Sussex. In novels like *From Doon with Death* (1964) and *Shake Hands Forever* (1975) Rendell mixes strong characterization with social criticism. P. D. James (b.1920) is noteworthy for her modern settings, such as a home for incurables in *The Black Tower* (1975) and an East Anglian forensic laboratory in *Death of an Expert Witness* (1977). Her series detective is Commander Adam Dalgliesh of Scotland Yard, a published poet, but she also used a young private investigator, Cordelia Gray, in *An Unsuitable Job for a Woman* (1972) and *The Skull beneath the Skin* (1982). Recent American writers include Charlotte Armstrong (1905–1969), whose series character MacDougal Duff probes moral questions in such stories as *Lay On, MacDuff!* (1942); Carolyn Heilbrun (b.1926), who, writing as Amanda Cross, has the university professor Kate Fansler solving crimes in works like *The James Joyce Murder* (1967); and Patricia Highsmith (b.1921), who is best known for *Strangers on a Train* (1950) and whose continuing character Tom Ripley is not a detective but a psychopathic killer, as in *Ripley's Game* (1974).

Women's detective fiction over the last century has shown marked differences from men's. Women use less violence and more characterization. Earlier they had, like their male counterparts, seen female detection strengths as intuition and observation; later, more than men, they emphasize women's logic, resourcefulness, and independence. Women favor male detectives, usually professional and upper-class, over female detectives, who tend to be amateurs and middle-class—a preference often attributed to snobbery but probably ascribable to the demands of realism and women's view of detection fiction as novels of manners. Women's choice of plots involving hidden identities may be connected to personal experiences of pressures to role-play: Braddon, for example, passed for years as the wife of a man already married; Sayers hid the existence of her illegitimate child from even her closest friends; Christie never explained her onetime "amnesiac" disappearance. Women writers often show their protagonist simultaneously solving a crime and resolving a private crisis; by unmasking an impostor, for example, Rinehart's heroine in *The Circular Staircase* comes to a sense of her true self, and Cross's heroine in *The Question of Max* (1976), like Sayers's in *Gaudy Night* almost a half-century before, reconciles her feminist principles with love and marriage in the process of unraveling a crime. The inherently conservative nature of detective fiction and the opportunities it allows for inventiveness within formulaic constraints have clearly proven congenial to women writers.

Further Reference. Patricia Craig and Mary Cadogan, *The Lady Investigates: Women Detectives and Spies in Fiction* (New York, 1981).

MARY ROSE SULLIVAN

DEVOTIONAL LITERATURE, MEDIEVAL. Probably the most popular of the various types of medieval literature, read or listened to by members of all classes of society; it is defined as literature written for the faithful and intended to develop or heighten feelings of devotion toward God or the saints. Devotional literature is not concerned with teaching theology, but it is didactic in its emphasis on the exemplary Christian life and on the relationship between the individual soul and the divine. Women were some of the best writers of devotional literature; we may also assume that they constituted a large proportion of its audience. Varieties included saints' lives, prayers, hymns or song cycles, guides to prayer, letters of spiritual encouragement, autobiographical narratives of personal spiritual growth, and accounts of women's visions and prophecies.

The prevalence of devotional literature by women attests to the near monopoly on education exercised by the church and to the misogyny in medieval culture that silenced all but the most holy or inspired women. Peter Dronke notes that writing by women "is a response springing from inner needs" resulting in a tone of immediacy; women "look at themselves more concretely and more searchingly than many of the highly accomplished men writers who were their contemporaries" (*Women Writers of the Middle Ages* [Cambridge, Mass., 1984], x). Women who learned to read and write usually did so in convent schools; for them to go on to become writers, they needed the conditions provided by women's communities: scholarly leisure, access to books and materials of book production, economic support, freedom from external responsibilities and from repeated pregnancies and childraising (Katharina M. Wilson, *Medieval Women Writers* [Athens, Ga., 1984], ix). Women without these advantages who felt called to be visionary writers strove to create comparable conditions for themselves so that their ideas and experiences could be written down, even if they had not learned to read and write (Elizabeth Petroff, *Medieval Women's Visionary Literature* [Oxford, 1986], 27–28).

Women are among the earliest writers of devotional literature. The autobiographical *Passion of Saints Perpetua and Felicity* dates from 203; Egeria's account of her pilgrimage to the holy land (*Itinerarium* or *Peregrinatio Aetheriae*) dates from the following century. In the eighth century, Frankish nuns write vitae of their famous contemporaries, a practice that continued in French and German convents until the end of the Middle Ages. At about the same time, Anglo-Saxon nuns active in the Christianizing of Germany and in charge of producing the books needed by this mission wrote letters and an epic account of the life of St. Willibald. More famous writers include the dramatist Hrotsvit of Gandersheim and the mystic Hildegard of Bingen.

The type of devotional literature in which women especially excelled is visionary or spiritual autobiography. The earliest example is St. Perpetua's account of her martyrdom, which describes an area of female experience—dreams and prophecies expressing the subjective experience of the divine—that by the twelfth century had become the dominant mode of women's religious writing. Visions, nurtured by the devotional meditations taught to women, provided the structure and content; the visionary was respected in medieval society, and a female visionary could teach others what God or one of the saints had taught her, even when as a woman she ought not to teach in public. Some of these writers are well known to students of mysticism: Mechthild of Magdeburg, Gertrude the Great, Hadewijch, Beatrijs van Tienen. Others were once influential but now forgotten: Umiltà of Faenza and Marguerite d'Oingt. Several—Marguerite Porete and Na Prous Boneta—were burned at the stake as heretics. Most of the famous mystics of the fourteenth and fifteenth centuries were deeply influenced by this female tradition: Angela of Foligno, Catherine of Siena, Julian of Norwich, Margery Kempe. These autobiographies are also models for the Christian life, prophecies of the future of the church, and guides to devotion. Many of women's devotional writings are among the earliest texts in the vernacular languages, a fact that suggests that these writings responded to a felt need among lay and religious people of both sexes for guidance to the spiritual life.

Similar autobiographies were often written in the late fifteenth and sixteenth centuries by radical reformers of existing monastic orders. The works of St. Teresa of Ávila are the culmination of this tradition and follow upon the earlier writings of Magdalena Beutler of Freiburg, Catherine of Genoa, and Catherine of Bologna. Scholars are only now identifying and translating women's devotional literature. Many questions remain to be explored: the importance of women writers' bilingualism (their ability to think and/or read and write in both Latin and their own vernacular language), their combination of oral and written methods of composition, their audience, their awareness of a female visionary tradition.

Further References. Susan Groag Bell, "Medieval Women Book Owners: Arbiters of Lay Piety and Ambassadors of Culture," *Signs* 7 (1981–1982): 742–769. Lina Eckenstein, *Women under Monasticism,* (Cambridge, Eng., 1896; still useful). Kurt Ruh, "Beginnenmystik: Hadewijch, Mechthild von Magdeburg, Marguerite Porete," *Zeitschrift fur deutsches Altertum und deutsche Literatur* 106 (1977): 265–277. Paul Szarmach (ed.), *An Introduction to the Medieval Mystics of Europe* (Albany, N.Y., 1984).

ELIZABETH PETROFF

DOMESTIC NOVEL. Includes works in the traditional canon, works just on the fringe of it, and scores of second-rate works of popular fiction. This variety reflects the confusion between the use of *domestic novel* as a literary term and its use as a popular one. As a specific term of literary criticism, *domestic novel of manners* is preferable to *domestic novel*. The domestic novel of manners is largely a phenomenon of nineteenth-century British literature and includes a number of texts that have been variously categorized as domestic fiction, domestic romance, social problem novels, governess novels, religious novels, and novels of manners.

The earliest novels that unequivocally idealize domesticity are by Maria Edgeworth, notably *Belinda* (1801) and *Patronage* (1814). The works of Jane Austen share many of the conventions of the domestic novel of manners, although Austen works within the framework of family life without actually idealizing it. The next major works of domestic fiction come in the 1840s and 1850s with the works of Charlotte and Anne Brontë and Elizabeth Gaskell. The novels of all three women show variations on the conventional pattern of the genre yet remain solidly within it. Two novels by George Eliot (*The Mill on the Floss* [1860] and *Middlemarch* [1871–1872]) mark the end of the genre as a major literary category.

The conventional idealization of domesticity is prefigured in *Pamela* (1740), *The Vicar of Wakefield* (1766), and *Evelina* (1778), to cite only three better-known and more substantial examples. These novels in turn draw upon an earlier tradition of sentimental romance, the conventional roots of which lie in the Middle Ages and, in the case of some conventions, beyond. Within the sentimental tradition the good female character, the heroine, is a series of negations—purity, ignorance, passive dependence—that must be preserved. This conception of ideal female character is the cornerstone of the primary component of the conventional pattern of the domestic novel of manners: the idealization of domesticity and the sanctification of middle-class, Christian, and family-centered values that dominate characterization, plots, and themes.

The central character, the imaginative heroine, is both an avid reader and a teller of tales, habits that link her closely to her author, reinforcing the textual interpenetration of the genre and its characteristic combination of reading and writing. These texts are not only implicitly parasitic upon earlier texts (and one another) but explicitly so. In early domestic novels of manners self-referentiality is manifest primarily as a preoccupation with literature, especially novels. As the convention evolves during the nineteenth century, it is increasingly preoccupied with language itself, as medium, metaphor, method. Heroines are regularly compared to heroines of fiction and then evaluated in terms of their ability to fulfill conventional requirements. The narrative never fails to call attention to them and consequently to itself, whenever they fall short of or positively contravene conventional ideals.

Love is at the heart of all domestic novels of manners in the sense that the plot always revolves around the vicissitudes of the heroine's preparations to love and be loved. The fact that the romantic love she seeks is sanctioned only within the confines of marriage is perhaps the most blatant instance of the idealization of domesticity. Happiness rewards only those characters who love in the right place at the right time, and surprisingly few characters actually achieve this ideal. There are, moreover, very few happily married couples in these texts. The happiest couples are those just on the threshold of married life, as though the conventional ''happy ending,'' the wedding, were actually the end of happiness. As a plot device, the heroine's marriage persists as the traditional closure of the domestic novel of manners long after the authors of these texts have begun to acknowledge its ambivalence explicitly.

The thematic focus of the domestic novel of manners shifts according to subgeneric category. The earliest examples of the genre are often attacks on sentimental or gothic romance. Maria Edgeworth's *Belinda* and Jane Austen's

Northanger Abbey (1818), for example, parody the conventional characterization of the heroine without seriously questioning traditional standards of female conduct or the pivotal role of marriage in a woman's life. Yet both novels represent a step forward in the concept of female character in that the passivity of absolute purity and ignorance is replaced by the necessity for moral development. Moral development follows the loss of romantic fictional illusions for both Belinda Portman and Catherine Morland. Marriage retains its thematic and narrative importance as both goal and closure.

Between 1830 and 1870 a handful of themes dominated Victorian fiction in general and the domestic novel of manners in particular. The three most pervasive of these themes were the status of women, social reform, and religion. The controversy surrounding the status of women at this time was very often addressed through the character of the governess and the closely related problems of the "fallen woman" and prostitution. Questions of social reform were more various but concentrated on industrial relations, public versus private charity, and the education of the working class. The crucial religious concern of the period might be characterized generally as the struggle between faith and doubt, a struggle that took numerous forms, both publicly and privately.

These three themes became loci for the reformation of many of the conventions of the domestic novel of manners, reformations that contributed to the creation of recognizable subgenres: governess novels, social problem novels, and religious novels. The last category is best represented by the works of Charlotte Yonge, whose domestic novels read rather like Evangelical tracts. In spite of Yonge's achievement, the religious novel, unlike the other significant variants of the domestic novel in this period, contributed little of lasting value to the mainstream tradition.

The governess novel was one of the most common vehicles for literary treatment of the woman question, a unique social problem crossing class lines, regional boundaries, and occupational categories. Although other kinds of working women are occasionally depicted in novels of this period (Elizabeth Gaskell's *Mary Barton* [1848] and Anne Brontë's *The Tenant of Wildfell Hall* [1848], e.g.), the plight of the working woman and her salvation through marriage are most often treated in governess novels. Lady Blessington's *The Governess* (1839) is in many ways the prototype of this subgenre, but its influence pales beside the sensation made by Charlotte Brontë's *Jane Eyre* (1847).

Elizabeth Gaskell's *North and South* (1854–1855) is the best example of the social problem novel informed by domestic standards and values. It is much superior to Gaskell's earlier novels in this vein, *Mary Barton* and *Ruth* (1853), and is even more successful than *Jane Eyre* as a novel of manners. In *North and South* Gaskell domesticates the conventions of social relevance in two important ways. First, the explicit analyses of social problems so central to this subgenre are placed in a domestic setting rather than in a mill, in the streets, or in a neutral narrative limbo. Second, household goods and family relationships are used to illustrate the effects of abstract social problems on individual human families.

The ultimate development of the domestic novel of manners comes in the works of George Eliot. *The Mill on the Floss* might be described as a mirror image of a domestic novel of manners, inverting as it does the major conventional mode of the genre, the idealization of domesticity. The traditional characteristics of the ideal female character (passivity, ignorance, purity, renunciation) are still in evidence, but the valuation of these traits has been reversed. Acquisition and preservation of these "virtues" reward Maggie Tulliver not with marriage but with death, the epitome of passive self-effacement. Throughout the novel marriage and family life are associated with images of oppression, self-immolation, and death.

It is in *Middlemarch* that Eliot most clearly achieves her desire to render the profound complexities of human character and the lamentably elusive nature of human dreams, including the dream of domestic bliss. The novel's most important themes—marriage, the egoism of perception, and imagination as illusion—shatter the conventional domestic ideals of the genre beyond redemption. Specifically, earlier perceptions of marriage as culmination and conclusion are consistently undermined. Even the marriage of Will and Dorothea fails to provide the conventional perfect fulfillment.

The patterns of characterization, plot, and theme in the domestic novel of manners reveal the close association of that genre with the concept of female *Bildungsroman* (a novel concerned with the formation of the hero's character) in nineteenth-century British literature. The loss of romantic illusions that is so often equated with the heroine's moral development in domestic novels of manners was itself an illusion. Romance was not truly discredited or overthrown; it was institutionalized in the "ideal marriage."

Further References. Lynne Agress, *The Feminine Irony: Women on Women in Early Nineteenth-Century English Literature* (Cranbury, N.J., 1978). Jenni Calder, *Women and Marriage in Victorian Fiction* (London, 1976). Vineta Colby, *Yesterday's Woman: Domestic Realism in the English Novel* (Princeton, N.J., 1974). Susan Siefert, *The Dilemma of the Talented Heroine: A Study in Nineteenth-Century Fiction* (Montreal, 1977).

ELIZABETH BOYD THOMPSON

DRAMA, MEDIEVAL: IMAGES OF WOMEN IN, represent those regarded as important agents in Christian history. The Virgin Mary and female saints played central roles in the drama of salvation enacted in hundreds of plays of biblical history and saintly deeds during the later Middle Ages. As vehicles for divine power and intercessors for human sinners, these holy females are so important that one can speak of a "feminization" of late medieval piety that is reflected in the drama.

Although all plays draw on the large body of exegetical, apocryphal, and folk material to interpret the women's actions, principles of selection also reflect the ideology of the social group producing the play as well as ideologies implicit in different dramatic genres. As the place of women in these ideologies varied, so images of women in the plays could vary widely.

The earliest and most widespread scenes with women characters were enactments of the angel's announcement of Christ's resurrection to the three Marys at the tomb (the *visitatio sepulchri*). We call these scenes "liturgical dramas," but since they usually took place within the celebration of the Easter matins office, were sung in Latin, and acted by and for clerics, they are more appropriately regarded as liturgical expansions than as "drama." The gender of the three Marys is unimportant for they are spiritual icons, representing all worshipers who seek Christ.

However, in a number of Easter plays, usually from the fourteenth or fifteenth century and in the spoken vernacular, the three Marys who come to anoint Christ's body are referred to as "weeping women." Attention is drawn to their gender by a spice merchant who, like a quack apothecary, promises that the ointments he sells them will act as aphrodisiacs or cosmetics to heighten their erotic appeal. One of the three Marys, Mary Magdalene, was especially associated in medieval drama with female sexual misconduct. She was portrayed as a beautiful, vain, and lecherous young woman who abandoned her worldly sins and became an example of Christ's mercy to those who demonstrated true penitence and ardent love of him.

In some scenes, the Marys are greeted with scorn when they bring news of the Resurrection to the apostles; Peter, Thomas, and others scoff that they cannot believe women's words since everyone knows that women love to spread idle tales. The function of this dramatic denigration of women is to critique conventional wisdom and worldly status. Just as the first announcement of Christ's birth was given to poor shepherds, so the first news of his Resurrection comes to women who are socially inferior. The devotion of the Marys or the exemplary penitence of Magdalene represents possibilities outside the normal structures of life, but possibilities available to all in their spiritual or social condition. Within the context of late medieval communal festivity, plays with gender symbolism expressed alternatives to the status quo.

Other representations of the Marys in drama might emphasize the theme of female kinship. In apocryphal legend Mary Salome and Mary Jacobi were said to be half sisters to the Virgin Mary through earlier marriages of their mother, St. Anne. The cult of St. Anne, part of popular piety of the fifteenth century, celebrated the female lineage of Anne and her daughters. Plays in which the kinship of these "holy women" is emphasized often are connected to lay devotional groups with largely female membership.

Cycles and passion plays produced for an urban bourgeoisie in which male civic and craft guild patronage predominated tended to portray biblical women as wives, workers, and neighbors. Many scenes of Joseph and Mary demonstrated proper marital relations as described in contemporary conduct books, while Noah's wife and the wives of other characters like the spice merchant, Pilate, or the smith who made the nails for the Crucifixion provided comic examples of disordered female behavior. Mary Magdalene's sister Martha—who in monastic and mystical literature had represented the less elevated "active life" of service in the world (whereas Mary represented the "contemplative")—now took on status as the busy housewife who entertained the men of God and gave alms. Martha earned salvation not by rejecting the world but by using its goods properly, with pious economy. She could be a role model not only to the housewife but to her bourgeois husband as well.

Eve as archetypal disobedient female is always portrayed with women's weaknesses of vanity, manipulativeness, irrationality, and perversity in plays of the Fall. The image of Eve in the medieval drama draws on antifeminist satires, while the portrayal of Mary, who redeems mankind from the effects of the Fall, draws on a corresponding literature of profeminist praise.

Although the typical medieval morality play casts a male as protagonist, at least one from Holland portrays a girl who is seduced into a Faustian pact with the Devil. The virtues and the vices are often female in the morality tradition, whose iconography is indebted to the visual arts.

Despite the variety and importance of female figures in medieval drama, acting was, with few exceptions, an activity only for males until the Renaissance. When a play was performed in a convent, the nuns took all the parts, male and female. In the late fifteenth century, too, dramas produced by the urban bourgeoisie occasionally cast young women, daughters or wives of important men in town, in female parts. Otherwise, female roles were probably filled by young men whose pubertal changes were still taking place, about age 18–20 in this period of later maturation.

KATHLEEN ASHLEY

DRAMA, RESTORATION AND EARLY EIGHTEENTH-CENTURY: IMAGES OF WOMEN IN, varies widely from classic antifeminist stereotypes to tough-minded portraits of women confronting complex problems in a society that grants them no genuine authority.

At the beginning of the period, the Restoration belle is a self-assured, independent, and witty young woman reluctant to give up the pleasures of single life. She likes the city and its freedom to come and go, to select her acquaintances and pastimes, to feel, in a way, free. Harriet in Etherege's *The Man of Mode* (1676) epitomizes the type. In a milieu where cleverness is the ultimate virtue, only she possesses the sangfroid and intellectual strength to hold her own in verbal combat with the libertine hero. Harriet shares Dorimant's pleasure in the control and conquest of the love chase, but ultimately she differs from other women whom Dorimant pursues in the self-control and wit that allow her to hold out for marriage. Though the witty belle may be libertine in attitude, unlike the beau, she must be chaste in action.

Excused some from this stricture are young country girls, who, like amoral animals, are free from the pretenses of society. Brought to town by a jealous old husband, Margery Pinchwife, in Wycherley's *Country Wife* (1675), does not conceal her pleasure in the omnivorous Horner's advances. The "natural" Miss Prue in Congreve's *Love for Love* (1695) freely proclaims, "Now my mind is set upon a Man, I will have a Man some way or other" (5.1). However, most women unable to control their sexual needs are fair game for ridicule. Their names proclaim their image: Lady Cockwood in Etherege's *She Wou'd if She Cou'd* (1668), Mrs. Loveit in Etherege's *The Man of Mode* (1676), Mrs. Termagant in Shadwell's *The Squire of Alsatia* (1688), Mrs. Wittwoud in Southerne's *The Wives' Excuse* (1691), and Lady Wishfort in Congreve's *The Way of the World* (1700). The wits ridicule those who are unable to suppress sexual desires beneath a mask of prudery or who fail to maintain a predatory coolness and so allow themselves to be victimized. A superannuated belle like Lady Wishfort is ridiculous for not realizing that she is no longer a beauty, yet she is also pathetic, trapped in a society that compels her to paint on the bloom of youth.

Judging from the couples they see around them, many young women in Restoration comedy do not expect much from marriage. Alithea, though otherwise the brightest woman in *The Country Wife*, feels obliged to marry her foolish suitor because she mistakes his self-absorption and negligence for genuine love and trust. But more often, aware of the real consequences of loveless marriages of convenience, women seek to marry someone not only attractive but also perhaps compatible. Hellena in Aphra Behn's *The Rover* (1677) finds conventional marriage unattractive and so, along with Willmore, hopes to transform the institution to suit herself. And countless heroines engage in witty "proviso scenes." In the most famous of these scenes (in *The Way of the World*), Millamant tries to carve out with Mirabel ground rules for daily coexistence to ensure her "dear liberty" before allowing that she "may by degrees dwindle into a wife" (Act 4).

By the 1690s playwrights turn their attention from public courtship to the private consequences when couples wed without choosing carefully. Generally husbands cope with unhappy marriages by philandering or gaming; without legal or economic protection, women had fewer options. In Colley Cibber's notorious *Love's Last Shift* (1696), Amanda's husband Loveless, absent for ten years, returns only when he believes her dead. After enduring what the epilogue calls his being "lewd above four acts," this patient wife finally reclaims him on his terms with a variation of "the bed trick." Discovering that the delightful woman in bed is not a courtesan but his disguised wife, Loveless vows to reform, praising "the chaste Rapture of a Vertuous Love" (Act 5). (An unconvinced Sir John Vanbrugh followed up on the Amanda/Loveless story later that season in *The Relapse*.) More often, wives—such as Lady Easy in Cibber's *The Careless Husband* (1704) and Mrs. Bellamant in Henry Fielding's *The Modern Husband* (1730)—rely on the strength of their virtue and forbearance to retrieve wayward husbands.

Particularly telling, however, are the images of unhappy wives in plays that offer no easy solutions. In Thomas Southerne's *The Wives Excuse* (1691), Mrs. Friendall holds off tempting advances while covering for her lascivious and mean-spirited husband. But at play's end, when Friendall is discovered in bed with Mrs. Wittwoud, the Friendalls agree to part, granting Mrs. Friendall a separate maintenance. He is pleased with his new freedom, but she recognizes her position: "The unjust world . . . condemns us to a Slavery for Life: And if by Separation we get free, then all our Husband's Faults are laid on us. . . . I must be still your Wife, and still unhappy" (Act 5). Lady Brute in Vanbrugh's *The Provoked Wife* (1697) and Mrs. Sullen in Farquhar's *The Beaux' Strategem* (1707) face in some ways a harder condition: their husbands, unlike the loathsome Mr. Friendall, are merely bored and boring. Though Mrs. Sullen is promised a "divorce" that will allow her to remarry, an option not available to women in the audience, Lady Brute's circumstances remain unresolved at play's end.

The portrayal of women in tragedy of the period is apparently far removed from these quotidian problems. In spectacular heroic drama, women often fit simple cultural stereotypes: Lyndaraxa and Almahide in Dryden's *Conquest of Granada* (1670–1671) and Nourmahal and Indamora in his *Aureng-Zebe* (1675) offer variations on standard contrasts between the manipulative seductress and the long-suffering wife. But the latter image of woman—as the civilizer whose noble love attempts to turn man's drive for power toward socially acceptable goals—gains increasing prominence. As Jaffeir says to his wife, Belvidera, in Otway's *Venice Preserved* (1682), "Oh Woman! lovely Woman! Nature made thee/To temper Man: We had been Brutes without you" (Act 1.1).

With growing frequency, women characters begin to dominate tragedy that is moving toward pathos. Following the lead of such plays as Otway's *The Orphan* (1680), Banks's *Vertue Betray'd* (1682), and Southerne's *The Fatal Marriage* (1694), Nicholas Rowe produced what he called "she-tragedies," centering on the undeserved distresses and domestic woes of their heroines: *The Fair Penitent* (1703), *The Tragedy of Jane Shore* (1714), and *Lady Jane Grey* (1715). Modern readers admire the spirited Millwood, in George Lillo's *The London Merchant* (1731), who says she learned from men that money secures one from contempt and dependence. "You [men] go on deceiving and being deceived, harassing, plaguing, and destroying one another," she tells her accusers, "but women are your universal prey" (Act 4.2). Yet contemporary audiences prized the play's Maria Thorowgood, who dutifully suffers "generous distress" when her beloved is revealed as a murderer. Like the good women trapped in bad marriages in comedy or bereft maidens like Indiana in Steele's *Conscious Lovers* (1722), good-natured Maria Thorowgood is the image of woman that carries into the great novels of the eighteenth century.

Further References. Shirley Strum Kenny, "'Elopements, Divorce, and the Devil Knows What': Love and Marriage in English Comedy, 1690–1720," *South Atlantic Quarterly* 78 (1979): 84–106. Susan Staves, *Players' Scepters: Fictions of Authority in the Restoration* (Lincoln, Neb., 1979).

SUSAN K. AHERN

DRAMA AND THEATRE, BRITISH (NINETEENTH-CENTURY), reflected the changing status of women in society and offered unusual career opportunities at a time when occupations open to women were severely limited.

While melodrama was the dominant genre of the period, the immensely popular pantomime, burlesque, and extravaganza also provided a subliminal means to explore complex, often contradictory attitudes toward power relationships and sexual boundaries. Frequently based upon classical myth or fairy tale, these entertainments combined archetypal image with topical reference and emphasized the physical charms of its female performers, who appeared in elaborate costumes often more revealing than contemporary dress. From the 1830s, the breeches role (inherited from the previous century) became a standard feature in these productions as the young male hero was played by an attractive actress (called the "principal boy" from the 1870s). In contrast, the "dame"—an unattractive female character middle-aged or older, often portrayed as a shrew—was frequently played by a male low comedian. Transvestite performance in general was a prominent feature of this period, as women performers played boys and men in both serious and comic, old and new plays.

The public nature of the actress's work made her a conspicuous social figure, as age-old objections to the itinerant nature of the life-style, along with the low ebb of theatrical fortunes in the first half of the century, contributed to a general consensus that acting was not a respectable occupation. When a decorous middle-class life-style emerged with Victoria's ascension to the throne in 1837, a heavy emphasis on feminine domesticity further highlighted the actress's anomalous position. Exhibition of her talents for gain condemned the average performer to a social category only slightly above the prostitute, but if her profession was shameful, it was also alluring. While she suffered ostracism from most polite circles, the actress enjoyed economic independence and a sexual and social freedom denied to more respectable members of her sex. The life was, in many cases, grueling, but those above the profession's lower ranks might enjoy the benefits of a potentially stimulating and lucrative profession that demanded the energetic application of creative talent. In the public imagination, at least, the actress offered a psychic release from the demand that women be self-sacrificing, self-effacing, and confined to the home.

In the first half of the century, most new performers came from the theatrical families that dominated the profession. Actresses frequently married other theatrical personnel and continued to work, often raising large families simultaneously. At mid-century, as financial stability increased and stage performers were successful in luring a respectable audience back to the theatres, women from middle-class backgrounds began to enter the profession in greater numbers. While the morality of the actress was still under debate late in the century, the most highly suspect were those who performed in light entertainment.

Throughout the period, the great tragediennes were often given the special dispensation of "high art." Undoubtedly, the most revered actress of the period was Sarah Siddons (1755–1831), whose career spanned the late eighteenth and early nineteenth centuries. A member of the Kemble family, she performed in their particular classical style noted for stateliness, dignity, and grace, though she was said to possess greater emotional intensity than the most famous of her siblings, John Philip Kemble. Helen Faucit (1817–1898), who debuted in London in 1836, was particularly concerned with illustrating acceptable feminine qualities in her portrayal of Shakespeare's heroines. Late in the period, the public was willing to overlook the unconventional living arrangements of Ellen Terry (1847–1928), whose liaison with Edward Godwin produced the important twentieth-century theorist, Edward Gordon Craig. Terry became the first actress to be named Dame Commander of the British Empire, in 1925, following by 30 years the knighthood of her leading man, Henry Irving, the first actor ever to receive such an honor. Such awards are now considered an indication that public opinion of the acting profession had risen considerably by the end of the century.

The majority of theatrical enterprises in the nineteenth century were controlled by men, but very popular actresses might influence staffing decisions as well as repertoire, while a significant number of women entered the realm of play writing or management. Dramatic writing was more difficult for women than other, more private forms of authorship, since it required public interaction and collaboration with theatre artists, but women were nonetheless represented as authors, translators, and adapters in the commercial theatre as well as in the "closet" dramatic literature never meant to be performed. Joanna Baillie (1762–1851), perhaps the most widely known female playwright of the period, experimented with the construction of dramas based upon one dominant emotion. Her "Plays of the Passions" were greatly admired by readers but achieved only limited success on the stage. The tragedies of Mary Russell Mitford (1787–1855) were performed successfully during the 1820s and 1830s, and *Quid Pro Quo*, by novelist Catherine Grace Frances Gore (1799–1861), was selected as the best comedy submitted to a panel of judges and produced at the Haymarket in 1844.

The hiring, firing, authoritative delegation of work, and financial planning that running a theatre entailed were normally considered masculine responsibilities. In 1831, however, Lucia Elizabeth Bartolozzi Vestris (1797–1856) assumed control of the Olympic Theatre and publicized herself as the first woman manager. This statement was not technically true, since several women, both in London and in the provinces, had managed theatres already, but Vestris was by far the most visible and the most important up to that time. A highly successful actress and singer known particularly for transvestite roles, Vestris converted the dirty Olympic into a highly fashionable place of entertainment and reigned there successfully until 1839, building a reputation for innovation in the integration of all production elements and the use of realistic props and detail. With her husband, Charles Mathews, she later managed the Covent Garden (1839–1842) and Lyceum (1847–1856) theatres, mounting several noteworthy Shakespearean revivals and numerous elaborate holiday entertainments.

By the mid-Victorian years, female managers were not uncommon, as women ran theatres alone and with husbands or other family members. Marie Wilton

(1839–1921), also a popular breeches role performer, renovated a theatre so filthy that it was known as "the dust hole" and opened it in 1865 as the elegant Prince of Wales'. Two years later she married her leading man, Squire Bancroft, and together they managed the Prince of Wales' until 1879, then the Haymarket from 1880 until their retirement in 1885. Their work with playwright T. W. Robertson marked a new era of realistic production style in Britain, and their managerial methods set the standard for much twentieth-century theatre practice. Noteworthy in a very different context was Sara Lane (1823–1899), who ran the Britannia Theatre in Hoxton with her husband, Sam, until his death in 1871 and then managed it successfully alone until her own death over a quarter of a century later. Revered by the neighborhood working-class people who made up the Britannia audience, Lane wrote eight plays for her own theatre between 1873 and 1881 and played the principal boy in the annual Christmas pantomime until she was in her seventies.

At the end of the century, popular entertainment continued to emphasize female display and sexual fantasy, while women performers, managers, producers, and playwrights participated in the intellectual and theatrical ferment that preceded World War I. In 1889, Janet Achurch (1864–1916), with her husband, Charles Charrington, presented the first significant production of Henrik Ibsen in England when *A Doll's House* was given a private showing. Actresses such as Achurch, Elizabeth Robins (1862–1952), and Florence Farr (1860–1917) found new, challenging roles as complex heroines in Ibsen and the Ibsen-inspired "new drama," often in performances that they themselves produced. Mrs. Patrick Campbell (Beatrice Stella Tanner, 1865–1940) made her reputation as the woman with a past in Arthur Wing Pinero's *The Second Mrs. Tanqueray* and later created Eliza Doolittle for George Bernard Shaw. Of great importance in the renaissance of Irish theatre were Lady Augusta Gregory (1852–1932), playwright and a managing director of the Abbey Theatre, and Annie Elizabeth Fredricka Horniman (1860–1937). After furnishing a permanent home for the Abbey, Horniman formed her own company in Manchester, which became significant in a revival of the repertory system. Theatre was enlisted in the campaign for social and political change when the Actresses' Franchise League, founded in 1908, sponsored plays and entertainments designed to further the cause of suffrage. The sweeping changes that came with World War I brought to a close a century of contradictions and evolution in the depiction of women in dramatic literature as well as in the actual contributions of women to the stage.

Further References. Christopher Kent, "Image and Reality: The Actress and Society," in Martha Vicinus (ed.), *A Widening Sphere* (Bloomington, Ind., 1977), 94–116. Allardyce Nicoll, *A History of English Drama 1660–1900* (Cambridge, Eng., 1955 and 1959); see vols. 4 and 5 for a handlist of authors and plays. Jane W. Stedman, "From Dame to Woman: W. S. Gilbert and Theatrical Transvestism," in Martha Vicinus (ed.), *Suffer and Be Still* (Bloomington, Ind., 1972), 20–37.

KATHY FLETCHER

DRAMA AND THEATRE, BRITISH (TWENTIETH-CENTURY). Drama
and theatre in Britain have undergone great change and expansion in the twentieth
century. Theatre was dominated by a handful of actor-managers at the turn of
the century. Prominent among them was Ellen Terry, who, with Henry Irving,
operated the Lyceum until 1902. Terry managed the Imperial between 1902 and
1907 and continued to exercise great influence on theatre by writing and lecturing
until her death in 1928. Major actors of this period include Elizabeth Robins
(also a playwright), Madge Kendal (also a manager), and Beatrice Stella (Mrs.
Patrick) Campbell.

The repertory movement generated new theatres throughout Great Britain.
Among them were the Kingsway, started by Lena Ashwell in 1907, and the
Little Theatre, begun by Gertrude Kingston in 1910. The most influential of the
new theatres included the Old Vic in London, the Gaiety in Manchester, and
the Abbey in Dublin. Annie E. Horniman operated a repertory company in
Manchester from 1907 to 1921. Occupying the Gaiety Theatre from 1908, Horniman's company produced over 100 new plays, many by local dramatists. Lilian
Baylis founded the Old Vic in 1912, developed it into a major center for Shakespearean drama, and managed it until 1936. Baylis, who also presented opera
and ballet at Sadlers Wells, is credited with laying the groundwork for today's
national theatre, opera, and ballet companies in Britain. Dublin's Abbey Theatre
was cofounded by Augusta Gregory (with W. B. Yeats) in 1904. Gregory worked
with the Abbey until 1928, both as producer and writer.

After World War II, permanent companies devoted to the classics stabilized,
with the help of government subsidy. Major female actors of this period included
Peggy Ashcroft, Fabia Drake, Edith Evans, Wendy Hiller, Gertrude Lawrence,
Flora Robson, Sybil Thorndike, and Irene Worth. Irene Hentschl was the first
woman to direct full-time at the Stratford Memorial (later the Royal Shakespeare).
Pre-eminent among designers were Tanya Moisewitsch, who was known for her
innovative architectural settings, Barbara Heseltine, and the all-woman design
team known as Motley.

Theatre in Britain expanded in a new direction when Joan Littlewood moved
her Theatre Workshop to London's East End in 1953. Littlewood had founded
Theatre Workshop ten years earlier as a mobile company based in Manchester,
with the aim of creating plays that would attract and express the concerns of
working-class audiences. Littlewood's use of improvisation, adaptation of music
hall techniques, and legitimation of working-class perspectives inspired further
exploration and experiment. Best known of Littlewood's productions was the
collaboratively written *Oh, What a Lovely War!* (1963).

After 1956, the Royal Court Theatre moved to the forefront of new play
production in England. During the decade in which it focused on the group of
playwrights known as "the angry young men," the Royal Court also helped
launch several women in successful careers. Jocelyn Herbert is the best-known
designer to have emerged at this time, though Margaret Harris and Sophie Devine

of Motley also designed some productions, and Deirdre Clancy contributed costume designs. Jane Howell, an associate director from 1965 to 1969, staged major revivals as well as the premiere of Edward Bond's *Narrow Road to the Deep North* (1969). Ann Jellicoe directed a number of plays, while Miriam Brickman, Pam Brighton, and Nancy Meckler directed occasional ones. Female actors who earned acclaim at the Royal Court include Joan Plowright, Jill Bennett, Mary Ure, and Billie Whitelaw.

The political and cultural upheavals of 1968 found expression in the experimental and politically activist companies that performed in small or improvised theatre spaces and became known collectively as the Fringe. Women, active in Fringe companies from the beginning, have, since 1973, organized a number of feminist theatre groups. These include the Women's Theatre Group, Monstrous Regiment, Mrs. Worthington's Daughters, Bloomers, Spare Tyre, and (in Belfast) Charabanc. Almost Free, Joint Stock, Red Ladder, Gay Sweatshop, Freehold, Paines Plough, Tara Arts, Half Moon, and Wakefield Tricycle are Fringe groups that have produced some feminist work. Directors well known for their Fringe productions include Susan Todd, Pam Brighton, Carole Hayman, Pip Broughton, and Nancy Meckler. Sue Plummer and Annie Smart are among the Fringe's best-known designers.

Government support in the 1960s and 1970s permitted expansion of the Royal Shakespeare Company (RSC), stabilization of many regional companies, and establishment of the National Theatre in London. Buzz Goodbody organized and directed in the Royal Shakespeare Company's Other Place. Di Trevis and Sarah Pia Anderson have directed at the National, while Annie Castledine and Jenny Killick have held artistic director posts in regional theatres. Di Seymour, Alison Chitty, Liz da Costa, Linda Hemming, and Sally Jacobs-Brooks have designed for the National and the RSC. Female actors prominent at the two major subsidized theatres, as well as in West End theatre since World War II, include Suzanne Bertish, Claire Bloom, Sinead Cusack, Frances de la Tour, Judi Dench, Glenda Jackson, Barbara Jefford, Penelope Keith, Felicity Kendal, Sara Kestelman, Jane Laoptaire, Anna Massey, Helen Mirren, Vanessa Redgrave, Beryl Reid, Maggie Smith, Elizabeth Spriggs, Juliet Stevenson, Janet Suzman, Dorothy Tutin, and Zoe Wanamaker.

The development of drama in twentieth-century Britain has paralleled that of theatre, from early realism to contemporary experiment. Augusta Gregory wrote approximately 20 plays, most of which focus on Irish folk and nationalist themes; among the best known are *The Gaol Gate* (1906) and *The Rising of the Moon* (1907). Other pre–World War I plays include *Chains* (1909) by Elizabeth Baker, *Rutherford and Son* (1912) by Githa Sowerby, and two religious dramas by Dorothy Sayers. In the decade following World War II, both Agatha Christie and Enid Bagnold wrote popular plays; Christie's most famous are *The Mousetrap* (1952) and *Witness for the Prosecution* (1954), while Bagnold's best known is *The Chalk Garden* (1955). Productions in 1958 included Doris Lessing's *Each His Own Wilderness* at the Royal Court and Shelagh Delaney's *A Taste of Honey* at Theatre Workshop. Ann Jellicoe inaugurated a period of formal experiment with *The Sport of My Mad Mother* (1958) and *The Knack* (1962) at the Royal Court. Margaretta d'Arcy cowrote with John Arden a group of plays dealing with the situation in Northern Ireland. In 1969, conscious feminism made its appearance in two plays: *Rites,* by Maureen Duffy, produced by the National, and *Vagina Rex and the Gas Oven,* by Jane Arden, at the Drury Lane Arts Lab.

Since 1970, the number of works produced in Britain by women playwrights has increased. Caryl Churchill, foremost among current Royal Court dramatists, has had 15 plays produced, many of which have won awards in England and the United States. Best known of Churchill's plays are *Cloud Nine* (1979), *Top Girls* (1982), *Fen* (1983), and *Serious Money* (1987). Pam Gems has become known for plays about women, including *Piaf* (1978) and *Camille* (1984), both produced by the RSC's Other Place. Scottish playwright Olwen Wymark's *Find Me* (1977) has been widely produced. Anne Devlin won the Susan Smith Blackburn Award for *Ourselves Alone* (1985), about women in Northern Ireland. Other notable playwrights since 1970 include Nell Dunn, Marcella Evaristi, Catherine Hayes, Deborah Levy, Clare Luckham, Sharman Macdonald, Mary O'Malley, Louise Page, Jill Posener, Sue Townshend, Michelene Wandor, and Fay Weldon.

The Women's Playhouse Trust (WPT) was formed in 1981 to promote equality for women in theatre and drama. It has sponsored productions, training workshops, public debates, and a comprehensive study of women in theatre. The study, published in 1987, showed that women comprise only 15 percent of artistic directors in building-based theatre companies and control only 11 percent of the national arts budget. New playwrights encouraged by the WPT include Sarah Daniels, Winsome Pinnock, Heidi Thomas, and Timberlake Wertenbaker.

Further References. Hugh Hunt et al., *The Revels History of Drama in English,* vol. 7 (London, 1978). Catherine Itzin, *Stages in the Revolution: Political Theatre in Britain since 1968* (London, 1980). Helen Keyssar, *Feminist Theatre* (London, 1984).

                                                    AMELIA HOWE KRITZER

DRAMA AND THEATRE, U.S. (see also PLAYWRIGHTS, U.S. [TWENTIETH-CENTURY]). This field for women has inspired not only a popular list of actresses in a steady stream since 1752 but beginning with the American Revolution has provided a sporadic collection of important playwrights and managers and, more recently, creative directors and designers. Acting has long been for women a road to financial and creative independence. The other theatrical occupations have always been much more difficult to enter, and success within them has been an infrequent accomplishment. In two waves, however, c.1890–1929 and c.1960–present, women have made great strides in breaking the sexist barriers in the professional American theatre. Furthermore, it might be said in overview that from 1752 to c.1890 women were primarily working to establish themselves in the marketplace of the theatre.

With the arrival from England of Mrs. Lewis Hallam (d.1773) in 1752, colonists enjoyed the first prominent woman on the professional American stage. As the leading actress of the Hallam troupe, she was important in helping to establish the British classical and contemporary repertory, tastes, and performance styles that remained the prominent dramatic model in American theatres throughout much of the nineteenth century. Many more talented and popular British-born actresses, such as tragediennes Anne Brunton Merry (1769–1808) and Mary Ann Duff (1794–1857), followed in subsequent decades and dominated the stage until the rise of native stars in the 1840s. Merry even broke a masculine barrier briefly when her second husband died and she took his place in co-managing for two years the Chestnut Theatre, the most important American playhouse until after 1810.

Although the eighteenth century produced no professional female playwrights, the fervor of the impending revolution inspired Mercy Otis Warren (1728–1814) to join the propagandistic war of belles lettres with her satirical *The Adulateur* (1773) and *The Group* (1775).

Throughout much of the nineteenth century actresses found themselves in a disadvantageous social position. Recognized by many in church and society as immodest purveyors of deception and lasciviousness, working actresses might be ostracized from church services and the parlors of the best society, but economically they often worked on equal footing with men. Although avenues to management and play writing were more difficult, actresses grew in both numbers and prominence as the century progressed.

Despite the social and religious taboos, many women flocked to acting as a means of making a decent living, supporting a family, or attaining economic freedom. One of the most dynamic among those seeking independence was America's first native-born acting star, who not incidentally often portrayed male roles. Charlotte Cushman (1816–1876), who became a star by 1843, performed primarily from the standard repertory and was particularly admired as Lady Macbeth. Although many actresses in England and America habitually played breeches roles in the nineteenth century, Cushman's harsh physiognomy, deep voice, and authoritative manner led her to prominence in roles such as Cardinal Wolsey, Hamlet, and, especially, Romeo. Cushman made great strides in convincing the public that the stage could serve as a center for great artistic achievement.

Throughout the nineteenth century few American women writers ventured into drama, opting for other literary forms instead. Although few plays written by women were professionally produced before 1915, an unusually brave and talented woman, Anna Cora Mowatt (1819–1870), wrote *Fashion* (1845), a frequently revived comedy of manners effactually satirizing the nouveau riche and one of the finest plays of the century. Mowatt "betrayed" her social class by entering the acting profession in order to retrieve financial security after her husband lost his fortune. At the time she was accused of setting a bad, even depraved, example for women of gentle breeding.

The second half of the nineteenth century witnessed the advent of important actress-managers who forged successful careers at the head of large companies and controlled their own theatres. Laura Keene (c.1820–1873) and Louisa Lane Drew (1820–1897), both British-born, encountered difficulties from men who found the idea of women managers unseemly. Inspired by the example of Madame Vestris in London, Keene, also a successful actress, ran the Laura Keene Theatre in New York (1855–1863), apparently the first long-term solo management by a woman in America. Drew not only performed and ran an excellent stock company and the Arch Street Theatre in Philadelphia with resounding success for 32 years beginning in 1860 but also was the matriarch of the Barrymore theatrical dynasty.

As the nineteenth century approached its end, two actresses made important strides toward improving women's rights, Mary Shaw (1860–1929) as an activist and Minnie Maddern Fiske (1865–1932) as an independent actress/manager. Both were dedicated to important social issues in drama and nearly stood alone in championing the social dramas of Henrik Ibsen and Bernard Shaw in America. Under her own direction Fiske performed many of Ibsen's heroines, most notably Nora and Hedda, often giving the plays the only unbowdlerized versions available in this country. With her husband she managed a superior acting company in the Manhattan Theatre (beginning 1901), thus making inroads against the stranglehold that the conservative Theatrical Syndicate had on professional theatre from 1896 to 1915.

As a suffragist and feminist, Mary Shaw became an important public speaker and crusader while touring the country in Ibsen's *Ghosts* beginning in 1899. In addition, she was arrested for playing the title role in the first American version of *Mrs. Warren's Profession* (1905), adjudged grossly immoral by the New York police. After starring in a suffragist play, *Votes for Women* (1909) by Elizabeth Robins, she attempted to found the Woman's National Theatre, which, if successful, would have had an all-woman management and artistic staff.

Before the 1920s most women who wrote with any success for the stage created light comedies celebrating conventional values. As suffrage approached, however, and with the arrival of the little theatre movement, which encouraged women to write for the stage, talented playwrights such as Rachel Crothers (1878–1958; *A Man's World* [1909]) and Susan Glaspell (1882–1948; *The Verge* [1921]) began to explore seriously women's problems such as the double standard, professionalism versus a career, and madness grown from social patterning. Glaspell was also instrumental in founding the Provincetown Players in 1915, the same year that Irene (c.1894–1944) and Alice Lewisohn (c.1883–1972) established the Neighborhood Playhouse, both influential little theatres that gave impetus to the first serious advance of artistic theatre off-Broadway.

In the 1920s one of America's finest actress-directors emerged in Eva Le Gallienne (b.1899). Her privately subsidized Civic Repertory Theatre (1926–1932) and American Repertory Theatre (1946–1948), led by Le Gallienne with producer Cheryl Crawford (b.1902) and director Margaret Webster (b.1905), were dedicated to producing important revivals of modern classics like Ibsen and Chekhov, establishing permanent acting companies, and making the theatre affordable to all economic classes.

Le Gallienne's values and experiments anticipated the spirit of the regional theatre movement. Three of the most important nonprofit regional theatres dependent upon subsidy were initiated by intrepid women: Margo Jones (1913–1955), Nina Vance (c.1912–1980), and Zelda Fichandler (b.1924), who popularized theatre-in-the-round, developed new playwrights, and demonstrated dedication to the classics with Theatre '47 in Dallas; the still thriving Alley Theatre in Houston, begun in 1947; and the very active Arena Stage, founded in Washington, D.C., in 1950.

The only instance of federally subsidized theatre in the history of America was led by a woman. Hallie Flanagan Davis (1890–1969) directed the Federal Theatre Project (1935–1939) under the Works Progress Administration. During the Great Depression this project, which established theatres all over the country, employed thousands of actors, directors, playwrights, designers, and stagehands, who presented hundreds of productions. Davis insisted on including children's, black, classic, contemporary, and experimental theatre companies.

Undoubtedly America's most celebrated woman playwright, Lillian Hellman (1905–1984) stands as a symbol of the independent, professional woman both in her plays and her life. *The Children's Hour* (1934) presents particular suffering in the lives of two unmarried professional women at the hands of a malicious child. Despite attention drawn to Hellman's work, few women playwrights emerged before the women's movement of the 1960s. After growing beyond the retrenchment following the success of suffrage, the shock of the Depression, and the effort of World War II, women again became significant in all aspects of theatre with the performance groups and experiments in dramatic form characteristic of the 1960s. Megan Terry (b.1932), for example, appeared with the Open Theatre and produced not only strong feminist statements in her plays like *Calm Down Mother* (1965) but also explored transformational character. Following the example of Terry's experiments with form and style, feminist writers began to break away from the traditional forms followed by Hellman and her predecessors. As women have discovered that many of their problems with identity, personal and professional needs, and emotional stability differ significantly from men's, so have the playwrights departed from the structure and methods created by men. It is not only the subject matter which has changed in women's plays, but the methodology as well.

Much off- and off-off-Broadway activity in the 1960s was inspired by women such as actress/director Judith Malina (b.1926), who codirected the political Living Theatre (the primary inspiration for a host of performance groups), and Ellen Stewart (n.d.), who in 1961 opened La Mama Experimental Theatre, the home for a myriad of young playwrights. Among the most important new playwrights have been Rochelle Owens (b.1936; *Futz* [1967], a fable of bestiality and sexual confusion); Maria Irene Fornes (b.1930; *Fefu and Her Friends* [1977], an experiment in theatrical space demonstrating the effect of home environment on the female personality); and Marsha Norman (b.1947; *'Night, Mother* [1982], an examination of suicide and mother/daughter relations). A host of important black women have also commanded attention as playwrights, beginning with traditional Lorraine Hansberry (1936–1965) and continuing with the rituals and choreopoems of Adrienne Kennedy (b.1931) and Ntozake Shange (b.1948). See AFRICAN-AMERICAN PROSE WRITERS.

Since the early 1970s many feminist theatres, notably the Omaha Magic Theatre, At the Foot of the Mountain (Minneapolis) and the Women's Project of the American Place Theatre (New York), sometimes working completely outside the commercial and professional world, have emerged. The goals have been not only to create new plays by and about women but to escape the competitive nature of mainstream theatre and involve audiences in improvisational or testimonial performances.

Further References. Albert Auster, *Actresses and Suffragists: Women in the American Theatre, 1890–1920* (New York, 1984). Helen Krich Chinoy and Linda Walsh Jenkins, *Women in American Theatre* (New York, 1981). Claudia D. Johnson, *American Actress: Perspective on the Nineteenth Century* (Chicago, 1984).

RONALD H. WAINSCOTT

DUTCH WRITERS. Women from Holland or the Flemish part of Belgium who write in Dutch or "Netherlandic." Until recently, there was no female tradition in Dutch literature nor any genuine awareness of women's literary achievement. In 1920, however, Maurits Basse drew attention to numerous hitherto ignored women writers from the Middle Ages to the nineteenth century. In 1934 Annie Romein-Verschoor published her dissertation about female novelists after 1880. Lately Hannemieke Stamperius, Hanneke van Buuren, Truus Pinkster, Anja Meulenbelt, and others have been studying women writers from a feminist perspective.

Among the oldest Dutch texts preserved are the biography and some religious poems of Sister Beatrijs van Nazareth (c.1200–1268) and numerous letters, poems, and "visions" of the mystic Hadewijch, who wrote in the vernacular.

The Catholic sixteenth-century poet Anna Bijns (1493–1575), an Antwerp schoolmistress, produced three collections of poetry and a number of plays. *Mariken van Nieumeghen* has been attributed to her. She participated fully in the literary life of her day, knew the leading figures of the Chambers of Rhetoric, and wrote, in addition to very candid love poems, virulent polemical verse attacking the Reformation and, especially, Luther. Because it is inspired by deep personal feeling, Anna Bijns's poetry is better than that of most *Rederijkers* (members of the Chambers of Rhetoric). The poetry of her contemporary Katharina Boudewijn, who was out of touch with literary fashions, represents a weak, late blooming of medieval religious verse.

The seventeenth century produced the pious Anna-Maria van Schuurman (1607–1678), a scholar and artist known throughout Europe as a prodigy. She was a staunch Calvinist and extraordinarily learned, attended the University of

Utrecht, and wrote a Latin treatise discussing the usefulness of intellectual training for girls. It was immediately translated into French and English. She later
rejected the ideas of this *Amica dissertatio* (1638), however, and concentrated
exclusively on theology and biblical exegesis. In Dutch she published an explanation of the first three chapters of Genesis, *Uitbreidingsrer de drie eerste
capittels van Genesis* (1632); a contemplative essay about death, *Paelsteen van
den tijt onzes levens* (1639); and her autobiography, *Eucleria of Uitkiezing van
het beste deel* (1684; Eucleria or The Best Part).

After Anna-Maria van Schuurman there was a hiatus of about a century in
which no female voices were heard. Then the eighteenth century peaks with *De
Historie van Mejuffrouw Sara Burgerhart* (1782; The History of Miss Sara
Burgerhart) about a middle-class girl in trouble who needs help and moral instruction. This book is the first modern Dutch novel and the first book written
for and by women. The writers Betje Wolff (1738–1804) and Aagje Deken
(1741–1804) promoted reason and virtue and described Dutch life with revolutionary realism and naturalness. They were influenced by Samuel Richardson
and like him used the epistolary form. Before teaming up with Deken, Wolff
produced poetry and numerous prose pieces of which only *De Menuet en de
dominees pruik* (1772; The Minuet and the Minister's Wig) is still read. Together
with Deken she also wrote *Historie van den Heer Willem Leevend* (1784–1785;
The History of Mr. Willem Leevend), *De brieven van Abraham Blankaart* (1887;
The Letters of A. B.), and *Historie van Mejuffrouw Cornelia Widschut of de
gevolgen van de opvoeding* (1793–1796; Story of C. W. or The Consequences
of Education), all inferior to *Sara Burgerhart,* which provides an unsurpassed
portrait of Dutch life in the eighteenth century.

Wolff and Deken were realists, not feminists, but they were thoroughly in
touch with their time. Geertruida Bosboom-Toussaint, on the other hand, used
history and aristocratic settings in other countries to escape her own milieu. Well
known are her historical novels *Het huis Lauernesse* (1840; The House of Lauernesse) and the *Leycester* trilogy (1845–1855). The didactic novel *Majoor Frans*
(1874; Major Frans), about the "masculine" and independent young woman
Frans, seems modern but is hardly a denunciation of nineteenth-century morality.
That Bosboom-Toussaint had no direct followers may be significant, for in the
next 50 years novel writing by women increased dramatically. As the labor
movement spread, the women's question also surfaced increasingly and was
dealt with in novels by many women writers.

Mina Kruseman's *Een huwelijk in Indie* (1873; A Marriage in Indonesia),
though of doubtfull quality, is truly feminist and modern. It was the first of a
large number of "emancipation novels" that form the first wave of Dutch feminism and include Anna de Savornin-Lohman's *Het eenige nodige* (1897; The
Only Thing One Needs), Cécile Goedkoop's *Hilda van Suylenburg* (1898) and
Cornélie Huygens's *Barthold Meryan* (1897). This trend is continued by the
feminist Jo van Ammers-Küller (1887–1966) but stops as a general phenomenon
around World War II.

In the first half of the twentieth century the vast majority of writing women concerned themselves with the so-called small genres, especially children's books and religious and didactic work. Many contributors of the Catholic journal *Van Onzen Tijd* (Our Time) and the Protestant weekly *Ons Tijdschrift* (Our Journal) were women. Serious literature was still almost entirely a male preserve. Notable early exceptions are the novelist *Virginie Loveling* (1836–1923), a foremost representative of Flemish realism; the poet Hèléne Swarth (1859–1944); the realist novelist Carry van Bruggen (1881–1932); and the poet Henriette Roland Holst-van der Schalk (1869–1952), editor of the Socialist journal *De Nieuwe Tijd* (A New Time) and author of a vast oeuvre including the poetry collection *Tussen tijd en eeuwigheid* (1934; Between Time and Eternity).

World War II has been recorded in the diaries of two of its victims, Anne Frank (1929–1945) and Etty Hilesum (1914–1943), and is a major theme in postwar fiction, especially the novels of Marga Minco (b.1920), Hanny Michaelis (b.1922), and Mischa de Vreede (b.1936). Also important is a preoccupation with the colonial past and life in the colonies of Surinam (described by Miep Diekman, Sonia Germers, Bea Vianen, Thea Doelwijt, and Diane Lebacs) and Indonesia (Augusta de Wit, Maria Dermoût, Beb Vuyk, Margaretha Ferguson, and Marion Bloem). The novelist Anna Blaman (1905–1960), the author of *Vrouw en vriend* (1941; Woman and Friend), *Eenzaam avontuur* (1948; Lonely Adventure) and *Op leven en dood* (1954; A Matter of Life and Death), was influenced by the French existentialists and described unsatisfactory relationships of people afraid of loneliness and death. Her analyses of the psychology of sex and eroticism met with great resistance.

Serious modern poets of quality are Ida Gerhardt (b.1908), Clara Eggink (b.1906), Vasalis (b.1909; was awarded the P. C. Hooft Prijs and the Constantijn Huygens Prijs), Ellen Warmond (b.1930), Maria de Groot (b.1937), and the feminist poet Elly de Waard (b.1940).

The second wave of feminism has occasioned an outburst of female writing on topics ranging from divorce (L. Stassaert, A. Meulenbelt, Dolores Thijs), celibate motherhood (Aleida Leeuwenberg, Gertje Gort), and giving up a child (Christine Kraft) to lesbianism (Blaman, Burnier, Meulenbelt) and sex-change operations (Dirkje Kuik). There are two main tendencies: (1) social, where the focus is on the immediate, honest expression of lived or observed experience, as in Anja Meulenbelt's *No More Shame* (1976) and (2) literary, where the author's feminism is interwoven with her search for new forms and techniques, as in the novels of Andreas Burnier (b.1931) and Monika van Paemel (b.1945) and in the poetic feminism exemplified by Lucienne Stassaert (b.1936). Less academic but no less literary are Hannes Meinkema (b.1943), Mensje van Keulen (b.1946), Doeschka Meysing (b.1947), and Hester Albach (b.1954). The sales figures indicate that these young writers strike a responsive chord in the population.

MAYA BIJVOET WILLIAMSON

DYSTOPIAS. Literary works depicting an imaginary society in which conditions are worse than in the author's experience, as opposed to a *eutopia,* in which conditions are better. (*Dystopia* means "bad place" or "evil place," *eutopia* means "good place," and *outopia* means "no place.") While some dystopias by women deal with many of the same issues as dystopias by men, feminist dystopias focus upon how extreme forms of patriarchy affect women's lives.

Like the utopia, the dystopia uses certain traditional narrative strategies. One of the most basic is the fantastic journey to an alternative world, an unknown land, another planet, or, most frequently, to the future. Another is the philosophical dialogue. Also, the dystopia frequently uses satire and irony to contrast present with future conditions that, the dystopia implies, will occur if current evils go unchecked.

Two of the most important dystopian novels by women written before World War II are *Swastika Night* by Katharine Burdekin (pen name Murray Constantine; 1937, repr. 1985) and *Kallocain,* by the Swedish poet Karin Boye (1940; Eng. trans., 1966). *Swastika Night,* published 12 years before Orwell's *1984* (which it resembles), portrays a grim future three centuries hence in which Nazism has conquered the world. Burdekin draws a clear parallel between woman-hating and other forms of oppression. In *Kallocain,* a male chemist creates a "truth" drug that empowers the state to read minds and thus to destroy the last vestiges of individual privacy.

The 1960s, 1970s, and 1980s have seen a flowering of speculative fiction by women, including many utopias and dystopias. Although women's dystopias show many of the usual concerns of men's, they also focus upon women's lives under patriarchy. They deal with the rise of the religious Right, the loss of women's control over their bodies, the persecution of minorities, and the loss of women's recent political gains.

Women's oppression is justified by religious fundamentalism in *The Handmaid's Tale* by Canadian Margaret Atwood (1986) and *Native Tongue* by Suzette Hadin Elgin (1984). In English author Zoe Fairbairn's *Benefits* (1979), the state seizes control of women's reproductive ability. The legally sanctioned oppressing of minorities appears in *The Handmaid's Tale* and in *The Godmothers* by Canadian Sandi Hall (1982). Atwood and Elgin, in particular, show in nightmarish detail how the oppressive world they describe is already germinating in the 1980s.

Many utopian works also have dystopian elements, for example, Ursula K. LeGuin's *The Dispossessed* (1974), Joanna Russ's *The Female Man* (1975), Marge Piercy's *Woman on the Edge of Time* (1976), and Sally Miller Gearhart's *The Wanderground* (1979). Russ and Gearhart both show destruction of the environment, loss of individual freedom, and extreme polarizing of male and female gender roles, all occurring as male aggression goes unchecked.

Many women's dystopias, unlike men's, assume that women's oppression under patriarchy is related to other forms of oppression and that patriarchy oppresses men as well. Male authors often assume that the desire for power is part of human nature and that oppression is thus inevitable. As a result, they conclude that the desire for utopia itself leads to worse conditions than those it seeks to correct (e.g., Huxley in *Brave New World* and Evgeny Zamyatin in *We*

[*Nous autres*]). But because many women authors see the urge for power as stemming from patriarchal ideology and not as existing as an immutable part of human nature, they are frequently more optimistic about the possibility of change.

Further References. Carol Farley Kessler (ed.), *Daring to Dream: Utopian Stories by United States Women, 1836–1919* (crit. bib. and annot. bib. 1836–1983; London, 1984). Ruby Rohrlich and Elaine Hoffman Baruch (eds.), *Women in Search of Utopia: Mavericks and Mythmakers* (New York, 1984).

CHARLENE BALL

E

EAST CENTRAL EUROPEAN WRITERS. In eastern Europe political history has determined the place of women writers more obviously than in western European nation-states where unified languages simplified the growth of national literatures. The multinational Austro-Hungarian Empire included peoples with old cultures and languages but without political status. In addition, the Turkish Ottoman Empire occupied about half of the area for two to five centuries. When the discovery of sea routes to Asia ended the early prosperity of eastern Europe based on the "silk routes," economic stagnation and political conservatism created general problems crying out for commentary by women writers as well as by men. Thus, social themes tended to predominate.

The development of vernacular literatures in the Renaissance and Reformation stimulated women writers among the literate nobility. Research is still incomplete on this period, but more is known of the baroque period (seventeenth and eighteenth centuries), particularly of religious hymnists or memoir writers. Interesting examples of memoirists are the Polish versifier Anna Stanislawska and the Magyar Kata Bethlen, who was forced to a Catholic marriage in violation of her Calvinist conscience. The prayer book of Katarina Frankopan Zrinski (1625–1673), *Putni Tovarus,* expressing her hope and despair at the anti-Hapsburg conspiracy she took part in, was the first Croatian writing by a woman. Related by family connections to Zrinski and part of the same continuing conspiracy was Kata-Szidonia Petroczy, whose Magyar hymns written to Slovak melodies were followed by a political poem against the Austrian throne (1705–1708). Such a complex of political and cultural relations was characteristic of eastern Europe. Numerous women collected songbooks of anonymous authorship to which they may have contributed. Another group of women known to be literate and literary were the printers' wives working with their husbands, or in some cases as widows, but it is difficult to know whether they composed or edited the many anonymous hymns and poems they printed.

Two trends emerged in women's secular literature in the nineteenth century and continue to the present. Since both men and women writers tried to be prophets and guides in the struggle for national liberation, usually political and social themes predominated. Periodically, however, this engagé tradition was abandoned for intensely personal lyric expression of erotic, feminist, or domestic subjects indistinguishable from women's concerns elsewhere.

One of the earliest secular women writers was the Czech Bozena Nemcova (1820–1862), who can be compared to George Sand. Her stories and sketches are early examples of realism and Romantic feminism. After the failed revolutions of 1848 and with the increasing women's movement, Nemcova was followed by writers who explicitly sought women's function in the national movement. Katarina Svetla's first novel in 1861 pictured an inspirational mother of two Czech revolutionaries, and Elena Marothy-Soltesova showed a Slovak woman inspiring her renegade husband to return to his nation. In much fiction the nationalist heroines were schoolteachers maintaining their students' language and identity. The Czech poet Eliska Krasnohorska and the Slovak Terezia Vansova were also important as editors of the earliest women's magazines in their languages. Czech dramatist Gabriela Preissova depicted sharply realistic village women. Rebellious figures forced by financial need into unhappy marriages were characteristic of the Slovak Bozena Slancikova Timrava. Historical novels and nationalist poetry were chosen by Maria Kubasec and Mina Witkojc, respectively, the first women writers of the restored Lusatian Sorbian language in its tiny enclave in eastern Germany.

The first Polish woman writer to gain great popularity, Maria Konopnicka (1842–1910), wrote both realistic stories and social and political poems during Poland's last partition. This poetic tradition was renewed in the Nazi occupation; Wanda Zielenczyk's and Krystyna Krahelka's poems were sung to marching tunes in the Underground. Other poets writing of the horrors of war included Anna Kamlienska and Kazimiera Illakowiczowna, who published again during the liberal period after 1955. Anna Kowalska was interned in 1982 for her political and religious poems on the Solidarity movement. The prose tradition was followed by Eliza Orzeszkowa with positivist fiction campaigning for widespread social reform, by Zofia Kossak-Szczucka with historical novels, and by Maria Kuncewiczowa with psychological novels in the 1920s and 1930s. Gabriela Zapolska was a naturalist playwright in the early twentieth century.

Izadora Sekulic (1877–1958) wrote psychological novels and essays that helped develop modern Serbian prose, while Ivana Brlic-Mazuranic (b.1874) chose mythic themes. The Czech prose of Maria Payerova (1882–1969) showed her strong social concern. Queen Elisabeth of Romania (1843–1916), though not of Romanian descent, translated Romanian folk literature into French and German under the pseudonym Carmen Sylvia. A popular saga by Hortensia Papadat-Bengescu followed a single family. The first major Magyar novelist, Margit Kaffka (1880–1918), in what were apparently autobiographical portraits, created female characters unable to find a place in the slowly modernizing world.

Strong females also characterize the contemporary novels of Magda Szabo. Historical novels were written by Cecile Tormay and Eren Gulacsy, as well as the Slovak Margita Figuli during World War II. The Bulgarian Blaga Dimitrova (b.1921) writes fiction and poetry as well as essays, and emigré Julia Kristeva has become famous for her place in French psychoanalytic and semiotic literary theory.

The personal lyric tradition in Poland was influenced by French modernism, and Bronislawa Ostrowska spent most of her life in Paris as a follower of Mallarme. Kazimiera Zawistovna developed heroines from history and myth with believable human motivation. Maria Jasnorzewska-Pawlikowska, considered the most feminist and erotic of Polish women poets, expressed in succinct lyrics her horror at women's subjugation to biology. The Czech Maria Pujmanova (1898–1953) showed aspects of Expressionism in poetry as well as in prose. Ludmila Podjavorinska returned to the Slovak ballad as a vehicle of personal emotions, and the lyrics of the contemporary Masa Halamova condense the elemental experiences of love and death. The Magyar Minka Czobel cultivated symbolist poetry at the turn of the century, and Renee Erdos expressed erotic details in both poetry and fiction. The Serbian lyric poet Desanka Maksimovic (b.1898) published several volumes on highly individualized themes, then changed to patriotic poetry in World War II. The Bulgarian Elisaveta Bagryana (b.1893) wrote moving, intimate, and feminist poetry until the war also turned her to political concerns.

Socialist feminism, following Karl Marx and August Bebel, has traditionally considered sex discrimination to be a capitalist contradiction that Socialist society cures. Thus, the current governments in eastern Europe, including the Soviet Union, allow no women's studies as such. Although the existence of unofficial women's movements shows that perceived problems still exist, little is known of them besides the reflection in contemporary literature of typical working women's concerns with child care and domestic burdens.

Further Reference. Katarina M. Wilson (ed.), *Dictionary of Continental Women Writers* (New York, 1990).

NORMA L. RUDINSKY

EDUCATION. In Western civilization, education comprises, first of all, the traditional molding of character by which societies inculcate their mores into their young. With respect to women, the aim has been to produce obedient daughters, chaste maidens, willing workers, faithful wives, and nurturing mothers. Training has most often been given in the home and/or under religious auspices.

Athenian women of the Golden Age did not participate in the great intellectual advances of their time; daughters of citizens received no education at all. But among the Romans upper-class young women were often tutored along with their brothers in order to enhance their role as mothers of soldiers and statesmen. In the early Christian era, St. Jerome agreed that women should be educated, by which he meant schooled in their religion. During the medieval period convent life was the only source of learning for women. Some nuns were highly educated and were able to manage abbeys, corresponding with educated men. Some upper-class women during the Renaissance were also learned; their male relatives displayed them along with their palaces, their art, and their libraries.

Women's education, like that of men, varied according to the roles individual women were expected to play in the society—servant, court lady, bourgeois helpmeet, worker. The common denominator, however, for almost all women's education in the past was the intention of inculcating the religious virtues considered proper to their sex: chastity and obedience. Any additional learning was mainly for the purpose of enhancing the role of the males in their families.

Even when not tied to religion, in periods of enlightenment and change, the ideal aims of women's education remained the same. In the mideighteenth century, Jean-Jacques Rousseau wrote in *Émile* (1762) that women should be trained in relation to men "to please them, be useful to them, be loved and honored by them, raise them when young, care for them when grown, counsel them, console them, render life sweet and agreeable to them." This purpose might be interpreted more or less broadly in different periods but remained at the heart of the education afforded to women.

Instruction, formerly a secondary goal of education, assumed greater importance as the division of labor created more complex societies. But, for the most part, women were instructed only in domestic skills, including the handwork required for the family clothing or, later, for the trade practiced by the family. However, in early modern times upper-class young women of all countries were taught "accomplishments" (dancing, fine needlework, music, drawing, and foreign languages) in order to enhance their value on the marriage market. During the seventeenth and eighteenth centuries some women, after marriage, were able to further their education by opening salons that attracted learned men able to converse with them.

Reading was a luxury of leisured women until the Reformation prescribed elementary education for all in Protestant countries for the purpose of reading the Bible. From that time on, the primary education of women has been closely tied to that of the lowest classes in general. With individual exceptions, societies that did not educate the poorest males did not provide formal instruction for women.

The needs of an expanding economy arising from the commercial and industrial revolution in modern times led to the extension of secondary education for men, but not for women. As a result, the relative position of women declined in the centuries of modernization. Their lack of education made women lower-class, whatever their family, and unskilled workers, whatever their trade.

At the end of the Enlightenment Mary Wollstonecraft had challenged Rousseau's position that women should be trained only for their marital and maternal roles. In her *Vindication of the Rights of Women* (1792) she noted the frivolity and silliness of upper-class women and attributed them to the woeful inadequacy of their intellectual training. Others, from Christine de Pisan in the fourteenth century to Catherine Macauley Graham in the eighteenth, had made the same point. But Wollstonecraft was the first to call for a system of universal coeducation in which the intelligence of women would be trained equally with that of men. She maintained that women could not even be good wives and mothers without instruction. And she suggested that women who did not have family duties might become doctors, managers, even legislators if their faculties were fully developed.

During the French Revolution the Marquis de Condorcet submitted to the Convention a plan for primary-school coeducation on a national level. He maintained that without it there could be no equality within the family and therefore none in the society. But he also insisted that women be given equal access to education as a matter of simple justice. However, Rousseau's views on women continued to dominate, in some form, the nineteenth-century developments in women's education. Even those who admitted the theory of equality between the sexes insisted on differences in their training. "Separate but equal," the most liberal position on women's education for all but a few, ensured inferior education for women well into the twentieth century, even when the "women's sphere" was broadened to include practical subjects like home economics and business courses.

Western elites justified the inferior education given women, as they did that given the lower classes, on the basis of their supposed biological inferiority. Aristotle was only one of many to identify the male with form, the female with matter; the male as active, the female as passive. The brains of females were said to be either smaller or more fragile—in general, incapable of grasping abstract ideas. In early modern times the clergy was convinced that reading and writing would lead women only to moral harm; they would read evil literature and write love letters. In the nineteenth century women were admonished that exposure to higher education would render them unfit to bear children. Despite these strictures, women sought education, and the necessities of the modern world gradually increased the amount and quality of the education they received.

Progress differed among nations. In general, there was more awareness of the necessity to educate as many people as possible in those nations that were economically more advanced. But in the nineteenth century this awareness did not always extend to women. Nor did the other argument for universal education after the extension of suffrage—"educating our rulers," as Gladstone put it— apply to women. Therefore the adoption of female education in different countries or parts of countries was often tied to some particular situation.

The German states were far ahead in primary education because of their Protestant background; Russia, in need of doctors, gladly opened its medical schools to women. In France, women's secondary education was part of a republican effort to decrease the influence of the Catholic church because of the church's opposition to liberal political development; women's secondary education was not, however, intended to lead to higher education or careers. In

Spain and Italy, church influence maintained the traditional forms of female education, in home and convent.

This unwillingness to alter tradition was manifest in England and the United States, where education was not controlled by the national governments. Left to themselves, most communities did not choose to educate women beyond the three Rs. In England, where secondary education was primarily for elite males, women's education lagged far behind, despite the founding of a few colleges in London, Oxford, and Cambridge. Major American cities established high schools during the nineteenth century, serving both men and women, and women's colleges (really secondary schools) were founded under private auspices. Only in the land-grant colleges of some of the states did American women receive the same higher education as men. The relative deprivation of women in this area is often obscured by the large numbers of women who were attending school in the United States.

In general, the modern experience has shown that women, like minority groups, are ensured an equal education only when the national government is committed to an educational program that guarantees it to them. Germany ensured almost complete literacy of its population, male and female, by the end of the eighteenth century. However, it was not convinced of the value of female higher education; Germany was the last of the great nations to allow women into the universities. France initiated universal education in the late nineteenth century, including female secondary education. But women had great difficulty enrolling in French universities until after World War I. Russia, in great need of doctors and administrators, had allowed women to attend universities in the late nineteenth century but installed universal education only under the Communist regime.

Countries behind the Iron Curtain had equal numbers of men and women in universities by 1950, followed closely by France. Germany maintained the more traditional position on higher education for women well into the twentieth century. So did England and the United States. In the latter countries, where democratic local control of schooling prevailed, persistence of traditional views was responsible for the undereducation of females on all levels of the educational ladder.

The other important factor in equal educational opportunity for women is also related to government. Where schooling is provided without cost, the proportion of males and females at all levels moves toward equality, particularly if education to a certain level is obligatory. Where families must contribute, fewer girls than boys are enrolled in primary schools. Child labor laws must also be enforced to ensure attendance. The same principle applies to women's access to higher education. The proportion of women in higher education in the United States lagged behind nations where university education is provided by the state without cost, up to the middle of the twentieth century. Rectification of this situation in recent decades may be due to government loan and scholarship policies.

Even when the optimum conditions are met, traditional views of what courses of study are appropriate for women may result in educational inequality. Until very recently science and mathematics courses were considered less appropriate for women because the careers to which they lead were viewed as masculine. This cultural pattern may have affected the ability of women to excel in these fields, since fewer women than men do so at present. Even where the course material is similar, as in biology, and women do well, they have been encouraged to become nurses while men are assumed to be candidates for medical school.

Education of women for particular tasks in the society may also, because of the continuing assumption of female intellectual inferiority, result in the devaluation of these curricula and of the positions to which they lead (i.e., teaching in the United States, medicine in the USSR). However, the presence of large numbers of educated women in a society tends to break down the traditional views of gender roles and leads to better opportunities for the next generation of women. (See also HIGHER EDUCATION; WOMEN'S COLLEGES.)

PHYLLIS H. STOCK-MORTON

EPICS, HEROIC (MIDDLE HIGH GERMAN). About 20 epics based on material from the native oral tradition, popular in what later became southern Germany and Austria from the early thirteenth to the late sixteenth century. Women are depicted variously in the epics according to the purpose of the (usually anonymous) author and the expectations of the audience. The *Nibelungenlied* (Song of the Nibelungs), earliest and most influential, was meant to warn a noble audience steeped in Arthurian romance of real dangers of moral and political corruption. In contrast to Arthurian romance, in which a male hero perfects himself and then improves society, the hero of the *Nibelungenlied* is Kriemhild, a Burgundian princess, who, victimized by the corruption of her society, brings about its destruction as well as her own. Her marriage to Siegfried is allowed only because it is politically expedient. When this expediency is no longer the case, he is murdered, and his fortune is stolen from her. Only remarriage to King Etzel of the Huns gives her the means of avenging the murder and robbery. Brünhild, the *Nibelungenlied's* other important woman, is also the pawn of political interests. At first a powerful queen, she is duped by Siegfried into marriage to Kriemhild's weak brother, Gunther, whereupon she loses all strength. When she learns of the deceit, she instigates Siegfried's murder in order to protect Gunther's image.

Virtually all other epics respond explicitly or implicitly to the *Nibelungenlied*; the roles of women in them reflect a reaction to Kriemhild and Brünhild. The *Nibelungenklage* (Lament of the Nibelungs), composed in the first third of the thirteenth century, attempts to excuse Kriemhild because her revenge was motivated by love for Siegfried. *Der grosse Rosengarten zu Worms* (The Large Rose Garden at Worms), composed at the turn of the fourteenth century, parodies the *Nibelungenlied* and the Arthurian romance alike by depicting Kriemhild as a woman who issues unreasonable challenges, for which in one version (*A*) she is punished by having her face scratched by a hero's beard as she rewards him with kisses. By the sixteenth century the material had become completely trivialized: in *Das Lied von hürnen Seyfrid* (The Song of Seyfrid with the Horny Skin), circulated for popular entertainment, Kriemhild has become a stereotypical abducted princess, rescued by, then married to, Siegfried.

Kudrun, composed c.1230–1240, uses the abduction plot to present a courtly alternative to the *Nibelungenlied.* Womanly virtue is depicted as passivity coupled with efforts to reconcile opposing forces. Hilde, Kudrun's mother, allows her fiancé to stage elopement as abduction but later makes peace between her husband and father. Betrothed to Herwig, but abducted by Hartmut, Kudrun spends years at hard labor because she refuses to marry Hartmut. When Herwig rescues her, she makes peace between them. This is possible because her suffering has not been caused by Hartmut, but by his mother Gerlind, whose assertive behavior is severely punished.

Twelve narratives, including *Rosengarten,* are called Dietrich epics because Dietrich von Bern, a supporting character in the *Nibelungenlied,* plays an important role in them. Three were composed for the nobility of the late thirteenth century to protest the tyranny of princes over lesser nobles. The others, more literary than political in focus, either uphold or criticize courtly values. Many literary epics became staples of popular entertainment by the fifteenth century. Two non-Dietrich epics, *Ortnit* and *Wolfdietrich,* parallel this group in focus and transmission. Women's roles are small in all these narratives.

Epics of the political group, like the *Nibelungenlied,* depict the suffering of women as pawns of political interests. In *Das Buch von Bern* (The Book of Bern) Dietrich reluctantly agrees to marry Herrat in order to get military aid from Etzel. In *Alpharts Tod* (Alphart's Death) Amelgart, brought from Sweden to marry Alphart, cannot dissuade him from going to his death in battle. In *Die Rabenschlacht* (The Battle of Ravenna) Helche, Etzel's first wife, who, in implicit contrast to Kriemhild and Brunhild, maintains harmony at court at any cost, forgives Dietrich even though he is indirectly responsible for the deaths of her sons. In Dietrich epics of the literary group such as *Laurin, Virginal,* and Albrecht von Kemenaten's fragmentary *Goldemar,* which uphold courtly values, women do not transcend the abducted princess stereotype. The same is true of the non-Dietrich epics *Ortnit, Wolfdietrich,* and the fragmentary *Walther und Hildegund.* The maiden pursued by a monster in *Der Wunderer* (The Monster) is a partial exception. She recruits Dietrich to defend her, saying later that she is Lady Luck, thus implying she can reward him for his action. Like *Rosengarten A, Eckenlied d* (Song of Ecke) criticizes courtly values. Queen Seburg sends Ecke to duel with Dietrich, who has done no harm to either. Dietrich, unwilling to fight without just cause, nonetheless punishes both Ecke's foolishness and Seburg's unreasonable challenge.

Further References. Ruth Angress, "German Studies: The Woman's Perspective," in Walter F. W. Lohnes and Valters Nollendorfs (eds.), *German Studies in the United States: Assessment and Outlook (Monatshefte* Occasional vol. 1; Madison, Wisc., 1976), 247–251. Joseph R. Strayer (ed.), *Dictionary of the Middle Ages,* 9 vols. to date (New York, 1982–); for individual epics.

RUTH FIRESTONE

F

FABLIAUX. Medieval comic tales in verse, usually indecent or at least irreverent in language and spirit. In the strict sense the term *fabliaux* refers only to some 150 Old French poems composed between about 1200 and 1340, but these poems have obvious affinities with bawdy narratives told in other centuries and other languages, notably the tales of the Miller, Reeve, Summoner, Merchant, and Shipman in Chaucer's *Canterbury Tales*.

Fabliaux make extensive use of certain easily recognizable types of characters, including lecherous priests, poor but clever students (clerks), newly rich peasants, ignorant virgins, jealous husbands, and resourceful wives. The typical plot pits two of these types against each other in a contest for sexual gratification, power, money, or revenge—or sometimes all four. Victory tends to be won by some ingenious stratagem. The female characters are worthy adversaries in these contests; in sharp contrast with courtly literature, in fact, fabliaux generally portray women as formidably aggressive, clever, and determined to get what they want.

What are we to make of the aggressive women in fabliaux? Critics have sometimes interpreted them all as hostile stereotypes, expressions of deep-seated fears of female sexuality and power. And there are fabliaux that clearly exhibit this kind of antifeminism. In "Porcelet" (Piglet) and "La Dame qui aveine demandoit pour Morel" (The Lady Who Demanded Oats for the Black Horse), for example, crude, scatological punishments are devised for wives whose sexual demands are excessive. "Sire Hain et Dame Anieuse" (Sir Hate and Lady Scold) emphatically recommends that a husband tame a disobedient wife by beating her. "La Dame escoillee" (The Castrated Lady) relates a more imaginative and extreme use of violence to reform domineering wives and concludes with a general curse on women who defy men's authority.

Reassertions of traditional male prerogatives are less typical of this genre, however, than stories that encourage identification with the rebellious woman.

Thus a number of fabliaux use the motif of an intolerable husband whose wife eventually turns the tables on him. One nice example is the suspicious peasant in "Le Vilain mire" (The Peasant Doctor) who decides to beat his wellborn wife every day because she might be unfaithful if she weren't weeping. After a few days of this treatment, the wife retaliates by persuading the king's messengers, who are seeking a great physician, that her husband can cure almost any malady if he's given a good beating first. The boastful coward in "Berengier au lonc cul" (Berengier of the Long Ass) demands a more humiliating comeuppance: he lords it over his aristocratic wife, pretending that he is a great warrior, until she disguises herself as a knight and forces him to choose between meeting her in battle and kissing her ass.

To applaud such heroines obviously requires one to dispense, at least temporarily, with conventional notions of proper female conduct. Indeed, fabliaux seem to have their own ethos, one that has little in common with either courtly ideals of polite behavior or Christian ideals of virtue. This point becomes particularly important when one considers the largest and most controversial group of women in fabliaux: wives who get away with infidelity by tricking their husbands. In another context such behavior would be the stuff of bitter satire, if not tragedy, and even the tellers of fabliaux often include some conventional moralizing against female deceit. But recent critics have argued persuasively that the real thrust of these stories is aesthetic rather than moral: the delight in a great piece of invention for its own sake. Hence the recurrent note of competitiveness. Can the woman manage simultaneously to have her husband cuckolded, beaten, and pleased with her (as in "La Borgoise d'Orliens" [The Townswoman of Orleans])? Can she tell him the whole truth, in language that he won't understand ("La Saineresse" [The Female Doctor])? Can she rise to the occasion when he finds her lover's clothes ("Les Braies au Cordelier"[The Friar's Breeches])? Which of three women deserves the prize for most cleverly deceiving her husband ("Les Trois Dames qui troverent l'anel" [The Three Ladies Who Found the Ring])? The ingenuity celebrated in such stories is not confined to women, of course. There are similar fabliaux about the exploits of peasants and especially clerks—other disadvantaged members of medieval society who become heroes, in these comic tales, by completely outsmarting their betters.

Further Reference. Charles Muscatine, *The Old French Fabliaux* (New Haven, Conn., 1986).

SHERRY REAMES

FIBER ARTS. Women have always been involved in the making and embellishment of items for practical use. In the Middle Ages, much elaborate embroidery with silver-gilt thread and semi-precious stones was created for church use. The Church was also the repository of works such as the 230-foot Bayeux Tapestry, an elaborately embroidered frieze, almost certainly created by teams of women working from plans of a single, unknown designer.

The division "fine" and "applied" arts or "crafts" developed in the Renaissance, reflecting hierarchical patterns found in the society at large, with "women's work" being afforded a different status from men's accomplishments. Architecture, sculpture, and painting were arts restricted largely to men. The "home arts" of decoration of clothing and household furnishings became more nearly the limits of women's creative outlets and were assigned less value than the "fine arts." This division has modified within the twentieth century.

Fiber arts are founded on traditions. Late twentieth-century women make many objects, using similar material and processes, that were made by early American women, but while there have been many carryovers, there have also been notable developments. Changes have occurred in the status of these objects and their makers relative to the fine arts, in the materials and processes, in their value, and in the goals of their makers.

In early America women worked in traditional areas of weaving, quilting, embroidery, and needlepoint. In colonial times professional weavers, a few of whom were women, made coverlets and other things for the home and dyed the fibers. The efforts needed for survival left little time for leisure or for self-expression in decorative work. Products were intended for practical use to add to the comfort and decoration of the home.

The scarcity of textiles made every scrap of material precious. Homemakers joined scraps of fabric to make bed-covers. The odd-shaped bits were joined into random, varicolored patterns by stitching them together to form a top layer for the crazy quilt. The top, an insulating layer, and a backing were joined by knots of string tied here and there across the top or by rows of small stitches—the quilting.

The pieced quilt was composed of tiny pieces arranged in geometric patterns within squares that were then joined to make the top. The quilting stitches enhanced the pattern either by following it or by creating a kind of counterpoint in their own design. In school or at home, girls were taught at an early age to make the small, even stitches prized in quilting. The piecing of the squares was usually done alone, but once a top was finished, the quilting often became a collaborative effort. Quilting was an excuse to socialize with neighbors who might live hours away. Pioneer women centered a large part of their social life on the quilting bee, a purely American custom.

As life became more settled and prosperous, women had more time, and decorative detail became more prevalent. Country fairs encouraged competitiveness in design, color, and craft. One tradition for brides was a chest with 13 quilts. A girl would begin when quite young on her first quilt in a simple pattern and progress till the last ones, of greater intricacy, would show off the skills of the young woman. The thirteenth quilt was the wedding quilt.

While the geometric quilt remained a favorite, appliqué was also popular. In appliqué technique, a plain background cloth has pictorial pieces sewn onto the surface. They are sometimes elaborately quilted and may be embroidered as well. In the style called "whitework" (regardless of color), two fabrics are quilted together, and the design comes entirely from the stitching. Trapunto is a version of whitework in which the two pieces are quilted together. Shapes of the design are made to stand out by pushing an opening in the backing cloth and forcing small amounts of stuffing into the shapes, producing a sculptured effect.

In the 1870s home-crafted items and quilting were largely replaced with manufactured goods. However, an 1876 exhibit of eighteenth-century quilts brought a revival of interest. In the late nineteenth and early twentieth centuries, articles and books on needlework brought about an increase in popularity of quilting and other handwork. *Godey's Lady's Book* published quilting patterns frequently. The first author to devote an entire book to quilts was Mary Webster (*Quilts: Their Story and How to Make Them*, 1915). Journalist and feminist Ruth Finley collected quilts and told their stories in *Old Patchwork Quilts and the Women Who Made Them* (Newton Centre, Mass., 1929).

After World War I, women played major roles in reestablishing the relevance of their crafts both to the art world and to design, especially in industry. Much of what we now take for granted in design was developed at the Bauhaus Design School, founded in Germany in 1919. When the Bauhaus closed with World War II, many of its masters emigrated to America, settling at Black Mountain College in North Carolina. These European émigrés played important roles in art and fine arts education in succeeding years. Leaders in weaving, Anni Albers and Trudi Guermonprez influenced a reevaluation of the loom as a tool for expression in functional and nonfunctional works of art. Loja Saarinen, as director of the weaving school at the Cranbrook Academy in Michigan, carried on her commitment to the connection among art, crafts, and architecture. Educational programs, crafts organizations, and crafts guilds appeared all across the country: in 1922, the Boston Weavers Guild; in 1924, the Shuttle Craft Guild, founded by Mary M. Atwater; in 1930, the Southern Highland Handicraft Guild; and in 1943, the American Crafts Council, started by Arleen O. Webb. Some who kept the fiber arts alive were Berta Frey, Trudi Guermonprez, Gunta Stoltzl, Mary M. Atwater, and Harriett Tidball.

After World War II, industrial designers became trendsetters for the textile market. In the 1950s there was an explosion of interest. The textile industry turned to artists for ideas, engaging designers responsible for many exciting textiles produced for mass production, such as Anni Albers, Dorothy Lieves, Pola Stout, and Hella Skowronksi. A variety of materials was explored for home and architectural use: newly developed synthetics, plastics, metals, leather, beads, etc. In New York, the Museum of Modern Art held an exhibit of weavings by Anni Albers, breaking the old tradition of exclusive concentration on the traditional fine arts.

At the same time, there was a new awareness of Third World art objects. These objects, intended for practical use, were revalued as art and influenced the making of more art. Master of fine arts programs in weaving and textile design began to appear throughout the country. Ruth Asawa, a West Coast artist, was showing looped, three-dimensional, and wire-interlaced forms, the first indication of contemporary woven sculpture. The trend toward three-dimensional reliefs and sculpture in fibers included work by artists Kay Sekimachi, Sheila Hicks, and Lenore Tawney. In 1957, the Staten Island Museum in New York held a major one-person show by Lenore Tawney.

The boom in crafts activities is often credited to the 1960s counterculture, with its emphasis on handwork and crafts for everyone. But it also shares its genesis with the liberation of the homemaker, who, with more leisure time, education, and exposure to contemporary art forms, began to seek avenues of personal expression. Fibers were a natural choice of media because of familiarity with them in homemaking roles. Classes in fiber arts areas sprang up across the country. Crafts were everywhere. The 1960s and 1970s saw a slow growth of the acceptance of crafts media within the fine arts. By the middle 1960s fibers arts were often shown with other arts media. By the beginning of the 1980s, a number of New York art galleries, previously inhospitable to this work, began to hold exhibits by artists working in crafts media.

The 1980s crafts artwork reflects broader art trends in the use of a variety of materials and the crossing of old barriers, combining needlework with paper-making, painting, and quilting and using of plastics, wire, found objects, and other items. Many artists worked in ways that combine the old understanding of "craft" with the values of fine arts. The division of "arts" and "crafts" has been largely erased.

Weaving, for example, has become a generalized term encompassing all ways of constructing textiles, including the knotted structures of Diane Itter and the sculptural forms of Claire Zeisler. Materials have also changed. Arline Fisch and Mary Lee Hu apply textile technique to metal instead of to the traditional yarns and threads. Cynthia Schira uses an Ikat warp with brocading elements of predyed cotton tapes. Embroidery from past centuries is certainly the root of the technique but has little in common with the finished forms of Mary Bero's small, brilliantly hued, intricately embroidered and painted faces.

Papermaking, another craft from the distant past, has had a recent revival in work by artists such as Nance O'Banion. Her powerful basket forms that combine paper with sticks and other materials have been influential for other artists. Lissa Hunter makes constructions of handmade paper, using basketry structure and lamination; surfaces are embellished with drawing materials and pigments. The purity of the sculptural forms of Ferne Jacobs makes her work seem almost totemlike. Felting is another ancient craft revived in service of contemporary artists' work. Joan Livingstone makes three-dimensional forms by combining painted wood and felt.

Tapestry has a long European tradition, but little early history in the United States. Helena Hernmarck works from and uses imagery of photographs in huge photorealism tapestries.

The work of many of the artists could be called "mixed-media," as would Jane Lackey's wall relief images, made in combinations like wire and wood.

Neda Al Hilali, as if creating her own canvases, plaits with processed paper, then paints and dyes the resulting surfaces. Another trend is called "installations." Magdalena Abakanowicz makes molded body forms in multiples and arranges them to fill large gallery spaces, as well as making many woven forms, huge and powerful environmental pieces. Collaboration, as in the cooperative group efforts of the early quilters, is also seen in Judy Chicago's "The Dinner Party," with dozens of people working together to produce the multiple parts, including ceramic plates and embroidered runners, which together celebrate women in history. Shiela Hicks has been influential in getting fiber arts into the architectural setting. Thus we can see the change in women's fiber art from mostly utilitarian objects done primarily in isolation, such as a quilt top, to works that hang in art galleries.

Quilting still survives, now as an art form, with artists using the intense colors of fabrics to create pieced and quilted works. The collaborative team of Gayl Fraas and Duncan W. Slade uses architectural elements and landscape vistas in quilts. Nancy Crow's intense colors and intricate geometric designs make looking at her quilts like looking at a kaleidoscope.

By the 1980s fiber arts expanded in many ways. Artists have begun to deal with subjects beyond the decorative and to treat subject matter heretofore dealt with in the fine arts but not in those media often called "crafts." Fiber artists are using their media to express and interpret ideas, emerging as artists free to deal with all possible concepts and sources of creative energy, including humor. The issue of fine arts versus crafts should no longer be a problem. When one realizes that it is not technique or materials that make an object fine art, then any medium can be elevated to an art form if its concerns are with concepts, questions, and inner visions. Artists working in fibers deal with the same issues as artists working in other media—art is a matter of quality.

Further References. Mildred Constantine and Jack Lenor Larson, *Beyond Craft: The Art Fabric* (New York, 1986). Wendy Slatkin, *Women Artists in History* (Englewood Cliffs, N.J., 1985). J. Paul Smith and Edward Lacy Smith, *American Craft Today: The Poetry of the Physical* (American Craft Museum, 1986). Naomi Whiting Towner, *Filaments of the Imagination* (essay, catalogue for exhibition, University of Hawaii Art Gallery, 1981).

KAYE WINDER

FILMMAKERS. Women have, in one sense, been prominent in commercial filmmaking. From its beginnings the dominant cinema in America has used women's labor in just about every aspect of film production. Women have reached eminence as writers, editors, technicians, animators, even as producers, and of course as actresses. In that sense there are and have been many women filmmakers. But popularly it is a film's director who is its real creator, and very few women have been entrusted with that role. Women were perhaps more active in the industry's silent era than now, although the relative incompleteness of records and film archives makes it difficult to assess precisely their contribution.

A few women, such as Alice Guy-Blaché and Lois Weber, certainly attained considerable prominence at this time. Guy-Blaché was, in fact, a pioneer in cinematography, claiming to have started movie-making before even Meliés, and was perhaps the first to direct a fictional film in France. After immigrating to America, she produced and directed numerous two-reel movies for her and her husband's companies, with major financial and critical success. She stopped directing in 1920, at about the time when, according to Marjorie Rosen, Hollywood's increasing commercialization was pushing women out of reach of any influential positions in the industry (*Popcorn Venus* [New York, 1974]).

Only one female director, Lois Weber, remained a major force throughout the silent era. Her movies were mostly conservative in ideology and have even been called "morality message movies" (Louise Heck-Rabi, *Women Filmmakers: A Critical Reception* [Metuchen, N.J., 1984]). Weber often acted in her own two-reelers, of which the most well known was perhaps *Where Are My Children?* (1916), an antiabortion and procontraception film. A more accomplished movie is *The Blot* (1921), an anatomization of petty bourgeois culture from the point of view of the heroine. The career of Dorothy Arzner overlaps with Weber's, but Arzner continued into the sound era to become the only major woman director in Hollywood during the 1930s and 1940s. Her work has been much discussed by feminist critics and historians (see, e.g., C. Johnson [ed.], *The Work of Dorothy Arzner: Toward a Feminist Cinema* [London, 1975]). Arzner regularly worked with mostly female crews and depicted strong, active women in her stories, as, for instance, in *Christopher Strong* (1933), a movie based on the life of Amy Johnson, the aviator. Perhaps the most discussed moment in her work comes in *Dance, Girl, Dance* (1940) when Maureen O'Hara as a showgirl turns on the males in her audience and, in effect, berates them for their voyeurism. Although a few women (such as Frances Marion, Anita Loos, and Lillian Gish) directed commercially successful movies, Arzner is probably the nearest to a feminist director. Indeed, the only other woman director to make a very significant mark in Hollywood, Ida Lupino, has specifically repudiated any feminist component to her movies. The dozen or so movies she made in the 1950s await, however, a sustained analysis. Lupino has been succeeded by very few women directors in Hollywood. Most of the movies directed by women that have had large circulation in America were made by Europeans such as Mai Zetterling, Liliana Cavani, or Lina Wertmuller. Largely ignored by Hollywood, women directors have had to produce and distribute their movies mostly through independent channels. In recent years directors of feature films such as Claudia Weill (*Girlfriends*) and Barbara Loden (*Wanda*) or Susan Seidelman (*Desperately Seeking Susan*) and the Australian Gillian Armstrong (*My Brilliant Career*) have achieved some success in reaching audiences with their movies, but they are exceptional.

Outside Hollywood and its commercial constraints, women directors have been free to make more significant contributions to the cinema. Perhaps the most important woman director in film history is Maya Deren, who made a series of experimental movies in the 1940s. Her work is surrealistic in quality, investigating the boundaries between objective and subjective reality, and includes *Meshes of the Afternoon* (1943) and *Ritual in Transfigured Time* (1946). For contemporary avant-garde women directors, in America and beyond, Deren has remained a crucial influence. The tradition of avant-garde filmmaking by women has remained strong in America. Recent influences from European directors such as Marguerite Duras and Schantal Akerman have combined with the effects of the women's movement in the 1960s and 1970s to produce a unique American feminist cinema. Directors such as Yvonne Rainer, Michelle Citron, or Bette Gordon make movies that investigate not so much women's lives or psychologies but, rather, the way in which traditional systems of representation construct particular meanings in relation to women and their sexuality. Such movies often fragment and dismantle the conventional codes and structures of the filmmaking process and attempt to show how new and different meaning might be produced. While these avant-garde movies try to disrupt traditional ways of seeing women, another tradition of independent women's filmmaking has the aim of factually recording women's lives and attempting to understand women's specific situation in American society. This documentary tradition, coming to prominence in the 1960s and 1970s, is perhaps influenced by the cinema-verité movie-making of women such as Shirley Clarke and includes many autobiographical narratives and descriptions of women's lives and relationships between women. Some of these movies, for example, are Geri Ashur's *Janie's Janie*, Joyce Chopra and Claudia Weill's *Joyce at Thirty-Four*, Kate Millet's *Three Lives*, and Julia Reichert's *Union Maids*. The importance of each of these movies is, of course, political; each is concerned to provide women with a means to speak of and record their experience in a male-dominated society. Most of these documentaries—and, indeed, avant-garde films by women—are produced with budgets that are tiny in comparison to those regularly expended in Hollywood. Women's access to both the cinematic technology and the funding necessary to use that technology has been severely limited in the past. It may, however, be possible to predict that the relative ease and cheapness of video technology—and its increasing importance in relation to film itself—will open up greater possibilities for women's participation in the production of images.

Further References. Charlotte Brunsdan (ed.), *Films for Women* (London, 1986). Annette Kuhn, *Women's Pictures: Feminism and Cinema* (London, 1982). Sharon Smith, *Women Who Make Movies* (New York, 1975).

PAUL SMITH

FOLKLORE and *women* are terms that have been linked in scholarship only recently. Expressive, artistic behavior, whether verbal or plastic, used to be considered an activity exclusive to men. Women's expressive behavior was assigned categories such as "decorative" or "utilitarian," thus denying the conscious manipulation of form and content for effect or aesthetics.

In 1888 the American Folklore Society was founded; from the beginning women scholars were represented in its publications as well as in other popular and scholarly publications of the time. However, the perceptions of women's contributions, whether as scholars or consultant/informers, were limited by prevailing ideas about women and their abilities. Today, women are actively challenging the preconceptions about themselves and their scholarship, sometimes with a strident rhetoric, sometimes with a comical or ironic attitude, but always with a plethora of knowledge and references. Indeed, the adage of women having to be "better than" to be considered "equal to" is demonstrated repeatedly in women's reports of their difficulties in being taken seriously and being published in premier outlets. While we like to think that our times are considerably different from those of 100 years ago, in practice we now find many similarities to the situation obtaining when folklore first became a scholarly presence in the American scene.

Early collectors, whether men or women, preferred to gather stories from men, unless, of course, the stories concerned hearth and home, charms or lullabies, children's games or cooking, which were the province of women, it was believed. Despite the fact that the Grimm brothers reported collecting their fairy tales primarily from serving-women, it was men who were believed to be the bearers of the important and lengthy traditions while women were believed to be more capable of, and interested in, things that surrounded what was considered to be their primary role: household and child care. Even when women's knowledge was demonstrated to be superior to that of men in a particular genre, it was the words of men that were preferred.

Gradually, during the 1950s and 1960s, information about women in journals or books was expanded to include their roles in cultures other than those founded on Western European models. At times some of this information related to folklore. But usually it was folklore *about* women rather then the kinds of expressive behavior in which women engaged, whether in groups of women, women with children, or mixed gender groups. Occasionally there was a single publication focusing on the repertoire of this female storyteller or that woman singer; such publications were exceptions to an otherwise firm rule that significant folklore study was predicated on working with men's knowledge.

By the late 1960s and the early 1970s the situation was changing rapidly. It is not a coincidence that this change occurred coterminously with the so-called women's movement and court cases affirming the rights of minorities and women. Many graduate school programs, previously de facto closed to women, began to reserve slots for women in order to ensure the continuance of federal funding for other sectors of the university. Older women, those with children, and those who lived on the margins longing for the opportunities of their brothers and husbands were represented in disproportionate numbers in these early graduate classes. These women, predominantly in our country at the University of Texas in Austin, at Stanford University, at the University of Pennsylvania, and at Indiana University-Bloomington, had life experiences and artistic/folkloristic repertoires that were neither described in literature nor accorded legitimacy.

These women began to be heard in the mid–1970s, when there was a sudden explosion of literature about women, their folklore, their roles, their self-perceptions, and even their bawdy jokes, stories, and tales—more often than not with men as the butt. With the increasing availability of funding for women and their concerns, stories began to circulate of the women's folklore from this country or that and its similarities and differences compared with American folklore. Much of this cross-cultural work, however, was not published until the late 1970s and early 1980s.

It was also during the late 1960s and early 1970s that women's groups were formed; originally these were consciousness-raising or rap groups, but now they are termed support groups and have generalized to the society as a whole. Women delighted in finding their commonalities, especially in sharing their ways of relating experiences about such commonalities in these groups. Some of the earlier published and scholarly work in women's folklore grew from such associations of women.

The numbers of books, articles, and chapters on women and their folklore being produced in the mid- and later 1980s reached such proportions as to make it impossible for any one person to keep adequate track of the literature without devoting full time to it. Primarily the work has focused on women's roles, and women's expressions of and about them in cultures throughout the world as well as in our own country. There has also been a coming together of feminism and scholarship. Women have been freed, one hopes permanently, from the bonds of being passive to the recognition that women are active agents, and often agencies as well, for the enactment of their lives. Even in repressed situations, such as can be seen in some back-to-the-past Middle Eastern cultures, women scholars are demonstrating the expressive ways in which women manipulate and comment upon their condition through folkloristic resources.

Theoretical work in women's folklore currently follows the same trends and paradigms as does any other subject in an academic discipline. There are those studies that focus on ethnography, on a Marxist perspective, on a structural presentation, on a semiotic interpretation, or on a performance enactment, as well as those that take a tone of literary criticism; additionally, there are many works that reinterpret past canon on the basis of contemporary insight. Previously taboo topics, such as lesbianism, receive their fair share of scholarly attention and are now publishable, whereas a few years ago they were not—save in the so-called underground press. What were once accepted social "facts," as, for instance, the concept of universal male dominance, have recently been shown to be as much a product of our own mythology concerning proper roles of men and women as they were social reality. The genres and paradigms that have been utilized to discuss women and their folklore or to trivialize them both are more reflective of the scholars and the *zeitgeist* than they are of the actual situation obtaining in any one time or place.

In the late 1980s attention is being given to the effects of colonialism, of cultural recidivism, of feminism, of text versus performance, of performance of text, and of alphabetic literacy on the production, recording, and interpretation of folklore and women. The topic of folklore and women now encompasses folklore of women, folklore about women, women's folklore, and metafolklore— the folklore about the folklore.

In 1888 understanding of folklore and women was a foregone conclusion: everyone knew the kinds of folklore women had and the areas in which they could be expected to demonstrate competency, and everyone knew that real folklore was a possession of men. It took almost 100 years, until 1972, before the first scholarly session on women's folklore was presented at the American Folklore Society; two years later, in 1974, the interest was so intense that there was a double session (four hours of papers.) In 1986 the society's annual meeting featured an entire day of scholarly papers on women's folklore, with multiple sessions running concurrently. Unfortunately, few men attended the sessions. This précis of the American Folklore Society's record concerning folklore and women replicates the situation in other disciplines and scholarship in general.

There are four works that have had a significant impact upon the thinking of those who write about folklore and women. Barbara Babcock's (ed.) *The Reversible World* (Ithaca, N.Y., 1978) contains two of her essays, the Introduction and "Liberty's a Whole," which are seminal. My own *Women and Folklore: Images and Genres* (Claire R. Farrer [ed.], 1986 reissue, Prospect Heights, Ill.) has articles repeatedly cited. Marta Weigle's *Spiders and Spinsters* (Albuquerque, N.M., 1982) presents images of women from many cultures throughout history. Finally, *Women, Culture and Society* (Michelle Zimbalist Rosaldo and Louise Lamphere [eds.] [Stanford, 1974]), although an anthropological collection, provided the stimulus for much of the research now seeing the light of publication.

CLAIRE R. FARRER

FRENCH ACADEMIC ARTISTS painted in accordance with the standards of the French Royal Academy (Académie Royale de Peinture et de Sculpture), founded in 1848 as France began its cultural ascendancy in the reign of Louis XIV. For over 200 years it was the dominant force in French art; its École des Beaux-Arts trained artists in the approved styles, and its annual salons exhibited only art that met its standards. Very few women were members, and those who were members were not in full standing—they could not attend the École or compete for the Prix de Rome until the end of the nineteenth century, could not hold office, and from 1791 held only honorary rank—but to achieve success, women artists, members or not, adhered to its standards. There were no radicals until the Impressionist movement in the late nineteenth century.

The number of women professional artists was inconsiderable in the seventeenth century but grew thereafter. By the end of the eighteenth century not only were some women artists earning a good—sometimes an excellent—living from painting, but the idea that well-bred young ladies should have "accomplishments" (i.e., know something of music and drawing as well as needle-work) meant others could support themselves by lessons in private homes or convent schools.

Most women artists were painters who confined themselves to portraiture, still life, and genre scenes, which earned less prestige and less money than the large historical, religious, and allegorical works commissioned by public institutions. Their training was restricted: they could not attend art schools until after the midnineteenth century or study from live nude models until the 1870s; until the Louvre was opened to the public after the Revolution, most could not study the old masters. Few attempted large-scale multifigure works that required knowledge of male anatomy, and when landscape became popular, women could not travel freely through the countryside. But within their limited confines, women were successful. As long as they "kept their place" within the genres classified as minor and did not threaten male artists economically and especially if they were of pleasing appearance and manners, they were accepted. If, however, they successfully vied for commissions for large-scale works or made too much money, they might find themselves accused of having had men retouch, or actually paint, their canvases.

In the seventeenth century almost all women artists came from families of artists and were trained by fathers or other family members, but in the eighteenth century exceptions were more numerous. From the latter part of the century the atelier system of studio instruction evolved, and women sought instruction in the studios of both male and female artists. A few women artists remained single, often the sole support of their families. Most married, usually to other artists. For some, marriage ended their careers; others continued, but production often declined sharply as childbirth and increasing domestic duties interfered.

Although Royal Academy salons were open only to members, public exhibitions were possible through the less restrictive provincial academies and, in Paris, through the Academy of St. Luke (Académie de Saint-Luc), until its closure in 1777. St Luke's lacked the prestige of the Royal Academy, but women could earn a reputation and with it some financial success through its exhibitions.

The first woman elected to the Royal Academy was Catherine Duchemin in 1663. Over the next 20 years, six other women were admitted, then no others for almost 40 years. The best-known woman painter of the seventeenth century was not a member; Louise Moillon (1610–1696) had probably ceased painting before the academy was founded (her first child was born in 1642). She was one of the earliest French still-life artists, painting fruit (and sometimes vegetable) still life with an almost classic simplicity of arrangement. Other French women artists of the seventeenth century include Madeleine Boullogne, still-life artist, and her sister Génevieve, about whom nothing is known, academy members in 1679; Catherine Perrot, admitted 1682; Sophie Chéron, who is best known for her allegorical portraits and who supported her family by her art; still-life artists Charlotte Vignon and Marie Blancour; Suzanne de Court, enameler; and Claudin and Antoinette Bouzonnet Stelle, engravers.

From 1720, when Italian pastelist Rosalba Carriera was admitted, to 1769, four women were elected to the academy, only one of whom was French, miniaturist Marie Thérèse Reoul. When in 1770 admittance of two women— Anne Vallayer Coster and Marie Suzanne Girout-Roslin—meant there were four women academicians, fears were raised, and it was decided never to exceed that number. Not until 1783 were women again admitted: the very successful painters Adélaïde Labille-Guirard and Elisabeth Vigée-Lebrun.

Marie Suzanne Giroust-Roslin (1734–1772), one of the two finest French pastelists of the eighteenth century, in her short career painted mostly family and friends. She died of breast cancer at 38. Anne Vallayer-Coster (1744–1818), on the other hand, one of the best eighteenth-century still-life painters, had a long career: 26 when elected to the academy, she entered her last salon the year before her death. One of her finest works is *The White Soup Bowl* (1771), a steaming white bowl of soup with dark bread and wine.

Adélaïde Labille-Guirard (1749–1803) and Elisabeth Vigée-Lebrun (1755– 1842) were admitted to the academy at the same time and were apparent competitors. Both, because of their success and their life-styles, were accused of immorality and of having men paint or retouch their work. Labille-Guirard over her long career showed continued growth, moving on to another genre after succeeding in a previous one (from miniatures to pastels to oils), and at the time of the Revolution she was moving into large canvases. Her best work was her portraits in oils, but her lack of flattery meant that Vigée-Lebrun was more in demand than she. First winning success in the Academy of St. Luke, in 1785 she created a sensation at the Royal Academy with her *Portrait of the Artist with Two Pupils*. She moved easily from painter of royalty in the 1780s to painter of revolutionary leaders in the 1790s.

Elisabeth-Louise Vigée-Leburn was enormously popular. Beginning at age 15, her talents were exploited first by her stepfather, then by her husband, until she divorced him in 1794. Her highly flattering portraits, combining rococo and neo-classical style, made her the most sought after painter in Paris and, during 12 years of exile, 1789–1801, in whatever city she visited. As official painter of the queen she did many portraits of Marie Antoinette, the last *Marie Antoinette and Her Children* in 1778 having been an official attempt to counter the virulent attacks being made on the queen's morals. After her return from exile her career did not resume its former prominence.

Marie-Ann Collot (1748–1821) was one of the few eighteenth-century women sculptors. She did many portrait busts during a long stay in Russia, where she went with her teacher Etienne Falconet. Later, when Falconet had a stroke, she left her husband, Falconet's son, and her career to take care of him.

All prerevolutionary academies were abolished in 1793. When they were later reestablished under the Institut de France, the Académie de Pienture et Sculpture admitted women only to an honorary rank, as had been decided in 1791. Since they could exhibit in salons and since they had been little more than honorary members before, numbers of women artists gained a practical advantage at the expense of prestige for a very few. Throughout the nineteenth century there was a continued increase in the number of women who exhibited in academy salons. In the second half of the century, as opposition to the academy and its conservative standards grew, women found it easier to exhibit, and, as academy prizes became more meaningless, to gain more of them.

From the late eighteenth century the sentimental genre became highly popular with male and female artists. More women were also trying historical paintings now, especially pupils and followers of Jacques Louis David, although the first classes with nude models were not open to them until late in the nineteenth century. (See ART EDUCATION, EUROPE [NINETEENTH-CENTURY.])

Marguerite Gérard (1761–1847), sister-in-law and student of rococo painter Jean Honoré Fragonard, painted mostly genre scenes but without the excessive sentimentality of so many paintings of the period. Prints helped popularize her work and spread her reputation, as they did also for Antoinette Haudebourt-Lescot (1784–1845), whose early paintings, genre scenes set in Italy, were so much in demand her work suffered from haste. Later she turned to portraits and in her forties abandoned genre painting. Pauline Angou (1775–1835), who entered her first salon at 18, combined sentimental genre with history in paintings of Marie Lousie, commissioned by Napoleon as part of his efforts to promote the empire.

Of painters reputed to have been pupils of Jacques Louis David, one of the most gifted was Constance Marie Charpentier (1767–1849). Her work includes portraits of women and children, genre scenes, and allegory. Marie Guilhelmine Benoist (1768–1826), student of Vigée-Lebrun and David, is the painter of the outstanding *Portrait of a Negress* (1800). When her husband was given a high government post after the Restoration, he ordered her to retire from professional painting. She was then at the height of her success. Also associated with David was Nanine Vallain, painter of classical and allegorical canvases, whose republican sympathies are clearly marked in her *Liberty* (1793–1794).

Félicie de Fauveau (1802–1886), best woman sculptor of nineteenth-century France, was an active political supporter of the monarchy, imprisoned for her activity during the July Revolution (1830). Interested in the medieval, she is an early figure in the gothic revival.

The animal paintings of Rosa Bonheur (1822–1899), the most successful painter of the nineteenth century, were more popular in England and the United States than in France. Her realistic portrayal of animals, the result of thorough studies from life, found a wide audience. Her most famous paintings, *Plowing in Nivernais* (1849), *Horse Fair* (1853), and *Haymaking in Auvergne* (1855) gained her national and international fame. Through prints her paintings appeared in homes and schoolrooms all over Europe and America. When she was denied the Cross of the Legion of Honor because of her sex, Empress Eugenie, acting as regent for Napoleon III in 1864, got it for her and delivered it personally. She was the first woman to receive this honor and the first to be made Officer of the Legion of Honor. Her success and her unconventional behavior—she smoked, cut her hair short, and wore trousers—caused resentment and ridicule.

Among other painters of the eighteenth and nineteenth centuries are Gabrielle Capet, pupil of Labille-Guirard, best known for miniatures; Marie Victoire Lemoine, a student of Vigée-Lebrun; Marie Geneviève Bouliar, portraitist; Elisabeth Chaudet, painter of children with animals and other sentimental themes; Jeanne Philiberte Ledoux, painter of children and young girls; Marie Eléonore Godefroid, portraitist; Adrienne Marie Grandpierre-Deverzy, painter of interiors and literary subjects.

Further References. Elsa Honig Fine, *Women and Art: A History of Women Painters and Sculptors from the Renaissance to the 20th Century* (Montclair, N.J., 1978). Anne Sutherland Harris and Linda Nochlin, *Women Artists: 1550–1950* (New York, 1976). Charlotte Yeldham, *Women Artists in Nineteenth-Century France and England*, 2 vols. (New York, 1984).

FRENCH IMPRESSIONIST PAINTERS. In 1874 a group of dissident artists declared their independence from the French academic art world and held their own exhibition. The original group of Impressionists included Claude Monet, Pierre Auguste Renoir, Camille Pisarro, Alfred Sisley, Edgar Degas, Paul Cézanne, Jean Guillaumin, and Berthe Morisot (1841–1895). Others similarly dissatisfied later joined them, including Mary Cassatt (1844–1926) in 1879. Some, although associated with the group and sharing a similar aesthetic, did not exhibit with them, as was the case with Edouard Manet and Eva Gonzales (1849–1883). Suzanne Valadon (1865–1938) is a Post-Impressionist with strong ties to the Impressionists.

The artists loosely grouped under the label Impressionist shared a basic need to escape from the narrow confines of academic orthodoxy and an overriding interest in light and color. They shared a common interest in the contemporary, in painting figures caught in a moment of ordinary activity.

Berthe Morisot and Mary Cassatt were fully accepted by their male colleagues. The limitations placed upon them as women were the limitations they themselves subscribed to. They were professional artists and they were revolutionaries within their profession, but they were also thoroughly upper middle-class nineteenth-century women.

Berthe Morisot's *plein air* landscapes had been accepted for salon exhibition before, in 1868, she met Manet and, through him, the young rebels who gathered at the Café Guerbois. It is after this time that her interests turned to figures in landscapes and domestic settings. The often reproduced *Mother and Sister of the Artist* comes from this early period (1869). Her painting achieved full maturity in the 1870s. *The Cradle* (1872) is characteristic of her treatment of interior light, here filtered through drapery onto the netting over the cradle, and of her mother-child paintings, with the mother in a protective posture.

In 1874 Morisot helped organize the first Impressionist exhibition and also entered into a successful marriage with Eugéne Manet, younger brother of the artist. Their beloved daughter Julia was model for many of her paintings.

In the 1880s Morisot's brush stroke becomes more marked, detail fades away, and definition becomes minimal, as light threatens to dissolve all forms. In *The Dining Room* (1886) woman and room seem to meld into one. Then in 1890 she began to change her technique. She makes many preliminary sketches, colors become more brilliant, figures more defined (e.g., *The Cherry Pickers*). While she was not a commercial success in her own day, her reputation grew in the twentieth century while that of more successful nineteenth-century artists, such as Rosa Bonheur, declined.

Mary Cassatt, from a well-to-do Pennsylvania family, studied with the fashionable academic Charles Chaplin and in Holland, Spain, and Italy. Although she exhibited in successive salons from 1872 to 1876, two rejections soured her on the selection method. When Degas in 1878 invited her to exhibit with the Impressionists, she was ready to do so. Her entry in the 1879 exhibition is one of her best Impressionist paintings, *In the Loge,* with its play of gaslight on the figure and dress of her sister Lydia relaxing during intermission at the opera.

Cassatt's paintings show a cool, detached realism, the complete lack of sentimentality that marked her life as it did her work. Among paintings exhibited from 1879 to 1886 were *The Cup of Tea* (1880), the portrait of her mother reading *Le Figaro* (1883), and mother-child paintings, on which she concentrated in the 1880s and 1890s. Mother-child paintings were popular with artists, male and female, during the period. Her many paintings of children may reflect the fact that a proper Victorian maiden lady was limited in the subject matter available to her. The completely unsentimental renderings of children do not bespeak the deep maternal longings male critics tried to read into them. Among her best Impressionist works is *A Mother About to Wash Her Sleepy Child* (1880).

Like Morisot, she too grew dissatisfied with Impressionism. In the late 1880s and early 1890s her painting shows renewed concern for clear definition, disappearance of the obvious brush stroke, brighter color, more structure. And the effect of spontaneity is eliminated in favor of the timeless pose. Two outstanding mother-and-child paintings from this period are *The Bath* (1891) and *The Boating Party* (1893–1894).

Influenced by Japanese woodcuts, in 1891 she produced a set of color aquatints, using her own technique. These superb prints (e.g., *La toilette*) help establish Cassatt's place in the history of art. In 1904 the French government awarded her the Legion of Honor.

Eva Gonzales, also upper middle-class and, like Cassatt, a student of Chaplin, in 1869 met Manet and became his model, student, and protégée. Like Manet she exhibited through the official salon, refusing to join the Impressionists, but, like the Impressionists, she was interested in scenes from everyday life and the effect of light on figures in the open air. However, in the definition of figures and the use of color she does not follow their lead. One of her finest works is *Reading in the Forest* (1879). She died at age 34, after giving birth to a son.

Suzanne Valadon was of a very different background from Morisot, Cassatt, and Gonzales and lived the very different life of a Montmarte bohemian. Growing up on the streets and on her own from at least age ten, in the early 1880s she became a very successful model. It was from her association with artists, many connected with the Impressionist movement, that she picked up technique, and, when she began drawing c.1883, Toulouse-Lautrec and then Degas took an interest in her work.

Her earliest paintings date from 1892–1893, but until 1909 she did mostly drawings and prints. Her first prints, etchings of various phases of the toilette, were done in Degas's atelier under his direction. It was not until she was 44 that she turned exclusively to painting. Her nudes (she was one of the first women to paint male nudes), portraits, and still lifes were drawn and painted in an original style—she claimed not to have been influenced by any other artist— and her bold color, strong line, and earthy realism contribute a vitality and forcefulness that stamp all her work.

Further References. Elsa Honig Fine, *Women and Art* (Montclair, N.J., 1978). Ann Sutherland Harris, *Women Artists, 1550–1950* (New York, 1977).

FRENCH WRITERS have a history that begins in the twelfth century with Marie de France, whose *lais* (narrative poems) were probably written before 1167. Composed of octosyllabic couplets and variable in length, the *lais* were inspired by legends from Brittany. They take place in fairy tale settings and depict love stories in which the male lover (such as a valiant knight) must overcome many obstacles to conquer his beautiful beloved (often a woman married to an old and jealous husband). The *lais* are appreciated for their clear organization but sometimes criticized for their affected naïveté.

Two centuries separate Christine de Pisan (c.1364–1431) from Marie de France. A widow at the age of 25, Christine de Pisan became a professional writer at the court of Charles VI to support her three children. She first composed ballades in which love and solitude are recurrent themes. An innovative narrative technique used by the poet consisted in letting the heroine express her point of view, whereas at that time the woman's thoughts were perceived through a man, when not ignored. In her didactic writings, Christine de Pisan fought the traditional and antifeminist image of woman given by the misogynist male writers of her day. Her *Livre de la cité des dames* (The Book of the City of Ladies), published in 1404, addressed all women about their role in society. A poet and polemist, Christine de Pisan also played a political role, writing about peace.

The author of poems influenced by her belief in mysticism, Marguerite de Navarre (1492–1542), the sister of King François I, is remembered for a work entitled *Heptameron*. Published posthumously in 1559, it was inspired by the *Decameron* of Boccaccio, from which she borrowed the narrative technique of embedded stories. Ten persons confined to the same room because of floods tell each other stories. *Heptameron* is a valuable literary work because each novelette is followed by a discussion among the storytellers. The main advantage of this device is the plurality of voices ranging from the realistic to the idealistic. Another meaningful characteristic of the *Heptameron* is that the participants have been identified as contemporaries of Marguerite de Navarre, and their stories constitute an historical testimony.

A true woman of the Renaissance enamored of the new culture, Louise Labé (c.1524–1566) played an active part in the cultural life of Lyons, where she was friends with celebrated poets such as Ronsard and Marot. The originality of her own poetry is found in the twist she imposed on the traditional conception of love: the man is the erotic object while the woman is the desiring subject.

Marie de Gournay (1565–1645) is referred to as "the spiritual daughter of Montaigne," whose work she edited for posthumous publication. Like Christine de Pisan, she lived by her pen. A very independent woman herself, she fought for the cause of other women in *Egalité des hommes et des femmes* (Equality of Men and Women) and *Le Grief des dames* (The Complaint of Ladies).

In the seventeenth century women played a leading role in the literary world with their salons. The salon of Mme. de Rambouillet, in existence between 1620 and 1648, that of the courtesan Ninon de Lenclos (attended by Molière), and the one of Mlle. de Scudéry were among the most prestigious salons. Madeleine de Scudéry (1607–1701) was herself a writer known for her huge epic novels. According to the author, love was the only virtue capable of raising individuals above themselves. She also favored the emancipation of women. Women, she wrote, should remain single to preserve their independence.

The year 1678 marked the publication of *La Princesse de Clèves*, a masterpiece still acclaimed in world literature as the first modern novel and as the archetype of the psychological novel. The book was published anonymously, but the author was soon identified as Mme. de La Fayette (1634–1693), the hostess of a leading salon who thought that writing was beneath her noble status. As a regular at the court of Louis XIV, she borrowed elements from that setting for *La Princesse de Clèves*. The interest of the novel lies in the personality of the princess, torn between her obligation of fidelity to her husband and her fatal attraction to another man.

A good friend of Mme. de La Fayette, Mme. de Sévigné (1626–1696), is known for her correspondence. Her letters, addressed mostly to her daughter, describe the daily life at the court. Written with spontaneity and no transitions, they resemble our modern news flashes.

The literary tradition of the salons continued in the beginning of the eighteenth century. During the second half of the century, as the revolution of 1789 was approaching, women became politically involved. Women's clubs where the situation of women in society was discussed evolved from the salons. Olympe de Gouges (1748–1793), an active feminist, questioned male privileges in her *Déclaration des droits de la femme* (Declaration of the Rights of Women).

The very beginning of the nineteenth century is marked by the work of Mme. de Staël (1766–1817). Her extensive travels through Europe, especially Germany, inspired her famous reflections *De la littérature* (1800; On Literature) and *De l'Allemagne* (1810; On Germany). In these works, Mme. de Staël promoted the notion of comparative literature by drawing attention to the similarities and differences between diverse national literatures. She also introduced the great German authors such as Goethe and Schiller to her compatriots and contributed to the development of French Romanticism in glorifying qualities such as enthusiasm, individualism, imagination, and passion. In another work, *Corinne* (1807), the author reflected upon the place of women in a male society. In her eyes, women were superior to men but were always crushed by male pride.

The prolific career of George Sand (Aurore Dupin) (1804–1876) can be divided into four phases. In the 1830s she wrote romantic fiction in which she described the lives of women (e.g., *Indiana* [1832] deals with the position of women in marriage). Her writings of the following decade reflect her political activity: *La Comtesse de Rudolstadt* (1844) showed Sand's solidarity with the working class. The late forties and fifties were the years of the pastoral novels in which she abandoned the urban proletariat in favor of the peasantry (as shown in *La Mare au diable* [1846; The Devil's Pool]). After the revolution of 1848, during which she again supported the proletariat, she retired to the country and wrote mostly letters. A literary circle gathered at her home. When she died, her good friend Flaubert said of George Sand: "One had to know her like I did to know how feminine this great man was!"

While male poets had dominated the symbolist movement at the end of the nineteenth century, women were in the vanguard of the lyric genre at the beginning of the twentieth century. The poet Anna de Noailles (1876–1933) was influenced by a neo-classical tendency that, in reaction to the stylistic liberties of symbolism, advocated the return to rigid rules in versification. As far as the content goes, Anna de Noailles's poetry had inherited the pagan characteristic of the *Parnasse*, a poetic school of the previous century. Through her lyrical and romantic soul, she symbolized the essence of femininity.

Many women writers of the twentieth century embraced the epic genre. The career of Gabrielle Sidonie Colette (1873–1954) (known simply as Colette) is spread over six decades. But her masterpieces date from after World War I, when her dissolute life became more stable. The majority of Colette's novels deal with various aspects of love. *Le Blé en herbe* (1923; The Ripening Seed) is the story of a teenager and his sexual initiation by a mature woman, while *Sido* (1929) describes the relationship between the author and her mother.

Between 1939 and 1945, when France was at war with Germany, Elsa Triolet (1896–1970), often known only as the muse of the poet Louis Aragon, was an active writer in the Resistance. A collection of her novellas, published clandestinely in 1943, received the Goncourt Prize (a prestigious French literary award) in 1945.

Just as Elsa Triolet lived in Aragon's shadow, Simone de Beauvoir (1908–1986) is always associated with the existentialist philosopher Jean-Paul Sartre, her lifelong companion. A professor of philosophy at first, she devoted her life to literature after the success of the first novel, *L'Invitée* (1943; She Came to Stay*, 1954). Her study *Le deuxième sexe* (1949; *The Second Sex,* 1952) made Simone de Beauvoir a major feminist figure. In her work she showed how women had always been and were still considered inferior by men. Her famous statement "One is not born a woman, one becomes a woman" implies that the education and the formation women receive make them alienated beings. In 1954, de Beauvoir received the Goncourt Prize for *Les Mandarins* (*The Mandarins*, 1956). *Mandarins* is a term she used to designate the leftist intellectuals who were questioning the value of their political involvement. She is also famous for writing memoirs, a domain in which she excelled.

Marguerite Yourcenar (pseud. of Marguerite de Crayencour) (1903–1987) traveled extensively through Europe before settling in the United States, where she taught literature until 1967. She became famous with the publication of *Mémoires d'Hadrien* (1951; *Memoirs of Hadrian*, 1954). Combining history and psychology, the book is a faithful account of the life of the Roman emperor Hadrian. In 1981, Yourcenar was the first woman to be elected a member of the French Academy, the prestigious institution founded in 1635 to preserve the quality of the French language.

Nathalie Sarraute (b.1902) was a leading proponent of the so-called new novel, the aim of which was to avoid the traditional forms of the novel. Her first work, *Tropismes* (1939; *Tropisms*, 1963), is a collection of brief and untitled texts with no apparent action and with anonymous characters. These texts constitute a successful attempt at describing what lies beyond expression and communication. Along the years, Sarraute has published many novels, among which are *Portrait d'un inconnu* (1947; *Portrait of a Man Unknown*, 1958), *Le Planétarium* (1959; *The Planetarium*, 1960), and the autobiographical *Enfance* (1983; *Childhood*, 1984). She has also written plays and an essay, *L'ere du soupçon* (1956; *The Age of Suspicion*, 1963), dealing with the epic genre.

Marguerite Duras (b.1914) is sometimes associated with the new novel also. Fairly traditional at the beginning of her career, she turned to narratives called antinovels, such as *Moderato cantabile* (1958; Eng. 1960). Her novel *L'Amant* (1984; *The Lover*, 1986) won the Goncourt Prize.

While the new novelists were devising innovative writing techniques, other writers were still successful with plain storytelling and real characters. In 1954, the French public discovered Françoise Sagan (b.1935), who had just published *Bonjour Tristesse* (Eng., 1955) and become famous overnight. Scandal, idleness, and luxury are constant characteristics of Sagan's novels.

In the 1970s, the movements of women's liberation fought for the identity of women. The feminists insisted on women's specificity and differences, whereas Simone de Beauvoir had refused the notion that women were inherently different from men. The feminist writers agree on the necessity of creating their own language because the commonly used language has been created by and for men. Men are not the only enemies. Specific types of women are denigrated by the feminists: the poster-girls of whom all men dream, the femmes fatales, and also the mothers, accused of perpetrating the continuity of slavery. Of these feminist writers, one should be familiar with Benoîte Groult (b.1920), Marie Cardinal (b.1929), Hélène Cixous (b.1937), and Annie Leclerc, among many others.

DOMINIQUE THÉVENIN

G

GERMAN ARTISTS, as was the case everywhere in Europe until the late nineteenth century, generally have painted, but only as daughters or sisters of painters in their workshops, without affixing their own names to any painting. One of the earliest exceptions known is sculptor Sabine von Steinbach (fl. c.1300), creator of several fine statues at Strasbourg Cathedral, built by her father Erwin von Steinbach. While some noted Italian Renaissance artists were women, the Reformation tended to relegate females to traditional occupations so that in Germany it took until the seventeenth century before autonomous women artists appear. Sybilla Merian, who had the luck to be born into a Frankfurt engraver's family and the determination to enter the Labadist sect, which freed women from traditional marital obligations, produced several volumes of etchings and watercolors. These show European and Surinam fauna and flora in amazingly aesthetic and microscopic detail; she is also said to have discovered the metamorphosis of the butterfly. In the eighteenth century, several painters' daughters such as Barbara Krafft (1764–1825) or Anna Dorothea Lisiewska-Therbusch (1721–1782) were appointed court artists after one of their works had attracted attention—in Therbusch's case, at Stuttgart and later Berlin and in Krafft's, at Vienna, Salzburg, and Prague—where they excelled mostly as portrait painters. The most famous was Angelika Kauffmann (1741–1807), a cosmopolitan neo-classical allegorist, portraitist, and history painter. She was founding member of the London Royal Academy and a friend and protégée of Reynolds, and her beauty and artistic and musical talent fascinated Goethe, whom she portrayed in Italy.

Romantics adored women as creative spirits of almost redeeming power but took the women's creativity as homage to their own, at least as far as painting is concerned. Geniuses such as Anna Maria Ellenrieder (1791–1863), an excellent draftsperson, easily became victims of sexism and provincialism; Ellenrieder eventually ceased to paint because of chronic depression.

It is not until the end of the century that women are noticed again as painters, the 1880s and 1890s being the first period when art academies sporadically opened to women. After studying in Paris, Paula Modersohn-Becker (1876–1907), living in the artists' colony of Worpswede, superimposed on German naturalism the intensity of Van Gogh and Gauguin, depicting in heavy Cézann-esque strokes and bright colors the motherly simplicity of Westphalian peasant women and ruddy children. Her most daring painting is a self-portrait in the nude, in which, like Frenchwoman Suzanne Valadon at the same period, she abolishes the habitual division of woman in art as *either* artist *or* model/muse, a myth perpetrated by the male establishment. Because of her early death after the birth of her child, she ranks only as a highly important precursor of Expressionism, whereas Becker's senior, Käthe Kollwitz (1867–1945), became one of its significant representatives. Kollwitz was trained privately in Berlin, Königsberg, and Munich because she had been denied access to art academies. In many media, especially the older black-and-white graphic techniques (drawing, etching, lithography) that are reproduced relatively inexpensively, Kollwitz depicts the misery of wars, proletarian deprivation, and social exploitation, thus creating an art that is truly political and can be widely disseminated. She was not the only productive woman artist during the Expressionist period: besides many émigré women living at one time or another in Germany, such as the Russian Marianne Werefkin (1860–1938), Gabriele Muenter (1877–1962) was an important member of the "Blaue Reiter" circle of Munich. Many landscapes painted simultaneously by both Muenter and Kandinsky permit interesting comparisons. The Bruecke group in Dresden did not produce equally important women artists.

Surrealism was an international artistic movement that inspired an entire generation of women painters, sculptors, and photographers. Sophia Delaunay-Terk (b.1885 in the Ukraine) received her artistic training and married German art dealer Wilhelm Uhde in Karlsruhe. Later she moved to Paris, where her geometrical canvases were to rival in luminosity those of her second husband, Robert Delaunay. Together they created the "Orphist" movement, which was avidly received in Germany by Paul Klee and the "Blaue Reiter." Another creative woman from surrealist circles was the Swiss Sophie Taeuber-Arp (1889–1943), who worked as dancer and theatre director as well as artist in Zurich, where Hans (Jean) Arp was attracted by her many talents. She conceived her work as a synthesis of architecture, sculpture, and painting and later collaborated with Arp and Theo van Doesburg on larger projects. In 1931, she settled near Paris, becoming a member of the group "Abstraction Création." Even better-known, if not notorious, Meret Oppenheim (b.1913 in Berlin) worked in Paris as a model of surrealist photographer Man Ray. Her felt-covered tea cup entitled *Breakfast in Fur* (1936) with its quasi-Freudian ironic juxtaposition of incompatibles has become known as a rebellious act against clichés of femininity and fashion. Almost forgotten for years, Hanna Höch (1889–1978) was recently rediscovered through a retrospective in the Musée d'Art Moderne in Paris. Her incisive collages deal with machismo and the dehumanization of modern war and technology. Her later paintings are inspired by the technique of her own photocollages.

Although still not as visible as their male colleagues, postwar German women artists have been participating in every artistic movement, a few ignoring particularly feminist issues or themes, while most have formed groups supporting each other and publicizing issues of women in art. Particularly attracted to performance art have been women such as Gina Pane (b.1939), Carolee Schneemann (b.1939), Renate Weh (b.1938), and Hanna Frenzel (b.1957), treating feminist themes, consumerism, and body art. There is also a significant contemporary movement attempting to reformulate feminist aesthetics and to rewrite art history, as in the important volumes by Gisela Ecker (*Feminist Aesthetics* [Boston, 1985]) and by Marlis Gerhardt (*Stimmen und Rhythmen: Weibliche Aesthetik und Avantgarde* [Darmstadt, 1986]) and Renate Berger (*Malerinnen auf dem Weg ins 20. Jahrhundert: Kunstgeschichte als Sozialgeschichte* [Cologne, 1982] and *Der Garten der Lüste* [Cologne, 1985]), texts that would warrant translation.

Although encyclopedias like the present one are a welcome positive manifestation of the wave of research on women in recent decades, the results so far are bound to be tentative, since much if not most research is still in progress on previously "invisible" women artists who were active during all periods of German art history.

Further References. Germaine Greer, *The Obstacle Race: The Fortunes of Women Painters and Their Work* (New York, 1979). Joerg Krichbaum and Rein A. Zondergeld, *Kuenstlerinnen von der Antike bis zur Gegenwart* (Cologne, 1979). Roszika Parker and Griselda Pollock, *Old Mistresses, Women, Art, and Ideology* (New York, 1981).

UTE MARGARETE SAINE

GERMAN WRITERS (REFORMATION THROUGH BAROQUE PERIOD). With the reform of the church and the establishment of Roman law during the thirteenth century, there was a decline in women's status in Germany, so that women lost not only legal rights and the ability to hold official positions and to practice a trade within the guilds, but even the possibility to acquire a full education in the liberal arts. Consequently the following centuries saw a sharp decline in female literacy and authorship.

Although some people called for an educational program for girls from the time of the Reformation, these efforts died at the end of the sixteenth century. Only at the end of the seventeenth century did the movement to institutionalize female education gain momentum. Hence we rarely find German female writers among the large number of poets from the fifteenth to the eighteenth centuries, although women were not illiterate altogether.

High-ranking noble women appear as early as in the first half of the fifteenth century as translators of French courtly literature or as patrons of courtly poets. Famous among them were Elisabeth of Nassau-Saarbrucken (1379–1456); Eleanore of Scotland, wife of the archduke Sigismund of Tyrol; and Mechthild (1419–

1482), in second marriage wife of the archduke Albrecht of Austria, who created a remarkable literary circle in Rottenburg on the Neckar. The Augsburg nun Klara Hätzlerin (c.1430–after 1476) gained a reputation for her work as editor of more than 200 secular and religious verses in her *Liederbuch* of 1471.

With the Reformation the last resort for female literary productivity—nunneries and cloisters—was closed or deserted. Charitas Pirckheimer (1464–1532), however, energetically and with partial success, fought for the preservation of her convent in Nuremberg. Her correspondence represents an essential part of female literature in the sixteenth century. Another epistolary author was Argula of Grumbach (1492–after 1563), who composed famous public letters in defense of early members of the reformed church and addressed them to imperial cities, dukes, and princes. Various other women who were involved in the Reformation, such as Ursula of Münsterberg (1491–after 1534), Katherine Zell (1497–1562), or Elisabeth of Braunschweig-Lüneburg (1510–1558), left important letter collections and religious treatises, along with personal accounts of their conversion to Protestantism.

In the early seventeenth century several women writers emerged at the various territorial courts. Elisabeth (1620–1697), Anna (1617–1672), and Augusta Maria of Baden-Durlach (1649–1728) composed lyric poetry and song-texts for the reformed church in Baden. Pietism helped such women as Adelheid Sybilla Schwarz (1621–1638) to express their concerns in a literary form. Schwarz was, in particular, one of the first in Germany to follow Martin Opitz's influential poetics of German language and poetry (1624), using the natural accent of prosodic speech in her own works. Also Rosamunde Juliane of Asseburg (1672–1712) was an enthusiastic pietist poetess. Both were strongly influenced by seventeenth-century French female pietists such as Antoinette Bourignon and Madame Guyon.

A truly intellectual and highly educated representative of German women poets was Anna-Maria van Schurmann (1607–1678), who composed poems in Latin, Greek, and Hebrew in addition to German. In a famous treatise (*Amica dissertatio*) she defended women's right to advanced education (1641). Anna Ovena Hoyen (1584–1655), who also excelled in her learnedness, dedicated many of her poems and songs to the Anabaptist movement. Elisabeth Charlotte, Duchess of Orléans, originally Lieselotte of the Palatinate (1652–1722), wrote a highly interesting account of her experiences at the French court of Versailles in hundreds of letters to her friends and relatives in Germany. The poetry written by Catharina Regina of Grieffenberg (1633–1694) is highly acclaimed for its adamant stand against the Counter-Reformation and its expression of her strong belief in the Protestant movement. Philipp Zesen even invited her to become a member of the Rosengesellschaft, one of the many German societies of the baroque period concerned with the purification and development of the German language.

Many other women writers such as Susanne Elisabeth Zeidler (fl.1681–1686), Margaretha Susanna of Kuntsch (1651–1716), and Anna Rupertina Fuchs (1657–

1722) were active in the late seventeenth and eighteenth centuries. They predominantly dedicated their attention to lyric poetry. Christiana Mariana of Ziegler (1695–1760) was one of the first German women writers of the Enlightenment. The highest recognition as an imperial poetess was given to Sidonia Hedwig Zäunemann (1714–1740) by Göttingen University in 1738.

The first woman to be an independent writer living solely on the income of her own writing was Anna Louisa Karsch (1727–1791), who gained widespread recognition among leading contemporaries such as King Frederick II and the poet Johannes Wolfgang von Goethe. Friederike Karoline Neuberin (1697–1760), a famous actress and playwright, and Adelgunde Victorie Gottsched (born Kulmus [1713–1762]), highly acclaimed both for her participation in her husband's work on a German dictionary and for her poems, plays, translations, and letters, were the first outstanding female poets representing the postbaroque period.

There are three major problems with the history of women writers since the Middle Ages. First, since a large part of the literary work by women has not been published, it is practically impossible to assess objectively the share of female literature in the Reformation and the baroque period. Second, the literature written by women has not received any comprehensive attention in literary studies up to now because of male-oriented scholarship in German literature since the Middle Ages. Third, most women writers prior to the eighteenth century composed private poetry and letters almost exclusively. Since they lacked any possibility of publication, they did not venture into plays, novels, or essays.

Further References. B. Becker-Cantarino (ed.), *Die Frau von der Reformation zur Romantik, die Situation der Frau vor dem Hintergrund der Literatur-und Sizialgeschichte*, Modern German Studies 7 (Bonn, 1980). Gisela Brinker-Gabler (ed.), *Deutsche Dichterinnen vom 16. Jahrhundert bis zur Gegenwart* (Frankfurt, 1978). K. M. Wilson (ed.), *Dictionary of Continental Women Writers* (New York, 1990). Jean M. Woods and Maria Furstenwald, *Women of the German-speaking Lands in Learning, Literature and the Arts during the 17th and 18th Centuries, A Lexicon*, Repertoire zur deutschen Literaturgeschichte 10 (Stuttgart, 1984).

ALBRECHT CLASSEN

GERMAN WRITERS (MODERN). As in the rest of Europe, the few German women who wrote in the Middle Ages were aristocrats or nuns and often both, such as Hroswit (Roswitha) of Gandersheim, Hildegard of Bingen, and Mechthild of Magdeburg. During the Renaissance, there were women close to the humanists: Caritas Pirckheimer, Elisabeth of Brunswick-Lüneburg and Emperor Charles V's sister Margaret of Austria.

A very interesting early baroque writer is Anna Owena Hoyen (1584–1655), who deserves more research. While little is known about her life except her struggles, she has left much poetry; for her, there is no contradiction between writing religious poetry and writing satirical attacks on certain clergymen. Catharina von Grieffenberg (1633–1694) is a major mystical baroque poet who meditates on religious subjects in a highly unconventional diction.

In the eighteenth century, women became culturally active. There is not only the theatre woman and impresario, Friederike Caroline Neuber, called "Neuberin" (1697–1760), but there is also the learned Luise Gottsched, the "Gottschedin" (1713–1762), who found a congenial husband to support her writing. Anna Luisa Karsch (1722–1792), who had to struggle, forged a very intense language that was the envy of male poets and anticipated the nature lyrics of Klopstock and the young Goethe. Sophie Albrecht (1757–1840) and Friederike Brun (1765–1835) are also worth mentioning.

Although the Romantics idolized women, and there were many female geniuses in their circle (Bettina von Arnim [1787–1859], Sophie von Mereau [1770–1806], Karoline von Guenderode [1780–1806], Caroline von Schelling [1763–1809], and Dorothea Schlegel [1763–1839]), their impressive creativity has been woefully undervalued (and well-nigh unpublished) to date. Two nineteenth-century writers, aloof from literary groups, have traditionally received recognition: the Austrian Marie von Ebner-Eschenbach (1830–1916), known chiefly as a writer of novellas based on traditional folklore, and Annette von Droste-Hülshoff (1797–1835), a Catholic of Westphalian nobility, known for her intensely introspective poetry.

In the twentieth century, women can be said to have finally achieved an equal place with men. During the early literary movements of the century, they are still considered the companions of relatively better-known male writers, who sometimes silence their creativity; such is the case of the Ingolstadt novelist Marieluise Fleisser (1901–1974), a friend of Brecht's early years, and Claire Goll (1891–1977), whose writing underwent a crisis during Yvan Goll's relationship with poet Paula Ludwig (1900–1974). Overlooked for a long time and recently rediscovered have been Emmy Hennings (1885–1948) and Rahel Sanazara (1894–1936), companions of Hugo Ball and Ernst Weiss, respectively. Both Goll and Hennings authored autobiographical texts. The most important poets of the early part of the century are Jewish women who have combined the insights of a life of persecution, a fascination with religious themes, and a daring twentieth-century subjectivity with intense poetic experimentation: Else Lasker-Schüler (1876–1945), Gertrud Kolmar (1894–1943), Nelly Sachs (1891–1970), and Rose Ausländer (1907–1988). Hilde Domin's (b.1912) literary criticism, especially on poetry, is equally as interesting as her poetic works. Marie Luise Kaschnitz (1901–1974), who lived in Italy much of her life, is a poet, novelist, and short story writer for whom the classical tradition is relevant. Elisabeth Langgässer (1899–1950), barred from publication during the Third Reich, has written three cycles of religious poetry, but her most important accomplishment is the novel *The Inextinguishable Seal*. Another author who was successful right after the end of the war is the Austrian Ingeborg Bachmann (1926–1973); while her modernist poetry was highly acclaimed, her prose works, for instance, *Malina*, were first condemned by male critics as "improper" only to be profusely imitated later. Ingeborg Bachmann, in fact, is considered by many today to be the outstanding woman "classic" author of the German postwar period.

The two most important poets writing today are the highly experimental and eclectic Austrian Friederike Mayröcker (b.1924) and the whimsical Sarah Kirsch (b.1935), trained as a scientist, whose poetry and narrative are often imbued with magic and fairy tale, but also with harsh, contradictory reality, first that of the Democratic Republic and, since her emigration, that of the Federal Republic. East Germany has at least three great novelists. Anna Seghers (1900–1983), exiled for many years, has movingly written about political dilemmas and the life of simple people. Her novel *The Seventh Cross* is about an early concentration camp for leftists, with the main character managing to escape. The second novelist is Christa Wolf (b.1929), whose novels have shown that subjectivity cannot be absent from literature even at a time when the official literary ideology of the Democratic Republic prescribed a Socialist realism that devalued individual psychology. Wolf's main theme is childhood (*Patterns of Childhood*, 1977) in Nazi Germany and youth in the Democratic Republic (*The Divided Heaven,* 1963; *Thinking About Christa T.,* 1968), but she has also treated the same interpenetration of political history and private fate in her long historical novella *Cassandra* of 1983, in her novel *Kein ort. Nirgends* (1970; No Place. Nowhere) on the double suicide of author Heinrich von Kleist and Henriette Vogel, as well as in her Chernobyl text *Störfall* (1987; Out of Order), which blends essay, biography, and what might be called fantasy. Wolf has written interesting critical texts in which she attempts to come to terms with her own fiction. In a deliberately feminist vein, the third woman, Irmtraud Morgner (b.1933), in several related novels daringly combines the life of a female troubadour with modern life and science-fiction events.

The Federal Republic has a very active generation of women writers, among whom the best known are the satirist Gisela Elsner (b.1937); the politically and sociologically oriented Ingeborg Drewitz (1923–1986); the prolific, sardonic Gabriele Wohmann (b.1932); and the impressive Karin Struck and Verena Stefan (both b.1947), all of whom deal in their novels with problems of female sexuality, the mother-daughter relationship, machismo, and other themes of female/feminist relevance, often blurring the traditional division between fiction and reportage.

Austria has produced a prolific generation of women, whose themes have included feminine depression (specifically Marlen Haushofer, [1920–1970]); education and daughter-parent relationships (Barbara Frischmuth [b.1941] and Jutta Schutting [b.1939]); and the grotesque and funny relationship between the sexes throughout the ages, for the benefit of female revolt today (Elfriede Jelinek [b.1946]).

Although encyclopedias like the present one are a positive outcome of the wave of research on women's creativity during the last decades, so much work is currently in progress on previously "invisible" women authors of all periods that the data in this article must be considered tentative and as yet inconclusive.

Further References. Gisela Brinker-Gabler, *Deutsche dichterinnen vom 16. Jahrhundert bis zur Gegenwart* (Frankfurt, 1986). Heinz Puknus (ed.), *Neue Literatur der Frauen* (Munich, 1980). Jürgen Serke, *Frauen schreiben* (Frankfurt, 1982).

UTE MARGARETE SAINE

GOSSIP. Generally a derogatory term today applied both to "idle," moralistic, and speculative talk about persons not present and to people, usually women, who engage in such talk. Its Old English form was *godsibb*, meaning akin or related, and its now archaic definitions refer to important, ritually established relations between godparents themselves or between them and the parents of the baptized person. Middle English usuage designated familiar acquaintance or friends and applied to either sex, but especially to a woman's female friends invited to be present at a birth. Chaucer's Wife of Bath refers to such an intense, satisfying relationship with her female gossip. The importance of this nurturing and bonding is also implied, at least in relation to women, by Ralph Waldo Emerson in *Representative Men* (1860): "Our globe discovers its hidden virtues not only in heroes, and archangels, but in gossips and nurses."

The degradation of the term is found in the third *Oxford English Dictionary* definition, first noted in 1566: "A person, mostly a woman, of light and trifling character, esp. one who delights in idle talk; a newsmonger, a tattler." In the eighteenth century, Dr. Samuel Johnson unambiguously linked gender and a gossip in his third dictionary definition: "One who runs about tattling like women at a lying-in."

Anthropologists and sociologists have remarked on the prevalence and importance of adult women's and men's gossip in social life. It has been viewed as an informal means of teaching morality, of indirectly controlling aggression, of maintaining social control and solidarity, of covertly negotiating, of building and destroying reputations, of exchanging valuable information, of expressing sociability itself, and of offering entertainment. The powerful positive and negative potential in gossip is seen, for example, in its use by healers diagnosing and treating the social component of illness and by practitioners of malevolent witchcraft or those making accusations of witchcraft. Because gossip deals privately in particulars, personalities, and personal relationships, it is often seen as the province of those too weak or disenfranchised to deal publicly with social problems and as dangerous to the official group culture.

By 1811, according to the *Oxford English Dictionary, gossip* was used to refer to a kind of conversation, "idle talk; trifling or groundless rumour; tittle-tattle. Also, in a more favourable sense: Easy, unrestrained talk or writing, esp. about persons or social incidents." The "less favourable" sense is influenced by deprecation of interpersonal life as frivolous, irrational, and antithetical to serious spiritual, philosophical, political, and economic pursuits. It is encapsulated in official sanctions like the biblical injunction, "Thou shalt not go up and down as talebearer [later: slanderer] among thy people" (Lev. 19:16, King James 1611).

The art of gossip, which in any group requires various performance and narrative skills and involves a creative, ludic interaction, is rarely studied (except, e.g., Sally Yerkovich, "Gossiping; or, The Creation of Fictional Lives," diss., University of Pennsylvania, 1976). Although men certainly gossip—by any definition of the term—it is women's talk that in Western society has become virtually synonymous with gossip and with other derogatory sociolinguistic terms also associated with women like *chatter, prattle, natter, nag*, and *whine* (see OLD WIVES' TALES). Myths in oral tradition (see MYTHOLOGY) and novels, biographies, and social commentary in literary tradition have served as the measure of narration and social criticism, and much reevaluation must be done if gossip is to be viewed as equally significant storying.

Further References: John Beard Haviland, *Gossip, Reputation, and Knowledge in Zinacantan* (Chicago, 1977). Ralph L. Rosnow and Gary Alan Fine, *Rumor and Gossip: The Social Psychology of Hearsay* (New York, 1976). Patricia Meyer Spacks, *Gossip* (New York, 1985).

MARTA WEIGLE

GOTHIC FICTION (1780 TO 1830) was dominated by women writers and readers. Novels of domestic virtue (see DOMESTIC NOVEL), also extremely popular during this time, reinforced the roles assigned to women in late eighteenth-century English society. The gothic, however, became the expression of repressed fears and anxieties resulting from women's actual oppression in a male-dominated environment. The literary conventions these writers established reflected the ambiguity of their lives. Unwilling to jeopardize social reputation and respectability, they wrote conservative gothic novels that overtly accepted women's idealized moral virtues and social positions of legal and economic inferiority, yet within this framework they dramatized their sense of exploitation and persecution.

Horace Walpole changed the course of English fiction for 50 years when he wrote *The Castle of Otranto* in 1764 with the express intention of restoring imaginative, unreal elements to novels, which he thought had become tedious in their depiction of ordinary experience. His inclusion of the supernatural, the remote, medieval castles and ruins with subterranean vaults and secret passages, and the prolonged pursuit of an innocent heroine by a male villain became standard fare for creating a sustained mood of terror. While male writers like Matthew Lewis and Charles Maturin developed an erotic, sensational kind of gothicism, in which the reader identified with a villain-hero who eventually paid the price for his satanic indulgences and abuses of human decency, the women writers established the dominant tradition of a genteel, sublime gothic fiction where the reader identified with the female protagonist threatened and imprisoned by a male villain. In novels by Clara Reeve, "the great enchantress" Ann Radcliffe, Sophia Lee, Charlotte Smith, Regina Maria Roche, Eliza Parsons, and many others, the female protagonist was the key factor in the reader's overwhelming response to this fictional experience.

Over and over again, the central pattern of the action, often narrated in the first person, was imprisonment and escape. Emily St. Aubert in Ann Radcliffe's *The Mysteries of Udolpho* (1794) represented the typical heroine, who, left without family protection and guidance, fell victim to the greedy and tyrannical Montoni. Confined in a castle, she could rely only upon her virtue to protect her against threats to her person and fortune. During all of her trials, she remained steadfast, proper, and passive; she never acted aggressively by attacking her male pursuer to free herself. Usually the heroine's escape was provided by a miraculous turn of events, such as the discovery of true identify through a will, or by the villain's self-destruction. Her sufferings were thus rewarded by a restoration of property and a good marriage. The lengthy and emotional descriptions of settings intensified the fear of imprisonment, a feeling shared by women readers coping, in fact, with their restrictive environments. The escape was seen as a triumph of good over evil, defined in the gothic as female over male, a liberation achieved without violating the attributes that made women appealing to men, especially their naïveté, their uncomplaining passivity, and their propriety. For women writers, who might have led uneventful lives tending the hearth, with virtually no participation in worldly affairs, the lofty language of the gothic, with its focus upon natural landscapes and interior descriptions, was suitable for their talents. For their readers, the fictional experience provided a vital outlet for their own sensibilities.

No wonder that this pattern should have been repeated with few exceptions for over 200 years of gothic fiction. Rare were the writers who took liberties with the genre: Jane Austen in *Northanger Abbey* (1818), a satire of the gothic advocating common sense in women; Emily Brontë's *Wuthering Heights* (1847), an incorporation of gothic material into romantic, psychological portraits; Mary Shelley's *Frankenstein* (1818), a brilliant abandonment of the innocent heroine in favor of the villain-hero. Today, as evidenced by the thousands of "supermarket romances" written and read by women, the formulas established between 1780 and 1830 persist in endless variation.

Further References. Elizabeth MacAndrew, *The Gothic Tradition in Fiction* (New York, 1979). David Punter, *The Literature of Terror: The History of Gothic Fiction from 1765 to the Present Day* (London, 1980). Bette B. Roberts, *The Gothic Romance: Its Appeal to Women Writers and Readers in Late Eighteenth-Century England* (New York, 1980). Ann B. Tracy, *The Gothic Novel: 1790–1830: Plot Summaries and Index to Motifs* (Lexington, Ken., 1981).

                                                            BETTE B. ROBERTS

GREEK AND ROMAN ART (ANCIENT). Greek art shows women as mortals and figures from myth and allegory in sculpture and painted vases (seventh to first centuries B.C.E.). The monuments were usually made by men for male buyers; with few exceptions, they present an idealized view of women's forms and lives. Roman art in which women appear in sculpture and wall painting (first century B.C.E.–fourth century C.E.) was also made by men, but women are sometimes documented as patrons and buyers. Their representations are more varied and include not only naturalistic portraits but even, though more rarely, scenes of public life. Despite the richness of the evidence, no book has been written on the whole subject.

Greek art presents women as goddesses such as Hera, mythological figures such as Amazons, and idealized mortal women. Goddesses were shown with emotions controlled and bodies clothed in the art made between the sixth and the early fourth centuries B.C.E., but during the Hellenistic period (third to first centuries B.C.E.), both nudity (e.g., the *Venus di Milo*) and emotion appear. Stories of mythological women appear both in religious art, for example, on temples such as the Parthenon in classical Athens, and on decorated vases. These stories seldom offer clear information about the lives of real women, although they may be presented using the visual language of real life, as when mythological weddings occur.

The mortal women of Greece appear on gravestones of the fifth to the fourth centuries as deceased or mourners. On vases of all periods women are shown as wives, mothers, and servants in domestic settings or as prostitutes at parties. At home, the women weave and spin, play with children, or talk among themselves and with men. Occasionally they appear in weddings, funerals, and religious rituals.

Both in Greek sculpture and in vase painting, women normally do not have individualized features (except for a few servants and prostitutes on decorated vases); instead they are idealized according to the standards of beauty common in the period. In the Hellenistic period there are extremely naturalistic figurines and statues of old peasants, and images of Hellenistic queens like Cleopatra VII show individualized features, as do contemporary male portraits. In general, however, Greek art is not an especially good source of literal information about women's (or men's) lives and appearances because of its emphasis on convention and idealization.

Greek works of art indicate men's rather than women's ideas about beauty and social order. From myth and comparative evidence, we can assume that women produced works of textile art, but only in the Hellenistic period is there any secure evidence that a few women were considered artists. The literary sources (e.g., Pliny, *Natural History* 35.147–148) tell about no more than a dozen women, all of whom were painters, most of whom were the daughters of artists. There is also far less information about women than about men as patrons or buyers of works of art in the Greek world, although some wealthy women are known to have given money for public monuments like temples.

Roman writings give no evidence that women were artists in the Roman world, but they do tell about women as patrons and buyers of works of art. One of the most famous examples is Eumachia, a rich woman who endowed a large public building in the Forum of Pompeii. Less splendid but equally important are the many examples of women who bought funerary monuments for their family members.

Roman art tends to reveal more direct information about women's lives than does Greek art. Romans seem to have preferred images that commemorated the individual's appearance, status, and activities in the world. This preference encouraged artists to provide public and private monuments that documented the real as well as the ideal and mythic worlds. Figures from myth and goddesses such as Venus appear in religious art, on tombs, and in house decoration as at Pompeii. In addition, however, real women abound in the art of every part of the Roman Empire. Highly detailed portraits of wealthy women abound, and even women without much money, many of them former slaves, paid for decorated tombstones that showed them with their families or, less often, at work, for example, selling groceries or delivering babies.

Although Roman art seems more realistic than does Greek art, it was often just as concerned with expressing gender ideals. Whether in its frequent representation of women as younger and more attractive than men or its preference for women with their families rather than in public roles, Roman art offers a strong sense of the conventions of society. The representation of the female members of the imperial family provides a last example of this sense; such women seldom appear on the decorated public monuments paid for by the Roman state, for example, the triumphal arches. When they do, though, they are either shown on coins as divine figures like Salus (the health of the empire) or shown with their husbands and children, as on the *Altar of Augustan Peace* in Rome (13–9 B.C.E.). The crossover from the private, women's realm to the public, men's world takes place in Greek art only in religious and mythological art, but in Roman art it also occurs when the emperor needs to show that his dynasty is strong and his children healthy.

Further References. Christine Mitchell Havelock, "Mourners in Greek Art" and Natalie Boymel Kampen, "Social Status and Gender in Roman Art: The Case of the Saleswoman," in Norma Broude and Mary Garrard (eds.), *Feminism and Art History* (New York, 1982), 44–77. Diana E. E. Kleiner, "The Great Friezes of the Ara Pacis Augustae," *Melanges de l'Ecole Francaise a Rome* 90, 2 (1978): 753–785. Brunilde Sismondo Ridgway, "Ancient Greek Women and Art: the Material Evidence," *American Journal of Archaeology* 91 (1987): 399–409. Dyffri Williams, "Women on Athenian Vases: Problems of Interpretation," in Averil Cameron and Amelie Kuhrt (eds.), *Images of Women in Antiquity* (Detroit, 1983), 92–106.

NATALIE BOYMEL KAMPEN

GREEK WRITERS (ANCIENT). The early Greek women writers whose works are preserved are all lyric poets. Lyric poetry, unlike epic and drama, had a ritual setting or an informal audience; it was part of women's lives, and women were composers and performers as well as audience. The most important of these poets is Sappho. She lived in Mytilene on the island of Lesbos around 630–570 B.C. (all the dates in this article are estimates). We know almost nothing of her life. Sappho's work was collected by Alexandrian scholars into nine books. Papyrus fragments found in Egypt have restored good parts of about eight major poems; quotation provides three other long poems and many excerpts.

The major poetic form before Sappho's time was epic. Epic was oral poetry; bards learned traditional plots and formulas, which they used to improvise narrative poems on the deeds of heroes. Once writing was introduced (c.750 B.C.), creative epic began a long, slow decline, though not before several major epics (notably Homer's *Iliad* and *Odyssey*) were recorded in writing. Sappho's poetry comes out of the same large oral background as epic. She uses the Aeolic dialect, native to Lesbos, but a polished version. Her meters and forms are derived from tradition, from hymns, laments, and work songs. But, unlike epic, Sappho's poems were sung. The meter is more fixed than Homer's, the lines shorter because the rhythm must fit the music. Sappho often used the Sapphic strophe, a four-line stanza, but also a variety of other meters. Sappho may have composed melodies for the poems or may have used traditional tunes.

Sappho's poetry has a simple loveliness that engages the hearer immediately but unfolds to reveal richness of thought and emotion. Most of the extant poems are about love between women, a love that, for Sappho, reveals itself as a sense of beauty. "The most beautiful thing is what one loves," she says, and she expresses greater desire to see Anactoria's step and sparkling smile than an awesome massing of military force (E. Lobel and D. Page, *Poetarum Lesbiorum Fragmenta* [Oxford, 1955] hereafter LP). As proof, Sappho adduces Helen, most beautiful (for she was everyone's choice), who chose her lover above all else. The interplay with Homer and the complex logic of the poem (Helen as paradigm for both Anactoria and Sappho) give it resonance.

Through language and image Sappho suffuses poems with fragrant, fugitive sensuousness. In 96 LP a woman in Lydia outshines her companions as the moon does the stars, the moon whose erotic magic reminds Sappho of her. The woman evoked is absent, her seeming presence a trick of vivid memory. By writing, Sappho fixes passing moments of memory (whether real or imagined) into a permanent form. Sappho is perhaps the first poet for whom the act of writing is part of the meaning of the poem. She opposes the oral tradition, with its assimilation to the typical, in her specificity of recollection, in the naming and recorded detail that escape the passing of time and of memory itself.

Yet Sappho was a singer, and her poems found their natural expression in performance. For whom did she perform? The male poets found an audience at drinking parties and political clubs. Sappho, too, must have had a set of friends; the question (most vexed) is whether they formed an organized group, a circle including young, unmarried women. On the basis of ancient remarks that Sappho "taught," scholars posit a circle whose purpose is variously imagined as religious or educational or initiatory (including initiation into eroticism). There is little evidence in the extant poems for such a circle. A two-line fragment without context says, "I will sing these pleasant things beautifully to my (female) companions" (160 LP). The poems sometimes speak to one woman about another or use the plural "we" in reminding a woman of past friendships.

Sappho herself is elusive in the poems; the complexity of dialogue and imagined and reported speech, the often perceptible distance between poet and narrator, the dreamlike scenes and depicted intimacy with Aphrodite make locating an historical Sappho in the poems impossible.

Lyric poetry could be either monodic, sung by a single speaker, or choral, sung and usually danced by a group. Most of Sappho's extant poems are monodic. But Sappho was famous in antiquity for her wedding hymns, probably danced choral songs. No substantial fragments of wedding songs survive. Short quotations offer jocular or admiring references to the groom, laments of lost virginity for the bride. Other fragments may also come from choral songs, for instance the ritual lament for Adonis, which belonged to a festival of Aphrodite. One fragment (44 LP), perhaps for a wedding, gives a long description of Hector's return to Troy, bringing Andromache, his bride-to-be. The meter is similar to epic hexameter, and the language more like epic than in any other poem of Sappho's.

Women poets are known from the fifth century. There was Myrtis from Boeotia. She is said to have been a teacher of Corinna and of Pindar, the composer of victory odes, but we have no evidence that would confirm this statement. No fragment or quotation attributed to her survives, just a tale of a woman's rejected love and revenge, which Plutarch says she narrated. She is mentioned by Corinna.

Corinna herself is the most problematic of the women poets. Ancient sources assign her to the fifth century as a contemporary of Pindar, but some scholars date her to the Hellenistic period (after 323 B.C.) instead. Arguments about her language and meter are not decisive either way. Papyrus finds have yielded sizable fragments of two poems, narratives of Boeotian myth, and bits of others. In a small fragment Corinna claims to sing tales for the young women of Tanagra and to make the city rejoice, so she may have written songs for women's choruses at local festivals. The meters are song meters similar to Sappho's, and the poems are in stanzas. If Corinna is Hellenistic in date, then she was a gifted archaist in a period that valued archaic poetry and local color.

Also fifth-century are Praxilla and Telesilla, the first from Sicyon, the second from Argos. Praxilla was known as a writer of dithyrambs, elaborate choral songs. One line from a dithyramb on Achilles is preserved because it illustrates the meter named Praxillean after her. Telesilla, too, had a song meter named after her. She was, according to Pausanias, "famous among women for her poetry." From the few references we may gather that she composed narratives of the gods, probably choral poetry.

Erinna, a fourth-century poet, was almost as famous in antiquity as Sappho. Her major poem, "The Distaff," said to have been in 300 hexameters, was greatly praised. About 50 broken lines of "The Distaff" have now been found on papyrus. The poem is a lament for the death of a friend, Baucis, interwoven with reminiscences of childhood and references to Baucis's wedding. A major symbol of the preserved section is the tortoise. The word is spelled in the Aeolian way in apparently deliberate reference to Sappho, who used it to refer to the lyre. The tortoise figures also in myth and in a girls' game that Erinna and Baucis played, so it serves to link the themes of childhood, marriage, spinning, death, and poetry. The Sapphic technique of rendering memory present and an imaginative meditation on the sorrows of women's lives are finely combined.

Poetry in the Hellenistic period was meant to be read by the educated. The distinction between public, political poetry, performed by men, and informal or festival poetry, which women also composed, has broken down. A favorite form now was the epigram. Three women epigrammatists, Anyte of Tegea, Nossis of Italian Locri, and Moero of Byzantium, have poems preserved in a collection known as the Palatine Anthology.

Most of Anyte's 20 genuine epigrams purport to be inscriptions; possibly some were written for that purpose. Four of them, for instance, are ostensibly for the tombs of young women who died before marriage, all quite different but all through language or image referring to a Homeric scene. Anyte also has several epigrams describing pleasant places for travelers or country laborers to rest, early examples of pastoral poetry.

More unusual are Anyte's descriptive epigrams, a type that she shares with Nossis and that they may have been the first to develop. These epigrams describe genre scenes or artwork; Anyte has one of children riding a goat. While Anyte shows interest in the unremarked or inarticulate—children, animals, quiet places—Nossis is interested primarily in women. Her erotic poetry is lost, but in one epigram she is among those "loved by Cypris," while in another she asks the stranger going toward Mytilene to remember her to Sappho. Perhaps her erotic poetry was addressed to women. The epigrams we have describe women's portraits or dedications to Aphrodite. Nossis describes the portraits as true likenesses that reveal each woman's essence, whether sensuality or gentleness or wisdom. In her own style Nossis repeats Sappho's desire to fix in writing the effect of women on those near them, a woman's response to the epic "deeds of men."

Names of other Hellenistic women poets are known, for example, Hedyle. Several who lived in the third century B.C. wrote poems for various cities, perhaps on commission, or traveled to major festivals to compete in poetry contests. Inscriptions record their names. Melinno wrote a poem in praise of Rome that has survived, but we have no idea of her date. Education for women improved in the Hellenistic period, so women began to write treatises on philosophy, gynecology, and literary questions. Leontion, for instance, whose work Cicero read, was a philosopher and companion of Epicurus. Less is recorded, or invented, about these women than about the earlier poets. Hellenistic scholars, inevitably, sought out the "antique" poets and neglected their gifted contemporaries.

Further References. W. Barnstone (trans.) *Sappho: Lyrics in the Original Greek with Translations* (New York, 1965). J. Duban, *Ancient and Modern Images of Sappho: Translations and Studies* (Lanham, Md., 1983). A. P. Burnett, *Three Archaic Poets* (Cambridge, Mass., 1983). P. Jay (ed.), *The Greek Anthology and other Ancient Epigrams: A Selection in Modern Verse Translation* (New York, 1973). G. Kirkwood, "Sappho" and C. P. Segal, "Women Poets: Corinna, Myrtis, Telesilla Praxilla," in P.E. Easterling and B. Knox (eds.), *Cambridge History of Classical Literature: Greek Literature*, vol.1 (Cambridge, Eng., 1985). S. Pomeroy, "Technikai kai musikai," *American Journal of Ancient History* 2 (1977): 57–68. Jane Snyder, *The Woman and the Lyre* (Carbondale, Ill., 1989). E. Stigers (Stehle), "Sappho's Private World" and J. Winkler, "Gardens of Nymphs" in H. Foley (ed.), *Reflections of Women in Antiquity* (New York, 1981).

EVA STIGERS STEHLE

H

HAGIOGRAPHY. Inspirational literature that recounts the lives, deaths, and/ or posthumous miracles of holy men and women; also known as saints' legends. Although similar stories have been told about the heroes of other religions and cultures, hagiography is associated above all with Roman Catholic Christianity between late antiquity and the Reformation. From this long period, much of it otherwise sparsely documented, thousands of hagiographical texts survive—a vast body of potential source material for feminist theologians, social historians, and other reinterpreters of the medieval past. The main problem is learning how to use this material.

Most hagiographical sources bear little resemblance to sober, trustworthy biographies—and logically so, since most hagiographers were publicists, not disinterested historians. Their central task was to glorify the memory of particular saints, usually for such practical purposes as strengthening the morale of the saint's community, attracting recruits to the saint's way of life, and drawing pilgrims to the saint's shrine. In this context, advocates of a new saint might go to some lengths to prove him or her superior, or at least equal, to earlier heroes of the faith and advocates of earlier saints might respond by improving their own legends. Hence the genre is full of polemical exaggerations, and legend after legend uses the same proven formulas for success—verbal commonplaces, key images, sometimes whole incidents borrowed from the Bible or from influential early legends.

What can modern scholars learn from sources like these? If we work cautiously enough, attempting to strip away all the conventional and polemical material in the legends, we may find nuggets of reliable historical detail. Donald Weinstein and Rudoloph M. Bell give a large-scale demonstration of this procedure, with applications to medieval family history, in *Saints and Society: The Two Worlds of Western Christendom, 1000–1700,* part 1 (Chicago, 1982). Alternatively, and probably with even more fruitful results, we can focus on the hagiographical elements, seeking, for example, to understand what the conventional images tell us about the assumptions and aspirations of medieval people. Some of the most interesting recent research of this kind has dealt with the issues of gender roles, sanctity, and power.

As many scholars have pointed out, the prevailing images of sanctity in late antiquity were masculine. Women were represented among the martyrs, of course, but even the martyr was envisaged as fulfilling a prototypically male role, that of athlete or warrior, which was beyond the natural capacity of women. Thus the endurance of the female martyr Blandina, in the famous letter about the persecutions at Lyons, is depicted as miraculous: "Tiny, weak, and insignificant as she was she would give inspiration to her brothers, for she had put on Christ, that mighty and invincible athlete, and had overcome the Adversary in many contests, and through her conflict had won the crown of immortality" (from Herbert Musurillo [ed. and trans.], *Acts of the Christian Martyrs* [New York, 1972]). The other great model of sanctity in this period was the monastic ascetic who withdrew from the world, renouncing all earthly pleasures and possessions to seek God alone. And the conventional image of such an ascetic, like that of a martyr, was male. The strength of this gender identification is suggested by the way Jerome praises his already saintly, ascetical friend Paula when he describes her visit to desert monks in Egypt: "Her endurance [was] scarcely credible in a woman. Forgetful of her sex and of her weakness she even desired to make her abode . . . among these thousands of monks" (Letter 108, W. H. Fremantle [trans.], in Philip Schaff et al. [eds.], *Select Library of Nicene and Post-Nicene Fathers of the Christian Church*, 2nd series, vol. 6 [New York, 1893]). There were also hagiographical romances about idealistic women who disguised themselves as men in order to join such communities of monks and achieve sainthood.

During the first two-thirds of the Middle Ages (sixth to twelfth centuries) the Western Christians most likely to become saints were bishops, abbots, monastic founders, and kings—individuals, that is, who wielded considerable power in society because of their high office and (usually) aristocratic birth. Given the emphasis on public power in this model of sanctity, it is not surprising that new female saints were even rarer than in late antiquity and likelier to be honored chiefly because they were related to male saints. But there was at least one major exception: Anglo-Saxon monastic hagiography produced some remarkably strong, positive images of abbesses who left their mark on the church. Bede's (d.735) brief life of St. Hilda in the *Ecclesiastical History* is one example. Rudolf's life of St. Lioba (written c.835) includes miracle stories which testify even more memorably to the kind of benevolent, world-changing power that Anglo-Saxon monks were willing to credit to holy women as well as holy men.

Turning to late medieval hagiography (thirteenth to fifteenth centuries), one finds female saints suddenly prominent. Of the new saints recognized during this period, about 30 percent were women—approximately double the percentage in the preceding centuries. Moreover, the late Middle Ages saw the multiplication of stories about the Virgin Mary, especially in her role as last resort of sinners, and a great revival of romanticized legends about early virgin martyrs like St. Margaret, St. Cecilia, and St. Katherine of Alexandria. Some of these late medieval favorites are very authoritative figures, but almost never do they recall the androgynous public authority of an Anglo-Saxon saint like Lioba. Indeed, their legends tend to dwell on virtues that sound quintessentially feminine—chastity, long suffering (whether from persecution, penitential asceticism, or illness), respect for the clergy, and compassion for unfortunates—and on such private supernatural experiences as spiritual marriages to Christ and visits from angels. Some late medieval hagiographers go so far as to suggest that being female is actually an advantage, rather than liability, in the quest for holiness.

The late medieval emphasis on holy womanhood does not mean that some great feminist tide was sweeping through the church. In the thirteenth century, even more than the fourth or the seventh, the majority of hagiographers were celibate male clerics who had been conditioned to distrust and avoid women in general. The paradoxical attachment of such men to feminine images of sanctity has been explored most notably by Caroline Walker Bynum, who analyzes significant uses of imagery by spiritual writers of both genders in *Jesus as Mother: Studies in the Spirituality of the High Middle Ages* (Berkeley, 1982) and "Women's Stories, Women's Symbols" in *Anthropology and the Study of Religion* (Robert L. Moore and Frank E. Reynolds [eds.] [Chicago, 1984]). Bynum shows that the late medieval images of female sanctity were not developed specifically to inspire or indoctrinate women, as some modern readers have supposed; in fact, they seem to have been much more important to men who were ambivalent about their own privileges and power, hence the recurrent emphasis on those aspects of women's experience that posed the sharpest contrast to the traditional male paradigm of earthly authority and public achievements. One can see something of the same pattern in contemporary lives of male saints, a number of whom (like St. Francis of Assisi) were revered for having renounced the kinds of power that earlier medieval saints had used for the glory of God.

Even if designed primarily to meet the spiritual and psychological needs of men, conventional images of sanctity must have affected women too. Assessing their impact will be no easy task, however. Since most of our best sources on women's lives are themselves hagiographical, the obvious question is whether women's imitation of legendary models can be distinguished from the mere reuse of conventions by hagiographers. The most promising research in this area is being done by historians like Bynum and Jane Schulenburg.

Further References. Eleanor McLaughlin, "Women, Power and the Pursuit of Holiness in Medieval Christianity," in Rosemary Ruether and Eleanor McLaughlin (eds.), *Women of Spirit* (New York, 1979). Jane Schulenburg, "The Heroics of Virginity: Brides of Christ and Sacrificial Mutilation," in Mary Beth Rose (ed.), *Women in the Middle Ages and the Renaissance* (Syracuse, 1986).

SHERRY REAMES

HIGHER EDUCATION. Women have a young history in higher education compared to the general history of higher education in America, which began in 1636 with the founding of Harvard, a liberal arts college for men. The express purpose of college was to train the religious leaders and statemen of the new nation. Women, not included in the ruling elite, were not considered as potential students of higher education.

In the eighteenth and nineteenth centuries the purpose of men's colleges broadened to include preprofessional and, eventually, graduate training in medicine, law, and teaching. When, in the 1830s, coeducational experiments were introduced into American higher education and the first women's colleges were chartered, it was not the aim or purpose of higher education for women to produce civic leaders as such, nor to prepare women for the professions. By law and by custom no professional careers were open to women until well into the twentieth century. When "exceptional" women did earn law or medical degrees, their femininity was subject to considerable speculation. Regardless of sanctions against women in the professions, some women did practice law and medicine before the turn of the century.

The impetus for higher education for women derived from complex interactions among economic, social, and political factors in the nineteenth century, among them the following: industrialization with its consequent shifts in the role and status of the family and the growth of class differentiation; the diffusion of democratic ideals and institutions that nurtured the growth of public schools and fostered ideas of the dignity of labor; and the spirit of humanistic reform, spawned by the European Enlightenment and modified to deal with the economic and social institutions peculiar to nineteenth-century American culture.

Two schools of thought on advanced education for women emerged. First, advocates of education for women per se called for the education of women to fill their "true sphere" as wives, mothers, and guardians of the nation's morality. Actually, with rapidly changing economic structures, growing urbanization, and revolutionizing discoveries in natural science, the American family and women's role in it were in the process of major change. However, the assumption remained throughout the nineteenth century that every daughter of the middle class should be prepared thoroughly for her future as wife and mother. The impact of this domestic goal on vocational training in post-secondary institutions of learning, including colleges, was to introduce greatly expanded domestic curricula into departments of home sciences (home economics).

Opponents of higher education for women also fastened onto the issue of women's proper sphere; the best interests of society, the opponents said, are threatened by a college education that leads women away from their domestic duties. The elite women's colleges, offering curricula modeled on that of Harvard and Yale, were urged to raise domesticity to curricular emphasis, and to the extent that Vassar (1860), Smith and Wellesley (1875), Bryn Mawr (1880), and Mount Holyoke (1888) ignored that urging, they were attacked for unsexing their students, for endangering the frail health of young women, and for subversively intending to undermine the family and thus the nation.

Second, the nation's expanding systems of public elementary and secondary schools needed teachers. For the first time in the nation's history, women as a class, a separate group distinguished solely on the basis of gender, were assigned a "legitimate" public role and function as teachers.

The Civil War marked the critical point in women's participation in higher education. During the war and in the years following, colleges faced financial crisis. As male enrollment declined, revenues from student fees, the major source of income, shrank dramatically. Suddenly women emerged as the viable source of financial rescue for struggling men's colleges. Coeducational experiments at previously all-male bastions were inaugurated, and land-grant colleges that proliferated after the Civil War initiated coeducation as they opened. By 1890, 70 percent of female college students were enrolled in coeducational institutions.

Many women could pay for their own college education with earnings from teaching, dressmaking, and domestic work. Middle-class parents were "able and willing to finance daughters' advanced schooling in an era of smaller families, rising age of marriage, lessened domestic duties, and demographic imblances that left many women permanently unmarried" (C. J. Clifford, "Shaking Dangerous Questions from the Crease: Gender and American Higher Education," *Feminist Issues* 3 [1983]: 30).

Progress was tempered, however, by those who questioned the *value* of higher education for women, thus continuing the earlier debate into the first 60 years of the twentieth century. The debate evolved from the prescriptive ideal of womanhood, rooted in Victorian principles of separate domains for women and men, clouding the economic realities of women's lives on one hand and, on the other, highlighting those economic realities by offering separate kinds of education for class-distinguished women. The elite women's colleges expected to serve exclusively the daughters of the upper and upwardly mobile middle classes. The home economics and normal departments of state-supported institutions and second-echelon private colleges, normal schools, and trade institutes enrolled working girls and the daughters of less affluent families, as well as young women of middle-class affluence. Embedded within the argument about women's education was the corollary issue of the nature of learning itself vis-à-vis assumed biological sex differences.

By the early 1900s native white women were routinely accepted as college students by the public. Still the way was difficult for nonnative whites and for blacks. Black women comprised only 0.3 percent of the female student population in institutions of higher education in 1910. Liberal arts colleges rarely were integrated, and black colleges had few women in the liberal arts course. Those black women who did gain access to postsecondary education usually received teacher or industrial training (B. M. Solomon, *In the Company of Educated Women* [New Haven, 1985], 76–77).

The prescriptive ideal of womanhood prevailed in all echelons of higher education among black women as well as white as late as the 1950s. In reality, graduates of women's colleges were educated to become enlightened mothers and socially exemplary wives, models to inspire women of the working classes. Working-class women sought training to better their lot through access to the only occupations offering upward mobility to women: commerce, some trades, and above all, teaching. The interests of the state were best served by providing access to that training; thus, the status quo was protected. Women were granted access to higher education, but the most highly educated women by male-dominated standards of classical liberal education and its by-product of professional training in no way threatened male hegemony in the public sphere of law, politics, medicine, business, religion, and college teaching. While it is true that women pioneers emerged in all the professions, it was not until the 1970s that college-educated women made significant gains in professional fields outside of teaching. The early 1980s ushered in a new era as female undergraduate students became, for the first time in history, the majority of college students nationwide. (See also WOMEN'S COLLEGES.)

Further Reference. M. Newcomer, *A Century of Higher Education for American Women* (New York, 1959).

                                                                    CAROL O. PERKINS

HISPANIC DRAMA AND THEATRE, SPAIN AND LATIN AMERICA.

Women entered the theatre arena as actresses. Midsixteenth-century Spanish women performed in barnstorming troupes, having their position legalized by Phillip II's 1587 proclamation allowing women on stage, provided they were married and wore no male costume. Over three centuries later some actresses were heading their own companies. The Catalonian Margarita Xirgú (Spain/Uruguay, 1888–1969), who acted in Catalonian and Spanish, formed her own company, traveled to Argentina, and excelled at female roles created by Frederico García Lorca, some specifically for her. Xirgú became a director and founded a theatre school in Uruguay. María Guerrero (Spain, 1868–1928) formed a touring company that premiered about 150 plays throughout Europe, the United States, and Spanish America, contributing to the splendor of Spanish theatre. The Cervantes Theatre in Buenos Aires was built through her initiative and financial support. Virginia Fábregas (b. María Barragán, 1880–1950) and María Teresa Montoya (b. 1902) were two Mexican actresses heading their own companies. They toured Europe, the United States, and Spanish America. In Argentina several actresses affirmed their independence by forming their own companies: Angelina Pagano (1888–1962); Blanca Podestá (b. 1889); Camila Quiroga (1896–1942), who toured the United States with her company; Elsa O'Connor (b. Elsa Asunción Celestino de Hartich, 1906–1947); Lola Membrives (1883–1968), for whom Jacinto Benavente wrote several of his female roles; and Paulina Singerman (1910–1984) and her sister Berta Singerman (b. 1897), who specialized in solo poetry recitals and who founded and directed a chamber theatre group.

Many actresses created memorable female characters: María Luisa Robledo (Spain/Argentina); Nuria Espert (Spain); Argentine Eva Franco, president of Casa del Teatro; Mexican Carmen Montejo; and Chilean Delfina Guzmán, actress and codirector of the theatre group Ictus. Of the present generation, Argentine actresses Norma Aleandro and Soledad Silveyra have shown an interest in scripts that examine women's issues. Noted in their special fields are the bilingual (Yiddish and Spanish) actress Jordana Fain of Argentina; the actress and mentor Hedy Crilla (Germany/Argentina, b. Hedwig Schlichter de Crilla, 1899–1984); puppet creator and director Mané Bernardo (Argentina); the Chilean folklorist, performer, and writer of protest songs Violeta Parra; Argentine performer and songwriter María Elena Walsh; Venezuelan puppeteer Carmen Delia Bencomo; Brazilian Maria Clara Machado and Peruvian Sara Joffré, both devoted to children's theatre; and the Argentine dancer/choreographers Iris Scaccheri and Ana María Stekelman, the latter director of the Buenos Aires Municipal Ballet.

As directing opened to women, actresses became directors, showing an interest in sociopolitical concerns of which women's status is a part. Examples are the Argentines Inda Ledesma, Marcela Solá, Norma Aleandro, Laura Yusem, Beatriz Matar, and Alejandra Boero; the Cuban director and playwright Karla Barro; the Costa Rican Bélgica Castro; the Venezuelan Germana Quintana; and the Mexican Martha Luna. Film director and producer María Luisa Bemberg (Argentina), a dedicated feminist, earned international recognition for her films *Camila, Miss Mary*, and *Sor Juana*. Graciela Galán (Argentina), scene and costume designer for theatre and opera, collaborated in these films. Other scene designers who entered this mostly male-dominated arena are the Mexican Félida Medina and Argentines María Julia Bertotto, Mayenco Hlousek, and Renatha Schussheim, painter and designer.

The richest and most lasting contribution comes from playwrights. Sor Juana Inés de la Cruz (Mexico, b. Juana Inés de Asbaje, 1648–1695), often called the "first feminist of Hispanic America," entered a convent as the only means to assert her right to an education. Though her plays *Los empeños de una casa* (The Labors of Home), *El divino Narciso* (The Devine Narcissus), and *San Hermenegildo* conform to the "comedia" and miracle play format of her time, her feminism is implicit in her participation in a field restricted to men in the seventeenth century and explicit in her approach to writing. Alfonsina Storni (1892–1938), Argentine writer, teacher, and committed feminist, wrote children's plays and some controversial adult plays: *The Master of the World, Cimbelline in 1900*, and *Polixena and the Little Cook*. Two strong female voices are Clorinda Matto de Turner (Peru, pseud. Carlota Dimont, 1852–1909), who wrote *Hima Sumac* (1892), and Gertrudis Gómez de Avellaneda (Cuba, 1814–1873) author of *La hija de las flores* (The Flowers' Daughter), *Saúl*, and *Tres amores* (Three Loves). The Mexican Rosario Castellanos (1925–1974) is an important feminist voice. In *El eterno femenino* (1975; The Eternal Feminine) she uses verbal and theatrical clichés to expose and satirize engrained stereotypes of the Mexican culture.

A psychological rather than a social female perspective is typical of Elena Garro (Mexico) in *La señora en su balcón* (1960; The Lady at Her Balcony) and *La mudanza* (1959; The Move) and of Luisa Josefina Hernández (Mexico), author of *Los frutos caídos* (1976; The Fallen Fruit). The Argentine Griselda Gambaro's recurrent theme is the relationship between victim and victimizer, which she sometimes illustrates with a male/female dyad, as in *El campo* (1967) (*The Camp*, 1970), *La malasangre* (1982; Evil Blood), and *Del sol naciente* (1984; Of the Rising Sun). Gambaro has perceived the need to make her female characters less peripheral and more dynamic from a female perspective. Myrna Casas (Puerto Rico) deals with the problem of female roles in *Absurdos en soledad* (1964; Absurd in Solitude) and *Eugenia Victoria Herrera* (1964).

The following contemporary playwrights concern themselves with the larger sociopolitical issues of their times and environment, reflecting them in various styles: in Spain, Laura Olmo and Ana Diosdado; in Mexico, Maruxa Vilalta (Spain/Mexico), Carlota O'Neill, and Sabina Berman; in Argentina, Malena Sándor (1913–1968), Roma Mahieu (Poland/Argentina), Beatriz Mosquera, Marta Lehmann, Aida Bortnik, Nelly Fernández Tiscornia, and Rosa Diana Raznovich; in Chile, Isidora Aquirre and María Asunción Requena; in Venezuela, Elizabeth Schön and Mariela Romero; in Cuba, María Alvarez Ríos, Gloria Parrado, and Ingrid González; in Brazil, Maria Wanderley Menezes; in Haiti, Mona Guérin; in Paraguay, Josefina Pla; in Peru, Sarina Helfgott; and in Costa Rica/Salvador, Carmen Naranjo. Though these dramatists examine women's status only tangentially, their voices merit careful attention.

Further References. Luiza Barreto Leite, *A mulher no teatro brasileiro* (Rio de Janeiro, 1965). Doris Meyer and Margarita Fernández Olmos (eds.), *Contemporary Women Authors of Latin America*, 2 vols. (Brooklyn, 1983). Yvette E. Miller and Charles M. Tatum (eds.), *Latin American Women Writers: Yesterday and Today* (Pittsburgh, 1977). Lily Sosa de Newton, *Diccionario biográfico de mujeres Argentinas* (Buenos Aires, 1986).

EDITH E. PROSS

I

ICELANDIC WRITERS. Women belong to an ancient and rich literary tradition with roots in the Old Norse culture. The oral tradition in poetry can be traced to women's culture, particularly to such activities as healing and prophesying. The main poetic genres were visions and incantations, but there were also dreams, work songs, laments, and poems on healing. The most important remnants of the Old Icelandic oral tradition are the Eddic poems. This loose collection of poetry, composed before the eleventh century and preserved in a manuscript dated from c.1270, is characterized by fantastic stories of mythological figures, supernatural events, and a heroic world. (*Edda* means great-grandmother and can etymologically be related to óðr, or ode.) Many of the poems abound in female experiences such as giving birth, embroidering, doing laundry. They describe feelings of love, betrayal, mourning, and abandonment. Some are women's monologues, others dialogues between women. In *Sigurdrífumál* (The Monologue of Sigurdrifa), a woman is teaching a man healing verses. *Oddrúnargrátr* (The Lament of Oddrun) is a dialogue between a woman in labor and a midwife who shares her own sorrows. In *Grottasongr* (The Song of Grotti) two slave women are singing as they work at an enormous millstone called Grotti, grinding out death and destruction to their suppressors. *Völuspá* (The Vision of the Sibyl), the most celebrated poem of Old Icelandic literature, has traditionally been interpreted as a poem about the apocalypse of the pagan culture—or the end of the world in general. However, the powerful image of the sibyl sinking into the earth after giving over all her knowledge to Odin symbolizes a more specific apocalypse: that of women's culture.

A similar story of appropriation can be seen in the myth in which Odin steals the mead of poetic inspiration from a giantess by tricking her. The story appears in Snorri Sturluson's *Edda* (c.1230), a textbook of poetics in which young men are encouraged to learn the metaphors of the ancient oral tradition for use in their courtly verses. This work culminated a process, beginning with the coming of Christianity (c.1000) and then literacy, by which poetry was taken out of the realm of women's culture and transferred to what became the first Icelandic literary establishment: the schools, the scribes, and the monasteries. At the same time, the thirteenth century marks the rise of the Icelandic sagas, an anonymous but overtly masculine genre emphasizing feuds and battles. Of special interest is the famous *Laxdælasaga* (The Saga of the Laxdale Dwellers) because of its great interest in women's life. A curious female perspective runs through the story, frequently suppressed by the genre's demand for masculine action and enterprise.

Up until the nineteenth century specific women poets are mentioned only sporadically in literary sources, and the few surviving poems by women are fragmented. Nevertheless, women's literature survived for centuries in oral form alongside the dominant canon of men. Their genres were the more flexible ones: ballads, lyrics, occasional poems, folk songs, and folktales. When women attempted a genre with strict metrical rules, they tended to parody the genre.

The first literary work published by an Icelandic woman was the book of poems *Stúlka* (1876; A Lass), by Júlíana Jónsdóttir (1838–1918). In many of her poems she writes about women—their hard work and powerlessness, often parodying the masculine tradition with irony and grotesque imagery. Her strong awareness of being a woman in a patriarchal world, also expressed in the title of her book, is typical of Icelandic women writers up to the present day.

Unlike their counterparts in many other countries, early women writers in Iceland generally did not attempt fiction, perhaps because of the strong tradition of the sagas. The first to do so was Torfhildur Hólm (1845–1918), who experimented with historical novels based on the lives of eminent Icelandic bishops. Her first novel, *Brynjólfur Sveinsson biskup* (1882; The Bishop Brynjólfur Sveinsson), is not only the first Icelandic novel by a woman but also the first historical novel in modern Icelandic literature. Despite their originality, these novels are artificial and uneven. In her short stories, the first examples of this genre by a woman writer, she explores various aspects of women's rights.

Around the turn of the century a group of women writers emerged who developed a new form of *þulur* (cantos), a genre of oral litany characterized by fantasy and fragments of folk songs. The *þulur* express women's feelings and the clash between dreams and cold reality. The most prominent figure in this group was Unnur Benediktsdóttir Bjarklind (1881–1946), better known as Hulda (the fairy or hidden one). In addition to her contribution to the *þulur* genre, she became the main proponent of symbolism. Praised but misinterpreted in her own time, she had an enormous literary output. Her first book of poems, *Kvæði* (1909; Poems), contains powerful metaphors of nature that suggest the oppressed condition of women. Also associated with this group is Ólöf Sigurðardóttir (1857–1933), who published two books of poetry entitled *Nokkur smákvæði* (1888, 1913; Some Short Poems). Her work has an explicit feminist perspective, challenging the patriarchal society by examining women's desire for independence, love, and creativity. Her prose fragment *Hjálpin* (c.1887; Help), the first example of narrative filtered through the consciousness of a single character, reveals the anguish of a woman trapped in marriage.

The period from 1920 to 1950 saw the development of the novel among several women writers who were some of the most prolific of this century. Kristín Sigfúsdóttir (1876–1953) wrote novels and short stories about the exploitation of women, forced marriages, disillusionment, illness, and death. However, like many other women writers, she tends to end her works in reconciliation, concealing their rebellious content. The many novels and short stories of Þórunn Elfa Magnúsdóttir (b.1910) focus on the condition of women and the conflict between career and family. Ragnheiður Jónsdóttir (1895–1967), known as an author of children's books, has written psychological novels, significant in their use of ambiguity to expose the deceptive surface of daily life. The enormously prolific Guðrún Árnadóttir frá Lundi (1887–1973) wrote romances about rural life. Her best-sellers established a genre that has attracted numerous women writers up to the present day.

Overshadowed during this period by fiction, women's poetry began to show important changes around 1950. The first signs of modernism can be seen in the pointed satire of Halldóra B. Björnsson (1907–1968), published in *Ljóð* (1949; Poems). The real breakthrough occurred with Vilborg Dagbjartsdóttir (b.1930), most explicitly in her third book of poems, *Kyndilmessa* (1971; Candlemass). Her innovations, springing from an overtly feminist point of view, consist of colloquial language and images of daily life. These features, along with the blending of fantasy and ordinary reality as well as the use of unexpected points of view, characterize contemporary women's poetry. This style is apparent in the surrealistic epigrams of Þóra Jónsdóttir (b.1925), as well as in the poems by Nína Björk Árnadóttir (b.1941), Þuríður Guðmundsdóttir (b.1939), and Ingibjörg Haraldsdóttir (b.1942).

The highly original short stories of Ásta Sigurðardóttir (1930–1971), collected in *Sunnudagskvöld til mánudagsmorguns* (1961; Sunday Night to Monday Morning), mark the breakthrough of modernism not only in women's prose but in Icelandic prose in general. In a new literary language they describe women and other outsiders, with their utter alienation and fears that border on paranoia. The novels and short stories of Jakobína Sigurðardóttir (b.1918) describe the clash between rural life and urban culture from a Socialist point of view. The lyrical novels and short stories of Álfrún Gunnlaugsdóttir (b.1938) portray women fleeing from a threatening environment. One of the most original writers in recent decades is Málfríður Einarsdóttir (1899–1983). Her prose fragments, published when she was in her seventies, mix fantasy, memoirs, philosophy, lyricism, and grotesque imagery to create a strange and unreliable world. A similar mixture of genres is seen in the works of Steinunn Sigurðardóttir (b.1950). The nonchalant tone with which she juxtaposes lofty themes and ordinary phenomena like sexual relationships results in farcical but incisive statements about life. The most celebrated woman writer in Iceland today is Svava Jakobsdóttir (b.1930). Her novels, short stories, and plays reflect women's search for identity as ordinary reality is transformed through surreal and grotesque metaphors of fantasy and horror. Her first collections of short stories, especially *Veisla undir grjótvegg* (1967; Feast by a Stone Wall), are some of the most revolutionary works in contemporary Icelandic literature.

HELGA KRESS

INDIAN DEVOTIONAL POETS in Hinduism include the Tamil-speaking Āṇṭāḷ (ninth century C.E.) and Kāraikkāl Ammaiyār (c. eighth century C.E.); Mahādevi Akkā, who wrote in the Kannada language (twelfth century C.E.); and the princess Mīrābāi (sixteenth century C.E.), who composed in Hindi. Very little historical information is available about their lives, but from later hagiographical literature and legends, certain common patterns are discernible. The women are portrayed as falling in love with the deity at a young age, rejecting earthly marriage or barely tolerating an unhappy married life, being initiated by a male saint, defying social norms, composing poems that express a passionate romantic love for God, and eventually "merging" or "becoming one" with the Lord enshrined in a holy place.

Most of the poets did not aspire or live up to "traditional" norms incumbent on women by the code of the lawgiver Manu (first century C.E.). Rather than get married and beget children in this life, they longed to be wedded to, or continually serve, the god they were in love with. In cases where they were actually married to a human being, they still asserted their first loyalty to the deity and sometimes left their husbands to seek a spiritual life despite stern social disapproval. Abandoning societal norms, which enhanced family honor and provided a well-defined and secure social role, some saints sought the company of groups of other devotees, frequently male. The piety and poetry of these saints were greatly admired, and some of the saints were enshrined in temples and worshiped after their deaths, but women poets were *not* considered suitable role models for Hindu women in earthly life. Honor and fidelity to one's husband were perceived as governing values for most Hindu women. It was only in the realm of devotion to God that the women saints were held to be models whose passion could be selectively emulated. None of the saints was regarded as a guru or formal instructor who could initiate other devotees.

The songs of women saints are similar to many works of male devotees who were part of the medieval devotional (*bhakti*) movement in India. The poems contain themes of "bridal mysticism;" verses are addressed to the deity cast in the role of the lover, but the poems are not generally explicitly erotic. In Hindu *bhakti* poems, God was frequently portrayed as the "supreme male," and *all* human beings were women in relation to him. Therefore, even male poets sometimes spoke from the stance of a woman pining for "her" divine lover. Female poets, however, never identified themselves in a male role. The women poets (as well as some male devotional poets) long not so much for liberation from this life (*mokṣa*), considered to be a classical Hindu norm, but for a passionate union with the Lord. Many verses are spoken from the stance of a girl separated from her lover, and these are the most poignant in all the collections. Occasionally, a poet may identify herself as a cowherd-girl in a myth connected with Krishna and speak in her voice. In times of separation, some poets like Āṇṭāḷ sent birds and clouds as messengers to the God-lover, to convey their love for him. Mīrābāi and Āṇṭāḷ describe dreams in which the Lord came as a bridegroom and took their hands in marriage; other verses speak of ecstatic unions between the deity and the saint.

Āṇṭāḷ's poems were canonized and became part of daily and annual home and temple liturgy for the Śrīvaiṣṇavas. The poems of Mīrābāi, Mahādevi Akkā, and the fourteenth-century Kashmiri saint Lallā are sung by congregations of pious worshipers. Many of the poems have been set to music, and sometimes the correct melody is mentioned in the text of the verse by the composer. Unlike the Sanskrit *Vedas*, the most sacred Hindu scripture, which could only be recited by male members of the highest ("priestly") class of society (*brāhmaṇas*), the poems of the women devotional poets were in the vernacular. Anyone, regardless of caste or sex, had the authority to chant or sing them.

The poems of Mahādevi Akkā, Kāraikkāl Ammaiyār, and Lallā are addressed to the god Śiva. Āṇṭāḷ's passion is directed toward Viṣṇu, and Mīrābāi addresses her poems primarily to Krishna, an incarnation of Viṣṇu. Critical editions of the poetry are not always available, and while Āṇṭāḷ's poems (totaling 173 verses) have been critically edited and the canon fixed, estimates on Mīrābāi's poems range from 103 to 590 songs.

Further References. A. J. Alston, *The Devotional Poems of Mīrābāi* (New York, 1980). Dennis Hudson, "Bathing in Krishna: A Study in Vaiṣṇava Hindu Theology," *Harvard Theological Review* 73 (1980): 537–564. A. K. Ramanujan, "On Women Saints" in J. S. Hawley and D. Wulff (eds.), *The Divine Consort* (Berkeley, 1982), 316–324.

VASUDHA NARAYANAN

INDIAN WRITERS. Though the literary tradition of India has been dominated by men, there have always been women who were an integral part of it. The earliest religious literature, the *Vedas*, contain hymns composed by women. In medieval literature, there have been well-known female ascetics in both north and south India, for example, Āṇṭāḷ, Mahādevi Akkā, Lalded, Jana, Sahaja, and Mīrābāi, whose songs of love and devotion are still sung. The historical records also tell us of women bards who composed original verses as well as kept the genealogies for the queens of medieval India. However, the phenomenon of women writers who, on the literary scene in large numbers, make an impact is entirely modern.

India is a land of many languages, and each language has its own literature, which is marked by its own individuality. However, the totality is undeniably Indian. Although India is split in many religions and divided into different climates, regions, and life-styles, the different literatures share the same dreams and concerns. This commonality is nowhere more obvious than in the writings of the women. Whether the language is English or Bengali, Hindi or Tamil, the women writers show a certain unity of ideas because their concerns are unique.

The rise of modern Indian literatures generally took place simultaneously in the early nineteenth century. Later on, the schools and the colleges educated young generations of Indians who grew up with the same textbooks and similar curricula. An urban middle class began to emerge with a voracious appetite for literature in its own language. The writers abandoned religious and erotic poetry in favor of new genres, like fiction, which became popular in every modern Indian language.

This development provided an easy opportunity for women writers because they had their own oral traditions, which were particularly suited to the spoken, narrative form. The stories in the oral tradition were of a domestic nature, focusing on interpersonal relationships between family members, a woman's work inside and outside the house, and her place in the general scheme of things. Interestingly, these are the very concerns that dominate women's writing in the modern period.

Earlier, the women, especially the female saints and ascetics, sang of love and devotion to God. Most of them were considered unconventional because they did not follow the role given to them by the society; they were outside the mainstream and strongly criticized the restrictions placed on them by Indian society. This spirit of rebellion and a preoccupation with the problems of women are other characteristics of women writers in the twentieth century.

The first writers to make a name for themselves in modern times came from well-educated, progressive, and elite families. It was natural that they chose English as their language.

Toru Dutt (1856–1877) was educated in Europe and knew French and English well. Her first book, *A Sheaf Gleaned in French Fields, Verse Translations and Poems,* was published in Calcutta in 1876 and attracted wide attention for its originality, vigor, and selection of themes. However, Toru Dutt died in 1877, thus cutting short a promising career as a poet. Her posthumous volume of English poems, *Ancient Ballads and Legends of Hindustan,* appeared in 1885, containing poems on various topics, including her own impending death. Sarojini Naidu (1879–1949) began her writing career at an early age. Her first volume of poetry, *The Golden Threshold,* came out in 1905, *The Bird of Time* in 1912, and her third, *The Broken Wings,* in 1917. However, after her first meeting with Mahatma Gandhi, the poet went into the background, and the active freedom fighter emerged. The main theme of her poetry is romantic love and yearnings. Her poetry does not have a variety of emotions nor a wide range of subjects; its dominant note is joy, and it is filled with exuberance of life.

The two women writers who are well known and well established in postindependence Indian literature in English are Kamala Markandaya (b.1927) and Anita Desai (b.1937). Both of them introduced in their well-written and well-constructed novels the phenomenon of being women in modern India. Kamala Markandaya's early novels focused on the economical and sociological problems, for example, hunger and poverty (*Nectar in a Sieve, A Handful of Rice*), East-West encounter (*Some Inner Fury*), and the clash between the new and old ideas (*Silence of Desire*). Anita Desai, from her first novel, *Cry, the Peacock,* chose the psychological complexities of human personality, the delicate balance needed in family and interpersonal relationships (as in *Fire on the Mountain, Clear Light of Day*). Anita Desai has not shunned the violent aspects of life, and, therefore, alcoholism, arson, rape, suicide, and murder are all present in her writing.

Though highly acclaimed for the literary quality of their work in the English-speaking world, the women writers in English hold only a marginal appeal for the general Indian reading public. Their influence is also minimal. It is the women writers in Indian languages who enjoy large readership. It is in their writing that one finds the rawness of emotions and harsh realities of life. Their writing is a true mirror of modern society, its progress, and the changes that have affected women's lives.

Another interesting characteristic of this writing is that most of the women writers share a bond with each other whether they are writing in Tamil, Bengali, Punjabi, Urdu, or Hindi. There is a certain continuity of themes and ideas. Indian womanhood, in all its variety, is the center of their universe. There has been no theme that touched the life of a woman that we do not find included. The oppression of the woman, whether as a prostitute or as an economically dependent wife, was a recurrent theme in the fifties.

However, the most remarkable phenomenon of the later writing is the emergence of a New Woman. She has the courage to break the traditions, she may not be highly educated but can earn a living for herself, and above all, she can make a decision about her own life. Her lot may not be enviable, but at least she has fought for and gained equality with men. Many of the the novels portray women in the process of discovering themselves and their potentialities.

Fiction remains a popular genre, and most of the writers have developed their own style, ranging from poetic and romantic to analytical and minimalistic.

Some of the well-known women writers are Amrita Preetam (Punjabi); Ashapurna Devi, Mahashweta Devi, and Anurupa Devi (Bengali); Kandanika Kapadika (Gujrati); MK Indira and Anusuya Shankar "Triveni" (Kannada); Kausalya Devi Kodoori (Telugu); Ismalt Chugtai and Qurratul Ain Hyder (Urdu); Mahadevi Verma, Usha Devi Mitra, and Krishna Sobti (Hindi); and Kusumavati Deshpande (Marathi). Some of these are poets as well.

Amrita Preetam and Mahadevi Verma have received the Gyanpeeth Award, a prestigious award given to one Indian writer every year as a recognition of the writer's genius and his/her contribution to Indian literature.

USHA NILSSON

ITALIAN ARTISTS (FIFTEENTH THROUGH EIGHTEENTH CENTURIES).

Before the Renaissance women artists are found in convents or in workshops where, usually as wives or daughters of a master, they contributed to the shop's production. By the fifteenth century, however, as artists strove to promote

art to the level of music and poetry and themselves from craftpersons to professionals, convents were no longer cultural centers and guilds were banning or
restricting employment of women, even wives and daughters.

The few known fifteenth-century women artists were nuns. Most is known
about the abbess Caterina dei Vigri (St. Catherine of Bologna) because of her
sanctity, not her art. Her painting seems untouched by the changes sweeping
the artistic and intellectual world of Renaissance Italy. In the sixteenth century
the Florentine abbess Pautilla Nelli was the most gifted of a handful of nun-
artists, but her fresco *The Last Supper* in the Church of St. Maria Novella shows
that she too lagged behind current developments in art, and the strict enclosure
of convents under the Counter-Reformation cut them off even further from the
artistic and literary movements of the day. Although there will continue to be
nun-artists, from now on professional women artists are almost always laywomen.

Women artists worked within certain limitations. Training was still done in
workshops, but male students now traveled all over Italy to seek out the best
teachers. In some cities artists joined together to share the costs of models for
private drawing sessions. With rare exceptions, women could not travel freely
in search of instruction, nor could they attend a drawing class with men without
ruining their reputations. To study male nude models was, of course, out of the
question, leaving women seriously hampered in their ability to paint figures.

Another serious limitation was a restricted market. Italy, unlike the Netherlands, did not have a substantial middle class of individuals interested in buying
art to decorate their homes. Most art was public art—altar pieces, official portraits, ceilings, overdoor panels—commissioned by princes of church or state
and other very rich patrons and made according to their specifications from a
limited range of subjects in history, mythology, religion, and allegory—the kind
of art for which women were not trained. Most Italian women artists did portraits
and plant and animal pictures.

Generally, the attitude toward women artists was friendly, if patronizing. Until
the eighteenth century all women artists were described as attractive, and praise
concentrated on their virtue, charm, and fulfillment of domestic duties. In discussions of their art, the platypus effect was often evident (the wonder is not
that she paints well, but that a woman can paint at all). However if women vied
for, and received, the lucrative public commissions, resentment could result, as
in the case of Properzia di Rossi (c.1490–1530) of Bologna. (Bologna was a
center of female humanism with a tradition of women artists that went back to
Santa Caterina and continued through Elisabetta Sirani.) Rossi began as a carver
of fruit stones (peach, cherry, etc.), delicate carving suitable for women. When,
c.1520, she moved on to sculpture, she entered a male monopoly. Her reputation
was ruined by the slanders of a jealous artist after she won a commission for
several figures for a church facade.

Most women professional artists were daughters of artists, and most married,
usually other artists. A few continued active after marriage, in some cases

becoming the economic mainstay of the family, but for most, marriage ended or seriously curtailed their careers. Some daughters of artists were overshadowed by their more famous fathers or brothers. Marietta Tintoretto (1551–1590), daughter of Jacobo Tintoretto, worked on backgrounds of her famous father's composition but was also a popular portraitist.

The Bolognese Lavinia Fontana (1552–1614), on the other hand, was one of the several women whose success exceeded their fathers'. She achieved fame as a portraitist when quite young, and when she moved to Rome, her portraits commanded very high prices. After she married, she supported the household. Her husband helped her with backgrounds and domestic duties. She expanded beyond portraits to larger works, altar pieces, and other religious works.

A large number of the women artists who have been recorded were noted, like Fontana, for their precocity. Fede Galizia (1578–1630), daughter of painter Nunzia Galizia, by her late teens had an international reputation. Although that reputation was based on her portraits, she also did religious paintings and was among the earliest Italian still-life artists.

The most famous woman painter of the sixteenth century, Sofonisba Anguissola (1532/1535–1625) was the daughter not of a painter, but of a nobleman and was a phenomenon of her age. From an artistically talented family (three of her sisters were also artists until death or marriage interfered), Sofonisba was a child prodigy whose fame soon spread beyond Italy. She was invited to the court of Philip II of Spain (1559), where she became court painter and had gifts lavished upon her, including a royal dowry when she wed a Sicilian nobleman c.1570. Four years later she returned to Italy as a widow, remarried, and settled in Genoa, where royalty, aristocracy, artists, and intellectuals flocked from all over Europe. The adulation paid her must have encouraged other women to enter art. She is also important as an innovator. In addition to portraits, including a large number of self-portraits, she did "conversation pieces," group portraits in which the figures are engaged in some activity, usually domestic—the origins of genre painting.

Although women were generally trained by their father or another family member, sometimes nonrelatives were hired to teach them as well. In the case of Artemesia Gentileschi (1593–1652/1653) this practice had disastrous effects. Gentileschi is one of the outstanding painters of the seventeenth century, an important baroque artist who helped spread the new Caravaggesque realism to Florence, Genoa, and Naples. Yet she is best remembered for the 1612 rape trial of the man hired to teach her, Agostino Tassi. He was eventually acquitted, even though, to make sure she told the truth, her evidence was taken under torture. Her greatest works are biblical, and mythological scenes centered on strong female characters such as Judith, Esther, Lucretia, and Cleopatra. She did several paintings of Judith and Holoferens, a popular subject at the time. Her earliest-known rendition of the subject, perhaps influenced by her rape, is the violent, bloody *Judith Beheading Holofernes,* in which Judith has just thrust the sword through Holofernes's neck. Her third, *Judith and Her Handmaiden* showing Judith and her servant, with Holofernes's head in a basket, preparing to flee the camp, is often considered her greatest painting. She was one of the first women to paint female nudes. The subject of Suzanna and the Elders was popular with male artists, but Gentileschi's treatment is very different from theirs. Her almost completely nude Suzanna is frightened and cowers away from the two lecherous old men leaning over her.

Elisabetta Sirani (1638–1665) died unmarried at age 27, but by that time she had completed a large body of work, taught a large number of women students in her own studio, and made a lot of money. The precocious daughter of a Bolognese artist, she became the sole support of her family after her father's health prevented his continuing to paint. Not satisfied with doing just portraits, she gained important commissions for religious paintings and thereby aroused jealousy in her male rivals. When they accused her of having men, including her father, paint her pictures, she invited a group to watch her paint a portrait which she did in one sitting. She also did biblical and history scenes featuring heroines, but her slender, gentle women are far different from Gentileschi's vigorous heroines.

Among other seventeenth-century women artists are Sister Lucrina Fetti (given name Guistina; fl. c.1614–c.1651) of Mantua, who was taught by her more famous brother Dominico and who did portraits of her convent's patrons, the Gonzagas, and religious compositions for the convent and the church of Sant' Orsola; and Giovanna Garzoni (1600–1670), from Ascoli Picena, most interesting today for her studies of plants, insects, and small animals. In the accuracy of their detail they foreshadow the work of Maria Sibylla Merian (see GERMAN ARTISTS).

Eighteenth-century Venice produced the enormously popular rococo painter Rosalba Carriera (1675–1757), whose works are found in major museums throughout the world. In her early twenties she developed the pastel portrait and spread its popularity. She never married, and she cared for her mother and sisters, whom she taught to paint. After her father's death in 1719, she went to Paris to paint Louis XIV (then 10 years old) and created a demand for pastel portraits that lasted into the nineteenth century. In 1720 she became the first woman elected to the French Royal Academy in almost 40 years. In 1730 she was invited to the Hapsburg court and spread the popularity of pastel portraits to Vienna. Her portraits are meant to flatter, not reveal character. However, the superficiality reflects the values of the age. Her self-portraits display her ability to interpret the personality of the individual through the face.

Little is known of other Italian women painters of the eighteenth century. Marianna Candide Dionigi (1756–1826) painted landscapes in oils and wrote a book on landscape painting before she turned her interest to archaeology.

Giulia Lama (c.1685–after 1753) was a highly talented late-baroque painter and one of the first women to paint male nudes. She did some very large altarpieces in neomannerist style for churches in Venice, an achievement that may account for the resentment of male artists against her. She is also among the first women artists to have negative comments made about her looks.

The discovery of women artists that began with the second wave of feminism in the late 1960s continues. The basic spadework is completed, but a definitive history of Italian women artists is still to be written.

Further References. Elsa Honig Fine, *Women and Art* (Montclair, N.J., 1978). Ann Sutherland Harris and Linda Nochlin, *Women Artists, 1550–1950* (New York, 1976). Karen Petersen and J. J. Wilson, *Women Artists* (New York, 1976). Chris Pettys, *Dictionary of Women Artists* (Boston, 1985).

ITALIAN WRITERS (SEVENTEENTH AND EIGHTEENTH CENTU-RIES). In seventeenth-century Italy, women's literary output changed both in quantity and in character. The cultural splendor of the Reniassance courts had gone, as had the secular literary enclaves and the publishing trade they had fostered. We would look in vain for the social sanctuaries of female emancipation that existed in the sixteenth century. As a consequence, the greater part of the writing done by women in the baroque age deals with religious subjects, organized in neat thematic categories according to the theological teachings of the Counter-Reformation church.

With the loss of their political freedom to Spain, the Italian states surrendered the trade and banking supremacy to the northern Europeans. A new conservative economy, based on land property, had tragic consequences for the female population as, increasingly, more girls were, at birth, destined for the convent, in order to spare reduced and unproductive family holdings.

Convents became centers of social and cultural life. To edify and to entertain, the nuns, who were among the best-educated women of their time, wrote religious plays, poetry, and prose. We know the names of many authors, but their works remain mostly unresearched. Of the literature produced in seclusion, outstanding are the letters of Sister Celeste Galilei (1660–1734), not only for their historical value—they were addressed to her father Galileo and dealt with family and convent matters—but also for their vivid descriptions of people and activities around her, of the comforts and discomforts of monastic life, and for their direct and graceful style, remarkably free of the rhetorical excesses typical of baroque prose.

Galilei's good-natured acceptance of fate has its counterpart in the polemical stance of Sister Arcangela Tarabotti (1604–1652). Her works constitute the strongest denunciation of women's condition in her times. The underlying argument of *Antisatira* (1644; Antisatire) and of *Difesa delle donne* (1651; Defense of Women) is that the relative position of men and women in this world ought to be decided in the natural light of reason and that female dignity is fully consistent with religious beliefs. *La semplicità ingannata o Tirannia paterna* (1654; Simplicity Deceived or Paternal Tyranny) is a sharp study of the social and psychological causes of women's confinement, while *Inferno monacale* (Nuns' Hell) describes the effects of convent life on the unwilling nun. Sister

Arcangela was not the first woman of the period to defend her sex. In *Il merito delle donne* (1660; Women's Merit), Moderata Fonte (1555–1592) had organized her arguments in the form of a dialogue. In *La nobiltà e l'eccellenza delle donne* (1601; Nobility and Excellence of Women), Lucrezia Marinelli (1571–1653) used the form of the treatise; these last two works were new in arguing that women's position of inferiority was the result of the constraints imposed on them by a male society.

Lucrezia Marinelli also wrote historical and mythological epic poems. Throughout the century, the epic remained the most prestigious genre and an acceptable one for women to cultivate. Among those who contributed to it are Maddalena Salvetti Acciaiuoli, Angela Scaramuccia, Barbara Albizzi, and Margherita Sarròcchi.

Many women were acclaimed as female wonders of learning. The most celebrated was Elena Cornaro Piscopia, of a Venetian aristocratic family, who was a poet, was conversant in many languages, and was a philosophy graduate of the University of Padua. A woman of learning also was Sara Copia Sullam, author of a letter entitled *"Manifesto"* (1521), in which she rebutted Baldassarre Bonifacio, a priest, who had accused her of denying the immortality of the soul. The letter is dedicated to her father, who had answered for her orthodoxy before the elders of the Venetian ghetto where she lived.

In the theatre women could still enjoy some freedom of movement and lifestyle. Of Laura Guidiccioni Lucchesini only the oratorio *Rappresentazione di anima e corpo* (1600; Play of Soul and Body) has come down to us. Other works by her, now lost, were *Disperazione di Fileno* (1590; Fileno's Despair), *Satiro* (1591; Satyr) and *Il gioco della cieca* (1594; Blind Man's Bluff). They were set to music by Emilio Del Cavaliere and are reputed to have been the very first examples of opera. Isabella Andreini, celebrated poet and star of the *Commedia dell'Arte*, died on a tour of France in 1604. Following in her footsteps came Margherita Costa, acclaimed opera singer in Italy and abroad, author of satirical sonnets and of burlesque love lyrics.

Women's massive re-entry into the field of lyric poetry occurred at the end of the century. In 1690, to counteract the extravagance of baroque taste and promote a classically restrained style, a new academy, called Arcadia, was founded in Rome. Others followed in imitation everywhere in Italy. They fostered an affectation of refined feelings and a taste for artificial pastoral settings, at the center of which stood a female creature of coy flirtatiousness and rococo delicacy. Extraordinary is the number of women poets, mostly from the aristocracy, who wrote in the Arcadian fashion and were admitted to the academies. In general, however, their poetry kept closer in sobriety of content and expression to sixteenth-century Petrarchism than did the men's. The best known of these women poets is Faustina Maratti Zappi (1680–1745), as much admired for her talent as adored for her charm and sensuous beauty. Her poems, formally and thematically correct, occasionally show the emotions of a woman severely tested by life. The poetic output of the indomitable marchioness Petronilla Paolini Massimi was, on the other hand, directly inspired by autobiographical events suggestive of a gothic novel. A preromantic fascination with ruins and lugubrious landscapes is noticeable in the pastoral poems of Prudenzia Gabrieli and in the historical odes and romances of Diodata Saluzzo Roèro (1774–1840), while *Arcadia* still triumphed with Angela Veronese (1779–1847), whose poems have a graceful musicality and are full of flowers, shepherds, and shepherdesses. Among the most celebrated poets of the day were Maria Maddalena Morelli and Teresa Bandinetti Landucci, who improvised verse on a given topic at public events organized in palaces and in auditoriums.

By the second half of the eighteenth century the cultural life of many Italian cities revived. Private salons, hosted by cultivated ladies of the upper classes, became meeting places for intellectuals and literati. The limits of their education were discussed and extended. Diamante Medaglia Faini drew a plan of study for girls that included mathematics, politics, and the experimental sciences. Many women gained entry in professional fields normally reserved to men. The old quarrel about the relative capacities of the sexes had been revived in 1727, when Aretafila de' Rossi felt compelled to debate G. A. Volpi on women's intellectual powers and when, in a Latin speech, Maria Agnesi upheld their right to education. Such debates were gallantly settled in favor of the aristocratic women present. When Giustina Renier Michiel translated Shakespeare and filled five volumes with the history of Venetian festivals and traditions, she seemed to exercise a prerogative of her aristocratic class.

Middle-class women began modern literary careers. Luisa Bergalli (1703–1779), friend of the Carriera sisters, supported herself and her family in Venice by writing tragedies, comedies, and melodramas and by providing producers and publishers with translations. She also edited a comprehensive anthology of women poets and the collected work of Gaspara Stampa. To Elizabetta Caminèr Turra (1751–1796) goes the credit of being the first woman journalist in Italy. She was the founder and sole editor of *Nuovo giornale enciclopedico*. She also wrote a great number of theatrical adaptations and pedagogical texts for the young.

Further References. J. De Blasi, *Le scrittrici italiane dalle origini al 1800* (Florence, 1930). N. Costa-Zalessow, *Scrittrici italiane dal XIII al XX secolo* (Ravenna, 1982). G. Conti Odorisio, *Donna e società nel Seicento* (Rome, 1979).

RINALDINA RUSSELL

ITALIAN WRITERS (FROM THE NINETEENTH CENTURY). In Italy the end of the eighteenth century saw the first revolutionary movements aimed at the establishment of more modern regimes; at the beginning of the next century, the long struggle for the unification of Italy began and was achieved in the decade 1860 to 1870. Women participated with their writings and their money; many also fought on the barricades. In Naples, Eleonora Fonsèca Pimentel, poet and journalist, was imprisoned as a conspirator, fought with the Republicans in 1799, and, upon surrender, was executed with them. Isabella Trivulzio di Belgioioso wrote about the 1848 uprisings in Milan and Venice. She also embarked on advanced social experiments and described the conditions in which women lived in Italy and abroad. The connection between the form of government and the current regimes was theorized by Maria Giuseppina Guacci, and it was effectively illustrated in her memoirs by Henrietta Caracciolo, who, until Garibaldi's troops entered Naples, had been unsuccessful in her efforts to renounce the veil.

After the unification of the country, women writers graduated from political and social tracts to creative literature. In fiction, their output was consistent with the realism of the postromantic novel that depicted the depressed living conditions in the countryside. The first true realist writer was, in fact, a woman, Caterina Percoto (1812–1887), whose stories about the underprivileged in her native Friuli are free from the sentimentality and the paternalism that mar much of the European regional literature. In Naples and in Rome, Matilde Serào fought her way to a commanding position in the male world of journalism and left a masterpiece of nineteenth-century reportage in *Il ventre di Napoli* (1884; The Bowels of Naples). This is a collection of articles skillfully organized and written in rebuttal to a statement made in Parliament about the necessity of cleaning the poor districts of Naples by "disemboweling" the city. Of Serào's huge fictional production, the best stories are "La virtù di Cecchina" (1883; Cecchina's Virtue), "Telegrafi di Stato" (1884; State Telegraphs), "Scuola normale femminile" (1885; Normal School for Girls), and *Sorella Giovanna della Croce* (1901; Sister Giovanna of the Cross), all stories of women, of their hardships, courage, and weaknesses. An accomplished writer of fiction was Anna Zuccari Radius, better known by the pen name of Neèra. In Milan, where she spent most of her life, she earned the admiration of good society by becoming a professional writer without losing her femininity. Of her 18 novels, the most successful and significant are *Teresa* (1886), the story of a woman sacrificed by her family to her brother's right to a full education and life, and *L'indomani* (1890; The Day After), a pitiless analysis of a middle-class marriage from the wedding ceremony to the birth of the first child. Greater critical recognition went to the prolific Sardinian writer Grazia Delèdda, who in 1926 became the second woman to be awarded the Nobel Prize in literature. The conflicts that had arisen in Sardinia between medieval social structures and a new economic reality were instinctively and skillfully transformed by Delèdda into tales of innocence, sin, and expiation and were played out with inexorable inevitability in a landscape that seemed magical and foreboding.

Serào, Neèra, and Delèdda declared themselves against the militancy of the feminist movement, either out of conviction or the need to safeguard themselves against unwarranted hostility. Many, however, were the women whose work was directly inspired by the movement and by the social turmoil that the new country was experiencing at the turn of the century. Maria Antonella Torriani, alias Marchesa Colombi, informed the public about the condition of working women in her novel *In risaia* (1878; In the Rice Fields). A polemical thrust is also found in her books *La gente per bene* (1887; The Upright People) and *Un matrimonio in provincia* (1885; A Small-Town Marriage). E. Ferretti Viola's *Una fra tante* (1878; A Woman Among Many) created a scandal and brought about a parliamentary debate. Anna Franchi fought for divorce and in old age wrote *Cose di ieri dette alle donne di oggi* (1946; Things of Yesterday Told to the Women of Today). The most celebrated feminist writer of Italy is, deservedly, Sibilla Aleramo. When it was published in 1906, her autobiographical book *Una donna* (*A Woman*, 1906) created a sensation in Europe. It is the story of a young provincial wife who becomes progressively aware of women's oppressed condition in society and who, in the end, gives up her husband and child to live in the capital as a feminist writer.

In poetry, women were influenced by the decadent trends that dominated literary circles of the late nineteenth and early twentieth century. Contessa Lara (1849–1896), Regina di Luanto (1862–1914), and the younger Amalia Guglielminetti (1885–1941) were femmes fatales in life and in literature. They expressed their languid or aggressive sensuality in backgrounds of opulent interiors and in suggestive art nouveau imagery. In the lyrics of Vittoria Aganoor Pompilj (1855–1910), late romantic and decadent moods give way to modern themes of incompatibility and betrayal, while in Luisa Giaconi's musical poems we find muted, grey-toned, introspective sketches. In the 1890s, Ada Negri, a young woman of the servant class, appeared on the literary scene and sang the hopes and defeats of the workers who lived in the industrial districts of the North. In the 1920s, her proletarian muse was hailed and appropriated by the fascist authorities, but soon her voice turned into that of a sentimental and confused bourgeois woman.

After World War II, acclaim went to three fiction writers born at the turn of the century: Gianna Manzini (1896–1974), Orsola Nemi, and Lalla Romano. They shared a common base in a continued concern with style, in a tendency to fracture the story line by a free association of imaginings and reminiscences, and in the investigation of the inner life of characters that moved in bourgeois family settings. Similar techniques were employed in her best stories by Elsa Morante (1912–1985), whose major theme was the contrast between innocent childhood and distorted adult life, while in Natalia Ginzburg's novels the gradual moral disintegration of people is described by a subdued voice in a style that is simple but cumulatively effective. Outstanding narrative talent, as well as psychological and historical insight, is displayed in the novels of Maria Bellonci (1902–1986) and Anna Banti (1895–1985), who had been active since the thirties. To Banti, an art and literary historian of repute, history provided the social background for stories in which female characters are explored with all their inhibitions and outside constraints.

In a different atmosphere wrote Fausta Cialente, whose *Cortile a Cleopatra* (1939; Courtyard at Cleopatra) and *Ballata levantina* (1961; *The Levantines*, 1962) evoke the cosmopolitan multiracial milieu she knew in Alexandria, Egypt, where she lived in self-imposed exile during the fascist years. In a still different vein, the Italian stories of social denunciation written by Anna Maria Ortese—

Il mare non bagna Napoli (1953; *The Bay Is Not Naples*, 1955) and *Silenzio a Milano* (1958; Silence in Milan)—display an original brand of storytelling, beautifully poised among reportage, essay, and a detailed description that verges on the surreal.

In her novels published since the 1940s, Alba De Céspedes dealt with women's situations that were to be much argued about in the 1960s and the 1970s. The uncomfortable position and the limited role assigned to women by society, the difficulties in communicating with men, the hypocrisies and frustrations of family relationships are themes she artfully developed in convincing contemporary backgrounds. Among the novelists who were moved by the isolation of women and by their hardships in war and in peacetime were Laudomia Bonanni, Paola Masino, and Renata Viganò (1900–1976). More recently, Milena Milani has devoted her writing to explore female sexuality, Gina Lagorio has described women's coming of age in the family and in society, and Dacia Maraini has shifted from existential malaise to outspoken social commitment.

Women's poetry made its official entry into the twentieth century with Antonia Pozzi (1912–1938). Her themes of disillusionment and alienation—Pozzi died a suicide—are expressed in common language of remarkable symbolic power and can be placed between symbolism and hermeticism. In the same generation, Daria Menicanti is outstanding for her capacity to communicate moments of loneliness and desire with delicate and voluptuous imagery. The younger Luciana Frezza, Vera Gherarducci, and Rosanna Guerrini deal with their resentment toward conventional thinking in epigraphic and jarring snapshots of family life or spell it out in obsessive word phrasing.

Greater critical attention went to poets who were closer to the leading literary movements of their times: Margherita Guidacci, whose limpid vein confronts religious and ethical themes regardless of social and personal issues, and the doyenne of Italian women poets Maria Luisa Spaziani, who from a brief allegiance to the hermetic school moved to develop a personal voice of vibrant and evenly sustained high style. Guidacci and Spanziani are only two of a large group of poets who are academics or have been active as literary critics, essayists, and translators in the field of European and American literature. Their linguistic experiments are often typical of the concerns with language and techniques that characterized the new avant-garde of the sixties. Such is the case of Jole Tognelli, Amalia Rosselli, Anna Malfaiera, Rossana Ombres, Giulia Niccolai, Anna Oberto, and Piera Opezzo. The 1970s saw the rejection of the rigidly formalistic program of the new avant-garde, and themes related to everyday living were acceptable again. The poetry directly inspired by feminist issues and views came then to the fore. Of the many talented women who have been moved to write poetry in this context, we can mention here the names of Gilda Musa, Rosanna Guerrini, Iolanda Insana, Mariella Bettarini, Bianca Maria Frabotta, Patrizia Cavalli, and Marta Fabiani.

Further References. M. Bandini Buti, *Poetesse e scrittrici* (Rome, 1941). N. Costa-Zalessow, *Scrittrici italiane dal XIII al XX secolo* (Ravenna, 1982). B. Frabotta (ed.), *Donne in poesia* (Rome, 1976). G. Morandini, *La voce che è in lei* (Milano, 1980).

RINALDINA RUSSELL

J

JAPANESE WRITERS (CLASSICAL). Japanese women writers played a major role in creating their culture's classical, elite literary tradition. Although their significance lessened greatly in later centuries, around the turn of the second millennium A.D., women writers enjoyed pre-eminence unparalleled in any other premodern literary tradition worldwide.

The first compendium of poetry in Japanese, the *Manyōshū* (The Collection of Ten Thousand Leaves), compiled mideighth century A.D., includes significant verses by women from the earliest periods. *Genji Monogatari* (*The Tale of Genji*), often called the world's first novel, was the work of a woman. Women were viewed as the natural and appropriate creators of literature in the native Japanese vernacular. This position is clearly evidenced by an ironic contrast to Western literary tradition: the oldest extant example of Japanese narrative prose by an identifiable author is the *Tosa nikki* (Tosa Diary), a literary diary created by a man who wrote in the guise of a woman.

Several sociological factors help account for the prominence of women among the earliest Japanese authors. Mythological and historical evidence indicates the significant position of women in early periods of the culture. In *Kojiki* (712; The Record of Ancient Matters), a mythopoetic account of origins, the central deity is Amaterasu, the sun goddess, who is presented as the ancestor of the Japanese ruling house. The oldest foreign record of an encounter with people in the Japanese islands is a Chinese account describing a tribe led by a woman called Pimiko.

The overwhelming influence of political and religious systems and cultural values imported from the Asian mainland gradually brought a decline in the position of women, but one such cultural system, the Chinese system of writing and its subsequent adaptation in Japan, was crucial to the formation of literature in Japan and directly affected the role of women as writers. Prior to Chinese contact Japan had no written language, but by the fifth century written Chinese was already becoming well established in Japan, its function being in some ways analogous to that of Latin in Europe. It was the language of official written discourse in the realms of politics and religion. Following the Chinese Confucian model, women were excluded from official participation in politics, and though a few did learn some Chinese, they were discouraged from demonstrating such knowledge.

By the ninth century an indigenous Japanese writing system called *kana* was developed. It used a relatively small number of simplified Chinese characters to represent sound alone, detached from meaning. *Kana* made it possible for the first time to write in pure Japanese vernacular rather than in Chinese. *Kana* writing was used by both sexes to record poetry, and the written exchange of poems was an important part of social discourse and courtship among the aristocracy. As the classical poetic tradition developed, many of the characteristics of the earliest poetry of women—the expression of personal, private emotions and a predominantly melancholy tone—came to dominate the formal Japanese poetry of both men and women.

Literary diaries were the most common form of classical women's writing. The earliest of these is *Kagerō nikki* (Edward Seidensticker [trans.], *The Gossamer Years*). Written by a woman known to us only as "the mother of Michitsuna," it covers the years 954 to 974 and is a virtual autobiography recounting the author's unhappiness over her husband's diminished affection after his attentions shifted to a later secondary wife.

Another sort of diary is *Makura no sōshi* (The Pillow Book) by Sei Shōnagon, a woman in court service. Completed shortly after the year 1000, it takes the form of a collection of notes, lists, and comments, rather than a chronological diary or journal. The personal voice of Sei Shōnagon, witty and ascerbic, contrasts strikingly with the self-pitying attitude of Michitsuna's mother. *Makura no sōshi* is still judged one of the greatest masterpiece of literary style in the Japanese language, and its random essay form became a mainstay of later literary writing by men.

Among all the writing by premodern Japanese, male or female, undisputed pride of place goes to *Genji Monogatari*. Like Sei Shōnagon, but about a decade later, its author, Murasaki Shikibu, was also in service as a tutor to an imperial consort, apparently having achieved this position because of her established literary reputation.

Genji Monogatari is a vast work of narrative fiction, rather than a diary, more than 1,000 pages in English translation. Completed early in the eleventh century, it depicts an imaginary court of about a century earlier and centers around the amours of the idealized male hero, the prince Hikaru Genji, "Shining Genji." Its later, darker chapters shift, after the prince's death, to the amorous lives of two younger men, each a pale, partial reflection of Genji.

Though the work was read by both men and women, its primary audience was the women at court. It was written serially and circulated chapter by chapter, apparently read aloud and discussed among the women. For this audience *Genji*

Monogatari must have been both diverting and soberingly instructive in its depiction of many aristocratic female characters of varied personality. As in women's literary diaries, more outward social and political concerns scarcely appear. The psychological intensity of women's passion, the negative power of jealousy, and the importance of personal taste and grace are its major concerns. Despite vast cultural differences, the book has an extraordinary feeling of modernity and accessibility.

The canon of classical Japanese literature includes about a half dozen other significant diaries and works of fiction by women. The last important flowering of the women's courtly literary tradition came some 300 years after *Genji* in the diary entitled *Towazugatari* (The Confessions of Lady Nijō). Written by an imperial concubine, it describes both her years at court and her later life when she became an itinerant nun after falling out of favor. Not only is she writing in the tradition of earlier courtly women diarists, but also she shows instances in which court activities were modeled on scenes in *Genji Monogatari*.

The decline of the court, the rise of other genres of literature and drama, and the gradually declining social position of women in subsequent centuries shifted literary pre-eminence away from the brushes of women writers. Only in modern times has writing by Japanese women begun to regain significance.

Translations : *The Manyōshū*, trans. Nippon Gakujutsu Shinkokai (New York, 1965). *The Tale of Genji*, trans. Edward G. Seidensticker (New York, 1964). "A Tosa Journal," in *Kokin Wakashu*, trans. Helen C. McCullough (Stanford, 1985). *Kojiki,* trans. Donald L. Philippi (Princeton, 1969). *Gossamer Years,* trans. Edward G. Seidensticker (Rutland, Vt., 1964). *The Pillow Book of Sei Shonagon*, trans. Ivan Morris, New York, 1967). *The Confessions of Lady Nijō,* trans. Karen Brazell (Stanford, 1973).

Further References: Donald Keene, "Feminine Sensibility in the Heian Era," *Landscapes and Portraits* (New York, 1971). Ivan Morris, *The World of the Shining Prince, Court Life in Ancient Japan* (New York, 1964).

SUSAN MATISOFF

JAPANESE WRITERS (MODERN). In the closing years of the Meiji era (1868–1912), Japanese women began to re-emerge as major writers after centuries of comparative silence. Despite their brilliant performance as writers during the classical age, women's active participation in the national literature had reached its nadir in the Tokugawa age (1603–1867), at least in part because the Tokugawa ethic supported the masculine samurai code and the enforcement of neo-Confucianism's definitively subordinate position for women within the social hierarchy.

Two late Meiji figures, the short story writer Higuchi Ichiyō (1872–1896) and the feminist poet Yosano Akiko (1878–1942), symbolize the changing opportunities for women in the new age. Higuchi, whose tragically short life culminated in four years of intense literary activity, in her fiction captures the force of traditional roles as they conflict with the personal aspirations of characters, many of whom are drawn from the fringes of the then fading pleasure quarters of the Yosh-iwara. Her writing fully reveals the still existent constraints that Japanese society placed upon women. Yosano's poetry, in contrast, is the product of a career span-ning a life of social activism and of feminism with a strong maternalistic bent. Taken together, the two writers, both of whom rank among the greatest practi-tioners of their respective genres, foreshadow the level of achievement and the per-sistent themes and concerns that recur in the works of ensuing generations of women.

Women's writing has tended to be marginalized by the readiness of Japan's largely male critical literary establishment to consign it to a separate category of "women's style writing" (*joryū bungaku*) and to label it as privatized and emotional. However, any consideration of the actual works themselves shows the great variation and scope of twentieth-century Japanese women's writing.

Although women suffered from a de facto exclusion from many important literary circles (the *bundan*), especially those centering around major universities to which women were not yet admitted, they found more hospitable ground and support in a few social and literary movements and institutions sympathetic to feminist concerns. One of the earliest of these was the feminist literary magazine *Seitō* (Blue Stocking), which was founded in 1911 by Hiratsuka Raicho (1878–1971) and which published works by leading women writers, including Yosano and Okamoto Kanoko (1889–1939), the latter of whom was another exponent of maternalism in both her poetry and her prose. Although the magazine, which ceased publication in 1916, existed for only the last two years of the Meiji and the first four of the Taishō (1912–1926) periods, its emphasis upon the individual creative energies of women prepared the ground for the more economic- and class-oriented expression of feminist concerns by women writing within the proletarian literary movement. The left-wing literary magazines and circles that sprang up in the Shōwa (1926–1989) decades of the twenties and thirties became a seedbed for writers of Socialist and anarchist political convictions, many of whom were to have illustrious careers in the postwar years. Writers such as Hirabayashi Taiko (1905–1972), Miyamoto Yuriko (1899–1951), and Sata Ineko (b.1904) underwent imprisonment because of their political beliefs, with Mi-yamoto's confinement continuing throughout the war years. The social con-sciousness evident in the works of enormously popular writers such as Hayashi Fumiko (1903–1951) and Ariyoshi Sawako (b.1931) is clearly in sympathy with the economic and class issues advanced in left-wing circles. Enchi Fumiko, perhaps the leading "recognized" woman prose writer and literary aesthetician of the postwar period, began her prewar career as a left-wing playwright. In poetry, too, a proletarian consciousness is expressed in the works of such pow-erful writers as Ishigaki Rin (b.1920) and Ibaragi Noriko (b.1926); poets maturing in the postwar years, such as Kōr Rumiko (b.1932), Tomioka Taeko (b.1935), who is also a novelist of note, and Atsumi Ikuko (b.1939), combine concern for feminist issues with a perspective on Japan's postwar demoralization and ma-terialism.

The exclusion of women from most other established critical and literary circles had the effect of fostering a cross-generic and cross-movement solidarity among the writers themselves through such organizations as the Women Writers Association (Joryū bungakushakai), which awards a coveted literary prize. Published anthologies of prizewinning stories reveal an impressive range of stylistic and thematic treatment. In poetry, too, women have continued to produce works in an amazing range. The postmodern cosmopolitanism of novelists like Kurahashi Yumiko (b.1935) and of poets like Tada Chimako (b.1930) represents a final intellectual challenge to stereotypes of suitable and appropriate styles and themes in women's writing. So too do the eroticism and violence of the poetry and fiction of Kanai Mieko (b.1947), who sprang from the revolt against society of the sixties' generation.

Lack of translation remains a major obstacle to world recognition of the power and variety of works by Japanese women. Although increasing numbers of translations into English have begun to appear, the bulk of the work by these and other women writers, work of high literary value, remains untranslated. The full range of the resurgence of women's writing can only be suggested here, but the twentieth century has become a second great age of Japanese women writers and rivals the early glory of classical Japan (Heian, late eighth through twelfth centuries), which first gave rise to the concept of "women's writing."

VICTORIA V. VERNON

JAZZ: BEGINNINGS THROUGH 1950s. Not until 1987 did the U.S. Congress, in a concurrent resolution by both houses, express appreciation of jazz "as a rare and valuable national American treasure to which we should devote our attention, support and resources to make certain it is preserved, understood and promulgated." The rich contributions of women to this only recently recognized art form are just beginning to be acknowledged and researched.

Spirituals. Spirituals are precursors of jazz, black American religious folk music appearing in the southern states in the early 1800s, sung by male and female Christian slaves, in unison or two-part harmony, expressing suffering and prayers in slow laments or shouting hopes in lively jubilee songs. Both the laments and the jubilee songs reveal African characteristics also pervading blues, jazz, and gospel: intense emotional expression, spontaneous improvisation, a strongly syncopated rhythmic sense enhanced with hand clapping or foot stomping, and a call and response form. These African elements are melded with the 4/4 time and basic harmonies of the European diatonic scale, which slaves heard in the secular and sacred music of American whites in the early nineteenth century. From 1871 to 1878 spirituals were introduced throughout the United States and Europe by the Fisk Jubilee Singers, four young men and five young women.

Ragtime. Ragtime is piano music, fusing the syncopations of jubilee songs with the musical structure of marches (three, four, or five thematic sections and modulating interludes), flourishing 1895–1920. "Raggy" (syncopated) tunes for dancing were played by blacks on fiddles and banjos even in antebellum times;

by the 1880s raggy music, played by brass bands and orchestras, ushered in the era of the cakewalk, 1897–1900, the dance craze that captured the United States and Europe. Among the six or seven published cakewalk composers is one woman, Saddie Koninsky, with her "Eli Green's Cakewalk," 1896. By the late 1890s this raggy, syncopated style came to be particularly identified with piano music called "ragtime" (first piano rags published 1897). Played by black men in bordellos and sporting houses of the South and Midwest, popularized by piano rolls, commercialized by Tin Pan Alley, published in sheet music in million-copy lots to be sold in the new "five-and-ten cents stores," ragtime was soon taken over and genteelized by middle-class white women to play at home on their new pianos. (Sales of inexpensive uprights, perfected by the late 1880s, averaged around 300,000 per year in the first two decades of the twentieth century.) Among the millions of white, female piano players of rags, a few also composed and published rags: May Aufderheide, who wrote at least six rags, two of which were standards with New Orleans jazz bands; Gladys Yelvington; Julia Lee Niebergall; Adeline Shepherd, who wrote a hit rag that William Jennings Bryan used in his 1908 campaign for the presidency; Louise V. Gustin; Nellie M. Stokes; Irene Giblin; Irene Cozard; Maude Gilmore; Ella Hudson Day; Nina B. Kohler. Most versatile of the female rag composers was Muriel Pollock, who wrote songs and theatrical scores as well. Most creative of the piano-roll artists in the period 1918–1928 was Edythe Baker. Interest in ragtime, revived in the 1970s by the movie *The Sting,* was sustained through the eighties by ragtime festivals, clubs, and newsletters. Outstanding contemporary female ragtime pianists include Molly Kaufman, Kathy Craig, Yvonne Cloutier, Jo Ann Castle, "Sister Jean" Huling, Mary Green, Joan Reynolds, and Virginia Tichenor Gilseth.

Traditional Jazz. An improvised, 4/4 music, based on a melody with set harmonies, traditional jazz appeared about the turn of the century, a blending of jubilee and ragtime syncopations with the call and response form and individualized sounds of the blues (see BLUES), played by instruments from marching bands (cornet with melodic lead, clarinet with countermelody, trombone as lowest voice of this trio), with other instruments for rhythm (piano, drums, banjo, guitar, bass, or sousaphone). By 1915 the word *jass,* later *jazz,* replaced the term *ragtime* to designate this syncopated music.

The two most important female bandleaders in early jazz were also pianists. Lovie Austin toured in vaudeville, leading Lovie Austin & Her Blues Serenaders, and recorded extensively. Lillian Hardin Armstrong, pianist, composer, vocalist, and arranger, led bands, some all-male, some all-female, and also worked in King Oliver's band, where she met and married Louis Armstrong, 1924. She recorded the classic Hot Five sides with him in 1927. Lee Morse, vocalist, led Lee Morse & Her Blue Grass Boys, sometimes using a western cowboy yodel to enliven her jazz.

A third long-active pianist and blues shouter but not a bandleader, Billie Pierce, with her trumpeter husband, DeeDee, accompanied Ida Cox on tour, worked the tent circuit, and played with the Preservation Hall Jazz Band in New Orleans. The female band pianist with the longest continuous career in traditional jazz is Jeannette Kimbal, who began about 1923 with the Papa Celestin Band and continued to play for over 65 years.

Swing. Beginning in the mid–1920s and continuing into the 1950s, swing was played by big bands, usually 13 to 15 members (five reeds, five brass, piano, bass, drums), utilizing written arrangements including rhythmic riffs and a call and response between the brasses and reeds for the large ensemble, limiting improvisation to soloists.

Female vocalists were featured with most swing bands: Ivie Anderson, with the Duke Ellington Orchestra for 12 years, and Mildred Bailey, the "Rocking Chair Lady," part Indian, the first nonblack woman to absorb the blues style successfully, who sang with Paul Whiteman and Benny Goodman and co-led a band with husband Red Norvo ("Mr. and Mrs. Swing").

The supreme Billie Holiday, "Lady Day," with a highly individualized style, riding off the beat, composing unique songs, recorded more than 350 records, protested against racial hatred in her famous song "Strange Fruit," and sang with the bands of Benny Goodman, Teddy Wilson, Count Basie, and Artie Shaw.

Helen Humes, master of blues, ballads, jazz, rhythm and blues, bop, and pop, sang with Count Basie 1938–1942 and with the Red Norvo trio. Maxine Sullivan, with a relaxed but swinging, cool jazz style, worked with Claude Thornhill, with her husband, John Kirby, and in clubs and festivals until her death. Lee Wiley sang on radio with Paul Whiteman, with the Dixieland groups of Eddie Condon, with Pee Wee Russell, and with Jess Stacy's big band. Helen Forrest was featured with Artie Shaw, Benny Goodman, Harry James, and with singing star Dick Haymes on a long-lasting radio series. Anita O'Day, considered one of the top ten female jazz singers by critic Leonard Feather, was featured with the Gene Krupa band, with Stan Kenton, and with Benny Goodman and influenced later jazz singer June Christy, who followed O'Day with Stan Kenton.

Two all-woman big bands starred in this period, one all-white and feted in the press, one racially integrated and ignored by all but the black press. Female bands and orchestras had appeared as early as 1884, but the first to earn national fame was Ina Ray Hutton and Her Melodears, led by the "Blonde Bombshell of Rhythm," pianist and gyrating vocalist Hutton, who later led other all-female and all-male bands.

The International Sweethearts of Rhythm, the first racially integrated women's band, was the hottest female jazz band of the forties and the most enduring (1938–1955). They made a "Swing Battle of the Sexes" tour with the Fletcher Henderson band, were broadcast by shortwave to every theatre of war, and played for domestic black troops and for troops in Europe. By 1947 key players of the group, Ernestine Tiny Davis, trumpet, and Vi Burnside, tenor sax, withdrew to form their own women's bands.

Several other women's bands, both black and white, functioned during World

War II, but only Eddie Durham's All Star Girl Orchestra was in a class with the Sweethearts. Pianist and blues singer Georgia White led a female band in Chicago and later worked with Big Bill Broonzy, recording about 100 songs.

Outstanding jazz instrumentalists of the swing era include several pianists. Norma Teagarden alternated leading her own band with playing piano in brother Jack Teagarden's band. The child prodigy Hazel Scott, pianist and vocalist, was noted for jazzing the classics. Barbara Carroll, composer and pianist, led a trio, then continued as soloist into the seventies. Dorothy Donean worked as a hot jazz pianist/entertainer.

One of the all-time great jazz musicians is Mary Lou Williams, pianist, composer of over 350 pieces, arranger, and bandleader. In the John Williams band by age 15, in four years she was "The Lady Who Swings the Band," soloist, arranger, and composer with Andy Kirk's Twelve Clouds of Joy. She made arrangements for Benny Goodman, Louis Armstrong, Cab Calloway, Tommy Dorsey, Glen Gray, Earl Hines, and Duke Ellington. She arranged her "Zodiac Suite" for the New York Philharmonic and performed it with them—the first jazz musician to appear with a major symphony; she played her "Mary Lou's Mass" in St. Patrick's Cathedral, New York City, the first jazz played in a non-black church; and she was awarded a full professorship by Duke University, perhaps another first.

Among many excellent female instrumentalists, Valaida Snow, trumpeter, singer, and dancer, stands out. She played with Earl Hines in Chicago, in revues in London and Paris, and in bands in Russia, Germany, the Near East, the Far East, Stockholm, and Copenhagen, was imprisoned in a Nazi camp, then resumed her career in the United States. Marge Hyams, able vibist with Woody Herman in 1944–1945, the year his band was voted "best swing band" by *Downbeat*, led combos, then joined the George Shearing combo. Mary Osborne played guitar, recording with Mary Lou Williams, Coleman Hawkins, and Ethel Waters, led combos, and played with Jean Wald's all-female orchestra; with Russ Morgan; with Joe Venuti; and on a long-running radio show. Melba Doretta Liston, jazz trombonist, composer, and arranger, toured with Dizzy Gillespie, Count Basie, and Billie Holiday, later led her own all-female quintet, and wrote arrangements for Mary Lou Williams and others. The first woman elected to the Songwriters' Hall of Fame, lyricist Dorothy Fields, collaborated for her greatest jazz successes with composer Jimmy McHugh. Unlike the vocalists and pianists of swing, who are given due credit in jazz histories, the outstanding female instrumentalists have been almost completely ignored.

Gospel. Strongly rhythmic and emotional black American religious music, gospel is the modern form of the spirituals, differing from the swinging syncopations of jazz and the blues only in the subject matter of the gospel lyrics, based on the Christian religion. That important difference led many churches at the turn of the century to forbid their congregations to join in "sinful" secular music. As a corollary, most jazz musicians did not play hymns or spirituals in clubs. Although Mahalia Jackson, "queen of the gospel singers," as a child loved to listen to the records of Bessie Smith and Ma Rainey, she refused ever to sing the blues and only after much persuasion agreed to sing gospel music outside the church in jazz festivals and concerts. In contrast, Sister Rosetta Tharpe, accompanying herself on guitar, gladly made gospel famous in the forties in nightclubs and with record hits, but the sad price of her success was a virtual shunning by the Holiness church congregations. Other well-known gospel singers were Clara Ward and Roberta Martin.

Although the differences between sacred and secular black music have been emphasized by the churches, the musical style of these two strands of development is the same. A strikingly different musical style began to appear in black music in the early forties (see JAZZ: MODERN DEVELOPMENTS).

Further Referencess. Rosetta Reitz, Liner Notes for Records in Women's Heritage Series 1980–1987, Rosetta Records, 115 W. 16 St., New York, N.Y. Eileen Southern, *The Music of Black Americans: A History* (New York, 1971).

JEAN KITTRELL

JAZZ: MODERN DEVELOPMENTS. In the bop years 1940 to 1948 and the "cool" years 1949 into the 1960s, musicians moved toward a more sophisticated style: from familiar harmonies and singable melodies to unexpected dissonances and melodic phrases difficult for listeners to remember; from impelling two- and four-beat rhythms inviting toe tapping, hand clapping, and dancing to subtle, nondanceable rhythms; from traditional or big band instrumentation to smaller groups, often without piano, using nontraditional instruments; from "rebop" to "bebop" to "bop" to "cool jazz" to "modern" to "progressive" to "new."

The incredible Ella Fitzgerald, the "First Lady of Song" among jazz singers for more than half a century beginning in the 1930s, with a virtuoso range and command of intonation, mastered a variety of styles, swinging to fame with "A Tisket A Tasket" and the band of Chick Webb (which she led for a year after his death), brilliantly scat singing in bop style in the forties, evolving her own jazz ballad style. She toured nationally and internationally with Jazz at the Philharmonic 1946–1950, then with her own groups through the 1980s.

Singer-pianist Sarah Vaughn, first with Earl Hines, then as bop vocalist with Billy Eckstine, rose to international fame as a soloist with unique piano styling and innovative vocals, performing in over 60 countries and appearing with major U.S. symphony orchestras. Roberta Flack continued the same demanding dual performance of vocals with keyboard accompaniment. Pianist Marilyn Mc-Partland developed a style much richer harmonically and melodically than that of ragtime or stride piano. She presides over a weekly national public radio series, begun in 1979.

Singers continue to outnumber instrumentalists among present-day female jazz musicians. Nancy Wilson, major star throughout the 1960s, touring the United States, Europe, and Japan, now appears on television as singer, actress, and host. Odetta, a big woman accompanying her big voice with guitar, considers herself a folksinger who does not attempt to distinguish folk ballads from blues, work songs, and popular music. Cleo Laine, one of the greatest living jazz singers, displays astonishing originality, an incredible range, agility of movement from lower to higher registers, and a variety of musical styles.

International superstar Aretha Franklin epitomizes the artistic and popular fusion of jazz, popular music, blues, gospel, and soul, with six gold LPs and 14 gold singles, each signifying 1 million records sold, a fusion continued by Tina Turner and Diana Ross.

The innovations of modern jazz disturbed performers and devotees who preferred earlier jazz forms (see JAZZ: BEGINNINGS THROUGH THE 1950s). A traditional jazz revival, begun in San Francisco in 1939, continued into the 1990s through jazz clubs that had memberships almost completely white and that supported concerts, newsletters, and festivals featuring traditional bands and female vocalists, predominantly white, often strongly influenced by Bessie Smith, vocalists like Barbara Dane, Pat Yankee, Carol Leigh, Joanne ("Pug") Horton, Jean Kittrell, Ruby Wilson, Jan Sutherland, Terrie Richards, Paulette Pepper, and Banu Gibson.

The bifurcation between modern and traditional jazz is obvious in the production of American and European jazz festivals and publications, which generally feature either traditional or modern jazz but not both. Although earlier forms of jazz, especially the blues (see BLUES), were the progenitors of rock in the sixties, and all blues bands and festivals proliferated in the eighties, most bands from the fifties on preferred the modern style of expression, leaving to a minority of traditional bands the early forms.

Most major female jazz musicians from the 1950s to the present, however, more flexible than band units, are neither extremely avant-garde nor simply traditional. They defy categorization into such separate stylistic modes and make irrelevant most fine distinctions among jazz, popular music, folk music, gospel, rhythm and blues. They fuse past and present, combining modern harmonies and syncopated rhythms, continuing the emotional passion of the blues and the joy of jubilee songs.

Further References. Sally Placksin, *American Women in Jazz: 1900 to Present* (New York, 1982). Eileen Southern, *The Music of Black Americans: A History* (New York, 1971). See also the monthly publication, *The Mississippi Rag* (ed. and publ. by Leslie Johnson, Minneapolis, Minn.).

JEAN KITTRELL

L

LATIN AMERICAN ARTISTS (TWENTIETH-CENTURY). Many well-known women artists of the twentieth century have had a formal education in the arts. They attended schools of art in their countries and also went to art institutes in France and the United States, receiving instruction from famous painters and sculptors. Returning to their homeland, these women introduced the new art trends, such as cubism, surrealism, and Expressionism, that expressed reality in a different way.

The new European art trends were adapted to Latin American reality, resulting in unique art expressions and particular personal styles. European surrealism, for example, became a reality in Latin America, where artists and writers found what Cuban writer Alejo Carpentier called magical realism. This magic reality is present in the exuberant nature of the Latin American tropical landscapes and, among other things, in the richness of Latin American myths, folklore, and cultures. Women artists of Latin America were also socially aware and were determined to express themselves strongly as women with progressive ideas. Although there are many excellent women artists in Latin America, here only a few representative ones can be mentioned.

Tarsila do Amaral (1886–1973) and Anita Malfatti (1896–1964), both from São Paulo, were among the pioneers of modern art in Brazil. Amaral studied art in Paris from 1920 to 1922, first at the Academy Julien and later with Emile Renard. At home and abroad she became involved with modernism, cubism, and primitivism. In her search for authenticity and Brazilian themes, she visited different parts of Brazil and observed the festivities and the people. Nativistic themes are portrayed in *The Negress* (1923), *Abaporu* (1928), and *Antropofagia* (1929). The latter two are also examples of "tropical surrealism," that is, the representation of the exuberant vegetation of the tropics in a surrealistic way.

Malfatti studied Expressionist painting with Lovis Corinth in Germany and became interested in cubism in New York. In December 1916 she exhibited her paintings in São Paulo. This was the first exhibit of modern art in Brazil and one of the first in Latin America. She caused a scandal with paintings such as *The Woman with Green Hair* (1916) and *The Man of Seven Colors* (1917), which demonstrated her position against the traditional expression of reality.

Maria Martins (1900–1973), Djanira da Mota e Silva (b.1914), and Lygia Clark (1920–1988), all Brazilian, also had an impact on modern Latin American art. Martins studied painting in Paris in 1930 and sculpture in Belgium under Oscar Jasper in 1939. She cofounded the Fundação do Museu de Arte Moderna do Rio de Janeiro. Her sculptures, also an example of tropical surrealism, show the immense flora of the Brazilian jungle.

Mota e Silva is a primitivist whose paintings re-create scenes from daily life and folklore. She has also done religious paintings mainly inspired by saints. Some of her works are *Tea Plantation in Itacolomi* (1958) and *Saint Peter and the Station of the Cross* (1943).

Lygia Clark, a member of the neo-concrete movement and cofounder of the Brazilian Neo-Concretist Association (1959), studied art in Rio de Janeiro and Paris (1950–1952). She also taught at the Sorbonne, Paris, from 1970 to 1975. Her sculptures are essentially "abstract constructivist." Some of her sculptures are *Space Bird, Project for a Planet, and Fantastic Carriage*.

Another influential figure in Latin American contemporary painting was Frida Kahlo (Mexico, 1907–1954), who was married, off and on, to the famous painter Diego Rivera. Their association lasted some 25 years. Most of Kahlo's paintings are autobiographical, expressed in a surrealistic and fantastic way. Her paintings show an obsession with pain and death and a strong attraction to eroticism, aggression, and procreation. The obsession with pain and death in her poetry can be explained in large part by her health problems. When she was a child, she had polio and as a teenager was in an accident that left physical and emotional scars. Some examples of her many paintings are *The Two Fridas* (1939), *Self-Portrait with Diego in My Mind* (1943), and *The Broken Column* (1944).

Tilsa Ysuchiya (Peru, 1932–1984) was inspired by the Indian cultures of her native land. After studying at the School of Fine Arts of Peru (1954 to 1959), she studied at the Sorbonne and attended classes at the École des Beaux Arts in Paris. Her works are based on her imagination and on Quechua legends and myths, all combined in a fashion reminiscent of dreams or a surrealism of Indian motifs. Representative paintings are *Myth of the Tree* (1976) and *Myth of the Woman and the Wind* (1976).

Beatriz Gonzáles (Colombia, b.1936) studied fine arts and art history at the University of the Andes and in 1966 studied graphics in Rotterdam. In *The Last Table* she represents da Vinci's *The Last Supper* on a large coffee table. *The Parrots* (1986) expressed a political message. It is a 40-foot frieze oil painting on paper that shows the heads of the Colombian president and his advisers, arrayed and colored like parrots.

Raquel Forner (b.1902), Noemi Gerstein (b.1910), Alicia Peñalba (b.1918), Sarah Grilo (b.1921), and Marta Minujín (b.1943) are distinguished Argentinian artists.

Forner studied art at La Academia Nacional de Bellas Artes of Buenos Aires and in Paris from 1929 to 1930. She is a cofounder of Cursos Libres de Arte Plástico, the first private academy of modern art in Argentina. She has painted a Space series, an Astrobeings series, and an Astronauts series. Gerstein and Peñalba have distinguished themselves as sculptors. Gerstein is attracted to metallic constructions, as, for example, her *Constellation* (1963), in which she used small tubular segments. Peñalba won the International Sculpture Prize at the sixth biennial exposition of São Paulo. In her earlier work she made totemlike structures inspired by primitive sources, but her more recent compositions are asymmetrical. These latest ones suggest motion in space. An example is *Absent* (1961).

Sarah Grilo and her husband, José Antonio Fernández Muro, became leaders of the abstract movement in Argentina. Sarah was a self-taught artist. After coming to New York in 1962, she included in her painting signs, graffiti, letterings, and numerals. Examples of that period are *Charge* and *Inferno*, both of 1964.

Marta Minujín came to New York on a John Simon Guggenheim Memorial Fellowship. There she excelled as a multimedia artist of international renown. She has staged environmental "happenings," transient artistic events, and has done experiments in interactive and dynamic art. For example, in *El batacazo* (The Long Shot) there are smells, sounds, and sights.

María Luisa Pacheco (1919–1982) studied in her native city of La Paz, Bolivia, and from 1951 to 1952 in Madrid with Daniel Vázquez. In 1957 she established her home in New York. She was three times awarded a fellowship by the John Simon Guggenheim Memorial Foundation and has won many national and international awards. She has used themes from her native land in cubist, Expressionist, and abstract styles.

Amelia Peláez (Cuba, 1897–1968) from 1927 to 1934 studied art in Paris at the École des Beaux Arts, École de Louvre, and under Russian artist Alexandra Exter. She was the first Cuban painter to be an advocate of contemporary art in her country. She searched for a syncretic style: modern, personal, and Cuban. An example of her work is *The Hibiscus* (1943).

Finally, Myrna Báez (Puerto Rico, b.1931) studied art in the Academia de San Fernando, Madrid (1957). She expresses social criticism in her art, as, for example, in *Barrio Tokyo* (1962), a scene of poverty.

Further References. Erika Billeter et al., *Imagen de México. La aportación de México al arte del siglo XX* (Dallas, 1988). Luis R. Cancel et al., *The Latin American Spirit: Art in the United States, 1920–1970* (New York, 1988). Gilbert Chase, *Contemporary Art in Latin America* (New York, 1970). Halliday T. Day and Hollister Sturges, *Art of the Fantastic in Latin America, 1920–1987* (Indianapolis, 1987).

AMALIA MONDRÍQUEZ

LATIN AMERICAN WRITERS. See BRAZILIAN WRITERS; SPANISH AMERICAN WRITERS

LESBIAN LITERATURE depicts love between women in a positive manner, but until the 1960s virtually none of it described sexual activity as part of the love relationship. Although women have always written about love between women, silence about sexual activity at times was the result of their inability to acknowledge sexual relationships between women. But more important was the fear of patriarchal sanctions, especially in the late nineteenth and early twentieth centuries.

The poetry of Sappho (sixth-century B.C. Greece) is the oldest extant literature containing passionate declarations of love for women. The earliest known lesbian literature in English (this article deals only with English language literature) is Katherine Phillip's *Poems* (1967), which also contains passionate declarations of love, but the author's soul is inflamed, not her body. Platonic friendships, a development of Renaissance Italy, by the seventeenth century had spread to England. Since the love in platonic friendships was considered to be spiritual, these relationships became socially acceptable between men and women.

In the eighteenth century, romantic friendships continued to develop in England and spread to America. Society encouraged these relationships among women because chastity had become a woman's most valued possession. Lesbian literature was therefore not considered unusual. Women could openly declare their love for each other as long as sexual activity was not mentioned. Indeed, romantic friendship became a popular theme in eighteenth-century literature (Lillian Faderman, *Surpassing the Love of Men* [New York, 1981]). Characteristic of this period is a female couple's desire for economic independence.

Mary Wollstonecraft's *Mary, A Fiction* (1788) is considered "the first novel on female variance to be written by a woman" (Jeannette Foster, *Sex Variant Women in Literature* [Tallahassee, 1985]). It is strongly biographical, another characteristic of lesbian literature in the eighteenth and nineteenth centuries. Works such as Sarah Scott's *A Description of Millenium Hall* (1762), the anonymous poem "Danebury: or The Power of Friendship" (1777), Helen William's *Anecdotes of a Convent* (1771), and Ann Seward's poems about Honora Sneyd (1770–1790s) consider romantic friendship superior to love between men and women.

Victorian society, subscribing to the idea that women lacked sexual desire, continued to encourage romantic friendships between women because they kept women confined to a female world and out of the affairs of men. This strategy, however, backfired. Romantic friendships brought women closer together, and involvement in reform movements was often a result. Women, finding their efforts to better their position validated only by other women, sought each other's company for encouragement and sympathy. Toward the end of the nineteenth century, lesbian literature began to reflect the attitude that romantic friendship could satisfy a woman's emotional needs better than marriage. Romantic friendships were glorified in works such as Sarah Converse's *Diana Victrix* (1897) and Sarah Orne Jewett's *Deephaven* (1877), and "Martha's Lady" (1897).

Permissive attitudes began to fade in the 1830s and 1840s when romantic friendship was viewed as an alternative to traditional marriage. In the late nineteenth century, sexologists' identification of same-sex love as a congenital abnormality and of lesbians as women who rejected traditional roles increased the attack on romantic friendships. By century's end they were no longer encouraged by English society, and lesbian literature declined. In America, however, lesbian literature still flourished, partly because sexological theories had not yet crossed the ocean. Mary MacLane's *The Story of Mary MacLane by Herself* (1902) and Clarissa Dixon's *Janet and Her Dear Phebe* (1909) still depicted romantic friendships in positive terms. Short stories such as Helen R. Hull's "The Fire" (1918), Jeannette Lee's "The Cat and the King" (1919), and Catherine Wells's "The Beautiful House" (1912), published in popular periodicals, still treated love between women in an unself-conscious manner. But early in the twentieth century attitudes changed. "Love between women, openly treated, was dead as a popular literary theme by the 1920's" (Faderman, 308).

Lesbian literature that sufficiently masked its theme was still published. Gertrude Stein's short story "Miss Furr and Miss Skeene" (1922) used a coded language. Edna St. Vincent Millay's play *The Lamp and the Bell* (1924) was placed in the distant past. Virginia Woolf's *Orlando* (1928) and *Mrs. Dalloway* (1925), Radclyffe Hall's *The Unlit Lamp* (1924), and Elizabeth Bowen's *The Hotel* (1928) all escaped opprobrium because of the subtlety with which they portrayed lesbianism. But most lesbian literature began to reflect the theories of the sexologists.

The most famous novel to incorporate sexology's definitions of lesbianism was Radclyffe Hall's *The Well of Loneliness* (1928). Accepting Havelock Ellis's theory that "inversion" is congenital, Hall attempted to defend lesbianism, arguing that there was nothing a lesbian could do about it except hope for sympathy and tolerance from society. Her book was attacked in the London *Express* and banned in England. The scandal was caused by the defense of lesbianism, not by any overtly sexual content. Ellis's theory of "congenital inversion" provided a major deterrent to the writing of lesbian literature since few women wished to be labeled a "freak."

After World War I, most fiction dealing with lesbianism portrayed it as evil. Among the few sympathetic treatments were Naomi Mitchison's "The Delicate Fire" (1932) and Victoria Sackville-West's *Dark Island* (1934), which avoided scandal by placing their stories in the past. After 1935, censorship groups, spurred by a crop of sensationalist literature that exploited sex of every kind, made the publication of lesbian literature even more difficult. However, a handful of lesbian novels managed to escape: Djuna Barne's *Nightwood* (1936) in England and, in America, Gale Wilhelm's *We Too Are Drifting* (1937) and *Torchlight to Valhalla* (1938), Helen Anderson's *Pity for Women* (1937), Elisabeth Craigin's *Either Is Love* (1937), and Kay Boyle's "The Bridegroom's Body" (1938).

From 1929 to the late 1960s, most lesbian literature continued to reflect society's negative label. Sexual activity was slowly becoming more overt, but with the exception of Mary Renault's *The Middle Mist* (1945) and Claire Morgan's *The Price of Salt* (1951), lesbianism was depicted as unnatural, and the works pointed a moral warning to society. Usually, the characters ended up "converted" to heterosexuality or dead. Paperbacks in the 1950s and 1960s exploited lesbianism as a theme to "titillate while upholding conventional values" (Faderman, 355). Even *The Ladder* (1956–1972), published by the Daughters of Bilitis, although intended as a lesbian magazine, promulgated prevailing psychological theories about homosexuality.

It was not until the 1960s' Women's Liberation movement, when the connection between lesbianism and feminism was acknowledged by women, that lesbian literature began to appear all over the United States and England in all literary genres. What separated the new wave of lesbian literature from its predecessors was its open defiance of society's views that lesbianism was an illness and was evil. The new literature reflected the lesbian's newly awakened awareness of herself as a woman loving women, neither abnormal nor sick. In addition, description of sexual activity was no longer skirted. Lesbian journals such as *The Lesbian Tide* (begun by the Daughters of Bilitis, 1971) and *The Furies: Lesbian-Feminist Monthly* (begun 1972) helped to spread the new, positive self-image. Most lesbian literature in the 1960s was published by lesbian-feminist presses, such as Kitchen Table, Crossing, Naiad, Persephone, and Spinsters, Inc. In the 1970s, the floodgates opened and lesbian literature poured off both lesbian-feminist and, increasingly, commercial presses.

Lesbian novels rapidly increased in the 1970s. In Rita Mae Brown's *Rubyfruit Jungle* (1973) a lesbian successfully copes with the problems encountered in an uninformed, bigoted society. Brown introduced humor into the lesbian novel, humor resulting from society's misconceptions about lesbianism. Novels such as June Arnold's *The Cook and the Carpenter* (1973), Sharon Isabell's *Yesterday's Lessons* (1974), and Elana Nachman's *Riverfinger Woman* and *Sister Gin* (1975) emphasized the lesbian's struggles to come to terms with herself, not as a lesbian, but as a woman with problems unrelated to her sexuality. Mary F. Beal's *Angel Dance* (1977) brought the lesbian into the detective novel. Short story anthologies found a large readership. In 1976, Barbara Grier and Coletta Reid published *The Lesbian Home Journal*, a collection of short stories from *The Ladder*, and Judy Grahn edited *True to Life Adventure Stories*. Lesbian poetry proliferated as well, and collections such as Adrienne Rich's *Twenty-One Love Poems* (1976) found an eager market.

In 1956, *Sex Variant Women in Literature* listed 324 titles. In 1975, *The Ladder* published a bibliography, *The Lesbian in Literature*, listing over 2,000 titles. In the 1980s, lesbian literature proliferated to the point where it would be virtually impossible to compile a comprehensive bibliography; lesbian literature has evolved into a recognized literary genre.

VICTORIA L. SHANNON

LITERARY CRITICISM, FEMINIST, analyzes texts with respect to the ideology of gender. In its preoccupation with how women in particular are represented in the system of gender relationships, feminist literary criticism may also share characteristics with other kinds of criticism, such as Marxist, psychoanalytic, and poststructuralist criticism. Its scope encompasses all world literatures and is not limited to the canonical genres of fiction, poetry, and plays.

Feminist literary criticism emerged in America in the 1960s, although its precursors can be found in the self-reflexive comments of women writers who discuss their circumstances as literary producers. Virginia Woolf, the first modern feminist critic, provides a more direct impetus to feminist critical activity in her explorations of woman's economic, artistic, sexual, political, and educational position in a society characterized by patriarchal dominance. Simone de Beauvoir's monumental work *The Second Sex* (1949; Eng., 1952) signals the emergence of an interdisciplinary, contemporary discourse on women. Beauvoir's claim that "one is not born, but rather becomes, a woman" (H. M. Parshley [trans. and ed.] *The Second Sex* [New York, 1974], 301) still preoccupies feminist work today.

The activity of feminist criticism assumes various nonevolutionary forms in the latter half of this century. Kate Millet's *Sexual Politics* (New York, 1971) represents feminist criticism's initial activity: the exposé and critique of women's representations in works by male authors in the literary canon. More than an obvious "first phase," this strategy of rereading, an important part of feminist critical activity, has become increasingly refined and sophisticated through the contributions of reader-response and post-structuralist criticism.

The work of recovering, reassessing, and reissuing lost and forgotten texts by women writers, a major enterprise within feminist literary criticism, has resulted in rich discoveries of writers whose analyses of sex, race, class, and sexual orientation challenge conventional delineations of "the literary" with respect to genre, author, subject matter and style. The publication lists of the Feminist Press and others in the United States, of des femmes in France, and of Virago in England demonstrate the feminist effort to forge a new critical tradition or to supplement the inherited one. These texts contribute significantly to the investigation of a female literary tradition and document relationships among women writers.

A number of works characterize feminist interest in women's writing and writing about women. Ellen Moers' *Literary Women: The Great Writers* (Garden City, N.Y., 1977) was one of the first important considerations of a women's literary tradition. Sandra Gilbert and Susan Gubar's *The Madwoman in the Attic: The Woman Writer and the Nineteenth-Century Literary Imagination* (New Haven, 1979) represents a provocative and controversial theory of female creativity. These and other critical studies illustrate the benefits of what Elaine Showalter terms "gynocritics," which she describes as "the study of women *as writers* ... the history, styles, themes, genres, and structures of writing by women; the psychodynamics of female creativity; the trajectory of the individual or collective female career, and the evolution and laws of a female literary tradition'' (''Feminist Criticism in the Wilderness,'' in Elaine Showalter [ed.], *The New Feminist Criticism: Essays on Women, Literature, and Theory* [New York, 1985], 248). Showalter contrasts ''gynocritics'' with what she calls the ''ideological'' mode of *''feminist reading* or the *feminist critique,''* which ''offers feminist readings of texts which consider the images and stereotypes of women in literature, the omissions and misconceptions about women in criticism'' (245), as well as considerations of woman-as-sign in discursive systems. Showalter's problematic opposition is being challenged for its assertion that one kind of feminist criticism is ''ideological'' whereas another is not and for its advocacy of some areas of investigation while excluding others.

The circle of activity needs to be drawn large enough to encompass feminist criticism that also reflects Marxist, poststructuralist, black, lesbian, and psychoanalytic concerns. The new work resulting from feminism's alliances presents an occasion for rethinking the underlying assumptions and strategies of feminist literary criticism. Margaret Homans, in '' 'Her Very Own Howl': The Ambiguities of Representation in Recent Women's Fiction'' (*Signs* 9 [1983]: 186–205), describes the differences between French and American feminist literary criticism in terms of critical attitudes toward language's capacity to represent women's experience:

The French writers who accept the premise that language and experience are coextensive also understand language to be a male construct whose operation depends on women's silence and absence, so that when women write they do not represent themselves as women. In contrast, more recent feminist criticism in this country has pragmatically assumed that experience is separable from language and thus that women are or can be in control of language rather than controlled by it, making women capable of self-representation (186).

Although this description of difference is generally useful, the explanation in terms of a French/American opposition is misleading and results in classificatory aberrations.

On the whole, Toril Moi in *Sexual/Textual Politics* (London, 1985) presents the best current overview of feminist literary theory today. Her study encompasses theorists such as Annette Kolodny, Myra Jehlen, Elaine Showalter, Hélène Cixous, Luce Irigaray, and Julia Kristeva, resulting in an expanded view of what feminist criticism accomplishes when it retains its full political potential through the inclusion of psychoanalytic, Marxist, and linguistic theory. The recurring concerns of poststructuralist inquiry—to deconstruct the oppositions of Western metaphysics, to enact a decentering that refuses new oppositions in unimproved structures, to unsettle the myth of the unified, singular ''self,'' and to discover how language writes ''the self,'' experience, and politics—all find productive application in feminist literary criticism.

Several other varieties of feminist criticism deserve special mention. Feminist literary scholarship concerned with psychoanalysis is currently gaining impressive strength, offering feminist rereadings of Freud and Lacan, of canonical authors and texts, and of works by women writers. Critical writing focusing on lesbian and black women's literature is beginning to catch up with the wealth of literature available for study. *Sturdy Black Bridges: Visions of Black Women in Literature* (Roseann P. Bell, Bettye J. Parker, and Beverly Guy-Sheftall [eds.] [New York, 1979]), which includes discussions of African, Caribbean, and African-American culture and women writers, has been supplemented by monographs like Gloria Wade-Gayles's *No Crystal Stair: Visions of Race and Sex in Black Women's Literature* (New York, 1984), which examines works by such authors as Alice Walker, Toni Morrison, and Gwendolyn Brooks. Several new works contribute to the consideration of lesbian literature, some with a specific focus on women of color: Cherrie Moraga and Gloria Anzaldua (eds.), *This Bridge Called My Back: Writings by Radical Women of Color* (Watertown, Mass., 1981); Gloria T. Hull, Patricia Bell Scott, and Barbara Smith, *All the Women Are White, All the Blacks Are Men, But Some of Us Are Brave: Black Women's Studies* (Old Westbury, N.Y., 1982); and Margaret Cruikshank (ed.), *Lesbian Studies: Present and Future* (Old Westbury, N.Y., 1982). These last works represent significant efforts to explore the complex nexus of exclusion, inviting feminist criticism to continue to supplement, challenge, and rewrite the terms upon which past literary critical activities have been based.

Further References. Elizabeth A. Flynn and Patrocinio P. Schweickart (eds.), *Gender and Reading: Essays on Readers, Texts, and Contexts* (Baltimore, 1986). Jane Gallop, *The Daughter's Seduction: Feminism and Psychoanalysis* (Ithaca, N.Y., 1982). Gayle Greene and Coppélla Kahn (eds.), *Making a Difference: Feminist Literary Criticism* (London, 1985). Elizabeth A. Meese, *Crossing the Double-Cross: The Practice of Feminist Criticism* (Chapel Hill, N.C., 1986). Marjorie Pryse and Hortense Spillers (eds.), *Conjuring: Black Women, Fiction, and Literary Tradition* (Bloomington, Ind., 1985).

ELIZABETH A. MEESE

LOCAL COLORISTS. Writers of the latter nineteenth and early twentieth centuries whose work is characterized by use of authentic local settings, regional dialects and characters, and historically accurate details of custom and habit. Their vision—especially in the early period of the New England school—was of a rural matriarchy that was counterposed to industrialism and Calvinism, which were seen as patriarchal systems inimical to women. Thus, their fiction often presents strong women characters in preindustrial milieus and focuses on rural women's cultural traditions and practices, some now largely forgotten, such as herbal medicine. The form the local colorists favored was the short story, although there are a few notable local color novels, for example, Harriet Beecher Stowe's *Minister's Wooing* (1859), *Pearl of Orr's Island* (1862), and *Oldtown Folks* (1869).

The women's local color story in the United States derived from the "village sketch" tradition pioneered in the 1820s by an Englishwoman, Mary Russell Mitford (1787–1855). Her focus was on eccentric personalities caught in humorous predicaments, and her sketches, which were enormously popular, were filled with specific local detail.

In this country the local color tradition may be distinguished from the other dominant women's literary tradition in the nineteenth century, sentimentalism or domestic realism, more recently labeled "woman's fiction" by Nina Baym (*Women's Fiction* [Ithaca, N.Y., 1978]). Local color literature was much closer to realism in its use of authentic character and local detail and in its avoidance of hyperbolic rhetoric and idealistic and romantic plot (all features of sentimentalism).

Caroline Kirkland was one of the first American women writers to develop realist literature. In her preface to *A New Home—Who'll Follow?* (1839), which describes pioneers' experiences in Michigan, Kirkland states that she is consciously emulating Mitford's sketches. But it was Harriet Beecher Stowe (1811–1896) who was the first to formulate the classic American women's local color story with several New England "sketches" published in the 1830s. The first novel by a black woman, *Our Nig* (1859), by Harriet E. Wilson, which is set in New England, is an interesting hybrid that reflects a local color and sentimentalist influence along with that of the black slave narrative.

The other pioneer of the women's local color movement was Rose Terry Cooke (1827–1892), whose stories are set mainly in Connecticut. The best of these are collected in *Somebody's Neighbors* (1881) and *Huckleberries Gathered from New England Hills* (1891). Probably the greatest of the New England local colorists was Sarah Orne Jewett (1849–1909), whose *Country of the Pointed Firs* (1896), set in Maine and focusing upon a powerful rural matriarch, is considered a classic of American literature. The other major New England local colorist was Mary E. Wilkins Freeman (1852–1930), whose *Humble Romance and Other Stories* (1887) and *New England Nun and Other Stories* (1891) include several masterpieces of the genre.

Other women who wrote important northeastern local color works include Elizabeth Stuart Phelps (Ward) (1844–1911), Alice Brown (1857–1948), Celia Thaxter (1835–1894), Constance Fenimore Woolson (1840–1894), Harriet Prescott Spofford (1835–1921), Elizabeth Oakes Smith (1806–1893), Annie Trumbull Slosson (1838–1926), Esther B. Carpenter (1848–1893), Harriet Waters Preston (1836–1911), Alice B. Neal (1827–1863), Elsie Singmaster (1879–1958), Margaret Deland (1857–1945), and Helen Reimensnyder Martin (1868–1939). The latter three set their material primarily in Pennsylvania. Peripheral to the local colorists were the women humorists Frances Whitcher (1813?–1852) and Marietta Hoxley (1836–1926).

The local color tradition was transported to the South by Mary Murfree (1850–1922), whose *In the Tennesee Mountains* (1884) is considered her most important work, and Grace King (1851–1932) of Louisiana. Kate Chopin (1851–1904), whose work, like King's, is set in the Delta region, is the best known of the southern regionalists. Her novel *The Awakening* (1899) is now regarded as a feminist classic. Other important writers of the southern school include Katherine McDowell (1849–1883) and Ruth M. Stuart (1849–1917).

Alice Cary (1820–1871) was among the earliest to set their works in the Midwest. The midwestern tradition included Mary Catherwood (1847–1902), Alice French (1850–1934), and Zona Gale (1874–1938) in her early works, such as *Friendship Village* (1908). Mary Hallock Foote (1847–1938) treated the Far West.

Later writers such as Willa Cather (1873–1947), Ellen Glasgow (1873–1945), or Mary Austin (1868–1934), who set their material in specific regions, are not considered local colorists because their work lacked what Edith Wharton called the "rose-coloured" tint associated (in many cases incorrectly) with the nine-teenth-century school.

Further References. Josephine Donovan, *New England Local Color Literature: A Woman's Tradition* (New York, 1983). Lina Mainiere (ed.), *American Women Writers: A Critical Reference Guide*, 4 vols. (New York, 1979–1982).

JOSEPHINE DONOVAN

M

MAGAZINES, WOMEN'S (NINETEENTH-CENTURY), in both Britain and America tended to reinforce the status quo, though their content and readership changed to reflect changes in society. Early in the century, the typical reader of women's magazines was a member of the upper classes, seeking light entertainment to fill her leisure time. The most popular British periodicals at this time were the "society" or "quality" journals such as *The Lady's Magazine or entertaining companion for the fair sex* (1770–1847), *The Ladies' Monthly Museum* (1789–1847), and *La Belle Assemblee* (1806–1847); these three shared identical content from 1832. Supposedly devoted to the improvement of readers' minds and the encouragement of virtue, they generally included reader-written sentimental poetry and romantic fiction with titles such as "The Fatal Fortnight" or "Secrets of the Confessional," sheet music, needlework patterns, question and answer pages dealing with love and family, etchings of the latest Paris fashions and detailed descriptions of clothing worn by court beauties, and— before about 1825—exchanges on current issues and some national and international news. But even limited treatment of public affairs largely disappeared from such magazines as the increasingly powerful ideal of the devoted wife and mother, untainted by knowledge of the world, led to greater emphasis on the "womanly virtues" of propriety, innocence, and docility. More space was devoted to fashion as clothing became more elaborate; women's magazines became an important source of information on appropriate dress for women of the nouveau riche. The fiction took on a more sober tone, and there was less reader involvement. The intellectual level was generally lower than in women's magazines of the previous century.

Of a somewhat higher caliber was the first long-running women's magazine in America, Sarah Josepha Hale's *Ladies' Magazine and Literary Gazette* (1828–1837). Though known as "the American lady's magazine," it differed significantly from its British counterpart in its more realistic fiction, its absence of fashion features, and a good deal of editorial content advocating improved education and legal status for women. Mrs. Hale went on to edit the enormously popular *Godey's Lady's Book* (1830–1898). Together with its competitors and imitators, *The Ladies' Companion and Literary Expositor* (1834–1844) and *Peterson's Ladies' National Magazine* (1842–1898), *Godey's* exerted strong influence on national tastes in literature, home furnishings, and domestic life. Many outstanding writers of fiction and poetry, including Poe, Hawthorne, Longfellow, and Stowe, were published in the major women's magazines, though these same writers sometimes decried the frivolity and sentimentality of the magazines' usual material. Serious-minded American women could find suitable intellectual fare in *The Ladies' Repository and Gatherings of the West* (1841–1876), one of several magazines out of Cincinnati; associated with the Methodist Episcopal church, the *Repository* reviewed some of the best new literature and offered intelligent, in-depth essays on literary and religious topics.

Social and economic upheavals in mid-century broadened the content of women's magazines on both sides of the Atlantic. The reform-minded editor Camilla Toumlin, for example, described for the upper-class readers of *The New Monthly Belle Assemblee* (1848–1870) the terrible living and working conditions of the seamstresses and shop girls who slaved to produce the fashions glorified in the magazine's own pages. The better American magazines also took up social causes such as temperance and public health but tended to avoid the subject of women's rights and often opposed women's suffrage. It was thus left to smaller feminist publications such as the British *Woman's World* (1866–1869) to challenge the cult of domesticity. The Langham Place feminists published *The Englishwoman's Journal* (1858–1865) to encourage greater employment opportunities for women, but even they found the suffrage issue too controversial to cover. The first wave of American feminism produced magazines such as Amelia Bloomer's *The Lily* (1849) and Mrs. E. A. Aldrich's *The Genius of Liberty* (1852–1854), later published as a regular feature in *Moore's Western Lady's Book*. Lucy Stone's *Woman's Journal* (1870–1917) provided a weekly voice for the suffrage fight. However, the readership for such magazines was relatively small.

In the latter part of the century, a revolution in printing technology and marketing techniques—particularly the acceptance of advertising as a major component of every magazine's content and cash flow—combined with an increase in literacy to encourage the creation of affordable magazines for middle-class women with few or no servants and limited income. Setting the pattern was Samuel Beeton's *The Englishwoman's Domestic Magazine* (1852–1881), a monthly offering guidance on domestic economy, courtship advice, information on hygiene and nursing, and such innovative features as paper dress patterns, as well as the usual mix of fashion and fiction. Of course, the more expensive and sophisticated fashion magazines continued to flourish, such as Beeton's society weekly *The Queen* (1861–   ) or the American *Harper's Bazar* (1867–1913), which combined light, entertaining essays and features with extensive fashion coverage. But the dominant magazines were clearly the many low-cost, practical monthlies for the home-centered woman, a good number of which have survived to the present day. Best known in America are *McCall's Magazine* (1873–   ), *The Ladies' Home Journal* (1883–   ), and *Good Housekeeping* (1885–   ), which provide thorough, scientific information on gardening, cooking, sewing, interior design, and child care to housewives who increasingly viewed themselves as professionals. By 1900, *The Ladies' Home Journal* would have a circulation of over a million subscribers, greater than any other American magazine.

The last two decades of the century saw enormous growth in the magazine industry; in Britain alone, 48 new women's magazines were founded between 1880 and 1900, and the diversity of the new publications reflected the increasing diversity of women's lives. Magazines were designed for women of various age groups, social classes, educational levels, and occupational groups. Particularly interesting to the feminist scholar are those designed for working women, such as the *Woman's Gazette, or news about work* (1875–1880), later titled *Work and Leisure* (1880–1893), which included information on job opportunities as well as fiction and light entertainment. In America, a *Business Woman's Journal,* completely owned and managed by women, was published in the 1890s. But for the most part, the important women's magazines of the nineteenth century focused on concerns seen as appropriate to "woman's sphere" and encouraged the maintenance of this separate sphere. Advertisers found the traditional home-centered woman to be an excellent customer for their clothing, cosmetics, and household products, and so they preferred to patronize publications that would not lead women to question their functions as consumers and caretakers. While the women's magazines did a great deal toward defining household management as a trade requiring skill and intelligence and helped women to develop those skills, they did very little to help and often directly hindered the movement toward opening other trades for women and defining womanhood in less restrictive ways.

Further References. About American Magazines: Helen Woodward, *The Lady Persuaders* (New York, 1960). About British Magazines: Irene Dancyger, *A World of Women: An Illustrated History of Women's Magazines* (Dublin, 1978); Cynthia Leslie White, *Women's Magazines 1693–1968* (London, 1970).

NAOMI JACOBS

MANNERS, NOVEL OF. The novel of manners, which developed in the nineteenth century, portrays with detailed realism the social customs, conventions, traditions, mores, and habits of a given social group at a particular time and place and explores as well as demonstrates the powerful control that these social constructs exert over characters in the novel.

Because it focused attention on the domestic arena and its emotional impact on the fictional characters, the novel of manners naturally attracted women writers. Many of these writers, however, wrote a type of fiction called the novel of sensibility or sentiment, which stressed the intensity of the characters' emotional responses frequently beyond the limits of the rational. Some excellent women writers of novels of manners also wrote novels of sentiment or satires of such novels. It is important to note that the true novel of manners examines objectively the impact of social gestures and constructs on character with strict attention to verisimilitude in an attempt to assist the intellect more than the heart in grasping social and psychological profundities.

Not only was Jane Austen (1775–1817) a novelist of manners, but her novels gave definition to the genre by bringing to culmination the artistic structure (including the perfection of an objective narrative technique infused with irony, wit, and perspicacity) and themes of the mainstream eighteenth-century novel. She wrote her major works in a remarkably short time. Her first novel, *Sense and Sensibility*, appeared in 1811, *Pride and Prejudice* in 1813, *Mansfield Park* in 1814, and *Emma* in 1816. (*Northanger Abbey* and *Persuasion* were published soon after her death but were written much earlier.)

Austen's novels are often criticized for what is seen as a too narrow range of interests. She concentrates on the country life among the upper middle class in southern England near the end of the eighteenth century to the exclusion of interest in even major national and international events. On the other hand, Austen is the subject of almost unbroken praise for the complex portrayal of what she called "the delicacy of mind," captured only by a supreme concentration on looking and listening. Many critics and readers go further to praise Austen's moral concerns, which they feel give her themes the highest significance. She is further praised by feminists for what Ellen Moers in *Literary Women: The Great Writers* (Garden City, N.Y., 1977) calls Austen's "deep concern with the quality of a woman's life in marriage" (107); other critics note her depiction of society's lack of concern for unmarried women.

Among Austen's precursors were Fanny Burney (1732–1840) and Maria Edgeworth (1768–1849). Three of Burney's novels were novels of manners: *Evelina* (1778); *Cecilia* (1796); and *Camilla* (1796). Although all three have many of the characteristics of Austen's major novels, *Cecilia* is least susceptible to being classified as a novel of sentiment. At the same time, in Wilbur L. Cross's *The Development of the English Novel* (London, 1899), *Evelina* is described as "the novel in which we move from the old to the new manners" (94). Cross also remarks, "Before Fanny Burney, the novel of manners had been cultivated almost exclusively by men" (95). Austen paid Burney homage by taking from one of her works the title and theme of *Pride and Prejudice*.

Maria Edgeworth wrote novels of manners that exposed false sentiment and frivolous nonsense in fashionable London society (e.g., *Belinda* [1801]). Edgeworth spent her childhood in England but moved to Ireland, a set of circumstances that allowed her to write fiction contrasting the manners of two societies (*Ennui* [1809] and *The Absentee* [1812]) and thus create the international novel.

Among novelists following Jane Austen was Elizabeth Gaskell (1810–1865), who wrote various kinds of novels, but her subject was always women. Several of her novels, including *Cranford* (1853), *North and South* (1855), and *Sylvia's Lovers* (1857), are aptly called novels of manners. In all her novels, characters struggle to understand their social circumstances and moral obligations, but none struggle more than women within the context of marriage.

Charlotte Smith (1749–1806), Elizabeth Inchbald (1753–1821), Frances Trollope (1780–1863), Susan Ferrier (1782–1854), Catherine Gore (1799–1861), and Harriet Martineau (1802–1876) are other women novelists of the period who worked in the genre.

Later in the nineteenth century, certain works by the realist George Eliot (1819–1880), such as *Middlemarch* (1872) and *Daniel Deronda* (1876), as well as vast parts of *Mill on the Floss* (1860), mark her as an important recorder and analyst of social manners. Harriet Beecher Stowe (1811–1896) wrote short novels about New England that are explorations of the society of the region. Sarah Orne Jewett (1849–1909) wrote almost all short fiction, but it concentrates on the intense and subtle ways society's manners and conventions dominate people. Kate Chopin's *The Awakening* explores the manners of Creole society in the South and its various methods of controlling characters' intentions and actions.

The woman novelist of manners of the twentieth century who is always mentioned because she worked extensively within the genre is Edith Wharton (1863–1937). Wharton's province was upper-class New York Society, and her fiction depicts and contrasts the manners of both the old and new monied families. She also wrote international novels, contrasting American and European manners. Wharton's novels share with other novels of manners a moral concern for the characters as well as for the effects of moral and immoral behavior of the societies involved. Her novels show Western civilization before and then after World War I, and they latterly suggest that the war and the modern world have destroyed tradition and ritual and thus the very kinds of manners that had been the basis for this popular form of fiction. At the very least, perhaps civilization needed to rest and rebuild for a while.

Further References. Marilyn Butler, *Jane Austen and the World of Ideas* (Oxford, 1975). LeRoy W. Smith, *Jane Austen and the Drama of Woman* (New York, 1983). Tony Tanner, *Jane Austen* (Cambridge, Mass., 1986). James W. Tuttleton, *The Novel of Manners in America* (Chapel Hill, N.C., 1972). Merryn Williams, *Women in the English Novel, 1800–1900* (New York, 1984).

GLORIA STEPHENSON

MUSIC BUSINESS (CLASSIC). Traditionally, those who have succeeded in music recognize their field as both an art form and a business. Musicians, composers, and conductors must be their own bosses and manage their own careers at a stage critical to their professional growth: the beginning. Those who lack the initiative to do so rely on talent alone to attract the attention of managers and patrons who will run their affairs, and inevitably the artists lose control. They are less prepared to take advantage of opportunities as they arise, and their instincts with regard to professional growth are untested and underdeveloped.

This entrepreneurial spirit is characteristic of women who have had a significant impact on the music business as we know it today. Most music histories ignore the contribution of women because musicologists focus on the development of style rather than the sociology of music. Women were not leaders in style changes because they were excluded, for the most part, from professional positions. Their music was fostered and appreciated only in domestic circles. Playing was considered one of the social graces and teaching was respectable and appropriate for women who chose to work, but it was also deemed a profession of low status; in 1870, 60 percent of music teachers were women (see Christine Ammer, *Unsung: A History of Women in American Music* [Westport, Conn., 1980]).

After the Nineteenth Amendment granted suffrage to women in 1920, American women became increasingly vocal about their status and contributions as musicians. The country's economic boom during the 1920s made way for a surge in the growth of American music. More concert halls were built, performance seasons were expanded, and orchestras increased in number. Women were still excluded from symphony jobs though, so some 30 women's orchestras were founded to provide a vehicle for artistic expression and growth. Female players and conductors sought recognition and professional status in hopes of creating a "mixed" orchestra. They did not want to make music alone; they wanted to play with their male counterparts. In the early 1920s women constituted the majority of U.S. music students but were barred from the professional mainstream, with the exception of a select few who achieved in opera, solo concert, and choral work. Yet women continued to play a critical role in the management of musical organizations like "Symphonic Ladies." It was these patrons and support groups that assumed responsibility for fund-raising, public relations, and ticket sales, which were critical to the survival of orchestras, opera companies, and other organizations. Women, in essence, defined the role of our first music managers. Then, shortly after the United States entered World War II, the work of these women was formalized with the creation of the American Symphony Orchestra League—a service organization that continues a strong presence today.

Discrimination against women players remained prevalent through World War II. With the Depression, many resorts and restaurants were forced to dispense with their orchestras, and theatre orchestras became obsolete with the introduction of talkies. Women's orchestras continued to emerge, however, in response to the number of fine female players and conductors. In the 1940s many of the women's orchestras disbanded as World War II enabled women players to get jobs in traditional male settings because of a shortage of civilian men.

Women conductors and composers also suffered from a lack of opportunity. In order to be heard, many of them formed their own ensembles and composers groups. For example, in 1926 Margaret Dessoff (1874–1944) was the first woman to conduct a major New York choral concert; she also founded a women's chorus and mixed chorus in New York to provide some consistency for her work and her career. A decade earlier, Mrs. Davenport Engberg was cited by *Etude* as the "only lady conductor of a symphony orchestra in the world" (quoted in

Ammer, 211). She was also the founder of a symphony in Bellingham, Washington.

As managers and especially teachers, women musicians have been more visible—to a point. Orchestras have hired women managers since the late nineteenth century, though as the urban musical organizations grew in influence men assumed the decision-making posts. In 1969, Helen Thompson became the first woman to manage a major orchestra, the New York Philharmonic. Already a leader in her field, she was one of the founders of the American Symphony Orchestra League.

In music education women were allowed to shine, partly because male performers found education beneath them. Women taught privately in the early nineteenth century and taught in the full-scale conservatories when they were being established in mid-century. But once recognized by society at large, these institutions began hiring more men than women. As late as the 1970s, although women students still outnumbered men in conservatories, faculties were predominantly male. Ammer (233) cites the ratio of men to women hired for teaching positions in the 1970s at 4 to 1, while the ratio of those with full professorships was 9 to 1.

Today the struggle of women in music continues toward equality in the workplace. Statistically, the percentage of women in professional jobs is increasing, but the numbers are still disproportionate to the working population. In the decade ending with 1975, female players in 27 U.S. orchestras increased by 36 percent (*Boston Globe*, June 16, 1976). Although more than half of all music students are female and some 45 percent of all American women are in the work force, only 10 to 15 percent are in the top echelons of professional music (Ammer, 223). Furthermore, full-time, male music administrators with comparable responsibilities, education, and years in the field are earning salaries averaging 20 percent higher than their female peers. As in other fields, some women have attempted lawsuits to rectify these inequalities, but discrimination has been very difficult to prove. The assessment or evaluation of one's musical abilities and talent is most often viewed as a subjective matter. In the 1970s, when all major orchestras began conducting blind auditions aided by the use of a screen, the percentage of women hired increased substantially.

The search for recognition of women in music is reflective of a struggle for women's rights in general, and there are indications that the situation is changing. For example, the salary discrepancies between men and women in music administration are decreasing among those entering the field. Of particular note, however, has been the tendency of women to take the initiative to forge their own careers where more traditional opportunities may not have existed. This tendency was true in the 1920s and 1930s with the cultivation of women's orchestras, and it is true today with the prevalence of women's ensembles, festivals, and composers groups. Those women in music who take control of their careers by creating new opportunities will have a better chance of being fulfilled artistically and professionally. Music, as an art form, is reflective of the world in which we live, and its ambassadors—male and female—must always find new ways of being heard and appreciated.

Further References. *Association of College, University and Community Arts Administrators Bulletin* 3, 7 (July/August 1987). Jane Bowers and Judith Tick (eds.), *Women Making Music: The Western Art Tradition 1150–1950* (Urbana, Ill., 1986).

ROBIN WHEELER

MUSICIANS (PRE–TWENTIETH-CENTURY). Although Sophie Drinker's conjectures that the art of music may have begun in the singing of magic by women and that women were the first musicians cannot be substantiated, cave paintings illustrate prehistoric women musicians. Among the oldest records of organized and systematized music, Sumerian texts from the third millennium B.C. speak of several classes of ecclesiastical singers and players, both male and female. Sumerian art also depicted female singers, and in certain royal tombs both male and female musicians were buried with their master.

From ancient Egypt we have pictures of women dancing, singing, and taking part in religious services as priestesses. A 5th-Dynasty (2563–2423 B.C.) tomb at Saqqarah depicts Iti, a prominent woman singer, accompanied by Hekenu, the first woman harpist to be known by name. Members of sacred women's choirs were led by a highly placed person such as the wife of the high priest, and at the beginning of the 18th Dynasty (1575–1352 B.C.) Queen Ahmes-Nefretere was leader of the singers of Amen, the protecting god of Thebes. Sacred female musicians are frequently depicted singing, hand clapping, and playing the sistrum, the instrument of sacerdotal potency. During the 18th Dynasty female musicians were brought in large numbers from Semitic lands and placed in harems at court and in the palaces of the nobility.

In ancient Greece women took part in religious rites as priestesses and members of religious societies, dancing and singing hymns. They also ritually lamented the death of a family member (or sometimes female musicians were hired for this responsibility), a tradition still maintained in parts of Greece today. Out of the rich musical life of Greece came a number of female poet-musicians, most famous of whom is Sappho of Lesbos (b. c.612 B.C.). Little but legend is preserved of her life, yet she is credited with being the first to use the pectis, a plucked string instrument, and with inventing the Mixolydian mode and Sapphic stanza. Later women known for music making were the hetaerae, courtesans who by the fourth century B.C. were devoting themselves to philosophy, literature, and the arts, including the playing of musical instruments and dancing. Manumission records from fourth-century Athens give the occupations of three freedwomen as harpist and aulos players.

In pre-Islamic Arabia, music was practiced mainly by women, especially by singing girls (*gaināt*) attached to upper-class households or employed at places of entertainment. With the rise of Islam, the male musician came to the fore, yet Jamila (d. c.720), a famous singer who gained her freedom, led her orchestra of 50 singing women with lutes on pilgrimage to Mecca in splendid litters, one of the great musical events of the Umayyad period (A.D. 661–750). During the following Abbasid period (A.D. 750–1258), the caliph, princes, and wealthy Arabs in Baghdad maintained harems of highly skilled women slaves (*al-Jawari*) who sang and played instruments such as the ud (lute).

In some places, the harem musician had a religious counterpart. In India, from around the third century A.D., *devadasis* (maidservants of God) were trained in music and dance and dedicated to Hindu temples. With the destruction of the great temples by Muslim invaders, the institution of *devadasis* began to decline in north India. But in south India, it flourished into the nineteenth century and was outlawed only in 1947.

In ancient China the aristocracy kept scores, even hundreds, of private "sing-song" girls, who danced, sang, and played musical instruments. During the Tang Dynasty (A.D. 618–907), sing-song girls conversant with arts and letters moved among poets, artists, scholars, and officials, entertaining them in the capacity of hostesses. Paintings from both the Tang and Song (A.D. 960–1279) dynasties depict entire female orchestras. Under Emperor Ming Huang (713–756), an institution for the performance of music and dance by female court musicians, the *chiao-fang,* was established; during this period, it had more than 3,000 female musicians. As late as 1900, sing-song girls still performed in places of public entertainment, but soon after that their activities were restricted. As with the *devadasis* in India, their status declined considerably; toward the end they were classed with prostitutes of the lower ranks. In Korea, the *kisaeng,* professional female entertainers active at court over many centuries, formed a counterpart to the Chinese sing-song girl, as did the *geisha* in Japan.

In the West after ancient times there was virtually no comparable development of female musical ensembles or courtesan musicians. Still, during the early centuries of the Christian church, women were active in sacred music and in singing at divine worship. But as the church grew, so did opposition to women's participation; the performance of church music increasingly became the province of trained male singers and priests. For more than a millennium, women were excluded from music making in the church. In convents, however, women sang, and the first extant works by a woman composer are liturgical compositions and a few other works by the ninth-century Byzantine nun Kassia; the second, the liturgical plainsong compositions and a liturgical morality play by the twelfth-century abbess Hildegard of Bingen. While women of other classes occasionally made their living as itinerant performers and household musicians, aristocratic women frequently sang and played for their own pleasure. A handful of them (the *trobairitz* [see TROUBADOUR LITERATURE]) and female *trouvères*) also wrote and set courtly poems to music. For the Middle Ages as a whole, nevertheless, women were excluded from advanced musical training and musical positions of high status.

During most of the Renaissance, a similar situation obtained. Women of the classes from which most male musicians emerged, unless born into musical families, had virtually no chance of acquiring a thorough music education.

Likewise, the principal music professions were closed to them. Nevertheless, a few women, primarily singers, made their living in low-status jobs, and girls born into noble or wealthy families were frequently provided with private music teachers and as adults continued to perform within their private social circles.

Toward the end of the sixteenth century the participation of women in professional singing began to increase radically as the result of the establishment of small ensembles of women musicians at northern Italian courts. During the next century, the rapid growth of opera and musical establishments in upper-class households provided work for a substantial number of women singers, some of whom reached the very apex of the profession. During the same period, women composers began to emerge from obscurity. The first published compositions by a woman—madrigals of Madalena Casulana—appeared in Venice in 1566, and throughout the rest of that century and the next, numerous other works by Italian women followed. The emergence of women composers at this time seems closely linked to four principal factors: (1) the development of careers for women singers; (2) the increased cultivation of polyphonic music in convents; (3) the growth of private music instruction; and (4) the growth of music printing. Some women, such as Francesca Caccini, Barbara Strozzi, and Isabella Leonarda, composed seriously over a long period of time. Still, women did not benefit from many of the advances in music making during this period, and their achievements in composition remained considerably slighter than those of men.

The burgeoning of public and private concerts in the late seventeenth and eighteenth centuries brought about the next significant increase of professional women musicians. This took place first in Paris where, at the Concert Spirituel (est. 1725), before the century was out women sang and performed on the harpsichord, organ, fortepiano, flute, violin, harp, and horn, sometimes playing their own compositions. As increasing numbers of aristocrats and bourgeoisie took up singing and playing, Frenchwomen also moved into private music teaching and, as demand for printed music increased, into music engraving and publishing. But they did not benefit from many of the routine employment opportunities open to men; for example, they were not hired to play in the orchestras that accompanied soloists at public concerts, even though these soloists be women.

Elsewhere during the eighteenth century, women joined the expanding ranks of touring virtuosos. Some, late in the century, were occasionally appointed church organists; finally, the barriers to women's performing in church were beginning to break down, although it would be some time before mixed choirs became common. As women entered music professions in increasing numbers, more began to emerge as composers. In France this trend was under way by 1700; in countries such as England, Germany, and Austria, it began primarily after 1750. It was principally the smaller instrumental genres and solo songs—mainly intended for domestic consumption by amateur musicians, many of whom were also women—that women cultivated, few symphonies or concertos coming from their pens. The exceptional Elisabeth-Claude Jacquet de la Guerre, however, composed over a wide range of genres and styles and was the first woman to compose a complete opera (1694).

During the nineteenth century, a crucial change was the establishment of public music conservatories, a number of which were open to women. As women increasingly gained advanced instruction in music, composers set their sights higher than domestic music. In France, for example, Louise Bertin, Louise Farrenc, and Augusta Holmès tackled some of the largest genres of their day— grand opera, symphonies, symphonic poems, and dramatic odes. In the last decade of the century, Amy Beach in the United States and Ethel Smyth in England began to astonish audiences and critics with powerful orchestral and choral works, which in no sense exhibited the limitations normally associated with women's work.

Women made great strides as performers as well. Although singing, both in opera and on the concert stage, remained the major outlet, more women became prominent instrumental virtuosos, first as pianists and later as performers on other instruments, such as violin. Some reached the very peak of their profession—among them, Clara Schumann, indisputably one of the greatest pianists of the century. Women also began to be appointed as teachers, like Farrenc and Schumann, at major conservatories of music and even, like Caroline B. Nichols, entered the conducting field. But while opportunities for professional musical employment increased, they did not keep pace with the new kinds of training women were receiving as musicians. One response to the sense of frustration women felt under these circumstances was to form women's orchestras and chamber music groups. But, women did not achieve their goal of joining established groups of male musicians until after the beginning of the twentieth century.

Women's advances also brought about a sort of backlash. Ideas about musical creativity solidified into a rock of masculine prerogative. Music was a "masculine idea," and music criticism of women's works used gender for leverage: "One will scarcely encounter a bold turn or startling episode with this woman, and should she nevertheless once fall into a distant modulation, so genuinely female, she ponders immediately how she can most quickly find her way home again" (Eduard Hanslick on Luise Adolpha Le Beau).

By 1900, while the idea of music as an "accomplishment" for women still lingered on in part, it was no longer the principal manner in which women could choose to relate to music. This change was signaled in 1904 by James Huneker, an American critic, who wrote:

Passed away is the girl who played the piano in the stiff Victorian drawing rooms of our mother. . . . The new girl is too busy to play the piano unless she has the gift; then she plays with consuming earnestness. We listen to her, for we know that this is an age of specialization, an age when woman is coming into her own, be it nursing, electoral suffrage, or the writing of plays; so our poets no longer make sonnets to our Ladies of Ivories, nor are budding girls chained to the keyboard.

Further References. Jane Bowers and Judith Tick (eds.), *Women Making Music: The Western Art Tradition, 1150–1950* (Urbana, Ill., 1986). Aaron I. Cohen, *International*

Encyclopedia of Women Composers (New York, 1981). Sophie Drinker, *Music and Women: The Story of Women in Their Relation to Music* (1948; rep. ed., Washington, D.C., 1977); should be used with caution.

JANE BOWERS

MUSICIANS (TWENTIETH-CENTURY). See COMPOSERS; CONCERT ARTISTS; CONDUCTORS; MUSIC BUSINESS (CLASSIC)

MYTH, REVISION OF. The publication of two critical texts has signaled a new focus on mythology as a source of feminist energy: Charlene Spretnak, *Lost Goddesses of Early Greece: A Collection of Pre-Hellenic Myths* (Berkeley, 1978) and Diane Wolkstein and Samuel Noah Kramer (eds.), *Inanna, Queen of Heaven and Earth* (New York, 1983). The Spretnak text brings together, in clear and straightforward versions, images of the Greek goddesses that long anticipate the patriarchal distortions firmly entrenched by Hellenic times and perpetuated through much of British and American literature and classics study. Wolkstein and Kramer's text brings to nonspecialists the first full translation and interpretation of the cycle of stories and hymns devoted to the Sumerian goddess Inanna, whose tarnished image previously came to us in the forms of Ishtar and Aphrodite, goddesses of war and of love. Current feminist theory, especially that of Marilyn French and Gerda Lerner, asserts that a key series of events in the transformation of culture from matrifocal to patriarchal must have been the shift from worship of powerful goddesses to dominant male gods.

Much feminist thought and research are now devoted to study of the cultural transformation, rather than solely to the recovered images, of the ancient goddesses. In 1985, Heide Gottner-Abendroth acknowledged the early research and reconstruction of goddesses by such scholars as J. J. Bachoven and Robert Graves, while going on to chart the regular and predictable transformation of goddess worship into god worship; her article, "Thou Gaia Art I: Matriarchal Mythology in Former Times and Today" (*Trivia, A Journal of Ideas* 7 [Summer 1985]), not only serves as an expression of what is now known about the transformation of worship but identifies as well a new interest in the rediscovery of goddess worship for contemporary feminists. A consistent pattern has been identified by many scholars. It consists of worship of a female principle of creation, followed by a battle for control between male and female creation principles, and succeeded by joint rule or male dominance. The creation mythology of many cultures has been demonstrated to follow such a pattern, testifying to invasions by successful, usually warlike, patriarchal cultures such as the early Greek.

The revision of mythology owes much to the integration of several disciplines, including art history, political theory, and classics. So urgent does reconsideration of myth appear to contemporary feminists eager to make sense of their current status within a patriarchal culture that specialists within disciplines have taken risks to study the new information about early goddess worship across disciplines. The importance of myth in the development of culture has long been clear. However, the proliferation of studies within the past ten years, including the reissuing of Philip E. Slater's much disputed *The Glory of Hera: Greek Mythology and the Greek Family* (Boston, 1968), demonstrates the growing awareness that proper understanding of myth is a precondition for full awareness of the sources for gender images over time and for contemporary religious practices.

Mesopotamia, long identified as the cradle of Judeo-Christian civilization, and Hellenic Greece, regularly claimed as the source of Anglo-American political structure, are of crucial importance in the current attempts to uncover and rein-terpret long-suppressed information about goddesses and goddess worship. Dis-agreement among scholars persists about the meaning of the prevalence of powerful goddesses such as Inanna and Hera; some scholars believe that religious myth and imagery attest to female power in the social and political world, while others insist on a distinction between myth and history. As scholars, especially feminists, uncover more information about the earliest goddesses, classical texts long understood in patriarchal context take on new meaning. Goddesses such as Athena and Artemis, important throughout classical literature, acquire new forms of identity and power, new archetypal implications, when studied in the light of recent feminist inquiry. It seems certain that such disciplines as psychology and literary criticism must be affected by the current determination to investigate and uncover the earliest forms of myth as well as the meaning of the supplanting of goddess worship by the worship of male gods.

Further References. Marilyn French, *Beyond Power: On Women, Men, and Morals* (New York, 1985). Gerda Lerner, *The Creation of Patriarchy* (New York, 1986). Barbara G. Walker, *Woman's Encyclopedia of Myths and Secrets* (San Francisco, 1983).

RUTH NADELHAFT

MYTHOLOGY. Both the study of sacred symbols, narratives, and rites, and their dynamic expression in human psyches and societies and also the collective term for myths from a specific group or about a certain entity. As generally understood and undertaken, mythology is based primarily on extant documents, field data, and interpretations by male scribes, scholars, artists, and "informants" and thus concerns men's myths and rituals. Far more is known about women *in* mythology, about the female figures who people male narratives, enactments, philosophies, theologies, and analyses, than about women *and* mythology or women's mythologies—the stories they recount among themselves and in the company of children, the rituals they perform, and the elaboration, exegesis, and evaluation of their own and men's profoundly moving and significant sym-bolic expressions.

Creation myths, particularly cosmogonic accounts, are accorded high status by mythologists. Female creator deities are rare. In ordinary, contemporary English usage the verb *to create* means *creatio ex nihilo* (creation from nothing) by thought, dream, spirit, laughter, or speech, or the crafting of the world and its inhabitants by an artisan or architect. "To create," then, is not the same as "to give birth to" or "to mother," so (symbolic or spiritual) creation is not equivalent to (natural or biological) procreation. Thus, emergence myths that tell how in the beginning people, animals, plants, and so on ascend through and emerge from the womb or wombs of the earth mother are seldom considered as significant as myths telling of creation by the word and by a *deus faber* or craftsman god, for example, in Genesis 1 and 2. Most such deities are portrayed as male or bisexual/androgynous, in which case the male aspect tends to predominate linguistically and/or mythologically. Whether worship of goddesses or gods is prior and primary historically or developmentally continues to be debated. In any case, worship of strong goddesses does not necessarily mean women enjoy social power.

Culture heroes bring or bring about valuable objects, teachings, and natural changes that make possible human survival and society. Fire, weather, agriculture, hunting techniques, rituals, and the healing arts are important among such benefactions. The feminine forms of *culture hero* and *creator, culture heroine* and *creatrix,* are awkward, marked terms, reflecting the relatively weaker roles women play in creation, transformation, and origin myths—when they appear at all in such accounts of ordering the world. Despite their natural procreative ability, goddesses, human women, and female animals are much more likely to be depicted in myth as destructive or static monsters than as creative benefactors.

In the beginning is also the end, that is, the *telos* or destiny. Origin myths—whether of the cosmos, humans, animals, plants, or customs—are used to validate and charter contemporary social and natural order, a theory attributed to British anthropologist Bronislaw Malinowski. Women's position in society is thought to derive from how they originated and their behavior in mythic times, as in the well-known Western myths of Lilith, Eve, and Pandora. According to this view, myths of matriarchy and Amazons would be used to justify present patriarchy by portraying women as losers in the crucial mythic power struggles and thus as unfit for present social status. Viewed from a feminist perspective, such myths present compelling, imaginative explorations of alternate lifeways.

Rites of passage, especially those associated with birth, puberty, marriage, death, and initiation into mysteries, are important in mythology. The lunar (and in women, menstrual) cycle serves as a ready measure for months and human lives and is almost paradigmatic for a woman's life, even though she may menstruate for only part of that time. The related measures of moons, months, and menses have more usually been viewed as dark and dangerous to the diurnal solar, which is generally equated with the masculine, than as sources of fructifying power for either women or men. On the whole, in Western tradition the lunar has come to be associated with the feminine and the unconscious, the solar with the masculine and the conscious and thus the more valuable domains.

Death is a passage requiring gnosis, or spiritual knowledge, and heroism. Death is sometimes depicted as a female figure like Ereshkigal, Sumerian goddess of the underworld, or Doña Sebastiana, the skeletal *memento mori* in Hispanic

New Mexican folk tradition. Although the central experience of Demeter's Eleusinian Mysteries has remained secret, like many other mysteries, it apparently involved revelations about dying and the afterlife.

Heroic journeys often entail a confrontation with death. Western notions of heroism are basically masculine, influenced by the Homeric epics and feudal ideas of kingship and military prowess. In his influential *The Hero with a Thousand Faces* (New York, 1949, 1968), Joseph Campbell almost exclusively uses male exemplars of the "monomyth" (departure, initiation, and return) of "the adventure of the hero," a "man or woman who has been able to battle past his [*sic*] personal and historical limitations to the generally valid, normally human forms." These normative biographical patterns usually say little about women's life stories, and in collections and analyses of myths women more often appear as passive and auxiliary like Odysseus's wife Penelope than as agents of their own and others' destiny like Psyche.

Much of the difficulty in discussing women and mythology comes from the differential evaluation of *mythos*, derived from Greek words relating to the mouth, speech, and oral story-telling, and *mundus*, this world, the mundane. Mythology as presently defined deals with time beyond time, the otherworldly, the extraordinary, but not with the present, flux, the everyday, the commonplace and ordinary. *Mundus* has been devalued, and *mythos* exalted as the cherished expression and object of study.

In many societies, women have been silenced altogether, or their speech, especially that dismissed as mere gossip (see GOSSIP) or old wives' tales, (see OLD WIVES' TALES) has been disregarded. When more is known of women's speech, narration, song, and ceremony with one another, it may be that gossip in its best sense will be seen as the mundane equivalent of supernatural myth narration. Mythology as heretofore defined and studied—as a public, collective, male-dominated means of communication pertaining to cyclic time and metaphysical, numinous being—will then be seen as but one aspect of all powerful human expressions of inter- and intrapersonal realities.

Further References. Barbara G. Walker, *The Woman's Encyclopedia of Myths and Secrets* (San Francisco, 1983). Marta Weigle, *Spiders & Spinsters: Women and Mythology* (Albuquerque, 1982).

MARTA WEIGLE

N

NATIVE AMERICAN WRITERS, after the establishment of reservations in 1851, attended reservation schools where they learned English as one of their first written languages (most Native languages were not written). Many were sent to schools off the reservation such as the one founded in Carlisle, Pennsylvania, in 1879. Even before the turn of the century, a number of Native women were highly educated, and some had college degrees. These writers took elements of the oral storytelling tradition that had always been an integral part of their culture and incorporated them in the genres of novels, short stories, essays, and poetry. In the traditional cultures, the stories both preserved values of the culture, ensuring solidarity, and also entertained. In most tribes, the art of storytelling was practiced by both men and women, and in some, particularly in the Southwest, the grandmother carried on the storytelling tradition. Native writers extended such elements into their writings as the sacredness of language, attention to place and landscape, and concern for tribal welfare as opposed to concern for the individual. Storytelling is a participatory event, and a good storyteller draws the story from the audience. A novel by a Native American writer is not so much fiction as witnessing significant events through time.

Sophia Alice Callahan, a highly educated Creek, is thought to be the first Native woman to write a novel. *Wynema* (1891) was intended by the author "to open the eyes and heart of the world to our afflictions, and thus speedily issue into existence an era of good feeling and just dealing toward us." Although *Wynema* has a romantic plot, the novel is quite political, criticizing the slaughter of women and children at Wounded Knee, and even has a passage supporting suffrage.

Other Native women wrote articles, stories, and poetry for the many Native journals and newspapers of the time period. For example, at age 20, Ora V. Eddleman Reed, a Cherokee, was the editor and a contributor to *Twin Territories: the Indian Magazine* (Washington, D.C.) beginning in 1916. Zitkala-Sa also wrote a collection of stories for children, *Old Indian Legends* (1901), and in 1921 published *American Indian Stories*, which are mostly autobiographical.

Sarah Winnemucca Hopkins, a Piute, wrote one of the first personal narratives by a Native American woman, *Life Among the Piutes* (1883). Like other writers of the time, she hoped to generate sympathy among her readers for the conditions in which her people lived. Other narratives of Native women such as the 1936 *Autobiography of a Papago Woman* by Ruth Underhill were told to and recorded by anthopologists in response to questions. A more recent example is the 1981 *Mountain Wolf Woman* by Ojibway storyteller Ignatia Broker, who relates the story of one of the grandmothers of her parents.

Emily Pauline Johnson, Mohawk, was a prolific writer of short fiction, essays, and poetry at the turn of the century. Some of her works include *Canadian Born* (1903), *Flint and Feather* (1914; poetry), *Legends of Vancouver* (1911), and *The Moccasin Maker* (1913).

Another important writer, Humishuma (Mourning Dove), an Okanogan, used her tribal traditions to create a novel examining the contemporary problem of being a mixed-breed person. To make up for her lack of education, she collaborated with Lucullus V. McWhorter, a student of Indian history and lore, in writing *Cogeweam, The Half Blood* in 1927.

In recent years, critics have noted that Native American literature has had a renaissance. As part of this revival, Native women have created an entire body of literature—novels, poetry, short stories, and the attendant critical essays. Leslie Marmon Silko, Laguna Pueblo, has volumes of poetry, and her *Storyteller* (1981) is a collection of poetry, family history, and stories. In her widely acclaimed novel *Ceremony* (1977), Silko has woven the traditional mythology of the Laguna into a modern story that shows how the values of the past can be pertinent to the present. Silko's novel has more than a little suggestion of the healing power of words, coming from the Native tradition of the sacredness of words.

Paula Gunn Allen, Laguna Pueblo/Sioux, has written one of the first novels since *Cogewea* to have a Native woman as its central character. Her *The Woman Who Owned the Shadows* (1983), which explores the role of a Native woman in contemporary culture and the influence of the past, has a lesbian-feminist theme. In addition to being a prolific writer of poetry (see for instance, *Shadow Country* [1982]) and fiction, Allen is also a noted scholar and critic. Her *Studies in American Indian Literature* (1983) and *The Sacred Hoop* (1986) are invaluable for the feminist scholar. In her work, Allen points out the inherent feminism in many Native cultures.

The resurgence of Native writers includes many other excellent women writers. Louise Erdrich, Turtle Mountain Chippewa, has received national recognition for her poetry, *Jacklight* (1984), and her novels, *Love Medicine* (1984) and *The Beet Queen* (1986). Linda Hogan, Chickasaw, writes short stories and has numerous volumes of poetry including *Eclipse* (1983), *Daughters I Love You* (1981), and *Calling Myself Home* (1979). Janet Campbell Hale, Sioux, has a volume of poetry, *Custer Lives in Humbolt County* (1978); a youth novel, *The Owl's Song* (1974); and another novel, *The Jailing of Cecilia Capture* (1985). Maria Campbell, Metis, writes of her personal experience of the pain of growing up a mixed breed in *Halfbreed* (1973). Anna Lee Walters, Pawnee/Otoe, has a collection of short stories, *The Sun Is Not Merciful* (1985). Shirley Hill Witt, Akwesansne Mohawk, writes of the intersection of Native culture and Hispanic culture in her stories and poems anthologized in Rayna Green's *That's What She Said: Contemporary Poetry and Fiction by Native American Women* (1984). This volume by Green, who is a Cherokee poet, scholar, and editor, is one of the best collections to date of Native women writers and contains a good bibliography.

Beth Brant, Mohawk, edited the ground-breaking collection of fiction, poetry, and narratives, including work of Native lesbians, *A Gathering of Spirit* (1984), and has a book of personal narrative and poetry, *Mohawk Trail* (1985). Writing of Native lesbians is also anthologized in *This Bridge Called My Back* (1981), edited by Cherrie Moraga and Gloria Anzaldua.

Poetry seems to be the dominant genre for a number of Native writers. Joy Harjo, Creek, is the author of *She Had Some Horses* (1982) and *What Moon Drove Me to This* (1978). Wendy Rose, Hopi/Miwok, has written *Academic Squaw* (1977) and *What Happened When That Hopi Hit New York* (1983), among others. Other poets of note and their works are Mary Tall Mountain, Athabaskan, *There Is No Word for Goodbye* (1982); Roberta Hill Whiteman, Oneida, *Star Quilt* (1984); Anita Endrizze-Danielson, Yaqui, *Claiming Lives* (1983); Diane Burns, Anishinabe/Chemehuevi, *Riding the One-Eyed Ford* (1981); and Elizabeth Cook-Lynn, Sioux, *Then the Badger Said This* (1977) and *Seek the House of Relatives* (1984). Carol Lee Sanchez, Laguna Pueblo/Sioux, has several books of poetry, among them *Coyote's Journal* (1981), *Message Bringer Woman* (1977), and *Morning Prayer* (1977).

Further Reference. Rayna Green, *Native American Women: A Contexual Bibliography* (Bloomington, Ind., 1983).

ANNETTE VAN DYKE

NETHERLANDISH ARTISTS (1600–1800). Nearly 250 women artists, amateur and professional, were recorded in the Low Countries (present-day Holland and Belgium) between the midsixteenth and the late eighteenth century. A small number were well known in their native Holland or Flanders, although they never enjoyed international distinction. These artists include such figures as genre/portrait painter Judith Leyster and watercolorist Margaretha de Heer. An even smaller group, including still-life specialists Maria van Oosterwyck and Rachel Ruysch, won international artistic recognition. Their accomplishments were discussed in the major biographies of Netherlandish painters by Arnold Houbraken (*De Groote Schouburgh der Nederlantsche Konstschilders en Schilderessen,* 3 vols. [1718, 1719, 1721; facsimile ed., Amsterdam, 1976]) and Johan van Gool (*De Nieuwe Schouburgh der Nederlantsche Kunstschilders en Schild-*

eressen, 2 vols. [1750–1751; facsimile ed., Soest, 1971]), and their work attracted the patronage of European nobility.

Unlike Italy, France, and Spain, where artwork was almost exclusively made-to-order for the very wealthy, in seventeenth-century Holland, art became a portable commodity affordable to the middle class. This development encouraged a diversity of subjects and techniques, and consequently Dutch painters were the first Europeans to develop fully the genres of still life, seascape, townscape, landscape, and scenes from everyday life.

Women artists, however, tended to avoid certain subjects. Unable to study anatomy from the nude, most could not acquire enough proficiency to compose groups of human figures in action, as was necessary for painting successful historical or religious subjects. Seascapes or town views were seldom popular subjects, perhaps because women needed chaperones to study them. With the exception of wax modeling and silhouette cutting, few women produced much sculpture.

Beginning in the late seventeenth century many women took up printmaking. Most made reproductive prints of works by old masters and by their male relatives. Geertruyt Roghman (d. after 1658), however, made original engravings depicting women's chores and occupations—a subject characteristic of contemporary women's genre painting as well. A few artists, such as Antonyna Houbraken (1686–1736; daughter of the famous artistic biographer), Rachel Ruysch, Michaelina Wautieres, and Henriette Wolters had their works engraved by men.

Although there were exceptions, the majority of Netherlandish women painters practiced still life and/or portraiture. For women artists of the north, the portrait tradition seems to have peaked not in the Golden Age of painting, but in the century preceding it with Levina Teerlinc (Bruges, c.1520–1576) and Caterina van Hemessen (1528–after 1587, Antwerp).

According to Houbraken, Anna Françoise de Bruyns (1605–after 1629) of Brussels was the best woman painter of her time. Her uncle and teacher, Jacques Francquart, presented her to the Infanta Isabella of Spain, for whom she painted religious scenes. Although she is recorded to have produced 245 portraits, de Bruyns's work is known only by engravings made after her paintings.

The few known portraits by Michaelina Wautiers (b. Mons, before 1627); Gertrude van Veen of Antwerp (1602–1643), daughter of Rubens's teacher, Otton van Veen; Catherina Pepijn of Antwerp (1619–1688), daughter of Rubens's rival, Martin Pepijn; Aleijda Wolfsen of Zwolle (1648–after 1690); and Margareta van Huyssen (fl.1688–1706) show a high degree of competence. On the basis of such a small number of works, however, it is difficult to determine the precise nature of each painter's achievements.

Judith Leyster (1609–1660), one of the outstanding artists of her time, created portraits and genre scenes that sparkle with the spirited brushwork characteristic of the work of fellow Haarlemmer Frans Hals. Her subject matter, however, adopts a woman's viewpoint. She excelled in renderings of children with their pets and musical instruments, and perhaps her most notable painting, *The Prop-*

osition (1631; Mauritshuis, The Hague), is a sympathetic portrayal of a harassed woman repulsing the advances of a drunk. The psychological poignancy of this work is enhanced by the sophisticated color harmonies and the use of the candlelight to reveal the woman's expression of annoyance. Leyster was elected member of the Haarlem painters' guild in 1633 and married the genre painter Jan Miense Molenaer in 1636. Her productivity declined after her marriage.

Henrietta Wolters (1692–1741) of Amsterdam, daughter of painter Theodor van Pee, was an extremely popular portrait miniaturist. Despite exceptional offers from Peter the Great and the king of Prussia to work at St. Petersburg and Berlin, Wolters chose to remain in her birthplace.

While only a few excelled in portraiture, Netherlandish women produced many of the most spectacular examples of still life in all of Europe. They generally preferred fruit, flower, and banquet pieces. At the beginning of the eighteenth century, when the flower piece reached the height of its popularity, flower painters of both sexes were paid astronomical sums for their richly detailed bouquets.

Clara Peeters (Antwerp, 1594–n.d.) was a major innovator of still-life painting in the north. We know nothing of her training, but the technical virtuosity of her early work (1608–1612) makes it most unlikely that she was self-taught. Her paintings belong to two categories of still life that were virtually undeveloped at the time she began to paint—"banquet pieces" and "breakfast pieces." Her early works are of the banquet type and include a great variety of expensive objects: Venetian glasses, rare shells, artichokes, knives with ornate handles, and vases of flowers. After about 1620, Peeters painted in a much plainer style, employing the monochromatic schemes then favored by Haarlem painters Pieter Claesz and Willem Claesz Heda. These later works depict simple meals featuring stacks of cheese, pretzels, and stoneware jugs. Four of her magnificent banquet pieces are in the Prado Museum, Madrid.

Maria van Oosterwyck (1630–1693), a painter of floral still lifes and vanity pieces, was born in Nootdorp near Delft, six years before Delft painter Johannes Vermeer. She studied still-life painting with Jan Davidsz de Heem, who brought about an exchange of still-life trends between the northern and southern Netherlands in the midseventeenth century. Van Oosterwyck's paintings possess the sumptuousness of De Heem's work plus a sharp, almost porcelain finish characteristic of the work of Delft-born flower painter Willem van Aelst, with whom she may also have studied. Houbraken reported that Van Aelst courted her, but this report cannot be verified; it is known that she never married. She was an extremely devout woman. She used some of her money to buy freedom for Dutch sailors captured by Barbary pirates and enslaved in Algiers.

The royalty of several countries, including Louis XIV of France, William and Mary of England, Emperor Leopold I, and the king of Poland, paid high prices for Van Oosterwyck's paintings.

Rachel Ruysch (1664–1750), whose exquisite fruit and flower extravaganzas sold for more than Rembrandt's work, served as court painter to the elector palatine in Düsseldorf from 1708 to 1716. Her fame spread to Italy when the elector sent two of her pendant still lifes to the grand duke of Tuscany. In 1723, Ruysch, her husband, and their son Georgio split a lottery jackpot of 60,000 guilders—equivalent to about a million dollars today. She continued to paint until the age of 83, two years before her death.

Ruysch's floral compositions possess a graceful, sweeping S-curve; a knot of brightly illuminated roses at the heart of the design; a plethora of butterflies, inchworms, and beetles among the flowers; and a snail on the ledge. Her bouquets frequently include exotic horticultural specimens that she would have seen in Amsterdam's botanical garden, where her father was supervisor for 46 years.

Maria Sibylla Merian (1647–1717) was born in Frankfurt-am-Main. When she was a very young girl, her father, Matthaeus Merian, produced magnificent engravings for one of the earliest catalogues of different flower species. Perhaps it was this early experience that sparked Maria Merian's interest in recording the natural world. After her father died in 1650, she took her first lessons in flower painting with her stepfather, Jacob Marrel, and subsequently with one of his most talented students, Abraham Mignon. Although Merian painted a few competent flower pieces, her work as a naturalist and scientific illustrator is her most distinguished contribution. She studied entomological, zoological, and botanical species in Europe and the Dutch South American province of Surinam and published the results of her research in magnificently illustrated books. Her three-volume work, *Der Raupen wunderbare Verwandlung und sonderbare Blumennahrung* (The Wonderful Transformation of Caterpillars and [Their] Singular Plant Nourishment) (1679, 1683, 1717), presented her revolutionary discovery that caterpillars and adult butterflies were the same species of insect at different stages of development. Previously, the life cycles of insects were so mysterious that people believed the creatures to have sprung fully formed from dirt and mud. Merian died in Amsterdam.

A number of women, including several with enormous reputations in their lifetimes, experimented with a variety of pursuits. They achieved notice not simply through the excellence of their work, but through its range and variety.

Johanna Koerten was a multitalented artist from Amsterdam (1650–1715), contemporary with Rachel Ruysch. She not only painted and drew but also was a silhouette cutter, embroiderer, etcher on glass, and wax modeler. She gained wide international fame and many honors, particularly for her silhouettes. Peter the Great, the queen of England, the empress of Germany, and other royalty paid high prices for the landscapes, seascapes, animals, flowers, religious subjects, and portraits she cut from white paper and mounted on black. Unfortunately few of her works are known today.

Anna Maria von Schurman (b. Cologne, 1607; d.1678, near Leeuwarden, Friesland) was perhaps the greatest Renaissance woman living in the Low Countries during the Golden Age. Her artistic pursuits included oil painting, wood and ivory carving, wax modeling, silhouette and paper cutting, and engraving and etching on copper and glass. Patronized by Queen Christiana of Sweden, Von Schurman was the first artist in Holland to work in pastel. Von Schurman was also a musician, celebrated linguist, scholar, and poet, and she agitated for improved educational opportunities for women; she never married.

Elisabeth Ryberg (Rotterdam, fl.1710) was a cut paper artist whose exquisite flowers, landscapes, architectural subjects, and seascapes attracted the attention of Johann Wilhelm of Düsseldorf, Rachel Ruysch's great patron. He bought a number of Ryberg's cut paper pieces for his enormous art gallery, which included paintings by Rembrandt and Rubens.

Before 1800, most women artists were born into artistic families and learned their craft from male masters who were relatives, usually fathers or brothers. Unfortunately, the work of these well-trained women has often been credited to their teachers or to the most famous men of the familial artistic dynasty because of the work's general stylistic similarity.

The problem of misattribution of works affected even the most celebrated women artists. Until recently, Leyster's genre scenes were credited to Frans Hals. In 1723, one year after her election to the French Royal Academy of Art, flower painter Margaretha Haverman (1693–after 1750) was expelled; the academicians (all men) ruled that her *morceau de réception* was the work of her teacher, Jan van Huysum. Contemporary scholars agree, however, that the painting was from her hand.

It was common for women artists to marry artists. Most married women from the Netherlands signed their work with their maiden names—a bride was not required to forfeit her maiden name and assume her husband's. Although pastel portraitist Anna Charlotte van der Haer (1748–1802) and Judith Leyster produced little art after their marriages, many other Netherlandish women were able to sustain a steady artistic production throughout their lives. One extraordinary case is that of Rachel Ruysch. Ruysch painted for some 65 years and bore ten children to her husband, portraitist Juriaen Pool II, who in mid-life apparently gave up his painting career to support and promote his wife's much more brilliant one. Ruysch painted her finest pictures during her childbearing years.

By the beginning of the eighteenth century, it was no longer unusual in the Low Countries for a woman to practice art as a living. Painters' guilds had numerous women members, particularly the Confrerie [Brotherhood] Pictura in The Hague.

Further References. Germaine Greer, *The Obstacle Race* (New York, 1979). Chris Petteys, *Dictionary of Women Artists: An International Dictionary of Women Artists Born before 1900* (Boston, 1985). Ann Sutherland and Linda Nochlin, *Women Artists: 1550–1950* (Cat. for exhibition, Los Angeles, 1977). U. Thieme and F. Becker, *Allgemeines Lexikon der bildenden Künstler,* 37 vols. (Leipzig, 1907–1950).

MARIANNE BERARDI

"NEW WOMAN" IN VICTORIAN LITERATURE. During the 1890s a group of popular English writers focused on women's issues, including careers, education, alternatives to marriage and motherhood, and freedom for women to express their sexuality. Their works feature women who take advantage of the changes during the nineteenth century and adopt nontraditional roles—New Women. The emphasis on all aspects of women's psychology and sexual behavior opened areas that had been taboo and had a profound impact upon modern English fiction.

Favorite subjects of these writers are the ways the feminine role (including innocence about sexuality, marriage, and motherhood and subordination to men) oppressed women. Thus, works by New Woman writers show women trapped in unhappy marriages and innocent women and children ravaged by venereal disease as well as more sensational subjects, including adultery, free love, and prostitution.

While contemporary readers and reviewers consistently label certain authors New Woman writers, the authors do not set out to establish a school, and their works do not present a consistent view. Some, working from a feminist perspective, suggest that human relationships would improve when more people adopt the ideals of their heroines while others demonstrate that the New Woman is a threat. Furthermore, while all New Woman writers are frank about sexual matters, some want women to be better informed while others want them to be experienced too.

As a result, H.E.M. Stutfield divided New Woman writers into two groups ("The Psychology of Feminism," *Blackwood's Magazine,* January 1897). The "purity school" consisted of Sarah Grand (pseud. for Frances McFall), Iota (pseud. for Kathleen Caffyn), and Grant Allen while the "neurotic school" included George Egerton (pseud. for Mary Chavelita Dunn), Emma Frances Brooke, Mona Caird, and Menie Muriel Dowie (pseud. for Mrs. Henry Norman).

In addition, Olive Schreiner, Thomas Hardy, George Meredith, and George Gissing are sometimes classified as New Woman writers because they treat the same subjects and focus on the same kind of heroine. The heroine of Schreiner's *The Story of an African Farm* (1883) proposes marriage to one man when she is pregnant by another. Sue Bridehead in *Jude the Obscure* (1896) argues for free love and has four illegitimate children. Gissing's *The Odd Woman* (1893), *In the Year of the Jubilee* (1894), and *The Whirlpool* (1897) and Meredith's *Lord Ormont and His Aminta* (1894) and *The Amazing Marriage* (1895) have characteristics usually associated with the New Woman.

The "purity school" seeks to establish an ideal of feminine purity that is derived not from innocence of the world but from knowledge and even experience of it. Grand's *The Heavenly Twins* (1893), usually considered the first New Woman novel, focuses on three women. The innocent, Edith Beales, dies after contracting syphilis from her husband; Evadne, learning of her husband's former mistress, refuses to consummate her marriage; and Angelica proposes to her future husband and dresses in masculine clothing to learn more of the world. Other works of the purity school are Iota's *A Yellow Aster* (1894) and Allen's *The Woman Who Did* (1895), *The British Barbarians* (1895), *A Splendid Sin* (1896), and *Miss Cayley's Adventures* (1899). *The Woman Who Did,* the most sensational of New Woman novels, features a heroine, Herminia Barton, who not only advocates free love but practices it as well.

Works of the "neurotic school" are more diverse, but a common theme is that women suffer because they struggle alone against a corrupt society, and heroines of these works often succumb to suicidal depression or madness or give up the struggle to achieve anything genuinely new. *Keynotes* (1893) by Egerton, the first of this school, features openly sensual women as well as those who rebel against conventional roles. The publisher, John Lane, was so impressed that he made it the first of a series and commissioned Beardsley to design a cover. *Keynotes* was followed by *Discords* (1894), *Symphonies* (1897) and *Fantasies* (1898), but the latter two volumes were less popular. Other works of this school are Brooke's *A Superfluous Woman* (1894); Caird's *The Daughters of Danaus* (1894), *The Morality of Marriage* (1897), and *The Pathway of the Gods* (1898); and Dowie's *Gallia* (1895) and *The Crook of the Bough* (1898).

Despite obvious differences, all these works feature women who feel free to initiate sexual relationships, to explore alternatives to marriage and motherhood, to adopt careers in nontraditional professions—medicine, nursing, and business—and to discuss sexual matters. New Woman heroines rarely achieve lasting happiness and almost never achieve lasting change, but the emphasis on these subjects and characters helped to destroy the idealized feminine character of earlier Victorian fiction and, therefore, had a liberating effect on twentieth-century English literature.

Further References. Gail Cunningham, *The New Woman and the Victorian Novel* (New York, 1978). Lloyd Fernando, *"New Women" in the Late Victorian Novel* (University Park, Pa., 1977). Elaine Showalter, *A Literature of Their Own: British Women Novelists from Bronte to Lessing* (Princeton, 1977).

CAROL A. SENF

NORWEGIAN WRITERS trace their roots back to Dorothe Engelbretsdatter (1634–1716), the first woman both to publish and to make writing her career. She wrote in the popular genres of the seventeenth century, that is, poetry, psalms and songs, and was in turn one of her time's most popular poets. Two hundred years later Camilla Collett (1813–1895) established the popular genre of her century with the publication of *Amtmandens døttre* (1854–1855; The District Governor's Daughters), the first modern novel of Norway. Prose became the medium par excellence for writers of the nineteenth and twentieth centuries, though they experimented with the drama and developed the poetic tradition of Engelbretsdatter.

Amtmandens døttre is a sociopolitical portrayal of the inhibiting influences of society, the family, and marriage on the growth of young women. Collett's Sophie yearns to discover herself. But external and internal pressures to become the dutiful wife of a superior man defeat her, and, relinquishing herself, she retreats into a traditional marriage. Criticized for painting an uncomplimentary picture of the family, Collett replied that people were not yet ready for the truth. *Amtmandens døttre* became the prototype for the novel of women's "education" for the next 100 years.

Amalie Skram (1846–1905) was one of the great prose writers of the nineteenth century, if the public was even less ready for her truth. Collett had defined the novel. Skram defined the naturalistic novel, depicting bourgeois society as not only inhibiting but deadly to women's growth. Her debut novel was *Constance Ring* (1885), a scathing portrayal of marriage and the patriarchal family and an open examination of female sexuality within their confines. Skram's focus was Constance, who takes her own life after a series of painful confrontations with men, and, through them, her repressed sexual longings. Skram wrote three other marriage novels, all of them brilliant, if disillusioned, psychological studies of women whose natures are fatally corrupted by traditional norms. In her two *romans à clef, Professor Hieronimus* (1895) and *På Sct. Jørgen* (1895; At St. Jørgen's) Skram exposed the misuse of modern medical science by men of power to control the minds of women. In Skram's hands the novel became a sophisticated instrument through which she probed the pathology of both society and female psychology.

Twentieth-century writers have built on the strong prose tradition of Collett and Skram. Representative among them are, first of all, Sigrid Undset (1882–1949), one of five women to win the Nobel Prize. She debuted in 1907 but first roused public attention and ire with her novel *Jenny* (1913), about a young Norwegian painter in Rome, longing to find fulfillment as a woman and an artist. Ending with Jenny's suicide, the novel is a Freudian exploration of a woman's crippling ambivalence toward her own creativity and sexuality. Undset is best known for the epic trilogy, *Kristian Lavransdatter* (1920–1922), in which she richly re-created medieval Norway, torn between pagan and Christian traditions. But once again she took up the question of a (modern) woman's creative/procreative/erotic nature in the more robust character of Kristin, torn like her country between her duty to herself as lover (the pagan) and her duty to others as wife and mother (the Christian). Undset remained ambivalent throughout her own life as to which role provided a woman her greatest fulfillment. Publicly she disassociated herself from the feminist movement. At the same time she was one of the most prolific writers of the first half of the century, writing contemporary and medieval novels, short stories, plays, essays, and cultural history.

Cora Sandel (Sara Fabricius, 1880–1974), like Undset, worked in several different genres. She debuted with her trilogy, *Alberte og Jakob* (1926; *Alberta and Jacob*, 1962), *Alberte og friheten* (1931; *Alberta and Freedom*, 1963), and *Bare Alberte* (1939; *Alberta Alone*, 1965). An immediate, extraordinary success, the Alberte books are a feminist "novel of education." With psychological and sociological insight equal to Skram's, if not so disillusioned, Sandel traces Alberte's journey: struggling to express herself as she comes of age in northern Norway, traveling to Paris, where she confronts herself as an artist and a sexual woman, and returning to Norway, where she leaves her husband and child to write on her own, rather than risk losing herself to others. In 1927 Sandel published *En blå sofa* (A Blue Sofa), the first of five short story collections, generally dealing with women, but also with men of little power in confrontation with a conventional, discriminating society. In 1945 she published the magnificent *Kranes konditori* (*Krane's Cafe*, subtitled "Interior with Figures"; Eng. publ. 1968). Stylistically her most radical work, it is a study of the narrow-minded, middle-class milieu at its worst. One day a timid seamstress sits down in Krane's Cafe and refuses to sew any more dresses for the rich ladies of the town. In this nice cafe for nice people, her revolt is a scandal. Sandel's brand of realism, sharp but understated, sympathetic but unsentimental, is unrivaled in Norway.

Torborg Nedreaas (1906–1987), like Sandel, was a master both of the novel and of the short story. She debuted in 1945 with a collection of short stories, *Bak skapet står øksen* (The Ax Is Behind the Cupboard), dealing with the daily life of occupied Norway, most poignantly with the *tysketøser* (the Norwegian girlfriends of German soldiers) who fall victim to the brutality of the occupiers. Nedreaas's first novel, *Av måneskinn gror det ingenting* (1947; *Nothing Grows by Moonlight*, 1987), again about a woman as victim, but also about men and patriarchal society in general, is a cry against sexual oppression. In 1950 Nedreaas published *Trylleglasset* (The Magic Prism), one of the finest short story collections of the decade. In it she introduced her character, Herdis, an artistic child, torn between her aesthetic calling and societal demands and responsibilities. Nedreaas followed Herdis's development in the later novels *Musikk fra en blå brønn* (1960; Music from a Blue Well) and *Ved neste nymåne* (1971; By the Next New Moon). The Herdis books are as central to the postwar years as Sandel's Alberte books are to the years between the wars.

In the 1960s Bjørg Vik (b.1935) was one of the major writers to emerge with three collections of short stories, followed by a novel, *Gråt elskede mann* (Weep Dear Man), in 1970. Writing from an increasingly feminist perspective, Vik for the most part portrays girls and women and their yearning for love in relation to the alienating society that has created and rejected them. The prose tradition has continued to flourish in the 1970s and 1980s. Liv Køltzow (b.1945), working, like Vik, with both the novel and the short story, published the classic, modern feminist "novel of recognition," *Historien om Eli* (The Story of Eli), in 1975. In a clipped, flat prose style, Køltzow relentlessly depicts the conditions that hinder women's liberation. Herbjørg Wassmo (b.1942), preoccupied, too, with the oppression of women, but also their capacity for hope and survival, published the first volume of her Tora trilogy in 1981, *Huset med den blinde glassveranda* (*The House with the Blind Glass Veranda*, 1987), exploring the growth of Tora, a sexually abused child who survives, for a time, on her fantasies. Cecilie Løveid (b.1951) is one of the most experimental and vital writers of the 1970s and 1980s, working with a unique prose/poetry, as in *Sug* (1982; Suck). The title suggests her obsession with the human capacity—constructive and destructive— for longing and love.

The dramatic tradition is slight by comparison to the prose tradition, though women of the late nineteenth century did write plays, generally about women's precarious position in a man's society. Prominent among them were Laura Kieler (1849–1932), Ibsen's model for Nora in *A Doll's House* ; Alvilde Prydz (1846–1922); Hulda Garborg (1862–1934); and A. Skram, whose *Agnete* (1893) is the most crafted drama of the period. It is a deeply pessimistic play about the inexorable differences between women's and men's value systems. Twentieth-century writers who have experimented with the drama form are, among others, the prose writers S. Undset and B. Vik, whose *To akter for fem kvinner* (1974; *Two Acts for Five Women*) has been performed in Europe and off-Broadway. C. Løvied is again the most experimental with her acclaimed radio and stage plays such as *Måkespisere* (1983; Seagull Eaters), providing a model for women in the theatre arena of the future.

Poetry has been a more expressive medium than the drama. Magdalene Thoresen (1819–1903) published *Digte av en dame* (Poems by a Woman) in 1860. To poetry what Collett was to prose, Thoresen explored the theme of female eros with radical honesty. Twentienth-century poets have elaborated in individual ways upon the themes of love and eros, from the earlier Aslaug Vaa (1889–1965), Inger Hagerup (1905–1984), and Halldis Moren Vesaas (b.1907) to the later Marie Takvam (b.1926) and Sidsel Mørck (b.1937). Woman's longing to merge juxtaposed to the reality of being alone is a pervasive paradox. Poetry has also been a source of humor, for adults and children, as in the hands of Hagerup; or a political weapon, registering the loneliness of the emigrants, as in the hands of Ingeborg Refling Hagen (b.1895); or our "thing" society, as in Mørck's; or discrimination, as in Takvam's. In their styles these writers have been as varied as the women themselves, from the modernist Kate Næss (b.1938) to the antimodernist Tove Lie (b.1942). They share, however, their deep conviction about the preciousness of life. Nature mysticism, common to the Norwegian spirit, strongly informs her women poets.

Further References. Ed. Englestad et al., *Norsk kvinnelitteratur historie* (Oslo, 1988). Mary Kay Norseng, "A Child's Liberation of Space: H. Wassmo's Huset med den blinde glassveranda," *Scandinavian Studies* 58, 1 (1986). Virpi Zuck, "Cora Sandel, A Norwegian Feminist," *Edda* 1 (1981).

MARY KAY NORSENG

NOVELISTS, BRITISH (EIGHTEENTH-CENTURY). Feminine novelists articulated the concerns important to women's lives and fates, 1715–1798. The majority of these novelists present us with a femiocentric story, a text that codes female sexual vulnerability as the controlling motive in female and male behavior; they do so, however, in categorically different modes. Penelope Aubin and Elizabeth Rowe, for example, code this vulnerability in the pious polemic, and Delariviere Manley and Eliza Haywood (in her satiric pieces like *The Court of Caramania*) do so in the *chronique scandeleuse*; Mary Collyer explores female passivity through epistolary fiction. The majority of the writers, however, turn to the romance, the novella, and later to the three-volume romance-novel for their metaphoric investigation of the femiocentric state. In the years before 1740 (Richardson's *Pamela; or, Virtue Rewarded* serves as a watershed even for this feminine fiction), all of these modes were used; the years after 1740 witnessed a movement away from these earlier, pure forms, first to parodies and satires of them, then to more serious reproductions of the forms combined with the educational novel and political fiction. By the last decade of the century, the novel of manners had become the prime feminine mode.

In the earlier years, the novelists were concerned with confronting and combating the two controlling feminine ideologies of the age: that of romantic love based on the assumption that female life gains value only through romantically conceived marriage, and that of female powerlessness, a vision of female life that presents the reader with a very low ceiling of female expectations and aspirations. Romantic love was the reason, it was argued, that women were powerless.

The ideologies were founded on tenets that defined woman as subordinate, submissive, passive. In the opinion of the majority of the feminine writers of the period such acquiescence was no longer viable (if it ever was), either for themselves, for their heroines, or for their readers. They combat these ideologies and assert themselves and their fictions in several ways, most importantly in the presentation of heroines who are split into two selves: virgin and virago. The virgins profess the controlling ideology: they are submissive and acquiescent. The viragos, though minor figures in the early fiction who grow into larger, more complex roles in the later works, express their author's frustration and the antithetical ideology as they display aggressive, independent, even feisty natures. Predictably, however, such characters are not allowed to predominate and survive; the end of their fictions finds them denied any positive state. Yet even the virgins, in the majority of cases, are not permitted a pleasant, happily-ever-after conclusion; instead their lives, too, end in exile, despair, madness, or death. Through seemingly inane, yet actually highly sophisticated, femiocentric texts, these eighteenth-century feminine novelists detail the state of the divided female in an effort to present an accurate picture of the feminine eighteenth-century world.

A second way these writers combat female trivialization is through their use of the masquerade set piece. (The masquerade, introduced by Count Heidegger in the very early years of the century, was an established and ubiquitous feature of English life by the 1720s.) The very raison d'être of the masquerade defines its efficacy for these novelists: a disguise, by its very nature, allows one to be an "other," to participate and be someone other than one's real self. Thus the docile heroine could hide behind the aggressive mask of the gypsy, the submissive shepherdess could become a tyrannical amazon, the quasi-conforming novelist could actually speak her mind. The disguise displays a spirit of liberty, and though an "illusion," the mask is really the true face of the female. The use of the virgin-virago duality, together with the masquerade set piece, allows these novelists to adopt what Nancy K. Miller has labeled a "posture of imposture" ("Emphasis Added: Plots and Plausibilities in Women's Fiction," *PMLA* 96 [1981]: 36–48), a stance that permits them the "cover" of the romance story for their more aggressive, femiocentric texts. They tell a romance story that contradicts the usual expectations. They engage in a process of double writing. Not content merely to adopt a masquerade technique in terms of their female protagonists, these novelists use the cover story of their romance plots to mask their feminist, aggressive intentions and to unmask the facile and fatuous fictions they are supposed to be writing as members of the weaker sex.

Penelope Aubin's (1685–1731) women, for example, are besieged, abducted, seduced, trappaned, raped—there seems to be no crime of which they are not victims; disguise becomes a necessity for existence, and this pervasiveness of the evil is startling even by twentieth-century tastes. Jane Barker (1688–1718) and Mary Davys (1674–1732) exceed all expectations of the genre with, for example, Barker's *Love Intrigues* (1713) when the heroine, Galesia, actually chooses to leave the hero and pursue her own course of study. Mary Davy's *Familiar Letters* (1713) is equally outspoken. Berina clearly and forthrightly speaks of her love for Artander long before he does; the male is left weak and emasculated by such a woman. By far the ringleader is Eliza Haywood (1693–1756), the most popular and prolific of these writers with about 60 novels and romances to her credit. (She was also the editor of the first magazine written by and for women.) Though she couches her revolutionary tales well within romance confines, she was able to impose her own feminine rhetoric on the forms. Thus it was that the very popular *Philidore and Placentia; or, L'Amour trop Delicat* (1727) was able to have a happy ending; yet Placentia, the heroine, was extraordinarily aggressive, virtually seducing the shy, reserved Philidore. The majority of Haywood's novels, however, do not end happily; *Idalia; or, The Unfortunate Mistress* (1723) is the best example of this tale of horror for the female. Seduced and raped by Floreo, Don Ferdinand, Henriquez, and Don Myrtano, Idalia has no self but functions only as the female mask these men have forced her to adopt. Similarly, tales like *The Perplex'd Dutchess* (1725) or *The Injur'd Husband* (1728) that feature the aggressive, domineering Gigantilla and the Baroness de Tortileé explore the nightmare world of the aggressive female. Yet the conclusions revert back to conventional attitudes, and so Gigantilla and the Baroness are "punished" for their self-assertion. Such outspokenness continued with Sarah Fielding (1710–1768). Her concern with women's position and rights was so strong that she threw caution to the winds, as did her contemporary Charlotte Smith (1749–1806), by disregarding the forms and telling a story very much not of the romance convention. Fielding actually anatomizes the romance genre in *The Cry: A New Dramatic Fable* (1754). In *The History of the Countess of Dellwyn* (1759) she explores the "Circaen Transformation" of the docile Miss Lucum into the Amazonian Countess and clearly uncovers more than one cares to see. Smith even goes so far as to unmask her very own self in her novels, thus totally uncovering the feminine fiction. During both mid-

and late century, then, the romance form was meeting great opposition. The women writers with their aggressive texts were accepted enough that Charlotte Lennox (1720–1804) was able to write *The Female Quixote* (1752) and parody the popular romance form while investigating the entire issue of female power. Late in the century, Elizabeth Inchbald's (1753–1821) *A Simple Story* (1791) continues this analysis of the romance form and rings the death knell on the aggressive text. With Jane West (1758–1852) the eighteenth-century feminine writers had mellowed. Late in the century there was less assertiveness in the telling of their stories, together with less aggressive use of the romance form. The way was paved for Jane Austen (discussed in MANNERS, NOVEL OF, and ROMANTIC PERIOD LITERATURE) and her nonthreatening novel of manners.

MARY ANNE SCHOFIELD

NOVELISTS, BRITISH (VICTORIAN). Generally middle-class women who found writing a form of self-expression and a means of financial support. In spite of the impression that women were flooding the market with books, female novelists made up only about 20 percent of the literary profession. This incidence remained true until well into the twentieth century, when opportunities for women's education expanded. It also was held that women took up writing merely for amusement; in fact, many supported themselves and their families with their work. Most managed to balance their domestic and professional duties, since writing could be done at home. To ensure that their fiction would be treated with the same critical objectivity as that of their male counterparts—and to allow a wider range of expression—Victorian women novelists sometimes adopted male pseudonyms.

Of the women who published novels in the Victorian period, four are generally ranked with the major novelists of the day. Charlotte (1816–1855) and Emily (1818–1848) Brontë, Elizabeth Cleghorn Gaskell (1810–1865), and George Eliot (Mary Ann Evans, 1819–1880) are given the same critical attention as Dickens, Thackeray, and Trollope.

The daughters of a Yorkshire clergyman, the Brontës drew much of their imaginative energy from the Yorkshire moors. This atmosphere permeates Emily Brontë's only novel, *Wuthering Heights* (1847). Although not a popular success, its mystical vision of transcendent passion established it as a masterpiece that goes beyond the gothic romances it superficially resembles. Emily Brontë's reputation as a novelist rests on this single work of genius.

Charlotte Brontë's novels are more realistic, but they too are unconventional in their handling of passionate love and female self-definition. *Jane Eyre* (1847) was an enormous popular and critical success, although one contemporary critic, Elizabeth Rigby, condemned it as un-Christian and refused to believe that any decent woman could have written it. *Shirley* (1849), Brontë's one attempt at an industrial novel, was based on an 1807–1812 conflict with Yorkshire mill owners. The least successful of her novels, *Shirley* is of interest because of its strong-willed protagonist, Shirley Keeldar. *Villette* (1853) and Brontë's first novel, *The Professor* (published posthumously, 1857), are seen as versions of Charlotte's unrequited love for her Brussels professor, M. Heger, a married man. In 1854 Brontë married her father's curate, Arthur Bell Nichols; she died a year later.

Elizabeth Cleghorn Gaskell was the wife of a Unitarian minister and the mother of four daughters. She was encouraged to write fiction after the death of her infant son, William. Her first novel, *Mary Barton* (1848), draws on her work in the slums of Manchester and empathizes with weavers in their conflict with mill owners. Later in *North and South* (1854–1855) she provides a more sympathetic picture of the manufacturers. A third social-problem novel, *Ruth* (1853), centers on an unmarried mother and argues for a single standard of sexual morality.

Mrs. Gaskell's *Cranford* (1851–1853) was published serially in Dickens's *Household Words*. It began as a series of sketches about a group of elderly widows and spinsters living in genteel poverty in a provincial town. Frequently viewed as a nostalgic look at a dying way of life, *Cranford* suggests the tensions of the emerging industrial age; its domestic realism foreshadows *Wives and Daughters* (1864–1866), which examines family relationships and generational and class conflicts. Mrs. Gaskell's fiction also includes *Sylvia's Lovers* (1863) and *Cousin Phyllis* (1863–1864). A friend of Charlotte Brontë, Gaskell wrote her *Life* in 1857.

Too intellectual to achieve wide popularity, George Eliot used the novel as a vehicle for serious ideas. In spite of her strongly Evangelical education, Eliot became an agnostic and developed a positivistic, humanistic philosophy that her novels reflect. She lived out of wedlock for nearly 25 years with George Henry Lewes; after Lewes's death she married J. W. Cross (1880).

Most of Eliot's early fiction centers on the ordinary people from her Warwickshire background. *Scenes of Clerical Life* (1857), a collection of three stories, was followed by *Adam Bede* (1859), set in rural preindustrial England. *The Mill on the Floss* (1860) presents the psychological development of Maggie Tulliver; it often is seen as semiautobiographical, reflecting Eliot's own spiritual and emotional struggles as a young woman. *Silas Marner* (1861), also set in rural England, develops Eliot's humanistic morality in a simple, almost Wordsworthian, manner.

Romola (1862–1863), Eliot's only historical romance, is set in fifteenth-century Florence. *Felix Holt, the Radical* (1866) moves back to modern England and the politics of the Reform Bill. Eliot's masterpiece, *Middlemarch* (1871–1872), illustrates her theories of character development and personal responsibility through a focus on several groups of characters rather than a single individual. It also addresses the issue of women in the nineteenth century. Her last novel, *Daniel Deronda* (1876), applies her theories to society life; its overt didacticism is a characteristic weakness. All of Eliot's novels show characters confronted with significant moral choices; her primary concern is with their complex inner lives.

Many female novelists of the period were both more prolific and more popular than the Brontës, Gaskell, and Eliot. Writers of sensational fiction Mary Elizabeth

Braddon (1835–1915) and Mrs. Henry Wood (Ellen Price, 1814–1887) produced enormous quantities of work. Braddon, whose *Lady Audley's Secret* (1862) sold nearly a million copies, wrote over 80 novels during her career; in addition to sensational novels, she wrote historical fiction and novels of manners. Mrs. Henry Wood wrote over 50 novels; her sensational *East Lynne* (1861) was a best-seller. Both Braddon and Wood were known for their unusual combination of domestic conventions and sensational matter.

Writers of romantic fiction included Ouida (Marie Louise Ramee, 1839–1908) and Marie Corelli (Mary Mackay, 1855–1924). Ouida's most popular romances were *Under Two Flags* (1867) and *Moths* (1880). Corelli, one of the best-selling novelists of the late nineteenth century, was best known for *The Sorrows of Satan* (1895), which sold more copies than any previous novel in English.

Female novelists often used the novel for moral purposes and for encouragement of social reform. Harriet Martineau (1802–1876) expressed her interest in Utilitarian political philosophy in didactic stories and somewhat more tempered novels, including *Deerbrook* (1839) and *The Hour of Man* (1841), an historical novel. Dinah Maria Mulock Craik (1826–1887) wrote a best-seller, *John Halifax, Gentleman* (1856), which chronicled the rags-to-riches story of a morally superior young man. Charlotte Mary Yonge (1832–1901), strongly influenced by the Tractarian movement, published nearly 75 novels and donated the profits to charity; *The Heir of Redclyffe* (1853) was a best-seller.

In addition to her travel books and other writings, Frances Trollope (1780–1863) supported her family with her novels. Mrs. Humphry Ward (Mary Augusta, 1851–1920) was active in the literary world and saw herself as a successor to George Eliot; *Robert Elsmere* (1888) was a best-seller, and she produced numerous other novels in the last part of the century. One of the most prolific writers of the period, Margaret Oliphant (1828–1897) was another example of a woman who supported her family (and her brother's) with her writing. She wrote novels of Scottish life—*Katie Stewart* (1853) and *Kirsteen* (1890)—and an acclaimed series of novels, *The Chronicles of Carlingford* (1863–1876). Scores of other female novelists wrote for a combination of pleasure, purpose, and profit in the Victorian period.

Further References. Sandra M. Gilbert and Susan Gubar, *The Madwoman in the Attic* (New Haven, 1979). Ellen Moers, *Literary Women* (New York, 1977). Elaine Showalter, *A Literature of Their Own* (Princeton, 1977). Michael Wheeler, *English Fiction of the Victorian Period* (New York, 1985).

SHARON LOCY

NOVELISTS, BRITISH (TWENTIETH-CENTURY). The most important British woman novelist of the century is, without doubt, Virginia Woolf (1882–1941). She is best known for her special adaptations of stream of consciousness to a form of interior monologue that grows increasingly experimental from *Mrs. Dalloway* to *The Waves*. Using what she called her tunneling method, she gives temporal dimension to characters depicted in the immediacy of their present existence by providing them with a rich consciousness of their own past. Since the 1970s the political concerns of her novels that were once ignored have been recognized, especially by American feminists who reevaluated her less acclaimed novels *The Voyage Out* (1915), *Night and Day*, (1919), *The Years* (1937), and *Between the Acts* (1941). The same preoccupations with the economic oppression of women and the relation between social institutions and war that are clearly articulated in her book-length essays *A Room of One's Own* and *Three Guineas* have now been recognized as informing elements in all her novels. Nevertheless, her greatest achievement as a novelist is the creation of her characters' sensuous apprehension of reality. Woolf uses language to get closer and closer to the experience of felt life: sailing off the coast of England, walking out into Bond Street on a June morning, watching the stroke of light from a lighthouse on a floor, looking into the heart of a crocus. In some of the most arresting moments of her most successful novels, *Mrs. Dalloway* (1925), *To the Lighthouse* (1927), and *The Waves* (1931), she has almost obliterated the distinction between poetry and prose.

Actually, Dorothy Richardson (1873–1957) preceded Woolf in her experimentation, publishing in 1915 the first novel in a series that eventually grew into 13 volumes of fictionalized autobiography called *Pilgrimage*. (After the publication of Richardson's first 3 books, May Sinclair applied the term *stream of consciousness* to them, using William James's phrase for the first time in literary criticism.) In 1938, when 12 of the books were published together for the first time in a 4-volume edition, the heroine Miriam Henderson's adventures extended from *Pointed Roof* to *Dimple Hill*, from her experiences as a teacher at Fraülein Pfaff's school in Hanover to her life with a Quaker family in Sussex. The most engrossing and sustained excursion into stream of consciousness is Miriam's long walk in *Revolving Lights*. In 1967 a new edition of *Pilgrimage* came out, including for the first time a final book, *March Moonlight*, which rounds off Miriam's experiences through her encounter with Mr. Noble, the man who will become her husband.

May Sinclair (1865–1946) and Rose Macaulay (1881–1958) were both popular novelists of the same period. At great length in *Mary Olivier* (1919) and in small compass in *Life and Death of Harriet Frean* (1922), May Sinclair writes about unmarried daughters' relations with their tyrannical parents. Rose Macaulay treats similar situations more satirically. Her essay-novels (such as *Told By an Idiot* [1923]) are full of speculations as well as very articulate and comic characters. Perhaps her best novel is a much later one, *The Towers of Trebizond* (1956), which combines fiction and the travelogue.

One of the most promising novelists of the 1920s and 1930s, Winifred Holtby (1898–1935), died young. Her posthumously published novel *South Riding* (1936) has been an "underground classic" for generations. The novel documents the functioning of county government in Yorkshire, but it also embodies a conflict between passion and a lack of shared values, the struggle between a thinking woman like Sarah Burton and a traditional man like the fox-hunting Carne, whom she loves. *The Crooked Street* (1924), another Yorkshire novel, depicts the same kind of conflict between Muriel Hammond and Godfrey Neale. In both novels women's relations with each other as fellow workers occupy a large place.

Ivy Compton-Burnett (1884–1969) has created one of the most distinctive styles of the century. From the 1920s through the 1960s, she produced approximately four novels each decade. Among the most important are *Pastors and Masters* (1925), *A Family and a Fortune* (1939), *Parents and Children* (1941), and *Mother and Son* (1955). All of her novels are family-centered and take place in late Victorian or Edwardian England. They are composed almost entirely of highly stylized dialogue and culminate in scenes of revelation and discovery. Letters and photographs contribute to almost Wildean moments of hilarious exposure of human foibles; meals create the ebb and flow of action and talk in which money uncovers hidden hypocrisies. Fairy-tale qualities combine with dry, psychological analysis to undermine any sense of human control of events, and people become wooden pieces in the chesslike movements of her elaborately structured plots.

Although the Anglo-Irish novelist Elizabeth Bowen (1899–1973) has received less critical attention than she deserves, at least two of her novels have become widely known: *The Death of the Heart* (1939), a funny and touching novel about an adolescent girl who goes to live with her married brother after the death of her mother, and *The Heat of the Day* (1949), one of the finest depictions of life in London during the blitz of World War II. Both works dramatize the painful encounter of the inner demands for the ceremonies of love and loyalty with a dessicating and unresponsive world. Betrayal and the wreckage wrought by innocence are always linked up in Bowen with the places in which they occur, for example, the burning of a great manor house in Ireland in *The Last September* (1929) and the suspension of two children's fate in a house that reverberates with the past out of which they were created in *The House in Paris* (1935).

The four most important novelists to have emerged since World War II are Muriel Spark, Doris Lessing, Iris Murdoch, and Margaret Drabble.

Muriel Spark (b.1918) specializes in the short novel with rapidly sketched-in characters who plunge into parable situations that test their moral fiber. As a Catholic, she is a religious humorist who explores some of the most perplexing social problems of the day. In her two best-known novels, *Memento Mori* (1958) and *The Prime of Miss Jean Brodie* (1961), neither old ladies nor children are sentimentalized; they are people always in their prime if *prime* means the moment we are made for, the moment of crisis and choice. Her theological perspective on old age and dying, on sex and war permits her to treat tragedy as comedy.

Doris Lessing (b.1919), an author who achieved literary fame in the 1950s and 1960s, continues to explore new possibilities of fiction. Her most recent novels of fantasy, the Canopus series, combine mythology and science fiction in a vision of the future that transforms the present into a past. But her two most substantial achievements so far are her five-volumed *Children of Violence* (1952–1969) and *The Golden Notebook* (1962). Like Richardson's *Pilgrimage*, Lessing's *Children of Violence* is fictionalized autobiography. Martha Quest, the heroine who grows up as the author did in Southern Rhodesia (now Zimbabwe), leaves for England after breaking away from marriages and love affairs. There, again like the author, she becomes disillusioned with Communism after the Hungarian uprising. Throughout the series, violence pervades private and public life. In *The Golden Notebook* madness replaces violence as a metaphor for contemporary society: here Anne Wulf experiences her own personal madness as a counterpart of the splitting off of one area of life from another that characterizes the world she lives in. She keeps a series of notebooks (black, red, yellow, and blue) that underscore the compartmentalization that afflicts both the individual and society. Lessing's novels are always richly textured, full of the data of racial and sexual relations, political events, fads in the arts, social changes in food, clothing, modes of travel. Out of the chaos of that experience *The Golden Notebook* attempts to shape wholeness rather than flounder in fragments.

Iris Murdoch (b.1919) is rather an oddity in English fiction, a philosophical novelist. The influence of Sartre and of existentialism in general is felt in all her novels (for example, *Under the Net* [1954], *The Severed Head* [1961], *Bruno's Dream* [1969], *A Fairly Honorable Defeat* [1970]), where life is solitary although always "in company" of others.

Margaret Drabble (b.1939) raises the ordinary and the commonplace to the level of poetry through her emphasis on the human capacity to rescue beauty from dehumanizing circumstances. Her morality is rooted not in any religious tradition, but in respect for human affection and responsibility. Her most successful novel to date, *The Needle's Eye* (1972), endorses a kind of moral resilience that allows each individual to turn chance into choice. Drabble lacks the thickly textured, political analysis of Lessing, the theological assurance of Spark, the philosophical sophistication of Murdoch. Her emotional immersion in the gritty facticity of life aligns her with earlier twentieth-century writers such as Winifred Holtby and Arnold Bennett.

Further References. Diva Daims and Janet Grimes, with ed. assist. from Doris Robinson, *Toward a Feminist Tradition: An Annotated Bibliography of Novels in English by Women, 1891–1920* (New York, 1982). Sydney Janet Kaplan, *Feminine Consciousness in the Modern British Novel* (Urbana, 1975).

                                                        JO O'BRIEN SCHAEFER

NOVELISTS, U.S. (TO WORLD WAR I). The earliest American women novelists, publishing in the 1790s, wrote primarily the seduction novel, modeled upon British examples but having a North American setting, or the frontier romance, a new genre detailing European settlers' experiences of abduction by Indian natives. Continuing to appear until the Civil War, these two genres merged afterward into literary realism.

During the seventeenth century, authors of captivity narratives, in recording their experiences, had initiated the tradition of writing about the frontier wilderness. In 1779 Ann Eliza Bleecker wrote *The History of Maria Kittle* (1791), the earliest-known frontier romance, an innovative blend of epistolary novel and fictionalized captivity narrative with its obligatory Indian abductors. Lydia Maria Child's *Hobomok* of 1825 was followed two years later by Catharine Sedgwick's *Hope Leslie*. Whereas Bleecker depicted Indians as wild savages, Child and Sedgwick both explored miscegenation, and Sedgwick's white character even preferred Indian to European ways. By 1839, Caroline Kirkland in *A New Home— Who'll Follow?* replaced an idealized, romantic view with an experiential, realistic view of frontier living as she revealed the deprivations women endured as they followed male relatives westward—often as nearly captive as any earlier heroines were of Indian abductors, or as African slaves were of their owners. The first known novel by a black woman, *Our Nig* (1859) by Harriet E. Wilson, derived from the slave narrative, as the frontier romance had from the autobiographical captivity narrative. Helen Hunt Jackson's *Ramona* (1884), a sympathetic, idealized romance between Spaniard and Indian, is laced with harshly realistic depictions of European treatment of Native American Indians. Later expressions of frontier romance and realism appear in utopian writings (see UTOPIAS, U.S.). By the end of the century what had begun as frontier writing became local color or regional realism, while social or psychological realism had its roots in the novel of seduction.

Also appearing during the 1790s, seduction novels too revealed women's subordinate role. The first North American best-seller, *Charlotte, a Tale of Truth* (1794) by Susanna Rowson, combined the titillation of a seduction with the didactic intent of warning naive female readers. Three years later Hannah Foster published an epistolary novel, *The Coquette*. Both Rowson and Foster warn readers in accounts of heroines' being punished in deaths associated with childbirth, but Foster depicts manners more realistically.

Both novels contained seeds of the "woman's novel," which reigned between 1820 and 1870. Plots of the woman's novel concern the trials the heroine, orphan, or heiress must overcome as she develops her capacities so as to triumph over inner and outer obstacles, rather than succumb as in the seduction novel (Nina Baym, *Woman's Fiction* [Ithaca, 1978]). As the first American novel to sell 1 million copies, *The Wide, Wide World* (1850) by Susan Warner (pseud. Elizabeth Wetherell) indicates the popularity of this genre. It depicts the education of a strong-willed heroine to submit to patriarchal authority and to know good from evil. In a variation of the genre, *Ruth Hall* (1855) by Sara Parton (pseud. Fanny Fern), a writer not only triumphs over cruel relatives, but also rises above dependence upon marriage and family. *The Hidden Hand* (1859), by the widely read E.D.E.N. Southworth, sports a lively heroine, Capitola, who defies authority, assumes male prerogatives, and earns rewards for such behavior. The novel's melodramatic plot suggests British gothic thrillers. Women's fiction after the Civil War continued to be written for a juvenile audience or by black women. Louisa May Alcott's *Little Women* (1868) is the outstanding example of the former, while in works by black women, heroines surmount the trials of women living in a racist society and triumph as advocates of their race. Frances E. W.

Harper in *Iola Leroy* (1892) and Pauline E. Hopkins in *Contending Forces* (1900) follow this pattern.

Works by the outstanding U.S. novelist before the Civil War, Harriet Beecher Stowe, partake of women's fiction features and anticipate literary realism. *Uncle Tom's Cabin* (1852) argues that maternal values should supplant masculinist views prevalent in society, thereby eradicating slavery and permitting black families to exist intact. *The Pearl of Orr's Island* (1862) describes gender stereotyping in the education of youth while minutely delineating a regional environment. Her most carefully wrought novel, *Oldtown Folks* (1869), provides a fictional portrait of New England village life at the turn of the last century. Stowe's fictional designs reveal both her wish to change radically the arrangements between the races and between the sexes and her awareness of the impact of specific geographical regions upon human lives.

The next generation of writers completes the transition from amateur to professional. The domestic priority of the previous generation disappeared as plots and heroines more frequently extended beyond the home. Stowe's immediate literary descendants include Elizabeth Stuart Phelps, Sarah Orne Jewett, and Mary E. Wilkins Freeman. All three produced works of regional, social, and psychological realism. Jewett's *The Country of the Pointed Firs* (1896), the most centrally regional of their works, eulogizes a lost world of maternal values. Phelps's *The Silent Partner* (1871) and Freeman's *The Portion of Labor* (1901) critique masculinist, urban industrialization within New England. New roles for women appear in the same setting: Phelps's *Doctor Zay* (1882) and Jewett's *A Country Doctor* (1886). Tragic psychological realism informs Freeman's *Pembroke* (1894).

As the maternal and domestic focus in women's fiction moved toward the wings, the artistic and literary purpose stepped forward to replace it. Phelps's *kunstlerroman* (artist novel) *The Story of Avis* (1877) portrays one woman's inner strife between domestic and artistic vocation. St. Louis author Kate Chopin in *The Awakening* (1899) pushes this strife to a tragic outcome in Edna Pontellier's renunciation of life rather than loss of self. Californian Mary Austin in *A Woman of Genius* (1912) and midwesterner Willa Cather in *Song of the Lark* (1915) created heroines who find artistic success by choosing to avoid domestic commitment.

The literary generation arising at the turn of the century extended well beyond New England. Cather, following the regional example of Jewett, wrote of immigrant survivors on her own midwestern plains in *O Pioneers!* (1913) and *My Antonia* (1918). Ellen Glasgow began in *The Battleground* (1902) an exploration of Virginia history and society. Edith Wharton in *House of Mirth* (1905) and *Custom of the Country* (1913) revealed how upper-class, New York society ravaged its women. And from Paris Gertrude Stein looked homeward to create in *Three Lives* (1909) stylistically experimental and ethnically diverse psychological portraits of women. By the turn of the century women had come of age as literary artists. Abandoning the prescriptive mode of the previous century—

idealistic, romantic, or moralistic—they adopted realism, a descriptive mode that set characters within a regional setting and sought to reveal their inner psychological and outer social development.

Further References. Lucy M. Freibert and Barbara A. White, *Hidden Hands, the Anthology of American Women Writers, 1790–1870* (New Brunswick, N.J., 1985). Mary Kelley, *Private Women, Public Stage: Literary Domesticity in Nineteenth-Century America* (New York, 1984). Annette Kolodny, *The Land before Her: Fantasy and Experience of the American Frontiers, 1630–1860* (Chapel Hill, N.C. 1984). *Legacy: A Journal of Nineteenth-Century American Women Writers*, 1– (1984–   ).

CAROL FARLEY KESSLER

NOVELISTS, U.S. (Twentieth-Century). The twentieth century has been marked by revolution, chaos, and despair. Ours is a century of firsts: the first world wars, the first atomic explosion, the first technologically produced holocaust, the first humans in space, the first babies in test tubes. Ours is the first century to attempt life without God and to substitute science, psychoanalysis, and politics in His/Her place. To some extent, the artistic response to these historical and cultural occurrences enacts itself through two major literary movements in the century, modernism and postmodernism, the former dating roughly from the opening years of the century through the twenties and the latter from the sixties through the eighties. While women writers have participated in these movements, they have worked predominantly in the realistic tradition through fiction dramatizing aspects of quotidian reality—emotional connection, childrearing, housekeeping.

In the opening years of the new century, three women writers produce influential prose that establishes them, by the thirties, as major literary figures: Edith Wharton (1862–1937), Gertrude Stein (1874–1946), and Willa Cather (1873–1947). Wharton, best known for her incisive, realistic portraits of upper-class society and the demands its superficiality and materialism make upon women, represents this world most successfully in *The House of Mirth* (1905). Other well-known novels of hers include *The Custom of the Country* (1913) and *The Age of Innocence* (1920). If Wharton is the consummate novelist of manners, then Gertrude Stein is the consummate innovator, the most radical of the modernists, whose best-known fiction, *Three Lives* (1909), remains her most accessible. Unlike Stein's reputation, Cather's has, until recently, been based upon an ostensible regionalism, presumably because the setting of a number of her novels is the Midwest—*O Pioneers!* (1913), *Song of the Lark* (1915), and *The Professor's House* (1925)—and her greatest, set in Nebraska, is *My Antonia* (1918). As critics now acknowledge, her texts are not limited by regional focus, for she explores a number of themes and issues vital to the modernist enterprise: the conflict over traditional values and modern technocracy, the connections between the mythic and the modern, the role of the artist and her relationship to society.

Three additional writers deserve mention in this period. The most innovative of these is Djuna Barnes (1892–1982), whose *Nightwood* (1937) remains enigmatic and difficult. Mary Austin (1868–1934) publishes *A Woman of Genius* in 1912, an early portrayal of the woman artist and an influence upon Cather's characterization of Thea Kronborg in *Song of the Lark*. Finally, Evelyn Scott (1893–1963) deserves greater notice for attempting to meld an extreme realism with her own version of stream of consciousness in *The Narrow House* (1921).

By the thirties, modernist experimentation is established as a literary option. One writer who utilizes it yet contributes her own African-American perspective is Zora Neale Hurston (1901?–1960), who comes to literary maturity and prominence in the thirties with the publication of her strongest novel, *Their Eyes Were Watching God* (1937). Hurston's emphasis upon a particular community is echoed in other women writers who turn to radical politics and the writing of committed literature as a way out of the global misery created by the Great Depression and the rise of fascism. In fact, Agnes Smedley's *Daughter of Earth* (1929) probably inaugurates proletarian fiction, which may be defined as a simplified realism emphasizing working-class characters, social themes, and, all too often, a melodramtic tone. Josephine Herbst (1892–1969)—*Rope of Gold* (1939)—and Meridel LeSueur (b. 1900), *The Girl* (written 1939, published 1978)—are two of the more effective writers in this tradition.

The post–World War II period may be looked at in two phases. The first ends in 1964, the year of Flannery O'Connor's death and the beginning of America's active involvement in Vietnam, and may be viewed as a time of consolidation. The second phase may be more accurately viewed as a time of innovation with post-modernism its most dominant feature.

Carson McCullers (1917–1967), Eudora Welty (b.1909), and Flannery O'Connor (1925–1964) constitute an influential triad of writers, who also happen to be southern, active in the forties, fifties, and early sixties. They enlarge the realistic tradition, with McCullers emphasizing the irremediable losses of childhood in *The Heart Is a Lonely Hunter* (1940); Welty emphasizing the endurance of human character in *Delta Wedding* (1946), *The Ponder Heart* (1954), and *The Optimist's Daughter* (1972); and O'Connor, the most ambitious female writer in the period, emphasizing the mysterious relationship among action, spirit, and grace in *Wise Blood* (1952) and *The Violent Bear It Away* (1960).

If the term *postmodern* resonates with any significance at all, it may be in its designation of an aftermath, the "sensibility" defined by an extreme self-reflexivity that is always aware of its own belatedness. Literally, postmodernism most often defines itself through a rejection of modernist aesthetics and values while attempting to promote its own kinds of experimentation with literary tradition, genre, and structure. In revising the literary past, writers may utilize parody and pastiche. Joyce Carol Oates (b.1938) revises the gothic romance tradition in *Bellefleur* (1980) and *A Bloodsmoor Romance* (1982), while in a quite serious vein Marilynne Robinson (b.1944) produces a neo-Romantic novel in *Housekeeping* (1981). Both Joanna Russ (b.1937) and Amanda Cross (b.1926) extend the possibilities of their respective generic options, the former in science fiction (*The Female Man*, 1975; *The Two of Them*, 1978) and the latter in detective fiction (*Death in a Tenured Position*, 1981; *No Word from Winifred*, 1986).

In the sixties, competing impulses dramatize writers' differences from one another as well as from postmodernism. Certain writers, susceptible to the burdens of history, present overtly political responses, for example, Marge Piercy (b.1936) in *Woman on the Edge of Time* (1976), *Vida* (1979), and *Braided Lives* (1982). Ann Tyler (b.1941), on the other hand, portrays the traditional story of family dynamics in a uniquely quirky and contemporary way most successfully in *Dinner at the Homesick Restaurant* (1982).

Perhaps the strongest impulse countering postmodernism is the "tribal." Ethnic/cultural identification serves as the necessary vehicle to dramatize social/historical/personal connectedness. Thus Maxine Hong Kingston (b.1940) presents Asian-American experience in *The Woman Warrior* (1976); Leslie Silko (b.1948), that of Native Americans in *Laguna Woman* (1974), *Ceremony* (1977), and *Storyteller* (1981); and Cynthia Ozick (b.1928), that of Jewish Americans in *Trust* (1966); while a growing number of black writers—Marshall, Bambara, and Walker, for example—present the African-American experience. From this latter group emerges, arguably, one of the most important writers of the last decades of the century—Toni Morrison (b.1931), author of *The Bluest Eye* (1970), *Sula* (1973), *Song of Solomon* (1977), *Tar Baby* (1981), and *Beloved* (1987), an evocative novel of women and slavery. It is a tribute to her particular genius that what the reader gains from the text is a sense of triumph, great compassion, and love.

See also AFRICAN-AMERICAN PROSE WRITERS; AMERICAN CLASSICAL CANON; LESBIAN LITERATURE; NOVELISTS, U.S. (TO WORLD WAR I).

SUSAN HAWKINS

O

OLD WIVES' TALES. The sayings, popular beliefs, precepts, and narratives once valued as the wisdom and wit of experienced, older women but now applied metaphorically to discredit forms of women's and men's speech as idle untruths. Both the *Oxford English Dictionary* definition, "a trivial story such as is told by garrulous old women," and that in *Webster's New World Dictionary*, "a silly story or superstitious belief such as might be passed around by gossipy old women," promulgate the common, sexist usage. There is no equally derogatory literal or metaphoric term commonly associated with old men's/husbands' verbal arts and lore. (See GOSSIP.)

Social recognition of older or otherwise knowledgeable women as persons of substance, spirit, wisdom, and valued verbal/nonverbal performance skills varies historically and cross-culturally. In many societies, postmenopausal women are freed from social restraints over those capable of childbearing and may participate fully in public ritual, politics, licentiousness, and entertainment. Often, older and younger women who practice healing, divination, midwifery, and other skills based on physical/social observation and analysis are considered valuable members of society by both women and men. This opinion is not the case either in Western scientific tradition, which generally has denounced women's traditional lore as irrational "old wives' tales," or in official Christian tradition, as reflected, for example, in Paul's injunction (1 Tim. 4:7, Tindale, 1526): "Cast away vngostly and olde wyves' fables," later translated as "Have nothing to do with godless and silly myths" (Revised Standard Version, 1971). (See MYTHOLOGY.)

Women verbal artists generally do not enjoy wide acclaim. Folklorists and anthropologists for the most part have assumed that women possess speaking and narrating competence informally with children but have ignored skills displayed with each other or in mixed adult audiences. However, there is historical evidence for the latter, like George Peele's 1595 play, *The Old Wives Tale*, framed as "a merry winter's tale [that] would drive away the time trimly" for three male pages spending the night with the blacksmith Clunch and his old wife Madge, who narrates the story within the drama until "cock's-crow." Among the Xhosa of South Africa, women are considered the best performers of valued dramatic narratives called *ntsomi* (Harold Scheub, "The Art of [Mrs.] Nongenile Mazithathu Zenani, a Gcaleka Ntsomi Performer," in Richard M. Dorson [ed.], *African Folklore* [Bloomington, Ind., 1972], 115–142). Nevertheless, women's enlightenment and entertainment of each other, their skillful, artistic use of old wives' tales to educate, constrain, and/or enable other women are matters still in need of study.

Further References. Mary Chamberlain, *Old Wives' Tales: Their History, Remedies and Spells* (London, 1981). Barbara G. Walker, *The Crone: Women of Age, Wisdom, and Power* (San Francisco, 1985).

MARTA WEIGLE

P

PAINTERS, BRITISH (VICTORIAN), worked throughout the latter half of the nineteenth century to achieve professional acceptance. Although most middle- and upper-class Victorian women learned how to draw and paint as part of their education, serious women found it nearly impossible to gain the additional education necessary for professional recognition.

Victorians divided the universe neatly into separate spheres; accordingly, women and men followed different educational programs and strove for different goals. While men worked for financial security, women were expected to adorn their homes, not just through cleaning and tidying, but through their artistic exertions. To this end, women learned decorative crafts such as embroidery, lacemaking, drawing, and painting. Also, Victorians expected women to demonstrate "genteel" accomplishments, particularly music or drawing. Most Victorian upper- and middle-class women could copy engravings or casts, draw landscapes, and dabble in watercolors.

Serious women painters had few educational options. Victorians believed that women were unsuited to strenuous intellectual or physical efforts. In theory, women were capable of copy work, in which they simply had to reproduce the greater productions of men artists; women could also produce watercolor paintings of flowers and gentle landscapes—oil painting was deemed too messy and strenuous. Most of all, popular belief was that women could not match men's genius: men could be great, women only good. For these reasons, women were excluded from serious study or competition. Painters need training and, even more importantly, need a supportive community of colleagues and a responsive public. If a Victorian woman was wealthy, she could gain the necessary experience by traveling to Rome and studying with famous artists, or she could hire a Royal Academy member to provide private lessons. A middle-class woman, however, had to rely on the few available art schools for education. Although women were not allowed to study in the Royal Academy of Arts until 1860, some schools provided the requisite artistic training for women painters. The Royal Female School of Art (founded in 1862) provided traditional "feminine" art education for amateurs; unfortunately, the Royal Academy Council forbade women to study in its classes because of the Royal Female School's existence. Henry Sass's School of Art, Dickinson's Academy, and the Slade School of Art focused on educating amateur painters but did help ambitious women achieve professional status. Laura Herford (one of the first Royal Academy women students), Kate Greenaway, Louisa Starr, Frances Fripp Rossiter, and Anna Blunden studied in various "female" schools.

Despite severe educational handicaps and enormous public prejudice, many women painters won public acclaim and financial security, often by defeating men painters on their own territory. Once women gained entrance into the Royal Academy, they quickly won student honors: Catherine Adeline Sparkes won a £10 prize in 1865; Louisa Starr won a silver medal in 1865 and a gold in 1867; Emmeline Halse won two silver medals in the 1880s. Women's success in the academy led to the council's refusing to admit any further women in 1863. When prominent women painters protested, the Academy grudgingly allowed 13 women students to attend all except nude life-study classes.

In the most important exhibitions, women painters were seriously under-represented: until about 1870, only 5 to 10 percent of the works at any major show were by women. The Royal Academy Exhibition, Society of British Artists, British Institution, and Portland Gallery preferred historical, classical, or portrait paintings in oil, which women rarely attempted. Watercolors of any kind, flower or genre paintings, landscapes, and works in alternative media, like embroidery or tapestry work, were not well received. The Society of Female Artists (founded in 1857) and the Manchester Society of Women Painters (founded in 1879) sponsored exhibitions dominated by amateur works. Usually, professional women painters sent their works to men-dominated exhibitions. Many of the works accepted for exhibition in the prestigious shows attracted massive critical and public attention. The most famous instance is Elizabeth Thompson Butler's overnight success with *Roll Call* (1874), a large oil painting depicting a scene from the Crimean War. Hung well at the Royal Academy exhibition, her painting increased in value from £126 to over £1,200, not counting income from the copyright. Queen Victoria insisted upon buying the painting from the original owner, but Butler kept the copyright.

Although the stereotype of a Victorian woman painter is a genteel woman who takes time from her household duties to paint delicate flowers on china or wispy landscapes in watercolors, women handled oil painting quite well, and they conquered a variety of subjects. Elizabeth Thompson Butler, Fanny Corbaux, and Henrietta Ward produced large historical and classical paintings, often portraying biblical, classical, or literary scenes in which women suffer or mourn. Margaret Sarah Geddes (Mrs. William Carpenter), Ambrosini Jerome, and Mrs. James Robertson excelled in portraiture; each of these painters received royal commissions. With financial support from John Ruskin, Elizabeth Siddal painted suffering, dying women. Many women excelled in landscape, still life, or genre painting: Helen Paterson (Mrs. William Allington); Alice Squire; Mary Rossiter; Eloise Harriet Stannard; Charlotte, Eliza, Louisa, and Mary Ann Sharpe; and Louisa and Fanny Corbaux. Women pushed beyond the boundaries imposed upon their art until they achieved a modest professional status.

In the last decades of the nineteenth century, women painters won access to nude life-study classes, gained better—but not equal—representation in exhibitions, and, in the 1920s, finally won membership in the Royal Academy. Unfortunately, as many feminist historians have noted, women won acceptance by institutions like the Royal Academy just as the institutions were losing prestige. Young artists, studying abroad, particularly in France, rejected traditional English values, education, and methods. The most brilliant, on their return to England, worked without Royal Academy acceptance. The Pre-Raphaelite Brotherhood broke away from the Royal Academy and its exhibitions to begin a splinter group and competing exhibitions. And women found it impossible to become members of the Pre-Raphaelites, or other such groups, except as models, wives, and lovers. Just as it was no longer fashionable to gain academic approval, women began to produce acceptable institutional art. They were doomed to second rank again.

Further References. Ellen Clayton, *English Female Artists* (London, 1876). Rozsika Parker and Griselda Pollock, *Old Mistresses: Women, Art, and Ideology* (New York, 1981). Charlotte Yeldham, *Women Artists in Nineteenth-Century France and England*, 2 vols. (New York, 1984).

JULIA M. GERGITS

PAINTERS, U.S. (BEFORE WORLD WAR I). Women painters, often self-taught, were active participants in the arts of the new American republic as folk artists, miniaturists, and, later, landscape, history, and genre painters.

The work of self-taught women helped meet the need for wall decorations. One of the most original painters was Eunice Griswold Pinney (1770–1849) of New York State. In strong two dimensional watercolors, such as *Two Women* (c.1815), the flattened perspective and careful arrangement of objects contribute to the design. Among numerous other folk painters are Mary Ann Willson (fl.1810–1825) of Green County, New York, who used crude, homemade paints in brightly colored scenes from the bible, history, and literature; Ruth Miles Bascom (1772–1848) who did profile portraits of friends and neighbors in rural Massachusetts; and anonymous Shaker women, whose "spirit drawings" were inspired by the spirit of their deceased leader Ann Lee.

Although art academies opened at the beginning of the nineteenth century, women were not admitted as students for several decades, but had to rely for training on private lessons, usually with a family member. Nonetheless, the American academies were more open to women than were their European counterparts. The Pennsylvania Academy of Fine Arts in Philadelphia (opened 1805) included women in its first exhibit in 1811. Approximately 6 percent of the artists who exhibited between 1826 and 1860 at the National Academy of Design (founded in New York, 1825) were women and 11 associate, 4 honorary, and 1 full membership were held by women. The New York academy accepted women on a regular basis from 1846. Anna and Sarah Peale were elected to the Pennsylvania Academy in 1824 and Jane Sully in 1831; the first evidence that women were regular students comes in 1844.

Admission as students did not include attendance at life classes with nude models. Beginning in 1844 the Pennsylvania Academy closed its antique sculpture gallery for three hours a week so women could study the figures. In 1856 gallery attendance was desegregated, but close fitting fig leaves had been added to male figures as necessary. Live female models were introduced into women's segregated life classes in 1860; male models in 1877. The National Academy allowed women in life classes in 1871.

Miniatures were considered most suitable for women painters in the early nineteenth century, as they had been in the eighteenth when Henrietta Johnston (d.1728–29) became the first American woman professional artist. Sarah Goodrich (1788–1853) of rural Massachusetts did miniatures on ivory of portraitist Gilbert Stuart, leading members of Boston society, and government leaders in Washington. Gilbert Stuart taught students, including Goodrich, but not members of his own family. Jane Stuart (1812–1888), his youngest, was able to pick up information from his instruction of others while filling in his backgrounds and grinding paints. After his death in 1828, she supported her mother and three sisters by making copies of his work, especially his Athenaeum Head of George Washington, and by her original portraits. She also did biblical and literary scenes.

Ann Hall (1792–1863), miniaturist from Connecticut, was the first woman to be a full member of the National Academy of Design (1833). Her group portraits of upper-class women and children had a delicacy and flattering "sweetness" highly admired at the time.

The "Painting Peales" of Philadelphia were the most famous family of painters in early America. Several daughters of James Peale became professional artists. Anna Claypoole Peale (1791–1878), who learned painting on ivory from her father, shared a studio in Washington, D.C., with the most famous Peale, her uncle Charles Willson Peale, and painted such worthies as General Jackson and President Monroe. She retired during her second marriage, then continued her career in Philadelphia when widowed.

Sarah Miriam Peale (1800–1885), the most successful of the Peale women, did full-size portraits during a long career. In Baltimore she competed successfully with some of the leading male portraitists of the day. After 22 years in Baltimore she went to St. Louis for a rest and stayed over 30 years. In her late seventies she returned to Philadelphia and continued painting, principally still lifes. Her portraits show people in their best light, dignified, but not idealized.

Other female "Painting Peales" include still-life artist Margarette Angelicia Peale (1795–1882), another daughter of James, and, in the next generation, Mary

Jane Simes (1807–1852), granddaughter of James, miniaturist, and Mary Jane Peale (1827–1902), granddaughter of Charles Willson, portrait painter.

By mid-century the increasingly affluent middle class provided a new group of art patrons looking for paintings that satisfied their taste for the romantic and the sentimental and reinforced their moral values. Women painters turned increasingly to genre, history, and allegory.

Herminia Borchard Dassel (d.1858), born in Germany, studied in Dusseldorf and Italy, leaving Italy for America when revolution broke out in 1848. In the United States, she turned to the American scene for her genre paintings, including romantic paintings of American Indians.

Lilly Martin Spencer (1822–1902), from Ohio, was a leading American genre painter of mid-century. In 1848 she moved to New York, where she supported her husband and large family by her painting (Benjamin Spencer assisted his wife and did much of the running of the household). Mrs. Spencer was interested in allegorical and literary subjects and used the portrait as a vehicle for allegory (*We Both Must Fade* [1869]), but her reputation rested on her genre paintings. She met the public taste for sentiment by domestic scenes, often with a vein of humor (*Peeling Onions* [c.1852]). Prints from engravings and lithographs of her work entered homes all over America, and sometimes abroad, but she had difficulty keeping her family afloat financially—she was paid only for the original painting. After the Civil War, as buyers of art preferred European paintings, her financial plight grew even worse; she sometimes had to barter her paintings for food.

Representative of the many women painters active in the second and third quarter of the nineteenth century, and of the subjects women painted, are the following: Charlotte Buell Coman (1833–1924) of New York was a "tonalist" landscape artist whose quiet, misty scenes were designed to create a mood in the viewer. Typical are her *Early Summer* (1907) and *Clearing Off* (1912). Fidelia Bridges (1834–1932) of Massachusetts, nature artist, did close-up studies of grasses, ferns, flowers, birds, as in *Daises and Clover* (1871) and *Thrush in Wild Flower* (1874). Anna Elizabeth Hardy (1839–1934) of Bangor, Maine, was a still-life artist whose best works are the well-defined fruit and flower studies of her early career. Susan Moore Waters (1823–1900) of Binghamton, New York, was an animal painter especially noted for her pictures of sheep.

During the "Gilded Age" (1876–1900) affluent Americans looked to Europe for culture and found things American inferior. Art students traveled to Europe, especially to Paris, international mecca of the arts. In the art academies open to women (the École des Beaux Arts and the Royal Academy in London did not open until the last decade of the century), women's life classes were segregated, cost more, had inferior models and lower standards, but women flocked to them nonetheless. Most women went to Europe for a few years; a few remained for the rest of their lives, returning to America only for visits.

The expatriates include one of the century's greatest artists, Mary Cassatt (discussed in FRENCH IMPRESSIONISTS). Another expatriate was Elizabeth

Gardener (Bouguereau) (1833–1922), the first American woman to receive a gold medal at the Paris Salon. Living in Paris, she painted sentimental genre and allegory and finally married William Bouguereau after his mother, who opposed the marriage, died (he was 71, she 58). Among other expatriate women artists were Ann Lea Merrit (1844–1930) and Sarah Paxton Dodson (1847–1906), academic painters who settled in England, and Cecile Smith de Wentworth (1853?–1933), best known for her portrait of Leo XIII, and Elizabeth Nouse (1859–1938), noted for her outstanding studies of European peasant women, who settled in France.

Growing dissatisfaction with American art schools not only gave impetus to the flight to Paris, but led to the formation of the progressive Art Students League in 1875 (see ART STUDENTS LEAGUE) and in 1877 the Society of American Artists, one of whose aims was to encourage women artists. As the number of women artists continued to increase, a sign of the art schools' growing dependence upon women students was the Pennsylvania Academy of Fine Arts' hiring of Catherine Drinker (Janvier) (1841–1922) in 1878 as part-time lecturer and Cecilia Beaux as the first full-time woman instructor in 1895.

Susan Macdowell Eakins (1851–1938) of Philadelphia, realist painter and first recipient of the Pennsylvania Academy's Mary Smith Award (1879), married her teacher Thomas Eakins in 1884. During their marriage she placed his career first, greatly reducing her own production, but after his death in 1916 she immersed herself in painting again. Her work (*Two Sisters* [1879] and *Portrait of a Lady* [1880] are among her best) is marked by strong characterization and lack of sentimentality.

Cecilia Beaux (1855–1942), was a leading portraitist of the late nineteenth century. She achieved success with her first major work, *Les Derniers Jour d'Enfance* (1883–1885), which won the Mary Smith Award and was accepted at the Paris Salon in 1887. Another of her finest paintings, *Fanny Travis Cochran* (1887) dates from her early period. After study in Europe she established a New York studio and joined the world of the New York social and intellectual elite. There in the 1890s she did a series of double portraits, including *Mother and Daughter* (1898), her most highly acclaimed and honored work. A major triumph of the early twentieth century is *After the Meeting* (1914).

Anna Elizabeth Klumpke (1856–1942) was born in San Francisco but received her education in Europe. She won honorable mention in Paris salons in 1885 and 1887, the latter for her portrait of Elizabeth Cady Stanton, then 71. She was teaching and painting in Boston when she wrote Rosa Bonheur (see FRENCH ACADEMIC PAINTERS), asking to do her portrait. In 1898 she went to By, Bonheur's estate at Fontainebleau, where a deep friendship developed and Bonheur asked her to remain and to write her biography. The portrait of Bonheur in 1898 is Klumpke's finest work. The biography was published in 1908. Klumpke's last years were spent between San Francisco, Boston, and By.

A few of the many other American women artists of note during the last quarter of the nineteenth century include Mary Lizzie Macomber (1861–1916), pre-Raphaelite painter; Lucia Fairchild Fuller (1870–1924), one of the few miniaturists of the period; Anna Richards Brewster (1870–1952), landscape artist; Lilla Cabot Perry (1848–1933), impressionist; Mary Oakey Dewing (1845–1927), and Claude Raguet Hirst (1855–1942), still-life painters; Jennie Augusta Brownscombe (1850–1936), commercial artist and American history painter; Alice Baker Stephenson (1858–1932), one of best-known illustrators in America at the time; and Grace Carpenter Hudson, painter of American Indians.

Both the Philadelphia Centenniel Exposition in 1876 and the World's Columbian Exposition in Chicago in 1893 provided a showcase for women's accomplishments in the arts. In both, a separate building housed exhibitions of women's accomplishments, in the arts as well as in other areas, and in both, women's art works were not limited to the women's building. The works on display demonstrated the rich variety and the quality of nineteenth-century art by women.

Further Reference. Charlotte Streifer Rubinstein, *American Women Artists: From Early Indian Times to the Present* (Boston, 1982).

PAINTERS (TWENTIETH-CENTURY). Although there had been internationally successful women painters since the 1500s, our own century has seen a tremendous increase in the number of European and American women supporting their families and making important cultural contributions through their art.

During the first decades of the twentieth century educational and societal barriers confronting female art students began to fall. At the same time, an explosion of scientific and technological discoveries, along with the traumas of World War I, led to an unprecedented questioning of traditional values and beliefs about all aspects of the world. Women painters played important roles in the radical "isms" that followed one another in rapid succession, including that most remarkable break with the art of the past: abstraction.

Fauvism and Expressionism—which originated c.1905 in France and Germany, respectively—were the first two revolutionary movements in twentieth-century art. Both of these influential styles evolved from the Post-Impressionist paintings of Cézanne, Seurat, Van Gogh, and Gauguin, and both feature images taken from the real world but stylized through the use of heavy outlines, intense colors, thick pigment, and flattened space. In general, Fauve art stresses joyous sensuality, while Expressionism evokes a darker mood. The Fauve-inspired art of Suzanne Valadon (1865–1938) celebrates the human body, often unashamedly nude and made up of solid, powerfully modeled forms and shocking juxtapositions of violent hues. Fauvism was a significant influence on the late northwestern landscapes of Canadian painter Emily Carr (1871–1945) and on the American Lois Mailou Jones (b.1905), whose work also reflects her interest in Haitian and African tribal art.

Among the most important German Expressionist artists was Gabriela Münter (1877–1962). Barred from the official art academies in Munich and Dusseldorf, Münter studied at the coeducational Phalanx School, established by Kandinsky. Münter's highly colored still-lifes, landscapes, and figure studies were denounced by the Nazis as "degenerate," along with the art of her countrywoman, Käthe Kollwitz (1867–1945).

Probably the most influential modernist style to develop during the first decade of the twentieth century was cubism. Coinvented by Picasso and Braque, cubism, with its distorted spaces and often illegible subject matter, challenged many of the basic tenets of Western art and spawned numerous offshoots, from England's vorticism to Italian futurism. A French variation known as orphism was developed around 1911 by Sonia Terk Delaunay (1885–1979) and her husband, Robert Delaunay. Russian-born and German-trained, Delaunay was strongly affected by the avant-garde artists she encountered on moving to Paris; her mature paintings feature complex arrangements of brightly colored, interlacing arcs. A number of modern art pioneers came from prerevolutionary Russia. One of these was Natalya Goncharova (1881–1962), who, along with Mikhail Larionov, developed a cubist offshoot called rayonism, in which highly stylized forms are crisscrossed by a series of diagonal lines, or "rays."

The work of the American painter Georgia O'Keeffe (1887–1986) is related to, but not directly influenced by, early twentieth-century European experimental art. Best known for her compelling images of flowers and sun-bleached bones, O'Keeffe is significant in art history primarily because of the spare, elegant watercolor abstractions she produced as early as 1915.

During the late 1920s and 1930s, surrealism became a powerful force in avant-garde literature and visual and performing arts. Like their male counterparts, American painters Kay Sage (1898–1963), and Dorothea Tanning (b.1910), Spaniard Remedios Varo (1913–1963), British artist Leonora Carrington (b.1917), and the Argentine Léonor Fini (b.1908) created irrational, often erotic and/or violent compositions juxtaposing unrelated objects derived from their subconscious minds. The art of Frida Kahlo (1910–1954) is also surreal, combining Christian symbols with references to the folk art of her native Mexico.

In the United States the 1930s and early 1940s were dominated by American scene painting—realistic representations of identifiably American subjects. In painting the landscape of New York City, Isabel Bishop (1902–1988) lovingly describes such ordinary moments as two office workers on their lunch break or a man getting a shoeshine.

At mid-century American art underwent an unprecedented change. The international art world shifted its center from Europe to the United States—specifically, New York, with the development of abstract expressionism: a radically new kind of abstraction—less cerebral than cubism, visceral, highly personal, and more appropriate to the post–World War II environment. While traditionally regarded as a male phenomenon—exemplified by the hard-drinking, chain-smoking, aggressively macho figure of Jackson Pollock—there were many important female abstract expressionists. Chief among these was Lee Krasner (1908–1984), whose "Little Image" paintings of the late 1940s were quintessential examples of this style. Other important abstract expressionist painters include Elaine Fried De Kooning (b.1920), Grace Hartigan (b.1922), Joan Mitchell (b.1926), and Helen Frankenthaler (b.1928).

The generation of painters who matured during the 1960s tended to react against what they perceived as the emotional excesses of abstract expressionism by moving either toward a form of realism that stressed the brandname, throwaway nature of American culture (pop art), or toward an exploration of emotionally neutral abstraction—using simple forms, unmodulated colors, and smooth surfaces (postpainterly abstraction). Prominent among the latter group is the English artist Bridget Riley (b.1931), who made her reputation with a series of sophisticated canvases in which repeating black, white, and grey shapes curve in and out through illusionistic space.

The tremendous growth of the women's movement during the 1960s was reflected in the new prominence of openly feminist artists such as Toronto-born Miriam Schapiro (b.1923). Trained as an abstract expressionist, Schapiro developed what she calls "femmage"—a technique combining colorful, commonplace materials traditionally associated with women, such as scraps of lace, sequins, and tea towels—into elaborate compositions. Along with Judy Chicago (b.1939), Schapiro organized the first feminist art program in the United States at the California Institute of Arts.

A popular phenomenon of the early 1970s was photorealism—extraordinarily detailed paintings that painstakingly reproduce the optical effects (including out-of-focus areas) seen in actual photos. Audrey Flack (b.1931) is a New York painter known for her large-scale, photorealistic still-lifes, which include a remarkable amount of iconographic content.

The many and varied approaches that have characterized avant-garde painting in the 1980s—including Neo-Expressionism, serial repetition, image appropriation, and the incorporation of three-dimensional objects into canvases—have all been explored by important women artists, notably Susan Rothenberg (b.1945), Jennifer Bartlett (b.1941), Sherrie Levine (b.1947), and Elizabeth Murray (b.1940).

Further References. Ann Sutherland Harris and Linda Nochlin, *Women Artists: 1550–1950* (Los Angeles, 1976). Randy Rosen and Catherine C. Brawer et al., *Making Their Mark: Women Artists Move into the Mainstream, 1970–1985* (New York, 1989).

NANCY G. HELLER

PATRONS AND COLLECTORS, U.S., have yet to undergo serious study. At this time only a random sample of women's contributions, through patronage, to U.S. cultural life is possible.

In Europe women of royal and aristocratic families, as part of their social and political roles, served as patrons of arts and letters. Since the French Revolution, as monarchies were eliminated, their art collections were opened to the public (e.g., the Louvre in Paris, the Hermitage in Leningrad), and the new republican governments took over the function of promoting and supporting the arts. Where monarchy persists, although royal influence can be important in promoting cultural forms, as the powers of the monarch were transferred to elective governments, so too was the support of the cultural life of the community.

In the United States, where republican government was established under Enlightenment ideals that restricted the government's role to the protection of life, liberty, and property and where there was no royalty or titled aristocracy with a tradition of patronage, promotion of the arts was slow to develop and fell to private individuals and groups. State and local governments became involved, beyond granting tax exemptions to cultural organizations, only from the latter nineteenth century, when they began to include art and music in school curricula and sometimes helped to support concert halls, museums, and libraries originally established by private means. It was not until the midtwentieth century that the federal government became involved, indirectly through the Works Progress Administration during the Depression and, since the 1960s, through the National Endowments for the Arts and Humanities.

Patronage of the arts in the United States, then, has been, and continues to be, primarily private, often by the combined efforts of people of relatively moderate wealth. Women's clubs, since the latter half of the nineteenth century organized by women for personal and social betterment, have been responsible for much of the promotion of the performing arts.

Mutual interest in music led to the formation of women's music clubs; the oldest was the Rossini Club of Portland, Maine, founded in 1868 by five women for the advancement of music in their community. These women's clubs gave concerts by their own members and by professional artists. The clubs booked the artists, rented the hall, promoted the event, sold tickets, and sometimes did the janitor work as well. The Mozart Society of New York City in the 1920s sponsored monthly Saturday musicals, evening concerts, a women's chorus, and social events. The women's music club in Oklahoma City organized a string orchestra and engaged a conductor. By 1927 the Oklahoma City Symphony Orchestra had 68 players. Women's clubs, by combining, could arrange a tour that brought great artists to smaller cities. For example, in the early twentieth century the Peoria music club, under Emily Roderick (Mrs. William Fisher), a public school music teacher, brought in the best talent of the day, including orchestras such as the Boston Symphony. The clubs also showed interest in making good music affordable to the poor in their cities and in music education for children. At the turn of the century, the Women's Philharmonic Society of New York sponsored concerts at low prices in tenement districts, music classes for children, and a children's orchestra.

The financial support given by women's committees and associations has been vital to symphonies since 1898, when women in New York founded a committee to support the New York Symphony Orchestra. By the mid–1970s there were over 75 women's symphony orchestra associations in the United States. In 1983 Constance Hoguet, first woman president of the New York Philharmonic Symphony Society, founded and cochaired the Friends of the Philharmonic, which raised $2.675 million for the symphony in 1983. To raise funds and to "democratize" opera, in 1935 Eleanor Elise Robson Belmont founded the Metropolitan Opera Guild. Scaled membership in the guild helped raise funds and also gave members a sense of ownership and a share in its privileges.

Many of the major cultural institutions in the United States owe their foundation to men and women of great wealth who established museums, conservatories, art institutes, concert halls, festivals, etc. They and others of lesser means have also supported the arts by establishing scholarships and competitions, acting as sponsors of young artists and musicians, becoming collectors—often later giving some or all of their collections to museums or founding museums to house them—and in other ways.

Only a few women patrons and collectors can be mentioned here, but they represent the many women whose support has helped to enrich life in the United States.

Irene Lewisohn, with her sister Alice, established one of the earliest "little theatres" in the United States, the Neighborhood Playhouse in New York, a major center of experimental theatre from 1915 to 1927. In 1928 she became cofounder and codirector of the Neighborhood Playhouse School and in 1937 founded the Costume Institute, now part of the Metropolitan Museum of Art.

Marie Leontine Graves Bullock in 1934 founded the Academy of American Poets to increase the appreciation of poetry, reward excellent poetry, and encourage new poets. The academy awards scholarships, prizes, and book awards. Elizabeth Kray, executive director of the academy from 1963 to 1981, founded with poet Stanley Kunitz the Poets House as a meeting place for poets.

Mary Curtis Bok Zimbalist founded the Curtis Institute in Philadelphia in 1924. Elizabeth Sprague Collidge devoted her energies and her fortune to the promotion of chamber music. From 1918 to 1925 she put on seven Berkshire festivals of chamber music and from 1923 also arranged festivals in European cities. In 1925 she set up the Elizabeth Sprague Coolidge Foundation at the Library of Congress and donated an auditorium to the library for chamber music concerts. The foundation then became her principal philanthropy, but she continued to encourage chamber music through other avenues as well.

Martha Baird Rockefeller, a former pianist, set up a fund for young musicians and was a major supporter of music institutions in New York and New England. Betty Freeman, a patron of new music, subsidized about 30 composers, including John Cage and Daniel Lentz. She helped finance concerts of new and minimalist music and in 1981 began monthly musicales in her home. A patron of jazz who moved to the United States in the 1950s, Baroness Pannonica de Keonigswarter befriended Charlie Parker and Thelonious Monk and helped finance Barry Harris's Jazz Cultural Theater.

It was through the advice of painter Mary Cassatt to wealthy friends that many of Europe's most outstanding paintings made their way to America and, eventually, into its museums. One of these wealthy friends was Bertha Honoré Palmer, social arbiter of Chicago and one of the first to introduce French Impressionists to America. On her death in 1918 she left $100,000 in objets d'art to the Chicago Art Institute. Louisine Waldron Elder Havemeyer was introduced to French Impressionist art by Cassatt when she was a young girl. She and her husband assembled a remarkable collection of moderns and Spanish paintings. When they left 142 art objects to the Metropolitan Museum of Art, that museum, which had refused to buy moderns, suddenly became one of the world's greatest holders in this area.

To the Havemeyer's dismay, their daughter Electra Havemeyer Webb began quite early to collect what they considered "junk." The result is the Shelburne Museum in Vermont, founded in 1947. It is a 45-acre, open-air museum containing American art, artifacts, and regional architecture: c.27,000 pieces in 37 buildings, a steam engine, private railway car, and the SS *Ticonderoga*.

Many collections of art were built by husband and wife teams, but other collections have been built entirely by women. Etta and Clara Cone's collection of twentieth-century art is in the Baltimore Museum of Art, and Ola Hirshhorn's is in the Hirshhorn Museum and Sculpture Garden, now part of the Smithsonian. Abby Aldrich Rockefeller, one of three women instrumental in founding the Museum of Modern Art in New York, gave it a large collection (over 2,000 objects) and an unrestricted fund for future purchases. The Abby Aldrich Rockefeller Folk Art Center at Williamsburg attests to her interest in utilitarian arts. Eleanor Biddle Lloyd was a founder of the Washington Gallery of Modern Art in 1950 and Institute of Contemporary Art at the University of Pennsylvania. Gertrude Vanderbilt Whitney, sculptor and patron of artists, with Juliana Force in an association that lasted from about 1907 to Whitney's death in 1942, promoted American art and living American artists, culminating in the Whitney Museum of American Art.

Progeny of philanthropists often continue the family interest in a foundation and may add to it or found new institutions in the same or related fields. Helen Clay Frick served as trustee of the Frick Art Museum (Pittsburgh), founded by her father. She also founded the Frick Art Reference Library in 1924 in New York City and in 1927 financed the Henry Clay Frick Fine Arts Department of the University of Pittsburgh. Flora Whitney Miller, daughter of Gertrude Vanderbilt Whitney, served as chairperson and president of Whitney Museum. Under her leadership the museum and its activities gained national stature.

One of the most avid collectors was Peggy Guggenheim. Her interest peaked to a frenzy of buying in the summer of 1941, when she went through Europe averaging a painting a day, despite the war raging at the time. After her return to America in late 1941 she established a gallery, Art of This Century, which quickly became the center of avant-garde art in New York. She gave generously to many museums in the United States, then in 1947 settled in Venice, where the Peggy Guggenheim Museum is today located.

Collectors of the latter twentieth century include Alice Dresel Beal Van Santvoord of Newburgh, New York, benefactor for artists Childe Hassam, Walt Kuhn, and Timothy Cole. Florence Lacaze Gould and her husband, Frank Jay

Gould, were literary patrons and collectors of art of all periods. Later in her life Mrs. Gould became interested in Impressionist and Post-Impressionist painters. Edith and Robert Scull (divorced in 1974) were among the most important collectors of the late 1950s and 1960s. They collected pop art.

There have also been women who collected women's art. Henrietta Louisa Koenen specialized in collecting engravings, etchings, and lithographs by women from 1848 to her death in 1861. In the early 1960s Louise Noun began to collect art by women, and Wilhelmina Cole Holladay, with her husband, Wallace, began specializing in women's art in the late 1960s. Chris Petteys began her collection in the early 1970s. Marge Greenbaum specializes in art by nineteenth- and twentieth-century American women artists. "Billie" Holladay's collection became the core of the National Museum of Women in the Arts, which opened in April 1987, with Holladay as first president.

HELEN TIERNEY WITH MELISSA HENSLEY

PATRONS OF THE ARTS (MIDDLE AGES AND RENAISSANCE). Although Herbert Grundmann convincingly argued as early as 1936 that the development of vernacular literature in the Middle Ages can be credited to the patronage of women and to their need to have Latin works translated into the vernacular, little attention has heretofore been given to the role of women patrons for medieval literature. Recent studies, however, have unearthed a wealth of new information about female patronage in the early and high Middle Ages. A comprehensive picture is nevertheless still missing.

Judith (d.843), empress and wife of Louis the Pious, was highly acclaimed for her literary interests. Hrabanus Maurus, Bishop Prudentius of Troyes, and Walahfrid Strabo dedicated their works to this woman. Matilde (d.968), mother of Emperor Otto I; Empress Adelheid (d.999), Otto I's second wife; and her two daughters, Mathilde (d.999) and Gerberg (d.1011), continued this tradition of patronizing poetry and the arts. Widukind of Corvey and Hrotsvit of Gandersheim dedicated their poems to the Empress Mathilde.

Throughout the Middle Ages needlework provided women with vast opportunities in the visual arts. Women's activity as embroiderers, weavers, and makers of tapestry is well documented, for instance, in the highly acclaimed Bayeux Tapestry (1066), commissioned by Mathilda, wife of William the Conqueror, and the opus Anglicanum, embroidery work from England in the twelfth and thirteenth centuries. Queen Margaret of Scotland (eleventh century) was at the center of a highly productive workshop of textiles and their ornamentation. Particularly, abbesses of many convents gained a high reputation for their support of these skills. Book production and illustration were almost exclusively in the hands of monasteries and convents. Gisela, Charlemagne's sister, directed the first Carolingian convent scriptorium at Chelles. *The Gerona Apocalypse* from 975 was produced and signed by a woman painter.

In the twelfth century, Maud of Scotland (d.1118) and Adeliza of Brabant, both wives of the English king Henry I (d.1135), established an important cultural circle at their courts. Adeliza in particular is famous for being the patron of the first vernacular English poems, whereas Maud commissioned *The Voyage of Saint Brendan* in Latin and later in Anglo-Norman translation.

Best known as a patron of the arts was, however, Eleanor of Aquitaine (d.1204), wife of both King Louis VII of France and King Henry II of England, because she was particularly responsible for the development and promotion of the Arthurian romances in England and France. Her two daughters Marie and Alice followed in her path. Marie, countess of the Champagne since 1164, supported Chrétien de Troyes; and Alice, Countess of Blois, supported Gautier d'Arras. Modern research has, however, dismissed the theory that Andreas Capellanus composed his famous treatise *De amore* at Marie's court. At the suggestion of another of Eleanor's daughters, Mathilde, the duchess of Saxonia since 1168, the French *Chanson de Roland* was translated into German by the cleric Konrad. She was probably also responsible for having arranged the translation of the *Roman de Tristan* by Eilhart of Oberg.

The court of Margarete of Cleve in northwest Germany made possible the first major translation of the French *Roman d'Eneas* into Middle High German through Heinrich von Veldeke. The philosopher and theologian Vincent of Beauvais wrote his treatise *De eruditione filiorum nobilium* (c.1247–1248) at the request of Queen Margaret of Provence. In 1328 she commissioned John de Vignai to translate Vincent's famous *Speculum historiale*. When in 1382 Anne of Bohemia arrived in England to marry King Richard II, she brought with her, along with a large library, a host of book illustrators. Very soon afterward she ordered an English translation of the gospel. Critical of Chaucer's antifeminist *Troilus and Criseyde,* she also inspired the poet to compose his *The Legend of Good Women.* Most didactic and instructional reading materials (primers, psalters, gospels, etc.) were ordered by women who were in charge of their children's education.

From the thirteenth century, legendary literature became the favorite object of female patrons, such as Guta (d.1297), wife of King Wenceslaus II of Bohemia. She was glorified by Ulrich von Etzenbach in his romance *Wilhelm von Wenden.* Other texts particularly popular among women, and thus often commissioned by female heads of royal households, were *Books of Hours.*

Elizabeth (d.1231), wife of Duke Louis of Thuringia, deeply influenced Wolfram von Eschenbach's composition of his *Willehalm* and his *Titurel* fragment around 1220. Possibly Duchess Agnes, wife of Duke Otto I of Wittelsbach, was the patron of the heroic epic *Kudrun* (c.1250). Well known as a patron of poetry was Mahaut, countess of Artois, who commissioned and collected a large library between 1300 and 1330. Especially important for our understanding of late medieval French literature is the patronage Queen Bonne extended to Guillaume de Machaut after her marriage to the future King Jean le Bon in 1332.

Late medieval women patrons can be detected at the various courts all over Europe and need not be listed in detail. However, Duchess Mechthild of Austria (d.1482), a leading personality for the development of German literature in

Swabia, deserves mention here. While she lived in her widowhood residence in Rottenburg near Stuttgart, her dedication to poetry opened the door for the first major German adaptations and translations of Italian poetry. Her sister-in-law Margarete of Savoy can be credited with stimulating her interest in literature, because she also gained a high reputation for her patronizing poetry and the arts.

Countess Elisabeth of Nassau-Saarbrücken (d.1456) was active both as author and patron. Her close family connections with the royal court in Paris helped to introduce a large body of prose romances into Germany. Equally important was Eleonore of Austria (d.1480), daughter of the Scottish king James I, who imbued the court of her husband Siegmund of Tyrol with a new literary spirit. Eleonore, mother of the emperor Maximilian I, entertained lively contacts with scholarly writers such as the astronomer Johannes Regiomantibus. Margaret of York, while duchess of Burgundy, encouraged William Caxton to translate from French and to print *The History of Troyes* in 1476. From 1473 when Eleanor of Aragon married Ercole I d'Este of Ferrara, she established another important Renaissance court with strong cultural interests. Her highly educated daughter Isabella d'Este, Countess of Gonzaga (1474–1539), also became a leading patron of literature and art. Her patronage, which reveals the guidance of humanist advisors, earned her general and high praise and made her court at Mantua one of the most famous cultural centers of the Italian Renaissance.

Further References. Susan Groag Bell, "Medieval Women Book Owners: Arbiters of Lay Piety and Ambassadors of Culture," in Mary Erler and Maryanne Kowalski (eds.), *Women and Power in the Middle Ages* (Athens, Ga., 1988), 149–187. Joachim Bumke, *Mäzene in Mittelalter* (Munich, 1979). William C. McDonald, with Ulrich Goebel, *German Medieval Literary Patronage from Charlemagne to Maximilian I* (Amsterdam, 1973). David Wilkins, "Women as Artists and Patrons in the Middle Ages and the Renaissance," in Douglas Radcliffe-Umstead (ed.), *The Roles and Images of Women in the Middle Ages and the Renaissance* (Pittsburgh, 1975), 107–125.

ALBRECHT CLASSEN

PLAYWRIGHTS, U.S. (TWENTIETH-CENTURY). While women dramatists in the United States have a history as old as the republic, women as playwrights have come to prominence in the twentieth century. Career women playwrights who have made a success of the commercial stage are relatively few in number and are a small proportion of the century's women dramatists. The principal support for production of women's drama has been in regional and little theatres. Magazine publication, while generally rare for plays, has fostered a number of playwrights, and prize competitions offered early validation for women as dramatists. Less commercial forums allowed for and encouraged experimentation with nontraditional subjects and techniques.

Throughout most of the century, women playwrights who have achieved commercial success have written in established genres—the social comedy, the farce, the problem play. Clare Kummer, for example, found success in the commercial theatre with farces like *Good Gracious Annabelle* (1916). Experimental techniques and form have found their place in regional theatres where playwrights have often been involved in production and selection of plays. Regional companies noted in theatre history, especially the Provincetown Players, have been especially important for women's drama.

Women playwrights have often focused on historical situations, recapturing our collective and individual past, including celebration of both famous and typical women as sources of courage and fortitude and as reminders of the oppression of women. Historical focus has been most prominent at critical junctures of social history: in the suffrage movement; in works by minority women during the twenties, including historical plays for children; in feminist drama of the seventies and eighties. Social problems have focused on the constraints impacting individual women's lives.

Early twentieth-century women's plays used domestic settings, employing easily staged, confined interior sets as emblematic of women's usual environment and stage for action. Even in plays that directly challenged the appropriateness and comfort of the domestic sphere, traditional settings (the table, the kitchen, the living room) and scenarios (receiving guests) served to question the reality and facade of women entrenched in domestic life.

Alice Gerstenberg's short plays—especially the often-anthologized *Overtones* (1913), an early feminist play—used innovative techniques of internal monologues and imagined characters to establish a woman-centered world rejecting traditional, sentimental valuations of marriage and domestic life.

Innovative subjects, problem plays, and experimental techniques evolved through regional and little theatres, which developed along with the little magazines. Edna St. Vincent Millay, while principally known as a poet, was instrumental in founding the Theatre Guild and extended both subject matter and technique with a number of verse plays. She also directed her successful, antiwar play *Aria da Capo* (1919).

Women's drama centered on social and political issues was also fostered by social organizations' and magazines' encouragement of minority voices. The National Association for the Advancement of Colored People (NAACP) produced Angelina Weld Grimke's *Rachel* in 1916. Georgia Douglas Johnson developed as a significant black playwright with works like *A Sunday Morning in the South* (1925), on the effects of lynching on a southern family, and her *Opportunity* prizewinner, *Plumes* (1927), a metaphoric play on burial customs.

Of all the early twentieth-century women, Rachel Crothers was the most consistently successful, serious, career playwright. Not only a writer, but also a director, set designer, and actress, Crothers established a genre of problem plays on women's issues and helped to develop a popular and critical audience for plays by women. *A Man's World* (1909) and *Mary the Third* (1923) were among her plays that focused audiences' attention on modern women's issues of equity and choice.

Zona Gale, Susan Glaspell, and later Lillian Hellman continued the tradition of *A Man's World* with serious problem plays focused on women's situation, building an increasingly forceful portrait of society's destructive pressures. Zona Gale won the Pulitzer Prize in drama in 1921 for an adaptation of her own novel, *Miss Lulu Bett*. Dramatizing the constricted role of the dependent spinster who becomes a servant to her family, *Miss Lulu Bett* indicts the family's relations with the dependent woman, as well as the traditional wife's forgetting of sisterhood.

Susan Glaspell was a founder of Provincetown Players and, like Crothers, a director and actress as well as a writer. Glaspell's plays, most notably *Trifles* (1916), *Women's Honor* (1918), and *Bernice* (1919), directly confronted contemporary women's issues, often using innovative techniques to reinforce her dramatic points. Glaspell's *Alison's House* won the Pulitzer Prize for Drama in 1931.

Not all early women's plays provided positive women's images or critiques of the golden cage of domestic life. Clare Boothe's *The Women* (1936) is exceptional in its vitriolic portrayal of women characters, but Boothe's capacity to identify the types of cages women willingly enter and the types of terror they inflict on other women parallels other women's drama. The sense of awakening benighted sisters and of showing the destructiveness of male identification pervades the drama of the era.

Lillian Hellman's *The Children's Hour* (1934) raised new subject matter and controversy with its lesbian theme and was the first of her three decades of finely crafted, well-made problem plays focused on evil in individuals and society. *The Little Foxes* (1939) and *Another Part of the Forest* (1946), two parts of a planned trilogy on the southern Hubbard family, and Hellman's anti-Nazi *Watch on the Rhine* (1941) remain among the best American plays of their kinds.

In comedy, Mary Chase's *Harvey*, the 1945 Pulitzer prize-winner that had a major Broadway revival in 1970, established her capacity for sensationally popular fantasy. Chase followed *Harvey* with two additional Broadway hits in 1952: *Mrs. McThing* and *Bernadine*.

The 1950s marked a new era in Britain and the United States of exceptional young women playwrights. Carson McCullers's dramatization of her novel *The Member of the Wedding* (1950) won the New York Drama Critics' Circle Award. Filmed in 1953, *Member* inaugurated a series of women's plays that dominated their seasons and went on to become major films of enduring popularity and significance. Lorraine Hansberry became the first black woman to have a play produced on Broadway. *A Raisin in the Sun* brought the black experience and black actors to prominence with mainstream, national audiences and won the Drama Critics' Circle Award as the best play of the 1958–1959 season.

In the 1960s, the numbers of women playwrights began to grow, and by the 1970s and 1980s, women had made substantial gains in commercial theatre, though women's theatres and feminist theatres supported the largest volume of new playwrights and productions. Women's plays of the sixties, like Megan Terry's *Calm Down Mother*, self-consciously and angrily recorded images and roles of women, overtly attacking stereotypes. Alice Childress's plays presented more complex visions of black life and history. *Wedding Band* portrayed the difficulties of a genteel, poor, black/white couple; *Wine in the Wilderness,* set in the racial conflict of the sixties, showed a black woman confronting the stereotypes of the artist who treats her as a symbol rather than a person. The number of exceptional plays, innovative subjects, and techniques mushroomed in the 1970s and 1980s, as women dramatists explored the conflicts between expectations and women's realities. Marsha Norman's *Getting Out* presented the same woman in two characters, her mature self and her rebellious teenage past. Wendy Wasserstein's *Uncommon Women and Others* carried her story to national audiences. Emily Mann's *Still Life* brought home the effects of the Vietnam War, and Mann was the first woman to direct her own play on Broadway. Norman's *'Night Mother* continued the story of generational differences. Beth Henley, winner of Pulitzer and New York Drama Critics' Circle awards, had major plays with *Crimes of the Heart* and *The Miss Firecracker Contest.*

The number and diversity of women dramatists in the 1970s and 1980s provide a dramatic antidote to the decades of sparse representation. Playwrights like Mary Irene Fornes attract critical acclaim and productions in previously male preserves. Institutional support has also come to encourage women dramatists. The Women's Project's Directors Forum of the American Place Theatre encourages supportive, noncommercial production and has worked to discourage the isolation of the woman dramatist by establishing active collaboration and instituting concepts of company and repertory. Among Women's Project plays are Lavonne Muller's *Little Victories,* which created a kind of pas de deux with Joan of Arc and Susan B. Anthony, and *Killings on the Last Line,* a working-class, assembly line drama; and Kathleen Collins's *In the Midnight Hour* and *The Brothers.*

The 1970s and 1980s have also seen a phenomenal development of feminist drama and theatres that include and extend traditional definitions of drama. Much feminist theatre has highlighted consciousness-raising technique: overt use of sex-role reversal, realistic portrayal of women's oppression, and historical characters in and out of historic context as role models of feminism.

Children's drama also came to prominence in the twentieth century, and women playwrights have been especially involved in the creation of significant, new plays for children, including historical treatments by black women writers of the 1920s, Charlotte Chorpenning's dramatizations of traditional stories in the 1940s and 1950s, and contemporary works giving serious treatment to individual and social pressures.

Further References. Helen Kirch Chinoy and Linda Walsh Jenkins (eds.), *Women in American Theatre* (New York, 1981). Dinah Luise Leavitt, *Feminist Theatre Groups* (Jefferson, N.C., 1980). Karen Malpede (ed.), *Women in Theatre, Compassion & Hope* (New York, 1983; repr., 1985).

CAROL KLIMICK CYGANOWSKI

POETESS entered the English language in 1530, according to the *Oxford English* Dictionary. Its form indicates its debt to the French, via Middle English: *poet* + the feminizing -*ess*; the word means "a female poet." Ironically, *poetess* derives from the Latin *poeta,* which means "poet" and which incorporates grammatical gender—feminine; *poeta* itself derives from the grammatically masculine Greek term *poētēs,* "poet." A related English word, *poetress,* was perhaps more common up to the nineteenth century. Of course, the "generic" term *poet,* variants of which have always been current, indicates that men's poetry, the standard, requires no sexist distinction. However, from the sixteenth to the nineteenth centuries, when *poetess* was most used, the majority of publically successful poets were men, and the sex-specific feminine term allowed for a dubious distinction often perceived as one of quality rather than kind. *Poetess* carries an inherent sexist slur, for it connotes that sex lies at the center of art and that sex is as important as genre in defining a writer.

Unfortunately, during the currency of *poetess,* femaleness was equated with various diminutive perceptions of femininity: domesticity, emotionalism, weakness, virginal purity, etc., and these qualities were transferred onto or demanded in the "poetess' " work. Twentieth-century consciousness-raising has provoked several changes in the preferred term for a female poet—from *poetess* to *lady poet,* to *woman poet,* to, simply, *poet.* Further, the range of subject matter (and style/language) has broadened; many contemporary female poets might better be called "women's poets," because they have intentionally explored territories particularly interesting to or concerning women themselves—territories hitherto often considered inappropriate or socially unacceptable. A fine example of this alteration may be studied in the lifework of Adrienne Rich, who began her career as an academic, mainstream poet often writing from a (false) male perspective and who had thereby achieved literary Establishment acceptance and acclaim. Rich has, like many women, transformed her worldview and poetic perspective over the past several decades; she now identifies herself as a lesbian, a feminist, and an activist, and her poetry has been strengthened by its resultant honesty. Similar in principle are the careers of such poets as Judy Grahn and Susan Griffin, whose published works have sprung from a feminist milieu and have demonstrated a peculiarly women's perspective openly and from the outset, but their acknowledgment by the literary Establishment has been hindered, perhaps purely because of this failure to disguise either their female identities or concerns, for the literary power structure remains largely in male hands. But *poetess* has been, happily, an early casualty of the war against linguistic sexism; concurrently, the numbers of poets who are women have increased, and women rarely hide behind male pseudonyms or initials to gain acceptance, as once was necessary to avoid the typecasting of being a "poetess."

Further References. Angela Carter, "The Language of Sisterhood" and Alicia Ostriker, "Body Language: Imagery of the Body in Women's Poetry," in Leonard Michaels and Christopher Ricks (eds.), *The State of the Language* (Berkeley, 1980). Elaine Showalter (ed.), *The New Feminist Criticism* (New York, 1985).

PENELOPE J. ENGELBRECHT

POETS, BRITISH (ROMANTIC). Numerous Englishwomen wrote and published poetry between 1789 and 1837 as part of the literary movement known as British Romanticism. To some degree, their work exhibits the same general philosophical concerns and poetic characteristics as the major male Romantic poets—Blake, Wordsworth, Coleridge, Byron, Shelley, and Keats. These philosophical concerns include a belief in the healing power of nature, a regard for the simple life of common people, and a faith in the possibility of human transcendency through divine inspiration or the poetic imagination. Typical genres include ballads, sonnets, odes, elegies, and verse dramas. Romantic poems are often set in exotic, medieval, or fantastic locales; they modulate from intellectual to emotional, from gothic to sentimental in tone and plot.

The women poets of this era are not as well known today as the men, partly because of the general disrespect for women's writing, but also partly because the women's poetry was not as successful artistically and intellectually as the men's. An exception to this generalization is Emily Brontë (1818–1848), the only woman of the period to be considered a major poet. However, her poetry was not well received upon publication (in 1846), and her philosophical orientation to Romanticism is sometimes questioned; often she is grouped with the Victorians. Also a figure of renewed interest today, though overshadowed in her own lifetime by her brother William's achievements, is Dorothy Wordsworth (1771–1855), whose relatively few poems were not published until 1940, except as incorporated into her brother's work.

Women's lesser degree of artistic success is attributable to various social conditions of the period. Most women did not receive the classical education that prepared the major male poets for their careers; though the women could and did write in the vernacular, as Wordsworth recommended, they lacked the advantages of his long and careful study of poetics. Socially, it was still considered somewhat unladylike to be in print, and it was hard for a woman to maintain a comfortable self-concept as a professional writer. Contemporary literary critics judged women's poetry differently from men's, restricting women to a conventional style and subject matter and condescending to them as "lady poets" in reviews of their work. Finally, women's opportunities for experience in the world were limited to domestic and social routines, creating serious problems of authenticity and credibility when women attempted to write about issues or scenes of general public interest with which they could not be personally familiar.

Despite all of these disadvantages, many were considered successful poets by their contemporaries. Among the best known and most respected were Joanna Baillie (1762–1851), Felicia Dorothea Hemans (1793–1835), and Letitia Elizabeth Landon (1802–1838). Baillie's best work was in the form of poetic dramas, including a series of *Plays on the Passions,* wherein one central facet of human psychology was illuminated in each play. Hemans was admired as a domestic and patriotic poet, quintessentially feminine in style and subject; in *Records of Woman* she sympathetically portrayed women's lives across barriers of space and time, nationality and class. *Songs of the Affections* contains her most popular poems. As for Landon, one critic dubbed her "the female Byron" for the melancholy tone and heightened emotionalism of her poetry. Overpraise led her to write profusely and abjure revision; as a result, little remains of her Romantic reputation today besides the mystery of her unexplained death by poison in Cape Coast, Africa, where she had traveled with her husband, a sea captain named MacLean.

There were many other popular poets of the Romantic period whose work remains interesting today. Mary Tighe (1772–1810) is chiefly remembered for her lengthy poem *Psyche, or the Legend of Love,* which was said to have influenced Keats's "Ode to Psyche." Amelia Opie (1769–1853) is still admired for her "Elegy to the Memory of the Late Duke of Bedford." The sisters Jane and Ann Taylor (1783–1824 and 1782–1866) wrote memorable verses for children, including "Twinkle, Twinkle, Little Star." Similarly, Mary Howitt (1799–1888) wrote the nursery poem "The Spider and the Fly," as well as numerous popular lyrics and ballads. A group of Scottish nationals, including Anne Lindsay Bernard (1750–1825), Carolina Oliphant (Lady Nairne) (1766–1845), and Janet Hamilton (1795–1873), produced melodic and convincing Scottish ballads in the manner of Robert Burns. Lady Caroline Norton's (1808–1877) and her sister Helen Sheridan, Lady Dufferin's (1807–1867) many popular ballads, both humorous and sentimental, were set to music and performed in drawing rooms for half a century. Caroline Bowles (1786–1854), who later married British poet laureate Robert Southey, published a metrical autobiography "The Birthday," in which she lamented the restrictions placed upon women and girls in the nineteenth century. Sara Coleridge (1802–1852), daughter of Samuel Taylor Coleridge, published the poetic tale *Phantasmion* in the manner of her famous father's fantastical poetry.

Many of these popular women poets published in the annuals, yearly illustrated collections of contemporary poetry and prose by diverse writers. Often these volumes were edited by aristocrats such as the Countess of Blessington (1787–1855) or Catherine Norton; they generally contributed a few pieces of their own and procured one or two poems by established writers like Wordsworth or Sir Walter Scott. Two other popular women poets who contributed regularly to publications like the *Keepsake, Forget Me Not,* and *Friendship's Offering* were Mary Russell Mitford (1787–1855) and Maria Jane Jewsbury (1800–1833).

This overview is by no means exhaustive. Though these many women poets of the Romantic period have been judged "minor" when considered within the Romantic context, as a group they achieved the distinction of helping to normalize the profession of poet as an appropriate career for a woman, thus opening the way for Victorian poets like Elizabeth Barrett Browning and Christina Rossetti to excel in the field later in the nineteenth century.

Furthermore, if viewed not in the context of the male Romantic movement, but in the framework of women's writing throughout the centuries, the English women poets of the Romantic period will be seen to participate in many female literary traditions. For example, a recurrent theme is social or political protest, including poetry criticizing the slave trade; lamenting the exploitation, poverty, and displacement of workers caused by the industrial revolution; or supporting the struggles for freedom in Greece. Woman's particular lot in life—with its burden of chastity, marriage, motherhood, and sorrow—is a frequent topic, with special attention to the double standard of love and sexuality. The women poets repeatedly express a love or yearning for freedom, a frustration with restriction and imprisonment, and an empathy with rebellion, all characteristic of the Romantic political stance. Yet at the same time they express a strong disapproval of Romantic self-exile and social alienation and resolve these postures with conventional Christianity. These and other differences from the philosophical stance generally accepted as Romantic illustrate the fallacy of subsuming women writers in masculinist periodizations of literature and history.

Further References. Janet E. Courtney, *The Adventurous Thirties: A Chapter in the Women's Movement* (1933; repr. Freeport, N.Y., 1967). Kathleen Hickok, *Representations of Women: Nineteenth-Century British Women's Poetry* (Westport, Conn., 1984). Margaret Homans, *Women Writers and Poetic Identity: Dorothy Wordsworth, Emily Brontë, and Emily Dickinson* (Princeton, N.J., 1980).

KATHLEEN HICKOK

POETS, BRITISH (VICTORIAN). Although many Victorian women wrote and published poetry, only Christina Rossetti and Elizabeth Barrett Browning have entered the received canon of British poetry. Novelists Emily and Charlotte Brontë and George Eliot have also received recognition as poets. Of the three, Emily Brontë is the most powerful and varied poet.

Women poets had an ambivalent relationship to poetic tradition. Like male poets, they were struggling with the weight of Romantic tradition, but their struggles were more acute. As Mrs. Adby, a writer for the annuals, wrote, "Never may Woman's lays their service lend/Vice to encourage, soften, or defend . . . No, may we ever on His grace reflect/To whom we owe our cherished intellect."

As Sandra Gilbert and Susan Gubar have argued in *The Madwoman in the Attic* (New Haven, 1979), this inclination to moralize the "cherished intellect" reveals the Victorian woman poet's sense that to be a "woman poet" or a woman intellectual was in itself psychically risky if not financially impossible. Women of all classes were generally not well educated. Among those writing verse a classical education or even a systematic education in literature was unusual. A notable exception was Elizabeth Barrett Browning, an accomplished classicist who also studied Hebrew and modern European languages. Lack of education, lack of a tradition of women writing poetry, and the general misogyny of the critical Establishment were impediments to any woman wishing to reach an audience beyond that of the newspapers and albums.

Despite these difficulties, Victorian women wrote about classical subjects in dramatic lyric and dramatic monologue. The classical subjects women chose, however, were often not those central to received tradition. In 1840 Caroline Norton meditated on "The Picture of Sappho," and in 1889 Michael Field (joint pseudonym of Katherine Harris Bradley and Edith Emma Cooper) published

"Long Ago: Based on Fragments of Sappho." A different kind of reinterpretation of classical and poetic tradition came in dramatic monologues spoken by women, as poets emphasized previously neglected perspectives on history. Mary Russell Mitford celebrated the heroism of Antigone and emphasized her opposition to tyranny and slavery. More interesting are Mrs. Augusta Davies Webster's dramatic monologue "Circe" and Amy Levy's "Xantippe: A Fragment." Levy's poem took the part of Socrates's wife, deliberately making sympathetic a woman who had been for centuries the object of antifeminist diatribe. Other dramatic poems took the points of view of contemporary subjects. Barrett Browning's "The Runaway Slave at Pilgrim's Point" invites compassion for the slave who has murdered the child she was forced to bear after being raped by her master. More common were less politically charged dramatic monologues, represented by Caroline Bowles Southey's "The Dying Mother to Her Infant." Though treating a potentially sentimental subject, Bowles makes real the threat of death in childbirth, and the emotional strength of the poem comes from the dying mother's fears for her infant daughter's own probable future in marriage. A still more striking treatment of this common Victorian subject is Christina Rossetti's "The Last Look," in which the lament for the dead child concludes austerely: "If I remember her, no need/Of formal tokens set;/ Of hollow token-lies indeed/ No need, if I forget."

Perhaps the most ambitious and successful attempt at transforming literary tradition and at taking up contemporary subject matter was Elizabeth Barrett Browning's combination of novel and epic in *Aurora Leigh*. Barrett Browning deliberately defended the possibility of epic and the responsibility of the Victorian poet to "represent the age." She implied that the modern long poem could be epic and at the same time contemporary and womanly.

Although *Aurora Leigh* was enormously popular with readers, running to five editions in five years, and was praised by poets as different as Walter Savage Landor, D. G. Rossetti, and Algernon Charles Swinburne, it was less well received by the critics, who generally found the plot melodramatic, the treatment of rape and prostitution unladylike, and its epic ambitions disconcerting. The *Saturday Review* labeled it an interesting study for those who would explain "feminine misadventures in art." Nonetheless, *Aurora Leigh* is, along with William Wordsworth's *The Prelude,* the major nineteenth-century treatment of what Wordsworth called "the growth of a poet's mind."

Usually not claiming epic scope, Victorian women wrote historical narratives or narrative romances on subjects ranging from Charles I to Margaret of Anjou; equally popular were lyric poems on a variety of topics—the beauties of nature, death (especially deaths of infants or mothers), the domestic affections, social injustice, religious experience, and moral sentiments. Much Victorian poetry and fiction, by women and men, treated these subjects in ways that seem to modern readers sentimental and that no doubt reinforced what one anthologizer of poetry by women called the "beautiful conservatism which so gracefully distinguishes women" and which curbs the "levelling tendencies of the opposite sex." Nonetheless, poetry about death of parents, about infant or maternal death, and about orphans not only elaborated the ideology of maternal virtue but spoke to the real situation of Victorian women, who typically were responsible for the care of children, for their sisters in childbirth, and for their aged or dying parents. Such poets as Mary Elizabeth Coleridge, Caroline Norton, Emily Pfieffer, and Caroline Bowles Southey, moreover, were sometimes openly critical of the sentimental treatment of domestic affections.

A great many Victorian women poets confronted more or less honestly the considerable social problems of their day. Among these women were the many who participated in the Chartist movement, especially between 1838 and 1843. However, poetry by Chartist women and by Victorian working-class women generally remains to be studied.

Many middle-class women also wrote about social injustice, especially poverty and slavery. Mary Anne Browne's "The Embroideress at Midnight" details the sacrifice and suffering of a poor young woman who embroiders finery for the rich to support her invalid mother, and even Laetitia Elizabeth Landon (L.E.L.), who usually dwelt on morbid and sentimental subjects, recorded the effects of industrialization in "The Changed Home." "The Children" by Mary Howitt is an interesting contrast to Elizabeth Barrett Browning's "The Cry of the Children" on the inhuman treatment of children in the mines and to Browning's anti–Corn Law poem "The Cry of the Human." After cataloguing the children's suffering, Howitt ends with a divine voice proclaiming, "The Children's prayer is heard!" Browning was less interested than Howitt in heavenly compensation for earthly suffering and more scornful of the callousness of the powerful. "The Cry of the Human" concludes with this stark image: "The poor die mute—with starving gaze/On corn-ships in the offing." Slavery was also opposed, notably by Eliza Cook in her poem on George Washington, by Maria Jane Jewsbury, by Elizabeth Barrett Browning, and by "the blind poetess of Ulster," Frances Brown.

At least as common as domestic themes and social commentary were poems on religious subjects. Many women wrote hymns, some, such as Sara Flowers Adams's "Nearer, My God to Thee," still popular today. By consensus, the greatest writer of religious poetry was Christina Rossetti. Rossetti's religious life as a devout Anglican was essential to much of her greatest poetry. The keynote of her religious experience was resignation, though she could be cele-bratory too. For clarity of diction and perfect control of poetic design, her work has no equal in Victorian poetry, except perhaps in the later poetry of Hardy. In poems such as "Up-Hill," "A Better Resurrection," and "The Heart Know-eth Its Own Bitterness" Rossetti uses the traditional imagery of the English Bible and of Anglican belief and liturgy to create a poetry of passionate resignation and of longing for union with God.

Rossetti wrote on other subjects as well. Like Barrett Browning, whose *Sonnets from the Portuguese* is still popular, Rossetti wrote sonnets, including one ex-traordinary sequence, "Monna Innominata." In addition to religious and devotional verse, sonnets, and poems on secular subjects, Rossetti, like many other Victorian women, wrote children's poetry.

Victorian women poets worked in a variety of forms: narrative, dramatic monologue and dramatic lyric, expressive lyric, hymn, and epic, and they took up the common themes of Victorian culture, particularly those associated with womanhood and the domestic affections. As they worked within the often restrictive conventions of their culture and within financial and educational limitations, many women, not just those few we now most commonly read, wrote with an artistic integrity grounded in personal and social honesty.

Further Reference. Kathleen Hickok, *Representations of Women: Nineteenth-Century British Women's Poetry* (Westport, Conn., 1984).

MARY ELLIS GIBSON

POETS, BRITISH (TWENTIETH-CENTURY). Work by women poets of British origin in the twentieth century may usefully be scrutinized in terms of several discrete—if imprecise—periods of activity. The century begins with a divided moment in which the majority of British women poets arrayed themselves with a less experimental tradition, while a small minority, sometimes expatriate, experimented with abstract and discontinuous forms or explored new concepts of the self and consciousness.

The second third of the century was a period of consolidation for women poets. T. S. Eliot's influence was widely felt, and some of the aspects of modernism, like free verse, a fragmented narrative line, and use of an associative symbolic method to suggest the flow of consciousness, were included in the array of techniques used by British poets, women and men alike. For the most part, however, the relatively few women who were able to command the attention of critics sought to continue traditional British poetic modes and forms, experimenting relatively little with Continental forms like surrealism or American revisions of syntax and sense.

In the years immediately after World War II, the number and visibility of women poets began to swell appreciably, with some women appearing among the membership of British coteries like "The Movement" or "The Group." Emphasis usually was on the very precise and nuanced rendering of limited, often personal subjects, usually within traditional verse forms, often with an understated irony and almost always with careful avoidance of rhetorical excess.

A major efflorescence of women's poetry began in the late 1960s, with substantial experiment in new forms, regular examination of highly charged political and emotional material, and exploration of feminist subjects or formerly suppressed elements of women's experience. Participating in this surge of vital poetic production were the women of a new, feminist generation born after World War II, as well as many women born in the 1920s or 1930s, whose careers had been delayed (a pattern that can be noted in a significant number of women poets) or marked by a less visible volume or two. Anthologies designed to showcase the strength of new women's voices played an important role in gaining significant recognition for powerful new women poets, whether they were adopted by the critical Establishment or not. The efflorescence of poetry was accompanied by decisive new critics who used both feminist and Marxist theory to demonstrate the ways in which literary expression is gender-inflected or reflects class positions. As a consequence, the early anthologies were followed by selections and reprints of the work of women poets from the first half of the century, who appeared, in the light of feminist theory and the explosion of women's poetic energies in the last half of the century, to exhibit unrecognized strengths and to be overlooked harbingers of a woman's vision. The effect of these developments has been to make a surprising range of women's voices from throughout the century virtually contemporaneous (an appropriate effect for a literature that often rejects linear orders) and to make visible the strength and extensiveness of female poetic traditions in the twentieth century.

British women associated with the modernist experiment in the first part of the century included Mina Loy (1882–1966), Edith Sitwell (1887–1964), Nancy Cunard (1896–1965), and Iris Tree (1897–1968). By far the most important British woman modernist poet was Edith Sitwell. Her most experimental work fell chiefly in the decade immediately following World War I, while she was editing the important avant-grade annual, *Wheels* (1916–1921) and publishing *Twentieth-Century Harlequinade and Other Poems* (with Osbert Sitwell, 1916), *Clowns' Houses* (1918), *The Wooden Pegasus* (1920), *Facade* (1922), *Bucolic Comedies* (1923), the ambitious long poem cycle *The Sleeping Beauty* (1924), *Troy Park* (1925), *Elegy on Dead Fashion* (1926), and *Rustic Elegies* (1927). She saw her poems as "abstract patterns," and the result was a poetry that sometimes suppressed semantic sense or invoked deliberate non sequitur. Sitwell's work notably demonstrates the modernist tension between order and disorder, between the drive for coherence and the celebration of the noncoherent. Her later work fell back from syntactic or narrative disorder; now Sitwell sought to recast traditional myth in terms of a female vision that rejected the violence and destruction of World War II. See *Collected Poems* (1965).

Growing attention is now being devoted to Mina Loy's and Nancy Cunard's contributions to the formation of modernism. Loy's early poetry was published in *Lunar Baedecker* (1923); she was revived in 1958 (*Lunar Baedecker and Time Tables: Selected Poems*), and her unpublished poems appeared in 1982 (*The Last Lunar Baedecker: The Poems of Mina Loy*). (Loy became a naturalized American citizen in 1946.) Cunard's contribution as printer and proprietor of the Hours Press is best known, but her early poetry, which drew criticism for obscurity and for expressions of revolt, was also part of the modernist movement. Her collections include *Outlaws* (1921), *Sublunary* (1923), *Parallax* (1925), and *Poems* (1930).

Among the early figures whose work was regarded as more traditional are Alice Meynell (1847–1922), Katharine Tynan (1861–1931), Charlotte Mew

(1869–1928), Margaret Sackville (1881–1963), Anna Wickham (1884–1947), Frances Cornford (1886–1960), Elizabeth Daryush (1887–1977), Rose Mac-Caulay (1889–1956), Dorothy Wellesley (1889–1956), Vita Sackville-West (1892–1962), Vera Brittain (1892–1970), Sylvia Townsend Warner (1893–1978), Ruth Pitter (b.1897), and Frances Bellerby (1899–1975). Contemporary feminist critics are rediscovering the quieter originality of some of the ostensibly less experimental figures like Mew (*The Farmer's Bride*, 1915; *The Rambling Sailor*, 1929; *Collected Poems*, 1953), Wickham (*Selected Poems*, 1971; *The Writings of Anna Wickham: Free Woman and Poet*, 1984), Daryush (collections from 1911 to 1971; major work from the thirties; *Selected Poems*, 1972; *Collected Poems*, 1976), Bellerby, and Warner (*The Espalier*, 1925; seven other volumes o poetry including the posthumous *Twelve Poems*, 1980; *Collected Poems*, 1982; *Selected Poems*, 1985). Newly attentive readers recognize these writers' decentered and self-reflex visions, unrhymed or rhythmically disrupted forms, and non traditional views of female roles or sexuality as important expressions of women's experience.

Among the poets whose birth dates place their production in the second third of the century (and sometimes later) are Stevie Smith (1902–1971), Sheila Wingfield (b.1906), E. J. Scovell (b.1907), Kathleen Raine (b.1908), Helen Adam (b.1909, now resident in the United States), Phoebe Hesketh (b.1909), Kathleen Nott, Anne Ridler (b.1912), Laurie Lee (b.1914), Jean Overton Fuller (b.1915), Betty Parvin (b.1916), and Muriel Spark (b.1918). The difficulty of securing publication during the war, the lack of critical encouragement for women poets, and the different patterns for women's lives delayed the careers of all but a few of these women until well after World War II, when their work appeared nearly simultaneously with that of the cohort of women born in the 1920s—Denise Levertov (b.1923, a U.S. citizen since 1955), Shirley Toulson (b.1924), Patricia Beer (b.1924), Elizabeth Jennings (b.1926), Molly Holden (1927–1981), Gerda Mayer (b.1927), Anne Beresford (b.1929), and Freda Downie (b.1929). In the years before the war Raine experimented briefly with techniques popularized by the surrealist movement; Lee experimented with the Neo-Romanticism that was more broadly practiced in England; and Ridler explored the possibilities of religious verse drama. Jennings, chiefly in postwar years, made important use of the confessional mode and used Expressionist methods to represent the experience of madness. Most continued to use rhyme and traditional meters a significant part of the time, although in the hands of a poet like Stevie Smith a traditional ballad or nursery refrain could be used with disquieting results. Among these poets, Raine, Jennings, and Levertov are in the vanguard of those with long-established reputations; Smith, Fanthorpe, and Beer have come to prominence with more recent, current generations.

The first cohort of women to enjoy from the beginning of their careers the stimulation of the greatly expanded presence of women writing poetry and assertive critical inquiry into the theory and content of women's writings was born in the thirties: Elaine Feinstein (b.1930), Ruth Fainlight (b.1931), Jenny Joseph (b.1932), Anne Stevenson (born in 1933 of American parents but now resident in England), Fleur Adcock (b.1934), Anne Cluysenaar (b.1936), Sally Roberts (b.1935), Gillian Clark (b.1937), and Frances Horowitz (1938–1983). Of these, Adcock, Fainlight, Feinstein, Joseph, and Stevenson comprise a "senior establishment" of women who forthrightly seek to express a gender-inflected (though not necessarily feminist) vision. Cluysenaar, trained in linguistics, has experimented with genre and themes in ways that reflect an acute feminist theoretical awareness (e.g., *Double Helix*, 1982, a joint mother-daughter text that explores the continuities of women's lives through a mixture of poetry and documents—letters, notes, and photographs).

The contemporary generation is a cacophony of powerful voices, many lifted in assertion of feminist themes, lesbian awareness, and the demonstration of poetry as both politically engaged and performative. Among the strong figures in this cohort are Judith Kazanztis (b.1940), Michelene Wandor (b.1940), Jeni Couzyn (b.1942), Nicki Jackowska (b.1942), Wendy Mulford, Sally Purcell (b.1944), Carol Rumens (b.1944), Eavan Boland (b.1944), Wendy Cope (b.1945), Valerie Sinason (b.1946), Penelope Shuttle (b.1947), Liz Lochhead (b.1947), Denise Riley (b.1948), Michéle Roberts (b.1949), and Alison Brackenbury (b.1953). There is no single thread. The range includes the complex and powerful title poem in Brackenbury's 1984 collection, "Breaking Ground," a long narrative poem that explores the problems of expressing or even establishing both identity and historical "truth"; Jackowska's feminist recuperation of myth in a brief poem like "Un-Fairytale" (from *Letters to Superman*, 1984); Michéle Roberts's riposte on Jacques Lacan: "Women's entry into culture is experienced as lack" (*Selected Poems 1975–1985*); and Carol Rumens's achingly political "Outside Oswiecim" from *Direct Dialling* (1985) or her philosophically sophisticated reflection of a mystical experience in "In the Cloud of Unknowing."

Three important anthologies in this period sought retrospectively to establish the existence of a rich and varied tradition in women's poetry (both British and American): *The World Split Open: Four Centuries of Women Poets in England and America, 1552–1950* (Louise Bernikow [ed.], 1974, repr. 1979), *Salt and Bitter and Good* (Cora Kaplan [ed.]), and *Bread and Roses: An Anthology of Nineteenth and Twentieth-Century Poetry by Women Writers* (Diana Scott [ed.], 1982). *One Foot on the Mountain: An Anthology of British Feminist Poetry 1969–1979* (Lilian Mohin [ed.], 1979) first gave wide recognition to the feminist poetry movement, and other volumes have highlighted various feminist or political subgroups or writing collectives, for example, *Cutlasses & Earrings: Feminist Poetry*, edited by Michelene Wandor and Michéle Roberts (1977); *A Dangerous Knowing: Four Black Women Poets*, by Barbara Burford, Gabriela Pearse, Grace Nichols, and Jackie Kay (n.d. [1984?]); *Beautiful Barbarians: Lesbian Feminist Poetry*, edited by Lilian Mohin (1986); *Angels of Fire: An Anthology of Radical Poetry in the 80s*, edited by Sylvia Paskin, Jay Ramsay, and Jeremy Sliver (1986); and *The New British Poetry*, edited by Gillian Allnutt, Fred D'Aguiar, Ken Edwards, and Eric Mottram (1988).

Nearly simultaneously, women's poetry was more broadly recognized by commercial publishers in such volumes as *Making for the Open: The Chatto Book of Post-Feminist Poetry 1964–1984* (Carol Rumens [ed.], 1985), *The Bloodaxe Book of Contemporary Women Poets: Eleven British Writers* (Jeni Couzyn [ed.], 1985), and *The Faber Book of 20th Century Women's Poetry* (Fleur Adcock [ed.], 1987). By this time most of the poets of the postwar generations have produced a number of volumes and many—like Adcock, Stevenson, Rumens, Fanthorpe, Roberts, and Lochhead—are available in collections of selected or collected poems.

CYRENA N. PONDROM

POETS, U.S. (BEGINNINGS TO WORLD WAR II). Includes more than 200 women from Anne Bradstreet to H. D. (Hilda Doolittle). This topic should be considered together with entries for AFRICAN-AMERICAN POETS; CHICANA WRITERS; NATIVE AMERICAN WRITERS.

Anne Bradstreet, America's first major poet, was the only woman to publish a substantial body of verse in the seventeenth century. Bradstreet was born in England, received a good education, and came to Massachusetts in 1630. She wrote many kinds of poems, quaternions, elegies, dialogues, love poems, religious meditations, even an unusual poem about mothering her eight children. "Contemplations"—a long work celebrating God and nature—is generally considered her best. Bradstreet celebrated women. Though seemingly content with her lot, she occasionally reveals a darker side, as where she remarks caustically: "I am obnoxious to each carping tongue/Who says my hand a needle better fits." Women poets were not always greeted affectionately in the colonies.

In the eighteenth century the number of women poets increased exponentially. American women had their volumes published and found opportunities to print their works in the burgeoning number of colonial newspapers. A list of the more prolific among these women, provided by Pattie Cowell (*Women Poets in Pre-Revolutionary America* [Troy, N.Y., 1981]), includes 11 poets. Jane Turrell, Phillis Wheatley, and Mercy Warren are probably best known, Turrell because she preceded the others, Wheatley because she was black and had been a slave, and Warren because of her political connections to the revolution. As a group these women sometimes followed Bradstreet's poetic lead, but they extended the range of women's forms to include political satire and verse drama. Many of them knew each other and corresponded about literary matters. However, the strongest influences on these women's poems were male. References to Milton, to Pope, and to classical writers abound.

By 1873 a revised edition of Rufus Griswold's famous *Female Poets of America* included 116 women, and this number excludes some important figures like the black poet Frances Harper and Emily Dickinson. The growing association of the spirit of poetry with women, the marked increase in the number of literate female readers, and the advent of widely distributed women's magazines like

Godey's Lady's Book all contributed to creating a society in which women could not only publish but also support whole families on the proceeds of their pen.

Maria Brooks, highly respected in England and America for her verse play *Zophiel: Or, The Bride of Seven,* is the first in a series of distinguished women poets. By mid-century conventional women poets like Lydia Sigourney, Sarah Helen Whitman, Anne Lynch, and the Carey sisters were joined by women less conventional and more outspoken on a whole range of issues, like Margaret Fuller, Elizabeth Oakes-Smith, Lucy Larcom, and Frances Osgood. Though few women were critical of men in their poems, many bemoaned the limited sphere of women's lives and the unequal distribution of sorrows and joys. The lyre came to represent not only poetry but the female sensibility: sensitive, thrilling, and melancholy. Yet these "nightingale poets" could occasionally write pungent poetry, as Lucy Larcom does in her dramatic monologues and Frances Osgood does in her love lyrics. In general, the single biggest female influence on these women was the British poet Felicia Hemans.

Emily Dickinson (1830–1886) published only ten poems during her lifetime but is now generally regarded as one of the greatest poets America has yet produced. Living her entire life in Amherst, Massachusetts, some 20 years of it as a recluse, she nevertheless produced over 1,700 poems, most of them short, enigmatic, verbally playful considerations of nature, God, the inner life, love, and death. Dickinson was a premodernist. Critics continue to dispute about the meaning of her lyrics, which sometimes seem deliberately obscure. Her peculiar style combines abstractions with startlingly specific references to the phenomenal world, as when she describes a chill as "zero at the bone." Her life and her poetry have furnished much material for feminist critics who find in her wit, irreverence, and originality an inner strength that defied the narrowness of her circumstances.

The second half of the nineteenth century saw the work of women poets incorporated into the national literature. Emma Lazarus's "New Colossus" was inscribed on the Statue of Liberty, Katherine Lee Bates wrote "America the Beautiful," and Julia Ward Howe wrote "The Battle Hymn of the Republic." A martial ideal combined with religious fervor also informed the poetry of Louise Imogen Guiney. Guiney, together with Lizette Reese, Anna Branch, and the notorious Ella Wheeler Wilcox, author of *Poems of Passion* (1883), are the women poets usually used to represent the 1890s.

A new era in American women's poetry was ushered in by Amy Lowell (1874–1925). Wealthy, cultured, and ambitious, Lowell, like Gertrude Stein, went to Europe and was converted to modernism. Unlike Stein, who was also an important poetic innovator, Lowell came back to America and worked actively to spread the ideals of "imagism." She published many books of poetry, was very popular in her time, and helped to support the reputations of other women poets like Dickinson, H. D., and Elinor Wylie. Her most famous poem is "Patterns."

In the last years of her life, Lowell saw the poetry scene changing and beginning to be dominated by female lyric love poets. Sara Teasdale and Edna Millay were known especially for their clear, resonant expressions of sentiment. Millay, however, was the more shocking. She wrote openly of sexual love, participated actively in political causes, and defied Victorian conventions. She produced a large body of work, still in print today, but the last decade of her life was blighted by World War II, ill health, and difficulties with her writing.

Together with Lowell, Stein, Adelaide Crapsey, and Mina Loy, Marianne Moore experimented with poetic conventions. Though personally reserved, she earned herself the role of grande dame of the avant-garde. Her highly intellectual poems unite philosophical commentary with quotations from a wide range of reading materials (both literary and scientific) and vivid visual descriptions. Of poetry itself, she wrote: "I, too, dislike it." Many of her poems about animals, like "To a Snail," are justly famous.

The time between the two world wars also produced a number of leftist women poets like Genevieve Taggard, Lola Ridge, Muriel Rukeyser, Margaret Walker, and Babette Deutsch. Often concerned with the plight of the poor and disenfranchised, these women never received the critical attention or the acclaim given the love poets and the experimentalists. Yet their work is still admired by women who find in them models of the attempt to combine political engagement with the literary life.

Both Elinor Wylie and Louise Bogan were praised during their lives for the intelligence, musical quality, and lyric sophistication of their poems. Though both women were more strongly influenced by models from the past than by contemporary experiments, they modulated the female lyric voice into a tone memorable for its strength and intensity. They followed Dickinson in preferring condensation over exuberance, reticence over sentimentality, and form over free verse.

Though hardly known 10 years ago, the work of H. D. (Hilda Doolittle) has come increasingly to occupy a central place in considerations of modern female poets. H. D. (1886–1961) wrote poetry for 50 years, and her career goes well beyond World War II. Born in Pennsylvania, she left America in her twenties, never to make it a permanent residence again. H. D. was deeply involved with male modernists like Ezra Pound and D. H. Lawrence, but she was never long an apprentice. Her association with a wealthy and talented English heiress, Winnifred Ellerman, allowed her to move freely throughout Europe. Her early work was highly condensed, imagistic, and influenced by Greek precedents. However, she moved beyond these early forms to write verse epics in her later years. H. D.'s work is informed by her involvement with film, with psychoanalysis, and with hermetic traditions. In some ways, she belongs to all the categories mentioned above. She was a love poet, an experimentalist, an intellectual, bohemian and yet conservative, and her insistence on revising received traditions and giving women mythic embodiment has made her work an important resource for contemporary feminists.

Further References. Louise Bernikow, *The World Split Open* (New York, 1974).

Alicia Ostriker, *Stealing the Language: The Emergence of Women's Poetry in America*
(Boston, 1986). Cheryl Walker, *The Nightingale's Burden: Women Poets and American
Culture Before 1900* (Bloomington, Ind., 1983). Emily Stipes Watts, *The Poetry of
American Women 1632–1945* (Austin, 1977).

                                                                            CHERYL WALKER

POETS, U.S. (CONTEMPORARY). Women are responsible for much of the
experimentation that has invigorated American poetry in the last 25 years. Moreover, the development since the early 1960s of a feminist audience for women's
poetry has, by reinforcing the connection between poetic communication and
urgent social concerns, helped sustain and broaden the current audience for poetry
by both men and women.

Contemporary poetry by American women varies widely in poetic form and
language, in subject matter and themes, and in approaches to women's experience. Some poets, such as Marilyn Hacker or Maxine Kumin, appropriate the
closed poetic forms of patriarchal traditions. Others, like Denise Levertov or
Adrienne Rich, search for new open forms and a new "common" language.
Some limit their political concerns to feminist issues. Others, such as Carolyn
Forché, Gwendolyn Brooks, Audre Lorde—particularly those who have experienced oppression based on class and/or race as well as gender—speak on behalf
of other groups or engage a wider range of political issues. Many, including
May Swenson, May Sarton, Jorie Graham, Mary Oliver, Sharon Olds, and Tess
Gallagher, leave feminism and politics in the background. A few, Louise Glück
or the late Elizabeth Bishop, for instance, have resisted being classed and anthologized as women poets while others, such as Judy Grahn or Adrienne Rich,
now speak as explicitly lesbian feminists addressing a specifically female or
lesbian audience. Probably the majority of women poets today are eager to speak
as and for women while addressing an audience that is both male and female,
heterosexual and homosexual. Because women inevitably write from their own
social contexts and points of view, which are significantly shaped by gender,
because they are inevitably conscious of being outsiders in a predominantly male
literary tradition shaped by patriarchal patterns of thought and language, and
because they are conscious of their affinities with other women writers, one can
generalize about contemporary women's poetry or speak of a single women's
poetry movement.

Contemporary poetry has tended to be more personal than the modernist poetry
of the first half of the century. The "confessional" movement that began in the
late 1950s (associated with such male poets as Robert Lowell and John Berryman)
helped women such as Sylvia Plath and Anne Sexton feel free to expose very
private anguish in poetry. The individual suffering and fury they were exploring
was intimately bound to social expectations of women in the 1950s and early
1960s. While their suicidal energy no longer predominates, women's poetry has
remained intensely personal. Thus, although feminist critics debate whether
language is capable of representing women's experience (either because of its

inherent nature as sign system or because of its roots in patriarchal culture), many poets have devoted themselves to presenting women's experience as directly and forthrightly as possible. Often invoking personal conversation or passionate outpouring, they involve the reader closely in intimate details of their sexual and emotional lives. Since women traditionally have been the object in poems, not the speaking subject, this candid self-expression is also a means of artistic self-creation and self-definition.

In the mid–1960s, involvement in the antiwar movement stimulated writers such as Denise Levertov and, more influentially, Adrienne Rich to insist on the continuity between their private struggles and public events. Since then, women poets have tended to treat their private experience as indivisible from larger political experience. The political dimension of their writing has grown more visible, and the personal details in their poems have assumed increasingly obvious political significance. In taking as their subjects women's experiences previously regarded as trivial—crafts such as weaving or embroidery, domestic tasks, child rearing, the bonds among women—they foreground the traditionally unrecognized dignity and significance of ordinary women's lives. In this way, they offer critiques of patriarchy as well as models for more harmonious society.

Many women poets today place their work within a female literary tradition. Among twentieth-century poets, they look to the daring innovations of Marianne Moore and Gertrude Stein, to the mysticism of H. D., to the political force of Muriel Rukeyser. Inspirational models from earlier centuries include Anne Bradstreet, Emily Dickinson, the Brontë sisters, Elizabeth Barrett Browning, Dorothy Wordsworth. Because women in the past wrote more novels than poems, recent poets also draw upon the achievements of women novelists, who often excelled as recorders of social and domestic details. The poets are equally conscious of the innumerable women diarists and letter writers whose creations may assist in the discovery of distinctively female voices and female language. The burgeoning of women's history has fostered interest in previously neglected women writers and in a range of women's historical achievements. Thus, a common type of contemporary women's poem imaginatively recreates the voices of earlier historical women. Matrifocal cultures, matriarchal rites, and myths about supernatural females have provided imagery and subject matter for contemporary women poets. Many, including Mona Van Duyn, Marilyn Hacker, Olga Broumas, and Alicia Ostriker, have revised patriarchal fairy tales to represent more fully and sympathetically the witches, evil stepmothers, old maids, dangerous sirens, and trapped maidens portrayed there. Revisionary mythmaking has become a major strategy for challenging gender stereotypes.

To the extent that they choose to stand outside the male tradition, women poets seek alternative forms, alternative approaches to poetic language, alternative subjects, and alternative treatments of poetic themes. Feminists who approach poetry as a tool for political change and empowerment, such as Marge Piercy and Judy Grahn, aim for accessibility; this approach contrasts sharply with the elitist sensibility dominant in the modernist period and still much in evidence among male poets. Women's recent tones have often been harsh, angry, and defiant, their forms loose and talky. The title of Rich's selected poems, *The Fact of a Doorframe,* suggests the widespread impulse not only to root poetry in the commonplace but to keep it true to the tangible details of domestic life. Women's bodies and the experiences of female sexuality, pregnancy, parturition, menstruation, and menopause have become important topics as well as sources of imagery in women's poems. Recent women poets have generally favored short lyrics or lyric sequences, showing less interest than their male counterparts in massive epics on conventionally grand subjects.

Further References. Suzanne Juhasz, *Naked and Fiery Forms: Modern American Poetry by Women, A New Tradition* (New York, 1976). Diane Wood Middlebrook and Marilyn Yalom (eds.), *Coming to Light: American Women Poets in the 20th Century* (Ann Arbor, 1985). Alicia Suskin Ostriker, *Stealing the Language: The Emergence of Women's Poetry in America* (Boston, 1986).

LYNN KELLER

PRÉCIEUSES. Women of seventeenth-century France who flaunted an excessive refinement and affectation of language and manners known as preciosity. Beginning among the aristocracy in Paris, the movement peaked to a fad that swept all France after mid-century, then died in ridicule in the 1660s. Dismissed as a silly pretentiousness of conceited, pedantic women, it has also been identified as a feminist search for identity and self-expression.

The pattern of manners and behavior adopted by the *précieuses* began to form early in the seventeenth century at the first French salon of Catherine d'Angennes, marquise d' Rambouillet, who, repelled by the vulgarity of the French court, set about providing an alternative gathering place. She had a house near the Louvre rebuilt to her own design and there, in the *chambre blue,* provided a setting and tone that soon attracted the female aristocracy and their satellite gentlemen, including the men of letters of France.

After the social upheaval caused by the Fronde, the last revolt of the aristocracy, 1648–1653, a seven-year period of peace and social stability saw the climax of the phenomenon. Salons multiplied, and members of the bourgeoisie, not just in Paris but all over France, took up the style and mannerisms of précieuses.

But in late 1659 and 1660, Moliere's one-act *Les Précieuses Ridicules* had Paris laughing at their affectations. Other attacks followed. More importantly, Louis XIV's personal rule, which gathered the aristocracy into a tight social system centered at the court, finished off the *précieuses.*

In reaction to the coarse behavior and speech of the day, the women of the Hôtel de Rambouillet cultivated a deliberate artificiality and stylization of social intercourse. The spirit of refinement in language and literature led to efforts of the women and their satellite literary men to make the language more precise and orderly, a movement taken up and furthered by the newly founded French Academy. The chance to exercise their wits in the shaping and twisting of language led to the exaggerated metaphors, conceits, and circumlocutions for which the *précieuses* were ridiculed. Similar experiments in Spain and England, influenced by the French, led to similar results: Gongorism in Spain and euphuism in England.

The interest of the *précieux* in literature led not only to the reading and discussion of poetry and novels, but to composition as well. The marquise de Sévigné and the comtesse de La Fayette represent the movement at its best. Madeline de Scudéry, the leading spirit of *préciosité* at its zenith, is not up to their literary standards, but her novels, read by all the *précieuses,* are important for their feminist protest.

The *précieux* phenomenon can be seen as a woman's movement, a search by women, married at or near puberty to strangers chosen for political and economic reasons, to affirm their identity as something other than brood mares. Their protest and their desire to express their own feelings underlie their experiments in startling dress and behavior as well as in the creation of their own language and can also be seen in the proposal of such radical ideas as trial marriage, divorce, and birth control, in a negative attitude toward marriage expressed by many, and in the *refus de l'amour*. The artificial atmosphere of the salon emphasized the chivalric and pastoral traditions that idealized women and exaggerated their influence. The ladies, using Arcadian pseudonyms (no lady could be called by her given name in public), discussed many things, but chiefly love. However, it was a love devoid of passion. The possibility of platonic love, an invention of the Renaissance, attracted them. The possibility of enjoying a spiritual relationship with a man, devoid of the dross of materiality, or of enjoying a purely intellectual relationship with a male admirer while keeping for her husband the only part of her he was interested in anyway, her body, was debated endlessly. Hence, despite the preoccupation with love, the *précieuses* were called the Jansenists (French puritans) of love. It was alleged that love did not arouse their passions but was a kind of religion with them (St. Evremond in his correspondence with Ninon de Lenclos).

Seventeenth-century thought tried to fit everything in the universe, including human nature, within universal laws or types. As females were thought of in terms of sex, all women were classified as either prudes or *galantes* (flirts). And as any woman who valued her reputation had to be chaste, the *précieuses* chose to be prudes, or at least to be thought of as such. With the topic of love dominating salon conversation, it had to be made very clear that such talk was not misunderstood; hence, the *précieuses* became celebrated for their prudery. While this was as exaggerated as their circumlocutions and conceits, it does not negate their serious wrestling with and trying to find answers to the very real problems of women's sexuality in the seventeenth century.

Further Reference. Dorothy A. L. Baker, *Precious Women: A Feminist Phenomenon in the Age of Louis XIV* (New York, 1974).

Q

QUERELLE DES FEMMES. Debate about the social role of women in modern Western society that began in France at the beginning of the fifteenth century. The *querelle* was part of the larger literary debate of the Renaissance that was initiated by Petrarch and Boccaccio, who championed "classical" models of human behavior grounded in the misogynist platonic tradition. The *querelle* was women's rebuttal of the "humanistic" ideals that denigrated the role and nature of women. Though the debate was literary, its participants addressed all of the areas in which women were being excluded by the consolidation of postmedieval society: politics, economics, and religion.

Christine de Pisan (1364–1430?) was one of the earliest and best-known writers who defended women from the increasingly misogynist attacks levied against them by church polemicists and spokesmen for the modern European states that were forming as patriarchal monarchies. She was an Italian scholar who traveled to Paris when her father was appointed to a position in the French Valois court. Widowed at an early age, Christine de Pisan used her humanistic training to support herself and her family and set an important precedent for women's participation in public discourse.

Christine moved from writing courtly literature to the arena of Renaissance humanism when she entered the *querelle de la rose*, a debate about *The Romance of the Rose*, a thirteenth-century poem that had been reworked by Jean de Meun at the beginning of the fifteenth century. Jean de Meun's version scorned the medieval ideals of courtly love while glorifying realism and logic. In denying the power of heterosexual love, he ridiculed the qualities of women. Writing in the same rhetorical style as other Renaissance writers, Christine de Pisan rebutted his vision and presented her case to the queen of France, thereby introducing the role of women into both scholarly and political debates throughout Europe.

In her analysis of the *querelle* Joan Kelly (*Women, History and Theory* [Chicago, 1984], 66) identified the debate as "the vehicle through which most early feminist thinking evolved.'' According to Kelly, the nearly 400-year-long debate was essentially static in character, though texts were composed by writers throughout Europe at different times (see Kelly's notes for bibliography.) For women living under the cultural hegemony of patriarchal society, the *querelle* served as a vital public forum in which they could develop and share their literary talent. If the endless discussion of essential qualities such as reason by mythological and noble characters gives the *querelle* an ahistorical quality, it is because the *querelle* was the collective voice of the loyal opposition that resisted secular changes that threatened the welfare of women.

Though its title suggests that the *querelle* was exclusively about women, the debate was a correction of other transformations that were taking place in European society between the fourteenth and nineteenth centuries: the shift to centralized nation-states, religious dissent and the secularization of society, and the development of a market economy—all of which subordinated the social role of women.

The attack on women was part of the attack on nature that characterizes modern Western culture. Renaissance writers vilified female reproductive and nurturing capacities that seemed to be antithetical to the ideals of reason, logic, and the ostensible objectivity of science. By denying nature, men felt free to plunder the environment in search of material wealth and to subject other human beings to economic and political exploitation. This view of the natural world changed in the eighteenth century when philosophers again saw a common nature in human beings and formulated a more egalitarian social doctrine based on natural rights. Although women were ironically excluded from the Enlightenment view of natural rights, they participated in the debate with the same vigor that characterized the *querelle*. Mary Wollstonecraft's *Vindication of the Rights of Women* (1792) generally marks the beginning of modern feminism, when the *querelle des femmes* moved from the rhetoric of moral allegory to the heated political argument that characterizes modern democratic society.

JANE CRISLER

R

RENAISSANCE LITERATURE, ENGLISH: IMAGES OF WOMEN IN.

Culminates in the image of Milton's Eve in the epic poem *Paradise Lost*. Although Milton's Eve comes, in the midseventeenth century, at the end of the Renaissance in England, her image builds upon and perpetuates Renaissance antifeminist commonplaces, while it also questions and undermines them.

Milton emphasizes Eve's subordinate position in his description of Adam and Eve in Book 4: "For contemplation he and valor formed, /For softness she and sweet attractive grace; /He for God only, she for God in him" (11.296–299). Eve herself articulates and generalizes that subservience: "God is thy Law, thou mine; to know no more/Is woman's happiest knowledge and her praise" (11.638–639). When she rebels against her secondary position, she separates herself from Adam in their Edenic tasks and thus is vulnerable to Satan's temptations.

Yet Milton's Eve also embodies some of the Protestant reformer's ideas about companionate marriage. Eve's sinfulness is not hers alone. While she falls tempted by Satan, Adam falls out of desire for her love. Eve's influence leads to the couple's mutual education. Through her pleas to Adam for forgiveness, Adam learns of the need for reconciliation and mercy, the Christian teaching of Milton's epic. As the mother of humankind, Eve learns that "by me the Promised Seed shall all restore" (12, 1.623). When the poem ends, Adam and Eve are "hand in hand" as they meet the world all before them. Although Milton's Eve becomes a more complex figure than her first presentation in *Paradise Lost* suggests, the dominant impression of woman's representation in Milton's poetic career and corpus remains that of a subordinate, shadowy figure.

When the Renaissance in England was at its height, in Edmund Spenser's Elizabethan world, the great epic poet of the 1590s presents images of women that contrast with the shadowy or negative women of Milton's epic poem. While antifeminist views of female nature are embodied in the allegorical Error in Book

1 of Spenser's *The Faerie Queene*, other females throughout the epic serve to celebrate women.

In part because Spenser's poem was written in praise of his own Queen Elizabeth, the positive images of women range widely. They include the gentle, yet forceful Una, whose cry, "Fie, fie, faint harted knight" (1. ix. 465) shocks the feeble Redcrosse Knight into action against the temptations of Despair. In the third book of *The Faerie Queene*, the virtue of Chastity is exemplified through the woman warrior Britomart. In this portrait, Spenser tells Queen Elizabeth that he is disguising praise of her, his own queen, since explicit celebration would be inadequate: "But O dred Soveraine/ Thus farre forth pardon, sith that choicest wit/ Cannot your glorious pourtraict figure plaine/ That I in colour showes may shadow it,/ And antique praises unto present persons fit" (3. i. 23–27).

Throughout her reign, Queen Elizabeth provided a strong positive image of a woman, through which poets from Peele's play, *The Arraignment of Paris*, through William Shakespeare's *Henry VI*, Part 3 found opportunities to create dominant roles for woman. Yet Queen Elizabeth herself perpetuated some of the misogynist stereotypes that haunted her at her accession in 1558, in such tracts as John Knox's *Blast of the Trumpet against the Monstrous Regiment of Women*. Queen Elizabeth ruled through her own alienation from her womanliness. She ruled as the Virgin Queen, continuing the idea of chastity as the norm, and replacing in her still newly Protestant country the lost ideal of the Virgin Mary. The artifice of her costuming and the artfulness of her speeches both contributed to her power.

During Elizabeth's reign from 1558 to 1603, positive images of women include the female characters of Shakespeare's comedies, like Rosalind of *As You Like It* and Beatrice of *Much Ado About Nothing*. After James I's accession, however, the Jacobean theatre explored female characters who achieved tragic, heroic stature, like John Webster's *The Duchess of Malfi*. In her closet drama, *The Tragedy of Mariam*, Elizabeth Cary explored the dilemmas facing strong women. In addition, in this later period of the Renaissance, such women writers as Elizabeth Grymeston, the author of the *Miscelanea*; Lady Mary Wroth, the author of the poetry and prose epic romance *Urania*; and Amelia Lanier, the author of a poetic defense of Eve, became creators of rich images of women, which we are only now beginning to recover.

Further References. Mary Beth Rose (ed.), *Women in the Middle Ages and the Renaissance: Literary and Historical Perspectives* (Syracuse, 1986). "Women in the Renaissance," *English Literary Renaissance* 14 (1984): 253–439.

NONA FIENBERG

RENAISSANCE LITERATURE: ENGLISH LYRIC POETRY. Ranges from celebrating the creative generosity of the muse who inspires male authorship to postulating a realm of civilized discourse into which the language of woman intrudes as a barbaric or infantile disruption. With Sir Thomas Wyatt's introduction of the Petrarchan tradition into English lyric poetry in the midsixteenth century, Petrarch's representation of woman as the poet's Laura, his beloved, and his object to be scattered into verses becomes established in England. Yet poetry's attachment to the changing circumstances of England's court through the Renaissance also modifies the Petrarchan legacy. Wyatt's question "What vaileth truth?" echoes through the period, and exposes the problematics of changing values in the court world. Whether the court was dominated by Henry VIII, Elizabeth I, or James I, court poets attached their uncertainties about their position to their representation of woman's mutability and woman's power. In the poetry of Sir Philip Sidney, John Donne, and Ben Jonson, male ambivalence about a woman's power renders the representation of woman all the more complex.

In Sir Philip Sidney's sonnet sequence, *Astrophil and Stella*, that ambivalence is revealed in the two dramas of the sequence: the emergence of Stella, not simply a projection of the speaker's desires, and the speaker's reification of Stella. Although Sidney fails to dramatize a "real" beloved, involved in a relationship of mature mutuality, he does risk confronting an affective presence with a poised, articulate voice, in short, a woman with language. The sonnet sequence does, particularly in the Eighth Song, give space to Stella, a woman with her own story. This song inscribes Sidney's imaginative empathy with woman's culturally imposed muteness. Such empathy contrasts with Shakespeare's dominance over the Dark Lady's voice in his sonnets, a dominance that marks an effort of "will" to control or order his mutable world.

While John Donne's love lyrics celebrate the woman who inspires his love, his desire to return home in "A Valediction: Forbidding Mourning," and his longing to create a universe of two in "The Sun Rising," that woman remains tied to her limited world as he leaves to explore court advancement. While the wit of his metaphysical language compliments his beloved's intellect, the vituperative speaker of "Elegy VII" condemns his beloved as "Nature's Lay Idiot," whose entry into the world of love means no more than complicity in the deceits of love language.

As Queen Elizabeth aged without a dynastic successor and died in 1603, leaving James I, son of Mary, Queen of Scots, on the throne, the poets of the court circle adjusted the rhetoric of their love lyric to a new hierarchy of values. No longer were the final arbiter of worth and the ultimate source of identity a woman. When Ben Jonson demonstrates his worth as heir to his classical models, he does so at the expense of his "lady friends." Such poems as "Inviting a Friend to Supper" and the "Cary and Morison Ode" posit an exclusively male world, troubled at the fringes by sexual and political instability. Female generation itself is undermined in the troubling portrait of the "brave infant of Saguntum" as the "Cary and Morison Ode" opens.

While Jonson praises the poetry of Lady Mary Wroth, we must examine her lyric poetry, particularly the sonnet sequence presenting love from the woman's perspective, *Pamphilia to Amphilanthus*, to see a woman reflect on the representation of woman in the English Renaissance lyric. As Sir Philip Sidney's niece, Wroth stood in a critical relationship to the sonnet tradition. Wroth uses her sonnets to articulate the difficulty of adapting love language and the sonnet form to a woman's experience. In contrast to a tradition of woman's faithlessness, in Wroth's work, the male beloved, Amphilanthus, is the lover of two women. Pamphilia's pain and conflict in love, then, derive in part from her suffering loyalty to a disloyal man. In addition, however, Wroth's songs and sonnets begin to create the new discourse necessary for the new voice she is presenting. That discourse begins with a woman alienated "from knowledg of my self" but finds the forms, myths, and language to end in repose: "My muse now hapy, lay thy self to rest." Wroth's achievement offers readers the opportunity to reevaluate the lyric tradition.

Further References. Josephine Roberts (ed.), *The Poems of Lady Mary Wroth* (Baton Rouge, La., 1983). Nancy Vickers, "Diana Described: Scattered Woman and Scattered Rhyme," *Critical Inquiry* 8 (1980–1981): 265–281.

NONA FIENBERG

RENAISSANCE LITERATURE: ITALIAN WRITERS. Divided into two groups: humanists and poets. In the fifteenth century many women, especially those of the upper classes, were given the same humanist education available to men. Educated in Latin, Greek, philosophy, and literature as young girls, they were regarded as prodigies by their established male counterparts, with whom they corresponded. However, upon reaching adulthood they either married or entered the convent, abandoning their writing. Such was the fate of Ginevra Nogarola (1417–1465) of Verona, Battista da Montefeltro Malatesta (1383–1450?) of Urbino, her granddaughter Costanza Varano (1426–1447), and Laura Cereta (1469–1499) of Brescia. Two exceptions were Isotta Nogarola (1418–1466), the sister of Ginevra, who chose to live in her family home and dedicate her life to scholarship; and Cassandra Fedele (1465–1558) of Venice, who as a young girl gave orations before the University of Padua, the Venetian people, and the doge. Seventeen years after marrying, Cassandra took up the pen once again.

In Florence, Alessandra Scala (1475–1506) wrote a Greek epigram in response to one written by her teacher, Poliziano. Using the vernacular, Alessandra Macigni Strozzi wrote 72 letters to her exiled sons. Lucrezia Tornabuoni d'Medici (1425–1482), the wife of Piero and mother of Lorenzo the Magnificent, wrote five short poems on biblical and evangelical themes and several lauds and hymns based on the life of Christ. Antonia Giannotti Pulci (1452?–?), the wife of writer Bernardo Pulci, wrote four *sacre rappresentazioni* (miracle plays).

In the sixteenth century many women rose to prominence as poets, imitating the style of Francis Petrarch, as did their male counterparts. Veronica Gambara (1485–1550) from Pratalboino (Brescia) wrote love poetry in her youth and passed to religious themes in maturity. Her sonnets, madrigals, and *stanze*, together with her correspondence, were published for the first time in 1759.

Vittoria Colonna (1490–1547) from Marino, Colli Albani (Rome), is known for her long-standing friendship with Michelangelo Buonarrotti and Galeazzo di Tàrsia. Her poetry was published on several occasions during her lifetime. In the 1544 edition of her *Rime* the poetry is divided into two sections: poems dealing with the death of her husband and poems on religious themes.

Gaspara Stampa (1523?–1554) from Padua moved to Venice in 1531, where her home became a musical and literary center frequented by Varchi, Vernier, Alamanni, and Domenichi. She was a member of the Accademia dei Dubbiosi. Her poetry (Venice, 1554), dedicated to her lover, Collaltino Collalto, consists of 311 poems divided into two parts: love rhymes and various rhymes.

Isabella di Morra (1520–1548) from Favale, Basilicata, wrote 13 poems, first published in 1559. She corresponded secretly with Diego Sandoval de Castro, who sent her poetry and letters. Upon discovering their correspondence, Isabella's brothers killed first her, then Sandoval.

Laura Bacio Terracina (1519–1577?) from Naples was a member of the Accademia degli Incogniti. She published seven collections of poetry, of which the first (1548) was reprinted five times in the sixteenth century, twice in the seventeenth. Her themes ranged from love expressed in Petrarchan terms to religious mysticism. In her *Discorso sopra tutti i primi canti di Orlando Furioso* (Venice, 1549; Discourse on All of the First Cantos of Orlando Furioso), the final line of each stanza was drawn from the first stanza of the corresponding canto of Ariosto's epic poem. A sequel followed in 1567. She also wrote *Sovra tutte le donne vedove di questa nostra città di Napoli titolate et non titolate* (Concerning All of the Widowed Ladies of Our City of Naples, Titled and Not Titled), an elegiac poem published in 1561.

Chiara Matraini (1514–1597?) of Lucca was a poet and scholar of philosophy and history. She wrote poetry in the Petrarchan style along with religious literature. *Rime e prose* (Lucca, 1555) was followed by *Rime e lettere* (Lucca, 1595) and *Lettere con la prima e la seconda parte delle rime* (Venice, 1597). Among her religious works are *Meditazione spirituali* (Lucca, 1581), *Considerazioni sopra i sette salmi penitenziali* (Lucca, 1586, Considerations on the Seven Penitential Psalms), *Breve discorso sopra la vita della Beata Vergine* (Lucca, 1590; Brief Discourse Concerning the Life of the Blessed Virgin), and *Dialoghi spirituali* (Venice, 1602).

Olimpia Morato (1526–1555) from Ferrara moved to Germany following her marriage to Andreas Grunthler. Deep Lutheran convictions permeate her letters, important documents in the history of the Reformation. The humanist training of her youth led her to write several other works: three Latin *proemi* (introductions) to a commentary of the *Paradoxa* by Cicero; a translation into Latin of the first two tales of the *Decameron*; two dialogues in Latin; and eight *Carmi* (odes), three in Latin and five in Greek. Her complete works were published in 1558, 1562, and 1570.

Laura Battiferri Ammannati (1532–1589) from Urbino, moved to Florence following her marriage to Bartolomeo Ammannati. She was a member of the Accademia degli Assorditi of Urbino and of the Accademia degli Intronati of

Siena. Her poetry, acclaimed during her lifetime, was first published as *Primo libro delle opere toscane* (Florence, 1560, First Book of Tuscan Works). In 1564 she published a translation into the vernacular of the seven penitential psalms of the prophet David. Her correspondence with Benedetto Varchi was published in 1879.

Renaissance society had a special place for the so-called honest courtesans, women renowned for their beauty and culture who moved in the highest circles and presided over salons. Two of these courtesans were writers. Tullia d'Aragona (1508?–1556), born in Rome, was the lover of the writers Girolamo Muzio and Bernardo Tasso and was friendly with Benedetto Varchi and Piero Mannelli, to whom she dedicated many of her sonnets. Because of her poetry (Venice, 1547), she was excused by Cosimo I, duke of Tuscany, from wearing the yellow veil required of all courtesans. She also wrote *Il Meschino altramente detto il Guerrino* (Venice, 1560; Meschino, Also Called Guerrino), a romance in 36 cantos; and *Dialogo dell'infinità di amore* (1552, Dialogue on the Infinity of Love), a disputation on platonic love.

Veronica Franco (1546–1591) from Venice was admired and beloved by the princes and intellectuals of her time. Her portrait was painted by Tintoretto, and she was mentioned by Montaigne in his *Jornal de voyage*. She helped to found the Hospice of S. Maria del Soccorso in Venice for abandoned young girls and reformed courtesans. Her literary works consist of *Le terze rime* or *Capitoli* (1575), 18 rhymed letters written by Veronica and 7 written to her; and *Lettere familiari a diversi* (1580), 50 letters dedicated to the cardinal Luigi d'Este. Unlike Tullia d'Aragona, Veronica never attempted to hide her "profession" from the public.

Further References. Natalia Costa-Zalessow, *Scrittrici italiane dal XIII al XX secolo: testi e critica* (Ravenna, 1982). Margaret L. King and Albert Rabil, Jr. (eds.), *Her Immaculate Hand: Selected Works by and about the Women Humanists of Quattrocento Italy* (Binghamton, N.Y., 1983).

JOAN H. LEVIN

RENAISSANCE LITERATURE: TRANSALPINE WRITERS. Perhaps the most seminally important contribution of Renaissance humanism to the burgeoning of female literary activity was the availability, on a large scale, of a diversified education to laywomen fortunate enough to have had access to books and teachers. Indeed, the education of women was one of the most persuasively argued topics in the famous Renaissance debate on women's worth, the *querelle des femmes*. The availability of education created a large class of men and women who mastered the rudiments of humanist learning: proficiency in Latin, competency in Greek, knowledge of ancient and patristic literature, history, and moral philosophy, as well as the conventions of Petrarchism and Ficinian Neoplatonism. In particular, ladies of the upper classes and women relatives of the humanists profited from the humanist curriculum.

Marguerite of Navarre attracted leading poets and scholars; Marguerite of

Navarre, educated with her brother Francis, the future king of France, was herself polyglot and wrote in many genres; the Dames des Roches consciously dedicated their lives to the pursuit of learning; and the Lyonnese school boasted such learned women as Louise Labé and Pernette Du Guillet. In England, Queen Elizabeth's philological training and knowledge of the classics dazzled the ambassadors at her court, and the erudition of Lady Jane Grey, Mary Sidney, and Margaret More Roper, to mention only a few, was eulogized by their contemporaries. Margaret of Austria and Louise of Savoy, both avid readers of the classics, ruled their realms with political and administrative acumen and their literary salons with erudition and wit. In Germany, Caritas Pirckheimer corresponded with the leading humanists of her day, and Margaret Peutinger was a noted biblical scholar. As during the Middle Ages, so in the Renaissance, a large portion of the works by women were of devotional or religiopolitical nature, but the ratio of religious versus secular texts became a great deal more balanced as time progressed.

Renaissance women writers could conveniently be categorized in six groups: the *grande dame*, the woman scholar, the nun, the religious or political activist, the *cortigiana onesta*, and the patrician. By and large, *grande dames* wrote secular and even public works, with lyric poetry, letters, translations, orations, and novelistic texts predominating, though some, notably Marguerite of Navarre and Vittoria Colonna, did compose devotional poems and Elizabeth I penned several homilies. By and large, they wrote in the vernacular, and almost invariably they were held in high literary esteem by their contemporaries. Second, the woman scholar, occupying perhaps the most Renaissance of the six categories, was almost invariably related to a literary man and was frequently of well-to-do but not necessarily aristocratic descent. Renaissance women scholars devoted themselves to philological pursuits: translations, essays, letters, dialogues, and even invectives, both in Latin and the vernacular. It is this group, together with the writers of the urban patriciate (that is, women for whom humanist education was not a matter of self-evident necessity), that seems most concerned with educational opportunities for women and with the obligations women have to take advantage of these new opportunities. Women scholars were occasionally attacked and ridiculed, and they were the most vociferous advocates that women should learn for learning's sake. Third, the nun, the major representative of medieval women writers, no longer occupied that pre-eminent position in Renaissance letters. Writing in Latin and the vernacular, she came from all social classes, and her compositions include not only visions, revelations, and *vitae*, as in the Middle Ages, but also translations, biographies, and autobiographies. Fourth, the *cortigiana onesta*, the Italian Renaissance brand of the Greek hetaira, exemplifies the single woman's other alternative. Cultured, though rarely, if ever, of aristocratic descent, she most often wrote vernacular lyric poetry. Fifth, the religious political activist, militant descendant of the medieval Margery Kempe, often belonged to the urban poor, invariably wrote in the vernacular, and was seldom rewarded for her activism and pamphleteering.

Finally, the gentlewoman writer was usually a member of the provincial urban patriciate and was a Renaissance novelty. She was ordinarily learned as well as cultivated, she could be either single or married, she was rarely related to a literary man, and she composed almost always in the vernacular and in a variety of devotional or fictional forms. Conspicuously absent from this catalogue of Renaissance women's writings are the learned commentary or treatise and the original epic or secular drama.

Further References. R. Kelso, *Doctrine for the Lady of the Renaissance* (Urbana, Ill., 1956). P. H. Labalme (ed.), *Beyond Their Sex: Learned Women of the European Past* (New York, 1980). M. E. Weisner, *Women in the Sixteenth Century: A Bibliography* (St. Louis, 1983). K. M. Wilson, *Women Writers of the Renaissance and Reformation* (Athens, Ga., 1987).

KATHARINA M. WILSON

ROMAN POETRY, WOMEN IN, is of necessity the study of the role of women in the works of male Latin poets, since only one woman poet, Sulpicia, has survived, and her meager poetic remains are of minor merit and interest.

Drama. In the comedies of Plautus and Terence, women play a large part, but, despite some sharply drawn characters, the numerous female figures can be reduced to a handful of stock types: the wily maidservant, the predatory prostitute, the prostitute with the heart of gold, the nagging wife, and (kept mostly offstage) the virtuous young girl. A special case is the heroine of Plautus's *Amphitryon*. A faithful wife, she is seduced by Jupiter in the guise of her husband and becomes an almost tragic character amid the comedy.

Lucretius. Lucretius, the epic poet of Epicurean philosophy, deals extensively with women in his treatment of love and sex. Love is an unhealthy distraction from Epicurean detachment and serenity of mind in which the lover torments himself and blindly transforms the vices of a woman into virtues. Sexual desire and its satisfaction without emotional attachment or complications, on the other hand, are natural and permissible.

Catullus. The lyric poet Catullus, with a truly revolutionary attitude toward women, idealizes his mistress and the love of a man for a woman to a degree unparalleled by previous ancient authors. In an important group of poems he expresses and analyzes his overwhelming love for an aristocratic Roman matron named Clodia (given the pseudonym Lesbia). He pays tribute not only to her beauty but to her intelligence, learning, and wit.

Catullus's love for Clodia has an intensity heretofore found in ancient poetry only in homosexual attachments. Flouting the traditional notion that passionate love of a woman was acceptable only as a passing stage in adolescence but folly and madness for an adult male, he makes the woman the center of his life. Since Romans could not be expected to comprehend this novel conception of love (and Catullus seems to have some difficulty in understanding it himself), he struggles to describe something that was not a part of accepted Roman values by expressing it in terms that the Romans did understand and respect: religion, friendship, law, international relations, and business.

Unfortunately Clodia, a very independent woman, seems not to have been interested in such a confining relationship. Catullus took this attitude as betrayal and responded with some brilliant, but often violently obscene, poems attacking her. Another attack on her came in a speech by Cicero, Rome's greatest orator, made in his defense of a man in whose prosecution Clodia was instrumental; Cicero defended his client in exactly the same manner as a modern defense lawyer in a rape case, by destroying the woman's reputation. It is regrettable that most of what we know about this remarkable woman comes to us in the writings of a disappointed lover and a designing lawyer.

Horace. In the odes and satires of Horace women are frequent, but they are quite unsubstantial figures. An exception is his ode on the death of Cleopatra, which begins with the queen as the familiar monster of Augustan propaganda but ends by investing her with the nobility of those Roman statesmen who, like her, chose suicide over submission.

Love Elegy. Love elegy was a literary genre invented by the Romans, with no Greek prototype, and in it woman was of central concern. The leading elegists were Propertius, Tibullus, and Ovid. Propertius wrote many poems detailing his love for a woman whom he calls Cynthia, whose real name was probably Hostia. He spoke of her as a slave would speak of his mistress and idealized her by identifying her with the renowned heroines of the Greek legendary past. Although she is to a great extent a peg on which to hang his probings of his own emotions, a plausible portrait of a woman emerges. She was not only beautiful and temperamental, but also very well educated (she had to be to understand his constant allusions to Greek mythology) and accomplished in the arts. She was strong-willed and unwilling to be tied down. Like Clodia, she inspired a love that she refused to be bound by.

Virgil. Virgil, in the Roman national epic, the *Aeneid*, creates a powerful woman in Dido. She is in every respect the equal of the hero of the poem, Aeneas, but when he leaves her to resume his mission to found the Roman people, the poet makes her react in a stereotypically female fashion, and women are seen to be obstacles to the serious enterprises of men. In addition, human and divine females are identified in the poem with the irrational and with the chaotic forces of nature.

Ovid. Ovid, of all ancient poets with the possible exception of the Greek tragedian Euripides, tries hardest to understand women and their psychology and to express what he has learned in his poetry, although at the beginning the knowledge he has gained through his close observation of women is used to portray them in a rather cynical fashion. In his *Art of Love* he instructs men in the manipulation of women, although the final third of the work is devoted to advice for women. By means of the "art" Ovid professes to teach, and the Latin word meant both art and science, man must cultivate woman in the same sense that man cultivates nature in the art/science called agriculture. Like land, woman in a state of nature is rough, crude, and useless. A woman's "no" really means "yes," and the force a man may sometimes find it necessary to use is secretly welcome to her. On the positive side, the lover is exhorted to make himself worthy of love and to attend to his mistress's sexual satisfaction (even to the extent of ensuring mutual orgasm).

The *Heroides* (Heroines), a collection of letters in verse that Ovid imagines were composed by famous women at major crises in their lives, shows a good deal of psychological insight.

By the time of the *Metamorphoses* (Transformations), Ovid sees women in a new light. Of this lengthy collection of stories drawn largely from Greek mythology, many deal with encounters of men and male divinities with women. Ovid strips the stories of their glamor and romance and presents them as rape seen from the point of view of the victim. In contrast to the *Art of Love*, he now knows that women do not like to be raped. In addition, the poem, in its comprehensive analysis of the varieties of love and of the shifting instability of personal identity, constantly delves into the psychology of women.

Juvenal. Juvenal devotes a poem of over 600 lines to shrill, unrelieved misogyny. Although the encyclopedic listing of women's vices suggests a striving for exhaustiveness that may be rhetorical in inspiration, it is difficult to deny the presence of genuine hatred of women.

LEO C. CURRAN

ROMANCE, MEDIEVAL. A literary genre that flourished from the twelfth to the fifteenth century in the literature of France, England, and Germany; examples of romance are also found in Provençal, Spanish, Portuguese, Italian, Hebrew, Greek, Dutch, and Norse. The English word *romance* is taken from the Old French term *romanz*, which evolved from the Latin adverb *romanice*, used as early as the ninth century to mean "in the vernacular." Since much of the material written *en romanz* in the twelfth century consisted of fictitious narratives with particular themes and formats, the English word *romance* has come to refer to those compositions and to the tradition they generated, as distinct from the epic tradition exemplified by the *chansons de geste*.

A form of narrative featuring love, adventure, or chivalry as a theme, medieval romance first appeared in verse and later evolved into prose. The subject matter of the romance was described at the end of the twelfth century by Jean Bodel, who divided vernacular literature into three groups: the *metière de Rome*, the *metière de Bretagne*, and the *metière de Charlemagne*. This latter group, also known as the *metière de France*, forms the basis for the *chansons de geste*, while the other two groups provide the basis for much of the romance material. The *metière de Rome* refers to legends and stories of antiquity on which were based the *romans d'antiquité*. The *metière de Bretagne*, or Breton material, includes the legends of both Arthur and Tristram. To the two romance *metières* included in Bodel's classification should be added the body of Graeco-Byzantine material that serves as the subject matter for many *romans d'aventure* and the "matter of England," a category added by modern critics to refer to romances set in England or concerned with English heroes.

The Old French *romans d'antiquité* have their predecessors in the classical romances, such as the early Greek romance of Alexander the Great. Following in this tradition is the first vernacular romance, *Roman d'Alexandre* (c.1100), a Franco-Provençal fragment that later appeared as a composite work in 12-syllable lines, which consequently came to be called *alexandrins*. An adaptation of Statius's *Thebaïs*, the *Roman de Thèbes* (c.1150) was composed by an anonymous Norman author. Another Norman adaptation of a Latin work is *Roman d'Enéas* (c.1160), an imitation of Virgil's *Aeneid*. *Roman de Troie* (1154–1173), a long compilation by Benoit de Sainte-Maure, is based on chronicles of the Trojan War.

The legends of King Arthur and his knights of the Round Table make up the body of material most often brought to mind by the term *romance*. Early portraits of Arthur by William of Malmesbury (*Gesta regum Anglorum*, 1125) and Geoffrey of Monmouth (*Historia regum Britanniae*, c.1136) underwent considerable elaboration by the Norman poet Wace in his *Roman de Brut* (c.1155), later translated into Middle English by the twelfth-century Saxon poet Layamon. Some of the earliest and best-known Arthurian romances were written by Chrétien de Troyes, who composed his *Lancelot* or *Le Chevalier de la charrette* after 1164 for Marie, countess of Champagne. While Chrétien's romances, which also include *Erec et Enide*, *Cligès*, *Yvain* or *Le Chevalier au lion*, and *Perceval* or *Le Conte du Graal*, show both classical and Byzantine influences, it was his treatment of the Breton material in a new form of narrative that had the greatest impact on the development of the romance genre, inspiring many imitations. The symbolism of the Grail theme, first introduced into European literature by Chrétien, is continued in Robert de Boron's *Joseph d'Arimathie* (late twelfth or early thirteenth century) and in the series of prose Lancelot romances dating from the early thirteenth century. Chrétien's romances provided the sources for the Middle High German works *Erek* (c.1190) and *Iwein* (c.1200) of Hartmann von Aue and *Parzival* (c.1200–1212) of Wolfram von Eschenbach.

Marie de France, a contemporary of Chrétien, is the first known woman author of narratives based on the *metière de Bretagne*. Her *lais*, composed in the second half of the twelfth century, may be described as short romances dealing with Celtic and Arthurian themes. Written in octosyllabic couplets, Marie's *lais* contain strong elements of the supernatural (as in *Guigemar* and *Bisclavret*) and treat both happy and unhappy love; *Lai du Chèvrefeuil*, one of Marie's most popular poems, presents one episode of the legend of Tristram and Isolde. Influences from Marie's *lais* may be seen in Gautier d'Arras's romance *Ille et Galeron* (c.1170), thought to be based on Marie's *Eliduc*, and in Hue de Roteland's *Ipomedon* (c.1185), which has parallels to the *lai Milun*.

The tragic love story of Tristram and Isolde first appears in the latter part of the twelfth century in the *romans* of Béroul and Thomas, as well as in a lost version by Chrétien de Troyes. The Norman poet Béroul's fragmentary work, written before 1191, most closely follows the lost Old French original (c.1150–1160); a parallel version exists in German by Eilhart von Oberge (c.1170). The *Tristan* of the Anglo-Norman Thomas (c.1155–1178), also a fragment, presents the more courtly version of the legend, later continued by the German author Gottfried von Strassburg (c.1210), by Brother Robert in the Norwegian *Tristrams saga* (1226), and by the anonymous author of the Middle English *Sir Tristrem* (c.1300).

Romances with Graeco-Byzantine themes include the *Eracle*, written after 1164 by Gautier d'Arras, and *Floire et Blancheflor*, (c.1170), later translated into Middle High German, Middle Dutch, Norse, and Middle English; the early thirteenth-century *chantefable Aucassin et Nicolette* shows influences from *Floire et Blancheflor*. Other *romans d'adventure*, such as the twelfth-century works *Partonopeus de Blois* and *Robert le Diable*, are likely based on folk motifs.

The English romances developed in the thirteenth century with the early works *King Horn* and *Havelock the Dane*, followed by dozens of romances in the fourteenth century, including *Sir Orfeo* (c.1320), a Celticized version of the myth of Orpheus and Eurydice, and the *Alliterative Morte Arthur* (c.1360); *Sir Gawain and the Green Knight*, written by an anonymous Midland poet around 1375, and Chaucer's *Troilus and Criseyde* (c.1385) are considered by some to be the greatest of the English verse romances. Although the romance genre declined in England in the fifteenth century, Sir Thomas Malory's prose *Morte d'Arthur* (1469) presented a synthesis of various Arthurian tales that would later serve as the basis for Tennyson's nineteenth-century reworking.

The Spanish *libros de caballería* appeared in the fourteenth century with the Castilian *Zifar* (c.1300), taken from Oriental sources, and *Amadís de Gaula*, a neo-Arthurian work whose central plot parallels that of *Lancelot* and that later inspired Cervantes's *Don Quixote* (1605). In Italy the *metière de Charlemagne* is treated as romance in heroic epics such as Matteo Boiardo's *Orlando innamorato* (1483) and Ludovico Ariosto's *Orlando furioso* (1516).

Representing a vast collection of women's literature, the romance frequently features powerful female characters whose importance is seen not only in their interaction with other characters but also in their influence on the development of the plot. Their power, however, usually comes from an external source, such as the world of magic or the fateful love malady inflicted on male and female protagonists alike. The transfer of power from such strong female characters to the male hero is an enabling process that sustains narrative tension by provoking action and contributing to the resolution of the hero's quest for self-realization.

In Marie's *lai Lanval*, the fairy mistress possesses such power and exerts a controlling force on the plot. It is she who seeks out Lanval and supports him both financially and emotionally. Similarly, in Chrétien's *Yvain*, Lunete transfers power to Yvain through her magic and moves him toward the accomplishment of his goals. In the *Chevalier de la charrette*, the lovesick Lancelot's obsession with Guinevere gives her such control over him that she is able to dictate his behavior. In the Provençal romance *Jaufré* (c.1225), the hero's search for adventure and self-definition becomes inextricably bound up in his pursuit of the beautiful Brunissen, whose power comes from her ownership of some 100 châteaus. Christine de Pisan's courtly romance *Le Livre du duc des vrais amants* (1405) features an influential female character who brings about the end of the love affair between the married princess and the anonymous duke.

One of the best-known female characters of romance is Isolde, who often precedes Tristram in initiating action and moving episodes toward resolution. Wonderfully adept at creating ambiguous oaths, she saves both herself and Tristram from punishment by the court. Isolde's magic healing ability, a link to Celtic tradition, gives her real and symbolic power over Tristram's life and death, a power dramatically illustrated in the tragic ending of the romance.

Further References. R. S. Loomis (ed.), *Arthurian Literature in the Middle Ages: A Collaborative History* (London, 1959). Eugene Vinaver, *The Rise of Romance* (London, 1971). Katharina M. Wilson (ed.), *Medieval Women Writers* (Athens, Ga., 1984).

MARYLOU MARTIN

ROMANTIC PERIOD LITERATURE: IMAGES OF WOMEN IN. Most commonly thought of in terms of the poetry of men (Blake, Wordsworth, Coleridge, Byron, Shelley, and Keats) and prose fiction by such men and women as Mary Shelley, Austen, and Scott. The images of women in the poetry of the great Romantics contrast significantly with the depiction of women in prose fiction. In the first, we see the female in terms of male aspirations and desires; in the second, women characters are generally more developed human beings.

Typically, the Romantic poet-persona seeks the ideal in terms of sexual union with a mysterious and elusive female, who often turns out to be a reflection of his desire for self-fulfillment. Because the poet considers this often exotic female as the Other and, primarily, in terms of his own male ego, women appear as idealizations, not individuals. This pattern emerges in Shelley's *Alastor* (1816) and in Keats's *Endymion* (1818), with variations such as Coleridge's Abyssinian maid and her magical dulcimer in "Kubla Khan" (1816). But if the female represents the object of the male quest, she also threatens the male as the femme fatale, who, like Keats's belle dame, seduces and destroys the pale knight and is thus blamed for the failure of imaginative vision. In the most narcissistic and nihilistic form of the quest, the desired female is the quester's sister, and the incestuous relationship is doomed to failure. We see this pattern in Byron's *Manfred* (1817), where we learn that Astarte had been destroyed by her brother's love, a supreme form of self-love. And although presumably without incestuous longing, in "Tintern Abbey" (1798) Wordsworth looks into his sister Dorothy's wild eyes and sees, not her hopes and fears, but his own "former self."

Also in Romantic poetry nature is depicted in female terms in opposition to male powers of imagination. Blake envisions nature as the deceptive goddess Vala, and Wordsworth, although a worshiper of nature, also reveals the darker shades of her power and influence in such works as the Lucy poems and the "Intimations Ode" (1807). Individual women in Wordsworth's poetry often become subsumed in nature and its processes so that they have no voice, no identity apart from the male poet's perception of nature: Lucy dies and is "rolled round in earth's diurnal course / With rocks, and stones, and trees" ("A Slumber Did My Spirit Seal"). Readers have noted the particular association between nature and motherhood in Wordsworth's poetry, generally concluding that Wordsworth sought the guardianship and protection in nature that he lost with the death of his mother when he was a young child. Wordsworth perceptively describes the natural process of the mother-infant bonding in a noted passage in Book 2 of *The Prelude* (1850).

Although a male-centered solipsistic vision prevails in much of the poetry, the Romantics also strive to place male-female relationships in the context of the fundamental human rights and freedoms inspired by the French Revolution. In *America* (1793), for instance, Blake dramatizes the intrinsic relationship between political and sexual liberation; following Mary Wollstonecraft's *Vindication of the Rights of Woman* (1792), he sees the analogy between political and marital tyranny. In a renovated world, the "doors of marriage are open," and females glow "with the lusts of youth" (15:19, 15:22). Like Wollstonecraft, Blake sees female liberation also liberating men from the self-destructive relationships based on power and jealousy. And Shelley, despite the contradictions in his own life and art, also claims in his *Defense of Poetry* (1840) the "abolition of personal and domestic slavery" and the "emancipation of women" to be the highest hopes for humankind.

The Romantic poets do on occasion acknowledge and even criticize their own self-absorption, but one of the strongest critiques of Romanticism comes from Mary Shelley, daughter of Mary Wollstonecraft and wife of the poet. In the character of Victor Frankenstein, Mary Shelley reveals the dangers of egotistical self-absorption, even when accompanied by genius. The more caring, sociable, and "human" monster (identified by some readers as feminine), created and destroyed by Frankenstein's ego, challenges the justice of Frankenstein's ambition. But *Frankenstein* (1818) is full of unresolved problems, and Mary Shelley seems both to condemn and desire Frankenstein's God-like creative powers.

The Romantics generally aspired to the great masculine, prophetic tradition of Miltonic poetry, in which the male bard as God-like creator sought the inspiration of his female muse. Such a concept of creativity and authorship excluded the female writer, as Mary Shelley suggests in the introduction added to the 1831 edition of *Frankenstein*. But the relatively new form of the novel was congenial to women both because of its "newness" and because the female writer could focus on the moral and ideological issues arising out of daily life and basic human relationships and institutions.

Jane Austen, of course, knew that she had been excluded from a male tradition. She has Anne Elliot argue in *Persuasion* (1818) that "men have had every advantage of us in telling their own story. Education has been theirs in so much higher a degree; the pen had been in their hands" (Chapter 23). Through close and sympathetic portrayal of characters like Anne Elliot, Emma Woodhouse

(*Emma*, 1816), and Elizabeth Bennet (*Pride and Prejudice*, 1813), Austen presents women who change and develop as they discover knowledge of themselves and their social world. We sometimes see her women characters through men's eyes, but we are almost always allowed to focus on the heroine's developing consciousness.

In his historical novels, Scott presents a wider panorama of society than does Austen, focusing less on a developing consciousness than on the larger forces and movements of society. In so doing, he creates a variety of male and female characters, ranging in social class from royalty to low-life criminals. Generally speaking, Scott is more successful in depicting native Scottish characters—often peasantry who speak in dialect—than ladies and gentlemen. While Scott's ladies are often as stiff and conventional as their language, his lower-class women have a flesh-and-blood liveliness. A good case in point is Jeanie Deans (in *The Heart of Mid-Lothian* [1818]), who refuses to save her innocent sister's life by telling a lie in court but undertakes a solitary and dangerous journey on foot to London to obtain a royal pardon. Behind Jeanie's courage lies the Scottish Presbyterian tradition, perhaps narrow-minded and at times fanatical, but asserting itself in Jeanie as an absolute moral standard.

Despite the working generalizations between poets and novelists, we should acknowledge that the images of women across genres are as varied as the authors themselves. The Romantic period constitutes less a consistent school of thought than an historical span that includes such diverse writers as Byron and Austen. And even within the work of individual authors, often unresolved and contradictory images of women abound, revealing the ambivalent attitude toward women and their place in late eighteenth- and early nineteenth-century culture.

Further References. Sandra M. Gilbert and Susan Gubar, *The Madwoman in the Attic* (New Haven, 1979). Margaret Homans, *Women Writers and Poetic Identity* (Princeton, 1980). Barbara Schapiro, *The Romantic Mother: Narcissistic Patterns in Romantic Poetry* (Baltimore, 1983). Irene Taylor and Gina Luria, "Gender and Genre: Women in British Romantic Literature," in Marlene Springer (ed.), *What Manner of Woman* (New York, 1977), 98–123.

JUDITH W. PAGE

ROYAL ACADEMY OF ARTS. The most prestigious British art organization, offering education, exhibition opportunities, and exclusive membership to aspiring painters, sculptors, and architects. Founded in 1768, the Royal Academy hoped to raise the level of British art by encouraging, according to its constitution, "men of fair moral characters, of high reputation in their several professions." Two prominent women painters were founding members of the academy: Angelica Kauffman (1741–1807) and Mary Moser (1744–1819). Unfortunately, from the beginning, women were excluded from holding any office within the organization and from assuming lectureships or attending life classes. Johann Zoffany's painting, *The Academicians of the Royal Academy* (1772) aptly portrays Kauffman's and Moser's roles in the early academy. Zoffany depicts most of the Royal Academy members (RAs) arranging a nude model and drapery; Kauffman and Moser are represented only by portraits on the right-hand wall. After Kauffman and Moser died, the Royal Academy discouraged women from studying art in its school and failed to invite another woman painter to join until 1922, when Annie Louisa Swynnerton (1844–1933) achieved Associate Royal Academy membership.

Excluding women from studying art and from full membership doomed women painters to second rank in England. Although painting was part of all educated women's regimen, women acquired primarily decorative skills. A typical middle-class woman learned to draw tolerably, paint landscapes, and copy artworks. Women painters excelled in watercolors, not oils, and focused on flower paintings, genre scenes, and touching love scenes suggested by literature. Although these paintings might gain a modest income for the artist, they could not successfully compete in Royal Academy exhibitions or gain support for membership. The Royal Academy valued large oil paintings, particularly historical or classical scenes, that displayed a painter's technical virtuosity and knowledge of human physique. Successful artists had to study anatomy and practice drawing nude models; women were not allowed this education.

Many art schools trained women to be lower-level artists; some of the most effective were the Female School of Design (founded in 1843)—which became the Royal Female School of Art in 1862—Henry Sass's School of Art (1842), Dickinson's Academy (1848), and the Slade School at the University of London (1871). The Royal Academy remained the school for serious painters, particularly for men intent on winning fame and titles. Although women were not expressly forbidden to enroll in Royal Academy classes, none tried until 1860. Sir Charles Eastlake suggested that Laura Herford, a prominent woman painter, apply for acceptance as a student. She submitted the requisite drawings under the name "L. Herford." She was accepted, as were 13 other women over the next few years, but women were restricted to studying from casts, reproductions, and clothed figures, never from living nudes. In 1863, the Council of the Royal Academy decided that its constitution did not allow women students. After protest from professional women painters, the Royal Academy allowed 13 women students to enroll.

Although many Victorian women became prominent painters, the Royal Academy remained adamant about not accepting women into full membership. Women were grudgingly allowed to study in separate classes, but not to teach or govern the institution. Artists of the caliber of Louisa Starr, Kate Greenway, and Elizabeth Thompson Butler were systematically ignored. Some intrepid RA members nominated prominent women for membership, but women lost every vote until 1922. Women were deemed less able to fulfill the necessary RA duties. Royal Academy membership entailed teaching and administrative responsibilities and guaranteed a painter's financial success. Victorians believed it improper for women to compete with or supervise men.

In 1903, the Royal Academy allowed mixed classes for most of its curriculum, and women were allowed to study nude figures in separate classes. Annie Laura Swynnerton and Laura Knight won associate membership in the 1920s. When, in 1936, Laura Knight achieved full status, the Royal Academy had, after 170 years, finally granted full rights and responsibilities of membership to women.

Further References. Ellen Clayton, *English Female Artists* (London, 1876). Sidney Hutchinson, *The History of the Royal Academy 1768–1968* (London, 1968). Charlotte Yeldham, *Women Artists in Nineteenth-Century France and England*, 2 vols. (New York, 1984).

JULIA M. GERGITS

RUSSIAN WRITERS. Women appear relatively late in Russian letters. Up to the eighteenth century the cultural conditions in Russia, overwhelmingly molded by an Orthodox Christian worldview, restricted women's activities to domestic cares in unconditional obedience to the master of the household. Peter the Great (1682–1725) drew women from seclusion into participation in social life. Catherine the Great (1762–1796) followed up by founding educational institutions for girls. Despite these measures, however, a basic patriarchal attitude dominated the Russian way of life well into the twentieth century in spite of social and political upheavals. This attitude explains in part the modest literary value of early women's writing.

The first known work by a woman, *The Memoir of Princess Natalia Borisovna Dolgorukaia* (1767), was soon followed by several autobiographies of formidable Russian women: Empress Catherine II; talented, erudite Princess Ekaterina Dashkova (1743–1810), one of the first women to hold public office in Russia (president of the Academy of Science, 1783); and the "Cavalry Maiden," Nadezhda Durova (1783–1866) who, disguised as a man, served in the tsarist army during the Napoleonic Wars. Durova later wrote hyperromantic novels and tales.

During Catherine's reign some 70 women tried their talents at writing, yet professional women writers appeared only in the first half of the nineteenth century. Many adopted male pseudonyms to avoid conflicts with publisher and reader prejudice. They represented the trend known as George Sandism, advocating the right to a meaningful education and free choice of husband but, at the same time, reflecting the sad reality of women's position. Elena Gan (1814–1842, pseud. Zinaida R-va) in *The Useless Gift* (1842), Maria Zhukova (1804–1855) in *Society's Judgment* (1840), and Julia Zhadovskaia (1824–1883) in lyric poetry and prose lament the plight of intelligent women forced into loveless wedlock and constrained to a life of banality.

Karolina Pavlova (1807–1893), respected by literary contemporaries, including Pushkin and Mickiewicz, died forgotten and in poverty only to be fully appraised as a significant writer by the symbolists at the turn of the century. Her elegaic poetry is marked by bold, innovative rhymes, rhythms, and intellectual brilliance. Pavlova's novel *A Double Life* (Barbara Heldt [trans.] [Ann Arbor, 1978]) shows a sensitive girl's struggle to rise above the emptiness of society's life-style. Pavlova contrasts her daily routine, described in prose, with her ideal nightly dreamworld, rendered in verse. The shallow, hypocritical behavior of the upper classes is also castigated and ridiculed by the successful and prolific countess Evdokia Rostopchina (1811–1858; e.g., "Rank and Money," in Helena Goscilo [trans. and ed.], *Russian and Polish Women's Fiction* [Knoxville, Tenn., 1985], 50–84) and Lidia Veselitskaia (1857–1936; pseud. Mikulich) in her *Mimochka* (1883–1893) stories.

Writers like Evgenia Tur (1815–1892; pseud. of Elizaveta Salias de Tournemir); Avdotia Panaeva (1820–1893; pseud. N. Stanitsky), remembered for her novels *The Talnikov Family* (1848), *A Woman's Lot* (1862), and *Memoirs* (1890); Marco Vovchok (1834–1907); Vera Figner (1852–1942); and Sofia Kovalevskaia (1850–1891), first Russian woman professor of mathematics, protest vigorously against discrimination and social oppression of women. In contrast, the gifted Slavophil Nadezhda Sokhanskaia (1823–1884) glorifies traditional patriarchal values. She draws bright pictures of the landed gentry's harmonious life in a spirited, colorful Russian.

After the turbulent 1860s and 1870s, with their stress on utilitarian literature, Russian modernism searched for new spiritual values and different artistic expression. Women participated effectively in all modernist trends: with the symbolists, Zinaida Hippius (1869–1945; emigrated to Paris 1919), Poliksena Solovieva (1867–1924; pseud. Allegro), and Mirra Lokhvitskaia (1869–1905) explored the "other Reality," the Absolute, the duality of human existence; Elena Guro's poetry was connected with cubo futurism; Anna Akhmatova (1889–1966; pseud. of Anna Gorenko) in her early stage the foremost representative of acmeism, favored precision of form and the esthetics of reality. With Marina Tsvetaeva (1892–1941), whose idiosyncratic, lyrical voice defies any categorization, Akhmatova belongs among the greatest twentieth-century poets. Akhmatova's and Tsvetaeva's verse, memorializing the dramatic events of their times, appears in most anthologies of women's poetry. As modernism crested, Anastasia Verbitskaia's (1861–1928) voluminous novels popularized the themes of women's emancipation and free love with considerable success, despite their second-rate quality. These themes were picked up by Aleksandra Kollontai (1872–1952), a true feminist, who undertook to make women aware of their rights officially sanctioned by the 1917 Bolshevik revolution. Kollontai's heroines are totally devoted to party ideology and consider love affairs unimportant as "drinking a glass of water."

The typical heroine in the following decades of Socialist realism, the dominant literary dogma since 1934, shares equal rights and equal duties with her male partner: she is industrious and successful in building Socialism and, as an efficient homemaker, lives up to the high standards of the new Soviet family. The heroines of Galina Nikolaeva (1911–1963), of Vera Panova (1905–1973), and of the later fiction of Marietta Shaginian (1888–1982) approximate this ideal.

Many outstanding women writers fled Russia after the 1917 revolution and during World War II, joining émigré literary centers in the West. Lidia Chervinskaia (b.1907), Anna Prismanova (1898–1960), Galina Kuznetsova (1900–1976), Nina Berberova (b.1901), Lidia Alekseeva (b.1909), and Olga Anstei (1912–1986) are among a score of remarkable women who have contributed brilliantly to the treasury of Russian literature in exile (see Temira Pachmuss, "Emigré Literature," in Victor Terras [ed.], *Handbook of Russian Literature* [New Haven, 1985]).

The Soviet totalitarian system has stifled literary initiative because the slightest nonconformity would meet with disapproval of dire consequence. Even after Stalin's death, when restrictions were somewhat slackened, no interesting experimentation took place in official literature. Yet many women writers have dealt with the horrors of Stalin's purges in shattering poems and memoirs: thus, Akhmatova's "Requiem"; Lidia Chukovskaia's (b.1910) *The Deserted House* and *Going Under* ; Nadezhda Mandelshtam's (1899–1980) *Hope Against Hope* and *Hope Abandoned* ; and Evgenia Ginzburg's (1896–1980) *Journey into the Whirlwind* and *Within the Whirlwind* have been translated into most world languages but have not as yet been published in the Soviet Union.

World War II has inspired much of women's writings. Akhmatova, Olga Berggolts (1910–1975), and Vera Inber (1890–1972) wrote patriotic war poetry, particularly about the 900-day siege of Leningrad. The single, self-supporting, usually professional war widow, bravely coping with all odds of life, discrimination included, hoping for a reliable, strong man for moral support, appears frequently in the postwar fiction of I. Grekova (b.1907, pseud. of Elena Ventsel), Margarita Aliger (b.1915), and Olga Forsh (1873–1961). In contrast, Maia Ganina (b.1927) and Victoria Tokareva (b.1937) picture liberated, independent women who proudly reject any encroachment on their freedom. Natalia Baranskaia's (b.1908) novelette *A Week Like Any Other* (1969) addresses candidly the emancipated woman's dilemma: how to pursue a career and simultaneously run a family.

Some innovative experimentation in prose can be detected in the latest works of writers born in the 1950s: Liudmila Petrushevskaia, Nadezhda Kozhevnikova, and Tatiana Tolstaia, the most original and exciting master of form. Poetry, a more suitable medium to obviate party restrictions, has shown revival in form, language, and motifs since the 1960s. The newest avant-garde includes first-rate talent: Bella Akhmadulina (b.1937) and Novella Matveeva (b.1934), as well as the dissident, now émigré poets Natalia Gorbanevskaia (b.1936) and Irina Ratushinskaia (b.1954), both victims of Soviet hard-labor camps and renowned for their unforgettable, poetic prison diaries. The avant-garde's most prominent member, though, is the exceptional Elizaveta Mnacakanova (b.1922; emigrated 1975), who combines musical structures with transrational language to create a singular, evocative view of the world in her poetry, none of which was published in the Soviet Union.

Finally, frank discussions of unsolved feminist issues, muffled and discreet in official women's literature, are widely taken up by Tatiana Mamonova, Tatiana

Goricheva, Julia Voznesenskaia, and other feminists who emigrated in 1980 in their book *Women and Russia. Feminist Writers from the Soviet Union* (Tatiana Mamonova [ed.] (Boston, 1984).

Further References. Barbara Heldt, *Terrible Perfection: Women and Russian Literature* (Bloomington, Ind., 1987). Temira Pachmuss (ed.), *Women Writers in Russian Modernism* (Urbana, Ill., 1978). *Russian Literary Triquartlerly: Women in Russian Literature,* no. 9 (Spring 1974).

MARINA ASTMAN

S

SCHOLARS AND INTELLECTUALS (MEDIEVAL). Women whose careers reflect the opportunities available to women for intellectual and creative pursuits, c.500–1400. More educated women are known by reputation than by surviving works: records show women who were teachers, students, patronesses, librarians, doctors, and lawyers. In the earlier Middle Ages, the abbeys provided most of the education for women in Latin and traditional school subjects, while noblewomen were taught at court, as were the daughters of Charlemagne. Latin education for women became increasingly rare toward the end of the period, although the convent of Helfta, which produced several important mystics in the thirteenth century, combined teaching of university subjects and devotional practice. Women known principally as scholars and intellectuals are the following:

Leoba. Leoba (Leobgyd; 700–779) was an Anglo-Saxon nun in the monastery of Barking and a missionary with St. Boniface in Germany. The nuns of Barking were well educated. On the evidence of Aldhelm's *De Virginitate,* which was addressed to them, they studied Scripture, law, history and chronicles, grammar, and poetry. Only one letter written by Leoba exists, but it shows the influence of Aldhelm's complicated Latin and her pleasure in composing poetry. She was praised in her "Life" for her learning and love of scholarship. Boniface established her as abbess at Bischofsheim, where she proved a wise administrator.

Dhuoda. Dhuoda (b. c.803,) was a Frankish noble woman who wrote a *Manual,* a handbook of instruction for her son. Out of the harsh circumstances of Dhuoda's life and her concern for the upbringing of her son, from whom she had been forcibly separated, comes her treatise that reflects a particularly medieval way of looking at the world. Dhuoda draws on sapient lore, accumulated from church teaching, patristic exegesis, folk wisdom, quotations culled from the classical texts of the Middle Ages, and Scripture. Her *Manual* offers a unique view of a laywoman using her knowledge out of her fervent desire to prepare the life and the soul of her son in a difficult time.

Hrotsvit. Hrotsvit (Hrotsvitha or Hrotswitha) of Gandersheim (b. c.935, d. after 973) was a Saxon canoness, one of the most prolific medieval women writers, who wrote Christian legends, plays modeled after the Roman dramatist Terence, and epic poetry. This activity has seemed to some incongruous or phenomenal, but Hrotsvit was a well-educated woman in an abbey that allowed an unusual degree of personal freedom and access to the outside world. Gandersheim, founded for noblewomen, who ruled it autonomously, maintained an excellent school and library and had close connections with the Ottonian court. The details of Hrotsvit's life come only from her prefaces and comments in her works, but it is possible that she was educated at court and participated in the intellectual life there as well as at Gandersheim. Her work shows that she was well versed in both the ancient and Christian authors; characters in her plays speak scholarly disquisitions on subjects drawn from medieval learning. Disproving her use of the commonplaces of feminine frailty and inadequacy, Hrotsvit accomplished an ambitious plan of works.

Her legends and plays together make up a double cycle of stories in a scheme with thematic parallels and symmetries. Hrotsvit uses tales of fall and conversion, martyrdom, and triumphant virginity to illustrate the Christian ascetic ideal. Her particular genius in the plays is her wit and imagination in combining the serious and the comic. She shows the sincere heroism of the believers, most often women, while tempering the fates of the villains with comedy, thus revealing their absurdity in the light of the ideal of Christian life.

Anna Comnena. Anna (1083 to 1153–1155?) was a Byzantine princess who chronicled the reign of her father, Alexios I. Her work is one of the primary sources for the history of the Crusades. Inspired by epics and classical histories, she combined in the *Alexiad* good historical method, using official papers and oral sources, with her knowledge of Greek classical poetry. Anna was educated in the palace, rather than in schools, and records that she studied the traditional course of subjects: rhetoric, philosophy, grammar, mathematics, church teaching, literature, and history. Her contemporaries held her in high esteem for her learning and her medical knowledge.

Héloise. Héloise (c.1100 to 1163) was renowned for her learning at a young age; she had been educated by nuns and by her uncle, a canon in Paris, who hired Peter Abelard to be her tutor. In a scandalous episode that has put them into the ranks of legendary lovers, Héloise and Abelard married secretly, then separated and entered monastic life. Her story is known to us through her correspondence and Abelard's *Historia calamitatum*. Three of her four surviving letters are addressed to him, as is her series of scriptural questions called the *Problemata*, written from her position as abbess of the monastery at the Paraclete. Through these letters, Héloise displays the literary knowledge for which she was famous, and her skillful use of the rhetorical art of letter writing emphasizes the emotion from which the letters spring. They move from personal topics to theological and philosophical problems, which she argues ably. In addition, she is concerned with devising an appropriate monastic rule for women. Foremost in these letters is the sense of a woman in pursuit of truth through her philosophical inquiries in personal, practical, and spiritual matters.

Hildegard of Bingen. Hildegard (1098 to 1179) was a German abbess whose visionary works place her in the first rank of medieval intellectuals. At age 8 she entered the Benedictine monastery of Disibodenberg, where, 30 years later, she was elected abbess. Frequently ill all her life, she had kept her visions hidden until she was 40, when her physical suffering pressed her to make known what she had seen. A part of her first visionary work, the *Scivias,* was read by Pope Eugene and approved as prophecy at the Synod of Trier in 1147. This recognition of Hildegard as a prophet accorded her a freedom and an authority that other women in the Middle Ages were rarely able to achieve. She credited her vision with having given her understanding and knowledge of theological and philosophical works as well as her knowledge of Latin and music. But while she claims little education, her writing reflects broad knowledge of the intellectual works important to her time; she is capable of writing complex and fluent Latin; and above all, she brings astonishing powers of intellect to every endeavor. From the time she began to record her visions to the end of her life, she engaged in prodigious activity, corresponding with religious leaders and heads of state, undertaking extensive preaching journeys, and engaging in an investigation of all aspects of humanity and divinity and the relationships among them. She wrote two more visionary works, hymns and sequences, and a play, now regarded as the first liturgical drama. Hildegard wrote on natural science and medicine, including discussions of women's physiologies and sexuality that appear to be completely original. A secret language and its alphabet complete the whole body of her works. All of Hildegard's achievements are remarkable, but her visions are her principal work and are striking in their beautiful imagery and her interpretations of them, transforming the mystical experience into poetic experience and spiritual understanding. Hildegard's visions are encyclopedic, making up the whole of human history in relation to the divine, incorporating the spiritual and physical worlds, everything necessary for the understanding of the soul's ultimate end in God.

Further References. Peter Dronke, *Women Writers of the Middle Ages* (Cambridge, Eng., 1984). Joan Ferrante, "The Education of Women in the Middle Ages," in Patricia H. Labalme (ed.), *Beyond Their Sex: Learned Women of the European Past* (New York, 1980), 9–43. Katharina M. Wilson (ed.), *Medieval Women Writers* (Athens, Ga., 1984).

CLIA M. GOODWIN

SCHOLARS AND INTELLECTUALS (ENGLISH RENAISSANCE). Writing in 1928, Virginia Woolf imagined a dreadful fate for Shakespeare's "sister," and explained cultural conditions as reasons why women did not write in the English Renaissance. In fact, Woolf was wrong in thinking there were no women writers of the Renaissance, but scholars have only recently discovered and appreciated much of their work and significance. And many of the women scholars and intellectuals were women of immense courage as well as talent, such as

Margaret More Roper, Katherine Parr, Lady Jane Grey, Elizabeth I, the Cooke sisters, and Elizabeth Cary, Lady Falkland. A woman who could read and write in the Renaissance was, however, unusual. It is difficult to know the literacy rates for women in this period, particularly since many people who could read could not write, and thus inability to sign names, one way of measuring lack of literacy, does not really work for this period. For both men and women, particularly in the countryside, literacy was probably low throughout the Renaissance. The work of English Renaissance women scholars and intellectuals was accomplished within a context where most of the population, but especially women, were illiterate. And we should not believe, simply because there were a number of learned women in the English Renaissance, that the culture believed in the concept of education for upper-class women.

Of the women scholars and intellectuals, most are of the aristocratic or gentry class; in fact, a number of women of these classes were highly educated. Yet the lives of aristocratic women, although less confined than those of women of the lower classes, were still restricted by the emphasis placed on their being chaste, silent, and obedient. We should not consider that education necessarily came from a belief in women's capabilities and their potential role in public life. Humanist education (which included a study of the classics and foreign languages) served a very different function for women than for men. In the early sixteenth century, English scholars and humanists debated the question of women's education and their public role. Some humanists believed education would make women better wives: the Renaissance ideal was for women to be in a private rather than a public role. When writers such as Juan Luis Vives argued for women's education, they still perceived that education would fit a woman for her *private* function. Few believed that education would make women ready to play a public role.

The first really to advocate a classical training for women was Thomas More, who provided such an education for his daughters and his female wards. In the 1530s and 1540s, Henry VIII appointed classical humanists as tutors not only for his son, Edward, but for his daughter, Elizabeth. This royal example caused several ambitious noble families to provide similar instruction to their daughters with the expectation this might lead to their making advantageous marriages. In the 1530s this argument over women's capabilities and their public position was mainly a theoretical issue; by the 1550s it had an immediate application, and John Knox called it a "monstrous" perversion for a woman to rule over men. Mary I's death in 1558, however, did not end this question, for her half-sister Elizabeth would rule for the rest of the century.

Yet even in the second half of the sixteenth century, when a highly educated woman, and one who was the author of some prayers and poems, was herself ruling, people did not use the example of Elizabeth to give other women more of a role in public life. Instead, other rationales were used for female education. For example, the education of women also came from a desire to allow them to participate more fully in a religious life. Protestants especially believed that everyone, female as well as male, should be able to read God's word. One result of this belief was that most of women's writings in the English Renaissance were restricted to religious subjects, either in original works or translations.

Religion, both Catholicism and Protestantism, did give some women such a strong sense of purpose as to justify their writings and their actions. Margaret Roper, daughter of Thomas More, not only corresponded with her father while he was in prison but did translations and wrote poetry and theological commentary. Thomas More was very proud of her, but he also warned her that she should restrict her learning to her home circle. Unfortunately, much of Roper's own work has been lost, and one wonders what else she might have accomplished but for the restrictions placed on educated women.

Later in the reign of Henry VIII, his last wife, Katherine Parr, encouraged his daughters Mary and Elizabeth to read and translate Christian works. Parr herself was the author of *The Lamentation of a Sinner*. She may also have encouraged their cousin, Lady Jane Grey, who was also briefly a member of her household and an intellectual prodigy. Lady Jane Grey, a passionately convinced Protestant, died on the executioner's block at the age of 16, a victim to an abortive coup in 1553 that would have made her queen in place of her Catholic cousin Mary. Though she died so young, she left behind a number of letters and prayers.

Anthony Cooke, a devout Protestant, like More provided his daughters (he had five) with a thorough classical training. His daughters showed a remarkable zeal for study: Mildred Cooke Cecil, for example, did Greek translations. Her marriage to Elizabeth's principal minister, William Cecil, was a mutually devoted and an intellectual partnership. Yet, because Elizabeth had no children, the emphasis on education from the royal household that had been so strong earlier in the century diminished. Educational treatises of the latter sixteenth century continued to tell women to be silent, chaste, and obedient. Despite this attitude, the end of the sixteenth and the early seventeenth centuries saw a number of brave, dedicated women, often inspired by religion, who used their scholarship creatively. For example, Elizabeth Cary, Lady Falkland, a converted Catholic, was the author of the play *The Tragedy of Mariam*. Cary's conversion led to her repudiation by her husband and great personal travail.

In Renaissance England there were a number of highly talented women who were scholars and intellectuals. Yet their accomplishments were attained within a context that was extremely restrictive for women. And the educated elite were often the more fortunate ones. Women of other social classes were economically marginalized and sometimes accused of witchcraft. Virginia Woolf was not so far off the mark after all. Shakespeare's sisters existed; they did not, however, have an easy time of it.

Further References. Margaret P. Hannay (ed.), *Silent But for the Word: Tudor Women as Patrons, Translators, and Writers of Religious Works* (Kent, Ohio, 1985). Retha Warnicke, *Women of the English Renaissance and Reformation* (Westport, Conn., 1983).

CAROLE LEVIN

SCIENCE FICTION. The relationship between women and science fiction (SF) encompasses women as characters in and as authors and readers of science fiction narratives and the critical attention that feminist science fiction has received. Each of these facets, as well as the overall relationship, differs in different countries. This article is confined largely to English-language science fiction. For a discussion of French-language SF the Canadian journal *Solaris* is recommended. Information on science fiction of all countries is available in *Science Fiction Studies, Extrapolation,* and *Fantasy Review.*

Until very recently, SF was perceived as a predominantly male genre, written by and for males. Therefore little attention was paid to possible differences that advanced technology might make in women's position and status. Women appeared as stereotypical excuses for males to stage rescue missions, as helpmates, lovers, mothers, and sisters to the world-conquering male heroes or as matriarchal monsters, aliens, or treacherous enemies who must be subdued or annihilated. (These images are still predominant.) Yet while Robert Heinlein, Andre Norton (Alice Mary Norton), and other writers of their generation gave stereotypical social roles to their women and girls, these same characters had adventures in space, performed their own rescues, and were often brilliant, energetic, exciting persons. To the generation of women now writing, reading, teaching, and criticizing SF, these stories, read during their childhood, gave hope in the imaginative space for which SF as a concept stood and represented possible alternative futures to those limited ones offered by day-to-day life. Depiction of women remained in this state until the publication of LeGuin's *The Left Hand of Darkness* in 1969, followed by many much more daring extrapolations and literary experiments in the early to mid–1970s. These extrapolations and experiments coincided with the influx of a significant number of women writers into science fiction.

There have been women writers of SF as long as science fiction has existed, its roots being traced back to E. A. Poe and Mary Shelley, H. G. Wells, Jules Verne, Francis Stevens, and Charlotte Perkins Gilman. But through the first half of this century, there was only a handful of women SF writers, such as C. L. Moore, Judith Merril, Andre Norton, and in the early 1960s, Anne McCaffrey, Marion Zimmer Bradley, and Zenna Henderson.

In the late 1960s, however, the situation changed. More women entered the scene and began to achieve recognition for the first time. From 1968 to 1984 women received more than ten Hugo (fan-presented) and Nebula (colleague-presented) awards.

During the 1970s and 1980s SF realized a potential that was always there: to explore either the implications of allowing the patriarchy to continue on its present course or the possibilities for a future where gender equality is a quotidian fact. Writers such as LeGuin, Russ, James Tiptree, Jr. (Racoona Sheldon), and Kate Wilhelm were among the earliest to explore this potential (as were a few male writers such as S. R. Delany).

By the mid–1970s excitement began to mount: four major anthologies (Pamela

Sargent's *Women of Wonder* [New York, 1975], *More Women of Wonder* [New York, 1976], and *The New Women of Wonder* [New York, 1978); and Susan Anderson's *Aurora Beyond Equality* [New York, 1976]) included stories by feminist novelists who were to become prominent in the latter part of the decade. The first panel on Women and Science Fiction was held at the 1976 World Science Fiction Convention in Kansas City. An amateur magazine, *Khatru*, had been printing letter interchanges on the issue of women in SF. A Canadian journal, *Witch and the Chameleon*, focused on that subject, and devotees in Madison, Wisconsin, who had just started an SF group and amateur magazine, founded an annual conference where a large percentage of the programming was specifically about women, feminist issues, and SF literature and where sexist programming would be discouraged. This conference continues despite early predictions of doom. Attention to women writers has also been drawn by the two journals *Aurora* (fan-oriented) and *New Moon* (critically oriented), both outgrowths of *Janus*, a fan magazine begun in 1975.

In the late 1970s major talents such as Octavia Butler, Suzy McKee Charnas, C. J. Cherryh, H. M. Hoover, Elizabeth Lynn, Vonda McIntyre, Kit Reed, Pamela Sargent, Joan Vinge, Chelsea Quinn Yarbro, Pamela Zoline, Elizabeth Vonarburg, Katia Alexandre, Joelle Wintrebert, and Monique Wittig (French) joined the earlier writers, but women were still responsible for less than 15 percent of the SF published in any one year.

In the mid–1980s some critics and writers were attempting to dismiss the importance of women writers and feminist issues in contemporary SF, saying alternately that women writers are disappearing or that their work is uninteresting. Nevertheless, established writers from other genres, such as Lessing, Atwood, and Piercy, as well as many new, excellent writers (e.g., Lois Bujold, Catherine Cooke, Zoe Fairbairns, Cynthia Felice, Mary Gentle, Megan Lindholm, R. A. McAvoy, Meredith Ann Pierce, Joan Slonczewski, Linda Steele, Sherri Tepper, Connie Willis, Cherry Wilder, Patricia Wrede) added their works to the existing corpus. The anthology *Despatches from the Frontiers of the Female Mind* (Green and LeFanu [eds.] [New York, 1985]) provides an introduction to some of them. With these new writers portrayals of both male and female characters have become more innovative as the powers of the imagination are stretched to encompass myriad possibilities such as alternative divisions of labor for the birth and nurturing of children, the provision of day-to-day needs, and the governance of societies or cautionary scenarios in which societies become more patriarchal, militaristic, or in other ways oppressive.

Critical studies began to appear with more regularity during the late 1970s and early 1980s, with ground-breaking articles in academic journals such as *Extrapolation* and *Science Fiction Studies*. Bibliographies, essay collections, single author studies, dissertation-cum-critical texts, all of which are phenomena of the late 1970s, continue. Notable among these is Roger Schlobin's *Urania's Daughters: A Checklist of Women Science Fiction Writers, 1692–1982* (Mercer Island, Wash., 1983); Betty King's *Women of the Future: Female Main Char-*

acters in Science Fiction (Metuchen, N.J., 1984); Nathalie Rosinsky's *Feminist Futures: Contemporary Women's Speculative Fiction* (Ann Arbor, 1984); and a collection of essays from a 1985 conference on women and SF held in Texas: *Women Worldwalkers: New Dimensions for SF and Fantasy* (Jane Weedman [ed.] [Lubbock, Tex., 1985]). The activity woven around and through women writing science fiction is a fact of the present as well as the future.

JANICE M. BOGSTAD

SCULPTORS. There are literary references to distinguished women sculptors in the ancient world, and medieval guild records list several women sculptors active in Paris during the thirteenth and fourteenth centuries. But it is only with the Renaissance and its elevation of the status of artists that significant information about women sculptors begins to become available. Even so, compared to women painters, from the sixteenth through the eighteenth centuries there are relatively few well-known female sculptors, because sculpture—viewed as a complex, expensive process, requiring great physical strength, a familiarity with human anatomy, and collaboration with numerous technical assistants—was not considered a suitable occupation for women.

Despite this prevailing attitude, Properzia de' Rossi (c.1450–1530) won an important competition to produce marble sculptures for the western facade of San Petronio, a church in her native Bologna; the Spaniard Luisa Roldán (1656–1704) trained at her family's workshop in Seville and became court sculptor to Charles II; and Anne Seymour Damer (1748–1828), an English artist, made portraits of such distinguished sitters as Napoleon and King George III.

The nineteenth century marked the emergence of more internationally successful women sculptors than ever before. As the vogue for Neo-classicism reached its peak, a group of American expatriate sculptors, all women, came to the fore in Rome. Nicknamed "the white, marmorean flock" (after their preferred medium, marble), they included Harriet Hosmer (1830–1908), known for both ornamental works and historical subjects; Anne Whitney (1821–1915), who sculpted likenesses of important liberal politicians; Emma Stebbins (1815–1882), responsible for a number of major fountain figures; and the remarkable Edmonia Lewis (1845–after 1911). The orphaned child of a Chippewa Indian and a black man, Lewis attended Oberlin College, studied sculpture in Boston, and made her reputation with a 12-foot-tall *Death of Cleopatra* that was acclaimed at the 1876 Philadelphia Centennial.

Other notable nineteenth-century women sculptors are Vinnie Ream Hoxie (1847–1914), the first woman to receive a U.S. government commission for sculpture (at 15), and three more Americans—Anna Hyatt Huntington (1876–1973), who specialized in animal sculptures; Gertrude Vanderbilt Whitney (1876–1942), a student of Rodin's, who produced several important war memorials; and Malvina Hoffman (1887–1966), another Rodin pupil, who created intriguing portraits of dancers and a series of 105 figures for the Field Museum of Natural History of Chicago. The German sculptor Elisabet Ney (1883–1907)

established a successful career as a portraitist while Frenchwoman Camille Claudel (1864–1943), Rodin's longtime assistant and companion, made works that
demonstrate her mastery of expressive gesture and surface textures.

The pace of change has quickened enormously in all fields—from science to
the arts—during the present century. And twentieth-century women sculptors
have figured prominently in all the radical new artistic developments—most
notably modernism (abstraction). In fact, two of the most important pioneers of
modernist sculpture were women: Louise Nevelson (1899–1988) and Barbara
Hepworth (1903–1975). Nevelson was born in Russia and moved as a young
child to the United States, where, by the mid-1950s, she had developed her
signature approach—assembling discarded bits of wood into elegant and elaborate
wall sculptures, painted all black, white, or gold. Hepworth was raised in Yorkshire, England, whose hilly terrain had a strong influence on her art—eloquent,
curving shapes that suggest a human figure or a landscape. Most of Hepworth's
sculpture was carved of wood or stone—sometimes embellished with wire, string,
or paint.

Two French sculptors, Germaine Richier (1904–1959) and Louise Bourgeois
(b.1911), were also early modernist pioneers—Richier with her spectral, cor-
roded-looking, cast bronze forms suggesting humans or other animals and Bourgeois with open-space, rectilinear wooden works and, later, rounded, organic
shapes of stone, plaster, and rubber. The principal spokesperson for the surre-
alists, André Breton, was impressed with the fur-covered teacup exhibited by
Swiss artist Méret Oppenheim (1913–1986) at the Museum of Modern Art in
1937. Ohio-born Dorothy Dehner (b.1901) was trained as a painter but, beginning
in the early 1950s, concentrated on three-dimensional art—simple, forceful works
in metal or wood.

Pop sculpture is well-represented by the work of Marisol (Escobar) (b.1930),
born in Paris of Venezuelan parents. Her blocklike, painted wooden figures
reflect the artist's sense of sociopolitical satire. The "nanas" of French sculptor
Niki de Saint-Phalle (b.1930)—playful female figures with ungainly proportions,
exuberant gestures, and bright colors—stand in stark contrast to the cerebral,
minimalist rectangles sculpted by American Anne Truitt (b.1921).

A wide variety of nontraditional materials and techniques has been explored
recently in the works of such artists as Magdalena Abakanowicz (b.1930), a
Polish sculptor known for her haunting arrangements of repeated, humanoid
forms made from burlap and rope; a whole host of Americans, including Lee
Bontecou (b.1931), who created an intriguing series of reliefs by stretching
canvas fragments over welded steel frames; Greek-born Chryssa (b.1931), who
makes neon sculptures; and Americans Barbara Chase-Riboud (b.1939), whose
work is characterized by sensous, textural contrasts of fibers and metal, Nancy
Graves (b.1940), who made her reputation by constructing a group of lifelike,
life-sized, multimedia camels, Lynda Benglis (b.1941), noted for her unusual
combinations of materials (chicken wire covered with gesso and gold leaf), and
Judy Chicago (b.1939), who, in 1970, along with painter Miriam Schapiro,

established the first American feminist art program at the California Institute of Arts and who is known for her massive, consciousness-raising collaborative pieces, such as *The Dinner Party* (1979), a sculptural survey of women's history.

One of the most exciting late twentieth-century artistic developments is environmental sculpture—which, instead of being confined to a pedestal, projects into the viewer's space—like the eccentric abstractions of Eva Hesse (1936–1970), whose erotic, curved forms (made of rubber tubing or string dipped in fiberglass) were typically suspended from gallery walls and ceilings or laid across the floor. Judy Pfaff (b.1946) creates playful, room-sized environments filled with brightly colored, "found" materials (twigs, electrician's wire), while Alice Aycock (b.1946) invents large, complex machines with uncertain uses. Other examples are set outdoors, within the natural environment, either as permanent installations, like the startlingly original public parks developed by Nancy Holt (b.1938), or temporary ones, like Beverly Pepper's (b.1924) fabricated sand dunes on the northeastern Florida coast.

Further References. Charlotte Streifer Rubinstein, *American Women Artists from Early Indian Times to the Present* (Boston, 1982). Virginia Watson-Jones, *Contemporary American Women Sculptors* (Phoenix, 1986).

NANCY G. HELLER

SHAKESPEARE, FEMINIST CRITICISM OF. The first book-length work of American feminist criticism of Shakespeare appeared in 1980—a decade after Kate Millett's pioneering *Sexual Politics* demonstrated the relevance of the women's movement for literary criticism. However, a substantial body of work was published during the period 1980 to 1985, thus establishing a distinctive field with its own internal debate. The Modern Language Association (MLA) Bibliography Online confirms this growth of interest; in a September 1979 article in *Database,* Eileen M. Mackesy reported 16 records for a computer search combining the terms *Shakespeare* and *women,* while the same search covering material through 1984 retrieved 105 entries.

The study of women in Shakespeare has not been a self-contained, marginal enterprise. From the outset it has been clear that the reassessment of female characters has direct implications for the status of male characters and for the status of Shakespeare. The ultimate issue is succinctly formulated in the introduction to *The Woman's Part* (1980): "The extent to which Shakespeare aligns himself with patriarchy, merely portrays it, or deliberately criticizes it remains a complex question, one that feminist criticism is aptly suited to address."

One way to preserve the complexity and openness of this question is to assume that Shakespeare cannot be usefully labeled either misogynist or feminist since he occupies an intermediate position between these extremes. The dominant mood of a particular play may tilt toward one direction or the other without ever reaching the simple stance of either pole. Shakespeare's drama offers a mixture of uncritical investment in patriarchal structures and critical exploration of them, but the degree of awareness fluctuates and must be decided on a case-by-case basis. No one formula will suffice for all the plays, so the question is never settled in advance.

In order to assess Shakespeare's relation to the sexual politics in his drama, it is important to refine and clarify the concept of patriarchy—to see that the plays contain two sets of patriarchal values, not just one. A distinction between ruthless and benevolent versions of patriarchy avoids the claim that Shakespeare magically transcended patriarchal attitudes. Shakespeare's frequent undermining of tyrannical patriarchy demonstrates the existence of his critical standards and insight. His frequent endorsement of benevolent patriarchy shows that he remains enmeshed in the assumption that social harmony depends on male control, sensitively applied.

For example, the evaluation of male bonds in *As You Like It* leads to a reappraisal of comedy and of the links between genre and gender. The standard view that, whatever suffering women undergo at the hands of deluded men in the tragedies, female characters are allowed to come into their own in the comedies is revised. Rosalind's power has been overestimated because the countervailing force of male alliance has not been sufficiently taken into account. We cannot celebrate the occasions of Shakespeare's achievement of mutuality between men and women without also sharply noting that this mutuality is not unqualified but is strictly limited by a division of labor and power according to gender. Such mutuality does not constitute equality or independence for women.

In its first stage, feminist criticism of Shakespeare has produced fresh insights on a wide range of issues, including family roles, courtship and marriage, male bonding, female bonds, gender and genre, androgyny, and the boy-actor convention. The very success of this effort has led at the end of 1985 to a retrospective pause focusing on the questions, Has feminist criticism of Shakespeare finished its work? and What should be the next step? While it is impossible to predict the future course of the study of women in Shakespeare, there is a strong prospect for greater emphasis on cultural history and, in particular, on increased interaction between feminist criticism and new historicism—a line of development exemplified by Carol Thomas Neely's seminar on "Images of Gender and Power in Shakespeare and Renaissance Culture" at the World Shakespeare Congress in April 1986. Three preliminary observations can be made here about the possible combination of feminist and new historicist approaches.

First, current work suggests that the study of Queen Elizabeth as an enormously powerful woman cannot be used to disprove the fundamentally patriarchal character of Elizabethan culture and of Shakespeare's work. In "Queen Elizabeth I and the Persistence of Patriarchy" (*Feminist Review* 4 [1980]), Allison Heisch shows that Elizabeth exercised power by employing rather than resisting gender stereotypes, while Louis Adrian Montrose—in " 'Shaping Fantasies': Figurations of Gender and Power in Elizabethan Culture" (*Representations* 2 [Spring 1983])—analyzes how Shakespeare's emphatic patriarchal design in *A Midsummer Night's Dream* undercuts the nominal praise of Elizabeth.

Second, research on women in the period is a major trend, raising the question of how this material will affect our image of Shakespeare. Examples are *Women in the Renaissance* (special issue of *English Literary Renaissance* 14 [Autumn 1984]); *Half Humankind: Contexts and Texts of the Controversy about Women in England, 1540–1640* (Katherine Usher Henderson and Barbara F. McManus [eds.] [Urbana, Ill., 1985]); *Silent But for the Word: Tudor Women as Patrons, Translators, and Writers of Religious Works* (Margaret P. Hannay [ed.] [Kent, Ohio, 1985]); and *Women in the Middle Ages and the Renaissance: Literary and Historical Perspectives* (Mary Beth Rose [ed.] [Syracuse, 1985]). Though the eventual impact of this new work cannot be anticipated, the likelihood now is that the contrast between actual women and Shakespeare's fictional women will be decisive, a contrast that may highlight the filtering effect by which Shakespeare narrows the range of possibilities open to historical women to create his own restricted version of women.

Third, a general consideration of the proper use of historical context is needed. Nonfeminist critics may raise the historical issue to block feminist approaches to the study of gender in Shakespeare: these are ruled out of bounds because Shakespeare is presented as a product of his times for whom feminist criticism is anachronistic and invalid. To this charge, the feminist critic answers that gender was not invented in the twentieth century and that Shakespeare's powerful dramatization of conflict between men and women and the intensity of his language in this regard demonstrate his probing of gender conventions. This reply is necessary but not in itself sufficient, however. The ultimate level of analysis is located in the critic rather than in the character or author since it is the critic who provides the final perspective on patriarchal values—for a full discussion, see Peter Erickson's "Shakespeare and the 'Author-Function' " (in Peter Erickson and Coppélia Kahn [eds.], *Shakespeare's "Rough Magic": Renaissance Essays in Honor of C. L. Barber* [Cranbury, N.J., 1985]). The feminist critic must acknowledge that our twentieth-century vantage point helps to make this perspective possible and must therefore squarely face our historical difference from Shakespeare.

The crucial point is that there are two distinct ways to respond to the question of historical difference. One way is to suggest that coming to terms with difference means simply to accept Shakespeare's perspective. This "love-it-or-leave-it" logic implies that if one cannot be satisfied with the Shakespearean ethic and make the best of it, then it is illegitimate to keep working on Shakespeare, and one ought to shift one's interest to contemporary women writers whose values one can find more compatible. One sign that feminist Shakespearean critics are vulnerable to this pressure is the attempt to avoid this difficulty by striving to make Shakespeare more feminist or transcendent than he is, to reduce expectations and to settle for what one can get. Particularly with the late romances, the temptation can be strong to redeem Shakespeare and to make things come out right in the end. The result is that some feminist criticism becomes virtually indistinguishable from the traditional account exemplified by D. W. Harding in "Shakespeare's Final View of Women" (*Times Literary*

Supplement [November 30, 1979]), which asserts that the dramatist had "worked through" earlier problems with women. But the happy ending to Shakespeare's career is produced by a one-sided, idealized view that ignores the continuing problematic aspects of male-female relations. This false optimism may seem preferable when the price to be paid for accuracy and the full integrity of feminist critique is made to appear negative—when feminist criticism is alleged to lead to a sense of loss and sadness because one is cut off from emotional participation in Shakespeare's work and condemned to barren repetition of feminist attack. But we are not limited to these two unpalatable choices.

Another way to approach the question of historical difference is to view the use of historical perspective as a two-part process that involves not only attending to Shakespeare's historical position but also recognizing our own. Feminist criticism of Shakespeare engages the split between his past and our present by experiencing historical difference as a source of strength rather than weakness. One must make the negative criticisms of the literary tradition in order to take the positive step of revising it. Shakespeare will continue to hold a pre-eminent place in the canon of Western literature, but not as an unalterable fixture; our understanding of him will be decisively changed. Feminist criticism reexamines the claim that Shakespeare is "not for an age but for all time" by differentiating between what is enduring and what is not. Feminist Shakespeareans gratefully acknowledge and savor the lasting power of his verbal and dramatic brilliance, but without acceding to the pretense that his truths are permanent, as though one could find in Shakespeare an ethic that would be adequate to the lives we are living now. Feminist Shakespeare criticism thereby connects with, and contributes to, the larger feminist effort with its twofold task of redefining the canonical writers and of discovering new ones. As Adriene Munich argues in the final essay in *Making a Difference: Feminist Literary Criticism* (Gayle Greene and Coppélia Kahn [eds.] [Methuen, 1985]), both tasks are necessary to the overall goal of remaking the tradition.

Shakespeare is a field feminist criticism should not abandon. The cultural heritage we receive from Shakespeare remains positive in the sense that we learn from his complexity and his difficulties. His work provides not a body of timeless, unmodifiable knowledge but rather an historical baseline that helps us to measure our difference and change—we cannot do without this historical perspective.

Further References. Linda Bamber, *Comic Women, Tragic Men: a Study of Gender and Genre in Shakespeare* (Stanford, 1982). Juliet Dusinberre, *Shakespeare and the Nature of Women* (London, 1975). Peter Erickson, *Patriarchal Structures in Shakespeare's Drama* (Berkeley, 1985). Marilyn French, *Shakespeare's Division of Experience* (New York, 1981). Gayle Greene and Carolyn Ruth Swift (eds.), *Feminist Criticism of Shakespeare*, 9, nos. 1–2, *Women's Studies* (1981–1982). Lisa Jardine, *Still Harping on Daughters: Women and Drama in the Age of Shakespeare* (Sussex, Eng., 1983). Coppélia Kahn, *Man's Estate: Masculine Identity in Shakespeare* (Berkeley, 1981). Carolyn Ruth Swift Lenz, Gayle Greene, and Carol Thomas Neely (eds.), *The Woman's Part: Feminist Criticism of Shakespeare* (Urbana, Ill., 1980). Carol Thomas Neely, *Broken Nuptials in*

Shakespeare's Plays (New Haven, 1985). Marianne Novy, *Love's Argument: Gender Relations in Shakespeare* (Chapel Hill, N.C., 1984). Linda Woodbridge, *Women and the English Renaissance: Literature and the Nature of Womankind, 1540–1620* (Urbana, Ill., 1984).

PETER ERICKSON

SPANISH AMERICAN WRITERS (COLONIAL). The deficient education of women during the colonial period made New World literature predominantly the domain of men. Additionally, criticism tended to pay little attention to literature written by women and in some cases has even denied feminine authorship of works written under pseudonyms. Recent scholarship gives us a better perspective of the epoch, for it has revealed formerly unknown names and texts, most from religious centers.

Despite the lack of intellectual stimulation, women in religious orders produced creative works that deserve consideration. The most outstanding are, from Mexico, Sor Juana Inés de la Cruz (1648?–1695) and, from Colombia, the Venerable Mother Josefa del Castillo y Guevara (Mother Castillo; 1671–1742). Others whose names remain but whose works lack any great importance preceded and followed them. They and a few lay women writers are listed in catalogues and collections of the time, lists copied by Carlos Sigüenza y Góngora, José Toribio Medina, Manuel Orozco y Berra, and Alfonso Méndez Plancarte.

The 4,000 or more volumes in the library of Sor Juana Inés de la Cruz and the instruments she possessed for the study of mathematics, physics, and music made her cell an intellectual sanctuary that attracted the most notable men of that epoch. In a reactionary period of extreme distrust toward all scientific or technical activities, Sor Juana distinguished herself as a solitary figure of genius dedicated to speculation and to experiments that prefigured the Cartesian spirit of the age of Enlightenment. She was a feminist and since the seventeenth century has been considered one of the greatest geniuses of baroque poetry. She was also outstanding in drama and in prose. Her complete works were collected in four thick volumes by Méndez Plancarte.

The works of Mother Castillo were not published until a century after they were written. Menéndez Pelayo called her the St. Teresa of America: not only did she dedicate herself to the mystic life as did the saint of Avila, she also recounted her own life at the urging of her confessors. Moreover, her mystic-literary works reveal the obvious influence of St. Teresa, and, although she was not canonized, she was beatified. Her literary production, collected and published in 1968 by Darío Achury Valenzuela, consists of *My Life*, an autobiographical book, and *Spiritual Affections*, a mystic treatise. There are also poems attributed to her, but Méndez Plancarte has shown that some are adaptations of poetry by Sor Juana Inés de la Cruz. Therefore, although she is assured a place among American prose writers, there remains a question of whether she should be included among the lyric poets of the colonial period.

Santo Domingo, then known as the Athens of the New World, was the home of the first woman poet whose work can be seriously considered part of American literature, Sor Leonor de Ovando (?–1610?). Of her work only five sonnets and a composition written in blank verse are known.

Thomas Gage (*A New Survey of the West Indies*, 1655) was the first to speak of the "Tenth Muse," Guatemalan Sor Juana de Maldonado y Paz (1595–1665?). From then on her name was regularly included in histories of Guatemalan literature even though until recently we did not have a single poem as evidence of a talent worthy of the place given her among her country's lyric poets. The research of Ernesto Chinchilla Aguilar and Mariano López Mayorical brought to light some documents that might confirm Gage's assertions. They tell of the small but lavish palace that Sor Juana possessed in her convent in Guatemala; the protests throughout the city when she was named abbess; Montúfar's painting of her in the pose of St. Lucía, condemned by the Inquisition; her cell as the meeting place for the most prestigious poets, artists, and intellectuals among her contemporaries. However, the poems attributed to her in Fray Antonio de Arochena's *Catalogue of the Writers in the Order of San Francisco of the Province of Guatemala* have never been located. The little that has so far been retrieved is not sufficient proof of an exceptional literary talent. Much research must still be done before a definite conclusion is reached.

There are many more nuns in the annals of mystic poetry, for example, Venezuelan Carmalite Sor María de los Angeles (María Josefa Paz del Castillo [1750–?]), Capuchin Sor Juana de Hazaña, and Sor Paula de Jesús of the Barefoot Merced order. Poems of the latter two were included in Rubén Vargas Ugarte's anthology *Peruvian Classics*.

A flood of the Mapocho River in 1783 led Sor Tadea de San Joaquín (Tadea García de la Huerta [?–1827]) to write a long ballad to her confessor, who was absent from the city. The ballad relates how the lives of the nuns were threatened when the water beat against the walls of the monastery. It was published in Lima in 1784 and is considered the first poem by a Chilean woman.

Autobiographies were also written in the convents, some of questionable literary value. They do, however, provide valuable sociohistorical information. In addition to the brief but important autobiography of Sor Juana Inés contained in the letter she addressed to Sor Filotea and the autobiography of Mother Castillo, they include one written in 1757 by Sor Mará Marcella (1719–?) of New Spain in 1757; by Sor Sebastiana Josefa de la Santísima Trinidad (?–1757), in the form of epistles addressed to her confessor; by Sor María Anna Agueda de San Ignacio (1695–1756), author of several devout works of poor literary quality and doubtful spiritual value; and, by Sor Ursula Suárez (1668–1749) of Chile, the *Story of the Singular Mercies the Lord Has Shown a Nun, His Bride*, which, according to Toribio Medina, is a product of her imagination. Mother Inés de la Cruz, founder of the convent of San José de Carmelitas Descalzas de Mexico, wrote an autobiography, as did Ecuadoran Sor Catalina de Jesús Maria Herrera (1717–1795; *Secrets between the Soul and God*).

Of special interest is *The Life and Adventures of the Nun-Ensign, Doña Ca-*

talina de Erauso (1592–1648?), published in 1828. The novelesque character of the life this singular woman led induces the suspicion that it is an apocryphal text: from the age of 4 she was isolated from the world in a convent in San Sebastián de Guipúzcoa. At 15 she ran away and, dressed as a man, served several masters as a page for a couple of years, but, fearful of being discovered by her family, she sailed to Chile. There she fought against the Araucanian Indians as a valiant soldier and later in Peru became famous as a gambler and a swordsman. After 19 years of adventures she revealed her identity and was forced to return to her native country. Under the name Antonio de Erauso she immediately embarked for New Spain, where she worked as a mule driver transporting goods between Veracruz and Mexico City. Between 1648 and 1650 she disappeared mysteriously. The written account goes up only to 1626, the date of her return to her native land. In it there is a basis of truth that probably comes from the oral or written tale that Catalina de Erauso herself told; however, along with the passages verified by the Archives of the Indies appear many fictitious ones that seem to be interpolations by another author. A meticulous in-depth study could prove that a process of fictionalization has occurred, characteristic of the colonial narrative, a process noted in studies by Enrique Pupo-Walker. For that reason it could be called fictionalized autobiography. Regardless of the identity of the interpolator, the important thing is that the manuscript that has been preserved was written between 1626 and May 24, 1784, the date Juan Bautista Muñoz deposited it in the Royal Academy of History in Madrid. This is a text that should be taken into account in future studies dealing with the narrative of that period.

Some women writers of great literary talent hid behind pseudonyms. Perhaps because their works stood out as superior, it was contended that those fictitious appellations really hid the identity of men. Amarilis and Clarinda in Peru are two cases worthy of mention.

Of Amarilis's work only one excellent lyric poem has been preserved. Entitled "Epistle to Belardo," it was addressed to Lope de Vega in 1621, begging him to write the biography of Saint Dorothea; it recounts that the author is the descendant of Peruvian conquistadors, explains that she is in a convent in Lima, and, above all, expresses her tendency to love boldly the most impossible things, among which she counts "the hopeless love" that he awoke in her with his "peerless works." In 1630 Lope de Vega included this poem in his *Apollo's Laurels*.

Clarinda, called the "Great Anonymous Writer," became known for her poem "In Praise of Poetry." Diego de Mejía included it in his *Antartic Parnassus*, explaining that the author was "an illustrious lady in the Kingdom of Peru, well versed in Tuscan and Portuguese," whose name Mejía withheld following her order and out of due respect. Some critics agree with the Colombian poet Rafael Pambo that "in Spanish seldom has anyone pronounced a more practical and elevated discourse on poetry."

Women outside the convent also made their mark. In the baroque literature of Mexico, Catalina de Eslava (1534–1601) and María de Estrada Medinilla are recognized. The former dedicated to her uncle, dramatist Fernán González de Eslava, a sonnet, "The Laurel Wreathes Our Brow," which was included in the preface to his book *Spiritual and Sacramental Orations*. Méndez Plancarte considers María de Estrada Medinilla the precursor of Sor Juana Inés de la Cruz. Two lengthy lyric poems of hers were published in 1640.

In conclusion, in colonial literature mystic poems and autobiographies by nuns predominate. In drama, Sor Juana Inés de la Cruz was the outstanding figure. Of all the writers mentioned, only the complete works of Sor Juana, Mother Castillo, and Sor María Anna Agueda of San Ignacio have been published. In general the works are ruled by the literary codes of Spain and Europe; by patriarchal conventions; and by norms imposed by phallocentrism and by scholastic philosophy. The restless clairvoyance of Sor Juana did not conform to the latter, and it was for that reason the church silenced her lyrical voice and her spiritual anxieties—an intellectual death that caused her demise within two years, but the Mexican nun still towers over the panorama of colonial literature. In general, the rescue of texts written by women remains today a challenging task for researchers.

RIMA DE VALLBONA, TRANSLATED BY BETRIE ACKER

SPANISH AMERICAN WRITERS: POETS (NINETEENTH-CENTURY). The social status of women in Latin America regressed during the nineteenth century, and women found themselves even more confined than before independence. They were especially handicapped in that very few women received any schooling beyond the elementary level unless they entered a convent or came from the aristocracy.

Given the fact that very few women benefited from the fruits of higher education, it is not surprising, then, that one finds so few of them among the intellectual luminaries of the nineteenth century in Latin America. In countries as large as Brazil and Argentina, history, a history written by males, does not record a single woman poet in the nineteenth century. In some Spanish American nations, however, a few women made a significant contribution to poetry: Gertrudis Gómez de Avellaneda of Cuba, Dolores Veintimilla de Galindo of Ecuador, Isabel Prieto de Landázuri of Mexico, María Bibiana Benítez of Puerto Rico, and Salomé Ureña de Henríquez of Santo Domingo. Minor poets were María Josefa Mujía (1813–1888) of Bolivia, Mercedes Marín del Solar (1804–1866) and Rosario Orrego Uribe (1834–1879) of Chile, Josefa Murillo (1860–1898) of Mexico, and Carmen Hernández de Araújo (1832–1877) and Úrsula Cardona de Quiñonez (1836–1875) of Puerto Rico.

Gertrudis Gómez de Avellaneda (1814–1873), poet, novelist, and playwright, was a person who lived intensely the 59 years of her life. Twice she married and twice became a widow. Her love affairs were full of turmoil, and she often found haven in her Catholic faith. In fact, she seriously considered entering the convent. From 1836 to 1859 she lived in Spain, where she earned accolades and was treated by the Spanish intellectuals as one of their own. In 1863 she returned home to play an influential role in Cuban letters as a lyric poet. Her Romanticism is full of emotional intensity and conveyed in neo-classical form, for she was a disciple of Quintana and Meléndez Valdés. Her *Devocionario poético* (1867) reveals a deep faith and a soul thirsty for God. "Al Partir," one of her best sonnets, expresses her love for her homeland. The best of her poetry can be found in *Obras* (4 vols., 1914–1918).

The Ecuadoran Dolores Veintimilla de Galindo (1821–1857) is perhaps the most fascinating and certainly the most tragic of the nineteenth-century women poets. She married the Colombian physician Sixto Galindo and accompanied him to Quito and Cuenca, where she became well known by distinguishing herself in literary contests. In Cuenca, however, she dared to oppose the death penalty imposed on a man convicted of killing his father. She wrote and dedicated a poem to this man, Tiburcio Lucero, whom she did not even know. She was violently attacked in the press, mercilessly slandered, and her life was threatened. Alone in her desperate sorrow, she committed suicide at the age of 36. Veintimilla's Romantic poetry is passionate and poignant, as was her life. Called the "Sappho of Ecuador," she left not only vibrant and moving verses but also the example of a woman who stood alone for the basic human right to life against a society that constantly denied it. Her poems were published in *Producciones literarias* in 1908.

Mexico's Isabel Prieto de Landázuri (1833–1876) was born in Spain and died in Germany but was wholly Mexican in literary training, expression, and temperament. She arrived in Mexico at the age of five and moved with her family to Guadalajara. She was especially adept in expressing maternal love in moving lyricism and Romantic emotionalism. Her poems were assembled, edited, and published in 1883 by the Mexican poet and humanist José María Vigil. Her contemporaries were so moved by her poetry that they called her the "Twin Sister of Sor Juana Inés de la Cruz."

Puerto Rico's two most important women poets of the nineteenth century were María Bibiana Benítez (1783–1873) and her daughter Alejandrina Benítez (1819–1879). María Bibiana lived to be ninety, far outlasting most nineteenth-century women in Latin America. She began writing verses in her middle life and was the first woman to write poetry in Borinquen. She first came to public attention in 1832 with "La Ninfa de Puerto Rico," a poem dedicated to the installation of the Real Audiencia de Puerto Rico (Royal Court and Council). She modeled her neo-classical and Romantic poems after Calderón and Fray Luís de León without ever achieving much originality.

María Bibiana's daughter Alejandrina Benítez proved a better poet than her mother, singing the beauty of the Puerto Rican landscape and displaying her enthusiasm for modern inventions and the achievements of nineteenth-century science in beautiful verses. She also gave Puerto Rico its best Romantic poet in her son Gautier Benítez.

Another Latin American woman poet who expressed great hopes and optimism about the capabilities of science in creating a better world was the Dominican Salomé Ureña de Henríquez (1850–1897). Her education was extensive because of the privileged position of her family, for she was the wife of Francisco Henríquez, president of the Dominican Republic. Salomé began to show her poetic inclinations at the age of 15 while using the pseudonym "Herminia." Her *Poesías* were first published in 1880 and reveal a patriotic and Romantic soul. Her greatest contribution to her country, however, was the establishment of the first Normal School for Women, the equivalent of the first Dominican Teachers' College. Two of her sons, Max and Pedro Henríquez Ureña, became distinguished writers and novelists. Her best poems, "La gloria del progreso" and "La fé en el porvenir," can be found in *Poesías Completas,* published in 1950.

Further References. Isaac J. Barrera, *Historia de la literature ecuatoriana* (Quito, 1954). Enrique Anderson Imbert and Eugenio Florit, *Literatura Hispanoamericana* (New York, 1960). Carlos González Peña, *History of the Mexican Literature* (Dallas, 1969). Cesareo Rosa-Nieves, *La Poesía en Puerto Rico* (San Juan, 1958).

TARCISIO BEAL

SPANISH AMERICAN WRITERS: POETS (TWENTIETH-CENTURY). Latin American poetry offers a rich spectrum of themes and styles, yet it has not been easy for the woman writer to be recognized by the patriarchal establishment with its rigid, critical canons. Despite all adversities, the lyrical heritage left by the early women writers as well as by those who continue working today is vast and vital.

In the 1920s there emerged in Spanish America a group of four important poets who would have an impact on future generations. The year 1920 is in itself a key date, for in that year women begin to appear in the public and intellectual circles of their respective cities, emerging from the habitual, intimate, and cloistered privacy in which so many of their contemporaries had remained hidden and silent.

Alfonsina Storni (1892–1938), poet of Buenos Aires, is one of the pioneers who began to speak out without false euphemisms or modesty concerning the condition of women. One of her most famous poems, entitled "Tú me quieres blanca," (You Want Me White), emphasizes the fact that man demands perfection and especially chastity of the woman, while he himself is exempt from judgment. This critical stance toward the society in which she lived, in addition to her profound identification with the woman who transgresses, is demonstrated in another poem, "La loba" (The She-Wolf). Here Storni portrays a woman who chooses to lead her own life through the image of an animal that separates from the pack and chooses a life that is solitary but dignified. This image represents one of the principal tendencies in Storni's work: her poetry champions above all the creative woman's right to freedom and pleasure.

Storni's opus, including seven volumes of poetry, children's theatre, and prose poems, makes her a prolific yet little studied creator. Her subtle irony and sharp critique of Buenos Aires society (also found in Mistral's poetry) and her deep concern for the marginal, the weak, and the oppressed open the way for the new voices of the future.

Gabriela Mistral (1889–1957), contemporary of Alfonsina Storni and the first Latin American woman to win the Nobel Prize in literature, is also a fundamental lyrical voice that blazes paths for future generations. Mistral is characterized by a primal attachment to the land that surrounded her. Her poetry is rooted in her native Elqui Valley in northern Chile. A profound regional attachment characterizes all her work, especially her important *Poema de Chile* (Poem of Chile) of 1954, dedicated to the topography of her country, and the famous long poem "Sol del trópico" (Tropical Sun), dedicated to all of Latin America.

A language studded with powerful images, sober verse form, and expressive sensuality characterizes this extraordinary woman, who wrote of maternity, frigidity, madness, and children. Because of this array of themes, she was always labeled as a traditional Romantic "woman poet." Yet the rich language and the original focus of these themes put her ahead of her time and caused her to be misunderstood.

Delmira Agostina (1887–1914) and Juana de Ibarbourou (1895–1977) draw a pattern different from that of Storni and Mistral; they also belong to a different poetic generation. The poetic of Agostini is characterized by an expansive eroticism and a concern centered on the discovery of her own freedom and autonomy. Through her intensely sensual poetry, unlike Agostina, Ibarbourou exults in conforming to the patriarchal standards of her time and in praising her own body, always in relation to a masculine object.

The Mexican Rosario Castellanos (1925–1974) is without doubt one of the most brilliant voices of the period. Born just as the preceding generation was beginning to publish, Castellanos took on the dynamism and the impetus of her predecessors and went on to produce one of the most profound and seminal bodies of work of contemporary Latin American literature. From *Travectoria del Polvo* (1948) through the poems collected after her premature death in 1974, the theme of Castellanos's poetry is above all the condition of the Spanish American woman, to whom "things" have been "taught mistakenly." With this phrase Castellanos draws the first coordinate of her poetry: the reevaluation of female passivity and the championing of a new search for fulfillment and freedom. Just as Storni scoffed at the "hombres pequenitos" (the little men), who shut women up in canary cages, Castellanos exposes the cult of confinement and domesticity, that is, the Latin American female destiny.

Castellanos denounces woman's immersion in petty detail, her subjugation to the prescriptions of motherhood and the cult of eternal love. In so doing she casts doubt on almost all the values that have dominated Hispanic society. Her poetry, like that of Storni and Mistral, is rich in imagery conveyed by means of everyday language. The contribution of these women can be summed up as the exposition of new themes and the exposure of the female condition through the elaboration of a new language linked to feminist postulates.

The poetry of three very important and highly original poets, the Argentines Olga Orozco (b.1931) and Alejandra Pizarnik (1936–1972) and the Puerto Rican Rosario Ferré (b.1942), should also be mentioned. Orozco's poetic voice is unique in current Spanish American literature. It is occasionally obscure, though not in imagery but in the existential mystery of what is enunciated. Her copious and well-known poetic production possesses a coherence that reflects the recurrent ambiguity of the poetic word itself. She manifests a strong attraction to the unconscious and a desire to release and liberate its energy. Her first book, *Desde lijos* (From Afar), published in 1946, already conjures up that sense of an unknown and perilous game with an inverted world. Orozco's poetry is highly dreamlike, sculpted with perspectives where dream takes on the outlines of reality. The same could be said of her fellow Buenos Airean, Alejandra Pizarnik, who, like her, inhabits a world dominated by the surreal and the transfiguration of immediate reality.

There are many other important women poets in the Spanish American lyrical tradition, but it is primarily these women whose originality and daring mark an indelible path in poetry written by women of the twentieth century.

MARJORIE AGOSIN, TRANSLATED BY LORRAINE ROSES

SPANISH AMERICAN WRITERS: PROSE (NINETEENTH-CENTURY).

With independence and the formation of the new republics during the early decades of the nineteenth century came an invigorating commitment to women's education, which had a correspondingly invigorating effect on women's writing. The work of educators such as Juana Manso and Rosa Guerre in Argentina, Rita Lecumberry Robles in Ecuador, and Ana Roque de Duprey in Puerto Rico and the proliferation of schools for girls assured the literacy of a large number of women and their consequent increased participation in a variety of literary activities. Poetry, the novel, and the essay were cultivated, and periodicals by and for women proliferated, they being one of the most popular and accessible outlets for women to express themselves and communicate with one another. Among the periodicals were *El Album cubano de lo bueno y lo bello* (The Cuban Album of the Good and the Beautiful; Havana, Cuba, 1860), founded and directed by Gertrudis Gómez de Avellaneda; *El Album* (The Album; Lima, Peru, 1874), founded by Argentine exile Juana Manuela Gorriti; *La Mujer* (Woman; Bogotá, Colombia, 1878), founded by Soledad Acosta de Samper.

Letter writing, a common form of written expression during the colonial period, continued its importance as an outlet for women. Well-known correspondence is that of María de Sánchez (Mariquita) (1786–1868), who presided over an important salon in Buenos Aires in the early decades of the nineteenth century and corresponded with Esteban Echeverría, Domingo Sarmiento, and other political and literary figures, and that of Manuela Sáenz to Simón Bolívar. Many nineteenth-century writers maintained a lively correspondence with friends, family, and one another, but those that have perhaps most captivated readers are the love letters of two Cuban writers, Gertrudis Gómez de Avellaneda

(1814–1873) and Juana Borrero (1877–1896). Much work remains to be done in collecting and publishing the letters of Spanish American women. As Sergio Verqara Quiroz demonstrates in his ground-breaking publication *Cartas de mujeres en Chile, 1630–1885* (Chilean Women's Letters) (Santiago, 1987), the correspondence of women who have not been remembered for singular acts of bravery, for their relationships with famous men, or for other literary accomplishments can have great literary as well as social and historical value.

A number of women combined a prolific and varied literary output with an active involvement in education, women's rights, and social reform. Gertrudis Gómez de Avellaneda, who was born in Cuba but spent most of her productive literary life in Spain, wrote poetry, numerous plays and novels, travel narratives, letters, and essays. Besides her journalism, Soledad Acosta de Samper (Colombia, 1883–1903) wrote biographies, history, travel narratives, and essays, among them "La mujer moderna" (The Modern Woman), a book-length text of scholarly research that is still useful today as a source of information on women's contribution to the arts and sciences. Juana Manuela Gorriti's (Argentina, 1819–1892) voluminous production includes history, biographies, novels, stories, legends, an autobiographical narrative, and even a cookbook. Clorinda Natto de Turner (Peru, 1852–1909) was active in journalism and wrote several novels. *Aves sin nido* (Birds without a Nest) is considered a forerunner of the Peruvian Indianist novel. Her forthright attacks on the clergy and on government officials caused her excommunication from the Catholic church. Other women suffered similar punishments or ostracism for their bravery in criticizing the Establishment in their novels. Mercedes Cabello de Carbonera (Peru, 1845–1909) attacked the corruption of urban Lima society in her novel *Blanca Sol*. She spent the last ten years of her life in an insane asylum. In Honduras, Lucila Gamero de Medina (1873–1964), credited with writing the first Honduran novel, was excommunicated for her criticism of the clergy in *Blanca Olmedo*.

Juana Manso (1819–1879), Rose Guerra (d.1864), and Eduarda Mansilla (1838–1892) enriched the literature of Argentina with their novels, journalism, and travel narratives, while Lindaura Anzoátegui is considered a forerunner of the *costumbrista* (literature of manners) movement in Bolivia because of her text *Como se vive en mi pueblo* (Life in My Town). Ana Roque de Duprey (Puerto Rico, 1853–1933), besides her work in education, journalism, and women's rights, wrote 32 novels, including *Sara la obrera* (Sarah the Worker), an example of social realism. The Cuban Luisa Pérez de Zambrana (1835–1922), although best known for her poetry, wrote 2 novels and contributed to various periodicals.

Two writers who deserve special mention are María de la Merced Santa Cruz (la Condesa de Merlin) and Flora Tristan. La Condesa de Merlin was born in Cuba in 1789 but went with her father to live in France and thereafter made that country her home. She maintained an attachment, however, to her native land, and her works *Mes douze premieres annees* (My First Twelve Years) and *La Havane* (Havana) were translated into Spanish and are considered a valuable contribution to Cuban letters. Flora Tristan (1803–1844), born in Paris to a

French mother and a Peruvian father, at the age of 23 traveled to Peru to claim what she considered to be her rightful inheritance. The account of her travels through Peru and her descriptions of people, places, and events are a unique and fascinating text.

Further References. Lynn Ellen Rice Cortina, *Spanish American Women Writers: A Bibliographical Research Checklist* (New York, 1983). Meri Knaster, *Women in Spanish America: An Annotated Bibliography from Pre-Conquest to Contemporary Times* (Boston, 1977). Diane E. Marting (ed.), *Women Writers of Spanish America: An Annotated Bio-Bibliographical Guide* (Westport, Conn., 1987).

JANET N. GOLD

SPANISH AMERICAN WRITERS: PROSE (TWENTIETH-CENTURY).

In the period after World War I, when Latin American literature needed alternatives to highly rhetorical and ornamental modes, women writers helped develop a simpler prose. Gabriela Mistral of Chile (b. Lucila Godoy Alcayaga, 1889–1957; Nobel Prize poet, 1945) in her essays recognized women as teachers, mothers, and counselors. Alfonsina Storni (Argentina, 1892–1938), also a poet, was a noted journalist and passionate feminist. Teresa de la Parra (Venezuela, 1891–1936) focused on upper-class, Europeanized ladies in her novels *Ifigenia* (1924) and *Mamá Blanca's Souvenirs* (1929; Eng., 1959). Early recognized as a stylist, she was rediscovered as a student of women's culture.

In the 1930s and 1940s Buenos Aires, known for sophisticated, fantastic fiction, featured Chilean novelist María Luisa Bombal (1910–1980) of *The House of Mist* (1934; Eng., 1947) and *The Shrouded Woman* (1938; Eng., 1948), Victoria Ocampo (1891–1979), an influential editor, and her writer-sister Silvina (b.1903). Writers of realism at this time included Marta Brunet (Chile, 1901–1967), who showed rural women as more independent than traditional codes would suggest. Nellie Campobello (b.1909) depicted the Mexican Revolution through a small girl's eyes in *Cartucho* (Cartridge, 1931) and the lives of revolutionary era women in *Las manos de Mamá* (Mama's Hands, 1937). Women folklorists studied and popularized crafts and lore. Lydia Cabrera (Cuba–United States, b.1900,) adapted Afro-Caribbean tales. María Elena Walsh (Argentina, b.1930), folksinger and writer, used folk narrative conventions to help children understand such issues as shifting sex roles and environmental dilemmas.

Currently being rediscovered are women who pursued both learning and social change during the 1930s and 1940s: the literary critic and feminist Concha Meléndez (Puerto Rico, 1904); the Costa Rican short story writer, activist, and student of Central American society Carmen Lyra (María Isabel Carvajal, 1890–1949); and Yolanda Oreamuno (Costa Rica, 1916–1956), psychological novelist and legendary nurturer of intellectuals and activists.

By the 1950s and 1960s, many more women participated in literary life. Social novelists included Rosario Castellanos (Mexico, 1925–1974), whose *The Nine Guardians* (1957; Eng., 1961) gave an inside view of Tzotzil Indian and Hispanic cultures in rural Mexico. Castellanos was an important feminist voice. Marta

Lynch (Argentina, 1929–1985) developed a political and yet highly personal novel; *La Señora Ordóñez* (1967) analyzes a woman's confused attempts at autonomy. Elena Garro (Mexico, b.1920) veils social criticism in the enigmatic, lyrical novel *Recollections of Things to Come* (1963; Eng., 1969). Two best-selling Argentine writers, Silvina Bullrich (b.1915) and Beatriz Guido (b.1925), leaven social commentary with melodrama.

In Mexico, Elena Poniatowska (b.1933), Margo Glantz (b.1930), and María Luisa Mendoza (n.b.d.) practice innovative journalism. Poniatowski obtains revealing oral histories from actors in Mexican history (*Massacre in Mexico*, 1971, Eng., 1974). Mendoza's journalism and novels transmit, in eccentrically cluttered style, social criticism and examine women's culture. Glantz is a supporter of cultural experimentation and a feminist.

Newly prominent writers include the Argentine–U.S. Luisa Valenzuela (b.1937) and Silvia Molloy (b.1934); Chilean Isabel Allende (b.1942), author of *The House of Spirits* (1982; Eng., 1985); Lucía Guerra (Chile, b.1943); Rosario Ferré (Puerto Rico, n.b.d.); and Albalucía Angel (Colombia, b.1939); enjoying renewed attention are the Argentines Griselda Gambaro (b.1928), Sara Gallardo (b.1929), and Angélica Gorodischer (b.1929), Inés Arredondo (Mexico, b.1928), Claribel Alegría (Nicaragua/El Salvador, b.1924), and Armonía Somers (Uruguay, b. Armonía Etchepare de Henestrosa, 1917), as well as women essayists in anthropology, activism, and social thought. While today's writers are often feminists, women's studies should also reexamine earlier authors who, without open feminism, understood women's status and culture.

Further References. Fabienne Bradu, *Señas particulares: escritora* (Mexico City, 1987). Diane E. Marting (ed.), *Women Writers of Spanish America: An Annotated Bio-Bibliographic Guide* (Westport, Conn., 1987). Doris Meyer and Margarite Fernández Olmos (eds.), *Contemporary Women Authors of Latin America: Critical Essays*, 2 vols. (Brooklyn, 1983). Evelyn Picon, *Women's Voices from Latin America: Interviews with Six Contemporary Authors* (Detroit, 1986). Carmelo Virgillo and Naomi Lindstrom (eds.), *Woman as Myth and Metaphor in Latin American Literature* (Columbia, Mo., 1985).

NAOMI LINDSTROM

SPANISH WRITERS. Women writers, a rare phenomenon before the twentieth century, had to surmount numerous barriers in a conservative, male-oriented society. This achievement was feasible because the women often were aristocrats or had a foreign education. In the Golden Age, Renaissance idealism accompanied by religious fervor produced several great mystics, including Spain's first woman writer, Santa Teresa de Jesús (1515–1582), a Carmelite nun of exalted spirit. She adapted love poetry symbols into divine poetry: mystic experiences are sketched through images of worldly love. In addition to three autobiographical books, she wrote *Camino de perfección*, a spiritual guide for nuns, and *Las Moradas*, describing the mystic's path to God (*Way of Perfection* and *Interior Castles*, in *The Complete Works*, 1957). In a simple and sometimes humorous style, they are a major contribution to the mystical tradition.

In the baroque period María de Zayas (1590–1661), an upper-class feminist with, except in matters regarding women, aristocratic values, created some narrative masterpieces. Her collections, *Novelas amorosas y ejemplares* (Love and Exemplary Novels) and *Desengaños amorosos* (Love Disillusions), follow structurally the *Decameron* model, have a didactic purpose, and promote equality: they condemn male chauvinism and the intellectual oppression of women, who are urged to be independent.

The nineteenth-century Romantic movement brought a new subjective lyric expression, free from neo-classical norms. Gertrudis Gómez de Avellaneda (1814–1873) marked this transition with several elegies and nature poems of neo-classical pattern, followed by passionate love verses, nostalgic descriptions of Cuba's landscape, and religious exultations based on biblical themes. Carolina Coronado (1823–1911), also influenced by the Bible, wrote simple, spontaneous poems of love, nature, and religion. Her social awareness led to satirical and feminist compositions like "Libertad," or freedom everyone can enjoy—except women. Lyric poetry reached new heights with the Neo-Romantic Rosalía de Castro (1837–1885). Her metafictional "strange story," *El caballero de las botas azules* (The Gentleman in the Blue Boots), scrutinizes writers, readers, and popular literary genres. But Rosalía is, above all, a poet. *Cantares gallegos* (Galician Songs) and *Follas novas* (New Leaves) offer an idyllic vision of her native Galicia, while echoing the voice of its oppressed farmers. Social concerns develop into existential thought and tender compassion in her symbolist masterpiece *En las orillas del Sar* (*Beside the River Sar*, 1937) where she encompasses human suffering and loneliness with tears of desperation. Rosalía is a prominent precursor of contemporary poets.

Among novelists, Cecilia Bohl de Faber (1796–1877, Fernán Caballero), an ultraconservative, defended upper-class privileges. Popular customs and anecdotes provided raw materials for her narrative, heavily ballasted with strict moral principles. Idealized peasants stage colorful romantic scenes in *La gaviota* (The Sea-Gull), subtitled "original novel of Spanish customs" while *Cuadros de costumbres* is a collection of short stories portraying Andalusian folklore. Countess Emilia Pardo Bazán (1851–1921) was the first woman to hold a university professorship and a pioneer in the feminist movement. Complaints about double standards are a leitmotiv of her works, which include several volumes of literary essays and more than 500 short stories in a wide thematic range. A key essay, *La cuestión palpitante* (The Burning Question), molds literary naturalism to her religious beliefs. *Los pazos de Ulloa* (The Manor of Ulloa) and *La madre naturaleza* (Mother Nature), novels stemming from this version of Spanish naturalism, present a pessimistic view of life in a rural setting. *Una cristiana* (A Christian Woman) and *La prueba* (The Test), published together (1890), portray types: the frivolous little doll, the ideal Christian, the liberated "new woman." Russian narrative influenced her last novels.

A second Golden Age of rich lyric followed the avant-garde movement of the early twentieth century. But the Civil War (1936–1939) shattered the country, forcing into exile many writers such as Ernestina de Champourcín (b.1905), who produced most of her poems in Mexico. *Presencia a oscuras* (Presence in the Dark), inspired by her rediscovery of God, has deep religious roots. In *Poemas del ser y del estar*, trying to reconcile poetry with the poet, similar religious feelings surface. Carmen Conde (b.1907), prolific in several genres, is the first female member of the Royal Academy of Language. Her passionate verse celebrates love and life but also expresses grief for the broken dreams of postwar Spain. Tenderness defines her "Poemas a la madre."

Until the 1950s, social poetry appeared isolated and timid; thereafter it became a rebellious trend. To Angela Figuera (b.1902) poetry is a tool for improving the world. The mild tone of maternal love in *Mujer de barro* (Woman of Clay) turns anguished and fierce in *El grito inútil* (The Useless Shout) and *Los días duros* (The Hard Days), fiery cries of compassion and impotence. Another strong social poet, Gloria Fuertes (b.1918), evolves from self-pity in *Isla ignorada* (Ignored Island) to sarcastic criticism of the inane middle class in *Aconsejo beber hilo* (My Advice Is To Drink Thread). Her poems about daily life, naive at times, exude anguish and solitude. A new sensibility emerges from the voice of Ana María Moix (b.1947), defending absolute freedom of forms while rehabilitating materials judged apoetic before, in *Baladas para el dulce Jim* (Ballads for Sweet Jim) and *No Time for Flowers*.

The narrative fiction of Concha Espina (1877–1955), bridging the centuries, combines traditional realist techniques with a new social awareness. Her best novels are *El metal de los muertos* (The Metal of the Dead), about labor problems the miners face, and *La esfinge maragata* (*Mariflor*, 1924) concerning women's marginal lives. Because of the Civil War, however, the novel, isolated from current Western innovations, nearly suffocated in its own tradition of outdated realism. The recovery starts with Carmen Laforet (b.1921). In her early novel *Nada* (*Andrea*, 1964), a best-seller and winner of the first Nadal Prize (1945), the heroine's dreams clash with a sordid environment and anomalous family members. Although conventional in structure and narrative techniques, it reveals an acute feminine sensibility combined with a wide existential scope: life's ups and downs lead to disenchantment, to "nothingness," because of the uncertain future and lack of communication. Elena Quiroga (b.1921), member of the Royal Academy of Language, gained immediate fame with the rather conventional *Viento del Norte* (Northwind) (Nadal Prize, 1950). But her narrative prowess is evinced in *La sangre* (Blood), with its technical novelty of a centennial chestnut tree narrating its impressions of four generations of a family, and in her psychological novels, *Algo pasa en la calle* (Something's Happening in the Street) and *La careta* (The Mask), with multiple point of view and stream of consciousness. A champion of social narrative and recipient of prestigious literary prizes, Ana María Matute (b.1926) defends the novel as a vehicle for revealing human problems and striking society's conscience. The Civil War and its consequences give the historical background to her best novels, *En esta tierra*, (In This Land) a political, nonconformist defense of the poor, and *Los hijos muertos*

(*The Lost Children*, 1965), a message against hate. Like the previous novels, *Primera memoria* (*School of the Sun*, 1963) protests lack of justice, deceptive charity, and indifference to suffering. A fatalistic view leads her narrative to themes of envy, destruction, and loneliness. Carmen Martín-Gaite (b.1925), one of today's foremost novelists, writes introspective novels where existential queries find an answer in the meaning of writing. All human conflicts are related to the need for communication, and *Retahílas* (Threads) deals with the lack of it. *Entre visillos* (Between the Blinds) (Nadal Prize, 1957) criticizes the provincial narrow-mindedness of middle-class young people without a clear purpose in life. Innovative and abreast of current trends, *El cuarto de atrás* (*The Back Room*, 1983) (National Literary Award, 1978) is a mystery novel that weaves fantastic elements with memoirs and metafictional thoughts.

Further References. J. M. Díez Borque (ed.), *Historia de la literatura española* (Madrid, 1980). Carmen Conde, *Poesía femenina española* (Barcelona, 1967 and 1971). José Simón Díaz, *Manual de bibliografía de la literatura española* (Madrid, 1980). Janet Pérez, *Contemporary Women Writers of Spain* (Boston, 1988).

J. BERNARDO PÉREZ

STEREOTYPICAL HEROINE IN VICTORIAN LITERATURE. The portrayal of women as the angel in the house, the old maid, or the fallen woman. The stereotype functions to idealize the passive, self-sacrificing mother for the benefit of a patriarchy. Often contrasted with the motherly angel, the old maid, in her unattractiveness, bitterness, or dislike of her role in the home, is seen as deserving of her lonely spinsterhood. The fallen woman, though usually portrayed as a martyr, is an example of the consequences awaiting women who unheedingly choose love before marriage.

The angel in the house is the perfect helpmeet. She serves and obeys her husband, is moral adviser and guide to the children, and ensures peace and stability in her home. Beautiful, sweet, passive, and self-sacrificing, her identity is derived solely from her role as wife and mother. Charles Dickens's Agnes Wickfield (*David Copperfield*) and Esther Summerson (*Bleak House*), being loyal to family unity, embody Victorian domestic values. But in their passivity and tireless self-denial to men who are unworthy of them, such heroines as William Makepeace Thackeray's Amelia Sedley (*Vanity Fair*) and Anthony Trollope's Lily Dale (*The Small House at Allington*) become almost masochistic parodies of the feminine ideal. Even women novelists who portray female characters striving for a life of their own suggest an ambivalence about independence and domestic security. Charlotte Brontë's Jane Eyre (*Jane Eyre*), Elizabeth Gaskell's Margaret Hale (*North and South*), and George Eliot's Dorothea Brooke (*Middlemarch*), though achieving strength, individuation, and self-knowledge through deep and enduring psychological struggles, eventually marry and become primarily the stabilizing forces in their husbands' lives.

Wilkie Collins's Marian Halcombe (*The Woman in White*) and Dickens's Miss Havisham (*Great Expectations*) represent stereotypes of the old maid. Though self-sacrificing in her devotion to Laura Fairlie, Marian Halcombe is unattractive and masculinely active, intelligent, and willful, traits repugnant in a Victorian wife. In her cruel scheming to keep Pip and Estella apart, Miss Havisham embodies the bitter vindictiveness of the betrayed and solitary woman. Brontë's Lucy Snowe (*Villette*), however, is a portrayal of a heroic old maid. Lucy lives a drama based on lack and need because of her determined attempt to define herself in what is to her an alien world, but her discipline through despair as she achieves independence is equated with her re-emergence into society on her own terms.

The fallen woman is allowed more sympathy than is expected from a society that insisted upon harmony in the home and chastity in single women. Though she is an example of the woman who has, if only for an instant, strayed from morality and therefore must deal with both her own guilt and society's ostracism, she is often a passive innocent. Gaskell's Ruth (*Ruth*) and Thomas Hardy's Tess (*Tess of the D'Urbervilles*) suggest the double standard of a society that at once teaches innocence as womanly duty and virtue and punishes those who are seduced. In these novels, the authors twist the moral lesson so that, rather than blaming the innocent heroine for her mistake, they present her as a victim of society's standards for women. In death, both Ruth and Tess become martyrs to a society that fails to see its own lack of morality in its victimization of women. Nancy, in Dickens's *Oliver Twist*, too, though an accomplice to underworld characters, is presented sympathetically. She is a victim of circumstances, the product of a society that provides no work for the uneducated woman. Thus, with no status or options, Nancy falls into prostitution. In her loyalty to Sikes, though, Nancy parallels the angel because her self-sacrificial death to save Sikes expiates her sins. George Eliot is the least sympathetic to the fallen woman. She not only condemns the vanity and ambitious sexuality that engender Hetty's seduction (*Adam Bede*) but compounds her selfishness with infanticide. Hetty, too, is ostracized and isolated from society and dies alone.

In the Victorian novel, women were stereotyped to ensure the dominance of the patriarchy. Presented as a role model and ideal for the family fireside readers, the sweet and beautiful angel is the arbiter of domesticity in the face of an uncaring world. In return for her loving devotion, she is rewarded by a marriage that provides her security and identity. In contrast, those women who are too willful or intelligent or who are embittered and unlovable are punished through spinsterhood. Preferring independence to obedience, the old maid is destined for loneliness and, probably, guilt. The precarious sexual position of young single women is depicted by the fallen woman who is most often a victim of her own innocence. While presenting a warning to the adolescent female reader, however, the authors' sympathetic portrayals also suggest that society should be both more compassionate toward the innocent heroine and more wise in educating her.

Female authors tend to be more ambivalent about stereotyping their heroines as angels than do male authors because women authors' heroines often embody

conflicts within the authors themselves. While passionately striving for independence, the heroines also desire love, but society's inability to accept and
encourage autonomy in a woman blocks the heroines from resolving this conflict.
The solution is to show the heroine's growth through struggle, from which she
emerges as a stronger and more self-assured and assertive individual. But this
strength, instead of allowing her social autonomy, enables her to be a more
interesting, more worthy helpmeet to her husband. The heroine is still idealized
as the self-sacrificing angel, albeit a more admirable one.

Further References. Nina Auerbach, *Woman and the Demon: The Life of the Victorian
Myth* (Cambridge, Mass., 1982). Richard Barickman, Susan MacDonald, and Myra Stark,
Corrupt Relations: Dickens, Thackeray, Trollope, Collins and the Victorian Sexual System
(New York, 1982). Francois Basch, *Relative Creatures: Victorian Women in Society and
the Novel 1837–67*, Anthony Rudolph (trans.) (London, 1974). Katherine M. Rogers,
The Troublesome Helpmate: A History of Misogyny in Literature (Seattle, 1966).

LAURIE BUCHANAN

SUPERMARKET ROMANCES. Romance fiction, epitomized by such publishing giants as Harlequin and Silhouette, is a major literary phenomenon of
the world of contemporary popular culture. Softcover novels, sold in super-
markets, airports, bookstores, and pharmacies, constitute an enormous proportion
of the reading material chosen by women readers; romance book clubs cater to
a large and appreciative audience of readers, representing all social and economic
classes. Since the latter 1970s, feminist critics and researchers have begun to
explore and to speculate about the appeal of the supermarket romance, as well
as to examine the content and the dynamics of the books themselves.

Romance fiction is formula fiction; readers and critics agree that much of the
appeal of the supermarket romance comes from its predictability. Women, usually young, though a subset of romance fiction is now specifically devoted to
the "Second Chance at Love," encounter romance and a judicious amount of
violence or difficulty, which culminates in romantic fulfillment, usually marriage.
Close reading of many Harlequin Romances, a particularly long-lived and successful segment of the romance fiction market, reveals a deep streak of violence,
including sexual violence. Rape, near-rape, kidnapping, imprisonment, slapping,
and manhandling are regular features of many Harlequin and Silouhette romances. Blind rage, the ripping of fabric, cruel savagery, and the predictable
triumph of the "new and disturbing sensations" of sexual arousal are characteristic of appeal to heroines and readers alike. While recent examples of supermarket romances pay some lip service to the realities of women's changing
roles in the family and in the labor market, the young and beautiful heroines of
the tales regularly crave, succumb to, and become addicted to the sexual powers
of strong and traditionally masterful men. An apparent updating of the formula
offers the young heroine early success in a variety of careers, from concert
musicianship to academic achievement; usually, however, the heroine chooses
to relinquish her career in order to experience fully the delights of marriage and
the promise of motherhood.

The authors of supermarket romances, some of them men writing under women's names, confidently offer advice to aspiring newcomers. At regular conferences, such as the November 1986, 5th Annual Book Convention in New York City, readers, writers, reviewers, and publishers meet; a series of awards, presented by *Romantic Times Magazine,* recognizes achievements within many categories of romance writing, including westerns, fantasies, science fiction, and historical novels. An extreme and revealing example of the devotion to romance literature's annual festival has been committed to film: a woman from Southern California, as reported in a *New York Times* article of August 19, 1987, organized a Love Train, "an Amtrak special, to take romance-novel readers and authors from the West Coast to New York with stops in between" to attend such a conference. The filmed record, *Where the Heart Roams,* opened on August 19 in New York City.

The big business represented by the supermarket romance is demonstrated by the sheer amount of bookstore space devoted to the genre; the Canadian critic Margaret Ann Jensen in *Love's Sweet Return: the Harlequin Story* (Bowling Green, Ohio, 1984) reported that in one year (1981 to 1982) bookstores increased the space devoted to formula romances by half. For one major bookstore chain, romances made up nearly one-third of all mass paperback sales, Jensen attested.

Reviewers and critics differ about the significance and effect of the supermarket romance saturation of women readers. Some, such as Janice Radway in *Reading the Romance: Women, Patriarchy, and Popular Literature* (Chapel Hill, N.C., 1984), see strength and self-determination in women's choices of reading material and their accounts of the meaning they find in the stories. Others, such as Tania Modleski in *Loving with a Vengeance* (New York, 1984), see the rapes and near-rapes as testimony to the power of women to arouse men, saying that "romances to some extent 'inoculate' against the major evils of sexist society" by showing that vicious men exist but that women retain the power to attract and to exact pleasure. It seems at least arguable that, in their heavy emphasis on traditional marriage as the successful culmination to a compellingly sexual relationship, the supermarket romances are reinforcing a pattern of romantic domesticity with serious political implications.

Successful authors Rosemary Rogers, Tom Huff (who writes as Jennifer Wilde), Heather Graham (who writers as Shannon Drake), and others regularly urge readers of women's magazines such as *Family Circle* and *Women's World* to try their skill at writing romances. The appeal to determined individualism is strong. "Hard work is the only key," Tom Huff counsels in a *Family Circle* interview of February 26, 1985. "Writing and rewriting day after day, until the job is done. That's what it all boils down to."

The end product will be a paperback novel that will net the author some $5,000 for a sale, with the ultimate prospect of higher prices upon proven success (vocabulary beyond the level of the average 12-year-old's comprehension is risky). Though Harlequin sales flattened in the mid–1980s, the company purchased Silhouette from Doubleday with the expectation of enhanced profits.

Supermarket romances depend on a heavy proportion of violence, sexual titillation, and an overlay of traditional familial values to appeal to a large number of devoted readers. While critics may continue to differ over the significance of the romance phenomenon, it seems clear that the supermarket romance, in its various guises, is a major publishing phenomenon of the twentieth century. Its meaning must continue to engage feminist scholars in disciplines ranging from sociology to literary criticism.

RUTH NADELHAFT

SWEDISH WRITERS' literary history begins with religious writings in the Middle Ages, as exemplified by the revelations of Birgitta (1307–1373). Other signs of beginnings can be seen in Hedvig C. Nordenflycht (1718–1763), of aristocratic stock, who set pen to paper to support her family. Well aware of women's precarious position in society, she defends her sex, demanding acknowledgement of woman's intellect and capacity for deep emotion. But it is personal loss and grief that remain central to Nordenflycht's writing, evidenced in her collection of poems *Den sörgande Turtur-Dufwan* (1743; The Mourning Turtle-Dove), important for introducing the subjective into Swedish literature as well as for its lyrical and artistic style.

Anna M. Lenngren (1754–1817) continues the budding feminist tradition of Nordenflycht in her "Några ord till min k. Dotter, i fall jag hade någon" (1798; A Few Words to my D. Daughter, in Case I Had One). Lenngren in short satire, realistic idyll, comical portrait, song, and epigram records everyday life.

During the nineteenth century Swedish realistic prose is in part shaped by three women writers from widely different intellectual and social milieus (Sophie Knorring [1797–1848], Emilie Flygare-Carlén [1807–1892], and Marie S. Schwartz [1819–1894]). It is, however, Fredrika Bremer (1801–1865) whom Sweden claims as its first major woman novelist. She presents the reader with realistic portraits of everyday life of the middle class, examining relations between the sexes, between parents and children, and especially between father and daughter. During the 1830s Bremer shapes the Swedish family novel, strongly mirroring social reality in many works. Her early female portraits show women obedient to convention, humble, submissive, self-sacrificing, but by the time she finishes *Hemmet (The Home)* in 1839 this presentation has changed. Bremer here presents a provocative study of parents' and society's violations of a young woman's endeavor to develop herself. Her New Woman is still firmly rooted in the family, but *En Dagbok* (1843; *A Diary*), influenced by Bremer's visit to Harriet Martineau, attacks the patriarchal family in a bleak description of women's conditions. A penetrating analysis of society, its realist technique is clearly influenced by Balzac. In 1856 Bremer again returns to the theme of the home brutalized by the patriarchal father in *Hertha,* her best-known work. It describes a young woman's fight against overwhelming odds to gain a sense of self. The heroine, a teacher struggling to instill in her students the urge to become free and self-sufficient, transgresses radically and dies young. Bremer's vision of a future for woman is the beginning of a literary theme pursued by Swedish women writers to our own times. It must be stressed, however, that her women figures best exert their "natural" and important influence within the home as wives and mothers.

Truth seekers as feminists (Sophie Adlersparre, Alfhild Agrell, Ellen Key, Anne C. Leffler) or as a reluctant feminist (Victoria Benedictsson) dominate the literary and critical scene of the 1880s. With strong foremothers such as Bremer, Mathilde Fibiger (Denmark), and Camilla Collett (Norway) and encouraged by the intellectual ferment of the Modern Breakthrough, these women set out to rewrite marriage, the relations between the sexes, womanhood, and sexuality. Among the best known are Leffler and Benedictsson. Although Leffler (1849–1892) daringly analyzes the nature of female sexuality under patriarchy, it is the life and work of Victoria Benedictsson (1850–1888) that have attracted feminist scholars. She is by many recognized as second only to Strindberg as an innovator of Swedish realistic prose. Her diary *Stora Boken* (1884–1888; The Big Book) must be seen as a great contribution to Swedish memoir literature. Hers was a tragic life; her writing was her way out of intensely oppressive living conditions. *Från Skåne* (1884; From Skåne), a short story collection, presents life among the peasants and lower classes in the provinces. It has an unmistakably feminist perspective of the sex-war problematic and the oppression of women trapped within the marriage institution. Benedictsson's first novel, *Pengar* (1885; Money), launches the author as the new, fresh voice in Swedish literature. In step with the Modern Breakthrough she delivers a scathing attack on the sexual, social, and psychological conditions of women. *Pengar* is exciting as a novel about self-development and self-destruction. Benedictsson's unmistakable ambivalence, in spite of the often outright statements to the contrary in the diary, about man's inherent superiority over woman, remains at the core of her subsequent writing. *Fru Marianne* (1887; Mrs. Marianne), in a complete turn from *Pengar,* presents a harmonious, ideal family. The novel describes the education of a spoiled city belle who in the end shines as the worthy wife, lover, companion of the Great Man, and worthy mother of his son.

The greatest Swedish woman writer of the nineteenth century is Selma Lagerlöf (1858–1940). Her tales, legends, gothic thrillers, historical novels, and realistic short stories have won her enormous popularity as well as critical acclaim. *Gösta Berlings Saga* (1891) single-handedly rejuvenates a flagging narrative art. The novel's poetic, imaginative language with its archaic expressions, its borrowings from tale and legend language, and its very lively and emotional emphatic characteristics all made *Gösta Berlings Saga* appear as something entirely new in literature. A trip to Italy resulted in *Antikrists mirakler* (1897; The Miracles of Antichrist), the author's attempt to bring about a union of Socialism and Christianity. In *Herrgårdssägen* (1899; The Saga of the Manor) she returns to the world of *Gösta Berlings Saga,* but in spite of its fantastic elements the story is a manifestation of Lagerlöf's interest in psychology, especially theories of the split personality. Her favorite themes of madness and guilt and retribution return with a vengeance in the magnificent *Herr Arnes pengar* (1903; Lord Arne's Hord). The year before that she published *Jerusalem* (2 vols.), a penetrating and at times brilliant study of religious fanaticism and social disintergration in a northern province in Sweden. In her later work Lagerlöf ponders the nature of the occult and evil, the various destructive forces that wreak havoc with the individual and with society. To the end of her life, however, Lagerlöf believes in the possibility of a good, decent world order beyond the ugliness and chaos of World War I.

In the early part of the twentieth century Agnes von Krusenstjerna (1894–1940) is especially noteworthy for her effort to break down literary taboos by writing openly about female sexuality, as in her antifamily novel series *Fröknarne von Pahlen* (1930–1935, seven vols.; The Misses von Pahlen), which created a bitter feud among critics and social commentators. Krusenstjerna's work, with its emphasis on peace and matriarchal ideals and on motherhood and giving birth and its stance against patriarchy, fascism, and oppression of women, challenged many of the women writers who followed, among them Karin Boye and Ellen Wägner. The latter (1882–1949) uses realistic prose to describe concrete political and social issues, particularly those dealing with women's emancipation. Influenced by the writings of the feminist theoretician Ellen Key, Wägner becomes a pacifist, arguing that it is a specific female role to work for peace and freedom. One of her best novels is *Åsa-Hanna* (1918), the story of a woman torn among choosing self, choosing the family, or working for world peace. *Väckerklocka* (1941; The Alarmclock) reveals Wägner's belief in and search for an ancient matriarchy, and in *Fred med jorden* (1940; Peace Be with the Earth) she takes a strong environmental stance. Swedish feminist and environmental movements of the seventies and eighties are indebted to her work.

Although women are predominantly prose writers, there is one central female poet, modernist Karin Boye (1900–1941). As a member of the Clarté group she is an activist and a pacifist. Her poem collections are central to Swedish literature. She renews poetry with her absolute ethical loyalties, with her intrepid exploring of the unconscious. The collection *För trädets skuld* (1935; For the Sake of the Trees), containing the well-known "Prayer to the Sun," exemplifies her technical boldness, her intensity in insisting that nature is the source of life and energy, the Originator. To come to grips with her lesbianism, she underwent psychoanalysis, described in the novel *Kris* (1934; Crisis). Published posthumously were the important collection *De sju dödssynderna* (1941; The Seven Deadly Sins) and her antiutopian science fiction novel *Kallocain* (1941).

The feminine mystique that characterizes much of the writing during the thirties and forties is met head-on by the one major female proletarian writer, Moa Martinson (1890–1964). She gives a strong, clear, new voice to women's experience by allowing the maternal body to speak, specifically about sexual experience, giving birth, sagging breasts, scar-ridden stomachs, abortions, sterility, and aging. Best known is her *Kvinnor och äppelträd* (1933; Women and Apple Trees), with its two heroines, both in their fifties. It is the story of how life and brutal conditions have literally formed these two bodies, but it is also the story of how these unlikely leading ladies fight to make life meaningful, after all. Importantly, her works give Swedish literature unique mother figures.

Sara Lidman (b.1923), in a more global sense, continues the Martinson tradition of writing about women, about society's underdogs and marginal types, as in *Bära mistel* (1960; To Carry) about a homosexual musician. Lidman, as did Lagerlöf, writes about atonement, guilt, and responsibility toward others. In her fiction from the seventies and eighties the author returns to her own province and in a language that rejuvenates Swedish prose sets out to write the history of the proletarian movement of northern Sweden in broad, epic narrative.

Kerstin Ekman (b.1933) writes Sweden's most broad social epics with women in the central roles, as in *Häxringarna* (1974; Witches' Circles), *Springkällen* (1976; The Source), and *Änglahuset* (1979; House of Angels). Her novel *En stad av ljus* (1983; A City of Lights) is the study of a father-daughter relationship and the many shapes and forms love takes. Fredrika Bremer's father-daughter theme, combined with concerns with the relationship among language, self, and female sexuality, is still prominent in Swedish literature.

PAAL BJÖRBY

T

TROUBADOUR LITERATURE. The poetry of Occitania (modern-day Provence in southern France) from the end of the eleventh century to the final decade of the thirteenth. Written in the medieval language of the region (*langue d'oc*), it was influenced by Arab sources, Ovid's love poetry, and contemporary vernacular verse but constituted essentially a new literature. Fittingly, the word *troubadour* means "finder" or "inventor" in Occitanian. Of the 400 known troubadours, 20 were women (the *trobairitz*).

With the exception of the earliest known troubadour, Guilhelm VII of Poitiers (1071–1127), the male troubadours were generally sedentary poets attached to a court. The songs they wrote were extremely formulaic, despite the inventive use of a limited number of figures of speech known as conceits or *topoi*.

Troubadour poetry gave rise to the conception of *fin' amors*, loosely translated as courtly love. *Fin' amors* was not an established system of rules for behavior, but a mode of thought emanating from the literature itself. Within this courtly ethos, the usual roles of aristocratic men and women were reversed. In most cases, the troubadour addressed his poetry as a humble knight to the wife of his lord and, thus, to a woman of higher status than himself. He vowed eternal homage and obedience to this lady as his master (*midons*, literally "my lord"). Through his love, he hoped to ennoble himself to her level and, therefore, to that of his patron.

Unlike much medieval literature that regarded women as obsessively carnal, troubadour poetry venerated the lady as a sexual being. Although the love professed by the troubadour was rarely consummated, this consummation was the goal of each supplicant. Through the denial resulting from such frustrated desires, the troubadour hoped to better himself. In general, troubadours were without land holdings and came from a relatively new and fluid class of noble families. The courtly love ethic they developed negated the effects of birth and declared the troubadours the equals of their lords through the ennobling effects of their long-suffering love. In essence, the lady was the embodiment of the troubadour ideal and a passive means of offering homage to her husband.

Although we know little about the lives of the female troubadours, it is clear that all of them were from the aristocracy and, as such, the potential objects of troubadour veneration. Approximately one-third of them were patrons of the arts who had troubadours in their own courts, several were probably the sisters or cousins of male troubadours, and certainly all of them knew troubadours personally. Except for the relative autonomy of the medieval convent, which produced several great literary works by female authors (e.g., Hildegard of Bingen), Occitania was the only region during this period to generate such a flowering of female literature.

The twelfth century seems to have been a period of economic and political decline for aristocratic women in many regions of Europe. In contrast, Occitania was a pocket of somewhat greater female power. One of the reasons for this difference may have been the legal system in southern France. Unlike other parts of Europe, Occitania retained vestiges of Visigothic law. As a result, unmarried daughters of the aristocracy could inherit equally with their brothers, and when these women married, they ceded only the use of their property (usufruct) to their husbands and retained ownership themselves. Since land was the basis of wealth and power during the Middle Ages, the legal system allowed Occitanian women of the aristocracy more power than their sisters had in other parts of Europe. In fact, by the beginning of the tenth century several important southern French fiefs were in the hands of women, including Montpellier, Nimes, Auvergne, Toulouse, Béziers, Périgord, Carcassonne, and Limousin. When the Crusades began (1095), aristocratic women in southern France consolidated their positions of power. Wives were left in charge of their husbands' lands, and many remained in power when their men fell in battle.

Trobairitz poetry reflects the contradictory situation of the powerful woman within a male-defined culture. The female troubadours were ladies who had stepped down from their pedestals. No longer the passive object of male paeans, these women took an active voice in the troubadour love relationship, thereby neutralizing their supposed domination as the arbiters of love. As a result, one common theme of *trobairitz* poetry was the desire to be acknowledged and to have a controlling voice in the courtship. With the reversal of male-female relationships in the poems, however, the analogy to the courtly system was seriously weakened. There were no idealization of the suitor and no prize to be gained by the *trobairitz*. In fact, the *topos* of *mezura* (patience, discretion) is practically absent from the women's poems, since the *trobairitz* continued to define themselves as the object of pursuit. This definition gave rise to such convoluted constructions as the countess of Dia's portrayal of her beloved as "he whom I most desire to have me."

In extending the limits of courtly love, the old *topoi* called into question many of the values upon which *fin' amors* was based. For instance, the female troubadours made liberal use of newly coined mercantile *topoi* such as *pretz* (value) and *merce* (grace, salary), which for their male counterparts implied a love relationship based on a means of exchange. However, lacking the usual connotation of vassalage implied in the male poems, what resulted was a concept of purely sexual power. Thus, in employing the conventional troubadour conceits in a different context, the *trobairitz* disrupted the poetic structure developed by their male counterparts.

The 20 known *trobairitz* were the countess of Dia, Tibors, Almucs de Castinau, Iseut de Capio, Azalais de Porcairages, Maria de Ventadorn, Alamanda, Garsenda, Isabella, Lombarda, Castelloza, Clara d'Anduza, Bieiris de Romans, Guillelma de Rosers, Domna H., Alais, Iselda, Carenza, Gaudairença, and Gormonda de Montpellier.

Further References: Joan M. Ferrante, *Woman as Image in Medieval Literature: From the Twelfth Century to Dante* (New York, 1975). Marianne Shapiro, "The Provençal *Trobairitz* and the Limits of Courtly Love," *Signs* 3 (1978): 560–571.

NANCY VEDDER-SHULTS

U

UTOPIAS, EUROPEAN. A utopia is an imaginary society, either an imaginary "good place" (eutopia) or "no place" (outopia). More imaginary societies have been written about by twentieth-century women authors of the United States than by women in Britain or Europe. Yet the imaginary society has existed in European literature written by women at least since the fifteenth century, when Christine de Pizan, the first European woman to earn her living by her pen, wrote her *Cité des dames*, an account of a city occupied by women of virtue. An answer to Jean de Meung's attack on women in his *Roman de la rose*, *Cité* was Christine's contribution to the *querelle des femmes* of the late Middle Ages.

In 1611 in England, Emilia Lanier (or Aemilia Lanyer) published a book of poetry entitled *Salve Deus Rex Judaeorum*. The third part of this three-part volume contains dedicatory poems to titled ladies noted for their learning, a religious poem including a spirited defense of women, and one of the first country house poems in English literature: a description of a lost female paradise of tranquil happiness.

Three eighteenth-century English women authors, Mary Astell, Sarah Robinson Scott, and Clara Reeve, wrote descriptions of all-women societies that provided education and useful occupation, primarily for unmarried gentlewomen. Astell's *A Serious Proposal to the Ladies for the Advancement of Their True and Greatest Interests* (1694, 1697) presents a plan for an all-woman religious and educational community. Scott's *A Description of Millenium Hall, and the Country Adjacent* (1762) describes an estate owned and managed by women, and Reeve's *Plans of Education* (1792) presents a plan for women's education.

A number of futuristic nineteenth-century British novels by men deal with women's lives, and a few anonymous (thus possibly by women) books describe positive utopias in which women have achieved equality. *New Amazonia: A Foretaste of the Future*, published by Mrs. George Corbett in 1889, presents an Ireland revitalized by women's rule.

Twentieth-century European dystopias by men have most often focused upon technology and totalitarianism, attacking both fascist and Socialist states (Aldous Huxley's *Brave New World*, George Orwell's *1984*, Henri Barbusse's *We [Nous Autres]*). In contrast, twentieth-century utopias by women have shown more interest in challenging gender roles. Some see gender as a societal construct; others see it in essentialist terms. *A Woman's Utopia* (1931) falls into the anti-Socialist category. Published under the pseudonym of "A Daughter of Eve," it attacks Socialism and advocates a meritocracy of talent. *My Own Utopia*, by Elizabeth Mann Borghese (1961), constructs gender as a status unrelated to biological sex (children are genderless, all adults become "women" upon maturity, and a smaller number become "men" in later life). In Mary Gentle's *Golden Witchbreed* (1983) biological gender is not established until maturity, and no social gender roles exist. Among Doris Lessing's several novels of speculative fiction, her *The Marriages between Zones Three, Four, and Five*, suggest men's and women's values are essential and immutable; the allegory attempts a "marriage" between them.

Monique Wittig's *Les Guérilières* (1969) has had great impact on the international women's movement. An account of a women's revolution, Wittig's novel deliberately subverts expectations about language and structure, as does another French feminist utopia, *Archaos ou le jardin étincelant* (1972) by Christine Rochefort. Many of the new French feminist theorists have used language in new and subversive ways: Hélène Cixous in "La rire de la méduse" (The Laugh of the Medusa) and Julia Kristeva in *Des chinoises* (About Chinese Women) describe women's possible futures. A French Canadian poet, Nicole Brossard, describes women loving women in a transformed, utopian New York City in *Amantes* (1980; Eng. trans., *Lovhers*, 1986). And a satire from Norway, Gerd Brantenberg's *Egalia's Daughters*, subverts gender roles by reversing them.

In summary, although French feminist authors, influenced by structuralist and poststructuralist theory, have produced some of the most daring nonfiction works about the future and in spite of the works by Brantenburg and Lessing, Britain and Europe have not yet seen a flowering of speculative fiction by and about women like that which has occurred in the United States.

Further References. Elaine Marks and Isabelle de Courtrivon (eds.), *New French Feminisms: An Anthology* (New York, 1981). Lyman Tower Sargent, "Women in Utopia," *Comparative Literature Studies* 10 (1973): 302–316. Barbara Brandon Schnorrenberg, "A Paradise Like Eve's," *Women's Studies* 9 (1982): 263–273.

CHARLENE BALL

UTOPIAS, U.S. Works depicting imaginary societies: as *eutopia*, conditions for women are better than the author's world; as *dystopia*, they are worse; or as *satiric* utopia, inversion discredits women's conditions. Various utopian strategies appear: description of an ideal society, a dream of an alternative world, a voyage to an exotic land or distant planet, a romance of a frontier community, time travel to an ideal future, or a satiric dialogue exposing contemporary inequities.

Several contrasts emerge within utopian writing by U.S. women from the first known instance in 1836, *Three Hundred Years Hence* by Mary Griffith, to the present upsurge of the 1970s and 1980s. First, whereas earlier writers were more likely to conceptualize utopia as static, an already perfected community, writers of the last decades locate utopia in a process of becoming: the nineteenth-century utopias are closer to blue-prints; those since 1960 show values in the process of being realized in action. A second contrast concerns the understanding of freedom. Up until about 1960, freedom for women in utopia has appeared as freedom *from*—especially marital or familial strictures. From the 1970s, freedom has meant autonomy—freedom *to*—pursue self-defined goals and fulfill potential, with support coming less often from a heterosexual family than from a women's community. Third, location has varied. In keeping with the literary realism of the late 1800s, utopias too were likely to be set in the then-contemporary United States. Now, with women's utopias often exhibiting characteristics of New Wave science fiction, a common setting is a distant future on a distant planet.

Production has varied. Up to 1870 might be called a latency period, with slightly more than one utopia appearing each decade. Thereafter three periods emerge. The output of the first period—from 1870 to 1920, the year women received the vote—averaged somewhat more than one utopia each year. This increase coincided with a large outpouring of utopian writing by U.S. men as well. Charlotte Perkins Gilman's *Herland* (1915) is the important work from this period. Between 1921 and 1960, few utopias appeared—about one every other year. Postsuffrage complacency, Depression blues, and World War II mobilization turned energies elsewhere. The transitional 1960s returned to almost one utopia a year, but since then the output has averaged nearly two a year. Significant works from this period are *The Female Man* (1975) by Joanna Russ, *Weave of Women* (1978) by E. M. Broner, *Wanderground* (1979) by Sally Gearhart, and *Woman on the Edge of Time* (1976) by Marge Piercy.

The utopias of each period exhibit characteristics of the historical context: the suffrage movement, an interim quieter period, and the recent feminist movement. The period from 1836 to 1920 stresses such solutions for reducing men's control over women's labor and sexuality as paid work, education, suffrage, and cooperation. Paid work appears as a solution in many utopias by men as well as by women. Education appears more before than after the Civil War, when higher education for women became more accessible. Suffrage appears as a solution in less than a quarter of the utopias, a suggestion that mere votes would not lead to greatly improved lives for women. Cooperation appears as a solution in more than half the utopias (e.g., shared house- or child-tending or whole-scale communitarian experiment). Though few of the cooperative solutions imagined have come to pass, the problems they were designed to solve are currently receiving widespread study. Though not blueprints, these utopias were harbingers. Their nowhere of actual place became a somewhere of inner vision, a predictor of the strongly spiritual dimension of current utopias.

During the period from 1920 to 1960, few utopias were feminist—only 6 of 27 by women, and of these, half make sex women's central concern. Of the three that permit women broadly human needs, one makes happiness central, another critiques free love as simply another deception foisted upon women, while the third posits a war-free world where love is neither exclusive nor possessive.

Since the 1960s, a decade of cultural transition, a new paradigm of values has emerged from feminist utopias. This paradigm includes not mere acceptance but also nurturance of diversity and nonviolence as a solution to resolving resultant differences. Three value clusters exist—the communitarian, the ecological, and the spiritual. The first cluster stresses the interrelatedness of all people— the notion of a global village, where villagers must be aware of the impact upon each other of their choices and behavior, where family members must permit the needs of each member to be met. Half of recent feminist utopias are all-female societies, validating and explicating women's experience and knowledge. The second cluster, the ecological, focuses upon our human impact upon animals, landscapes, natural resources, and outer space. Finally, spiritual values receive stress: utopia becomes a healing state of mind where readers may retreat for renewal and empowerment, a *Gedankenexperiment* (thought-experiment). Two new utopias stress language as creating and transmitting culture, a mechanism like religion to bind society together (Suzette Haden Elgin, *Native Tongue* [1984] and a *Dictionary and Grammar of L'aadan* [1985]; and Ursula LeGuin, *Always Coming Home* [1986]).

Further References. Carol Farley Kessler (ed.), *Daring to Dream: Utopian Stories by United States Women, 1836–1919* (bibliog. to 1983) (London, 1984). Natalie M. Rosinsky, *Feminist Futures: Contemporary Women's Speculative Fiction* (Ann Arbor, 1984).

CAROL FARLEY KESSLER

V

VICTORIAN LITERATURE, IMAGES OF WOMEN IN: often stereotypic reflections of social realities in nineteenth-century Britain. The middle-class ideal of womanhood was a domestic one; the Victorian woman is seen as daughter, wife, and mother, with qualities men deemed suitable for the fulfillment of these roles. The highest manifestation of this ideal is "the angel in the house," a label derived from a poem written by Coventry Patmore between 1854 and 1860, extolling married life and the model wife, a competent manager of domestic affairs and an exemplar of all the moral virtues.

Charles Dickens consistently reflects the image of the angel in the house. In *David Copperfield* (1849–1850), Agnes Wickfield is the paradigm of this stereotype. She has control of the management of her father's household, her mother being dead, and she wears at her waist a basket containing the house keys. This image of Agnes is combined with the picture of her ascending the staircase, the light from a stained-glass window shining behind her. The image of the saintly woman pervades the novel; to the end, David sees Agnes as "ever pointing upward . . . ever directing me to higher things!" (chap. 60). The role is repeated in Esther Summerson, the domestic and moral anchor of *Bleak House* (1852–1853), whose emblem also is the basket of household keys. Esther is a model female—modest, loyal, self-sacrificing, caring, subordinate to men and nurturing of children.

Women who fall short of the domestic ideal do so because they are incompetent in some way to fulfill the role of housekeeper, wife, and mother; they lack the moral qualities considered essential for the role or they are psychologically unsuited to the passive, subservient character demanded by it.

Dickens presents many ineffectual angels. Often they are childish women like David Copperfield's wife, Dora, prized for her innocence and sweetness in spite of her very real deficiencies as housekeeper and wife. Generally Dickens treats such characters tenderly, torn between their attractive feminine qualities and their serious inability to manage for their husbands. Sometimes, however, he uses the indifference to good household management as a metaphor for a warped social vision and misplaced priorities. Mrs. Pocket (*Great Expectations*, 1860–1861) buries herself in the peerage, ignoring her children. Mrs. Jellyby's establishment in *Bleak House* goes to ruin, and her family is neglected as she sets her sights on philanthropy in Africa. Setting these irresponsibilities against the larger themes in the novels, Dickens implies that such women should be attending to their domestic duties.

Frequently, the angel in the house role is too limiting for independent-minded women of intelligence and spirit. In *Jane Eyre* (1847) Charlotte Brontë's heroine complains bitterly of the "restraint" and "stagnation" of the domestic role (chap. 12). In *Middlemarch* (1871–1872) George Eliot demonstrates the limitations of the traditional female role for Dorothea Brooke and Rosamond Vincy. Dorothea had hoped to be her husband's "lamp holder" (chap. 5) by helping him with his scholarly work. Limited by her female education, Dorothea does not presume to do such work on her own, but she is frustrated when Casaubon is incapable of sharing it with her. Like Jane Eyre, Dorothea Brooke is both psychologically and intellectually unsuited to find contentment as the passive household angel.

Rosamond Vincy is, typically, educated to be ornamental. Her "accomplishments" and her delicate blond beauty make her attractive to a variety of suitors but do not prepare her for the realities of married life, nor do they give her that spiritual dimension that a woman was expected to possess as if it were genetic. Her husband, Lydgate, expected her to be the angel in his house, gracing his life and assisting him in his career by being a careful manager and a sympathetic retreat from his worldly troubles. Lacking the practical education, common sense, and strength of character to fulfill Lydgate's expectations, Rosamond makes him and herself miserable as they struggle with their problems. His stereotypical view of womanhood is as much to blame for their unhappiness as she is.

Generally, aggressive women, old or physically unattractive women, women desiring to do traditionally masculine work, and unmarried women of a certain age are considered anomalous and inherently unfeminine. These characters sometimes are given a wider scope than the traditional heroine, their idiosyncrasies freeing them from the conventional role. Wilkie Collins's Marian Halcombe, the dark and unattractive sister in *The Woman in White* (1860), is resourceful, brave, and intelligent. She is given "manly" virtues to compensate for her lack of beauty. While men treat her as an intellectual equal, Marian is not an example of the "new woman" found in the later novels of the period. She has no ambitions to do men's work or to claim rights denied to her because of her sex.

Elizabeth Gaskell creates a sympathetic picture of elderly widows and old maids in *Cranford* (1851–1853), showing clearly the pressure of financial constraints on women with no men to provide for them. The genteel poverty and sexual paranoia of the Cranford ladies are handled with light comedy, but other novels provide a darker picture of women without men. George Gissing's pathetic Madden sisters (*The Odd Women,* 1893) show the desperation of husbandless females and the suffering of those who marry only to fulfill social expectations or to find financial security.

Some female characters fail morally. In Thackeray's *Vanity Fair* (1847–1848) Becky Sharp is conniving and ambitious; she manipulates men, and her sexual behavior is suspect. Skilled at many kinds of household management, she does not employ her domestic skills for the comfort of husband and child. Thackeray makes Becky amusing and interesting, but he also makes it clear that she is no model for his female readers. His most damning indictment is her lack of concern for her young son; a bad, unloving mother is an unnatural woman.

Few Victorian heroines are like Becky Sharp. Most fallen angels are portrayed as victims of adverse social circumstances or unscrupulous men. Female sexual purity is so fixed in the Victorian mind that few nineteenth-century novelists treat its lapses realistically. Most, like Charles Dickens, sentimentalize fallen women. David Copperfield's childhood playmate, Little Emily, is lured away by the magnetic villain Steerforth. Seduced and abandoned, Emily is saved through the help of another fallen woman, Martha, a stereotypical prostitute with a heart of gold. While Elizabeth Gaskell's *Ruth* (1853) may be seen as a plea for a single standard of sexual morality, her handling of the fallen woman echoes the sentimental view; Gaskell endows Ruth with superhuman virtues of forgiveness and self-sacrifice, almost canonizing her with a saintly death.

Traditionally the obverse of the saintly angel is the dark femme fatale, the dangerous fiend-woman who both charms and destroys men. Few mainstream Victorian novelists present this figure, although shadows of her haunt the sexual nightmares of the period. Normally passionate women such as Jane Eyre must wrestle to reconcile their strong sexual feelings with the conventional view that good women did not experience sexual pleasure. Brontë balances Jane's intense feelings with heavy doses of propriety, and she provides a hideous analogue for passion gone wild in the character of Rochester's mad wife, Bertha.

Comedy is a safeguard for the novelist who wishes to present a sexually attractive female. Anthony Trollope's Madeline Vesey-Neroni (*Barchester Towers,* 1857) is a flagrant flirt; the beautiful Madeline flatters, insinuates, and tempts. While protesting her lack of heart and her unfeminine love of manipulation, Trollope softens her image by making her a humorous adversary to the pompous, power-hungry Mrs. Proudie and the hypocritical Mr. Slope. He further restricts her power to do real harm to the good men of Barchester—enticing as she is— by confining her to her invalid sofa.

Later in the period novelists began treating women realistically. George Meredith satirizes the male desire for a wife who perfectly reflects the husband's ego. In *The Eqoist* (1879), Clara Middleton escapes marriage to a hopeless male chauvinist. Thomas Hardy's *Tess of the D'Urbervilles* (1891) illustrates the consequences of false male images of women and the sexual double standard. Tess is a victim not only of rape but of her husband's view that she is irreparably tainted by it. Angel Clare's inability to excuse Tess and her own acceptance of his view of her are at the heart of their tragedy.

Novels of the period present many examples of women for whom the Victorian ideal is a contining—sometimes deadly—trap. Jane Eyre, Dorothea Brooke, Tess Durbeyfield, and scores of their sisters show that the image was not resisted without physical, social, or psychological peril. The suffering women experience for their nonconformity reveals the potency of the image in the nineteenth century.

Further References. Patricia Beer, *Reader, I Married Him* (New York, 1974). Sandra M. Gilbert and Susan Gubar, *The Madwoman in the Attic* (New Haven, 1979). Elizabeth Hardwick, *Seduction and Betrayal* (New York, 1974). Carolyn Heilbrun, *Reinventing Womanhood* (New York, 1979). Martha Vicinus (ed.), *Suffer and Be Still* (Bloomington, Ind., 1972).

SHARON LOCY

W

WOMEN'S COLLEGES. Higher educational institutions for women, first founded during the nineteenth century and designed to provide women with a four-year course of study, usually leading to the bachelor's degree. According to data compiled by the Women's College Coalition in 1987, there are 98 women's colleges in the United States, including 30 Roman Catholic institutions. Women's colleges comprise approximately 4 percent of all U.S. higher educational institutions and currently educate about 2 percent of the total number of women undergraduates in the United States. Unlike coeducational institutions, the leadership of women's colleges is predominantly female: in 1980, 67 percent of all women's college presidents were women. Geographically, women's colleges are heavily concentrated in the East, with the Mid-Atlantic States accounting for 39 percent, New England 32 percent, the Midwest 14 percent, the South 12 percent, and the West 3 percent.

While recent trends show an 8 percent annual increase in applications to women's colleges, both the number of women's institutions and current enrollments represent a sharp decline since 1960, when 298 women's colleges existed and approximately 9 percent of all women students attended single-sex colleges. This decline is attributable in part to the closing of some women's colleges, but more importantly, it reflects a larger pattern of growth in number and size of coeducational institutions since World War II. All but two traditionally all-male colleges (Morehouse and Hampden-Sydney) have become coeducational since the 1960s, and a number of women's colleges (including Vassar, Goucher, and most recently, Wheaton) now admit men. Historically, the largest absolute number of women's college students was 106,000 in 1940, while the percentage of women enrolled in women's colleges has declined steadily since at least 1870, when it is estimated that 59 percent of all women students attended women's colleges. This last percentage had dropped to 30 percent by 1890 and continued steadily to fall during each decade of the twentieth century.

This pattern of decline, however, obfuscates the significance of women's colleges in the growth of American women's intellectual status over the past two centuries. Growing out of the female academies that began to flourish during the last quarter of the eighteenth century and the subsequent antebellum seminary movement, women's colleges represented an important new educational opportunity for nineteenth-century women and served, moreover, as a highly visible symbol of women's intellectual equality with men. Access to higher education was a central goal of the nineteenth-century women's movement, and men's exclusion of women from American colleges was incorporated by the Seneca Falls Convention in 1848 as a grievance in the *Declaration of Sentiments,* which observed: "He [man] has denied her [woman] the facilities for obtaining a thorough education, all colleges being closed against her."

By 1848, when the *Declaration of Sentiments* was framed, a number of female academies, seminaries, and colleges were, in fact, providing collegiate-level education to women, but their offerings often were not perceived to be as rigorous as those demanded by the leading men's colleges. A few coeducational colleges also had been founded, but women often were relegated to "ladies' courses" or other second-class programs. Oberlin, founded in 1833 as a coeducational preparatory and collegiate institution, had begun in 1837 to admit women to the regular degree program and had awarded the baccalaureate degree to a woman for the first time in 1841. A number of state universities began to admit women to some programs in the 1850s and 1860s. Still, it was not until the founding of degree-granting women's colleges modeled after the elite eastern men's colleges that the concept of women's intellectual equality and right to rigorous intellectual training was articulated as an institutional rationale. The early coeducational colleges and state universities, in most cases, admitted women in response to financial exigencies, and the institutional justification for educating women most often was to provide "helpmates" to the male ministers the colleges were training or to prepare some women to teach in the common schools. Women's intellectual ambitions and abilities rarely were discussed, and coeducational institutions often reduced or eliminated access for women to their programs when improved finances permitted. The women's colleges, on the other hand, represented women's education as a primary mission, and they served as a challenge to critics to justify the continued exclusion of women from the full privileges of higher education nationwide.

Arguments against the education of women beyond the secondary level held sway throughout the nineteenth century and, changing in form somewhat over the years, continued to condition beliefs about women's intellectual abilities well into the twentieth century. It was these denials of women's mental capacities that the nineteenth-century women's colleges (and some earlier academies) set out to disprove. Critics claimed that advanced education would "unfit" women for "the duties of their station," particularly their obligations as wives and mothers. It was argued that "man loves a learned scholar, but not a learned wife," that women's character would be "hardened" and "deformed" by a college education, and that the stress of intellectual activity not only would "unsex" women but actually would harm their reproductive organs and render them unfertile. Women's intellectual capabilities were denied throughout the century by prominent educational spokesmen such as President Charles W. Eliot of Harvard University, who argued in 1873 that "women differ more from men than men differ from each other" and that "there is a fundamental pervading difference between all men and all women which extends to their minds quite as much as to their bodies" (Address to the Social Science Convention, Boston, May 14, 1873). Eliot and others argued that women therefore should be educated differently than men, and the theories and prescriptions for such distinctive educations ran the gamut from minor curricular alterations, such as the substitution of French for Greek, to elaborate regimens such as those proposed by Dr. Edward H. Clarke in 1873, which supposed women unable to accomplish mental tasks during certain phases of the menstrual cycle (and only moderately able to function at other times).

In spite of such objections, women's colleges increasingly began to upgrade their curricula to conform to the requirements of comparable men's colleges. Elmira College, founded in 1855, compared favorable in both its admissions standards and course requirements to neighboring men's colleges except for the level of Latin required for admission and the exclusion of Greek grammar as a prerequisite. Vassar College (1865) required both Greek and Latin on a par with the elite men's colleges for admission to its classical program, but in deference to the poor preparation of many girls it also provided a scientific course that did not require Greek or advanced Latin. Smith College (1875) generally is credited with being the first women's college with both admission requirements and a course of study identical to those of the best men's colleges. Smith modeled its four-year program (as did Wellesley, which also opened in 1875) after the Amherst and Harvard curricula. Smith's admissions requirements were identical to those at Harvard, and Wellesley (which initially did not require Greek) matched the Harvard admissions requirements in 1881. These women's colleges insisted that women could meet the academic demands required of men, and the successes of their early generations of students provided substantial evidence that critics of women's higher education were wrong in their predictions.

The women's colleges continued to be attacked, however, as America moved into the twentieth century and as the number of women college students increased. Charges of "race suicide" were levied against women college graduates who had shown themselves less likely to marry than American women in general. (That the male graduates of Harvard and Yale also married at a lower rate than men in the general population during the late nineteenth and early twentieth centuries was deemed less alarming.) Attacks on women's colleges were particularly harsh, in part because of the colleges' visibility as symbols of women's educational attainments and also because their alumnae represented a certain educational and social elite. The social activism of many women's college students and faculty was condemned by conservative critics as was the pacifism that grew on women's college campuses prior to America's involvement in World War I. During the 1920s and 1930s, women's colleges faced a new assault as communities of women were charged with being "unnatural" or "sexually deviant" by Freudian critics, and public fears and prejudice against lesbianism found a convenient and symbolically powerful target in the women's colleges—a dynamic that has continued to the present. In defending their institutions against such attacks, therefore, women's college supporters historically have served as the defenders of women's education in general, and the importance of women's colleges as a social institution in American life has been much greater than the number of graduates would suggest. As the number of women's colleges has decreased, moreover, women have lost access to leadership positions as presidents, deans, and tenured faculty; women students, in turn, have lost highly distinguished role models.

Since the early 1970s, women's colleges have played a complex role in the contemporary women's movement. Criticized by many for lagging behind many coeducational institutions in adopting women's studies courses and programs, the women's colleges have responded to newly articulated feminist goals in diverse ways, reflecting differences in their institutional histories, religious affiliations, and economic needs. A number of women's colleges (most recently Mount Holyoke and Spelman) have renewed their commitment to feminist goals by appointing women to the presidency after decades of male leadership. The elite eastern women's colleges, which provided the first generations of college-trained women with new opportunities for advanced study and professional employment, have been in the forefront of curricular and pedagogical innovation since the 1970s as they have reexamined their programs and practices in the light of feminist theory and goals. Other women's colleges across the country have reformulated their traditional commitment to women's education by promoting both women's studies on campus and an array of professional internship and training programs for women in the larger community. In spite of their differing perspectives, most feminist observers and educational scholars agree that it is important to preserve these women's institutions and that women's colleges continue to serve as a symbol of women's intellectual worth.

Further References. Sally Schwager, "Educating Women in America," *Signs* 12 (1987). Barbara Miller Solomon, *In the Company of Educated Women* (New Haven, 1985). Thomas Woody, *A History of Women's Education in the United States*, 2 vols. (New York, 1929).

SALLY SCHWAGER

Selected Bibliography

A very limited number of bibliographic references are included in many of the articles in the encyclopedia. In addition, a few general works, bibliographies, dictionaries, and comprehensive works on women in literature, art, and music, which may prove useful as a starting point for study, are listed below.

Anderson, Jack. *Ballet and Modern Dance: A Concise History*. Princeton: Princeton Book Co., 1986.

Bowers, Jane, and Judith Tick, eds. *Women Making Music: The Western Art Tradition, 1150–1950*. Urbana: University of Illinois Press, 1986.

Cohen, Aaron I. *International Encyclopedia of Women Composers*. New York: R. R. Bowker, 1981.

Fine, Elsa Honig. *Women and Art: A History of Women Painters and Sculptors from the Renaissance to the 20th Century*. Montclair, N.J.: Allanheld and Schram, 1978.

Flynn, Elizabeth A., and Patrocinio P. Schweichart, eds. *Gender and Reading: Essays on Readers, Texts, and Contexts*. Baltimore: Johns Hopkins University Press, 1986.

Gilbert, Sandra M., and Susan Gubar. *The Madwoman in the Attic*. New Haven: Yale University Press, 1979.

Harris, Ann Sutherland, and Linda Nochlin. *Women Artists: 1550–1950*. New York: Alfred A. Knopf for the Los Angeles County Museum of Art, 1979.

Lablame, P. H., ed. *Beyond Their Sex: Learned Women of the European Past*. New York: New York University Press, 1980.

Lauter, Estella. *Women as Mythmakers: Poetry and Visual Art by Twentieth-Century Women*. Bloomington: University of Indiana Press, 1986.

Mainieri, Lina. *American Women Writers, A Critical Reference Gender*. 4 vols. New York: Ungar, 1979–1982.

Marting, Diane E., ed. *Women Writers of Spanish America: An Annotated Bio-Bibliographical Guide*. Westport, Conn.: Greenwood Press, 1987.

Meyer, Doris, and Margarita Fernandez Olmar, eds. *Contemporary Women Authors of Latin America*. 2 vols. Brooklyn, N.Y.: Brooklyn College Press, 1983.

Petteys, Chris. *Directory of Women Artists: An International Dictionary of Women Artists Born before 1900*. Boston: G. K. Hall, 1985.

Showalter, Elaine. *A Literature of Their Own: British Women Novelists from Brontë to Lessing*. Princeton: Princeton University Press, 1977.

Vicinus, Martha, ed. *Suffer and Be Still*. Bloomington: University of Indiana Press, 1972.

Walker, Barbara G. *The Women's Encyclopedia of Myths and Secrets*. San Francisco: Harper and Row, 1983.

Wilson, Katharina M. *Dictionary of Continental Women Writers*. New York: Garland, 1990.

———. *Women Writers of the Renaissance and Reformation*. Athens: University of Georgia, 1987.

Woods, Jean M., and Marie Furstenwald. *Women of the German-Speaking Lands: Learning, Literature and the Arts during the Seventeenth and Eighteenth Centuries, A Lexicon*. Stuttgart: Metzler, 1984.

Index

Page numbers set in *italic* indicate the location of a main entry.

and Greek writers, 152–54; and Italian writers, 176; and English Renaissance, 286–88; and Spanish American writers, 318, 322; and Spanish writers, 329; women in Roman, 292–93

Macaulay, Rose, 236
McCall's Magazine, 205
MacCarthy, Molly (Mary Warre-Cornish), 39
McCauley, Sue, 30
McCullers, Carson, 242, 263
McCullough, Colleen, 30
MacEwen, Gwen, 49
Mackintosh, Elizabeth (Josephine Tey), 87–88
MacLane, Mary, 35, 195
McPartland, Marilyn, 189
Magazines: and Australian and New Zealand writers, 29, 31; and popular writers, 15–16; and U.S. poets, 275–76; women's (nineteenth-century), *203–5*, 276
Magnúsdóttir, þórunn Elfa, 167
Magyar writers, 113, 114, 115
Mahādevi Akkā, 168, 169
Mailer, Norman, portrayal of women, 21
Maillet, Antonine, 50
Maksimovic, Desanka, 115
Maldonado y Paz, Sor Juana de, 319
Male: ambivalence of, 286–87; and female relations, 5, 39, 297–99, 316–17; network, 16, 314, 315; pseudonyms, 233, 301; as sex objects, 138
Malfatti, Anita, 44, 191–92
Malina, Judith, 106
Managers: music, 208–9; theatre, 99–100, 101, 102, 104–5, 162
Mander, Jane 30
Mann, Emily, 263
Manners: novel of, 90–93, *205–7*
Mannerisms of the *précieuses*, 280–81
Mansfield, Katherine (Kathleen Beauchamp), 29, 33
Manzini, Gianni, 179
Maoris of New Zealand, 28, 30
Mao Zedong, rules for writers, 68
Ma Quan, 60

Maraini, Dacia, 180
Marchessault, Jovette, 52
Margarete of Savoy, 261
Margaret (Queen of Scotland), 256
Marguerite of Navarre, 137–38, 290–91
Marie de France, 137, 295
Marie of Champagne, 76, 260
Marinelli, Lucrezia, 176
Marisol (Escobar), 313
Markandaya, Kamala, 170
Market: for American writers, 15, 16, 17; for Italian art, 172
Marriage: and art careers, 172–73, 225; Danish writers' views on, 83–85; and domestic novels, 91, 93; and Renaissance literature, 285; and Restoration comedy, 96
Marsh, Ngaio, 29, 87
Marshall, Paule, 52, 53
Martineau, Harriet, 33, 207, 235
Martín-Gaite, Carmen, 330
Martins, Maria, 192
Martinson, Moa, 337
Martyrs, and gender prototypes, 158–59
Marxism influence on Chinese writers, 68
Ma Shouzhen, 59
Masino, Paola, 180
Masked themes, in lesbian literature, 195
Masquerade set piece, 231–32
Massimi, Petronilla Paolini, 176–77
Matière de Bretagne, 294, 295
Matière de Charlemagne, 294, 296
Matière de Rome, 294, 295
Matraini, Chiara, 289
Matriarchy, rural, in New England school of writers, 199–201
Matute, María, 330
Mayamoto Yuriko, 184
Maywood, Augusta, 80
Mechthild, Dutchess, 143, 260–61
Medieval literature, 89–90, 93–95, 107–8, 255–58, 294–97, 305–7. *See also* Courtly love; Epic poems: (heroic middle high German); Fabliaux; Hagiography
Medieval patrons, 256, 339
Meireles, Cecília, 44
Meléndez, Concha, 327

About the Editor

HELEN TIERNEY is Professor of History at the University of Wisconsin-Platteville. She is the editor of *Women's Studies Encyclopedia Volume I.*